Academy Royal Irish

The Transactions of the Royal Irish Academy

Academy Royal Irish

The Transactions of the Royal Irish Academy

ISBN/EAN: 9783744741262

Printed in Europe, USA, Canada, Australia, Japan

Cover: Foto ©ninafisch / pixelio.de

More available books at **www.hansebooks.com**

[JUNE, 1880.]

THE
TRANSACTIONS
OF THE
ROYAL IRISH ACADEMY.

IRISH MANUSCRIPT SERIES.

VOLUME I.

PART I.—*On the Calendar of Oengus.* By WHITLEY STOKES, LL.D.

DUBLIN:
PUBLISHED BY THE ACADEMY,
AT THE ACADEMY HOUSE, 19. DAWSON-STREET.

SOLD ALSO BY

HODGES, FOSTER, & FIGGIS, GRAFTON-STREET,

AND BY WILLIAMS & NORGATE,

LONDON: | EDINBURGH:
Henrietta-street, Covent Garden. | 20, South Frederick-street.

1880.

On the Calendar of Oengus. By WHITLEY STOKES, LL.D.

[Read November 13, 1871.]

THE Irish metrical *félire*, or Calendar of Church festivals, now for the first time printed, is contained in several manuscripts, none of which appear older than the fourteenth century. It is, however, commonly attributed to Oengus the Culdee (*céle dé*, servus dei[*]), who is said to have flourished about the beginning of the ninth century after Christ. But the grammatical forms of the poem seem to show that it could not have been composed much before the end of the tenth century, when the Old-Irish language was becoming Middle-Irish.

I propose in the present paper, first, to enumerate the manuscripts in which the Calendar, or any considerable part thereof, is contained: secondly, to notice Oengus, the alleged author of the poem: thirdly, to consider some of the characteristics of its language, especially as bearing on the date of its composition: fourthly, to describe the metre in which it is written: fifthly, to give some account of its contents: sixthly, to notice the glosses by which obsolete words are sought to be explained; and, seventhly, of the notes added by the scholiast, to indicate those that are important as materials for a natural history of Irish society.

Lastly, I will set down the corrigenda and some of the addenda which have occurred to me in the course of the nine years during which this paper has been passing through the press. The corrigenda mostly refer to the translation, of which I wish to speak with sincere diffidence, as being merely a contribution towards a better understanding of the longest, and perhaps the most difficult,[†] relic of ancient Irish poetry. My version claims only a temporary and provisional value, and I confess my inability to render with certainty several portions of the text.

[*] The Welsh equivalent *meu-dwy* (= Ir. *mug dé*) now means a hermit.
[†] I here exclude intentional word-puzzles, like the Amra of Colombcille.

I.—*The Manuscripts.*

The Calendar of Oengus is now printed from four manuscripts:—

A, the so-called Lebar Brecc, or Speckled Book, a huge folio vellum codex, in the library of the Royal Irish Academy, compiled about the year 1400. A lithographic facsimile of this manuscript has been published by the Academy. Of this facsimile our poem occupies pages 75 to 106, both inclusive. The text of A is often very corrupt. For example, *ritroich*, Prol. 28, for *rith roraith: itáll céllin*, Prol. 316, *domair*, Feb. 16, for *domair, aidiu*, March 19, for *aite: propaci*, May 13, for *Probique*.

B is a double-columned folio vellum in the Bodleian, marked Laud 610. It contains ff. 146, and was written at different dates from (perhaps) the twelfth to the fifteenth century. The late Dr. Todd* thought that the part containing our poem was written in the middle of the thirteenth century. I should be inclined to put it at least a century later. There are in this text Middle-Irish corruptions—for example, *fororenait*, Prol. 87, *cumscaidset*, Feb. 6, *gan*, Nov. 8, *dodigset*, Ep. 24, and *congbaid*, Ep. 279—which could hardly be so early as the year 1250. In this manuscript our poem begins at fo. 59 a 1, and ends at fo. 72 a.

C is another vellum, also in the Bodleian, marked Rawl. B 505, and described in Macray's Catalogue of the Bodleian MSS., Part v., fasc. i., col. 723. It is a folio, containing ff. 220, of the beginning of the fifteenth century, and its chief contents are the Latin lives of thirty-eight Irish saints. This manuscript contains neither prose preface, prologue, nor epilogue; but the body of the poem is complete: it begins at fo. 211 and ends at fo. 220. This copy seems to have been transcribed from a good manuscript. Archaic forms, such as *arsil*, Sep. 29, are preserved, and the foreign proper names are given with exceptional correctness. For example, Gluceri, Jan. 14, Valerius, Jan. 22, Amphianus, Ap. 2, Saturnin, May 2, Cyriacus, May 12, Teraci Probique, May 13, Epeethiti, May 23, Lupus, Simplice, July 29, Bartholom, Aug. 25, Eleuther, Oc. 2, Baluina, Oc. 4, Merobus, Dec. 4. A peculiarity of the scribe is his fondness for 'irrational' vowels. Thus, ad*a*bal, June 26, aidb*i*le, March 26, c*a*rann, March 10, liber*e*n, March 11, for adbul, aidble, crann, libren. He writes *l* for *r* in damail, Feb. 16, and *r* for *l* in tempuir, Dec. 15. The medial *d* is aspirated in edhnig, Feb. 17.

* *St. Patrick*, p. 24, note.

D is a vellum manuscript, also in the Bodleian, marked Rawl. B. 512. It is a double-columned quarto, containing ff. 154, and written in the fourteenth or fifteenth century. The prose preface begins at fo. 53 a 1. The poem commences at fo. 53 b, but breaks off at line 60 of the prologue. At fo. 54 a begins the epilogue and it ends at fo. 56 b. This is followed by some misspelt verses commencing thus:—

    bendacht indrig donelaib rogenair omvire
    for anmum ganmire oengusa conglaine;*

   *The blessing of the King of Clouds, who was born of Mary,
   on the soul without madness of Oengus with purity;*

and the seven succeeding folios, from 57 a to 64 a, are filled with notes on the body of our poem, which unfortunately is not now in this manuscript. The scribe's name appears to have been Dubthach O'Duibgenan. The text of these fragments is respectable, but the corrupt Middle-Irish spelling prevails. Thus, ea for Old-Irish e is found in seacht, Prol. 2, ro-sealgatar, Prol. 29, teacht, Prol. 31: final a is written for u in surna, Prol. 44; and d is written for t in coméd, Prol. 6, fodaimdis, Prol. 51, ada-n, Ep. 34.

These four MSS. all offer the same text, and their disagreements in orthography (often very considerable) are due to the ignorance and carelessness of the copyists. By intercomparison and by attending to the rhymes the original text can generally be restored.

Besides these four there is a vellum copy of our poem, written by one Ruaidhri O'Luinin, formerly in the College of St. Isidore, in Rome, and now in the Franciscan Monastery, Merchants'-quay, Dublin. Of the part of this (with the notes and glosses thereon) dealing with the month of December, I possess a transcript made by the late Dr. Todd. There is also said to be a paper copy, made by Michael O'Clery, in the seventeenth century, and preserved in the Burgundian Library, at Brussels; and there is an imperfect copy, in a small folio vellum MS., belonging to the Royal Irish Academy, now marked $\frac{23}{F.3.}$ and written by Uilliam mac an Legha in the year 1467. The prologue here is missing, and also the calendar for the months of May, September, and December.

---

* This is apparently a verse in the metre of the Félire, and should run thus:

    Bendacht rig do nélaib
    rogénair ó Mairi
    for a maim cen mire
    Oengusa co nglaini.

Lastly, there are glossed fragments of our poem preserved in several Middle-Irish MSS. Those in H. 3, 18 (a codex in the Library of Trinity College, Dublin), pp. 616–622,* and in O'Davoren's Glossary,† have been already printed.

II.—*Oengus the Culdee.*

Nothing certain is known about the supposed author of our poem. It is alleged that he was son of Oengoba, and a descendant of Echaid Cobai; that he was a contemporary of Aed Ordnithe, overking of Ireland from the year 793 to the year 817, and of Fothud of the Canon an ecclesiastic of that time: that he was a member of the monastery of Cluain Eidnech (Clonenagh), on the banks of the Nore‡ in Queen's County, where he founded the church of Disertenos: that he afterwards joined the fraternity of Tamlacht (Tallaght), near Dublin: that at first he worked there as a slave in the drying-kiln, till the cornblades

* See *Three Irish Glossaries*, London, 1862, pp. 125–140.

† *Ibid*, pp. 47–144. The quotations from the Félire made by O'Davoren, are collected by Ebel in the *Revue Celtique*, II. 160–169.

‡ To this refers a poem of thirteen stanzas in the Lebar Brecc, p. 106ᵇ, which begins thus:—

Aibind suide sund amne
retaeb coire uarglaine.

*Pleasant to sit here thus,
beside the cold pure Nore;*

which tells how he miraculously restored his "gospel-hand," chopped off while he was cutting wood, and which contains the two stanzas whereof Mr. Matthew Arnold has said, with kindly exaggeration, "a Greek epitaph could not show a finer perception of what constitutes propriety and felicity of style in compositions of this nature." They are as follows:—

Ængus ahœnach nime
sund ata alecht 'sa lige
issund dochunid archeal
isináine conaemncam.
Isacluain eidnech roalt
hicluain eidnech roadnacht
hi cluain eidnech ilar cross
roleg asalmu artuoss.

*Aengus out of the assembly of Heaven,
Here are his tomb and his bed.
It is hence he went to death,
On the Friday, to holy heaven.
It is in Cluain Eidnech he was reared,
It is in Cluain Eidnech he was buried.
In Cluain Eidnech, of many crosses
He first read his psalms.*

grew through his hair by reason of the greatness of the service : that he was recognised by having, like S. Martin of Tours, 'imprudently committed a miracle' on behalf of an idle boy : that he composed the calendar now printed, moved thereto by seeing a flight of angels over the grave of a veteran who had done nothing good save recounting, twice a day, the saints of the world. These allegations, of which one, perhaps, is as authentic as another, are founded solely on the obviously unhistorical prose prefaces printed in pp. i.-xii. of the present volume—at least the statements about Oengus, made by O'Clery, Colgan, O'Curry, O'Hanlon, and other recent writers, have not been shown to rest on any higher authority. As regards Oengus' life or death, there is not the slightest notice in our Annals, and of his history, "the sole chronological notes which we possess are his connexion with St. Maelruain, and one or two other contemporaries, his pedigree and his obitual day [March 11] in the calendar.* Linguistic reasons, which will hereafter be adduced, tend to show that Oengus cannot have been the author of the poem now printed. Like reasons may be brought forward to prove that he could not have writen the *Saltair na Rann*, † which also is ascribed to him, though it contains such forms as those that are italicised in the following lines taken from it :—

    in muir serb suiges insluag.
    anduili *cestait* intsluaig.
    ona *cethri* retglannaib.
    each a mathair 'sa athair.
    betit ind angeil fom traig.

Again, the late Professor O'Curry speaks of "Pedigrees of the Irish Saints, compiled, it is believed, by Oengus Céile Dé at the close of the eighth century, as well as his celebrated Litany of the Irish Saints."‡ There is not, so far as I am aware, a particle of trustworthy evidence to show that Oengus ever wrote either of these works. Another treatise, *De Matribus Sanctorum Hiberniae*,

---

* Reeves' *Culdees*, p. 8.

† So far as I know, the only copy of the collection of poems so called is preserved in the Bodleian, in a codex marked Rawl. 502. It is headed Psaltair na rann inso sis dorigne oengus celide *Psalter of the quatrains this below, which Oengus the Culdee made*. It begins thus :—

    MOrise ri nime nair.
    My King is king of high heaven,

and is well worth publishing, though I doubt if any scholar could understand it all.

‡ A copy of this Litany, imperfect at the beginning, is said to be in the Lebar Brecc, pp. 23, 24 ª.

ascribed to him with equal confidence, refers to Maelbrigte, one of the abbots of Iona, who died in the year 927,* more than a hundred years after Oengus is said to have flourished. Again, the Martyrology of Tallaght, of which, on the authority of a rubric in the Book of Leinster, Oengus and Maelruain are asserted to be the joint authors, mentions Blathmac, who was slain A.D. 823, and King Feidilmid, son of Crimthann, who died A.D. 845. It mentions Cairpre, bishop of Clonmacnois, who died in the year 899, and it even gives the names of Oengus and Maelruain themselves, at 11th March and 7th July, the days on which they were commemorated as saints.† Lastly, Codex A of the Calendar now printed appears to refer, at March 26, to a second Sinchell, who died A.D. 982, and at March 11, actually commemorates the obit of Oengus himself, the alleged author.‡ The fact seems to be that the name of Oengus, like those of Benén, Colomb Cille, Cormac and many other names in Irish literature, has been prefixed to later compositions, by the pious fraud of the real author or his successors, and the reference in our Calendar, Ep. 64, 65, to abbot Maelruain, whom the poet calls his aite *fosterer*, *tutor*, is probably nothing but an ingenious attempt to father the poem on Oengus.

III.—*The Language of the Calendar.*

I proceed to state the linguistic facts which seem to me to prove that the Calendar could not have been composed much before the end of the tenth century. It must, of course, be admitted that most of the Middle-Irish corruptions visible in the texts now published are due to the transcribers. But the following modernisms can hardly be ascribed to anyone but the author :—

1°. The aphaeresis of *a* in '*nair*, Jan. 8, for Old-Irish *andir*, that of *i* in '*nambuidnib* Ep. 295, for Old-Irish *in-am-buidnib*, 'in their companies,' and that of *in* in *dadaig*, Feb. 15, for *ind-adaig*, ' in the night' :

2°. The occurrence of the transported *n* after *Marcellum*, Oct. 4, which shows that the use of this *n*, after the accusative singular, had, when the poem was composed, become merely syntactical :

3°. The nom. sg. of the neuter article (*an*, *a*) replaced by the masc. or fem. *in*. Thus : *in ydir*, Oct. 20, *in togu* Prol. 123 (Laud 610), for Old-Irish *angáir*, *atogu* :

* Reeves' *Columba*, 302.
† Todd, *Martyrology of Donegal*, Introduction. p. xiv.
‡ Compare Deuteronomy. xxxiv., 5.

4°. The nom. pl. of the masc. article (*ind, in*) replaced by the feminine *inna, ina, na*. Thus: *inna druing, ina druing* Ep. 285, *na tri maccain*, Aug. 2, for Old-Irish *in druing, in tri maccáin*.

5°. The occurrence of *hua*, June 21, as a monosyllable, whereas in Old-Irish the corresponding form *húae* is always dissyllabic.

6°. The constant use of the comparative for the superlative, or, perhaps, as an enhanced positive. Thus *isliu* Prol. 153, *glainiu* Prol. 246 A, *dilsiu, uaisliu* Prol. 262, 263, Jan. 18, *noebu, noemdu*, Jan. 20, May 27, *dixu* Jan. 18, *cadu*, March 20, *danu, daingniu* May 23.

7°. The use of the numeral *cethri, ceithri* 'four' with all genders, instead of the Old-Irish *cethur* m. *cetheoir, cethcora* fem. Thus *ceithri deich* Oct. 16, *cethri deich* Oct. 25, *cethri chét* Sep. 1, B.

8°. The occurrence, among the verbal forms, of the following:

bebais Prol. 95, Feb. 18, Ap. 23, for the Old-Irish reduplicated preterite *bebe, bebae*. Other instances of the addition in Middle-Irish of the endings of the s-preterite to reduplicated forms will be found in Kuhn's Beitraege vii., 44, and in Windisch's Kurzgefasste Irische Grammatik, S. 303. Compare Latin forms like *totondisti*.

do-rimemar, do-ruimdemar, Ep. 6, for the Old-Irish s-preterite *doruirmisem*. *conicsid*, Ep. 393, for the Old-Irish *conissid*.

berthair, trebthair, Prol. 175, 176, for the Old-Irish plurals passive *bertair, trebtair*.

asa, assa, 'whose is,' Prol. 50, 98, etc., *ata-n* 'whose are,' March 14, Ap. 6, June 27, Ep. 34, 82, 274, seem not to be Old-Irish formations.

9°. The government of the dative by the preposition *itir*, March 11, Nov. 23, and of the accusative by the preposition *iar*, Ep. 315. In Old-Irish *itir* governs the accusative and *iar* the dative.

10°. The pleonastic use of the possessive pronoun: *a thuath de* Prol. 142, *an itgi horum atque harum* July 17.

These phenomena will, I think, satisfy all competent judges that our Calendar could not have been composed before the time when Old-Irish was beginning to pass into Middle-Irish. On the other hand, the archaic forms which will now be mentioned, tend to show that it was not composed much after that time:

1°. The adjective *óac, óoc* Sep. 22, is still dissyllabic. So are *ua* Ap. 11, *siuur* Dec. 14, *deud* Prol. 220. *Nóis* Prol. 184, *déac* Sep. 23.

2°. The feminine numeral *teor* 'three' (=Skr. tisras) occurs at Sep. 1. This is older than the Zeussian *teora*, which form is due to a false analogy with the nom. and acc. pl. of fem. ā-stems.

3°. The adjectival i-stems make their gen. pl. in *-e*. Thus *áille* Ep. 83, gen. pl. of *álaind, blaithe* Sep. 18, gen. pl. of *blaith*, and *maithe*, July 23, gen. pl. of *maith*.

4°. The superlative in *m* still survives. Thus *ardam, arddam*, Mar. 23, Dec. 27, Ep. 207, 278, *amram* Sep. 24 (Rawl. B 505), *deodam* Ep. 498, *noemem, naebem* July 14.

5°. In the verb the Old-Irish distinction between the absolute and the conjunct forms is invariably preserved. Thus, confining ourselves to the 3d sg. pres. indic. active, we find the following absolute forms: *canaid*, Ap. 26, *marnid, mairid* Prol. 168, 204, 252, 255, *trógaid* Prol. 231, *móraid* Prol. 232, and the following conjunct forms:—

ā-stems (the Latin third conjugation): *ní mair* Prol. 199, 203, *ní dlig* Jan. 6, *na dlig* March 7, Ap. 25, *ar-dlig* Jun. 1, Aug. 5, *do-beir* March 31, Nov. 30, *con-gaib, con-geib* Ap. 1, Ep. 76, 279, *con-ó-caib* Ep. 208, *don-for-maig* Oc. 18, *de-for-maig* Ep. 195, 206, *mos-tic* July 9, *do-t-ic* May 25, *tair-ic* July 19.

ā-stems (the Latin first conjugation): *for-osna* Prol. 5, *ad-it-cialla* Feb. 23, *ar-don-sela* June 23, *ni-s-tarca* June 29, *for-tn-iada* July 31, *fu-t-botha* Nov. 15, *ar-it-léga* Ep. 178, *for-ceuda* Ep. 282.

ia stems (the Latin fourth conjugation): *at-sluindi*, Prol. 110, *do-don-fairci* Jan. 26, *fo-dom-gluaisi, fo-m-gluaisi* Ep. 376, 377.

6°. The reduplicated preterite is still in constant use. Thus:

Sg. 1. *adróithach* Ep. 300, 301,* from *ateoch, ro-gád-sa, ro-n-gad-sa*, Ep. 412, 421, from *guidim*.

Sg. 3. *cachain*, Dec. 8, from *canim, cechaing*, Jan. 25, from *cingim, geguin*, Oc. 23, from *gonaim, ro- leblaing*, March 5, from *lingim, d-r-braing* Ap. 2, 17. *selaig* (for seslaig), Prol. 101, *senaig* (for sesnaig) May 15, from *snigim, do-ro-chair, tor-chair* March 26, Ep. 361. With *á* in the root-syllable: *ráith* Jan. 6, Sep. 19 from *rethim, fo-raith*, Jan. 15, *fris-raith* Prol. 302, *ro-scáich*, Prol. 121, 177, 193 *ro-fir-*

---

* The MSS. have adroitheach, adroethech, atraethech, atroethech, atroitheeh; but the rhyme with soethar shows the true reading.

scáich Prol. 84, from *scuchim*. With the root-syllable and the reduplication-syllable combined: *ar-ro-chinir* Prol. 67, 127, from *erchrinim*.

3d pl. *gignetar, gegnatar*, May 19, *do-choemnachtar** Jan. 4, *selgatar* (for seslgatar, seslagatar) Prol. 29, *rathatar* Sep. 18.

tanic, Jan 11, Ap. 14, *ránic* May 2, Ep. 17, pl. *tancatar*, Ep. 88, *rancatar* Prol. 78, are also reduplicated preterites (*dnac* = Skr. ānāça).

7°. Deponential preterites are *damair* Feb. 9, 16, *ro-lamair* Prol. 58, *génair* Prol. 251, Sep. 24, Dec. 25.

8°. There are six or seven examples of the curious forms in -*ai* (= W. -*awd* now -*odd*) which may possibly be imperfects corresponding with Lithuanian forms in -*ójô*, Skr. -*ayat*. Thus *ro-pridchai* Prol. 164, *aibdai* Ap. 9, *do-n-gesnai* May 12, Oc. 25, *fris-m-brechtai* Nov. 29, *labrai* Dec. 22 (= W. *llafurodd*), *ternai* Ep. 544, *ad-r-annai* Sep. 6, and perhaps *gabai* Ep. 173.

9°. The reduplicated future is represented by the following absolute forms: active, 3d sg. *gébaid* Dec. 12, *méraid* Prol. 174, 1st pl. *regmai* Prol. 291, and the following conjunct forms: 2d sg. *at-um-didmae* Ep. 494, 3d sg. *at-béla* Ep. 116, *no-t-géba* Ep. 114, 166, 1 pl. *nad-célam* Ep. 86, 3d pl. *do-ragat* Ep. 115. Passive 3d pl. *do-génatar* Ep. 176.

10°. Of the absolute form of the s-preterite or s-aorist in the 2d sg. an example is *sóersai* (or *sóersi*) Ep. 447, 455, 459, 463, 471, 479, 491, 495, 499, 503.

11°. Examples of the s-future active are the following: absolute forms: 2d sg. *lilessai* (leg. *lilessi*) Prol. 311. Laud 610 has here the 1st sg. *li[le]issiu*: 3d sg. *ain(s)-sium* Jan. 30, 1st pl. *rosme, resmai*, Prol. 257: conjunct forms: 2d sg. *at-chóis* Prol. 182, *ro-is* Ep. 146, *com-éir* Aug. 26, 3d sg. *ar-sil* Sep. 29 (=ar-sisl), *do-m-r-or-bai* Prol. 25, *tecma* Jan. 10. *rom-ain* Dec. 22. 1st pl. *r-isam* Dec. 17, 2d pl. *con-icsid* Ep. 393, 3d pl. *t-isat, tisset*, Ep. 24, 295, *do-airset* Sep. 20. Secondary forms are: 2d sg. *tiastae* Ep. 470, 3d sg. *téised* Ap. 27, *no-t-gesed* Ep. 217, *nach-at-r-issed, nach-at-r-isad*, Prol. 284.

12°. Other rare verbal forms are *molatha, molotha* Sep. 2, the 2d sg. imperative of *molur, molmae* Aug. 31, a participle pret. passive of the same verb, *glanna* Oc. 13, a participle pret. passive of *glanaim*, and *melaid* July 12, the absolute form of the 3d sg. pret. passive of *melim*.

---

* The MSS. have docoemnagtar, docóemnacair, docoemnactar, infra p. xxvi.., docoemnichtar, dochóemhnichter, Three Ir. Glosses, p. 127.

So much for the grammatical forms.

The syntax of the Calendar is often highly archaic. Thus, before the dat. or abl. plural the governing preposition is omitted where in Old-Irish prose it would, as a rule, be found. Examples are:—

iarna foebraib fennad, 'after flaying them with sword-edges,' Prol. 48.

ind locáin rogabtha déissib ocus tririb, 'the little places that were taken by duads and triads,' Prol. 209 B.

is dallchéilliu dóinib, 'it is a . . . . to men,' Prol. 316.

asrala saeth sétaib, 'went from ways of tribulations,' Ap. 3.

Cyriacus crochtha tri cétaib donasenai 'crucified Cyriac, with three hundreds, went to him,' May 12.

Ciar trib cétaib cáinib, 'Ciar with three fair hundreds,' Oc. 16.*

Like constructions are *socrais cech fleid forcraid*, Sep. 25, *it gessi cech cobair*, 'they are to be asked for every aid,' Sep. 28, where A interpolates the preposition *im*, to the ruin of the metre.

Again, the genitive, singular or plural, often precedes the noun that governs it. Thus:

la jége frithguam, 'with diligence of sharpness' (i.e., with keen diligence), Prol. 331.

martra mórsus dorus, 'martyrdom's door magnified them,' Jan. 30.

Enan rois rind solus, 'Enan, Rossmore's bright star,' Jan. 30.

Locha Uair ard áige, 'Loch Uar's high pillar,' Feb. 7.

nél co himbel, 'unto the clouds' rim,' Feb. 16.

sern Iacoib ordan, Lucas lir uas trilis 'announce (?) James' sovranty and Lucas over the sea's foam (lit. hair),' March 15.

lir dar doe, 'over the sea's rampart,' Mar. 22.

Martai for sluaig saithiu, 'on the troop of the host of March,' Mar. 31.

saeth sétaib, 'from ways of tribulations,' Ap. 3.

fri cruche cretair, 'to the relic of the Cross,' Ap. 12.

in echdromma dairiu 'in Echdruim's oakwood,' May 7.

batir Érend arda, 'they were Ireland's heights,' June 25 (Rawl. B 505).

---

* Examples of this construction are quoted in Goidelica, 2nd edition, 154, 155. Others are *tuailfidir Medib limsa*, 'he will be celebrated in lays by me,' St. Paul, i., 6. *Rogenad glasaib slabradaib*, O'Dav. 96, *doglinn glasaib temrach*, ibid. 73.

for September (leg. *Septembir*) *kalaind,* 'on September's calends,' Sep. 1.
Luscai la macc cuilind, 'with MacCuilinn of Lusk,' Sep. 6.
Septimber (leg.-*bir*) *iar snithib,* 'after September's swarms,' Sep. 30.
in Ochtimbir etan, 'in October's front,' Oct. 1.
la taimthene talgud, 'at death's quieting,' Oc. 29.
Ochtimbir ardethre, 'October's high end,' Oc. 31.
ar Bledna baile bélaib, 'before strong (Slieve) Bloom,' (lit. 'before strong Bladma's lips,') Nov. 20.
Nouimbir for sluagu 'on November's hosts,' Nov. 30.
sluind Decimbir kaloind, 'declare on December's kalend,' Dec. 1.
illiglatha lestar, 'in the beautiful Kingdom's vessel,' Ep. 22.
tar salmuire sretha, 'over ranks of main seas,' Ep. 238.*

In the second edition of the *Grammatica Celtica,* p. 915, Ebel has noticed this construction. He quotes *ar colla cisu* 'nostrae carnis census,' Ult. h. 5, and in *domuin cathim* 'mundi esum' i.e., comedere mundum, Br. h. 8. To these examples may be added *fidbaidæ fál* 'dumeti sepes' Sg. 203, and *di Moisten mine mrugaib* 'from smooth Moistiu's plains,' St. Paul, i.

Another archaism in our Calendar which is worth noticing is the occasional position of the accusative before the governing verb. Thus : *ata saidbri saigte* 'there are those who seek (eternal) wealth,' Prol. 162, *ar Crist cech mbáis brenis* 'for Christ's sake he vanquished every lust,' Ap. 4, *aurgais dogné* Nov. 13, 'thou shouldst make supplication,' *lucht fris fáilte* (leg. *fáilti*) *feraim* 'those to whom I make welcome,' Ep. 49, *félire roscrutus* 'I have sought out a calendar, Ep. 109, and *mórfertai doriqnis* 'who hast done great marvels,' Ep. 506.

The linguistic phenomena here adduced have led me to the conclusion above indicated, namely, that the Calendar was composed towards the end of the tenth century; and this conclusion seems confirmed by two lines in the Prologue, vv. 219, 220.

> de niurt dé dianmedair
> indiu deud domain,

that is, 'by God's virtue is vehemently announced to-day the world's end.' Here the poet obviously expresses the belief, so prevalent in the tenth century after Christ, that the world would come to an end in the year 1000.

---

* Another example is, I feel pretty sure, the corrupt last line of the quatrain for April 6, which should apparently be *i fiadat find fini,* 'in fair God's vineyard.'

IV.—*The Metre.*

The elaborate metre in which the Calendar is written is described in the Irish prose prefaces. Its essential characteristics are as follows :—

(1.) Each line of the quatrain contains six syllables.

(2.) The second and fourth lines have a final double rhyme, generally assonantal.

(3.) Each line ends (like the Ovidian pentameter) in a dissyllable, except where the last word is a foreign proper name.* Irish verbs compounded with inseparable prefixes are, for this purpose, regarded as being *in tmesi.* Thus *con-sáidu* Jan. 23, *for-tn-iadae* May 31, *ar-don-sela, don-r-ema* June 23, are treated as if they were dissyllables. So the proclitics—the article, possessive pronouns, verbal prefixes, prepositions, verb substantive, negative particle, are not regarded as part of the word to which they are prefixed. Examples may be found in every quatrain. On the other hand, the pronominal enclitics *-sa,* *-sin, -siu,* and *-som* are deemed (for metrical purposes) to convert the monosyllables to which they are annexed into dissyllables. Thus *mór-sa, buan-sa, n-án-sa, nuall sa,* Prol. 301–306, *már-sin, da-sin,* June 20, *réir-siu* Prol. 269, *mind-som* Prol. 257.

(4.) In each quatrain two, three or more accented syllables begin with the same letter—all the vowels being, for this purpose, deemed identical.

When there are two of these alliterations [in the first half of the quatrain†] the metre is called *réid-rinnard dá n-ard* ' smooth *rinnard* of two alliterations' ; when there are three, it is called *réid-rinnard trí n-ard,* when four, *réid rinnard cethri n-ard.* The example of the first kind, quoted from the Calendar by the writer of the preface is,

For kalaind mis *M*arta
uit *m*árda frinn-guide, March 1.

His example of the second kind is,

Ro síl *d*álach *d*óine
toided in rí remain, Jan. 1.,

where *tóided* should apparently be *dóided* (=dofeded.)

---

* See for example, *M*órmartra *R*edanis, Jan. 3, Bás caid Aquilini, Jan. 4, Martra Luciani, Jan. 7, Etsecht Egemoni, Jan. 9. When a dissyllabic noun is compounded with an adjective, the adjective is disregarded—e.g. cain-ésce, Jan. 3, duib-réa, Jan. 5.

† The examples given in the Irish prefaces seem to justify the words in brackets.

His example of the third kind is,

>Lassar gréine áine
>apstol Erenn áge, March 17,

where the four vowels *a*, *a*, *é* and *ó* alliterate.*

Furthermore, there are two metrical phenomena, which though not essential, are of constant occurrence in our Calendar. One of these (the *conachlonn* of modern Irish grammarians) is what the writer of the Irish prose preface in Rawl. B. 512, calls *fidrad cubaid etir tosaichib na rann ocus deridib na rann eli* 'an harmonious *fidrad* (?) between the beginnings of the quatrains and the ends of the other (i.e. the preceding) quatrains.' This agreement may be either complete, as in the case of the third quatrain of the Prologue (the first line of which is identical with the last line of the second quatrain), or partial. Thus the beginning of the second quatrain of the Prologue—*a gel-grían*—partially harmonizes with *gréne gile*, the end of the first quatrain. Do *rígrad no-molur*, the beginning of the fourth quatrain, partially harmonizes with *ar molad dot rigraid*, the end of the third. So in the quatrains for the first seven days of February. *Erenn* and *Airitiu*, *aire* and *andreas*, each begin with a vowel; and each of the pairs *digrais* and *donroemat*, (Sim)*froni* and *Fronius*, *crésen* and *crochda*, *mile* and *Mellan*, begins with the same consonant. The object of this device is, of course, to aid the memory. There is something like it in a French poem quoted in Disraeli's *Curiosities of Literature*, and Mr. Gladstone, I think, has alleged that the Homeric Catalogue of Ships is so arranged that the end of each section suggests the beginning of the next one. I believe, too, that in Welsh poetry there is a similar device, called *adgymeriad*.

The other metrical phenomenon above referred to is an occasional ornament produced by making the final word of a third line rhyme with the first or second word of the fourth line. Thus, to confine ourselves to the Prologue and the months of January, February, and March.

>rom-berthar buaid *lére*
>a-rí *gréne* gile (Prol. 3, 4)
>conamraib cach *solad*
>ar-*molad* dot rígraid (Prol. 11, 12)
>cáin-popul cul-*lígdath*
>in *rígrad* im-rordus (Prol. 19, 20)

* As all these vowels are different, they would in **Anglo-Saxon** form a perfect vowel-alliteration, March, Comparative Grammar, p. 224.

is torba dian-*promam*
in *prolach* do-beram (Prol. 143, 144)
la sessilbe *mbuada*
cluana móir mac-núis (Prol. 183, 184)
it fása cen *adrad*
amal *lathrach* lugdach (Prol. 207, 208)
rolin flaith dé *athar*
uem *talam* la trethan (Prol. 215, 216)
dorónta col-*léce*
slébe dona glinnib (Prol. 239, 240)
German martir *uasal*
Cuanna credal crésen (Feb. 4)
Daman mil mind *martrai* (MSS. martra)
co-*macraid* cáin crochdu (Feb. 12)
dobreth brigach *nualann*
sil *m-buadach* lech n-érenn (Feb. 13)
la sceith scél a *annaich*
demon *damair* indel (Feb. 16)
for óenlith lán-*tene*
gene Tarcellorum (Feb. 26)
Carthach rígda *ruamach*
Ciaran *sluagach* saigre (March 5)
int-organ cét *buada*
Grigoir *Ruama* rolaind (March 12)
Abbán doss óir *aingl ch*
Finan *laindrech* lobar (March 16)
la Tiamda ro-*rímed*
fiche *míled* mochta (March 18)
Scire cáin car *tredan*
Mochta *credal* craibdech (March 24)

This ornament also occurs in Maelísu's hymn (Goid.² 174), one of the few other Irish compositions in *rinnard* which have yet been found:

a Ísu, ron-*nócba*,
ron-*sóera* do spirut.

In the quatrains for Sep. 9 and Nov. 28, the first and third lines, as well as the second and fourth, have final rhymes.

I have dwelt at some length on the characteristics of this metre, partly because nothing is more important for restoring the corrupt text of a poem than a right understanding of the metrical rules by which the author was guided; partly because observation of the technical skill of the writer of the poem now printed, is almost the only source of pleasure derivable from his work; and partly because Ezzardi's recent suggestion* that the metre of the Calendar of Oengus appears to have been the model of the Skaldic *dróttkvætt*, especially the *hattlausa*, makes this Irish *rinnard* matter of interest for Teutonic, as well as for Celtic, scholars.

V.—*The Contents of the Poem.*

After an invocation of Christ, who is called the king of the white sun, the poet adverts to the consolation which he, in his penitential sufferings, has found in celebrating the saints. He describes (vv. 29-48) the various modes of martyrdom which the soldiers of Jesus (*mílid Isu*) suffered with cheerful heroism. They now (unlike the great pagan kings) enjoy their eternal reward with Mary's Son, while their bodies are enshrined in sparkling gold (vv. 49-84). Herod and Pilate are then contrasted with Christ, Nebuchadnezzar with Paul the Monk, Herod and his Queen with John the Baptist, Nero with Peter and Paul, Pilate's queen with Mary the Virgin. Then come some reflections on the nothingness of earthly power and mundane potentates, as compared with the love of Mary's Son, and with the lowly soldiers (*amsáin*) of Jesus. In Ireland, for example, Tara has perished while Armagh remains with her crowd of champions of wisdom. King Loiguire's glory has departed; but St. Patrick's name lives on. Various ruined strongholds and cities of the Pagan Irish—Raith Cruachan, Aillinn, Emain, and others—are then contrasted with the monasteries flourishing in the poet's time. The forgotten renown of pagan chieftains, like Donnchad, Bran of Berba, Domnall, is contrasted with the abiding glory of Christ and divers Irish saints. The poet then breaks out into a laudation of Jesus, prays for success in the work in hand, and concludes by describing its nature (vv. 249-340).

Then comes the Calendar, which consists of 365 quatrains (or 366, if we

---

* In Paul und Braune's *Beitræge zur Geschichte der deutschen sprache und literatur*, 1878, ss. 583, 584. Ezzardi cites from O'Donovan's Irish Grammar the quatrain for March 17, and says "Dies versmass scheint das vorbild des dróttkv., zunächst der hattlausa, gewesen zu sein."

include the one for *bisextus* in the note at Feb. 23), commences with the feast of the Circumcision and ends with that of St. Sylvester (Dec. 31). With Sylvester, Lochan and Endae, two Irish saints, are commemorated. The entries are generally of the most meagre description, consisting of the name of the Irish or foreign saint commemorated, with some standing epithet or standing phrase tacked on so as to comply with the exigencies of metre, rhyme and alliteration. But sometimes brief reference is made to a tale, legend, or tradition. Thus at Jan. 27, the wild story of Liban or Muirgen, the mermaid, told in *Lebor na huidre* pp. 40, 41 ;* at Feb. 6 the legend of Lucia, who could not be dragged to martyrdom ; at Feb. 13, the tradition of the introduction of bees into Ireland; at Feb. 16 the legend of Juliana and the Devil; at March 9 the legend of the forty Cappadocian soldiers to whom the sun shone at the bottom of a lake; at April 14 the tradition (also mentioned in Fiacc's hymn) that Bishop Tassach gave the communion to the dying Patrick ; at Ap. 17 the pathetic tale of the martyrdom of Donnan of Eig ; at Aug. 7 the seven sleepers of Ephesus; at Sep. 4 the legend of the orphans playing round Ultan who saved them from starving; at Sep. 29 the legend of Michael and Antichrist ; at Oct. 23 the wounding of Christ by Longinus ; at Nov. 23 the legend of Clemens and the sea ; at Dec. 8 that of Egbert and the skinless coracle ; and at Dec 21 the death of St. Thomas in India.

After the Calendar comes the Epilogue. After referring generally to the Calendar and acknowledging Christ's help in composing it, the poet prays for eternal life along with the saints whom he has commemorated. It declares that they have blessed whomsoever shall sing it, and that they will come to attend him at the time he shall die. The poet then mentions the sources of his compilation—the *Pairt* of Ambrose ; the *Sensus* of Hilary ; the *Antigraph* of Jerome ; the *Martyrology* of Eusebius, and 'Ireland's host of books—the Calendars of the men of the Gael.' He again refers to the beneficial effects of reciting his poem, the last mentioned being—

> His soul without conflict
> In heaven with whiteness.
> Behind him, after attaining,
> His grave's dew shall heal.

* The Senchaid quoted in L.U. 40 b cites the very words of our poem: Muirgein is *gein com-baadaib*.

Like curative powers were ascribed to the grave of Colomb Cille (*ar noicad a drucht no a ur ar cach ngalar*, Amra Chol.), and see Grimm's *Deutsche Mythologie*, 1129.

The poet then classifies the persons commemorated—angels, prophets, apostles, martyrs, bishops, saints, priests, monks, and virgins of Ireland, who will all, he says, befriend him. After praying the saints to beseech Christ on his behalf, he adjures Jesus by the sufferings of saints and penitents, by the offerings of his Body and Blood, by his Manhood and Godhead, to grant him what he is contending for. The rest of the Epilogue is occupied with longings to pass from the afflictions of the world, and prayers to be saved like Elijah and Enoch, Noah, Abraham, Lot, Jonah, Isaac, Jacob, the people of Israel, Job, Samson, David, Susannah, the three children, Tobit, the people of Nineveh, Daniel, Moses, Paul, and Peter, John 'from the vat of fire,' Martin 'from the priest of the idol,' Patrick 'from the poisonous drink at Tara,' Coemgin 'from the falling of the mountain.'

The poem concludes with another prayer to be saved, and an entreaty that the saints commemorated may convey us to our solace.

It must be confessed that in all this long poem there is not a trace of imaginative power or of observation of nature. Here, as in almost all the Celtic poetry that I have read, substance is ruthlessly sacrificed to form, and the observance of the rigorous rules of metre seems regarded as an end in itself. Touches characteristic of the poet's time and country are almost wholly absent. I have already noticed his expression of the belief, current in the tenth century, that the world was about to come to an end. The quatrain for May 17, in which the poet treats three saints as if they were three Irish chieftains making a raid in their war chariots into heaven, is about the only passage that can be quoted as racy of the soil.* It is, perhaps, an adaptation of a formula inherited from earlier bardic poetry. The frequent metaphorical use of words meaning diadem (*mind*), flame (*breo, lassar, bith*), gold (*ór*), pillar (*áge, uaitne*), and sun (*grian*), may also be due to secular song.

---

* As to using the technical language of plundering for the expression of religious sentiment, see Miscellany of the Celtic Society, 338.

VI.—*The Glosses.*

That most of the glosses on our poem were written a long time (perhaps three hundred years) after it was composed, appears from the uncertainty of the glossographer as to the meanings of several words, and from the mistakes which he occasionally commits. Thus, *ciatcóis*, Prol. 182, is glossed by *cia etsi. no cia indise* 'though thou hearest or though thou declarest.'

rindaig, Jan. 12, is explained by *glicc* 'cunning' or *rinn cith* 'a sharp point.' In the Franciscan copy the glossographer has rightly .i. *ro-innestar runa crist* 'he related Christ's mysteries,' and the true reading is *Crist as rúna rindid*, a tmesis for *as-r-indid rúna Crist*.

digna, Jan. 22, is glossed by *cen táire no cen tróige no cen dimecin* 'without reproach, or without wretchedness, or without contempt,' and at Feb. 9 by *neimgné* 'non-form,' .i. *drochgne* 'bad form':

consádu, Jan. 23, is glossed by *comsaigim no comaidim iat isin rann* 'I mention or praise them together in the quatrain':

donrrnat, Feb. 3, is explained by *ronairimit no ro(n)nertat no robet romaind* 'may they protect us, or may they strengthen us, or may they be before us':

táthus, Feb. 5, .i. *rothinoil no ata duit* 'he collected or thou hast':

mor a laidib lamais, Feb. 27, .i. *mongenar dún lamthana a thabarta illaidib. no dia lamais a faisnes o laidib. no lamais nomen poetæ* 'happy for us to be allowed (?) to mention him in lays, or if we dare to manifest him with lays: or *Lamais* is the name of a poet.'

cotaruicset, May 8, .i. *fuarutar ruice ocus imdergtha ar crist. no ar crist catha ruicset .i. ro chathaigset ar crist no doroegsat .i. tanic ruice doib im crist. no cotaruibset .i. arrubart[at]ar ríth no roimchuirset anéri. ar crist* 'they found shame and reproaches for Christ.' Or [the right reading is] *ar crist catha ruicset* i.e. they fought for Christ. Or . . . . . i.e. shame came to them for Christ. Or [the right reading is] *cotaruibset* i.e. 'they enjoyed, or they bore their burden for Christ.'

oid, June 1, .i. *ceol no airfitiud no bindius. Oid menman rl. i. uigid. bid din. oid .i. uglud no aithiugud menman. no oid .i. indethmig .i. tabair dot aire. no oid. bindig. bid din. oda .i. adbond* et unde [leg. inde?] dicitur *od .i.*

binnes et melodia, 'music, or playing, or harmony.' *Oid menmun* etc., i.e., it sharpens: now *oid* is a sharpening or whetting of the mind. Or *oid*, i.e., consider, or give to thy heed. Or *oid*, i.e. make harmony. For *oda* is a song, et inde dicitur *od*, i.e. harmony.'

See also *bille*, Aug. 8, *ainbil*, Nov. 9. and many other cases in which the glossographer gives a variety of inconsistent explanations, leaving the reader to take his choice among them.

The following are instances in which the glossographer gives only one explanation, and this is obviously wrong:

ogri, Prol. 92 (a scribe's corruption of *óerí* 'young king,' 'prince,') is explained by *ríg comlan* 'a complete king.'

séntai, Prol. 100 ('was sained') is explained by *atchi*, 'sees.'

Lastly, rare words and forms, such as *dallchéilliu*, Prol. 316, *suacht*, Ap. 19, *toscai*, July 19, *cathor*, Aug. 15, *sobarthan*, Ep. 57, *colba*, Ep. 74, *at-um-didmae*, Ep. 494, *ar-dom-tíasi*, Ep. 374, *roach*, Ep. 129, are left unexplained, or (as in the case of *sudmach*, Oc. 27) an absurd legend is invented to account for the supposed meaning.

It is clear enough to any one capable of judging of such evidence, that the traditional explanations given by the Irish glossographers of their old poetry do not go back to the period of the production of the poetry itself, nor even to a time when that poetry was fully understood, and that these explanations (like those of the Hindú commentators on the Veda[*]) are not only insufficient, but to some extent misleading. In making these remarks, I do not mean to depreciate the native scholiasts, but only to furnish ground for the proposition that in interpreting the Calendar of Oengus it is necessary to apply the scientific processes of modern philology, and especially those of comparison of texts and of juxtaposition, that is to say, of placing together all the passages which are akin in diction or meaning. An attempt to do this latter will be found in the Glossarial Index, which occupies pp. ccix.–cccxxix. of the present paper. Inadequate as that Index doubtless is, it has at least enabled me to avoid the errors noted below, found in a copy of a translation of our

[*] See J. Muir, *On the Interpretation of the Veda*; Journal of the Royal Asiatic Society, New Series, Vol. II., p. 303: Whitney, *The Translation of the Veda*, Oriental and Linguistic Studies, 1st Series, p. 100.

Calendar made by an eminent Irish scholar, the late Mr. O'Curry, which is now in my possession, and to which I have constantly referred.*

* Prol. romberthar, 5, *that I may attain*. romain aratrogbus, 17, *to wash me from what I have contracted*. imrordus, 21, *I celebrate*. domrorbai, 25, *this hath been given to me*. ritroich [leg. rith romith] in slogsa, Prol. 28, *of which these hosts testified*. soréid, Prol. 30, *possible*. . iarrannaib, Prol. 38, *into divisions*. cenciniech, Prol. 42, *infuriated*. bithgobait bil-loscud, Prol. 62, *are suffering eternal scorching*. craibdig, Prol. 79, *afflicted*. hit aidble, Prol. 81, *in high places*. faroches, Prol. 86, *who crucified*. arngérait, Prol. 90, *our living son*. dorodbad, Prol. 96, *is oblivious*. sentai, Prol. 100, *he looks out upon*. réim culad, Prol. 107, *stern decree*. atsluinne, Prol. 110, *is heard in*. atchissiu, Prol. 150, *we see*. fororbairt incretem, 173, *the increase of the Faith*. ciatchois, 182, *are heard*. cit uallaig rig talman, 245, *the contentious Kings of earth*. ciarosme fomniudsom dorige aramsom, 257, 258, *though I wished to be silent on his greatness, it is necessary to rhyme him*. bad sonairt aru-airle, 261, *great shall be our reward*. nachatrissad münnter, 284, *whose family I shall not enumerate*. ismenand aruire, 289, *their chiefs are quite manifest*. regmai co[n]nach dichel cech dirinch don bliadain, 291, 292, *we shall select with all our endeavours all that is righteous in the year*. lilessai, 309, 311, *a sufficiency*. manithueni samlaid, 313, *if this did not adopt*. flaithem noem nanduile, 337, *heaven of the saints and creatures*.

January: imrordus, 7, *I now speak of*. án suba, 11, *the unpleasant*. crist as runaid rindaig (leg. rúna rindid), 12, *in the mysteries of Christ is acute*. frisrogabsat rige, 16, *with him they took sovereignty*. rousnadat dond rigu, 23, *they have passed into the Kingdom*. rousnadat diarn dilins, 29, *have gone to our inheritance*. ainsium ar lin amus enan rois rind solos, 30, *they abode with the number of soldiers*. Eman of Ross solus Point. benait . . . barr find, 31, *they carry Barrfinn*.

February. morait. 1, *they adorn*. caid, 1, *chosen*. tathus mor maith aire, 5, *that will bring much good to you*. hua án indecis, 8, *the grandson of An the Poet*. mainech, 19, *preceptor*. lanfrecra, 22, *abundant in works*. ronsnada, 23, *has gone*. fedba (leg. febda), 24, *widower*. mor alaidib [leg. mar ó laidib] lamais, 27, *great (our happiness) to be permitted in our poems*.

March. slan doe, 2, *full of godliness*. feil, 3, *the festival*. ronsnaidet, 6, *they passed*. nidlig diarnduain dignac, 7, *who on our poem will bring no contempt*. Hit coimti, 11, *he is the associate*. crochais colaind, 12, *his body was hanged*. ronsnaide mocormoc don bithcoemnu bias, 13, *Mochoemoc passed away to the good life that awaits us*. Patraic comeit mile, 17, *Patrick with many thousands*. mochta, 18, *that were sacrificed*. frisnig etla ainbech, 24, *who shed tears in abundance*. tusslucud, 27, *redemption*. Donrogra ronsnaidea sechpiana ronsena maria ronmora, 28, *to the Kingdom has she sped by pains she being sanctified, Maria the beatified*.

April. socrait. Kl. apreil ambrois comeit nglaine, 1, *he makes smooth the kalend of April, Ambrose of great purity*. gerait, 7, *acute*. bledech, 7, *bellowing*. Ronain moedoc mainech, 11, *Moedoc of Main fasted*. Dalais andsa opair, 12, *he consented to the obnoxious operation*. gerait crist caiu deochain pol deochain donrema, 13, *the acute in Christ was gently severed, Paul the deacon was made of the number*. doreith duit forsidit, 16, *who quickly flew on her being*

Before leaving these glosses, it seems worth remarking that they contain some negative evidence as to the place at which they were compiled. Thus,

summoned. co ibu. áu soad asuacht chorpain chriad, 19, *to Jesus the replenished with happiness, out of a cold body of earth.* Romain pilip aspal, 22, *Toru was Philip the Apostle.* sochla dine, 24, *has brought happiness to people.* cesais, 26, *passed through.*

May. and tindscan, 1, *the commencement.* carsat crist as diliu indeach dromma dairiu, 7, *they loved Christ most fervently, Indeach of Drom Dairiu.* ronsnada, 10, *has passed.* scorsit, 17, *they have rest.* Ronsuada cohainglin, 28, *by angels have been carried away.* ronsnadat, 29, *have been carried.* ingen aillen inmain *a beautiful, lovely virgin.* mi mái comet mile dia primfeil fortniadac, 31, *the month of May of many thousands, of its chief festivals we conclude.*

June. mor ndidnad, 8, *of great purity.* atmer, 13, *I should have been mad.* masa leir ronfethis, 24, *fully I have preserved.* lamluoc glan geldai, 25, *Lamluoc the pure and brilliant.*

July. moras matha, 1, *the magnifying of Matthew.* roir crist sid slemnn amorseirce la onnan, 5, *for Christ they smoothly watched in great love and fear.* Conrualaid co aingliu, 12, *with angels he eloped.* lamsiloc donrigraid, 13, *Lamsiloc unto the Kings.* fosduil, 15, *who were sent.* ron morat anitge, 17, *magnified be their prayer.* at meirb manit frescai, 19, *we are cowardly if we do not seek.* lambiu indsi causcraid, 22, *Lambin of Inis Causcraidh.*

August. doraraice mor mbrige, 1, *Doraraic of great power.* inmain feil conani, 3, *Inmain of the noble festival.* Rona[i]n ciriacus, 28, *invoke Ciriacus.* bid coleri, 29, *do it in full.*

September. Luscai la mac cuilind, 6, *Lusca with MacCuilinn.* la tiandai iar sótaib, 8, *nor of fatigue on the world's journey.* maire mur co talcu, 15, *the great, important building.* nuall cech genai, 16, *the pride of every chaste person.* arndala, 20, *our ways.* rohir, 23, *who sought.*

October. aslondud cech gena, 3, *is to be mentioned above all births.* raith ar-rém-sin, 16, *gifted was his career.* comeit meithle, 31, *with his numerous co-labourers.*

November. mind senaid, 3, *a sanctifying chief.* ccalmgur a slige, 7, *their death was fearful.* tindscau lexu leri, 14, *began the comprehensive Lex.* corgus mafutbotha, 15, *to the Lent if you submit.* arbledma bale belaib, 20, *a noble vessel with strong mouth.* uad duthain, 28, *without gloom.*

December. frem, 12, *tree.* donrogna hi righaith rig ronuc ar siuur, 14, *called into the royal kingdom was a king who espoused our sister.* atrovis, 16, *who were with him.* sluag mor imeradi, 20, *the great host of Imeradi.* inrrandaib, 21, *torn to pieces.* lamthemneoc don rigraid, 23, *Lamthemneoc one of the Kings.* lamchua caim cocrait *Lamchua the beautiful in concord.* arricfae, 30, *they reached to.*

Epilogue. fortsella, 4, *we have occupied.* ceuecmaingsem aurain, 7, *we have brought them in triumph.* cerobaige, 27, *though 'twere denied.* fomruirmius, 38, *of my enumeration.* mor dothorba, 74, *much of their suffering.* acht cuimbrigud indsce fosoas docuibded, 123, 124, *but in the strength of art with proper knowledge harmonize them.* la bethaid a anmae, 169, *with the food of his soul.* cocundai, 170, *shall he share.* romain gres anguide, 226, *I have earned their prayers.* condomraib itrigiu, 359, *who enjoy the wonders of thy Kingdom.* conicid mo chabair ol is mor forn gaire, 381, 382, *I deserve that ye help me, for much have I served you.* rocresiu uile, 427, *thou lovest in fulness.* dabaig, 540, *furnace.*

they were not written in Leinster, otherwise the glossographer would not have thought it necessary to say, as he does at Prol. 189, that Aillenn was a fort in that Province (*dún fil il-Laignib*). Nor were they written in Munster, otherwise he would not have said (Jan. 1) *sic dicit in muimnech. ni fuil erain duit and* 'so saith the Munster-man, 'thou hast not a superfluity there.' Nor in the Highlands, otherwise *cae* (June 10) would not have been glossed by *focal albanach* 'a Scottish word'; and the phrase *ni leic susten dam* would not have been introduced (July 10) by '*ut dixit int-albanach.*'

VII.—*The Notes.*

Every copy of the Calendar that I have seen contains a body of notes in Irish, or mediæval Latin, or a mixture of both, written between the lines of the poem, or on the margins, or immediately after the set of quatrains devoted to each month. They contain much matter of interest to the topographer and hagiologist. They have somewhat, too, for the writer (if ever he shall appear) of the natural history of Irish society.

There is little or nothing, indeed, to throw light on the civil government or military institutions of the country,* on social observances, on the relations of the sexes,† on the relations of parents to children, and fosterers to fostered.‡ on the industrial system, on the industrial arts§—facts which, as Mr. Herbert Spencer has pointed out,¶ are needed to enable us to understand how a nation has grown and organized itself. But there are legends illustrating not less essential facts, such as the religious ideas, discipline, and constitution of the Church. Consider, for instance, the story of Scothine and the two

---

* The journey of Oengus Maccu-Loigse, Jan. 20, to enter the service of the King of Connaught, may be noticed in this connexion.

† The story of Dubthach's wife and his handmaid, Feb. 1, and the legend of the freeing of women from liability to war-service, Sep. 23, may here be referred to.

‡ See the explanation of *mac nisse*, Sep. 3. The instances of naming persons after their mothers (Mac Cúla, Ap. 5, and p. lxxiii., Mac Lémna, p. lxxxiii.) may perhaps point to the time when paternity was uncertain, and there was a system of kinship through females only, see M'Lennan's *Studies in Ancient History*, 1876, pp. 101–171 and 176 (where he cites 'the tradition that in Greece, before Cecrops, children always bore the names of their mothers'); see also in the same book, p. 289.

§ See the story of Etchen's ploughing, Feb. 11, the passage about the cattle and horses kept by Ciaran, March 5, the mention of the practice of drying corn in a kiln, Aug. 19.

¶ *Education*: pp. 34, 35.

maidens, Jan. 2, which reminds one of the practice of the early Christian sect of the Apostolici, and of Robert d'Arbrissel, founder of Fontevrault:* the instance of saints exchanging their respective ailments, Jan. 16 : the horrible acts of asceticism attributed to Findchú, Nov. 25 : the stone kept in Ultan's mouth during lent, Dec. 22 : the dress of Ciaran and his dinner, March 5 : the lenten fare of the Welsh bishops, Jan. 31, S. Columba's nettle porridge, June 9 : the 'orders of penitence' conferred on S. Brigit, Feb. 1 : the worship of relics, Feb. 8, June 21. There are superstitions, too, which obviously originated in the times of heathenism, and justify M. Renan's statement as to the Celts : nulle race ne prit le christianisme avec autant d'originalité, et en s'assujettissant à la foi commune, ne conserva plus obstinément sa physionomie nationale. Consider only the legend of the birth of Ciaran of Saigir, March 5, the tale of Silán of the Hair, Sep. 11, the loathsome legend of Créd's pregnancy, May 22 (so like the story of the nymph Adriká and Uparicharas, Mahábh. Adi-parva, 2371-2392) : the too brief allusion, April 7, to Beenat and the golden salmon : the story of Fuinche the Rough, and her miraculous dive under Lough Erne, Jan. 21, the group of myths about Brigit, Feb. 1, especially that of the pillar of fire passing from her head to the ridge of the church : the story of the yew of Mughna, Dec. 10 : the practice of exchanging names in token of brotherly union, a practice which doubtless rests upon the notion, common among barbarous tribes, that a name is part of the person named, or, to use Mr. Spencer's words, vitally connected with the owner : whether the practice of giving names from events which occurred on or about the child's birthday rests on a superstition, I am unable to say. We have an early European example of this practice in the Odyssey, xix., 406-409, where Autolycus says—

γαμβρὸς ἐμὸς θύγατίρ τε, τίθεσθ' ὄνομ', ὅττι κεν εἴπω
πολλοῖσιν γὰρ ἐγώ γε ὀδυσσάμενος τόδ' ἱκάνω,
ἀνέρασιν ἠδὲ γυναιξὶν ἀνὰ χθόνα πουλυβότειραν·
τῷ δ' Ὀδυσεὺς ὄνομ' ἔστω ἐπώνυμον.

And many examples of it are found in the notes to our Calendar. See, for instance, the story of Féchín the 'little raven,' Jan. 20, of Giallán the 'pledgeling,' Oc. 2, of Moling, 'well-leapt,' June 17, of Mo-chua mac ochai, 'my

*See also *The Knight de la Tour Landry*, chap. cxxxiv., 'How the holy ladye approuved the heremyte.' And compare Todd's *Life of S. Patrick*, p. 91, an article in *The Saturday Review* for 13th July, 1867, p. 65, and Yule's *Marco Polo*, II., 353-357.

Kick, son of Armpit,' Aug. 4, of Colman duib Chuilind 'Colman (son of) Cuilenn's ink,' Nov. 24.

Special evidence of the intellectual condition of the nation is wanting; but the general impression produced by these notes is that the persons by and for whom they were written were, in the kind and amount of their education, and in their way of thinking, on a very low level. Whether this was due to the decay of an early civilization, or (as I believe) to the arrested development of Irish society, need not here be further considered.

Of the degree of aesthetic culture to which the Irish had attained, these notes supply but little evidence. Architecture is faintly illustrated by the three mentions of the *daurthach* (oratory?), which appears from the story of Derbfraich, April 4, to have been wholly or in part built of wood. Metal-work, caligraphy, and, apparently, illuminations, are referred to in the notes on Daig, son of Cairell, Aug. 18, and Cairnech the Bald, March 5. As to music, the notes are silent, save in the second quatrain, cited at June 23, which reminds one of the Birds of Rhiannon. See also the gloss on June 1. Poetry, or, to speak more correctly, the art of verse, is sufficiently exemplified by the metrical narratives of Itu and Jesus, Jan. 15, of the healing of Constantine, Jan. 18, of Ciaran's birth, March 5, of Créd's pregnancy, May 22, and by the numerous quatrains scattered through the annotations. As to the metrical narratives, it is worth observing that they are generally preceded by the story told in simple prose, and that this arrangement is exactly that of the stories among the brown Polynesians, and reminds one of the Buddhist literature, where we also find the same story told twice, once in metre (*gâthâ*) and once in prose.[*] The quatrains occasionally have some poetic value. I would instance the pair of verses about the murder in a mill of Cerball's grandsons (May 21)—

O mill
How much wheat thou hast ground!
This was not a grinding of oats:
Thou groundest Cerball's grandsons.

The grain the mill grindeth
Is not oats, but it is red wheat.
Of the fruit of the great Tree is
The feed of Maelodrain's mill.

[*] Max Müller, *Hibbert Lectures*, 75.

and the quatrain ascribed to Moling (June 17)—

> When I am among my elders,
> I am proof that sport is forbidden.
> When I am among the mad (young) folk,
> They think that I am the youngest.

Compare the scholion—

> σύν μοι πῖνε, συνήβα, συνέρα, συστεφανηφόρει,
> σύν μοι μαινομένῳ μαίνεο, σὺν σώφρονι σωφρόνει.

Still nearer is the boast of Theognis :

> ἐν μὲν μαινομένοις μάλα μαίνομαι, ἐν δὲ δικαίοις
> πάντων ἀνθρώπων εἰμὶ δικαιότατος.

There is nothing in the notes to throw light on the daily lives of the people—their food, their homes, and their amusements—unless, indeed, the reference to horse-racing in the ancient poem at Jan. 17, which is ascribed to the Devil, and of which, by the way, two quatrains occur in a codex of the 9th century, preserved in the monastery of St. Paul, Carinthia. Lastly, the picture of the national life of a people should, according to Mr. Spencer, exhibit the morals, theoretical and practical, of all classes, as indicated in their laws, habits, proverbs, deeds. In this connexion may be noticed St. Maelruain's reason, July 7, for not killing the man who stole his door-keeper's cow, which, it is to be hoped, is not a fair specimen of the ethical teaching of the old Irish ecclesiastics : the mention of *eric* or mulct (May 16) for slaying men under a saint's safeguard : the practice of giving *ratha* 'guarantees' or 'securities' (Feb. 21) : the four *cána* or laws of Ireland (March 17, Sep. 23), as to slaying clerics, slaying women, stealing (slaying?) oxen, and transgressing on Sunday : the old usage of women going to battle, so vividly illustrated by the story of Adamnán and his mother Ronait, Sep. 23 ; and the practice of exposing infants, of which the story of Molua, Aug. 4, seems to furnish an instance.*

---

* I take the following from Smith's *Dictionary of Christian Antiquities*: I am unable here in Calcutta to verify the reference.

"In a collection of Irish canons, ascribed to the end of the seventh century, is one on infants cast forth in the Church, which enacts, in very uncouth and obscure Latin, that such an infant shall be a slave to the Church unless sent away, and that seven years' penance is to be borne by those who cast infants forth.—(Bk. xli. c. 22.)"

VIII.—*Corrigenda and Addenda.*

Having thus roughly indicated the notes that seem of some importance for the natural history of Irish society ; having also mentioned the manuscripts of our poem, noticed its alleged author, considered its language and metre, given a précis of its contents, and criticised some of the glosses, it now only remains to set down the corrigenda and the more important addenda which have occurred to me during the last nine years. The list of errors is large, but I have no doubt that it should be larger, and that the researches of Professor Hennessy and of continental scholars, such as Windisch, Zimmer, and Ascoli, will soon clear up obscurities which are now to me impenetrable.

Page.
xiii. Text, col. 3, line 20, *for* 'inrórdus' *read* 'imrordus.'
      Translation, §17, *for* ' from [the evil] I have got' *read* ' for I have sung it.'
           " 25, *for* 'him bestow on' *read* 'let it profit.'
xiv.   " 33, *for* 'pierced' *read* 'impaled.'
          " 37, *read* 'they were torn, according to (historic) verses, with very rigid spearpoints.'
          " 45, *for* 'stretching' *read* 'persecution.'
          " 49, notwithstanding O'Clery, I suspect that *fiam* is here a substantive, and that the line in which it occurs should be rendered ' whose virulence is mighty.' Compare line 330.
xv. Text, col. 3, *for* ' 72 ' *read* ' 73.'
      Translation, §65, *for* ' champions' *read* ' sinners.'
xvi.   " 89, *for* ' perfect king' *read* ' prince (of the kings of the earth).'
          " 97, 101, } *for* ' hath been' *read* ' was.'
          " 105, *for* ' joyful multitude' *read* ' multitude of pæans.'
          " 109, *for* ' not worthy,' &c., *read* ' to a believer it seems unworthy that he should utter Nero's name.'
          " 113, *for* ' he was not godly' *read* ' it was not a consecrated thing.'
xvii.   " 117, *for* ' a centre ' *read* ' the forefront.'
          " 133, *for* ' we love them,' &c., *read* ' whom we love not, it is not known, nor has there remained, the name of one of them on earth.'
          " 137, *for* ' hath been' *read* ' was.'
xviii. " 149, *for* ' O man' *read* ' whose strongholds.'
             for ' servants' *read* ' soldiers.'
          " 169, *for* ' Was ' *read* ' Hath been.'

Page.		
xix.	Translation,	177, *after* 'Crúachan' *insert* 'it.'
	,,	185, *for* 'did it' *read* 'would perform:' *for* 'they' *read* 'ye' (the right reading is probably ni beth).
	,,	193, *after* 'burgh' *insert* 'it.'
xx.	,,	209, *for* 'with twos' *read* 'by twos.'
xxi.	,,	265, *for* 'have done' *read* 'would make.'
	,,	269, *for* 'have done' *read* 'would do.'
xxiii.	,,	329, *for* 'heedful attention' *read* 'keen diligence.'
xxvi.	,,	2, *for* 'Eirge' *read* 'Airic.'
	,,	3, *for* 'clergy' *read* 'train.'
xxvii.	,,	11, *for* 'From' *read* 'Out of.'
	,,	12, *for* 'clergy' *read* 'train.'
	,,	13, *for* 'their blessing be unto us' *read* 'we have their blessing:' *for* 'Poitiers' *read* 'Poitou.'
	,,	14, *for* 'Lord' *read* 'God:' *for* 'sage' *read* 'elder.'
xxviii.	,,	15, *for* 'underwent' *read* 'succoured.'
xxix.	,,	27, *after* 'Mœda' *insert* '(my God).'
xxix.	,,	§28, *for* 'seven' *read* 'eight.'
xxx.	,,	30, *for* 'of Ros(mór) (the) bright headland' *read* 'Rossmore's bright star.'
xxxiii.	Col. 2, line 2, *for* 'Kiu' *read* 'King.'	
xxxv.	Col. 2, line 21, *for* 'Demands' *read* 'Gives.'	
xxxvii.	Col. 2, line 15, *for* 'this' *read* 'that.'	
xxxviii.	Col. 2, line 11 from bottom, *for* 'it was tried' *read* 'they were proceeding.'	
xli.	Translation §3, *after* 'they' *insert* 'always.'	
xlii.	,,	14, *for* 'was' and 'were' *read* 'has been' and 'have been.'
xliii.	,,	15, *read* 'sing a Sunday's celebration on the morrow at night.'
	,,	18, *for* 'mention him' *read* 'whom thou mentionest.'
xlvi.	Col. 2, line 15 from bottom, *for* 'bandtree' *read* 'clapper.'	
liv.	Col. 2, line 3, *for* 'shall be' *read* 'is.'	
lvi.	Translation §13, *for* 'will be' *read* 'abideth.'	
	,,	14, *for* 'his clergy' *read* 'whose trains.'
lvii.	,,	15, *for* 'Of Christ they loved knowledge' *read* 'Muttered prayer to Christ they loved.'
	,,	18, *for* 'were not many faults' *read* 'whose faults were not many.'
	,,	20, *for* 'holiest' *read* 'noblest.'
lviii.	,,	23, *for* 'received ordination' *read* 'used to set forth nobleness.'
	,,	25, *for* 'shouldst link' *read* 'linkest.'
	,,	26, If 'sinchell' in Codex A is miswritten for sinchill, *for* '(the) two perennial Sinchells' *read* 'thy Sinchell the perennial.'
	,,	27, *for* 'from' *read* 'out of.'

Page.	
lviii.	Translation 31, *for* 'clergy' *read* 'train :' *for* 'troops' *read* 'swarm.'
lix.	Line 15 from bottom, *for* 'welcome to the' *read* 'welcome have I for the.'
lxi.	Col. 2, line 17, *for* 'as' *read* 'is.'
lxv.	Col. 2, line 19 from bottom, *for* 'dá Chellóc' *read* 'da-Chellóc (thy Cellóc).'
lxvii.	Translation §1, *for* 'an exceeding' *read* 'more than.'
	,, 4, *for* 'all' *read* 'every.'
	,, 6, *for* 'great is his thousand' *read* 'whose thousands are great.'
	,, 7, *for* 'was' *read* 'is.'
lxix.	,, 15, *for* 'he vanquished' *read* 'that vanquishes.'
	,, 17, *for* 'clergy' *read* 'train.'
	,, 19, *for* 'coldness of his' *read* 'weakness of a.'
lxx.	,, 27, *for* 'went' *read* 'would go.'
	,, 28, *for* 'of' *read* 'to.'
lxxi.	,, 30, *for* 'clergy' *read* 'train :' *for* 'I recount' *read* 'that thou recountest.
lxxv.	Col. 2, line 11, } *for* 'clergy' *read* 'train.'
lxxvii.	,, line 6, from bottom, }
lxxviii.	Translation §1, *for* 'began' *read* 'begin.'
lxxix.	,, 12, *for* 'who accompanied' *read* 'went to.'
	,, 14, *for* 'pious perennial' *read* 'an eternal sea.'
lxxx.	,, §15 and §19, *for* 'clergy' *read* 'train.'
	,, 17, *for* 'Basil' *read* 'Basilla.'
lxxxi.	,, 23, *for* 'torments' *read* 'sorrows.'
	,, 24, *for* 'Ermes' *read* 'Hermes.'
	,, 26, *for* 'Colman and Stelláin' *read* 'Colman Stelláin.'
	,, 27, *for* 'clergy' *read* 'train.'
lxxxvi.	Col. 2, line 12, *for* 'clergy' *read* 'train.'
lxxxviii.	Col. 2, line 16 from bottom, *read* 'How much wheat thou hast ground''
	Col. 2, line 14 from bottom, *omit* 'on.'
xci.	Col. 1. last line, *for* 'coniugem eius potentem' *read* 'coniugium eius potentem.'
xcii.	Translation §1, *for* 'Music of the mind is' *read* 'Behold.'
xciii.	,, 10, *for* 'met' *read* 'meet.'
xciv.	,, 13, *for* 'hear' *read* 'heardest.'
	for 'chaste' *read* 'noble.'
xcv.	Head line, *for* 'JAN.' *read* 'JUNE.'
xcvi.	Translation §27, *read* 'Proven by martyrdom, whose seas are very heavy.'
	,, 30, *for* 'strike a fair fetter' *read* 'draw (lit. strike) a fair bolt.'
cii.	Line 1, *for* 'airne, Airne' *read* 'airdne, Airdne.'
ciii.	Col. 2. line 9, *for* 'has the scholar leapt' *read* 'does the scholar leap.'
cx.	Translation §9, *for* 'diligence as to' *read* 'devotion unto.'
cxii.	,, 26, *before* 'train' *insert* 'fair.'

ON THE CALENDAR OF OENGUS.

Page		
cxiii.	Head line, *for* '1-15' *read* '31.'	
	Translation §31, *for* 'from' *read* 'out of.'	
cxxii.	„ 7, *for* 'beheldest' *read* 'preservedst.'	
cxxiv.	„ 15, *for* 'King's host' *read* 'host of Kings.'	
cxxvi.	„ 31, *for* 'overspread' *read* 'loosen.'	
cxxxv.	Col. 1, line 2 from bottom, *for* 'generi' *read* 'genserici.'	
cxxxvi.	Translation §2, *for* 'Molotha Theodota (Theotimus?)' *read* 'Praise thou Theodota.'	
	„ 4, perhaps this should be 'The great sinless Kingdom wherein are lovesome little ones' (cf. Matth. xix, 14).	
	„ 6, *for* 'divides' *read* 'shared.'	
cxxxvii.	„ 14, *for* 'Ciprian's' *read* 'Cyprian's.'	
cxxxviii.	„ 15, *for* 'of martyrdom' *read* 'to martyrdom.'	
	„ 18, *for* 'a hundred and seven thousand blossoms' *read* (with Rawl. B 505) 'six hundred lovesome soldiers.'	
	„ 20, *for* 'guard' *read* 'visit.'	
cxli.	Col. 2, *for* 'Molotha' *read* 'Praise thou.'	
cxlix.	Translation §2,	
cl.	„ 12, } *for* 'Oinme' *read perhaps* 'at the same time.'	
	„ 13, *for* 'young queen Glanna' *read* 'pure princess.'	
cliv.	Line 6 from bottom, *for* 'Sinéch' *read* 'Sinech.'	
clv.	Line 24, *after* 'Foilo' *insert* '(Fial?).'	
clvi.	Line 15, *for* 'Fiachrae's' *read* 'Fiacc's.'	
clx.	Line 19, *for* 'shapely, brown Abban' *read* 'Abban, shapely lord.'	
clxii.	Translation §6, *for* 'dissolved' *read* 'destroyed.'	
clxiii.	„ §10, *for* 'little—it was not more—(was) death (to him)' *read* 'he was almost greater than death.'	
	„ 13, *for* 'before Christmas,' &c., *read* 'before high Christmas thou shouldst make supplication at,' &c.	
clxiv.	„ 15, *for* 'colour, Lent if thou fear it' *read* 'hue, if Lent alarms thee.'	
clxvii.	Col. 2, line 15 from bottom, *after* 'Dimma' *omit* 'son.'	
clxxiv.	Translation §4, *for* 'sages' *read* 'noble elders.'	
clxxv.	„ 15, *for* 'chaste' *read* 'noble.'	
clxxvi.	Note i., *for* 'of Rath' *read* 'mention.'	
clxxix.	Col. 2, line 13 from bottom, *for* 'Inber' *read* 'Inbir.'	
clxxx.	Col. 2, line 13, *read* 'Tech da Goban.'	
clxxxi.	Col. 2, line 8, *for* 'of' *read* 'or.'	
	Col. 2, line 5 from bottom, *after* 'yew' *insert* 'of.'	
clxxxiv.	Col. 2, last line, *for* 'Let not thy voice be overloud' *read* 'Be not overloud of voice.'	
clxxxviii.	Translation §1, *for* 'take possession' *read* 'thou possessest.'	
clxxxix.	„ 37, *for* 'counted up—may I be above' *read* 'laid me down—let me have life.'	

Page.		
clxxxix.	Translation	49, *for* 'territory' *read* 'company.'
cxc.	,,	81, *for* ' much of high praises' &c., *read* ' many delightful alliterations (?) that give point to its melodies (?) ' Perhaps *rindi* here means metrical feet: cf. O'Cl. *rinne* .i. *cósa*.
cxcii.	,,	133, *for* 'milked' *read* 'rifled.'
cxciii.	,,	145, *for* 'wilt' *read* 'wouldst'; *for* 'is' *read* 'would be.'
cxciv.	,,	173, *for* 'clean' *read* 'penitent (?).'
cxcv.	,,	225, *for* 'urgency in beseeching them' *read* ' the urgency of their prayers.'
cxcvii.	Text, col. 3, *for* '357' *read* '257.'	
	Translation §257, *for* ' flame' *read* ' wheat (?).'	
cxcviii.	,,	289, *for* ' was' *read* ' hath been.'
	,,	305, *after* 'not' *insert* 'to be.'
cci.	,,	389, *after* ' have' *insert* ' had'; *for* ' may be' *read* ' should have been.'
	Note d, *read* ' B ' would have wrought.'	
ccii.	Text, col. 2, line 4, *for* ' naic' *read* ' maic.'	
	Translation §405, *read* ' For the intercession of this King to whom this cry is made, help him [*farith* = *fo-a-rith*] out of this sadness, this wretched mendicant.'	
	,,	417, *for* ' that I have said' *read* 'this supplication.'
ccv.	,,	493, *for* ' protect' *read* ' acknowledge (?).'
	,,	521, *for* ' censure' *read* ' spoiling.'
ccvi.	,,	541, *for* ' from' *read* ' out of.'
ccix.	Line 19, *add* ' imm-a-curtis Ap. 27, farith (= fo-a-rith) *succour him*, Ep. 407.	
ccx.	Line 14 from bottom, for '*protect*' read '*acknowledge*.'	
ccxii.	ailgis (from *ail* and *ges* ?) seems a *shameful* request. 1. aille seems fem. not neut. *for* ' gen. pl. aille Ep. 83,' *read* ' tre ailli Z.² 652.'	
ccxiv.	*after* ' airnecht' *insert* ' airther *see* oirther.'	
	álaind; after line 4 *insert* ' The gen. pl. occurs in Ep. 83: mór n-ard n-aille (for áilne).	
ccxv.	amus, acc. pl. amsiu Ml. 16 ª 2.	
	6. an. See Zimmer in Kuhn's Zeitschrift xxiv 523.	
ccxvi.	after anfut *insert* ' angim, aingim *see* anach.'	
ccxvii.	3 ar. *add* ' The forms or, for, ol are also found.'	
	archrinim. Add Skr. çrnāmi.	
	ard, s. seems to mean *alliteration* pref. The gen. pl. apparently occurs in Ep. 83: mór n-árd n- áille.	
ccxviii.	Line 1, for ' arfich *fregit*' read ' arfiuch *I vanquish*, *overcome* Z.²949, 3d sg. pres. indic. act. arfich *vanquishes*.'	
	Line 2, *for* ' vicit' *read* ' vi-n-cit.'	
ccxx.	*after* ' athlaech' *insert*	
	' atmaim (ad-damim) *I confess*. See ataim. Hence also atumdidmac (ad-dum-di-dmac), Ep. 494, 2d sg. redupl. fut.'	

Page.	
ccxxi.	Line 15, *after* 'from p' *insert* 'bece *little*=piccus, biáil *axe*=pialla, hóc *kiss*=pacem.'
ccxxi.	Line 4 from bottom, *for* 'bái' *read* 'báis.'
ccxxii.	*after* 'bart' *insert* 'Bartholom, Bartholomaeus, Aug. 25 D.'
ccxxiii.	bél (ex gvesla) is probably = χεῖλος.
	after 'benim' *insert* '1. beó s.=βιός *life* Ep. 39. dat. sg. biu, Fiacc.'
cxxv.	*for* 'bláith s. *blossom* c'c.,' *read*
	'blaith, adj. *blandus*, n. pl. m. blaithe (bláithi) Sep. 4, gen. pl. blaithe Sep. 18.
	bláithe, Aug. 19, is perhaps a noun meaning (and cognate with) 'bloom,' W. blodau *flowers* 2 Kuhn's Beitr. 174.'
ccxxvi.	breó : *after* 'Aug. 20,' *insert* 'Ep. 259 B. Root bhru in Lat. furor, OHG. brunst.
ccxxvii.	Line 21, *for* 'bruyn' *read* 'brwyn.'
ccxxx.	có s. .i. talam. Windisch regards this có as a demonstrative pronoun, and compares Goth. hi- in himma-daga, Lith. szis.
ccxxxiv.	cloor. *add* 'root klus.'
	cluinim. *omit* 'root klus.'
ccxxxv.	Line 4, *for* 'KAN, καινω,' *read* 'KNAT, vedic gnath durchstossen.'
ccxxxix.	Line 16, *for* 'conói *servare*' *read* 'conúim *servo*.'
	Line 5 from bottom, *for* 'cúraid n. pl. Prol. 65, gen. pl. corad' *read* 'coraid *for* curad *champions*, gen. pl.'
	before 'corann' *insert*:
	'cúraid s.m. *sinners*, Prol. 65, gen. pl. fri tabairt corad ocus eccraibdech int saegail documm nirse, Three Mid. Ir. Homilies, p. 42. Derived from cóir *a crime*.'
ccxliii.	Line 6 from bottom, *for* 'to' *read* 'l.'
ccxlviii.	Line 14, *for* 'didge' *read* 'digde.'
	Lines 17, 18, 19, *dele* these lines : *digni* in Prol. 254 (where it rhymes with *rig-ni*) is the gen. sg. of the substantive dígnae.

THE CALENDAR OF OENGUS.

THE IRISH PREFACES.

A.

[Lebar Brecc, fo. 28 a. 1.]

CETHARDAI CONDAGAR DA cechelathain .i. locc 7 aimser 7 persa 7 fáth airice. IS fisid cid armaid locc conesta artús 7 aimser isinlucc tannisi 7 persa isintres lucc 7 fath airice in fine. IS aire isloce artus aris fri cathardu 7 eclaisi domiditer luice .i. primluicc 7 cádus doibside. Fri rigu 7 tuatha din. domiditer aimsera. Locc tanaisse do suidib. Persa immorro isintress lucc aris ahecla is no atunith airethid cacha helathan. Tucait post ara frith fath remtechtais donafiledaib archena meretrix. No din. sechim nafellsam fil and .i. locc artús aris corpdai locc. Aimsear isinlocc tanaisse aris nemchorpdai. Persa isintress lucc arisóchurp 7 nemchurp doairis. Fath airic din. sicut dixit. no isord airic chrutai nandúl fil and .i. locc artús aris dia máirt dorignead talum. Aimser isinlucc thancaisi aris dia cétain dorígned grian 7 escai 7 isfriuside domiditer aimsera. Persa isintress lucc aris dia haine dorigned induine. Tucait immorro fo dera aris dia sathairn rosbendach dia nadúile 7 rofaillsig fath anairice.

IS hi immorro aimser indernai oengus[a] infelire .i. aimser æda ordnige maic neill frassaig. arise rogab rige ncrenn indiaid dondchuda maic domnaill. uair tice oengus isinbroluch thoisiuch infeliri lebás dondchada. Dofothud na canoine vero rotaispen oengus artus infelire diandechaid æd sluaiged dúin chuair hicocrich mide 7 laigen 7 diandechutar clerig erenn lais imchommnach comorba patraicc 7 isforinsluagadsin rossertha clerig erenn arfecht 7 slungad. arise fothud na canoine ruc inmbreith diarosærtha eculsa erenn amail atbert

    Eclás dé bíí
      leic díí nasnai
      bid acert forleath
      feib asdeach robui

    Cech fírmanach fil
      forachubus nglan
      doneclais dian dir
      gnid amail cech mog

    Cech dilmain iarsin
      fil cenrecht cen rer
      ccat ciatheis fri báig
      aeda mair maic neill

    Is hí in riagail chert
      sech nimor nibec
      fognad cách a mog
      cen on iscen ec . Eclas dé bíí.

[a] [IN MARGINE] Aengus immorro M. ængoband M. oiblein M fidrui M diarmuta M ainmirech M cellair M oengusa M uatsluaig M coelbuid M cruind badrai M cchach cobai.

Rosær tra red ordnige ceulsa erenn 7 aclerchiu forsluaiged osin immach. Rothaispen
din. fothud cetul nacanoine 7 cetul nacosaite do oengus . 7 daronsat anoentaig annsin.
7 rosbennach cach dib clathain aroile . 7 forfacsat ratha imda forintſi nosgebaḋ cumenic
iufélire. Hite em inso ratha infelire am*al* ata isinbróluch deghdinach don félire fessin.
IS fissid diu, cia aiste triasin ṅderuad infelire. niu.   Rindard. Caidhe em aichne rinnairde, nin, ui, sillaba ineach cethrumthain . 7 XII. isinlethrand .XX.IIII. im*mor*ro isinrand
chomlan . et si sit plus uel minusue error est (ispudar). Recomare im*mor*ro .i. desill*a*bach
ina rennaib isfuireside daroine oengus infelire 7 fortri gneib diu .i. for réid rindaird .i.
for rinnaird danard 7 for rinnaird tri nard 7 for rinnaird .IIII. nard.   Rinnard danard
c*et*amus inso . ut beccan mac cula dixit no ise crurach[a] indse móire

                        Diarmait maith m*a*c cerbaill
                        can nige[b] cenlaige
                        nirochluine meirlech
                        aeirlech atraite

Oc*us* am*ail* atbert oengus beos

                        For kal*ain*n mis marta
                        nit mordai frianguide[c]
                        senan moinend myse
                        dab*id* chille muine

Rinnard im*mor*ro tri nard inso

                        Fland tendalach temrach
                        tendrig fotla feraind
                        otha anall domuinin
                        isi achland dogegaind (.i. doga)

Oc*us* am*ail* atbert oengus beos

                        Re sil dálach doine
                        toided inri remain
                        luid forecht ard erail
                        cri*st* ikal*ain*n enair

Rindard .IIII. nard inso . ut fothu*th* nacanoine dixit

                        Aed ordnige obaid (.i. oliss obaig agaid inagaid fri
                        orflaith banba bledig   [boilech)
                        coich isferr imfalaig
                        inaectoir oilig

Oc*us* am*ail* atbert oengus

                        Lassar greine áine
                        apstol[d] erenn uaige
                        patraic cumeit mile
                        ropdítiu diartruaige

[a] Perhaps *rurach*.   [b] MS. cánaide.   [c] MS. frianguide.   [d] MS. as*p*ol.

Locens huius artis cuil bendchuir amuig reicheat . hicrich .h. failge aráithindscetail. hicluain éidnech im*morro* aermor hitamlachtu lilarén a forlm uile . ut alii. Persa dó oengus mac oengaband m*aic* ociblen domuintir cl*uana* éidnech. Isainsir cholathaig choeilbreag. Is he infochund . fecht dolluid oengus dochuil bennchu*ir* amuig rechet conu*s*facea lige and 7 balán doainglib it*er* neam 7 lar uasinlige . coro iarfaigsium dosacurt nacille cia ro adnoeht isinlige ucut. Senoir truag robui isinbaile olinsacurt . Cia maith dognid ol oengus. Nisfaicinnse annaith sunnraid ol insacurt. Cia rét it*er* dognid ol oengus. Nocim indomain dothuirem oliusacart doneoch ba cumain lais dib fo lige 7 fo érgi am*ail* ba bés do athloechaib indomain. Amo de nime ol oengus cipe dogneth tria filidecht trilig moltai dona nocmaib ropu mor alóg do intan isfor inathkech tanic rath naméti ucut. Rothinscain tra. oengus aféire indsin. Daroine din. amedonrind icluain eidnech. Hitamlachtu (.i. isinaith) im*morro* roforbad .i. inaimsir moelruain doronta he .xx.iiii. sill*aba* incach rand et si sit plus minusve sicut praedictus error est. etc.

A.
Translation.

' FOUR things are required by every work of art, namely, a Place and a Time and a Person and a Cause of invention.' It should be known why he thinks that Place should be required first, and Time in the second place, and Person in the third place and Cause of invention *in fine*. It is for this that Place is at the beginning, because it is by cities and churches that places are distinguished, to wit, chief places, and (there is) reverence unto them. By kings and peoples, then, Times are distinguished. The second place (is) to these. Person, however, (is) in the third place, for of (the) church or of (the) laity is (the) inventor of every work of art. Cause (is) *post* for cause of precedence was found for poets because of a harlot.[a] Or indeed it is a following of the (usage of) philosophers which is there, to wit, Place at first, for place is corporeal. Time in the second place, for it is incorporeal. Person in the third place, for it is from Body and Not-Body it consists. Cause of Invention then *sicut dixi*. Or it is the order of inventing the creation of the beings that is there, to wit, Place at first, for it is on Tuesday (the) earth was made. Time in the second place, for it is on Wednesday (the) sun was made and (the) moon, and it is by them that times are distinguished. Person in the third place, for it is on Friday the Man was made. Cause, however, at (the) end[b], for on Saturday God blessed the beings and manifested (the) cause of their invention.

Now this is (the) Time at which Oengus[c] made the Calendar, to wit, (the) time of Aed the Dignified, son of Niall the Showery, for it is he that took (the) kingdom of Ireland after Donnchaid son of Domnall, for Oengus came on the first prologue of the Calendar at Donnchaid's death. To Fothud of the Canon, now, Oengus first showed the Calendar when Aed led the Hosting of Dún Cuai into the border of Meath and Leinster, and when (the) clerics of Ireland went with him around Connmach, Patrick's successor. And it is on that hosting that the clerics of Ireland were freed from fighting and

---

[a] This passage is unintelligible and probably corrupt. [b] fo-*dera* for fo-*deirid*?
[c] [IN MARGINE] Oengus, now, son of Oengoba, son of Oiblen, son of Fidrui, son of Diarmait, son of Ainmire, son of Cellar, son of Oengus, son of Natslunig, son of Coelbad, son of Crund-Badrai, son of Echaid Cobae.

b 2

hosting, for it is he, Fothud of the Canon, that passed the judgment whereby (the) churches of Ireland were freed, as he said

 (The) Church of living God
  Leave to it the ....
  Let its right be apart
  As it is best it were.

 Every true monk that is,
  (Be it) on his pure conscience
  To the church whereto (it is) due
  Let him act like every servant.

 Every freeman afterwards,
  Who is without law, without submission,[a]
  (Hath) leave though he come to the battle
  Of great Aed son of Niall.

 This is the right rule —
  Forsooth, not great, not little:
  Let every one's servant serve him
  Without fault and without compulsion.

So Aed the Dignified freed the churches of Ireland and her clergy on hosting from that time forward. Then Fothud showed the poem of the Canon and the poem of the Complaint to Oengus, and then they made their union, and each of them blessed the other's composition, and they left many blessings on him who should sing the Calendar often. These truly are the graces of the Calendar as is [shown] in the last prologue of the Calendar itself.

It should be known, then, in what metre the Calendar was made. Not hard (to say). *Rinnard*. How is *Rinnard* recognised[b]? Not hard (to say). Six syllables in every fourth (of a stanza), and twelve in the half-stanza, but twenty-four in the whole stanza, and if there be more or less there is a mistake. It is *reomare* i.e. dissyllabic in its terminations. It is in this (metre) that Oengus composed the Calendar, and in three kinds, i.e. in *réid-rinnard* (smooth, easy *rinnard*), i.e. in *rinnard* of two alliterations and in *rinnard* of three alliterations and in *rinnard* of four alliterations. *Rinnard* of two alliterations, first, (is) this, *ut Beccán* son of Cula *dixit;* or it is Ruirech of Inis Mór.

  Diarmait maith mac cerbaill etc.

And as Oengus said also

  For kalann mís marta etc. [1 March]

Rinnard, however, of three alliterations is this:—

  Fland tendalach temrach etc.

  [a] i.e. Who is not bound by vows of obedience. E. O'C.
  [b] Lit. 'what then is the recognition of *rinnard?*'

And as Oengus said also:

  Ró síl dálach dóine etc. [1 Jan.]

Rinnard of four alliterations (is) this, as Fothud of the Canon *dixit:*

  Acd ordnigc obaid (i.e. from Liss Obaig face to face with Ailech) etc.

And as Oengus said

  Lassar gréine áine etc. [March 17]

 Locus hujus artis (was) Cool Banagher in Morett; in (the) territory of Offaly its beginning, in Clonenagh, however, its continuation (?), in Tallaght Libren its entire completion *ut alii*. Its Person (was) Oengus, son of Oengoba, of (the) monastery of Clonenagh. In the time of Cobthach Coelbreg. This is the cause: Oengus went once to Cool Banagher in Morett, and he saw a grave there, and all between heaven and (the) ground over the grave was full of angels. And he asked (the) priest of the church "who has been buried in that grave?" "A poor old man who was in the place," said the priest. "What good used he do?" said Oengus. "I used not to see any special good done by him," said the priest. "What thing at all used he to do?" said Oengus. "He recounted (the) saints of the world," said the priest, "such of them as he remembered, on lying down and rising up, as was a custom of (the) whilom-laymen of the world." "Ah my God of heaven!" said Oengus, "whosoever should make in poetry a song of praise for the saints, great would be his reward therefor, since grace of that greatness hath come upon this whilom-layman." So Oengus began his Calendar there. He made the middle part of it in Clonenagh. In Tallaght, however, it was completed. In (the) time of Maelrúain it was made. There are twenty-four syllables in every quatrain, *et si sit plus minusve sicut praedictus error est, etc.*

B.

LAUD 610. fo. 60. a. 1.

 CEATHARDAI connagar do cech cladhain .i. loc 7 persa 7 aimsir 7 cuis scribind. Atcuintesta dna doneladainsea.

Loc ém chitius di cuil bendchair immaig rechet ierich unfailge 7 indóith itamlachtain indernad dna ní de fcluain éidnech athindscetal hautem feúil bendchair 7 aforba issindaith ítamlachta.

Oengus im*morro* mac oengobann mic ocbléin mic fidhrui mic diarmata mic ainmire mic cellair mic oengussa mic natsluaig mic caelbaid mic cruind[badrai] mic cochach coba mic luigdech mic rossa mic imchatho mic feidlimtbe mic caiss mic fiachrach araide a quo dail naraide. nomenatur inpersu.

IShí hautem aimsir indernad .i. aimsir reda oirdnide arissé rogab rigi neire*nd* andiaid donnchada ártic oengus issinbroluch tóisech indfelire tar bás dondchada.

ISí im*morro* inchuis. Fecht nóen dorala [o disiurt oengusa] immumain co cúil bennchoir oetecht dogabail mailruain itamlachtuin danmcharait. conacca adhnacul isinchill 7 balán daingilb uassa conem. coro iarfaig oengus do sacart nacilli cia roadhnacht and. Araile athlæch truag bói isinbaile arinsacart. Cia maith dorigneside aróengus

Nífaicmis émh arinsacart naeǒhmaith dodenam dó acht nócim indomain do thuirim folighi 7 fóéirgi anaal ishés athlaech. Adé nime ar ængus cipé dogneth tririg molta do nóebaib ropad mór alóg dó. corothinnscain iarum inféilire annsin fochétoir. itamlachtain immorro roforbad. Ceithri sillaeba fichet fecchrand. diarñbé plus no minus is mell.

Dofothud nacanoine immorro rothaispen oengus artus in feileire diañdechaid arslóiged dúin chuair 7 cleirig heirend immaille fris inchonnmach comarba patraic 7 is dontsluaigedsin rosóertha cleirig arsluaiged. ar issé fothad ruc imñbreith diarosócrad ocailsi cirend amal isbert feisin

[60. a. 2] Eclas dé bí
leic día* nasnái
bith acert forleth
feib as dech robói
Cach firmanach fíl
fornchubus glon
dondeclais diantír
gnid ainal cach mod[b]
Cach dilmain iarsein
fil cenrecht cenreir
cet ciathes friabáig
reda [unáir maice néill
IShí inriagol chert
sech ní mór] ni bec
foghnad each dia mogh
cen on is cen ecc. Ecclas.

Rothaispen dna cetal nacanoine 7 cetal nacosaite do ængus 7 dorousat anæntaig annsin 7 robendach each dib eladhain araile 7 forfaesat ratha ratha imdai foriutí notoscebad comiuic. Ata imda ém ratha indféilire chitus amal tarmither isinbroluch déidenach. INtængus sin tra robo mog mnal inissel do dia hé 7 issé nochanad athsahau amlaid seo céin bói ic disiurt oengusa .i. l. isindabhaind 7 gat immabragait icengul don bile. l. dna fón ríbile feissin 7 .l. ina reicles. Roindsaig dna iartain comælruain corragbad hé danmcharait.

ISé immorro immælruainsin rochind nagebad feraud itamlachtain nócoñgabad michel fris amibe acharadrad[conid triasin cairdeþin atat minda cosseeartha domichel itamlachtain. Eccnaing tra fecht nóen iarsin cindiudsin cipisdil 7 fót imalle fria dochur de nim co mælruain corragbad ferann conidannsin iarum rogabad tamlachta.

Dornacht iarsin æengus irricht moghad clnice 7 roerb mælruain fris frestal na hatha.
Rogabsom sin dolaim 7 issed indister ann corofas in fochand trianafolt armét indfognuma. Dorála din fecht ann mae bec ocléigiunn atsahm lamælruain cohdeclaid inclcireǒh fecht nóen donelais corocrb donmae mebrugad aaiccepta comad erlam fria thaispenad arachind. Élaid immorro inmae ór nár tsáil annísin 7 issed dorala hé donáith cohængus. Iarfaigis iarum de cid rombói. indissigé inmae dó. Tair ille arængus 7 tabair do cheun for moglún 7 eotail. Dorigned amlaid. Eirgis inmac iarsin. isann atbert æengus geib thaiccept a mic. Gcibid iarum in mae nfba huilliu innás intaicept. Canét sin a mic arængus. Inléighind nile ocum ar in mae. Imthig ar ængus 7 na

^a leg. dí   ^b leg. mog   ^c leg. indissid

THE IRISH PREFACES.

hataim cia rustárnill. Téit iarum in mac 7 taispenaid intaiccept do maelruain 7 rathaigis maelruain coraibe aice ní bud mó. 7 iarfaigis de cia dotáraill a mic. Ní fetar arin mac. Brec ém sin ar an cleirech. abbair coluath. Ni fetar ar in mac acht domrala don áith 7 dochothus 7 mochend forglun fír na hatha. Is fír sin arse. ISé œngus in tairngertaig sin 7 tic amach cohopunn iarsin 7 ní thuc acht lethássa imme 7 rosoich innaith. Maith aœngais arse. nirbo chóir duit ar ihbrécad. uair ba córa sinde ic foghnam duitsiu inna thussa duiudne. Ruc maelruain leis hé iarsin cononoir moir 7 slechtais œngus dó. 7 dogniat anœntaig innœntaig innim 7 talmain. Conid amlaid sin iarum rofoillsiged oengus do maelruain.

IS fisid din cia hernail aisti trinsañdernad infeilire. niu. rindaird. Isfisid din caide aithne rindairde feissin. niu. Sé sillœba ina cethramnaib 7 adó déc ina lethrannaib 7 acethair .xx. ina rann[aib]chomlana. et si sit plus minusue is pudar. Recomarc immorro ina r[e]annaib. Recomraic .i. désillabach. frisinernail airigthi din donaistisco dianad ainm réidrinnaird danard doroine œngus infeilire 7 trignœ fuirriside .i. réidrindaird danard ut est becan dixit no inde ruirech indsi [móire] dixit

    Diarmait maith mac cerbaill
    can aige ganlaice
    ní rocluine meirlech
    acirrlech atraite

7 amal asbert œngus

    For kalaind mis marta
    nid morda friañguidhi
    senan moinend moysi
    dauid cilli muine

Ocus reid rindaird tri nard ut mœlmura fothna cecinit

    Fland tendalach temrach
    tend rí fodla feraind
    ótha amall dommuinim
    isi achland dogeogaind (.i. dothogfaind)

7 amal asbert œngus

    Re sil dalach daine .7 rl.

Rindaird ceithri nard immorro amal asbert fothud nacanoine

    Aed oirdnige obhaig
    for flaith banba blidig
    cuich is ferr imfalaid
    ina echtair ailig

B.
Translation.

Four things are required by every work of art to wit, a Place, a Person, and a Time, and a Cause of writing. They are required now for this work.

Place, forsooth, first for it: Cool Banagher in Morett in the border of Offaly, and it was the kiln in Tamlacht wherein some of it was made. In Clonenagh its beginning, in Cool Banagher, and its completion in the kiln in Tallaght.

Oengus, now, son of Oengoba, son of Oeblén, son of Fidrui, son of Diarmait, son of Ainmire, son of Cellar, son of Oengus, son of Natsluag, son of Coelbad, son of Crunnbadrai, son of Eochaid Coba, son of Lugaid, son of Rossa, son of Imchath, son of Feidlimid, son of Cass, son of Fiachra Araide *a quo* Dál n-Araide, *nominatur* the Person.

Now this is the Time at which it was made, to wit, the time of Aed the Dignified, for he it was that took the realm of Ireland after Donnchad, for Oengus begins the first prologue of the Calendar after Donnchad's death.

Now this is the Cause. Once upon a time he fared from Disert Oengusa in Munster, to Cool Banagher, coming to get Maelruain in Tallaght for his soulfriend. And he saw a grave in the church and (all) over it was full of angels even unto heaven. And Oengus asked the priest of the church, who was buried there? "A certain wretched whilom-layman, who was in the place," quoth the priest. "What good did he do?" quoth Oengus. "We used not to see," quoth the priest, "any good done by him, save that on lying down and rising up he recounted the saints of the world, as is the usage of whilom-laymen." "Ah, God of heaven!" quoth Oengus, "whoso should make a song of praise for the saints, great would be his reward!" So he then began the Calendar there at once. In Tallaght, however, it was completed. Four and twenty syllables in every quatrain, and if there be more or less it is an error.

To Fothud of the Canon now Oengus first showed the Calendar when he went on the hosting of Dún Cuair, and the clerics of Ireland together with him, about Connmach, Patrick's successor. And it on that hosting that clerics were freed from hosting. For it is Fothud that passed the judgment whereby the churches of Ireland were freed, as he himself said,

'The Church of living God,' etc.

Then he showed the poem of the Canon and the poem of the Complaint to Oengus, and they made their union there, and each of them blessed the other's composition, and they left many graces on him who should repeat it often. Many, indeed, are the graces of the Calendar, as is recounted in the last prologue.

Now that Oengus was an humble, lowly servant to God, and he it is that used to sing his psalms thus while he was in Disert Oengusa, to wit, fifty in the river and a withe around his neck tied to the tree; fifty, moreover, under the tree itself, and fifty in his chapel. Thereafter he came to Maelruain that he might take him for a soulfriend.

This is that Maelruain who decided that he would not take land in Tallaght until Michael [the Archangel], towards whom was his affection, should take it; and because of that agreement there are reliquaries consecrated to Michael in Tallaght. Now it happened once on a time after that decision that an epistle and a sod fell together from heaven to Maelruain, so that he took land, and then Tallaght was taken.

Thereafter Oengus, in the guise of a slave, came to him, and Maelruain entrusted to him the care of the kiln. He took that in hand, and this is related, that the cornblades grew through his hair by reason of the greatness of the service. It happened once that there was a little boy reading his psalms with Maelruain, and the cleric went to the church, and he charged the boy to learn his lesson by heart, so that he might be ready to repeat it before him. The boy, however, ran away, for he did not like that thing, and he came to the kiln to Oengus. So Oengus asked him what was the matter. The boy tells him. "Come hither," quoth Oengus, "and put thy head on my knee, and sleep." Thus was it done. Thereafter the boy arose, and then said Oengus, "Say thy lesson, O boy!" Then the boy says somewhat more than the lesson. "What is that thing, O boy?" quoth Oengus. "The whole reading I have," quoth the boy. "Go thou," quoth Oengus, "and confess not whom thou visitedst." Then the boy goes and repeats the lesson to Maelruain, and Maelruain perceived that he had somewhat more, and he asked him, "Whom didst thou visit, O boy?" "I know not," quoth the boy. "That is a lie, indeed," quoth the cleric, "tell (me) quickly." "I know not," quoth the boy; "but I came to the kiln, and I fell asleep with my head on the knee of the kilnman." "That is true," quoth Maelruain. "Oengus the prophesied one is that man," and he comes forth at once then, and he brought only one shoe on him, and he went to the kiln. "Well, O Oengus," quoth he, "it was not meet for thee to lie unto us, for meeter were it that we should be serving thee than thou us." Maelruain then brought Oengus with great honour, and Oengus knelt to him, and they make their union the union in heaven and earth. So thus it was that Oengus was manifested to Maelruain.

It is worth knowing what kind of metre the Calendar was composed in. Not hard (to answer): *Rindaird.* It is worth knowing, also, how to recognise *rindaird* itself. Not hard. Six syllables in its quarters, and twelve in its half-quatrains, and twenty-four in its complete quatrains, *et si sit plus minusve* there is an error. *Recomarc* (a dissyllable) in the desinences of its lines. *Rechommaic*, i.e. dissyllabic. In the particular kind of this metre named *Reid-rindaird danard* ('smooth-*rindaird* of two alliterations'), Oengus composed the Calendar, and three kinds are in it, i.e. smooth *rindaird* of two alliterations as Becan said, or Rubech of Inis (Mór) said '*Diarmait*,' &c. And as Oengus said, *For kalaind,* &c. And smooth *rindaird* of three alliterations as Maelmaire of Fathain sang, *Fland,* &c. And as Oengus said, '*Résil,*' &c. *Rindaird* of four alliterations, moreover, Fothud of the Canon said, '*Aed ordnigthe,*' &c.

D.

[RAWL. B. 512, fo. 53. a. 1.]

[C]ETHARDAI CONDAGAR DA CACH EALATHAIN .i. loce 7 aimsir persa 7 fath airice. ISfissid cid armad loc connesta artus 7 aimsir isinluc tanaisi 7 persa isintresluce 7 fath airice in fine. IS aire is loc connesta artus ar is fri catharda 7 cacailsi domiditer fuice 7 eadas (.i. primluice). Fri rigu 7 tuatha domiditer aimsera. loce tanaise do suidib. Persa isintresluce arisacaclais no tuaith airethig cach ealathan. Tucait post ar frith fath reimtheachtais donafidib (*sic*) archena meritrix.

No dno sechem na fellsom fil ::: .i. loc ardus ar is corpda loce. aimsir isin ::: tanaisi aris neamcorpdai. Persa isin :::::: ec arisochurp 7 oncamchurp doair :: :::: airic sicut diximus.

No is ord airic cruth ::: andul fil ann .i. loce artús arisdia ::::: dorigned talam. Aimsir isinluc tánaisi :::: dia cédain dorigned grian 7 easca 7 isfri ::::: domiditer

aimsera. Persa isiu tresluce áris : : : : : : : : dorigned duine. Tucait vero fodera aris : : :
sathairn robennach dia na duile 7 ro : : : : : sig fath anairic.
Locc em citus donealathainsi chuil beaunchuir inmuigh rechet : : :ich hua foilghe 7
indláith itamlachtain indern : : : dan no ní de ieluain cdnech. Atinnscet : : : : la icuil
bendchuir 7 aforba isindaith itamlachtain.
Aengus mac oiblein m. fidrúi : : diarmata m. cellair m. ainmire m. œn : : : : : m.
nadsluaig m. coelb. m. cruindbadrai m. echach c. m. lugdach m. rosa mc. : : : a m.
feidliuathe m. flachrach araide a quo dal naraidi nominatur. ISe aspersa doneladainsin.
ISí aimsir indernad. aimser æda oirdnige aris e rogab rig[e] nerend indegaid dondchada ar : : : : oengus isinbroluch tóisech [le] bas donnchada.
ISí vero a tucait. fecht dorala ængus : : disert immumain dochuil bennchuir icrich
ua failgi dogabail mailruain otamlachtain do anuecharnit anaea indadnacal isin : :ll . 7 ba
lan do ainglib uasa co neam coro iarfaig ængus dosacart nacille. Cia rondnacht ann.
Araile athlæch truag boi isin : :li arin sacart. Cia maith dognidside orængus.
Nifaicinnsi náeh maith dodenam dó orinsacart acht noiun indomain doguide foligo 7
foéirge. : :e ninne orocugus cipe dogenad trilig molta dib robad maith alogh do.
Corothinnscaiu iarum infeleri illic. itamlachtain vero roforbad ut prediximus.
Dofothud na canoine immorro rothaisben ængus artus indfelere diandechaid æd
sloiged duin evair icoicrich inide 7 laigen 7 dia ndechadar elerigh erenn lais um
chommnach comarba patraic 7 rl. 7 isforinsluaigedsin rosærtha elerig erenn forfeacht 7
sluaiged. arisó ruc in breth doib .i. fothud na canoine dia rosærtha elerig erenn 7
aheacailsi ut amal isbert

         Eglas dé bi. leig df inasnai
         bid a cert forleth. feib asdeach roboi
         Cach firmanach fial. fornchubus glau
         doneaclais diandír. gnidb amal eachmogh.
         Cachdilmain iarsin. fil cenrecht cenreir
         cet ciates fribáigh. æda mair maic neil
         ISi indriaguil cert. seach ni mór ni bec
         fognad each a mogh. cenon is cen eace. Eclais.

Rosærtha tra annsin ecailsi erenn lafothud nacanoine 7 laæd oirduide.
Rothaispen dna fothud cetal nacanoine 7 [cetal] na cosaite do ængus 7 doronsat
annsin amentaig . 7 robennach cach a cheli dib 7 ealathain araili 7 fornesat ratha imda
foriuti nomebraigfeadh 7 nogebad cominice infeleri. At imda immorro ratha indfeleri
amal tuirmidtir isinbrolach dedenach.
INtoengus vero roraidsemar ropa fognomaid maith dodin . 7 robo inog umal iniseal e.
ISe nochanad natri .l.tu cein bói oedisert noengusa .i. l[a] isindabaig 7 gat immo-
braigidsim icengul donbile . 7 l[a] fobun inbile 7 l[a] narechís.
ISe vero roinnsaig conærluain do thabairt anuecairdesa dó. ISe inmælruainsin
rocinn nagebad ferann italmain nogo gabad michel frisi raibe (sic) acaradrad conid
triasin cairdesin ata minua michil itamlachta.
Dorócht iarum oengus iricht inogad chuice . 7 rocarb frestul nahatha fris 7 rogabsom
sin dna dolaim . 7 ised innister ann gurfás fochann triana chend armed iudfognama.
Dorala dno fecht ann mac bece olegiund arnelud arcacla mailruain arni raibe aige
aaiccept adochum. Iarfaigis ængus de cid rombui. Innisid inmac beace do. Tair ille
or oengus 7 cuir dochend for mogluu 7 cotail. Dorigned amlaidsin. Ergis inmac beac
iarsin 7 isbert ængus fris geib taiccept. Geibid in mac beac ní ba huilli inda aicept

Cret sin amic aræng*us*. Indlegiund uili ocvm arinm*ac* bec. Imthig arængus 7 ná ataim
cia rotaraill. Teit iarum 7 taisbenaid aniceapt do maelruain. Iarfaigid de cia rotaraill
amic orsé. Nifetar or in m*ac*. Brec am sin ol in clerech. abair colluath. Nifetar or
in mac acht domrala donaith 7 rocotl*us* 7 mochenn forglun fir na atha. IS fir sin d*na*.
ise oeng*us* intairng*e*rtaigsin orse. 7 tice amach cohopunn. 7 nithucc acht lethassa vime.
7 rosaigh indaith. Maith sin a rengais orse. Nírbo cóir duit armbrégad. coru damsa
foguum duitsiu qu*am* duitsiu foguam damsa. Rug maelruain leis he iarsin 7 dogniat
amentaig atalmain 7 anim 7 dob*er*t maelruain onóir mór do 7 sleachtais ængus dó conid
unl*aid* sin rofaillsig*ed* æng*us* dó.
  IS fis*id* d*na* cía hernail aisti triasand*er*nai æng*us* infel*ire*. Nin. rinnard. IS fisid
dna caidhe aichne rinnairde feisin. Nin. Se sill*aba* ina cethramthaib adódéc ina
leith .i. isin lethrann a cethair xx" isinruun com*l*án. si sit plus minusue ispudar.
  Recomrac imm*orro* areannaib. Recomraic .i. désill*a*bach frisin hern*ail* airithe din
aistisin dianad ainm réidh rinuard doróine oeng*us* infelere 7 trignee fu*i*rriside .i. reidrinnard dá nard ut est bec*á*n mac cúla dixit no rurach innsi móire dixit

     Diarmaid maith m*ac* cerbaill
     can aige gan laicce
     nirocluine merlech
     anirleach itraiti

7 am*al* atb*er*t æng*us*

     For kl. mis márta
     nid morda friguide
     seanán moeneann móisi
     d*a*bid cille muine

7 Reidrinnard trínard ut moelmura athna cecinit

     Flaun tendal*ach* temr*ach*
     f. teannri fotla fe*r*nim
     otha innall domuinim
     isi achlann dogegainn

am*al* atb*er*t æng*us* bé*us*

     Re sil dal*uch* daine
     toided inri remain
     luid foreacht nard nearail
     xp. ikl. enair

Rinnard cethri nard inso ut est fothud na canoine

     Aed ord ord*nide* obaig
     órfl*aith* banba bleidhig
     cuich asfearr imfhal*aig*
     inda echtoir ailich

amal asbert ængus

Lasar gréine áine
apstol e. o.
p. g. m. m.
r. d. d. t.

Ata fidrad cubaid et*ir* tosaichib narann 7 deri*dib* narann eli*

---

* ‘There is an harmonious *fidrad* between the beginning of the quatrains and the ends of the preceding quatrains.’ As the rest of this preface contains nothing that is not in the other two prefaces, it seems unnecessary to translate it. The following quatrain occurs in B and D :—

B.

Taided remaind sligid sactraig
cosacraib sil gaeidil gairg
cosinnaigtech nóibind nethrach
rogab fine nechdach naird

D.

Taided remainn sligid sæthra*ig*
cosacraib sil gaidil gairg
cosinndaigthech noibind neathrach
rogab fine eachdach aird.

THE PROLOGUE.

D. Rawl. B. 512. fo. 53, b. 1.	B. Laud, 610. fo. 59, a. 1.	A. Lebar Brecc. fo. 28, a, 2.
1. [S]én acrist molabra achoimdi seacht nime romberthar buaid lére ari greine gile 5. Agelgrían forosna riched coméd noebe ari onic aingliu achoimdi nandoine 9. Achoimde nandoine ari tirian firmaith conainraib cachsol*ad* armol*ad* dotrigraid 13. Dorigraid nomolur olistu arruire doralus armaire gr*é*schi icanguide 17. Guide itge doaib romain aritrogb*us* cain popul colligdath inrigraid imrordos 21. [IM]rord*us* inrigraid umaurig uasnélaib aill uas laithib ligaib aill uas diannaib dérnib 25. Domrorbai domthéti olamtriamuin trogsai iartimnaib inrigsa rith r: raith inslógsa[a]	1. Sén acrist molabrad achoimdiu .uii. nime rofersam buaid léire ári gr*é*ine gile 5. A gelgrian forosnai riched comet nóimi ari conic aingliu achomdiu nanúini 9. Achoimdiu nanduine ari firen firmaith conomraib do solad armolad do rigrad 13. Dorigrad romolur ár istú arruri dora*lus* ar maire gr*e*scha icanguide 17. Guidiu itge doib rommain audorogb*us* cain popul coligdath inn rigrad imrordus 21. Imrordussa inrigraid immourig osnelaib aill uas lathib ligaib aill fo dianaib déraib 25. Domrorba domthete olamtriamain truagsa iartimnaib indrigsa rith ra reith inshuagsa	1. Seu acrist molabra achoimde .uii. nime romberth*ar* buaid leri ari gréni gile 5. Agelgrian fornosna riched cuméit noemi ari conic aingliu achoimdiu nandoine 9. Achoimdiu nandoine ari firian firmaith conainraib ca*ch* solad armolad dotrigraid 13. Dorigrad nomolar ol istu moruire doralus armaire gr*é*schi oc do guide 17. Guidiu itge d*ó*ib rómnin arat rogbus cain popul culigdath inrigrad im*ó*rdus 21. IMrordus inrigraid imuurig uasuclaib aill uas laithib ligdaib aill uas diannaib deraib 25. Domrorbai dom teti olamtriamain trogsa iartimnaib inrigsa ritroich inslogsa

---

TRANSLATION.

1. Sain, O Christ, my speech, O lord of seven heavens! Let the guerdon of devotion be given to me,[b] O king of the white sun!

5. O white Sun that illuminest heaven with much of holiness! O King that rulest angels! O Lord of the men!

9. O Lord of the men! O King righteous, truly-good! Let every solace[c] be mine for (my) praise to thy kings!

13. Thy kings whom I praise, for thou art my[d] sovran. I have put for my heed constancy in praying to them.[e]

17. I pray a prayer of them—may it preserve me from [the evil] that I have got! —a fair people with beauty, the kings I have commemorated.

21. I have commemorated the kings around the King above clouds, some on beautiful (feast-) days, others under[f] vehement tears.

25. Let him bestow on me for my comfort, for I am a wretched weary one, the course which this host ran, according to this King's mandates.

[a] MS. inrslogsa. [b] B. 'may we attain the guerdon,' &c. [c] B. 'thy solace.' [d] B. and D. 'our' [e] A. 'to thee.' [f] A. and D. 'over.'

RAWL. B. 512.	LAUD 610.	LEBAR BRECC.
29. Roscalgatar rotu nad soreid laboethu iarnateacht donrigraid rodamnatar soethu	29. Roselgtar rout na[b]darreith labœthu rianatacht dondrigu rodamdatar swethu	29. Roselgatar rotu nadsoreid la boethu iarna techt donrigiu rodamdatar soethu
33. Rosonnlta fiad sluagaib ate conambrigaib robruithe indálaib rohorta fia :::::::	33. Rosuindtca fiad sluaguib oté conambrigaib robruthea indalaib rohorta fiadrígaib	33. Rosonnta fiadslogaib ate conambrigaib robrúitea indalaib ro orta findrigaib
37. Roringthe corindib ratennib iarrandaib roloisethea nasteindtib forlnachtetib lannaib	37. Rorringthea corrindib rotinnit irrannaib roboisethea uas tentib forluachthithib landaib	37. Roringthe corinnib rotennib iarrannaib roloisethe uastenntib forluachtetib lannaib
41. Roláithe for biastaib laberga cencineach sroig :::::: scól calad triasnasurna teinead	41. Rolatha forbiasta laberea eencineach rosraiglithea calad tresnasurnu tened	41. Roláithe forbiastaib laberga cencineeh sroiglithe scol calad triasnasurnu teined
45. Douetha iearcraib icrochaib a senna : itsloig icasindad iarnafoebraib feu :::	45. Ronetha acarecraib icrocha asennad intsluaig icásonnad iarnafiubraib fendad	45. Douetha iearcraib icrochaib asennath itsloig oecasinnad iarna foebraib fennad
49. Failte fri each noidig (?) asafortren fiam fodaimdis án croan mór dorigaib r :::	49. Fœlte fri each náidid assa forthren fiam fotomtis án croan mor do rigaib riam	49. Failte fria cech nóedig asa fortren fiam fodamtis án croan mor do rigaib riam
53. Rodamatar nile nuallsa mor ngnim nga- ::: arfirthuillem buide fri ihu. mac maire	53. Rodamdatar huile nasluaig[a] mor gnim ṅgaile arfirtuillem buidhe fri ihu. mac maire	53. Rodannatar uile nuallsa mor ṅgnim ṅgaile afirthuillem mbuide fri ihu. mac muire

29. They hewed out roads, it is not very easy to foolish ones: after[b] their coming to the kingdom they suffered pains.

33. They were pierced before hosts: they were with their powers (of endurance): they were broken in assemblies: they were slain before kings.

37. They were torn with spearpoints into very rigid pieces :[c] they were burnt over fires on white-hot gridirons.

41. They were flung before beasts by robbers without mercy, they were scourged —a hard course—through the furnaces of fire.

45. They were cast into dungeons: on crosses (was) their stretching, the hosts reviling them, after flaying them with swordedges.

49. Welcome (there was) to every death exceeding violent, horrible : many kings before this used to suffer—noble prowess !

53. They all suffered—great this mighty deed of valour—for a true addition of reward with Jesu son of Mary.

[a] written in a later hand over 'nalsu.'   [b] B. 'before.'   [c] B. 'the hosts.'

THE PROLOGUE

RAWL. B. 512.	LAUD 610.	LEBAR BRECC.
57. Maire cach rodasortsum rolamair anguinsium iarnasocthor ngorsum ite cenasunairsium [Here this fragment ends]	57. Maire each rodanortsam rolamair anguinsom iarnasœthar gairsom ité canismvirsom	57. Mairg cách rodusortsam rolamair anguinsium iarnasœthear ngorsum ato cenesmarsium
	61. Mórrig inna[n]gente bithgolait illosceud sluaig ihu. anascour itfœilte iarcoscur	61. Morrigu naṅgennti bithgolait hilloscud sloig ihu. cenescor itfailte iarcoscor
	65. INchoraid lasrorta conimmud auduire arrochur anaine itfássaig andúine	65. INcóraid lasorta conimud aṅdúire arrochinir anaine it fása aṅduine
	69. ITé iarnarrethib rosiachtatar rigi airruama centathe it bortgala mile	69. Hite iarnasæthaib rosiachtutar rige aruama centáide itbordgala mile
	73. Milid rodos crochsat ciabdar baile ambressa apiana itbrassa allighi nífessa	72. Mílid rotus crochsat cebtar bailce bressa apiana itbrasa allige nitfessa
	77. Nimthat milid ihu. rancatar treib toidlig dianeiss acuirp chraibdig	77. Nimtat milid ihu. rancatar treib toidlig dianeis acuirp chraibdig
		imemraib óir oiblig
	81. ITtaidbli find scoraib rigrad *crist* iarfuilib ríg domain iartolaib roírscáich arsudib	81. Hitaidble fiadscoraib rigrad *crist* iarfuilib rig domain iartolaib roírscaich arsuidib
	85. Hiruath 7 pilait	85. Hiruath ocus pelait

57. Woe is everyone who killed them, who dared to slay them: after their short suffering they ARE, though they abide not (here).

61. The great kings of the Pagans wail ever in burning: Jesu's hosts without a fall[a] are blithe after triumph.

65. The champions by whom they were slain, with (the) abundance of their cruelty, their splendour hath vanished, their forts are desolate.

69. They after their afflictions[b] have reached (the heavenly) kingdom: their graveyards (are) without concealment: they are *bordguls* of thousands.

73. (The) soldiers who crucified them, though strong were their battles,[c] their pains they are great, their graves they are not known.

77. Not so are Jesu's soldiers: they have reached a radiant homestead: behind them their holy bodies (are) in shrines of sparkling gold.

81. They are grand before multitudes, Christ's kings after wounds: (the) world's kings after lusts passed away before these.

85. Herod and Pilate, by whom our Lord suffered, their powers have been ended: their pains ever abide.

[a] B. 'a splendid leap' [b] D. 'their careers'
[c] A. 'though they were strong, valorous.'

xvi   THE CALENDAR OF OENGUS.

Laud 610.	Lebar Brecc.
lasroches arfiada	faroches arfiadu
fororcnait ambága	forforcennta ambrígu
bithmarait apiana	bithmarait apiana
89. Ihu. ciarocrochad	89. Ihu. cerocroch*ad*
arcoimdiu arngerat	arcoimdiu arngerait
for c*ach* ńdúil doróssa	forcech ńduil dorosat
is ocgri asrúracht	is og rí asreracht
93. Ciarbo rí indomain	93. Cérbo rig indomain
nabcodon rúad roglach	nabgodon ruad roglach
ómbébais latheglach	obebais latheglach
aordan dorodbath	aordan dorodbad
97. Nimtha insruith seanpol	97. Nimta seanpól manach
assa dithrub dubach	asadíthrub dubach
fria nóemainm cororath	fria noemainim corrorath
séntai c*ach* sluag subach	sentai cec*h*slog subach
101. Cia rosclaig cloideb	101. Coroselaig claideb
eoin babtai[s]t mbrigach	iohen bauptaist brigach
forbithché romorad	forbith ché romorad
iflaith dé rorigad	iflaith dé rorigad
105. Hiruath conarigain	105. Hiruath co*n*arigain
lasrort colín ilach	lasort colín ilach
nírathgab reim calad	nirathgab reim calad
tal*am* na nem ninach	talam na neam ninach
109. Nóebanim petair ap*stail*	109. Noemainim petair aspoil
asluindi each senad	atsluinne cech senad
noco*n*tiu lacredal	noconfiu la credal
dorogra ainm nera[n]d	dogara ainim neran
113. Neir ní fes a ligh*i*	113. Neir nifess alige
dethbir nibu cretar	deithb*ir* nibocretair
inbith collin popal	inbith colín popuil
morait lectan petair	morait lechtan petair

89. Jesu, though he was crucified, our Lord, our champion, over everything that he set up, he arose a perfect king.

93. Though the king of the world was Nebuchadnezzar red, very valiant, since he died with his household his sovranty hath perished.

97. Not so is old Paul (the) monk,[a] whose desert is gloomy: by his holy name with great grace, every happy host hath been sained.

101. Though a sword hewed mighty John Baptist, on earth here he was magnified, in God's kingdom he was crowned.

105. Herod with his queen by whom he was slain with a joyful multitude, received not—a hard course—earth nor delightful heaven.

109. Apostle Peter's holy name, every synod declares: not worthy with a believer is he who utters Nero's name.

113. Nero not known (is) his grave, reason (is), he was not godly: the world with a multitude of people,[b] magnify Peter's tomblet.

[a] B. 'the senior.'   [b] B. 'peoples.'

THE PROLOGUE. xvii

Laud 610.	Lebar Brecc.
117. Primshuide donéran in aeriunch phene pol apstol ard áge adreth riched réde	117. Prímsuide do nerainn inairenach péine pól aspol ard áige adreth riched redi
121. Roscaich ordan nerain issærchiau oshudiu ainm póil bunin intogu attasom for tuiliu	121. Roscaich ordan nerainn iserchian ósuidiu ainim póil buan toga atason fortuiliu
125. Ciapu tholcda rigan phelait amnuir (no amúr) chlaine arrochiur aaine oluid iloc núire	125. Ciarba tolgdai rigain phelait amuir chlúime arrochiuir aháine ótluid illoc núire
129. Nimtha maire ingen inmain attún daingen sil ádaim ard nimel mórsus lasluag naingel	129. Nimtá muire ingean inmain andúnª daingen síl nadaim ard imel morthus laslog naingel
133. Ciabdar aidblí ili meic deice drece nadcharam niconfes nach romar ainm nach hé fortalum	133. Ciaptar nille ile mec dec dric nádcelam noconfess naromar anim nafortalam
137. Nimthá ciric maccan amorscel rosretha bacain geim achatha rolín brugu betha	137. Nimtá ciric maccán amorsceol nosretha buaid ceiiu cain achatha rolin buren inbetha
141. Bid armenma uile athuath de nícbelam istorba diafromam inbrolach atheram	141. Bid armenma uile atuath de nadcelam istarba dianpromam in prolach doberam
145. ISbrég bríg indomain	145. ISbrec bríg indomain

117. A chief seat to Nero in a centre of pain: apostle Paul—lofty pillar!—hath reached a kingdom of smoothness.

121. Nero's sovranty hath vanished: it is very far from this: Paul's name—a lasting choice[b]—this is a-flowing (like a tide).

125. Though haughty was Pilate's queen from abundance of down, her delight hath vanished since she went into a place of clay.

129. Not so is Mary Virgin, delightful her strong fortress: Adam's seed, a lofty border, magnifies[c] her with a host of angels.

133. Though fair[d] were many sons of wrathful Decius, we love them not, it is not known, nor very great, the name of one of them[e] on earth.

137. Not so is Quiricus the child: his great renown hath been spread: it was his battle's fair shout that filled the burghs of the world.

141. Let all our minds be from God's people whom we conceal not: it is profit if we prove it, the prologue which we give.

145. A lie is the might of the world to everyone to whom it is a stead: this is the whole might—great love for Mary's Son.

ª leg. a dún.   [b] B. 'lasting the choice.'   [c] B. 'magnified.'
[d] B. 'vast.'   [e] A. 'in heaven nor.'

d

LAUD 610.
dochach diambí baile
issí inbríg uile
serec mór domac maire
149. Ciat moir ríg indomain
aduini atchisiu
fachét cét atuaisliu
amsain ísil issu
153. Ciat islin laduiniu
condelnaim angretha
biattáird uas dind latha
tria bithu naihbetha
157. INbith truag itaam
is duthain arígi
inrí onic aingliu
iscoimdiu cach thíre
161. Céd atír itaam
atá saidbre saigthe
dincort de dehn sochla
fil and dun ropridchai*
165. Atbath brog throm temra
la tairthim atlaithi
collin choir cuairt sruithe
maraid ard mor machi
169. Romuchad mor tairbaid
miad legaire loglaig
ainm patraic án erdraice
atásom forforbairt
173. Fororbairt incretem
méraid co dó inbrátha
genti bidbaid berrthair
nithrebthair arratha

LEBAR BRECC.
doncoch dianitbaile
issi inbrig uile
serec mor domacc muire
149. Cid móir ríg indomain
andúinc[b] atchissiu
fo cét cét atuaisliu
auasáin ísil ihu
153. Ciatisle fiadainib
cundehnaim angrethai
bid ard uas dind flatha
triabithu na[m]betha
157. INbith truag hitaimne
asduthain árige
inrig conic aingliu
incoimdiu cech thire
161. Cid natire hitaimne
itasaidbre saigte
doucrt de deilm sochla
fil dunn and ropritcha
165. Atbath broc tromm témra
latarthim atlatha
colín corad sruithe
maraid ard mor macha
169. Romúchad mor tirbaid
miad loeguire roglaig
ainm patraic an aurdraic
ata sou sororbairt
173. Forforbairt incredium
meraid codea bratha
gennti bidbaid berthair
ni trebthair aratha

149. Though great are the world's kings, O man thou seest, a hundred, hundred times nobler are Jesu's lowly servants.

153. Though they are very lowly before men, with noise of their crying, they will be high above the Kingdom's height through worlds of worlds.

157. The wretched world wherein we are, transitory is its kingdom: the King that ruleth angels is the lord of every land.

161. Even (in) the lands[c] wherein we are, there are (those) who seek wealth: of God's might, a famous sound, we have (one) who preached there.

165. Tara's mighty burgh hath perished with her kingdom's splendour (?): with a multitude of champions of wisdom[d] abideth great Armagh.

169. Was quenched—a great anguish—very valiant Loeguire's glory. Patrick's name splendid, conspicuous—this is a-growing.

173. The faith has grown: it will abide till Doomsday: guilty gentiles are carried off: their *raths* are not dwelt in.

* l. dun nann roptechthc.   [b] leg. á duini.   [c] B. 'land.'   [d] B. 'with choristers, a court of sages.'

THE PROLOGUE.   xix

LAUD 610.

177. Raith chru[a]chan roscaiche
la hailill gein mbuada
cáin ordan uas flaithib
fil icathir chluana

181. Classa buana binde
imchiaran ciatchois
lasceselbe mbuada
cluana moir m (l. mnc) nóis

185. Niptá ní bas tilsiu
serc dé madaronaib
adrad inrig nélaig
is de nibdir brónaig

189. Brog aillinde huallach
atbath lasluag mbágach
is mor brigit buadach
is mor aruam dalach

193. Brog emna rotetha
acht mairit aclocha
isruam iarthair betha
glend dalach dalocha

197. Lochat lainrech lígach
ferna forthren cobail
nimair indro[u]g úabair
ratha bice maice cogain

201. Cid na decais uile
breatha in crist chetna
ní mair bécc mac cogain
maraid aed mac setna

205. Senchathraig nangeinte
immarocrad ruadrac
itfássa con adhrad
amal lathrach lugdach

LEBAR BRECC.

177. Raith cruachan roscaiche
lahailill gein buada
cáinordan uasflaithib
fil icathir chluana

181. Classa buana binne
imchiaran ciatcois
lasessilbe mbuada
chluana móir maice nois

185. Niuntá ni asdiliu
serce dé madorónaid
adrad inrig nelaig
is de nibet bronaig

189. Broc aillinne uallach
athbath liaslog bagach
ismor brigit buadach
iscáin aruam dálach

193. Broc emna roscaiche
acht mairde aclocha
isruaim iarthair betha
glennd dalach dalocha

197. Loichet lainnrech ligach
ferna fortren cobail
nimair indroug uabair
ráith bécce maice cogain

201. Cid nadéchaid uilo
bretha iurig cétna
nimair bece macc cogain
mairid aed macc setnai

205. Sencathraig nangennti
imaroraid' rudrad
itfasa cenadrad
amal lathrach lugdach

---

177. Raith Crúachan hath vanished, with Ailill offspring of victory: a fair sovranty above kingdoms is in Cluain's city.

181. Choirs lasting, melodious around Ciaran if thou shouldst mention him, with a chant of victory of great Cluain-maic-nóis.

185. Not so is that which is dearest, God's love if ye did it, adoration of the Cloudy King, it is thence they will not be mournful.

189. Aillinn's proud burgh hath perished with its warlike host: great is victorious Brigit: fair[d] is her multitudinous city.

193. Emain's burgh hath vanished,[c] save that its stones remain: the Rome of the west of the world is multitudinous Glendalough.

197. A lamp lucid, beautiful, is Ferna mighty, good-great: the vainglorious throng abides not in Bécc son of Eogan's *rath*.

201. Though all went not, the same king[d] was carried off: Bécc son of Eogan abides not: Aed son of Setnac abideth.

205. The Gentiles' ancient cities whereon great duration was wrought: they are waste without adoration, like Lugaid's house-site.

[a] leg. imarśirad   [b] B. 'great.'   [c] B. 'fallen.'   [d] B. 'Christ.'

d 2

LAUD 610.

109. Indlocain rogabtha
deissib 7 tririb
itruama condalaib
cocétaib comilib

113. Romillead ingeintlecht
ciabulighach lethan
rolín flaith dé athar
nem talam la trethan

117. Tathund ní asnessu
ararsúil salm solmail
di niurt dé dianmedair
indíu diaid indomain

121. Dondchad drec rí rogda
no bran buadach berba
nibeir dím snim lobrai
athigid ammembrai

125. Mælruain iarnagaire
grian mar desmaig midi
acalecht conglaine
ictar cnet cach cride

129. IScomiuir incoimdiu
cethurtir athreta
bithtrogaid a náimtiu
bithmóraid a gerta

133. INgormrig romuchtha
indomnaill roplagtha
inciarain rorigtha
incronain romartha

137. Namorsléibe annaig
rotesetha corindib
dorónta colléee
sléibe doua glindib

LEBAR BRECC.

109. Inlocáin rogabtha
condessib istrivib
itruama condálaib
cocétaib comilib

113. Romilled ingenntliucht
ciarboligda lethan
rolín flaith dé athar
neam talam latrethan

117. Tathum[a] ní isnessu
ararsuil salm solmail
de niurt de dianmedar
indiu deud domain

121. Donnchad dric rnad rogdai
no bran buadach berba
nibeir dím snim lobra
aithigid amemra

125. Moelruain iarnagaire
grian már desmuig mide
ocáleacht conglaine
icthar cneat cech cride

129. IS comiuir incoimdiu
cethuirtir athrétha
biththrógait anáintiu
bithmoraid ágértha

133. INgormrig romuchtha
indomnaill roplagtha
inciaráin rorigtha
incronain romártha

137. Namorslebi amlaig
rotesetha corindib
doronta colcci
slebti donaglinnib

109. The little places that were taken, with twos and threes, are Romes with multitudes, with hundreds, with thousands.

113. The paganism hath been destroyed, though fair it was (and) widespread: God Father's kingdom has filled heaven, earth and sea.

117. We have what is nearest, before our eyes a holy psalm, by God's virtue is vehemently announced to-day the world's end.

121. Donnchad the wrathful, ruddy[b] chosen, or Bran the victorious of Berbha, visiting their burial-places takes not from me the weariness of weakness.

125. Maelruain, after pious service of him, a great sun in Meath's south plain, at his tomb with purity is healed every heart's sigh.

129. The Lord is equally just, if his ... are scrutinized: He ever makes miserable his foes: He ever magnifies his champions.

133. The red kings have been stifled: the Domnalls have been plagued: the Ciaráns have been crowned: the Cronáns have been magnified.

137. The great mountains of evil have been cut with spearpoints: straightway mountains have been made of the glens.

[a] leg. Táthunn

[b] B. 'King'

THE PROLOGUE.   xxi

LAUD 610.

241. Cia ronbeth dochingecht
cath fridemon detla
diar fortacht ard áge
maraid ancri*st* cetna
245. Ciatuallaig rig talman
itlachtaib *con*glaini
atuclat iartuile
téit cach rianaraile
249. INrí cain *con*glaine
ihu. uas tuinn tuile
nodgeinair omaire
maraid diancis huile
253. Rolénad nert demuin
co*n*adubluag digna
bithmaraid indúagi
nert ruanaid arigui
257. Ciaresmai foa*n*indsom
dorigi arannsom
ol nítiamda tiusom
niféimdebthar annsom
261. Badsonairt arnárle
ascnam an*as* dilse
ol iscd as uaisliu
caram uile issu
265. A issu not guidiu
ar écnaire nasluagsa
dothol inmaith morsa
arinssi[a] dorónsa
269. Doronsa doreirsiu
arí sion sluagaig
rombith beo latrigraid
isin bithlaith buadaig

LEBAR BRECC.

241. Ciaronbeth dochingthecht
cath fria demun detla
diarcombair ard áige
maraid incr*ist* cétna
245. Cituallaig rig thalman
itlachtaib isglainiu
atfiadat iartuiliu
teit cách rianarailiu
249. INrig cain congairiu
ihu. uas tuind tuiliu
madgenair omuire
mairid dianéis uile
253. Rolenad nert demain
co*n*adubsluag dignai
bithmairid inuage
ne*r*t ruanaid arrigne
257. Ciarosme foa*n*indsom
dorige arannsom
olnitiamdai tiusom
nifemdibther annsom
261. Budsonairt arnáirle
ascnam an*a*sdilsiu
arisse*d* isuaisliu
carum uile ihu.
265. Aihu. notguide
arecnaire naslógsa
dothol inmaith morsa
arímsi doronsa
269. Doronsa dorersiu
arig sión sluagaig
robeosa latrigraid
isinbithlaith buadaig

241. Though we have evil championing, a fight against a bold demon, to aid us, a lofty pillar, the same Christ abideth.

245. Though haughty are the kings of earth in robes that are brightest, they shew abundantly that each goes before another.

249. The fair King with piety,[b] Jesus over a flooding wave, was happily born of Mary : he abides after them all.

253. The demon's power hath been wounded, with his black reproachful host: ever abides in perfection our King's mighty power.

257. If we should go under his diadem, his part will come : since he is not timid, feeble, there will not be denial there.

261. Let our will be firm, to visit what is dearest : because it is this that is noblest, let us all love Jesus.

265. O Jesus I beseech thee, for intercession of these hosts, thy desire (be) this great good, this numbering which I have done.

269. I have done thy will, O king of hostful Zion : may I be with thy kings in the eternal, victorious realm !

[a] MS. armissi   [b] B. 'purity'

Laud 610.	Lebar Brecc.
173. Rob beosa fortlnimsiu isindlaith imbísiu bendacht cacha brotgail forthordon aíssu	173. Robcosa fortlnimsiu isinflaith imbistu bendacht cecha bordgal forhordan aihu.
277. A issu conrocther dorigrad dorélad iarsindurd dochuad*ur* chuccut conem nélach	277. Aihu. conruidiur dorigrad dorélad iarsin urd dochuatar chucut forncam nélach
281. Nifíl issinbli*adain* acrist cianocluinter lathi issindalltar nachatrissed muinter	281. Nifuil isinbliadain acrist cenf cláinter laithe isinalltar nach atrisad múnnter
285. IS menand a ruri arí rimther flaithe sloindfimni conlothi socrcoindli cac*h*laithi	285. ISmenand aruire aríg rimther flaithe sluindfemne colluithe socrchoinnle cech laithe
189. Arlebran nosturfem^a frinech foraniarair regmai cen nach dichil cac*h*ndiriuch don bli*adain*	189. Arlebráin nostuirfem frinech foraniarair regmai cenach dichel cec*h* diriuch donbli*adain*
193. Bid hé corp arnaigde admat nab di tiamda comlin caibdel cóemda fo lín laithi i*n*bliadna	193. Bid he corp arnaicde admat na batlamdai comlin cáibtel cocmdai folín laithe blia*dnae*
197. Arnabé fo*r*erimniur don intliucht cosaichi cac*h* caibtel cosruithe sloind*fi*t feil alaithe	197. Arnabe forerindither doindtliucht cosaiche cech cáibtel colluithe sluinnfet féil cec*h* laithe
301. Laithe na mís mársa frisreith ingrian buansa araslnagad nánsa nibruifem anunalsa	301. Laithe nanús mórsa frisraith ingrian buansa arinsluaiged nánsa nibruifem annuallsa

173. May I be at thy hand in the realm wherein thou art—a blessing of every *bordgal* upon thy sovranty, O Jesu!

176. O Jesu, may I attain it, to manifest thy kings according to the order they went to thee to cloudy heaven!

281. There is not in the year, O Christ, though it is not heard, a day on which, into the other world, a family would not come to thee.

285. It is manifest, O Chief, O King that numberest princes, we will declare swiftly every day's noble lights.

289. Our books we will search them for everyone on seeking them: we will go without any neglect straightway to the year.

293. This shall be our building's body—timber that is not dark—a number of fair chapters equal to the number of a year's days.

297. That thou mayst not be falling, that thou mayst attain to understanding, every chapter swiftly^b shall declare every day's feast.

301. On days of those great months to which this lasting sun runs, for this splendid host we shall not forget their acclamation.

^a MS. nostfurem. ^b B. 'with wisdom.'

THE PROLOGUE.   xxiii

LAUD, 610.

305. Nónæ 7 idæ
rem kailne cofíre
fornargan comhbaine
biait ina líni
309. L[il]cissiu ditlaithib
itlebranaib leirib
lilesa iarlinib
coléir dina feilib
313. Manithuca samlaid
ord fil forarláidib
nondlomaim fia dálaib
is dallcheilliu dúinib
317. Denam tormach néolais
do intliucht cosaiche*
co tarlam cenloithi
fo leith feil cachlaithi
321. Laithi na mis gréine
nimfoersa asallann
diar laith arnapi[n]mall
acht da se (ii. kl. x.) kl.
325. On kalainn coalailiu
nimfoersa iarsetaib
acht cuic caibdil uasail
sescat ar tri .c.aib
329. Occuingid ua fele
assa forthren taitnem
túir la feige frithgnam
colleir ord na caibdel
333. INtord innacaibtel
conallaither leirib[b]
issé ord iarlínib
fili forsna feilib

LEBAR BRECC.

305. Nóna 7 ída
réim kalne cofíre
fort margan combáine
biait inaline
309. Lilessa dolaithib
itlebranaib lérib
lilessai iarlinib
colléir donafclib
313. Manithucai samlaid
ord fil forarláidib
notlomaim fiadalaib
itáll célliu doinib
317. Denum tórmach ncolais
doinntliucht cosaiche
cech caibtcal coluithe
sluinnfid féil cechlaithe
321. Laithe namís gréne
ni[m]fcirsa asalland
diarlaid aruápinmall
acht di .ui. cáin kalland
325. On callaind cóalaile
ni[in]foirson iarsétaib
acht .u. cáibtil uasail
sescat ar .ccc.aib
329. Occunchid naséile
asafortren taitncam
túir laségi frithgnam
coleir ord nacaiptel
333. Intord inacaiptel
conaleidib lérib
ise ord iarlinib
file forsnafélib

305. Nones and Ides, a series of calends with truth, on thy margin with whiteness shall be the lines.

309. Thou wilt follow the days in thy pious booklets, thou wilt follow according to lines the festivals piously.

313. Unless thou understand so the order that is on our lays, I declare it before assemblies, it is blind guidance (?) to men.

317. Let us make an increase of knowledge that thou mayst attain to understanding: every chapter swiftly shall declare every day's feast.

321. The days of the sun's months to sing them shall not delay me, that there be not sadness to our lay, but twice six fair calends.

325. From the one calend to the other this shall not delay me according to paths, but five noble chapters, sixty to three hundreds.

329. In seeking the feasts, whose radiance is full strong, search with heedful attention industriously the order of the chapters.

333. The order of the chapters with their pious lays, it is the order according to the lines which are on the festivals.

* no cach saite.

[b] no cona laidib léirib.

LAUD 610.

337. Flaithim nóeb nanduile
dia* macc maire nóebe
issu inmaine áge
toided re síl duine
Ré síl dalach dúine
Finit.

LEBAR BRECC.

337. Flaithem noem nanduile
cri*st* macc muire noeime
ihu. inmain áige
toided resíl doine

337. The holy Prince of the elements, Christ son of holy Mary, Jesus, beloved pillar, let him come before men's seed.

* no cri*st*.

GLOSS FROM THE LEBAR BRECC.

[NOTE: where the gloss refers to a whole line, that line is not here reprinted.]

Line 5. *fornosna* .i. soillsiges. 21, 22. .i. imraidim araile donoebaib filet ifla*thos* nime 7 araile filet indiamraib deiritib parrduis. 23, 24. .i. ro imraidim nanoebu hillathib aillib cosubai 7 nosimeraidim foderaib dianaib colchaire. 25 *domrorbai* .i. romtoirne no romtoirbire. *domteti* .i. domaibindius. 26 *triamain* .i. toirsech. *trog* .i. toirsech. 28. *ritroich* .i. roreith. 29. *roselgatar* .i. rosligsetar. *rotu* .i. slige. 30. *nad soreid* .i. nach roreid. 32. .i. rodamsat soethu .i. piana. 34. *conambrigaib* .i. cofoiditin moir. 37. *roringthe* .i. roreptha. *corinnib* .i. imblogaib tendib. 40 .i. for lannaib lauteib. *luachtctib* .i. lanteib. 42. *laberga* .i. la fergachu 43. *calad* .i. cocruaid. 46 *asennath* .i. aducit (?) .i. asinecht .i. amartraige .i. carcar artus 7 croch fadeoid. 47. *oca sinnad* .i. ocacained 48. .i. iarnafenulad cofoebraib. 50. *fiam* .i. grannai. no robui indfetheam feochair calma occu oclecud amarbtha ardia. 51. *croan* .i. cronugud l. crodacht. 52. *riam* .i. remund .i. isnabaimscraib rocaite remuind. 54. *nuallsa* .i. oll indso .i. mor indso. 57 *rodusortsum* .i. rodusoirg 59. .i. iarnasaethar gairitseom. 60. *ate* .i. isiat. *conesmarsium* .i. cid namarait .i. mairit ecin. 62. *hilloscud* .i. ifiirnd, 64. *failte* .i. aige .i. oegid muinnter de isintsoegul. no robotoegid indiu uair fuarutar failte oeged. no roboebind intoscor .i. inleim ruesat apianaib intsoegail bifailte fochraicce. 67. *arrochiuir* .i. roerchran. *anaine* .i. anailbnius. 69. *ite* .i. isiat 70. *rosiachtatar* no friscobsat 71. *centaide* .i. cenfolach. 72 *it bordgala* .i. it lana conice ambord domilib congail chrabuid necu. 74. *bailce* .i. calma l. tren. *bressa* .i. ambága 75. *itbrasa* .i. lithailcide .i. mora. 77. *nimtat* .i. nihamlaidsin atat. 78. *toidlig* .i. taitnemaig. 80. *himemraib* .i. hiscrinib. *oiblig* .i. solusta. 81. *hitaidble* .i. nime 7 talman. 82. *fuilib* .i. martra. 83. *tolaib* .i. acolla. 84. *arsuidib* .i. orru .i. forraib. 86 *arfiadu* .i. arfiaduaise cri*st* fil hifiadnaisi chaich 7 ita cach fiadnaise. 87. *forcennta* .i. roforbaide. 90. *arngcrait* .i. armae beoda. uair gerat artus .i. mac indiu 7 isris atherar gernt indiu risinti isbeoda. 92. *isegri* .i. isrig comlan forru uile. 94. *rogloch* .i. rogalnch .i. rofergach. 95. *bebais* .i. o atbath fen 7 o atbath atheglach. 96. *dorodbad* .i. rodibdad. 100. *sentai* .i. atchi .i. a anim each slog ernibdech. 101. *ocroselnig* .i. cia rodslig .i. rottesc. 102. *brigach* .i. ernibdech. 106 *ilach* .i. subai. 107 *calad* .i. cruaid. 108 *ninach* .i. gablach. 110 *atsluinne* .i. asluindid. 112. *neran* .i. neir. 114 *cretair* .i. creitmech. 119. *aige* .i. calma. 120. *adreth* .i. roét. *redi* .i. reid

122 *erchian* .i. adbulchian *osuidiu* .i. osin hille l. ondiu eosin 124 *tuiliu* .i. immed crabuid 125 *ciarba tolydai* .i. ciarbo diumsach 126 *amur* .i. ahitamed 127 *arrochinir* .i. roerchran *aháine* .i. ahaibnius 131 *ard imel* .i. imnda cohimbel indomain 132. *morthus* .i. moraid inní muire síl nádaim and 134 *mec dec dric* .i. fergaig 135 .i. nach romar fortalmain .i. isuathad fortalmain rofitir ainm neich dib 138 .i. rosreith fondomun achlu 139 *buaid ecim* (*no bo geim*) .i. geim aurdraice 142 *nadeelam* .i. nidichlem nanoebu 144 .i. dia triallum crabud istarba dún inni doberum isiumbrolachsa .i. dinsium intsoegail 146 *dianitbaile* .i. intí dianad árus and 150 *atchissiu* .i. atchí condat moir uarig isintáoegulsa 7 *condat* mo muinnter nime 154 .i. cid mó deilm fogur 7 gríth .i. gáir nandaine aflius bid mo gloir nanoeb thall 155. *uasdiud* .i. uas nimmard 161 *na tire* .i. heriu 162 .i. ata sochaid[e] snides a suidbre 163 .i. ise nert dé is erdareu 7 is shochlu inda cechnert 7 ise dobeir forsinsoegul erchrn 164 *ropritcha* .i. pritchas dún 174 *codea* .i. colaa 175 *berthair* .i. dontshoegul 179 *uaeflaithib* .i. uas cech rige indomain 182 *ciatcois* .i. cia etsi, *no* cia indisc 184 .i. cluain nois muor .i. *uomen* uiri. 189 *broc uillinne* .i. dún fil illaignib 194 .i. fogeba diarrís emain 197 *loichet* .i. locharn 198 *cobail* .i. iubail forsintsoegul 204 *aed mac setnai* .i. momoedoc feruai 206 *imaroraid* .i. immaroferad .i. inmu roguiad *rudrad* .i. rodurad .i. beith cofoda forferand comaithech 209 *rogubtha* .i. onanoemnaib artus 214 *ciarbo ligdu* .i. ciarbo halaind 216 *trethan* .i. fairrge .i. inmuir .i. oilena inmara 217 *tathum no tathurm ní is nessu* .i. ata dún erchrn is nessu ocund 218 .i. forcedul follus narfhindnaise. 219 *de niurt de* .i. nert dé dobeir erchra forinsoegul conaretaib 221 *Donnchad* .i. donnchad mac domnaill mide. rig mide. *rogdai* .i. roga sochaide he 222 *bran* .i. bran ardehend mac muiredaig ríg laigen 224 *a memra* .i. annducul 225 *iarnagaire* .i. oengus doroine agaire 226 *desmuig mide* .i. ri mag andes ata achell .i. tamlachtu 229 *is cominir* .i. is comdíriuch hic híce namnaithe 7 hietraethad nanole 233 *ingormrig* .i. uarig erdareu 234 *domnaill* .i. roges. 237 *andaig* .i. feirge 240 *donaglinnib* .i. donanoemaib 7 donacellaib 241 *dochingthecht* .i. dochalmacht 242 *detla* .i. dana 250 *uas tuind tuiliu* .i. uas inuud ard intsoegail 251 *nadgenaic* .i. ismadgenair duinne agein 254 *dignai* .i. dímienech 255 *inuaye* .i. inimlaine 256 *ruanaid* .i. roenid for cech cath *arrigne* .i. ihu. xpi. 257 *ciarosme* .i. tast .i. cia thairismit l. ciarismait *foamindsom* .i. auaisle, *no* foachroichsium difnes each 259 *tiamdai* .i. metta 260 .i. uifeimebthar arad eofil cech maith andsom 262 .i. tiagam co arndíles .i. cograd nde 7 conuolad 285 *menand* .i. follas 287 *colluithe* .id est cito .i. dian 299 colluithe .i. déni

[NOTE.—Besides the above glosses there are the following in a modern hand :—5 *riched* .i. righ fath 7 *eonic aingliu* . . . . da bhfuil cumachta orru 11 .i. goraibe agvm gach s . . . 17 doib .i. vaidhib 20 antsreith riogda roiomradus*]

* Facs. roiomrardus

RAWL. 505, fo. 211 a.

1. Re sil dalach doine
toided in ri remain
luid fo' recht nard nerain
crist hi kl. enair
2. Essodir intepscop
abb ocailse airde
manchene an airgge
scoithine mind[b] mairce
3. Marmartra rodanis
connchleir caineisce
findlug cofeib huasle
fintan derb duin bleisce
4. Bas caith aequilini
combuidin ba balcu
hifuil crist trenchurpu
docoemnagtar tlactu
5. Togairm semeon srotha
cocrist cruth ronglea
bacaingrian greit nua
ciar ingen duibrea
6. Raith corig rantoga
iulian ba baill nglaine
nidlig sar slan suba
baithis mar meice maire
7. Martra luciaui
coslog mar ba dixu
imrordus ashuasliu
tosach corguis issu

LAUD, 610.

1. Re sil dalach dáine
taided inri remain
luid forecht nard uerail
crist ikl. enair
2. Essodir intepscop
abb ecailsi airdi
mainchine anargge
scotheine mind mairge
3. Mommartra rodamais
conncleir cainesce
fintan cofeib huaisle
finnlug derb dunbleisci
4. Bas caid aquiline
combuidne ba balccu
hifuil crist trinchurpu
docóemnacair tlachtu
5. Tognirm semeoin srotha
cocrist cruth ronglea
ba caingrian greid nua
ciar ingen duibrea
6. Raith corig rantoga
iulian all nglaine
nidlig sar slan suba
bathes mar m. maire
7. Martra luciáne
coslúag már badixu
imrordus as huaisliu
tosach corgais issu

LEBAR BRECC, p. 79.

1. Resil dalach doine
taided inri remain
luid forecht arderail
crist ikll. enair
2. Esodir inteps[c]op
abb ecailse airde
mainchine ancirge
scuitline mind mairge
3. Mormartra rodanis
connacleir cainesce
fintan cofeib uaisle
finnlug derb duinlesce
4. Bas caid aquilini
combuidin babalcu
hifuil crist treacurpu
docoemnactar tlachtu
5. Togairm semeoin srotha
cocrist cruth ronglea
bacaingrian greit nua
ciar ingen duibrea
6. Raith coarig rantoga
iulian all nglaine
nidlig sar slan suba
baithes mar mc. muirc
7. Martra luciani
coslog mar badilsiu
imrordus isuaisliu
tossach corgais ihu.

TRANSLATION.

1. Before men's multitudinous seed let the pre-eminent King advance: Christ on January's calends underwent a law,[a] high bidding!
2. Isidorus the bishop, abbot of a high church: Mainchíne of splendid Eirge, Scoithíne diadem of Mairge.
3. Rhodon's great martyrdom, with his clergy, fair moons! Fintan with an age of nobleness, Finnlug the sure, of Dún Blesce.
4. Aquilinus' noble death, with a troop that was strongest: in Christ's blood through their bodies they washed garments.
5. Simeon the sage's calling unto Christ —a form that purified! A fair sun, a fresh champion, Ciar daughter of Duibrea.
6. Ran to his King—right noble choice! —Julianus, rock of purity. Deserves not outrage — perfect gladness! — the great baptism of Mary's Son[d].
7. Lucianus' martyrdom with a great host that was dearest.[e] I have commemorated what is noblest, the beginning of Jesu's lent.

[a] MS. fo   [b] MS. and   [c] circumcisio secundum legem Moysi.   [d] The Epiphany.   [e] B. and D. 'highest.'

Rawl. 505.	Laud, 610.	Lebar Brecc, p. 79.
8. Etsecht egimoni epscop etla arda ercnat hua[g] an orbla nechtan nair dealba	8. Etsecht egemoní epscop etla ardda érenait huag anorba nechtan ner dealba	8. Etsecht ecimoni epscop etla airdæ ercnait uag án orba nechtan nair dealbœ
9. Ailli geill conglaini argnuis rig roradis fœlan deoda digrais felix finn uitalis	9. Ailli geill conglaine fiadgnuis rig roradis fœlan deoda digrais felix find uitalis	9. Aildi geill conglaine argnuis rig roraidis fœlan deoda digrais felix find uitalais
10. Almini anitge arnantecema drochrann milit caid cain cathbarr diarmait inse clothrann	10. Almini itge nachamtecma drochrand milid cain caincathbarr diarmait indsi clotrand	10. Ailme itge ndichra nachintecma drochrand milid caid cain cathbarr diarmait indse clothraud
11. Croch in martir phetar cosintluag lan gailc ahegept an suba tanic macc mar maire	11. Croch inmairtir petair cosiusluag lán gaile aheigipt ánsuba tainic macc mar maire	11. Croch inmartir petair conasluag lan gaile ahegipt án suba tanic mac már maire
12. Martra mar muscenti conachleir chain chlannaich crist asruna rinnaid laicenn macc baith bannaich	12. Martra már muscente conachleir cain claunaig crist isrúna rindid laidgenn m. baith bannaig	12. Martra mor muscenti conachleir cain claudaig crist asrunaid rindaig laidcend mc. baith bandaig
13. Ambennacht ronbia balc itge cenalgais sulpicc sothnge suabais clair abb pichtadis	13. Ambennacht ronbia balcc itge cenalges sulpic sochla suabais helair ab pictanis	13. Ambendacht ronbia balc itge cenailgis sothnge sochla suabais clair abb pictanis
14. Pais gluceri deochain diarfiadait basereach sruth nola noeb sochlach felix fland find fechtnach	14. Pais gluceri deochain diarfiadait ba sereach sruth nola noeb sochlach feilix flann find fechtnach	14. Pais luceri deochain diarfiadait basereach sruth nolæ noeb sochlach felic fland find fechtnach

8. Death of Egemonius, a bishop of high penitence. Erenait a virgin, a noble heritage. Nechtán from the east, from Alba.

9. Beautiful hostages with purity before a King whom thou hast mentioned, Faelán godly, excellent, Felix the fair, Vitalis.

10. We pray a fervent prayer,[a] that an ill lot happen not to us: chaste[b] Miletus, a fair helmet: Diarmait of Inis Clothrann.

11. The cross of Peter Martyr, with his host full of valour. From Egypt—bright gladness!—came Mary's great Son.

12. The great martyrdom of Moscentius, with his clergy having fair offspring. Christ's mysteries Laidcenn, son of Baeth Bannach, interpreted.

13. May their blessing be unto us—a strong prayer without importunity!—Sulpicius famous,[c] gentle, Hilary abbot of Poitiers.

14. Deacon Glycerius' passion: to our Lord he was loving: Felix, sage of Nola, holy, famous: Fland fair, happy.

[a] D. "their prayer."   [b] B. "fair."   [c] D. "eloquent."

RAWL. 505.	LAUD. 610.	LEBAR BRECC, pp. 79, 80.
15. Foraith mur mór ngalar carais mortromtredau ingriau ban ban muman ite cluana credail	15. Foraith mor ñgur ñgal-ar carais mor troin tredau ingriau bán ban muman mide chluana credail	15. Foraid mor ngur ngalar carais mor troin tredan ingriau bán ban muman ite cluana credal
16. Craidbig hifeil fursa fris rocobsat rige noi mili[a] meith buada forfichit mar mile	16. Cradbig ifeil fursa frisrogabsat rigi noe mile meit buada forfichit mormile	16. Craibdig ifeil fursa fris rogabsat rige trimile meit buada for .xx.it mor mile
17. Nosmolammar menic folu nidatcalaid lucht cessais cenchinaid hifeil antoin manaigh	17. Nosmolomar menic fobith nibdar calaid lucht roches[b] cen chinaid ifeil antóin manaig	17. Nosmolamar menic fobith nidatcalaid lucht cesais cen chinaid ifeil antóin manaig
18. Morad petair epstail hiroim rad asdixu lasinlith ashuasliu tasc mar mathair issu	18. Morad petair epstail irroim róm asdixu lassin lith as uaisliu tasc mor mathar isu	18. Morad petair apstail iruaim rad isdixu lasinlith isuaisliu bás mor mathar ihu.
19. Etsecht maire marthæ coniugum nodnali lasinfeil cosaire senphol cain conani	19. Estecht muire ismartha sororum lazari lassinfeil cosaire senphoil cain conáine	19. Etsecht muire martha sororum lazairii lasinfeil conocbi senpoil cain conani
20. An cethrur conuagu foroenlith as noelu molocca moecca sabbaist ocus oenu	20. Ancethrur conhuagu foroenlith isnóibiu molacen moecca sabaist ocus oennu	20. An cethrur conuaige foroenlith asnoebu molaen mocca sapaist 7 oenu
21. Robat oin damsnadud[c] comrig reim as dixu fainche feim as huasliu agna ingen issu	21. Ropat oen domsnadug comrig reim as dixu fuinche feidm as uaisliu agna ingen issu	21. Robatoen domsnadud comrig reim asdixu fuinche feidm isuaisliu agna ingen ihu.
22. Etsecht ingen comgaill colman m[ai]cc huibeona ualerius cendigna felix fuair cuairt ceolda	22. Estecht ingen comgaill colman mc. huabeogna uale[ri]us cendigna feilix fuair cuaird ceolda	22. Etsecht ingen chomgaill colman mc. hui beona uarilius cendigna felic fuair cuairt ccolda

15. She underwent great grievous disease, she loved great, heavy fasting, the white sun of Munster's women, Ite of Cluain Credail.

16. Pious men on Fursae's feast ascended to the Kingdom, nine[d] thousand—greatness of victory!—and a score of great thousands.

17. We praise them often, because they are[e] not hard, the folk that suffered without crime on Monk Antony's feast.

18. Apostle Peter's magnifying in Rome —a saying[f] that is noblest!—At the festival that is highest Jesu's Mother's great death.[g]

19. The death of Marius (and) Martha the spouses, which thou invokest[h] on the feast with nobleness[i] of old Paul fair with splendour.

20. A splendid four I sew together on one feast that is holiest, Molaca, Mocca, Sebastianus, and Oenu.

21. May they be one to protect me to my King—course that is noblest!—Fuinche —effort that is highest ! Agnes, a daughter of Jesus.

22. Death of Comgall's daughters: Colmán son of aue-Beóna : Valerius without reproach : Felix found a melodious sojourn.

[a] l. tecra mile.   [b] l. cesais.   [c] MS. damspnadud   [d] A. 'three'   [e] B. 'were'   [f] B. 'course'
[g] The Assumption.   B. D. 'tidings'
[h] A. and B. "The death of Mary and Martha, sisters of Lazarus."   [i] A "holiness."

JANUARY.

Rawl. 505.

23. Cesad seueriani
clemati consadu
ronsnadat dondrigu
conandunud danu
24. Domanmaindomchorpan
ropmur arcech merblen
babaill bruth oir orlan
conatriur deiblen
25. Nidedbul alláithe
lith friscuirter gretha
coerist cechaing saithi
pol imbathis bretha
26. ISbrigach asluagad
larig dodanfarchi
sluag orta iargortai
lapais policarpi
27. Carais maeda muirgein
mirbuil gein combuadaib
bert glanbuaid fiadrigaib
agnetis deichnuagaib
28. La haccobran huanui
pais ocht nuag conani
gabsat buaid condirgi
sluag mar mesorani
29. Ain epscoip roradius
ronsnadat diarndilius
hipolitus paulus
gillas constantiuus

Laud, 610.

23. Cessad seueriani
clemati consadu
ronsnaidet donrigu
conandunad dana
24. Domanmain domchorpau
ropmur arcach meirblen
baball bruth óir orlan
conatriur dedblen
25. Nidedbol allathe
lith rochuirset gretha
coerist cechaing sathe
pol imbáithis bretha
26. ISbrigach allochet
larig dodonfairchi
sluag ortai iarngorti
lapais policarpi
27. Carnis moida murgen
mirbuil gein combaugaib
bert glanbuaid fiarigaib
angetes .x. nuagaib
28. La occobran huaine
pais ocht nuag conaine
gabsat buaid condirgi
sluag mor miseraine
29. Anepscop roraidius
ronsnadud diar[n]dirus
ipolitus paulus
gillas constantinus

Lebar Brecc, p. 80.

23. Cesad cebriani
clementi consadu
ronsnadut dondrigu
conandunad danu
24. Domanmaindomchorpau
ropmur ar cech meirblen
babaill bruth oir orlan
conathriur dedblen
25. Nidedbal alaithi
lith fris cuirther gretha
coerist cechaing saithe
pol ambáithes bretha
26. ISbrignach allochet
larig dodotfairci
sluaig orta iarngorta*
lapais policarpti
27. Carais moeda muirgen
mirbuil gein combuadaib
bert glanbuaid fiadrigaib
agna condeich nuagaib
28. Lahacobran uainni
pais .uiii. nuag conani
gabsat buaid condirge
sluag mor miseriani
29. An escoip roraidius
ronsnadut diarndilius
ipolitus paulus
gillas constantinus

---

23. Severianus' suffering (and) Clement's I set together: may they protect us to the Kingdom with their daring host!

24. To my soul, to my poor body be a wall against every weak woe Babylas, an abundant, glowing-mass of gold, with his three weaklings!

25. Not puny the day, a festival at which shouts are sent forth: to Christ went a troop: Paul was borne into baptism.[b]

26. Mighty is their lustre[c] with (the) King who guards us, hosts slain after famine at Polycarp's passion.

27. Moeda loved Muirgein ('sea-birth'), a wonderful birth with victories! She won a pure victory before kings, Agnes with ten virgins.

28. With Accobran from us, (the) passion of seven virgins with splendour: they got victory with righteousness, Messorianus' great host.

29. Splendid bishops whom I have mentioned—may they protect us to our possession! Hippolytus, Paulus, Gildas, Constantinus.

---

[a] The facsimile has *iarngngorta*   [b] conversio sancti Pauli ad fidem.   [c] 'hosting' D.

RAWL. 505.	LAUD, 610.	LEBAR BRECC, p. 80.
30. Seaca archet martir martra morsus doros ainsium arlin amus enan rois rind solos	30. Cóecca[a] ar .c. mairtir martra morsa dorus snaidsium iarlin amus enan ruis rind sol*us*	30. L. ar .c. martir martra morsus dorus ainsium arlin amus enan rois rind solus
31. Sluind ṡed fortren ferna mæl anfaid ainm remain benait com[b]rig romoir barr find forsluag enair	31. Sluind ṡed fortren ferna melanfaid ainm remain benaid combrig romoir barrfind forsluag enair	31. Sluind ṡed fortren ferna moelanfaid ainm remain benait combrig romoir barrfind forsluag enair

30. An hundred and fifty[b] martyrs: a door of martyrdom magnified them. May he protect me against a number of temptations, Enan of Ros(mór), (the) bright headland.

31. Declare strong Aed of Ferns (and) Maelanfaid a name pre-eminent: they strike, with full great Brig, a fair end on January's host.

[a] no xl [b] D. 'An hundred and sixty.'

January.
GLOSS FROM THE LEBAR BRECC, pp. 78, 79, 80.
[Figures in parentheses ( ) refer to the lines of each quatrain.]

1. (1) Resil dálach .i. hicotat dála .i. congregationes. (2) tóided .i. ueniat .i. ante omnes. (3) luid forecht arderail .i. uasal incrail shiansaide .i. esium féu forecht imdibe nam uis [leg. quamvis] uile opus quia ér uasal dicitur ut dicitur érlom .i. luam uasal. *no* erail .i. uasal ail. .i. incloch de quo facta est circumcicio apud ueteres. *no* eráin .i. forcraid. sic dicit innúiumech. nifuil crain duit aud. *no* uráin ab eo quod est urou i.e. ab urina .i. incroicend remaniusa rincach .i. réim uáiniusa. *no* romain .i. remṡamud infás bís acind inbaill ferrdai sis. *no* neraiu .i. furail .i. informad bec nothesta and

[The foregoing glosses are in p. 78, at the end of the prologue.]

1. (1) *resil* .i. ante omnes qui sequntur. *doine* .i. sancti. (2) *taided* .i. toet l. ticead. *remain* .i. remaigti ante omnes sanctos .i. sub circum[ci]cionim .i. remfaisnes *no* tossach (3) *ard* .i. uasal *ail* .i. uasal. *no* aurain .i. ernibind. (4) *crist* .i. a crismate .i. ab unctione[a] dictus. *no* urain .i. imarcraid dotheeht forecht nimdibe

2. (3) *aneirge* .i. annirgob .i. incladnaib be. *no* aband .i. fil ocnchill 7 airic abainm

3. (2) *cainesce* .i. esca cain *no* alaind *no* lucida. *esce* .i. escomlad (3) *cofeib* .i. cosægul .i. sægul fota *no* ernibdech

4. (1) *caid* .i. uasal (2) *balcu* .i. tressiu (3) *hi fuil crist* .i. immartra docuatar cum eo .i. arcrist dochuat[ar] imartra (4) *docoemnactar tlachtu* .i. ut dicitur lauaucrunt stolas suas .i. ronigset .i. rochoemnaigestar .i. ronigset *no* rochemnigset

5. (2) *ronglea* .i. rogleestur .i. roglauastar .i. acurpu (3) *greit* .i. gérait *no* gairit orobái

6. (1) *raith* .i. rorcith *ran* .i. uasal (2) *all nglaine* .i. ba ri maith *no* all .i. lan do glanecna he (3) *suba* .i. ondi as suauis.[c] (4) *baithes* .i. inbaithis roslanaig sind ní dlig sár fuirre

7. (2) *badilsin* .i. dodia .i. airdi *no* badixu [in marg.] ba dixu .i. airde. (3) .i. roimraides uí isuaisliu inás féli noem .i. corgus ibu. [in marg.] corgus quasi quadragés .i. a xl. *no* oní is coir gestum .i. gester (?) cordis.

8. (2) *etla* .i. ciamail congain chride *no* cridechair [in marg.] Etsecht ecimoni esp. etla 7rl. etla .i. craidechair .i. familiaris. *no* etla .i. congaine craide moire (3) .i. afoirb dia *no* do dia bi. *orba* .i. neam

[a] MS. uncircumcione [b] Facs. rochemigset [c] Facs. assua.

9. (1) *geill* .i. do dia (2) *argnuis* .i. arbelaib *rig roraidis* .i. risintí nolégfad lebar atbertsom so (3) *digrais* .i. dogrés *no* romaitb
10. (1) *ailme* .i. guidiu [leg. guidmi?]. (2) *drochrand* .i. hifern *no* errand do ule ifirn (3) *cathbarr* .i. icaliten illi
12. (2) *elcir cainelaudaig* .i. eland sualach accu. *no* clanmair propter multitudinis (3) *rindaig* .i. asglice *no* laideend me. bandaig baith isrinn aith irrúaib *crist*
13. (2) *balc* .i. tréu. *itye* .i. atach. *cenailgis* .i. ni heccan rouilges ríu (3) *sothnge* .i. sothenga sochla .i. suilbir. *snabais* .i. sobésach
14. (3) *sochlach* .i. imitge
15. (1) .i. fororéith fogallraib
16. (1) *eraibdig* .i. cróbethadaig. *no* cræbbethadaig .i. torad cræb nomeltís. *no* fochrælaib nobitís sine aliia doma [leg. alia domo]. *no* caradbethadaig .i. caraid cách ambethaid quia omnes amicos habent* ifeil fursa ebraldig
17. (2) *nidat calaid* .i. nidat e[ru]aide *frianguide*
18. (2) *isdixu* .i. isairdiu (3) *lith* .i. lúthach lacách (4) *bás* .i. tasc .i. atásc coróim tanic isinlósin
20. (1) *conuaige* .i. connaigim
21. (1) *robatoen* .i. robat ocntadaig
22. (3) *cendigna* .i. centáire *no* ccntróige *no* cendímecin (4) *ceolda* .i. ceol munntire nime .i. biud
23. (1) *cesad* .i. a cedendo. (2) *clementi* .i. [nomen] proprium. *consadu* .i. comsaigin *no* comúidim iat isiu runn (3) *ronsnadut* .i. dochum nime (4) *conandunad* .i. connsluagud *no* conanirt
24. (2) .i. arcech len meirb .i. arcech nenirte. (4) *dedblen* .i. óndí is debilis .i. cum tribus dis[c]ipulis paruis.
25. (1) *ni dedhal* .i. nideroil (2). *friscuirther gretha* .i. fricuirther ccill [oenaige 7 cluichi, Rawl. 505] *no* guire. (3) *cechaing* .i. ruc lais *saithe* .i. buiden .i. roching sochaide coc*rist* isinló robaisted pól
26. (1) *isbrigach* .i. isnertmar. *lochet* .i. issaignen *no* issutrall [*no*] is sét solusta .i. fil uasaind *no* donforsat *no* sutrall lasinrig ata gabar coimct .i. dia (3) *ortu* .i. romarbtha
27. (3) *bert* .i. berid *no* ruc
29. (1) *an escoip* .i. solam ifertaib he (2) *diarndilius* .i. dochum nime
30. (2) *morsus dorus* .i. mor indorus. *no* dorus riacach dodul amartra. *no* romorustar dorus na martra iatsom .i. ar is dorus dochum nime martra (3) *ainsium* .i. romainsct sin *no* ronáinset .i. imon senti
31. (1) *sluind* .i. indis (3) *benait* .i. doberait

Notes from the Lebar Brecc, pp. 78, 79, 80.

Translation of the Irish.

2. *Essodir* .i. in chulmin [p. 79] Essodir 7 rl. spana ciuitas eius isidorus etymologiarum[b] memoratur hic si uero alius est ut oengus refert cum[c] episcopum et martirem[d] nescimus eclesiam cius.
Mainchine ancirge .i. disirt mic cuilind hiláigis laigean. [p. 79] Mauchine .i. mac luimnig. *no* manchánі .i. aband fil aniarthar laigean .i. hiláigis 7 airic abaium et ab eo illo nominatur quia iuxta illam eclesia eius sita est .i. disert mic cuilind

2. ' *Isidorus*,' &c. of the *cuilmenn* ('book' O'Curry Lect. pp. 8, 31).

' *Mainchine of splendid Eirge*,' i.e. of Disert Mic Cuilind in Leix of Leinster. Mainchine i.e. son of Luimnech : or Manchání .i.e. a river that is in the west of Leinster, i.e. in Leix, and Airic its name.

[a] Facs. h. iit [b] MS. est esio doro sechem ologiarum [c] MS. rem [d] MS. martirum

Scuithine mind mairge .i. scuithine slebi mairge 7 iubail hita acholl innossa fochomair funid for narda siar isin fuirrge. atcither tond ocerg[i] doboind indaurrthige boos

p. 78]. Scuithine .i. othig scothine isléib mairge. ISéssid cid dianabar scothine *friss* .nin. arinseothail imlochta doguid .i. dul dorunim inoenlú 7 toidecht uathi inoenlo aile. uel ideo Scothene dictus est .i. fecht dorala he dobarra chorcaige. 7 essium ocimthecht inmara. 7 barra hillúing. Cid fodera inmuir doimtechtt duit olbarra. Ní muir it*ir*. *acht* mag scothach scothcimrach olscuthín 7 tocbaid [in]alaim scoth chorem 7 cuirid uad dobarrn isinluing. Ocus atbert scothin cid fodera long dosnám forinmag. Issin nguthsin sínid barra aláim isinmuir 7 atuaig bradan esti 7 telcid cu scothin. Conid onscoithsin ainmnigther scoithín do.

NOloigdís din. dí ingbin chorrcichecha imme cech nóidche comad móti incath dó. corohimraided aéliugud tritsin cotanic brenaind diafromad. conderbairt scothin laigod brenaind imlepaidsi anocht olse 7 laigidse uime a ingena. Orasiacht iarum cohnair chumsanta ann tecait nahingena isinteach iraibo brenaind 7 anurtlaige dogrísaig inacasslaib 7 nivosloisce intene eat 7 doirtit itiaduaise brenaind 7 tiaguit isinlepaid chuico. Créd so olbrenaind. isamlaid dogniam cech nóidche olnahingena. Laighit imbrenaind 7 nicocumnacair codlad it*ir* lahelscoth. ISanfoirbthe sin achlerig olnahingena. inti bis sund cech noidche ni mothaig ni it*ir*. Cid tái nach ergi isindabaig usqi aclérig diamad ussaite duit. arismenice athaiges incleroch .i. scothine. Maith tra. olbrénuind iscoir dún inderbudsa. arisferr intísea inaimne. Dogniat ancontaid 7 acodach indsin .i. brenaind 7 scothin 7 searait feliciter. Scothin mac setnai m. throbthaig m. dala m. laidir ara choncorb m. imrossa nitha m. firthluchtga m. fergusa m. rúig.

" Scuithine diadem of Mairge," i.e. Scuithine of Sliab Mairge, and the place wherein his church is now is opposite Fir Arda westward in the sea. A wave is still seen rising from the gable of the *daurthach*.

'Scuithine' i.e. from Tech Scothine in Sliab Mairge. It is worth knowing whence he is called Scothine. Not hard (to say). Because of the speed of the journey which he made, i.e. to go to Rome in one day and to come from it in another day. *Vel ideo Scothéne dictus est*, i.e. Once upon a time he met Barra of Cork, and he walking on the sea and Barra in a vessel. "What is the cause of thy walking on the sea?" says Barra. "It is not sea at all, but a plain flowery, shamrocked," quoth Scuithin, and he lifts in his hand a purple flower and casts it from him to Barra in the ship. And Scothin said "What is the cause of a vessel swimming on the plain?" At that word Barra stretches his hand down into the sea, and takes a salmon thereout, and casts it to Scothín. So that from that flower he is named Scoithín.

Now two roundbreasted maidens used to lie with him every night that the battle [with lust] might be the greater unto him. And it was proposed to accuse him on that account. So Brenaind came to test him. And Scothín said "Let Brenaind lie in my bed to-night," quoth he, "and do ye, O maidens, lie along with him." Now when he reached the hour of resting then come the maidens into the house wherein was Brenaind, and their lapfuls of embers in their chasubles, and the fire burnt them not, and they spill (the embers) before Brenaind, and they go into the bed unto him. "What is this?" quoth Brenaind. "Thus it is that we do every night," quoth the maidens. They lie down with Brenaind, and nowise could he sleep with longing. "That is imperfect, O cleric," quoth the maidens: "he who is here every night feels not anything. Wherefore goest thou not into the tub of water, O cleric, if it be the easier for thee? for it is often the cleric, to wit, Scothíne, visits it." "Well, then," quoth Brenaind, "it is unjust for us to make this assurance, for better is this man than we are." They make their union and their covenant then, to wit, Brenaind and Scothín, and they part *feliciter*. Scothín son of Setnae, son of Trebthach, son of Dal, son of Láidir, Cú-corb's charioteer, son of Imrossa Nith, son of Fertlachtga, son of Fergus mac Roig.

3. *Finnlug* .i. dalta dosinntan. *lesce* .i. andis indún [leg. amnis imdún ?] .i. aland .no blesc mucaid rig caisil is uad raiter incheall. ut dixit comgall

> Gébaid modaltán in múr
> finntan lasfaigebthar dún
> isi achaithir comall ngle
> diamba comainm dún blesco.

p. 78.] Mormartra rodauis 7rl.
Findlug .i. descipul. 7 brathair fiuntain he. et ideo cum eo uominatur et perigrinationem exiit in aquilonim. Conid he isnoem itamlachtu findlogáin icianachta glinde gemin.

Dunflesci vel lesci. vel blesc. vel lese nomen meretricis quae habitabat[a] in illo loco et ab cá[b] nominatur. vel nomen subulci[c] regis uacuanach ciamti [leg. qui ?] sanctum in illo loco habitabat et ab eo sic nominatur. vel flesci .i. flese nomen amnis[d] qui est iuxta urbim et ab eo nominatur

4. Bás cáid acilíne 7rl. Cáid .i. cáid 7 cádus[e] a cades dicta est .i. caithir dína ataig indesciurt treuc iuda

5. *Togairm semeoin srotha* .i. sacerdos .i. sruith he [in marg.] .i. sem[eoin] srotha 7 rl. .i. sacerdos qui cristum in templo inter ulnas accepit et qui prophetauit[f] de illo et qui sepultus est in ualle iosafath in una basilica cum iosep sponsato marie

Ciar ingen duibrea .i. icill chori amuscraide thire ata 7 dosil conaire di. [in marg.] Ciar ingean duibrea .i. a muscraige thire ata 7 dosil conaire mic messi buachai[lle] di

6. *Iulian* .i. [nomen] proprium uirginis. [in marg.] Raith coarig rán toga. Iulian all nglaine.i. all uasal a glaine. *no* is all uasal doglain taitnemaig iulian .i. pater monachorum et .x. m. monastriarum[g] et in terra egipti habitabat

7. *Martra luciani* .i. prespiter [in marg.] .i. lucianus prespiter.

9. in marg.] Aille geill conglaine 7 rl. .i. isaille 7 glaine nahetire ifiadnaise iurig

roraides .i. rorades isin memoria [h]orum in mente eius prius fuiset

Faelan deoda digrais .i. hi cluain mescna iferaib tulach ata [in marg.] Faelan .i. calue induib dortan ata achell pasa fæl .ix. .i. prius

10. *Milid* .i. miliates .i. abb róma he uel miligo

3. '*Finnlug*' i.e. a pupil of Finntan's. '*Lesce*' i.e. . . . by a fort i.e. a river. Or Blesc a kin of Cashel's swineherd: from him the church is called, ut dixit Comgall:

> My fosterling shall take the rampart,
> Finntan, by whom the fort shall be left.
> It is his city—bright fulfilment—
> Unto which was the name Dún-Blesco.

'Findlug' i.e. a disciple and a brother of Finntan (was) he.
And it is he that is saint in Tamlachta Findlogáin in Cianachta of Glenn Gemin.

4. 'Aquilinus' noble death.' *cáid* and *cádus* were said from Kadesh, a city of protection . . . . in the south part of the tribe of Juda.

5. '*Calling of Simeon the sage*' i.e. sacerdos, i.e. a priest was he.

'*Ciar daughter of Duibrea*' i.e. in Coll Chére in Muscraige Tire she is and of Conaire Mór's seed is she. [in marg.] 'Ciar daughter of Duibrea' i.e. from M. T. is she, and of the seed of Conaire son of Mess Buachaille is she.

6. [in marg.] 'Julian a rock of purity' i.e. a noble rock, or she is a noble rock of radiant glass. 'Julian' i.e. father of . . . . monks and of ten thousand nuns, *et* etc.

9. 'Beautiful hostages with purity' &c. i.e. most beautiful and pure are the hostages in the presence of the King.

'I have mentioned' i.e. I have mentioned in the &c.

'*Faelan godly, excellent*' i.e. in Cluain Moescne in Fir Tulach he is. [in marg.] Faelan i.e. Calue in Hy-Dortan is his church.

10. '*Milid*' i.e. Milites (Miltiades?) i.e. abbot of Rome (was) he.

---
[a] MS. habitabot [b] MS. eo [c] MS. subuilci [d] MS. mris. [e] MS. quidadus [f] MS. profitauit [g] MS. monustinarum

in marg.] A'ilme itge ndichra 7 rl. .i. milito episcopus laodiceae in assia minore.[a] uel milit ut oengus dicit. 7 cumad fria diarmait atbertha esside .i. Diarmait mac lugnai m. lugdach m. findbairr m. fraich m. catheon m. oengusa m. nathíí m. fíachrach. uel militiadis episcopus

11. [in marg.] Croch in martir petair 7 rl. quatuor uel quinque annis christus in egipto fuit fugiens herodem. elipoliu vel fomith [leg. Heliopolis vel Sotineu ?] vel hermopolis[b] nomen ciuitatis in qua christus habitauit[c] in egipto ubi ut aiunt in die aduentus[d] illius in urbem omnia idula eius comminuta[e] sunt cito[f] in terram. aphrodosius[g] uero nomen principis illius qui christum et parentes benigne su[s]cepit.

Cid fodera conid sollamain tidecht crist ahegipt 7 nach sollamain adul inuto. nin. árisinand egiptus 7 tenebro .i. dorcadæ 7 iscoru suba dothiachtain ueich esti ina dul inutib.

12. in marg.] Marttra mar 7 rl. Laidceann mac bœith bannáig .i. boeth bannach buadach ainmm aathar. ochluain ferta molua do laidcend 7 illic
13. Elair. hic mochonna insi patraic. pictauis .i. ciuitas
14. sruith nolœ .i. ciuitas amuig champain in etalia [in marg. infer.] Pais luceri 7 rl. .i. ciuitas felicis martiris in etalia. no sruith nolæ .i. o inber ueola icoerich tiro conaill 7 cogain 7 sruith intíí rogab furbrú amnis .i. noile

15. Ite cluana eredal .i. íta uirri imseree udé 7 dona dessib di .i. dalta benedicht 7 rorethside mor dogalaraib

in marg. infer.] Forail mor ngur ngalar 7 rl. .i. rofurtachtaig dia do íte. no rotroeothustar morgalar hi .i. bamor ingalar didoel ocadiul. Modithir oreni corchlai aletæb uile. niftir nech sin fuirri. Tétsi focht naud immach. tic indóel asa fochlai dia hessi. Atchiat nacaillecha he. Marbait din he. Tic íto iarsin 7 ona tanic indóel diasaigid iarfaigis cid dochoid modalta olsi. nagat neam fuirn olnacaillecha. sinne romarb he arnifetumar narbo hirchoitech he. Cid fil ann ol íte acht nígoba cailloch triabithu mochomorbusa isinng[u]imsin. Ocus nigebsa

'We pray a fervent prayer' &c. i.e. Milito, bishop of Laodicea, in Asia Minor. Or Milit, as Oengus says, and it may be that this was said of Diarmait, i.e. Diarmait son of Lugnae, son of Lugaid, son of Findbarr, son of Fraech, son of Cathchú, son of Oengus, son of Natl í, son of Fiachra.

What is the cause that Christ's coming out of Egypt is a solemnity and his going into it is not a solemnity ? Not hard (to say). Because *Egyptus* and *tenebrae*, i.e. darkness, are the same, and fitter is happiness at one's coming out of it than at going into them.

12. 'A great martyrdom' &c. Laidcenn son of Daeth Bannach i.e. Baeth Bannach the Victorious his father's name. Of Cluain Ferta Molua was Laidcend.
13. '*Hilary*.' Here Mochonna of Inis Patrice (is commemorated).
14. '*Priest of Nola*' i.e. a city in the plain of Campania in Italy.

or 'priest of Nola' i.e. of Inber ueola in the border of Tyrconnell and Tyrone, and a priest (was) he who kept on the brink of the river i.e. Noile.
15. '*Ite of Cluain Credail*' i.e. a thirst (*ita*) on her for God's love, and of the Desies was she, i.e. a pupil of Benedict, and she underwent (*l*) much of diseases.

'She underwent great grievous disease' i.e. God aided I'te, or a great disease overwhelmed her, i.e. great was the disease of a stag-beetle a-sucking her. Bigger than a lapdog (was it), and it destroyed the whole of one of her sides. No one knew that of her. She goes out once there. The beetle comes from his den after her. The nuns see him. Then they kill him. I'te comes thereafter, and when the beetle came not to her she asked "why has my fosterling gone ?" quoth she. "Do not rob us of heaven," say the nuns : "it is we that killed him, for we

---
[a] MS. episcopis ludaciæ in assiæ minoriæ   [b] MS. noerinim folis   [c] MS. habitabit
[d] MS. audentus   [e] MS. cominatu   [f] MS. tam cidu   [g] MS. afrodíus   [h] MS. egalia

din. omthigerna cotuca amac aricht noidean dia altram dam. Tanic iarum intaingel nognaithiged tinithirecht disse arnhamus. Mithid em din. olsi fris. condebairt intaingel fria. doberthar duit inní connige cotanic crist chuice aricht nóidean. ut dixit

ISucan
alar lium imdisirtan
ciabeth clerech colín sét
isbréc uile *acht* isucan.

Altram alal.* lium imthig
nihaltram nach doernthaig
ihu. coferaib niuc
rem cride cech noenadaig.

ISucan oc mobithmaith
éruid 7 ni maithmech
inrig conic nabuile
cenaguide bid aithrech.

Ihu. uasal ainglide
nococlerech dergnaide
clar lium imdisirtan
ihu. *mac* nahébraige.

Mec naruirech mcc narig
imthir cia dothisatan
níhuadib sailim soch*aide*
isdocha lium ihu. can.

Canaid cóir aingena
dúr dligi*us* bar cisucan
ata napurt uasucan
ciabeith anucht ihu. can. Ihu. can.

16. *Craibdig ifeil fursa.* dochuatar alii relicione ad celum in feria eius .i. lx. mile *for fichit* mile parona in gallis est. Ocus dochonallib muirthemne. im*urr*o do fursa.

in marg. inf.] Craibdig hi féil fursa 7rl. .i. ifeil fursa craibdig. Mellan im*mer*ro mac .h. chuind oiuis mic .h. chúind forloch oirbsen la condactu lahanmchara dofursa. Ecmaing tra. fursa comaignenn chille maignend. Cnüt ancentaid 7 claechloit atreblaite archomartba anoentad .i. galchind *no* doergalar róbúi forfursa

---

knew not that he was not hurtful." "However it is then," quoth I'te, "but nun shall not take succession to me for that deed. And I will not take (aught) from my Lord until he give me his Son in an infant's form to nurse it." Then towards her came the angel who used to tend her. "It is time, indeed," quoth she to him. And the angel said to her, "What thou askest shall be given to thee;" and Christ came to her in an infant's form. *ut dixit*

Jesukin
Is nurst by me in my little hermitage.
Though it be a cleric with a number of treasures
All is a lie save Jesukin.

A nursing that is nursed by me in my house,
Not a nursing of any base clown:
Jesu with (the) men of heaven
Before my heart every single night.

Jesukin at my eternal good
Demands and (is) not forgiving.
The King who rules all things
Not to beseech him will be repentance.

Jesu noble, angelic,
Not a carnal (!) cleric,
Is nurst by me in my little hermitage,
Jesu son of the Hebrew woman.

The sons of the Princes, the sons of the Kings,
Though they should come into my country,
Not from them I expect a host:
Likelier with me is Jesukin.

Sing ye a chorus, O maidens,
To Him who hath a right to your little tribute.
He is in his port above us,
Though Jesukin is in (my) lap.

16. '*Pious ones on Fursae's feast.*' Others in religion went to heaven on his feast, i.e. twenty-nine thousand. Peronne in Gaul is (Lis), and of the Conalli Muirthemne, moreover, is Fursa.

i.e. on the feast of pious Fursa. Mellán, now, son of Ua Cuind of Inis maic hui Chuind on Lough Corrib in Connaught was soulfriend to Fursa. Now Fursa chanced to visit Maignenn of Kilmainham. They make their union and they exchange their tribulations in token of their union, to wit, a head-ache, or piles (?),

* leg. alar

dobeth for máignenn. 7 béist robui himáig-
nend dodul ifursa comba he agnathugud cech
maitne tria bithu teora mírenda* saille do ithe
curathoirnead gal nabiasta. Ecmaing din.
fursa darmuir corocht aroile morcathraig. 7
gniidsium agnáthbes innte. Ocus berair co-
hespoc nacathrach dianotad. Nicrábud maith
dobethu olintespoc. ISecad duitsiu achlerig
olfursa afromad innf dobeir formsa sin. Lingid iarum innibéist focétoir inubragait inespuic.
Orafitir iarum cach sin gairmid fursa innbeist
chuice doridise 7 mortbar aium dó 7 fursa triasin firtsin 7 erpthar incathair uli conaferond
fognuma dodia 7 dofursa ;

18. [p. 80.] Mornd petair asp. 7 rl. .i. a
adnocul iróin árisanúig hatar athaisse conicesin
conidiarsin roherbad róiu do. Mornd petair .i.
quando reliquit constantinus filius elenne [e]am
.i. romam petro et quando*b* construxit constan-
tinopolim in regalem ciuitatem sibi*c* in catacumina corp[or]a apostolorum .i. petri et
pauli custodit[a] sunt anno uno et mensibus .uii. sed uerius [quod] cornelius papa as-
portaverat*d* ea a catacumina post multa [tem-
pora] post pasionem quia .xx.*e* 7 .i. reges a
neroine sub quo pasi sunt apostoli petrus et
paulus usque ad gullianum*f* sub quo corpora
eorum a catacumina duxit cornilius. Mornd
petair aspail unde dicunt

in marg. d.] Maithe tanic risinrig
reconstantín conabrig
donchathraig moir marbud deass
ruead coróim dialeiges.

Adrubratar lega friss
comad he leigess acniss*g*
fothrucad arsét a alt
afuil .ccc. mac nendac.

Cotanic petar ispól
sanaidche iarnatinol
dodín namac inbuilid inbind
7 dice inrig rogrind.

Eirg fobaithis arpetar
rissinrig narbutecal
dáig tiefa hícc archinaid
donbaithis báin buanidain.

a leg. tri mirenna as in Laud, 610.   *b* MS. anno   *c* MS. ciuitas l. ciui. sibui
d MS. papias pretauerat   *e* MS. icit   *f* MS. petri 7 pauli usque ad galliámi   *g* Facs. achiss

that was on Fursa to be on Maignenn and a
beast that was in Maignenn to go into Fursa,
so that it was his custom every morning for
ever to eat three bits of bacon so that he might
suppress the beast's violence. Fursa, then,
happened to go over sea and came to a certain
great city, and therein he observes his usual
practice. And he is brought to the bishop of the
city to be censured. "Not good devotion is thy
life," quoth the bishop. "Thou art permitted, O
Cleric," quoth Fursa, " to try that which inflicts
this on me." Forthwith, then, leaps the beast
into the bishop's throat. Now when every one
knew that, Fursa calls the beast back to him
again, and God's name and Fursa's are magnified through that miracle, and all the city with
its service-land is conveyed to God and to Fursa.

18. 'Magnifying of Apostle Peter,' &c. i.e. his
burial in Rome, for it is outside were his relics
thitherto, and it was after that that Rome was
granted to him.

A grief came to the King,
To Constantine with his might.
To the great City, as was right,
He was borne, to Rome, for his healing.

Said leeches to him
That his skin's cure should be
Bathing by way of his joints
In three hundred innocent children's blood.

So that Peter and Paul came,
In the night after collecting them,
To protect the children beautiful, melodious,
And to heal the very comely King.

"Get thee under baptism," quoth Peter
To the King, "be not afraid,
Because healing from sin shall come
Of the baptism, white, lasting, pure.

Siluestar abb nacatrach
city foaláim arismthmar
guím deoda triastoichfea neam
trínoit treoda dochredeam.

Dochuatar nahaspail ass
arfágbail nambriathar mbrass
rochomall inrig diancis
cechni daronsat dfaisnés.

Atgeoin cruth petair nambreath
7 poil codeligtech
rofaillsig othanic la
retáidbsin anecosca.

ISonscelsin tanic tair
morad petair primaspail
isleiss roim osin ille
7 lepol cinmaithe. M.

"Silvester, the abbot of the city,
Get thee under his hand,[a] for he is gracious:
A divine deed through which thou wilt reach
   heaven (is)
To believe the trinal Trinity."

The Apostles went forth
After leaving the swift words.
The King fulfilled after them
Everything which they had testified.

He recognised the form of Peter of the judgments
And of Paul distinctly.
He manifested when day came
Their countenances by showing.

It is from this tale that in the East came
(The) magnifying of Peter chief Apostle.
With him is Rome thenceforward,
And with Paul, without grief. A grief, etc.

19. *Etsecht muire martha* .i. muire martha coniugis nouali .i. coniugis marii .i. primi uiri[b] de romanis 7 martha aite tigidit.[c]

in marg.] Etsecht muire martha. *no* etsecht muire ismartha sororis mariae. Maria martha duae sorores lazari[d] hautem mariu magdalena sed a uico magdalo in quo nata est uel nutrita dicta est.

20. in marg.] Ancethrarconuaige 7 rl. Molaca .i. oc láind becuir imbregaib ata. *no* cumad he lochine mac duibalhigid .i. othelaig mín molaga iscruib muige isimmumain.

Moecca .i. fechine fabair [in marg.] Moecca immurro .i. fechin fabair. Fechin immurro dorada ris. ideo .i. ecmaing he occrein chnama inalenab ifhiadnaise amáthar conlebairt inmáthair mofiachan becsa sut olsi. inde fechin dictus est. Moecca hautem dictus est .i. urafeccaidecht arisdó dorala infeccaidechtsa ardesmbirecht .i. Diambui fechín ocdamairecht dochiaran chluana. Ecmaing achuit dofácbail dó forinimelach. Ferg din. fechín desin 7 teit amach iarum 7 facbaid inchell 7 teit esti sair. INnister dochiaran sin. inadeguid olciarán 7 minathi arais tucaid aróein he olciaran. Tiagar inadhegaid 7 atbert fechíne nisticfad 7 naigead roime. *conid* amlaid tucad he 7 achul remi.

19. '*Death of Marius and Martha*' i.e. of Marius and Martha his *conjux* beseech it i.e. of the wife of Marius, a chief man of the Romans and Martha mistress of his house.
'Death of Mary, Martha,' or death of Mary and Martha Mary's sister.

20. 'A splendid four I sew together' &c. Molacca i.e. at Lann Becuir in Bregia he is. Or it may be Lochíne son of Dubdliged i.e. from Telach mín Molnga in Fir Maige in Munster.
Moecca i.e. Fechíne of Fabar. [in marg.] Moecca, now, i.e. Féchín of Fabar. Féchín, now, was said of him *ideo*: he happened when a child to be gnawing a bone in his mother's presence, and the mother said to him "That's my little wee raven," quoth she. inde *Féchín* ('corvulus') dictus est. Moecca hautem dictus est i.e. for his backsliding, for it is to him happened this backsliding for example, to wit, when Féchín was ox-herding for Ciarán of Cluain it happened that his quota was left for him on the *imelach* (l). Féchín was wroth at that, and goes forth then, and leaves the church, and goes eastward thereout. That is told to Ciaran. "After him," quoth Ciaran,

---
[a] i.e. Confess to Silvester and get absolution from him.
[b] MS. mure .i. prím muire
[c] leg. aithech tige dit, and cf. *luige in aithig tige 7 na haithige tige*, O'Dav. 51.
[d] MS. lazaire

Forfeccaid iarum infersin olciaran. et inde mofecca nomen a[c]cepit.

in marg. inf.] Sabaist .i. sebbaist din. achoir quia sebastianus dolensis passus est.
Oenu .i. mac .h. Iffigne comorba cluana claran oengus nomen eius
in marg. dext.] Oenu .i. œngus mac h. laigse. do laigis laigean. Dochuaid 7 dígilla immaille fris for focht dodul inamsaine corig con[n]acht condechaid copurt innse clothrandictriall tarloch rib siar. Ecmaing din. ciaran isind[i]ndse tunc et adbert tabar amuig intoclæch ar bid fer corath dó he 7 bid he gebus mochomorbusa darmesi. Atnagar amuig din. oengus. Cia hairet ata doset olciaran. corig con[n]acht olingilla. Nach ferr lat dochur frivig nime 7 talman ol ciaran. masa choir din. olingilla isferr. issed immurro olciaran. Tescthar atolt indsin 7 ailtcar frissineclais 7 gabais comorbus ciarain iarsin. ut ciaran profetauit.

21. *Fuinche* .i. ingen coirill isintuaiscirt .i. oruss airther forloch erni. 7 fainche cluana cain incoganacht caisil. no fainche. no femi .i. iconernaide amuig itha atá .i. femin ingen coirill .i. derbsiur dodaig mac coirill.ª

in marg. inf.] Robot ocu dom snadug 7 rl. Fuinche feidm no fuinche femi et duæ anusᵇ sunt. no curaad fuinche cluana cáin in eoganacht caisil. no fuinche ruiss airthir itir ratha for loch érui 7 isfria ráiter fuinche garb. isaire atrubrad garb fria arrotrialled abirnaidm dofir 7 otchuala sí sin lingid illoch nérni 7 roimdig fousei Itir firusci 7 muir coturcaib aceaud aninis clothrann 7 comustarla dodiarmait hi. coriarfaid di ciahiintus formroibe. innissid din. ascela dó 7 isamlaid rombói 7 sligre 7 turrscar immara immlenmain. conid desin iarum atberar fuinche garb di. 7 atbert diarmait isgarb sin. Feime .i. fuinche garb ingen choirill [mic laisre] mic dallaiu mic eogain mic neill .ix. giallaig.

Agna ingen isu. [p. 81. in marg. sup.] Agna

ª Facs. dersiur .... corill ᵇ MS. amus

"and if he come not back, bring ye him by force," quoth Ciaran. They go after him, and Féchíne said that he would not come with his face before him, so that thus was he brought, with his back before him. "That man now has backslided," quoth Ciaran, and thence he got the name of Mofecca ('my-backslider').
'Sabaist' i.e. Sebbaist now (is) its proper (form).
'Oenu' .i. son of ua-Laigse, successor of Cluain Cluran. Oengus n.e.
'Oenu' .i. Oengus son of Ua-laigse of Leix of Leinster. He went, along with two gillies, on a journey to enter service, to a king of Connaught, and he came to (the) port of Inis Clothrann, passing over Loch Rib westwards. Now Ciaran happened to be in the island then and he said "Let in the young hero, for he is a man with God's grace, and he it is that will take my coarbship after me." Oengus then is taken on shore. "To what place is thy path?" quoth Ciaran. "To (the) king of Connaught," quoth the youth. "Were it not better for thee to put (thyself) with the King of heaven and earth?" quoth Ciaran. "If it be proper," quoth the youth, "it is better." "It is, forsooth," says Ciaran. His hair then is cut, and he is reared at the church, and he took Ciaran's coarbship afterwards, as Ciaran prophecied.

21. '*Fuinche*' i.e. daughter of Coirell in the north i.e. of Ross Airther on Lough Erne. And Fainche of Cluain Cáin in Eoganacht of Cashel. Or Fainche, or Femi i.e. at the Ernaide in Mag Itha she is, i.e. Femin Coirell's daughter i.e. sister of Daig son of Coirell.
'May they be one to protect me' &c. Fuinche feidm or Fuinche femi *et duæ anns* sunt. Or it may be Fuinche of Cluain Cáin in Eoganacht of Caisel. Or Fuinche of Ross Airther in Tír Ratha on Lough Erne and it is of her is said Fuinche (the) Rough. This is why 'Rough' was said of her, for it was tried to wed her to a husband, and when she heard that, she leaped into Lough Erne and went under water, both freshwater and sea, till she raised her head at Inis Clothrann and she came to Diarmait, and he asked her what adventure she was on. Then she tells her tales to him, and thus it is she was, both shells and weeds of the sea sticking to her. So that thereafter 'Fuinche (the) Rough' is said of her, and Diarmait said "that is rough." Feime i.e. Fuinche

uirgo in roma et ado[p]tiua filia iesu fuit[a] et xiii. annorum erat quando passa fuit[b] sub simpronio prefecto uirbis rome et uicario eius aspasiaro[c] nomine. per multa tormenta misa est et e his uiua[d] et sana rediuit et postea confictus[e] gladius nudus in ore[f] eius et usque ad interiora eius peruenit et sic uitam finiuit. Agna et tecla et maria mater domini tres uirgines et excelsisimae sunt inter uirgines scripturae.

22. *Etsecht ingen chomgaill* .i. .iii. hingena comgaill .i. blaisse 7 coma 7 boga 7 illetir dalaraide atat 7 dodálaraide doib

Colman mac hui beona .i. oliss mor

24. *Babaill* .i. babillus espoc inantoig cum suis tribus fili[i]s.

[p. 81, in marg. s.] Domanmain domcorpan 7 rl. babaill .i. martir et episcopus antiochia .i. ux. episcopus post petrum. cum hautem ueniset numerianus rex ad templum ut in eo sacrificaret dis suis .i. idilis tunc babillas conatus est introire in templum domini et stans in ostio templi resistit numeri[an]us dicens

26. [p. 80, in marg. inf.] ISbrigach alloichet 7rl. Policairpi .i. espoc .i. quidam episcopus in assia minore qui erat di[s]cipulus apostoloruin [et] hab ipsis ordinatus est in episcopatum[g] eclesiæ smirnæ. in tempore hautem marci et auirilii (*sic*) imperatorum pasuss est.

27. *Carais moeda muirgen* .i. moeda .i. modia no mofiada maith. *Muirgen* .i. iloch echach robui

28. *La hacobran* .i. donoemaib herenn do 7 icill roiss itermand indse cathaig icorcu baiscind ata som.

30. *Enan rois rind solus* .i. mac germainid[h] 7 momernoc glinde faidble[i] inuib garchon .i. oruss mor momernoc inuib dega *solus* .i. solus inrind .i. ross mor *no* comad iferna ata

31. *Sluind æd fortren ferna* .i. moædóc [in marg. sinist.] .i. aed .i. moædoc .i. moædoc 7 doferaib luirg oloch érni do .i. Moedoc mac sétnai m. eirc m. foradaig m. fiachrach m. amalgaid m. muredaig m. carthaind m. colla uais

in lower marg.] L. espoc dodechutar dochum moedóc ferna do bretnaib clille muine. ina[n]

[a] MS. fi.ii ih.u st.   [b] MS. post   [c] MS. aspassiora   [d] MS. uiba   [e] MS. comictus
[f] MS. mori   [g] MS. in episcopo pr.   [h] Facs. gemainid   [i] Facs. faidle.

(the) Rough daughter of Coirell son of Laisre, son of Dallan, son of Eogan, son of Niall the Nine-hostaged.

22. '*Death of Comgall's daughters*' i.e. three daughters of Comgall, i.e. Blaisse and Coma and Boga, and in Letir Dálaraide are they, and of Dálaraide are they.

'*Colman son of Ua Beona*' i.e. of Lismore.

24. '*Babylas*,' a bishop in Antioch with his three sons.

27. '*Moeda loved a seabirth*' i.e. Moeda i.e. *mo-dia* (my God) or my good God. *Muirgen*, 'Seabirth' i.e. in Lough Neagh was she.

28. '*With Acobran*' i.e. of the saints of Ireland (was) he, and in Cell Roiss in the sanctuary of Inis Cathaig in Corcu-baiscinn is he.

30. '*Enan of Ross* (mór), *the bright headland*' i.e. son of Germained and Mo-Mernóc of Glenn Faidble in Hui-Garchon, i.e. of Ross Mór Mo-Mernóc in Hui-Dega. *Solus* i.e. sunny the point i.e. Ross More ; or it may be in Ferns he is.

31. '*Mention Aed the strong of Ferns*', i.e. My-Aedóc i.e. Aed [in l. marg.] i.e. Aed i.e. My-Aedóc i.e. Moedóc, and of Fir Luirg of Lough Erne was he, i.e. Moedóc son of Setna, son of Erc, son of Feradach, son of Fiachra, son of Amalgad, son of Muiredach, son of Carthann, son of Colla Uais.

Fifty bishops of the Britons of Cell Muine went to Moedóc of Ferns. On their pilgrimage

oilithre dodechutar. arbadalta innoedoc ferna
do dabid chille muine. O aimsirᵃ dabid niructha
feoil iproinntech cille muine. conusruc comorba
moedoc ferna. is dornth 7 comsuide do fria
dabid donchomorba notbern 7 ana[d] dó isin-
proinntig .i. inabdaine chille muine uatcom-
raigfetᵇ acosan friular iccin bess imbethu.
Tauentar din. inailithre comoedóc. Ructha
iteach nóeigid icorgus erraig. dobreath doib
.l. bairgen 7 luss 7 mendgusce prainde. Cid
dint uendso olinespuic. dia thomeilt duibsc olinferthigis. ber lat iterum olinespuic. nicnith-
fither ní de sund cornib mucc ocus ágh and.
ISed olinferthigis. ccad olmoedóc. berair dóib.
ismaith olse. domelut infeoil. Bit ann coarn-
barach. bendachaid moedóc doib. Maith
olmoedóc ni furail barcursachud isinfeoil da-
thomailt ddib isinchorgus 7 inarán doobad. Ni
hassinlégiund turais sin amoedóc olinespuic.
Maith ol moe[d]óc. Nin. olinespuic. ass amáthar
atib inmucc 7 innágh tucad dunn 7 nocha duaid
acht fér intalman .u. oirbe ar tri .xx.ib ar .ccc.
ata iconbairgen 7 isaire narochaitsium.

Benait combrig romoir .i. ochill brige itæb
liss moir 7 itæb chille dara 7 i[ngen] cairpre h.
ciardai

[p. 81, upper marg.] Moelanfaid .i. abb
darindse. oc liss mór mochuda ata darinis .i.
ubi abunn mor in mare exit. ISbe inmoe-
lanfaidse itchonnaire inaroile ló én mbcc occái
7 ocdogra. Amode olse cid táraill siut. atgillim
tra olse nichaithiubsabiad corofaillsichthardam.
INtan din. bái and conacca aingel ina dochumm.
Maithsin aclerig olintaingel. nachateuired a-
sním ní bus mo. Molua mac ocha atbath. ocus
[is] aire nocháinit nahanmanna he. arniromarb
anmunna riam dobic ná domor. ar ní mo cháinit
nadáine he inát nahanmunda aile 7 intén mbec
atchisiu

ᵃ Facs. ainsir   ᵇ Facs. -fed

they went, for the Moedóc of Ferns was a pupil
of David of Cell Muine. From David's time
flesh was not brought into the refectory of Cell
Muine, until a successor of Moedóc of Ferns
brought it. Opposition and contumacy (?) towards David are (imputed) to the successor who
shall bring it, and remaining in the refectory, i.e.
in the abbacy of Cell Muine, so that his feet shall
not touch its floor so long as he is alive. Now
they [the bishops] came on a pilgrimage to
Maedóc. They were taken into the guesthouse
in [the] Lent of spring. There were brought to
them, fifty cakes and leeks and whey-water
for dinner. "Wherefore has this been brought?"
quoth the bishops. "For you to consume it,"
quoth the steward. "Take (it) away with thee
iterum : nought thereof shall be consumed until
there be a pig and an ox there." "Is it (permitted ?") quoth the steward. "Permission,"
quoth Maedóc. It is brought to them. "It is
well," quoth he; they eat the meat. They are
there till the morrow. Maedóc blesses them.
"Well," quoth Maedóc, "it is not superfluous
to reprove you for your eating the meat in Lent
and refusing the bread." "Not from reading
hast thou delivered that, O Maedóc," say the
bishops. "Well?" quoth Maedóc. "Not hard,"
said the bishops, "the pig and the ox that
were brought to us drank their mothers' milk,
and ate nought save the grass of the earth.
Three hundred and sixty-five *oirbe* (?) there are
with the cake, and therefore it is we consumed it not."

' *They strike, with full great Brig* ' i.e. of
Cell Brige beside Lismore, and beside Kildare,
and a daughter of Cairpre ua-Ciardai (was she).

' *Moelanfaid* ' i.e. abbot of Darinis, at Less
Mór Mochuda is Darinis, i.e. *ubi* a great river
in mare exit. He is that Maelanfaid who saw
on a certain day a little bird a-wailing and
lamenting. "Ah my God," quoth he, "what
has happened here? I vow," quoth he, "I will
not eat food until it is revealed to me." So
while he was there he beheld an angel (coming) to him. "That is well, O cleric," saith
the angel: "let (this) not give thee grief any
more. Molua mac ocha has died. And therefore it is that the living creatures bewail him,
for he never killed a living creature, whether
small or great. So that not more do the people
bewail him than the other living creatures,
and the little bird which thou seest."

Rawl. 503, fo. 211, b.	Laud, 610.	Lebar Brecc, p. 81.
1. Morait kl. febrai fros martir mar ngledenn brigit ban balc nualann cend caid cailloch nerenn	1. Morait kl. febrai fross mairtir mor gledenn brigit ban balcc nualann cenn caid chaill*ech* neir*enn*	1. Morait ka*laind* febrai fross martir mar ngledend brigit bán balcc nualann cend caid cailloch nerenn
2. Airitiu meic maire hitempul derb dinnais sluag marmartir suabais lafindig nduirn ndigrais	2. Airidiu m. muire itempul derb dinnis sluag mor martir suabais lafindig duirn digrais	2. Airitiu ma*ic* muire itempul derb dinnis sluag mor martir suabais lafinnich duirn digrais
3. Donroemat colanc dogres ar[ch]achtrogi sluagad find cofeli felicis simfroni	3. Donroemat collaine dogres arcach troigi sluaiged find cofeilc feiluxeis sinproinc	3. Donroemat colani dogrés arcach troige sloiged find cofeli felicis simfroni
4. Fronius is magnus gelaisa roffoser german martir huasal cuanda credal cresen	4. Froini*us* 7 magn*us* geleassa rofeaser german mairtir uassal cuana credal creissen	4. Fronius 7 magnas gelaisse rofeisor german martir uasal cuana credal cresen
5. Cro[ch]tha corp agatha ingerat conglaini la issu congili tathus mar maith airi	5. Crochta corp ncntha ingerait conglaine lahissu congile tathus mar maith aire	5. Crochda corp agatha ingerait conglaine la ihu. congile tathus mor maith aire
6. Andreas ard a ordan epscop mel mind rigi lucia conani nadchumscaigset mili	6. Andrias ard aordan espoc mel mind rigi lucia conaine nadcumscaidset mile	6. Andreas ard aordan espoc moel mind rige lucia conine natcumscaigset mile.
7. Mellan inse huaisle macc huichuind nadnale lomman locharn brige locha huair ard age	7. Meallan inse uaisle mc. huachuind conaile loman locharn mbrigi locha huair aird áigc	7. Mellan indse uaisle mac .h. chuind notnali loman locharn brige locha unir ard aigi

Translation.

1. They magnify February's kalend, a shower of martyrs, great, purecoloured. Brigit fair, strong, praiseworthy, holy head of Ireland's nuns.

2. Mary's Son's reception in the Temple sure, inestimable: a great host of gentle martyrs, with Finnech Duirn the excellent.

3. May they protect us fully against every misery, the fair host with modesty of Felix, of Symphronius!

4. Fronius and Magnus, Gelasius thou shouldst know. German, a noble martyr. Cuanna, pious, holy.

5. Crucified was the body of Agatha, the champion with purity: by Jesu with whiteness she hath much good upon her.

6. Andreas, high his installation! Bishop Moel, a kingdom's diadem. Lucia with splendour, whom thousands moved not.

7. Mellán of noble Inis maccu-Chuinn, thou beseechest him: Lommán, lamp of vigour, high pillar of Loch Uair.

RAWL. 505.	LAUD, 610.	LEBAR BRECC, p. 81.
8. Hua an indeciss ba imcrist alabra fiachra ba fer ferda ab birard[a] amra	8. Hoa án ineiceis ba imcrist alabra fiach[r]a ba fer ferrda abb ilarda amra	8. Hua an indecis ba um crist alabra fiachra bafer ferrda abb irarda amra
9. Mochuaroc indecnai noeb nadamair digna cairech dergan deoda epscop ronan rigda	9. Mochuaroc inecna naem nardamair dingna cairech dergan deoda espoc ronain rig[d]a	9. Mochuaroc indecna noem nadamair digna cocirech dergan dioda espoc ronain rigda
10. Retlu chain gein mbuada bruth oir etrocht age cronan caid cendigna grian gel glasse mare	10. Raetla chain gein buada bruth óir etrocht aghe cronan caid cendigna grian gel glasse maire	10. Retlu cain gein buada bruth oir etrocht aige cronan caid cendigna grian gel glaisse maire
11. Mogopnat conglanbnil imseire crist bahilmain maith leiss gres diagarmaim epscop etchen inmain	11. Mogobnat conglanbail imseire dé ba hi[l]main maithleis gress diagarmain espoc eithin inmain	11. Mogobnait conglanbail imsere de bahilmain maith lais gress diagarmaim espoc ethcen inmain
12. IMmonepscop simplex slechta primslog promtha daman mil mind martra comacraid chain chrochtha	12. Himon nepscop simplex slechta primsluag promtha daman mil mind martra comacraid cáin crochta	12. Himonespoc semplex slechta primslog promtha daman mil mind martra comacraid cain crochda
13. Hicurchan modomnoc anair darmuir ṅgledend dobert brigach nualann sil mbua[da]ch mbec nerenn	13. Hicurcan modomnoc anair tar muir ṅgledenn dobreth brigach nualann síl buadach bech neirenn	13. Hicurchan modomnoc anair darmuir ngledend dobreth brigach nualand síl mbundach beach nerenn
14. Hiroi ualentini marcellus roringed hiflaith crist roclannad ochtmoga caincinged	14. Hirroi ualentini marchellus rodringned hiflaith crist roclandad ochtmogha cáin cinged	14. Hiroi ualentine marcellus roringed iflaith crist roclandad .lxxx. cain cinged

8. [Onchu,] splendid descendant of the sage: his speech was concerning Christ. Fiachra was a manly man, a marvellous abbot of (Cluain) Irard.

9. My-Cuaróc of the wisdom, a saint who endured not reproach. Coeirech Dergan the godly. Bishop Ronain the kingly.

10. Fair star, offspring of victory, glowing-mass of gold, bright pillar, Cronán holy, without reproach, white sun of Glais Már!

11. My Gobnait with pure goodness, as to God's love was opulent. Of crying to him continually he is fain, bishop Ethchen the loveable.

12. About the bishop Simplex was slain a prime, proven host. Damianus a soldier, a diadem of martyrdom, with children fair, crucified.

13. In my Domnóc's little boat, from the east over a pure-coloured sea, was brought —vigorous praise—the victorious seed of Ireland's bees.

14. In Valentine's field, Marcellus was tortured: in Christ's kingdom were planted eighty fair champions.

RAWL. 505.	LAUD, 610.	LEBAR BRECC, pp. 81-82.
15. Cain celebrad domnaig iarnabarach ńdadaig lacesaid sloig brigaig buaid mc. de dianamaid	15. Cain ccilebrad domnaig ifeil beraig bágaig lacessad sluaig brigaig buaid mc. dé dianamait	15. Can celebrad domnaig arnabarach dadaig lacesad sluaig brigaig buaid maice dé dianamait.
16. Donduaig iuliana an ńainm nel cohimbel^a laisceith sccél ahannaig demon damail indel	16. Donduaig iuliana anainm nel cohimbel lasccith scel a annaig demon damair indil	Donoig iuliani anainm nel cohimbel lasceith sceeoil aannaich demon domair indel
17. Dlomthus each coholl- muir feil cormaice conglanboil	17. Dlomthus each coholl- muir feil chormaic conglan- bail	17. Dlomthus each coholl- muir feil chormaic conglan- bail
lafeil fintain fi[g]lich cluana odhnig adboil	lafeil fiutain figlig chluana eidnig adbail	lafeil findtain figlig chuana ednich anbail
18. Bebais incaid colman molipa nodnali hifeil fir onocbi rutuli siluani	18. Bebais in caid colman moliba nodrado hifeil cain connaili rutuli siluani	18. Bebais incaid cohuan moliba noradi ifeil cain conocbi rutuili siluani
19. Sluind lett lapais pupli pais maircill mind mbua- dach boethini mor maineeh mace caindelda cuanach	19. Sluind lat lapais pauli pais marcill mind buada baithine mor maineeh mc. caindelda cuanach	19. Sluind lat lapais pauli pais marcill mind bua- dach boethine mor maineeh mac caindelta cuanach
20. Gaius intepscop achesad nicelar immaslecht sccel dogar fiche trénar trebar	20. Gaius intescop achessad ni celar immaslecht scel dogar tricha trénfer trebar	20. Gaius intespoc accsad nicelar im[a]slecht scel dogar .xxx. trenfer trebar
21. Togairm fintain choraig post contemptum mundi hifeil fir colainni uiruli iocundi	21. Togairm fintan corach post contemptum mundi hifeil cain collainni uiruli iocunndi	21. Togairm findtain choraig post contemptum mundi ifeil cain collaindi uiruli iucundi
22. INantoig ahortan	22. INantuaig aordan	22. INantuaig aordan

15. Sing the celebration of Sunday, on the morrow after night (?),^b with a vigorous host's suffering. God's Son's victory over his enemy.

16. To the virgin Juliana, a splendid name as far as the clouds' rim, for whom a demon that endured yoking vomited tidings of his evil.

17. Every one proclaims them to a great sea, the feast of Cormac with pure goodness, with the feast of Finntan the prayerful, of vast Cluain Ednich.

18. The holy Colmán died, Moliba, mention him, on the fair feast with holiness of Rutulus (and) Silvanus.

19. Announce thou with Paul's passion the passion of Marcellus, a victorious diadem. Boethline great, treasurous, Cuana's shining son.

20. Gaius the bishop, his suffering is not hidden, around whom were slain—mournful tale!—thirty wise champions.

21. The calling of quireful Finntan, *post contemptum mundi*, on the feast fair, with sharpness, of Verulus (and) Jocundus.

22. In Antioch (was) Peter's installation: he used to make known wisdom. Laurence's birth, a full answer, with Thecla's radiant feast.

^a MS. choimbel.   ^b B. 'on warlike Berach's festival.'

RAWL. 505.	LAUD, 610.	LEBAR BRECC, p. 82.
petair adfet ecna gein lurint lanfrecra lafeil toidlig thecla	petair atfet ecnai gein laurint lanfrecra lafeil toidlig tecla	petair atfet ecnai gein laurint lanfrecra lafeil toidlig tecla
23. Mathias intapstul arcr*ist* cesais riaga dondrichiud ronsnada oneoch adidńgialla [a]	23. Madian intepscop ar cr*ist* cessais riaga donrichiud ronsnada coṅdeoch anithgialla [b]	23. Madian intaspa*l* arcr*ist* cesais riaga donrichiud ronsnaiden co*n*deuch aditcialla
24. Lapais luciani cruimther crochtha dem- na abb iro an ergna cunmini find febda	24. Lapais luciani crunther crochtha dem- na abb ie án ergnái cunmine find febda	24. Lapais luciani cruimth*ir* crochda dem- na abb hia an ergna cumine find fedba
25. Fofrid cenn poil apstail indanchińged chredlaig hifeil indfír chumrig teolis treoin tredṅaig	25. Forrith cenn poil apstail indánching[ed] credlaig hifeil indfír chumrig teoilis triuin tredṅaig	25. Fofrith ceand poil aspa*il* inanchinged credlaig ifeil infír chumrig teolis triuin tredṅaig
26. Togairm alaxandri bisosad sanctorum foroenlith lantene gene darcellorum	26. Togairm alaxandri issossad sanctorum foroenlith lan tene gene tarchellorum	26. Togairm alexandri isossad sa*n*ctoru*m* fo*r*oenlith lan teni geni tarcellorum
27. Lacessad habundi marolaidib lammais feil again cing innis airec cinn ioha*n*nis	27. Lacessad habundi mad arláidib lammais feil comgain cendinnis airee cind iohan*n*is	27. Lacesad abundi mor alaidib lamais feil chomgain cendindis airec cind ioha*n*nis
28. Hifeil sillain bendchoir deich noebuaga delbdai la cessad sluaig ferdai forcennat crich febrai	28. Hifeil sillain bennchoir .x. noebuaga delbdai lacessad sluaig ferdai forcennat cleir febra	28. Hifeil sillain bendchuir x. noebuaga delbdai lacesad sloig ferdai forcendait crich febrai

23. Matthias the apostle,[a] for Christ he suffered tortures: to the Kingdom may he protect us with every one who submits to him!

24. With the passion of Lucianus, a priest who crucified demons, (is celebrated) an abbot of Ili, a splendid intellect, Cumine, fair, aged.

25. There was found the head of Apostle Paul, the splendid, pious champion, on the feast of the man of the bond, Teolis (?) strenuous, abstinent.

26. Alexander's calling into the saints' station. On one festival, a full fire, the birth of the Tarcelli.

27. With Abundius' suffering, if we dare in lays, the feast of Comgan without reproach,[c] the finding of John's head.

28. At Sillán of Bennchor's feast, ten holy, shapely virgins, with the suffering of a manly host, end February's limit.

[a] no donneoch agialla

[b] Here follows a quatrain referring apparently to 24 February (=vi. cal. Mart.), which was doubled every fourth year:—

Pais chomarba petair
ioaindeis uassal iarraid
inla forsambí bisix
cach cothramad bliadain.

"The passion of Peter's successor, of John, ye nobly seek, the day whereon is *bisextus* every fourth year."

[a] B. 'bishop'

[c] D. 'a champion, relate!'

Gloss from the Lebar Brecc, pp. 81, 82.

Feb. 1. *morait* .i. ercait *no* noemait .i. dormitatio sancto brigit[tae]. (2) *mar nylcdend* .i. mor nglaine .i. dind taitnemach cech óen dib .i. aille glana dend .i. li glódend din .i. li glan *no* li glé. (3) *brigit* .i. brigait .i. isat ait abriga . *no* breo saigit .i. omnes *no* breo saigit .i. omnes. *no* brigit .i. brig oit .i. fótla. no breosaigit .i. omnes. *no* breosaigit .i. timetur. *balce* .i. treu. *nualann* .i. nuall ann *no* nuall án *no* uasal. *no* nuall an .i. is mor 7 isán nuall cáich o[c]cuiuchid itge forbrigit. *no* ismor nuall celebartha ocbrigit. *no* is an nuall o hoim [leg. hominibus?] ocmolad brigde 7 ocahatach

2. *airitiu* .i. forrigthib semioin .i. in octauo die ot .xl. ductatus est xps. ad templum secundum morem legis. (2) *dimis* .i. dameass dosemion. dimis .i. nifetar ameass. *no* mor indimess do abreith hitempul aruirabatar cinta aice. *no* isdoilig ameass. *no* díameass doratad fair in templo. Dimis .i. adbul miti purgatio [leg. purificatio] sancta[e] maria[e] memoratur in hoc die apud romanos et non ac[c]epti[o] christi in templus (sic). (3) *suabais* .i. omni is suauis .i. suailsoach.

3. (1) *donroemat* .i. rouairimet *no* ro[n]uertat no robet romaind *coluni* .i. cocomlau (3) *sloiyed* .i. sluag. *cofeli* .i. cum . . . . (4) *felicis* .i. folle lictus.

4. (1) *Fronius* .i. dikl. *magnus* .i. proprium [nomeu]. (2) *gelaisse* .i. proprium [nomen]. (4) *credal* .i. cretmech *no* craibdech. *no* credlach [i.e. crésen?] .i. sean a chré .i. sehior [leg. senior] *no* cresinech .i. faiscti .i. áintech.

5. (1) *agatha* proprium [nomen]. (2) *gerait* .i. beoda (4) *tathus* .i. rothinoil *no* ata duit

6. (1) *ordan* .i. ordinatio est. (3) *lucia* proprium [nomen] muli[oris] *comaine* .i. comairtitiud (4) *nateumscaiyset mile* .i. forendigset ilmile acúmscugud assin inud aroibe

7. (2) *notnali* .i. atach (3) *locharn* .i. lucerna. (4) *ard aigi* .i. uasal intaige he. *aigi* .i. tuir

9. (2) *nadamair digna* .i. neingné .i. drochgue. *no* nifodamair drochgue (3) *dioda* .i. cendimess *no* dimdatus.

10. (1) *retlu* .i. solas .i. sanctus. (3) *caid* .i. sanctus. caid dicitur a cades barna [nomen] proprium loci in monte sinay cádes interpre[tatur] scians. *digna* .i. *cendigna* .i. cendrochgne *no* cen dimess gnói a gnosia [γνῶσις] grece scientia latine. *no* odroch dignoi

11. (2) *ba hilmain* .i. baetir .i. illda a himnai[n]echt imseirec nde. no ahilmaine (3) *maith lais gress diagarmaim* .i. maith les agairm comenic .i. icamolad *no* occúnchid itge fair

12. (2) *slechta* .i. rosligthe .i. romarb[tha]. *no* atat sligida *no* slaite .i. lechta (3) *mil* .i. milid

13. (3) *dobreth* .i. tucad. *nualand* .i. nuallan mac. *no* gnir mor accu

14. (2) *rorinyed* .i. rorengad .i. roriagad. *no* rorinded .i. rogonad corindib. *no* dorata rinde trit *no* rorengad .i. doronta renga 7 bloga de. .i. isinreid roriagad marcellus .i. loc césta martirum ualentinum. (4) *cinyed* .i. treufir .i. calma .i. iarsinui chengait sech cach

15 (1) *can* .i. canta.

16. (3) *lusccith sceoil aannaich* .i. roindis fen aulcu di. (4) *damair indel* .i. rodamair aindlead di. *no* indlod .i. cengul *no* cuimrech

17. (1) *dlomthus* .i. indissid

18. (1) *bebais* .i. obith [leg. obiit?] .i. atbath. ne[s]cio ubi est. (2) *noradi* .i. ráid no ataig

19. (1) *sluind* .i. aisneid (4) *caindeltu* .i. taitnemach *no* lassardai

20. (3) *im[a]slecht* .i. uime roslaitea .i. romarbtha. *doyar* .i. toirsech

22. (1) *at[s]et ecnai* .i. indisid ecna icforcetul caich

23. (4) *condcuch aditeialla* .i. cocechoen rogiallustar dó *no* rochreit dia thrit

24. (2) *cruimther* .i. sacart .i. ainm dacech fir graid óntoirned thoirnes octabairt graid fair

25. (2) *inanchinged* .i. inanroith. *no* incing án ifertaib. *credlaig* .i. credmig (3) *feil infir chumrig* .i. ininfir (sic) cuimrechta himartra he. *no* robui icumrech ardia (4) *trednaig* .i. troscig

26. (2) *hisossad sanctorum* .i. in coelum. (3) lanteni .i. lán dothenid ratha inspirta noeim he

27. (2) *mor a laidib lamais* .i. mongenar dún lamthana athabarta illaidib *no* dia lamais afaisnes olaidib. *no* lamais nomen poeta[e]. (3) *cendindis* .i. cendinsem. *no* cendin[n]is proprium nomen collis in propria regióne comgan indál cais. (4) *airec* .i. fagbail *Iohannis* .i. bautiste.

28 (2). *delbdai* .i. sochar (4) *forcendait* .i. forbait

[in p. 82.] NOTES FROM THE LEBAR BRECC, pp. 81, 82, 83.

1. Morait kl. febra 7rl. berchan cecinit

IN ban a life nalerg
ingen dubthaig adruim derg
isamarmch teit cotrait
isdia laim audaecht patraic.

Ocht nespuic .x. tancotar cobrigit ahúibbr[i]uin chualand othelaig nanespoc coloch lemnachta hitoeb cille dara atuaid. corofiarfaid brigit diacoig .i. doblathnait inroibe biad aice. et dixit illa nou. 7 banár labrigit. condóbart intaingel nabái doblogan iterum coruablig brigit coroslínsat nadabcha 7 nolínfatis lesttra laigen uile. 7 condechaid inloin tarna lésttra condernai loch de. inde loch lemnachta dicitur.

Foglaid tanic codubthach cotuc assill isincoire dó 7 conderna .u. blogai de. rocarb dobrigit acoimet. cotanic cú truag eluicesi 7 cotarut na .u. bloga asincoire ifiadnaise inóclaich. 7 frith iarum na .u. bloga isinchoire rohindissed dodubthach sin. 7 dobert dubthach feraun di .i. rethet daurthige ituaith dámuige.

Macclerech domuintir fornai moire .i. dalta do brigit ticead condútnrachtaib dissi. Essim hipronntig lesi .i. friacaitheim biú. Focht ann din. iartecht doib dolaim benaid brigit baschrand. Maith ale ameícelérig thall olbrigit. infíl anmchara lat. ata immurro olinelerech. gaibem acenaire olbrigit. cidsin olinnac clerig. Atbath muritconnaresa intan roscaich deit leath dochota isand bamarb. Cid diata lat olin clerech. nin. olbrigit. atchonnaresa iutan roscaich leath dochota isitmedi'doberthea dochuit 7 tú cen chend fort itir. onuair bamarb hanmchara. Eirg ass olbrigit nacaith ni besuió corogaba annchara. ariscolann cencheud duine cenanmcharait.

1. 'They magnify February's calend,' &c. Berchan *cecinit*

The woman from Liffey of the slopes,
Daughter of Dubthach from Druim Derg,
To-morrow she goes to a combat;
From her hand is Patrick's bequest.

Eighteen bishops came to Brigit from Hui-Briuin Chualand, from Telach nan espoc to Loch Lemnachta beside Kildare on the north. So Brigit asked of her cook, to wit, of Blathnait, whether she had food, *et dixit illa nou*. And Brigit had shame, so the angel said that the cows should be milked *iterum*. And Brigit milked them, and they filled the tubs, and they would have filled all the vessels of Leinster; and the milk came over the vessels and made a lough thereof. *Inde* Loch Lemnachta *dicitur*.

A robber came to Dubthach, and he put a joint into the cauldron for him, and made five pieces thereof. He charged Brigit to keep it; and a wretched hound came to her, and she gave it the five pieces out of the cauldron in the champion's presence, and the five pieces were afterwards found in the cauldron. That was related to Dubthach, and Dubthach gave a land to her, to wit, the site (?) of an oratory in Tuath dámaige.

A young cleric of the family of Ferns, to wit, a fosterling of Brigit's, used to come with wishes to her. He . . . . . into the refectory with her, i.e. for eating food. Now on a time there. after they had come from confession, brigit strikes a handtree. "Well, O young cleric there," quoth Brigit, "hast thou a soulfriend ?" "I have, forsooth," quoth the cleric. "Let us sing his requiem," quoth Brigit. "Why is that ?" quoth the young cleric. "He died as I saw when half thy quota had gone from thee, it is then he was dead." "How is this with thee ?" quoth the cleric. "Not hard" (to say), quoth Brigit. "I saw when half thy quota had gone, that thy quota was put into thy trunk, and thou without a head on thee at all, since thy soulfriend was dead. Get thee hence," quoth Brigit, "eat no more till thou takest a soulfriend. For a man without a soulfriend is a body without a head."

Amra plea .i. cathir fil forbrú mara torren. no plea cathir fil do brigit forbrú inber mara 7 ise abordside fil ocmuintir brígte. et sic factum est id .i. brigit rofóid morfessiur unthi dofóglaim uird petair ocus póil. uair narochind dia di fen dul. 7 nithucsat inord. corofóid intresfechtsa sair 7 a mac dallsi leo. uair cech ní nochluinedside bamebar lais. INtan tra. rancotar muir nichtt tanic anfud dóib comór furri corolaiset sís anmgir corolean for bendchopar indaurtige corolaiset sortem inter se imthecht sís conid doudáll dorala techt sís. obsolbit ille iningair et sedit annsin cocend mbliadna ocfóglaim inuird cotorachtatar infiallach aile orúaim chuicesium. conustarla anfud dóib bcos isinbaile cétna corolecsot ingcorum sis cotanic inmac dall leo anís conurd plea lais 7 coclug taitnemach. ocus ise maires indíu .i. ord plea.

Robail din. dobrigit grada aithrige dothabairt fuirri. Dorocht cobrig éle 7 morfessiur cailleoch imaille fria. orochuala espoc moel dobeth and. ocus intan rancutar ní robi intespoc anu. acht dochuaid icrich .h. néill. Luidside din. iarnabarach ocus maccaille do eolas rempi darmónaid flathuig. Doroine brigit corba mag mínscothach doib inmóin. Orancotar ifochraib donbaile iroibe espoc moel. et dixit brigit fri maccaille corofoided caille foracind arnadicsed cenfial daracend cusnaclerchiu. 7 cumad he sin caille fornithmentar sund. Iarrochtain disse din. rolass colma teuntige diacind coclethi na heclaisi. Otconnaire din. espoc moel sin roiarfaid cuich nacaillecha. Atbert maccaille issi so inchaillech aurdoirc delaignib .i. brigit. Mocheu di ol espoc moel. isme olse dosrengart abróind amáthar 7 ismé dobéra grada furri.

Focht tanic espoc moel do [p. 83] thig dubthaig cofacaaid sé setig dubthaig fobrón coriar-

Amra plea, i.e. a city which is on the shore of the Tyrrhene sea. Or Plea, a city of Brigit's on the shore of Inver Mara,* and its Rule is that of Brigit's family; *et sic factum est id*, to wit, Brigit sent seven persons from her to learn the Rule of Peter and Paul, for God did not determine that she herself should go. And they brought not the Rule, till she sent this third time eastward, and her blind boy with them, for everything he used to hear he remembered. Now when they reached the Ictian sea, came a storm to them mightily thereon, and they cast down their anchor, and it caught on the roof of the oratory, and they cast a lot *inter se* as to going down, and it fell on the blind boy to go down. *Obsolvit ille* the anchor *et stetit* there till a year's end, learning the Rule, until the rest of the party came (back) from Rome to him, and a storm fell upon them again at the same place, and they cast down their *ancora*, and the blind boy came from below with them, with the Rule of Plea along with him, and with a beautiful bell; and it is this that abides to-day, to wit, the Rule of Plea.

Now Brigit was fain to have the orders of penitence conferred upon her. She went to Bríg Ele, and seven nuns along with her, since she heard that Bishop Moel was there. And when they came, the bishop was not there, but he had gone into the border of the Huí-Néill. So she fared forth on the morrow, and Mac Caille to guide before her, over Múin Fathuig. Brigit wrought so that the bog became a smoothflowery plain for them. When they drew nigh to the place wherein was Bishop Moel, *et dixit* Brigit to Mac-Caille that he should send a hood to meet her, so that she might not come to the clerics without a veil over her head; and it may be that this hood is commemorated here. Now after her arrival a fiery column went from her head to the ridge of the church. When Bishop Moel beheld this, he asked, "Who are the nuns?" Said Mac-Caille, "this is the conspicuous nun of Leinster, to wit, Brigit." "Welcome to her," quoth Bishop Moel. "It was I," quoth he, "that prophecied her from her mother's womb, and it is I that shall confer orders upon her."

Once upon a time Bishop Moel came to Dubthach's house, and he saw Dubthach's wife

---

* The Straits of Gibraltar.

faid cid das inbean. Ata liumm adbar bróin olsi. nair isdocha ladub*thach* inchumal fil ocíndlad dúibsi olsi indúsa. ISdethb*ir* detsiu ón ol espoc moel. arfogénaid dosílsa dosíl nacuma*ile* .i. dobrig*it*.

Cid dia tancut*ar* nacaille*cha* olespoc moel. dothabairt grád aithrige forbrig*it* olinmac caille. Iarsin rohirlégait grada forbrig*it*. 7 grada espu*ic* dorat espoc moel fu*i*rri. con*i*d indsin rogab maccaille caille forcind brigte. con*i*d osin ille dliges comorba brigte. grada espu*ic* dothabairt fu*i*rri. 7 cén búi oc airlégad grád fu*i*rri. isamla*id* búi brig*it* 7 coss na altóri inalaim. ocus roloisctheá uii. neclaisi 7 inchossin inntib 7 nícon-loisced si .i. sed seruata est per gratiam brigittae. Dicunt alii. cu*m*ad iferaib tulach ata ineclassin maritehuaid espoc moel. ita ut alii putaut.

[p. 81.]
2. La *finnich duirn digrais* .i. inatulcha sin illaignib icill findich.

Findech duirn .i. ochíll finche inosraigib .i. oath duirn buide .i. dorn buide nomen collis magne amuig raigne. *no* isinúib scellain slebe mairge ata findech duirn buide. ut alii putant. uel nomen uiri a quo nominatur inbali. no la nindid duirn d*igrais* .i. laimidain.

4. *Gelaisse rofesser* .i. anus gelasus papa romæ.
Cuana credal cresen .i. abb liss moir
5. *Agatha* .i. uirgo.

6. *Espoc moel mind rige* .i. inardachad itebtha ata espoc moel. darcrea siur patraic m*á*thair espu*ic* moel. 7 ise dorat grada forbrigit 7 ba-grada espu*ic* iatside 7 isiat bis foracomorba diabessi

[p. 81, in marg. inf.]
Lupait 7 tigris (proprium [nomen]) tend feib doruirmess is ric*ell* (proprium [nomen]) dárcrea is liamain na lend gabsat diamair cen d*í*chell. Anmand sin re sret[h]aib scall scath*ar* patraic nap*r*imchell

under grief; so he asked, "why sorrows (?) the woman?" "Cause of grief have I," quoth she, "for dearer unto Dubthach than I am is the handmaid that is washing your feet," quoth she. "Thou hast good reason," quoth Bishop Moel, "for thy seed shall serve the handmaid's seed," to wit, Brigit.
"Wherefore came the nuns?" says Bishop Moel. "To have orders of penitence conferred on Brigit," says the Mac-Caille. Thereafter orders were read over Brigit, and a bishop's orders Bishop Moel bestowed upon her, and it was then Mac-Caille set a hood on Brigit's head, and thence it is that Brigit's successor is entitled to have a bishop's orders conferred upon her. And while he was reading orders upon her, Brigit was in this wise—the leg of the altar in her hand; and seven churches were burnt, and that leg (was) in [one of] them, and it was not burnt, *sed servata*, &c. *Dicunt alii* that in Fir Tulach is that church, as Bishop Moel declared, *ita*, &c.

2. '*With Finnech Duirn, the excellent*' i.e of the Tulach (is) that, in Leinster in Cell Findich.
Findech Duirn, i.e. of Cell Finche in Ossory, i.e. of Ath Duirn Buide ('the ford of yellow Dorn'), i.e. Dorn Buide *nomen collis magni* in Mag Raigne, or it is in Hui-Scellain of Sliab Mairge is Findech of Dorn Buide, *ut*, &c. or [the true reading is] *la nindid duirn digrais* 'with Nindid of the undefiled fist.' i.e. pure-handed.

4. '*Gelasius thou shouldst know*,' i.e. Gelasius, a Pope of Rome.
'*Cuana pious, believing*,' i.e. Abbot of Lismore.

6. '*Bishop Moel, a kingdom's diadem*,' i.e. in Ard-achad in Teffia is Bishop Moel. Darerca, Patrick's sister, (was) Bishop Moel's mother; and he it was that conferred orders on Brigit, and they were a bishop's orders, and it is they that are on her successor after her.

Lupait and Tigris the strict,
As I have counted, and Ricell,
Dárerca and Liamain of the surplices,
They took ..... without decrease.
Those are the names by ranks of times
Of the sisters of Patrick of the chief churches.

x.uii. nespuic um espoc m.cárthaind rogénair
ó dárerca 7 dí óig . ut dixit [poeta]

Buadaig munter darerca retindrim
xuii. [nepscoip] dóib darlermuir
di oig ingin
Ocus is iat nahógu .i. aiche 7 lallóc. ut dixit.

Aiche craibdech rochar trédnu
duscid marbu. moraid lubru
lallóc osendliss iarm[b]ádgnu.

7. *Mellan indsc uaisle* .i. mellan indse mec
.h. chuind forloch noirpsean aniarthar chon*dacht.*
Loman locharn brige .i. o inis moir locha uair
inúib maic uais míde.
8. *Hua an indecis* .i. onchu *no* ternoc

ternoc tren atharba

[in marg. d.] Hua an indéis .i. onchú aninm
.i. isindertbig relgi aingel icluain mor moedoc
ata 7 docon[u]achtaib do. 7 f[ili] maith lais he.
Conid he ní forsutarla he .i. taisse noem erenn
dothinol. ocus nigaibed innách cill cenni dothaissib innocim sin dotabairt dó corothinoil
coroibe scrín móir nice dothaissib noem erenn.
Teit din cocluain moir moedoc .i. Móedoc .b.
dunlaing dolaignib. 7 nihe moedoc ferna.
Eccmaing moedoc beo forachind. Ni dottaissib
dit damsa aclerig olse corabut imaille frissna
taissib elesi. ISdoilig sin olinclerech. Adénam
arai arinfilid. Teascaid iarum inclerech alúdain
de 7 atnaig donfilid. Gortaigther iarum inclerech
desin conid de asbert inní rothinoilis olse.
isandso bias 7 isand bias dothaissi fén beos. ocus
issed ón rocomaillead.

uel onchu nomen eius qui uenit cofinan lobar.
ut perigrinarentur. et dixit finan lobar mor[i]ere
mecum qui tunc fuit in dolore.* et dixit onchu
uon sed colligam reliquias omnium sanctorum
hic ad te .i. co cluain mor moedoc. et sic factum
est.
Fiachra ba fer ferrda .i. o congbail glinde sáilige .i. nomen arinis [leg. amnis?]. irarda .i. a

* MS. idnio lore

Seventeen bishops, with Bishop MacCárthainn, were born of Dárerca, and two virgins,
as a poet said:—

Gifted the family of Darerca by conclusion:
Seventeen bishops of them over main sea,
Two virgin daughters.

And these are the virgins, namely Aiche and
Lallóc, as said [a poet]

Pious Aiche loved fastings:
She raises the dead,
She magnifies lepers,
Lallóc of Senliss after . . . .

7. '*Mellan of a noble isle,*' i.e. Mellan of
Inis mec bui Chuind, on Lough Corrib, in the
west of Connaught.
'Loman, a lamp of strength' i.e. from Inis
Mór of Loch Uair, in Hui-Maic-Uais of Meath.
8. '*Splendid descendant of the sage,*' i.e.
Onchu, or Ternóc ('thy Eruóc').

'Ternóc, strong his profit' [is the true reading.]

'Splendid descendant of the sage,' .i. Onchu
his name, i.e. in the oratory of Relic Aingel in
Cluain Mór Maedóc (i.e. Maedóc hua Dunlaing
of Leinster, and not Maedóc of Ferns).
Maedóc happened (to be) alive before him.
"Somewhat of thy relics (cut) off thee for me,
O cleric," quoth he, "that they may be along
with these other relics." "That is hard," quoth
the cleric. "It is to be done, nevertheless,"
quoth the poet. Then the cleric cuts off his
little-finger and gives it to the poet. Then the
cleric is pained thereby, so that he said, "What
thou hast gathered," quoth he, "it is here it
shall be, and it is here that thy own relics
shall be;" and this was fulfilled.
Vel Onchu nomen eius qui venit to Fínan the
Leper *ut, &c.*

'*Fiachra was a manly man,*' i.e. from Congbail of Glenn Suilige, i.e. a river's name. Irarda

nomine aba[ti]s. *no* ceall inúib dróna illaignib .i. inard uasruithe. aníb dróna fria berba aniar 7 mocholmog cluana iraird in *hoc die dicitur.*

9. *Mochuaroc indeena* .i. indésib muman ata qui cronau mac netsemon. isaire atberar mochuaroc nanona friss. arisó toisech rodelig ceilebrad nóna. quia cum media uel ora apudantiquos celebratur.

Coeirech dergan dioda .i. hicluain boirend forbrú sinda ata.

[p. 84, at the end of March]. Cairech dergáin. inúib maine forbrú sinda .i. hicluain boirend ata cairech dergain .i. Cairech ingen chonaill deirg mic doimeni doim argait .i. siur éndai áirne. IShe din. inconall roscur loch nerni fricennachtu 7 dubthor frialáignib 7 rothafuind ullta targleand rige sair. ocus isiatsin teora ferguimu conaill. INgen din. donchonallsin cairech. ut. diximus et derbráthair di endai áirne mac conaill deirg .i. intress athlœch naherend. ideo haec.

Cáirech dergain di[n]. Ecmaic di oc ascaid chind abrathar .i. éndai airne. Ecmaic din. áliud forsiumbrathair. INuister disse siu. indergthar impo asahaithle. conid assin cháir sin 7 assin indergad rolaad fuirri atberair cáirech dergain fria.

Espoc ronain rigda .i. illiss mor mochuda ata.

10. *Cronan caid cendigna* .i. hirose glaise. *no* cumad be mochua miliuca.

Grian gel glaisse maire .i. sinand. *no* isna desaib .i. ceall fas frisord ancs* .i. cronan mac mellan oglais moir indesaib muman 7 din ata illiss mor. *no* glais mor. ceall robui itóeb suird alla anessacotanentargaill indbírdomnand chuice cormarbsat amuinntir inoennaidche et nullus de familia eius euasit.

11. *Mogobnait coglanbail* .i. cailleeh gobger. *no* gob inait nahernaigthe. *no* cruaigthe ainm inbaile hita.

Espoc ethcen inmain .i. icluain fota boetain aba uenide ata.

p. 84, in marg. inf.]. Espoc etchein. din hicluain fotai boetain iferaib bile andescert inide ata. Ocus is fora amus dochóid colum

i.e. *a nomine abbatis.* Or a church in Hy-Drona in Leinster, i.e. in Ard na sruithe in Hy-Dróna to the west of the Barrow; and Mocholmóc of Clonard *in hoc die dicitur.*

9. '*My-Cuaróc of the wisdom*' i.e. in Desies of Munster he is, *qui* Cronan mac Netsemon. For this is he called 'my-Cuaróc of the None,' because he was the first who divided the celebration of None.

'*Coeirech dergan the godly*' i.e. in Cluain Boirenn on the Shannon's brink she is.

'*Cairech dergain,*' in Hy-Maine on the Shannon's brink, i.e. in Cluain Boirenn is Cairech dergain i.e. Cairech daughter of Conall Derg, son of Domene Doim-argait i.e. sister of Endae of Aran. He is the Conall that severed Lough Erne from Connaught and Dubthor from Leinster, and hunted the Ulstermen over Glen Rige eastwards. And those are Conall's three manly deeds. A daughter of that Conall was Cairech *ut diximus,* and a brother of hers was Ennae of Aran, son of Conall Derg, the third whilom-hero of Ireland.

'Cairech dergain,' again. She happened to be searching the head of her brother i.c. Enna of Arran, and it happened that a charge (was brought) against the brother. This is told to her. There is a blushing on her thereafter, so that from that blame and from the blushing that was brought upon her, she is called Cairech Dergain.

'*Bishop Ronain the royal,*' i.e. in Les mór Mochuda he is.

10. '*Cronan the chaste without reproach*' i.e. in Ros Glaise, or he may be Mochua of Milluc.

'*Fair sun of Glais Már*' .i. the Shannon; or in the Desies i.c. an empty church to the south of Sord i.e. Cronan son of Mellan of Glais mór in Desies of Munster, and moreover he is in Lismore. Or Glais mór a church that was beside Sord ['Swords'] on the south, and foreigners of Inver Domnann came thither, and slew its family in one night, *et, &c.*

11. '*My-Gobnait with purity*' i.e. a nun sharpbeaked, or a beak in the place of the prayer. Or *Ernaigthe* the name of the place wherein she is.

'*Bishop Ethcen the loveable*' i.e. in Cluain Fota Boetain Aba in Meath he is.

Bishop Etchein, now, in Cluain Fota Boetain iu Fir Bile in the south of Meath he is. And on a visit to him went Colum Cille to have a

---

* MS. *pris* ordanes.

cille dothabairt grad espuic fair. Suidig din. colam cille fón mbaisene friacill aniar. ocus iarfaigther uad cáit aubói incléirech. Acsin ol fer and forfairche inarathair tís he. ISdoig olcolam cille ni coir dún aircam dothabairt grád foirn. arái sin tra fromther ocaind he. Othancotar friss. cuingit cétus insoce fair prius. Domber dóib fochetoir ocus uilugnite roairset nadoim. ISfer maith incléirech oliat. Afromad beos ol colam cille. Cuingit intimechtraid fair. Atnaig dóib fochétoir ocus forcongraid espoc étchein fordam nallaid bói isinchoillid infeidmsin do dénum. 7 dogní fochétoir.

Téit iarum colam cille foramus inclerig iarnafromad 7 indissid dó inní foatánie. Dogentar olincléreeh. Atnagar din. grádai sacairt forcholam cille. ocus grádai espuic robail dó do thabairt fair. Ernaigid inclerech cóarabárach. Pudarsin achlerig ol colam cille ingrád tucais formsa. 7 arái niaithrégsa he hi céin ham beo. INa inad sin din. ni thicfa nech cobráth dothabairt grád fair cusincillsea. Ocus issed on chomailltcr beos.,

[p. 81]
12. *Himon espoc simplex* .i. m[o]diuid espoc ochill modiuit isogan

Daman mil mind martra .i. othig damain indib crimthandain. Daman. lithgen. miada. abban. senchan. duban. toimdenach. uii. germani sunt. Mell din. soror choemgin mater eorum. Dámnan mac laiguig mic coindig mic labrada mic imchada mic cormaic mic concorp

13. *Hicurchan modomnoc* .i. hifeil etsecta modomnoc .i. hitibrait fachtna inosraigib. et quies modomnocsa.
14. *Hi roi ualentine* .i. irré feraind inrocrochad ualintinu[s] isand doronta renga 7 bloga de mercello.
15. *Can celebrad domnaig* .i. canta .i. aranuaisle nafeil cincob ar domnach bct. *no* hifeil beraig bágaig .i. berach mac nemnaind m. nemangen m. finntain m. mail m. dobtha m. oengusa ra. crea derg mc. briain m. echach muidmedon. ocus coccigis derrach aféil 7 indítbrib cenel dobtha icon[n]achtu ata som .i. icluain cairpti. ut dixit angelus

bishop's orders conferred upon him. Now Colum Cille sat under the tree to the west of the church, and it was asked by him where was the cleric? "There he is," quoth a man there, "on the field of the ploughing below." "Meseems," quoth Colum Cille, "it is not right for us that a ploughman should confer orders upon us. However, now let him be proven by us." When they came to him they first asked the ploughshare of him. He gives it to them at once, and not the less did the oxen plough. "A good man is the cleric," say they. "Prove him still more," quoth Colum Cille. They ask the outer ox of him. He gives it to them at once, and bishop Etchein orders a hart that was in the wood to do that work, and he doth it at once. Then Colum Cille comes to the cleric after proving him, and tells him what he had come for. "It shall be done," quoth the cleric. A priest's orders are then bestowed on Colum Cille, and it was a bishop's orders that he wished to be conferred upon him. The cleric prays till the morrow. "A mistake is that, O cleric," quoth Colum Cille, "the order thou hast conferred upon me, and yet I will not change it so long as I shall be alive. In lieu of that, now, no one shall ever come to this church to have orders conferred upon him." And it is this that is still fulfilled.

12. '*Around the bishop Simplex*' i.e. My-Diuit, bishop from Cell mo-Diuit in Sogan.
'*Damian a soldier, diadem of martyrdom*' i.e. of Tech Damain in Hui-Crimthannáin. Damán, Lithgen, Miada, Abbán, Senchán, Dubán, Toimdenach, *septem germani sunt*. Mell, moreover, *soror* of Cóemgen *mater eorum*. Daman, son of Laignech, son of Cindech, son of Labraid, son of Imchath, son of Cormac, son of Cúchorp.
13. '*In my Domnóc's little boat*' i.e. on the feast of Domnóc's death, i.e. in Tibra Fachtna in Ossory. *et quies* of my-Domnóc.
14. '*In Valentine's field*' i.e. in the strip of land wherein Valentine was crucified, it is there shreds and pieces were made *de Marcello*.
15. '*Sing the celebration of Sunday*' i.e. *canta* .i. for the nobleness of the festivals, though it is not on Sunday that they are. Or [for the second line of this quatrain read] *hi féil beraig bágaig* ' in warlike Berach's festival,' i.e. Berach, son of Nemnann, son of Nenaingen, son of Finntan, son of Mal, son of Dobaid(?), son of Oengus, son of Erc Derg, son of Brian, son of Echaid Muidmedon, and a fortnight of

ᵃ Facs. inré

Berach is mochoem
rop mellach angnáis
cipé nosguid friheolu bais
niconrágba bás .i. hifirnd.

Berach and my-Coem
Pleasant was their presence.
Whoever beseeches them at the lips of death
Will not get death i.e. of hell.

16. Donóig iuliani 7rl. uirgo romana que ligáuit demonem[a] uno capillo capitis[b] sui .i. ethiar dub din. ainm indemainsin. 7 isinand he [ocus] lucifer et postea eum[c] posuit sub stercolinio. 7 roadaim annsin conidhe roaimsig adam 7 eua 7 cain 7 crist 7 iudam[d] et alios multos et iulianam[e] item.

16. '*To the virgin Juliana,*' &c. *virgo,* &c.
i.e. Black Ethiar then that demon's name, and he is the same as Lucifer, *et postea,* &c. and he confessed there that it was he that tempted Adam and Eve and Cain and Christ, *et Judam et alios multos, et,* &c.

17. *Feil chormaic conglanbail* .i. cormac espoc comorba patraic 7 inathtruim iloegaire ata.

17. '*Feast of Cormac with pure goodness,*' i.e. Cormac bishop, Patrick's successor; and in A'th Truim of Ua-Loegairi he is.

La feil findtain figlich .i. finntan mac gaibreni m. corcrain m. echach m. bresail m. dén. sund condric ocus brigit ut dixit fintan

'*At the feast of Finntan the prayerful,*' i.e. Finntan, son of Gaibrene, son of Corcrán, son of Echaid, son of Bresal, son of Dén. Here he and Brigit meet [in their pedigrees], *ut dixit* Finntan :—

Amra inindeoin buadusa[f]
dorala formitisi [leg. form mithis-si]
cipe impas sunn fotrí
derb doria doridiso

Wondrous this anvil of victory
Which has come on my time !
Whosoever turns here thrice
Will surely come again.

Oengus cecinit

Oengus sang:—

Fintan fial
nirothomail raré riam
ucht aran corna fodda
ocus usce créda criad.

Generous Fintan
Never ate during his time
Save woody bread of barley,
And clayey water of clay.

Alii dicunt cumad he colman mac œda fil in ardbó forbrú locha echach uel hoc quod nerius est [secundum] alios .i. colman mac fergusa. dicit oengus hic sed non sic sapio sed quod tue col. s. leige in scuchas.

Alii dicunt that he was Colman, son of Aed who is in Ardbó, on the brink of Lough Neagh.

Diomtus each 7rl. la féil fintain figlig uel uindium uel uindunus in libris uetustissimis[g] inuenitur et a uino dicitur eo quod fudit uinum doctrinae et religionis in cordibus monachorum[h] suorum et.uii.nu[n]is uinonutritus est. lege in senchas. xu. bl*iadna* 7 ui. xx. it sægul fintain oceantain *salm* mbuan mbind uas or thobair

Finntan cornch senach garb
colman mac comgaill condalb
tri dúilríg congliaid gaile
diaid indiaid inapdaine

Fifteen years and six score (was) the age of Finntan a-chanting lasting, melodious psalms over the edge of a well.

Finntan the quireful, Senach the rough,
Colman son of Comgall with guile.
Three great kings with warfare of valour
One after the other in the abbacy.

[a] MS. demenium [b] MS capatis [c] MS. p.team [d] MS. iuadam [e] MS. iulianum
[f] .i. incloch forarbaisted fintan ('.i. the stone whereon Finntan was baptized').
[g] MS. untis. q. uindunus in libri uetus ussimis. [h] MS. monucharum

18. *Moliba noradi* .i. inænach alti inuib echach ula*d* ata.
19. *Boethine mor mainech* .i. boethine mac cuanach m. coeim m. enda. othig boethin aniarth*ar* mide. Tri tige boethin ann .i. tech boethin immide 7 tech boethin itír conaill 7 *tech boethin* inairtiuch fria cruachain con-[n]*acht* aniar. ut dixit

> Cetri cómanmand rorimed
> boethine bulcc buadach
> mac brenaind mac findaig
> mac alla mac cuanach

20. *Gaius intespoc* .i. papa et sub* carullo u*el* caro [leg. Caracalla?] .i. pasus est
21. *Togairm fintain choraig* .i. fintan mac gaibren am*al* ata thuas. Fintan corach .i. dia oilithre dachoid icon[n]*ach*taib corgabsat ratha aire. arn beo no aramarb dotiachtain doridise. hilemchoill itir hua nduach 7 laigis ata fintan corach *no* iclúain aithchein hilaigis. *no* hiclúain ferta brenaind atá fintau corach .i. coir gabar oca lige 7 ni haille et ideo dicitur corach. no corach ima beo *no* ima marb doriachtain doridisi. *no* cuir rogabtha do intan [docuaid] dochum nime cotisad doridisi. *no* rola inscrín irabutar athaisi curu di. *no* ise dorigne cora inuird nuabcsa ut

> sancti columbæ merita
> ba[i]thinique dignisima
> ac adamnani omnia
> adiuuent nos celsisima.

uel quod uerius [est] hi cluain óidnech attat na .iiii. fintain

[*in marg. s.*] .i. comorba brenaind fintan 7 dochorco dúibne dó 7 do chorco dúibne *máthair* brenaind

22. *In antuaig a ordan* .i. anntiocia[e] rotescad folt petair 7 dorígne a *cét*procept 7 isinte .lin ariacht nahanmundsa .i. christiani[b] et eclesia *a ordan* .i. cathedra petri .i. oirdned petair hi cathair inantuaig.

Gein laurint .i. deochain iroim
23. *Madian intaspol* .i. madian asp*al* in ierusalem sepultus est 7 traian rosmarb he. 7 ernín lethglindi cum madiano

[r] *donrichiud ronsnaidea* .i. breath inaingil so donanoemaib imdala inbisecsa fribisec dothachur cech cethrumad bl*iadain*

* MS. sup   [b] MS. xp.c

---

18. '*Moliba thou relatest*' i.e. in Oenach Alti in Hy-Echach of Ulster he is.
19. '*Boethine great, treasurous*' i.e. Boethine, son of Cuana, son of Coem, son of Enna, from Tech Boethin in the west of Meath. Three *Tige Boethin* are there, i.e. Tech Boethín in Meath, and Tech Boethin in Tir-Conaill, and Tech Boethin in Airtech to the west of Cruachu of Connaught, ut dixit [poeta :]

> Four names that were counted,
> Boethine, stout, victorious,
> son of Brenann, son of Findach,
> son of Alla, son of Cuana.

21. '*The calling of Finntan the quireful*,' i.e. Fintan son of Gabran as is above. *Fintan corach* i.e. on his pilgrimage he went into Connaught, and they took securities from him to come again, whether alive or dead. In Lemcboill in Tír Hua nDuach and Leix is Fintan Corach or in Cluain Aithchein in Leix, or in Cluain Ferta Brenainn is Fintan Corach i.e. pledges (*coir*) are taken at his grave *et ideo dicitur corach*. Or pledged whether alive or dead to come back again, or pledges (*cuir*) were taken from him when [he went] to heaven that he would come again. Or the shrine wherein were his relics made circles (*curu*). Or it is he that made the adjustments (*cora*) of the order of the new rite, *ut*, &c.

Vel, quod verius est, in Cluain Eidnech are the four Finntans.
i.e. Finntan (was) Brenann's successor, and of the Corco Duibne was he, and of the Corco Duibne was Brenann's mother.
22. '*In Antioch his sovranty*,' i.e. at Antioch Peter's hair was cut, and he made his first preaching, and it is therein moreover, were invented these names i.e. *Christiani* and *ecclesia*. '*his sovranty*,' i.e. cathedra Petri i.e. Peter's installation on a throne in Antioch.

'*Birth of Laurentius*' i.e. a deacon in Rome.
23. '*Matthias the apostle*' i.e. Madian the apostle was buried in Jerusalem, and Trajan slew him: and Ernín of Leighlin (is commemorated) with Madianus.

'*To the kingdom protect us*,' i.e. this is the angel's sentence to the saints concerning the *bisextus*, to insert (the) intercalary day every fourth year.

Pais comorba petair
eoin uasail iarraid
inla forsmbi bisex
cech cethrumad bliadain

(The) passion of Peter's successor
Of noble John seek ye
The day whereon shall be *bisextus*
Every fourth year.

Bisextus hic oritur* in saltu lune celerius
a[s]cendit quam putatur in bisex vero tardius
a[s]cendit quam putatur. bisex namque retardat
saltus vero celerat.
24. *abb hia* .i. *cholum cille*
cumine find fedba .i. *cumin mac dinertaig ise
tuc taissi poil 7 petair lais codisiurt chumin
itermand ruis chré. corochaidset uad do russ cré*

24. '*Abbot of Hi*' .i. Colam Cille.
'*Cumine fair, aged*' i.e. Cumíne son of
Dínertach : it is he that brought the relics of
Paul and Peter with him to Disert Cumín in
the *termann* of Ros Cré, and they went from
him to Ros Cré.

25. *Fofrith cennd poil* .i. post .xl. annos.
Petronilla[b] filia petri apostoli inuenit *caput
pauli apostoli post .xl. annos post decollationem
eius a nerone.*
27. *Feil chomgain cendindis* .i. comgan oglind
buissen. comgan cum germanis. Comgán.
mernoc. moelchu. mirili. moeldub. teldub. tebard aidne .ui. *meic* uthendi ingen fedlimthi
tuir tuadmar *tri* gredel bed gradmair siur
coluim (.i. *cille*) choir dochloind clethig *conaill*
moir am*áthair*
Airec cind iohannis .i. bautiste.

27. '*Feast of Comgan without reproach*'
i.e. Comgan of Glenn Uissen. Comgan *cum
germanis*. Comgan, Mernóc, Moelchu, Mirili
Moeldub, Teldub Tebard of Aidne six sons of
Uthende Fedlimid's daughter . . . .
Sister of Colum Cille the just, of the eminent
race of great Conall was their mother.

[in marg. d.]
Tri .xx. it bliadan buan bil
.cc. treriaglad rimthir
iarfell forargtois infir
cend eoin baubtaist fodicheil

Three score years, lasting, good.
(And) two hundred by ruling are reckoned
After the treachery which the men . . . .
John Baptist's head (was) in hiding.

Bás chomorba petair
eoin uasail iarraid
inla forsmbi bisex
cech cethrumad bliadain.

(The) death of Peter's successor
Of John the noble seek ye
The day whereon shall be *bisextus*
Every fourth year.

[at foot of page 82]
Rabisex dothochar
incethrumad bliadain
ærrthig feil dontsluagsa
nárfuasna doriagail.*

There was *bisextus* to add
On the fourth year
. . . . festival to this host
Which has not disturbed thy rule.

28. *hi feil sillain bendchuir* .i. abb bendchuir
.i. sacerdos
p. 82, in marg. inf.]. Luna feb. inter mediam
noctem et galli cantum accendit. nox horarum.
xiiii. dies. x.

28. 'On the feast of Sillán of Bennchor'
i.e. abbot of Bangor i.e. a priest.

---

* MS. orit*us*   b MS. Petronillo   c The same quatrain is in p. 85, line 6 from bottom.

RAWL. 505.
1. For kl. mis marta
nitmordai friaṅguidi
senan moinen moysi
dabid cille muine
2. Mamemraig*ter* feli
hipais lucilia
gein senphoil slan doe
feil find fergna ia
3. Hipais florian[i]
fail daretlainn remain
cele cris*t* cain erail
moachru m*a*c senan
4. Sluinn cesad indepscoip
hiroim rigda cainlech
cosluag adbul aiṅglech
lucius les lainrech
5. Roleblaing nibalbda
aclu darsal sairde
carthach rigda ruamach
ciaran sluagach saigre
6. Ronsnadat iarleri
dolaith de fordirgi
sluag orta conani
hi feil uictorini
7. INmain decheng deoda
nadlig diarṅduain digna
felicitas noeb[da]
perpetua primda

LAUD 610.
1. For kl. mís marta
nid mordai friaguide
senan monenn moisi
dauith chille muine
2. Ma mebraig*ter* feli
hipais luciliæ
gein senpoil slandoe
feil find fergnæ iæ
3. Hipais floriani
fil diretlaind remain
ceile cris*t* cain erail
moncru macc senain
4. Sluindcessadindeps[c]oib
iróim rigda caindlech
cosluag adbul ainglech
luci*us* les laindrech
5. Roleblaing ni balbdai
aclu tar sal sairde
carthach rigda ruamach
ciaran sluagach saigre
6. Ronsnadet iarleire
do laith dé *for* dirgi
sluag orta conani
hifeil uichtoríni
7. Inmain decheng deoda
nadlig diarṅduain digna
felicitas noemdai
perpetua primdai

LEBAR BRECC p. 83.
1. For kl. mis marta
nitmorda friaṅguide
senan moinend myse
dabid chille muine
2. Ma mebraig*ther* feli
ipais luciliæ
gein senpoil slan doe
feil find fergna iæ
3. Hipais floriani
feil daretlaind remain
celi cris*t* cain aurail
momacru m*a*cc senain
4. Sluind cesad inespu*ic*
iruaim rigda coindlech
cosluag adbul ainglech
lucius less loin*n*rech
5. Roleblaing inbalbda
achlu darsal sairde
carthach rigda ruamach
ciaran sluagach saigre
6. Ronsnaidet iarleri
dofiaith de fordirge
slog orta conani
hifeil uictorini
7. INmain decheng deoda
nadlig diarnduai*n* dign*æ*
felicitas noemda
perpetua primdai

Translation.

1. On the calend of Mars' month—not haughty are they at prayer to them—Senán, Moinenn, Moses, David of Cell Muine.

2. If thou remember feasts on Lucilia's passion, (commemorate the) birth of Old-Paul a sound rampart, (and the) fair feast of Fergna of Hí.

3. On Florianus' passion are two preeminent stars. Céile Crist, a fair enjoiner, my-Macru, Senán's son.

4. Mention the bishop's suffering in Rome, regal, brilliant, with a host vast, angelic, Lucius a lucid light.

5. Unsilently his renown sprang over (the) eastern sea, Carthach royal, roman, Ciaran the hostful of Saigir.

6. May they protect us after piety to God's kingdom straightway, a host that was slain with splendour on Victorinus' feast.

7. Dear the godly pair of champions, that deserve not reproach from our song, sainted Felicitas, excellent Perpetua.

Rawl. 505.	Laud 610.	Lebar Brecc, p. 83.
8. Senan inse cathaig crothais* ecrait narach connadail cli buadach epscop beoœd bagach	8. Senan insi cathaig crochas ecrait narach coniñgin cli buadach epscop beodaid bagach	8. Senan indse cath*aig* crochais ecrait narach conandil clii buadach espoc beored bagach
9. Bas cethracat miled comorsluag basorchu diaduarcaib frihilchu grian hiluce dub dorchu	9. Bas cethrachat miled comorsluag basorchu dia tuargaib fri hulchu grian iluc dub dorcha	9. Bas .xl. miled comorslog basorchu diatuarcaib frihilchu grian illuc dub dorcha
10. Dorograd cohangliu constantin cain cainlech	10. Dorrograd cohañgliu *constantin* cain caindlech	10. Dorograd cohaingliu *constantin* cain coindlech
lassafrith [eo] ainglech carann cruiche inchoimded	lasafrith eo ainglech crann croiche inchoimded	lasafrith eo ainglech crand croiche incboimded
11. ITcoimti arfiadat isindlaith uasflaithib liberen senan suthain	11. Atcoomti arfiadat isindflaith uas lathib Oeng*us* libren senan suthain	11. Hitcoimti arfiadat oeng*us* itir flaithib libren senan suthain
constantin ri rathin	*constantin* ri rathin	*constantin* rig rathin
12. Rearichtain aferainn arcr*ist* crochais colainn intorgan chet buada grigoir ruama rolainn	12. Re riachtain aferaind arcr*ist* crochais colaind intorgan cet buada griguir ruama rolaind	12. Rerichtain aferaind arcr*ist* crochais colaind intorgan .c. mbuada grigoir ruama rolaind
13. Rousnada mochoemoc donbithchoemnu bias cuangus caid cosoas oliath mor maith dias	13. Ronsnáde mochoemóc donbithchaemnu bias cuang*us* caid cáin soas oliath mor maithdias	13. Ronsnaide mocoemoc donbithcoemnu bias cuangus caid cosons oliath mor maith dias
14. Dionis intepscop ataclinra cocma comainm cr*ist* rousnada	14 Dionis intepscop ata cleire céuna comainm cr*ist* ronsnade	14. Dionis intespoc atacleri cocma comainm cr*ist* ronsnaidea
saluator ronsoera	saluator ronscera	salualtur ronsoera

8. Senán of Inis Cathaig gibbeted (his) foe Nárach,[b] Conandil victorious prince (?), bishop Beo-áed the warlike.

9. Forty soldiers' death with a great host that was brightest, for whom arose with paeans a sun in a black dark place.

10. To (the) angels was called Constantine fair, luminous, by whom was found an angelical shaft, the tree of the Lord's Cross.

11. They are comrades of our God in the kingdom above kingdoms,[c] Librén, Senán the lasting, Constantine king at Rathin.

12. Before reaching his territory, for Christ he crucified (his) flesh, the organ of an hundred victories, vehement Gregory of Rome.

13. May my-Coemóc convoy us to the everlasting protection which will be, Cuangus holy, with science, from Liath mór, a goodly pair.

14. Dionysius the bishop, his clergy are loveable. May Christ's surname protect us, may Salvator save us!

[a] leg. crochais   [b] or perhaps '(his) shameful foe.'   [c] A. 'Oengus among princes.'

RAWL. 505.	LAUD. 610.	LEBAR BRECC, pp. 83-84.
15. Seru iacob ordan lucas lir huas trilis fricrist carsat sanais meice nessan ondinis	15. Serud iacoib ordan lucas lir huas trilis fri crist carsat sanais mc. nessain oninis	15. Seirn iacop ordan lucas lir uastrilis fri crist carsait sanais mcc nessan oninis
16. INmain acht lademon eugenia fordumun abban doss oir ainglech finan lainrech lobur	16. INmain acht lademon eugenia fordoman ablan dos óir ainglech finan laindrech lobor	16. INmain acht lademan eugenia fordoman ablan doss oir ainglech finan laindrech lobar
17. Lassar gréine ane apstal herenn huaige patraic comeit mile rop ditiu artruaige	17. Lassair greine aine epstal cirind oighe patraic comét mile robditiu diartróge	17. Lassar greni aine aspal crenn oige patraic comet mile ropditiu diartroige
18. Comorbuidin martra nabdar ili lochta latiamda rorimed sesca miled mochta	18. Commorbuidin martra nabdar ili lochta latimda rarimed fiche miled mochta	18. Comorbuidin martra naptar hile lochta latiamda rorimed .xx. miled mochta
19. Molachtoc lagrigoir ingradgreit as dixu ioseph ainm as huasliu aite alainn issu	19. Molachtóc lagriguir ingradgreit as dixu ioseph ainm asnaisliu aite alaind issu	19. Molachtoc lagriguir ingradgreit asdixu iosep ainm isuaisliu aidiu alaind ihu.
20. Etsecht policroni noibepscoip aschadu cechaing ceim as dirgiu comorsluag badanu	20. Eitsecht policroni noebepscop aschadu cechaing ceim as dirgu comorsluag badánu	20. Etsecht policroni noemespuic iscadu cechaing ceim asdirgn comorsluag badanu
21. Donbith ba mor mbuada benedicht balcc age forcenlith ler slúagda enna airdire airne	21. Donbith bamor bunda benedicht balc aghc forcenlith ler sluagda enna indraic airne	21. Donbith bamor mbuaide benidecht balcc aige forcenlith ler sluagda enda airdere airne
22. Ardchesad secundi ccnambriathraib bia balc les lir dardoe failbe aule ia	22. Ardchessad secundi conambriathra bire balceles ler dardoe failbe ainle ire	22. Ardcesad secundi cain imbriathraib bire balcc les ler dardoe failbe ainle ire
23. Ingen dalach dærmar feradaig asarddam	23. Ingen cosluag dermair feradaig asardam	23. INgen cosluag dermar feradaig isardam

15. Relate James' sovranty, Luke over sea's hair. Of Christ they loved knowledge, the sons of Nessan from the island.
16. Dear save to (the) demon (was) Eugenia on earth Abbán angelic bush of gold Fínan a leper lucid.
17. (The) flame of a splendid sun, (the) apostle of virginal Ireland, Patrick guard of thousands, be a protection of[a] our misery.
18. With a great troop of martyrs were not many faults. With Timothy was reckoned a score[b] of glorified soldiers.
19. My Lachtóc, with Gregory, the champion of rank who is noblest, Joseph (or) a name that is higher, Jesu's pleasant foster-father.
20. Death of Policronius, saintly bishop who is holiest, he went a step that is straightest, with a great host that is boldest.
21. To the world much of victory was Benedict a stout pillar. On one festival, a hostful sea, Enda of Arran (the) conspicuous.
22. High suffering of Secundus, fair in words of might (?), a strong light over a rampart of seas, Failbe the fair, of Hí.
23. A daughter, with an enormous host,[c] of Feradach who is highest. From Christ

[a] A. and B. 'to' [b] D. 'sixty' [c] D. 'multitudinous, vast'

lviii   THE CALENDAR OF OENGUS.   [MARCH 24-31.

RAWL. 505.	LAUD, 610.	LEBAR BRECC, p. 84.
ocrist adfet orddan	ocrist atfet orddan	ochrist arfet ordan
mo medoc mind nalban	momædoc mind alban	momoedoc mind alban
24. An lanamain liagach	24. Anlanamain lighach	24. An lanomain ligdach
frisnaig etla ainbech	frinig etla ainbech	frisuig etla ainbech
scire cain car tredan	scire caiu car tredan	scire cain car tredan
mochta credal craidbech	mochta credal craibech	mochta credal craibdech
25. Crochad ocus chompart	25. Crochad 7 compert	25. Crochad 7 compert
issu crist itcori	issu crist itcore	ihu. crist atcori
foroenlith coleri	foroenlith collere	foroenlith colleri
lapais iacobi	lapais iacoibi	lapais iacopi
26. Hiletha dorochair	26. Illetha dorochair	26. Hilletha dorochair
mochelloc iarlaithib	mochelloc iarlaithib	mochelloc iarlathib
feil intinchill suthain	feil intsinchill suthain	feil dasinchell suthain
cille aidbile achid	cilli aidble aichid	cille aidble achid
27. Hisexkl. aperil	27. Hisexkl. apreil	27. Hisexkll. apreil
iartuaslucud anman	iartuaslugud anman	iartuaslucad anman
asreracht secl ndermar	asraracht secl dermair	asreracht secl dermar
issu abru thalman	issu abrú thalmain	ihu. abrú thalman
28. Donrogra ronsoera	28. Danrogra ronsera	28. Donrogra ronsnaden
sechphiana ronsena	ronsnade sechphiana	sech piana ronsena
maria ronmora	maria ronmora	maria ronmora
inmor magdalena	inmormagdaléna	inmor magdalena
29. Lalith ingen mbaiti	29. Lalith ingen mbuiti	29. Lalith ingen mbaiti
bas sluaig mair cofeili	bas sluaig moir cofeili	pais sluaig moir cofeli
hifeil fir ohuagi	hifeil fir conuagi	ifeil fir conuagi
grigoir nazareni	griguir nazaréni	grigoir naz[a]reni
30. Sluind mochua balla	30. Sluind mochua balda	30. Sluind mochua balla
blog conordun ainbich	blog conordan ainbig	bolg conordan anbich
colman olinn ligaig	colman olaind ligaid	colman olaind ligaich
la feil tolai craidbith	lafeil tola craibdig	lafeil tola chraibdig
31. Croch ninach annissi	31. Croch ninach annisi	31. Croch ninach anissi
cocleir bain badaithiu	cocleir bain badaithiu	cocleir bain badaithiu
dober barr triabithu	dobeir barr trebithu	dobeir barr trebithu
martai forsluaig saithiu	martai forsluag sathiu	marta forsluag snigthiu

my Maedóc, diadem of Alba, received ordination.

24. A splendid lustrous couple, plenteous penitence washed them, fair Scire who loved fasting, trustful, pious Mochta.

25. Jesus Christ's crucifixion and conception thou shouldst link together, on one festival with piety with James' passion.

26. In Letha fell my-Celloc after (many) days. (The) feast of (the) two perennial Sinchells of vast Cell Achid.

27. On (the) sixth kalends of April, after loosing the souls arose—a mighty tale!— Jesus from earth's womb.

28. May she call us, may she protect us past pains, may she sain us! May Mary magnify us, the great Magdalena!

29. At (the) festival of Baite's daughters the passion of a great host with modesty, on the feast of a man with virginity, Gregory of Nazianzum.

30. Declare Mochua of Balla, a fragment (bag?) with abundant sovranty. Colman from beautiful Lann, with pious Tola's feast.

31. (The) forked cross of Anissus, with a fair clergy that was keenest, for ever puts a top on the troops of March's host.

GLOSS FROM THE LEBAR BRECC, pp. 83, 84.

1. (2) *nitmorda* .i. nit diumsaig
2. (1) .i. mádail féli dochonghail dó is coir so domebrugud (3) *slan doe* .i. [lan] dofis *no* diadachta *no* nirt [*doc*] .i. clad ard iarstair *no* iarnoebi
3. (3) *aurail* .i. do crail neich fordia
4. (1) *sluind* .i. indis (4) *loinnrech* .i. taitnemach
5. (1) *rolebluing* .i. roling *inbalbda* .i. nibalbda *no* ni hanerdaire *no* nitastach. (2) .i. de sair roling achlú (4) *sluagach* .i. buidneach
6. (1) *ronsnaidet* .i. ronditnet. *iarleri* .i. iarcrábud *no* dubtach dil condirge chrabuid .i. albanach (3) *orta* .i. argain
7. (1) *decheng* .i. daching *no* datrénfer. *dcoda* .i. diada. (2) *nadlig diarnduain dignæ* i. taire .i. cen achuimniugud inarnduain
8. (1) *indse cathaig* .i. cathach ainm na biast[e] *no* achathach hitoil dé *ecrait* [.i. escarait] .i. inboist. *no* cucuimroch
9. (3) *fri hilchu* .i. fri hilachu suba anernaigthi. *no* frigáire custodientium* .i. nacoimetaige.
10. (3) *eo* .i. lignum .i. crand
11. (1) *hitcoimti* .i. it cocmtechtaide. *no*
    guid ifeil maic oeibléu ["Beseech on the feast of Ocbléu's son
    oengus itirflathib. Oengus among princes.']
12. (1) *feraind* .i. nime
13. (2) *bithcoemnu* .i. coelum .cccc. xiii. (3) *soas* .i. airchedul
14. (1) *dionis* .i. oirdned *no* buaid .i. cicli ut alii putant. (2) *atacleri coema* .i. atachlerig *no* at cliara .i. coem a cliar familia dionis. *no* robochoem achliar .i. achráibdig
15. (1) *seirn* .i. sreath *no* aisnéd *no* sern oni i[s] sertum .i. is guath scirt imchend neich iarmbreth buada .i. dicloidem .i. suetaig *ordan* .i. aoirdned (2) *uastrilis* .i. uas moing in mara (3) *sanais* .i. sainfis fis sen *no* ernaigthe
17. (3) *mile* .i. filet isinlosa
18. (2) *lochta* .i. pecdai. (4) *mochta* .i. machtba *no* moigthe *no* tormaigthi. *no* tormochta .i. rotoiset comoch .i. mox mortui .i. quasi magis auctæ sunt vel macta .i. mactata sunt .i. occissa sunt .xl. milites. occisa sunt .xl. miliades.
19. (2) .i. robogerait uasal he ingrad crist
20. (3) *cechaing* .i. roching
21. (2) *aige* .i. tuir (3) *ler sluagda* .i. imad sluag imailli friu
22. (2) .i. cid arna bia imbriathraib ocaind he ara unisle. *no* cata briathra on aissneidfem he (3) *balce* .i. mor. *les* .i. slisse. *dar doe* .i. dar dó osmuir. *no* crich nafairrge. *no* doa .i. clad. dar doe .i. darfairrge *no* dar doss .i. dar nert ut dicitur

    Mochen linm don [*in left marg.*] dartan   'My welcome to the herd
    toet chucam dar in doa   That comes to me over the sea!
    mo mac fen mac mo mic   My own son, my son's son,
    mobrathuir mac moa   My brother, my grandson's son.'

23. (2) *ardam* .i. admirabilis .i. airde ina sochaide
24. (1) .i. an ifertaib 7 mirbuilib eat *lanomain* .i. uir et mulier .i. lánsomain .i. cendfuluirt cáich dib ocaroile *no* lánamain .i. lan homo .i. dui[n]e comlan .i. fer 7 bean. sic fuit ádam et cua una caro. (2) *etla ainbech* .i. déra iumda *no* colchaire imda (4) *credal* .i. creitmech
25. (1) *atcori* .i. atat hi córaid 7 cánin innse celltra. *no* is cóir a fiss *no* rofás mor dib desil ádaim (3) *leri* .i. soeri. *no* coléri .i. cocrábud. *no* isléir dochach conid forlith iacoip atat
27. (2) .i. a hifiurn (3) *asreracht* .i. atrácht
29. (3) *conuagi* .i. conglaine
30. (1) *sluind* .i. aisneid
31. (1) *nimach* .i. glacach *no* crechtach *no* nin gabul .i. ginol .i. glac nagabla (4) *saigthiu* [leg. *saithiu*] .i. sluagu

* MS. *cusdotientium*

NOTES FROM THE LEBAR BRECC, pp. 83, 84.

1. *Senan* .i. indsi cathaig bas obitus est in hoc die. no salmcetlaid esbog moinend

In marg. d.] Moinend .i. espoc 7 comorba cluana ferta brenaind he
myse .i. moyse mac amra no moyse manach a hedísa no abeg[i]pt.
in marg.] Dabid chille muine dobretnaib descirt et archiepiscopus britaniæ insolæ.

2. *lueilic* .i. lucius papa et episcopus .i. liado paissilcaud
fergna iæ .i. fergna brit abb iæ choluim.

3. *celi crist* .i. ochill céli crist intíib dúnchada ilaignib
mo macru mac senain .i. abb cluana hédnech iláigis 7 hitig thacra anuib dúnchada 7 itindmaig ifothartaib
in left marg.] hic memoratur muccin maigne

4. *lucius* .i. papa.

5. *carthach rigda* .i. hua rig muman. *ruamach* .i. doroim rofoid ciaran he iartecht icómdail mna [*in r. marg.*] .i. Carthach mac fiud mic noei. m. cellain m. tailcind m. firb a quo hui firb.

in r. marg.] Carthach din dalta chiaran saigre 7 mac rig eoganachta caisil 7 i cairpri hua ciarda a baile 7 druim fertain 7 inis uachtair for loch silend les beos ocus aide mochuda he. ut dixit mite

Ticfa carthach chucaib
fer conartrach cretim
berthar mac docharthach
noco marthar otir

ISe tra. incarthachsa .i. dalta ciarain rofúided laciaran coróim dia oilithre iartecht fcomdail mná dó ar is dó ba mac molua mac ocha*.

ciaran sluagach saigre. do dal birnd doosráigib do ch[i]aran

in r. marg.] Ciaran credal comorba soer sinnsear nanoem nem fograd amra gein iurig

1. March 1. '*Senán*,' i.e. of Inis Cathaigh his obitus (*bás*) is on this day. Or he was Bishop Moinenn's psalmist.
'Moinenn,' i.e. a bishop and *coarb* of Cluain ferta Brenainn was he.
'*Moses*,' i.e. Moses, son of Amra, or Moses a monk from Edessa or from Egypt.
David of Cell Muine of the Britons of the South, and archbishop of the island Britannia.

'*Fergna of Hi*,' i.e. Forgna Brit, an abbot of Hí of Colum (Cille).

3. '*Céle Crist*,' i.e. of Cell Céli Crist in Hui-Dúnchada in Leinster.
'*My-Macru son of Senán*,' i.e. an abbot of Cluain Ednech in Laigis and in Tech Tacra in Hui-Dúnchada and in Findmag in Fotharta.

5. '*Carthach royal*,' i.e. descendant of a king of Munster. '*ruamach*' i.e. to Rome Ciaran sent him for having come into a woman's company. i.e. Carthach, son of Find, son of Noe, son of Cellán, son of Tailcenn, son of Ferb, *a quo* are the Hy-Firb.
Carthach, now, a pupil of Ciaran of Saigir and son of a king of the Eoganacht of Caisel, and in Cairpre Hua-Ciarda his place (is), and Druim Fertain, and Inis Uachter on Loch Silenn (are) his also ; and he (was) Mochuda's tutor *ut dixit* my-Ite.

Carthach will come to you,
A man who upraises(?) faith.
A son will be born to Carthach :
He is not magnified thereby at all.

It is this Carthach, i.e. Ciaran's pupil, that was sent by Ciaran to Rome on his pilgrimage for having come into a woman's company, for it is to him that Molua mac ocha* was a son.
'*Ciaran the hostful of Saigir*' . of Dál Birnn of Ossory was Ciaran.

Ciaran the trustful, a noble successor,
Senior of the saints . . . .
Wondrous the birth of the king

---

* .i. molua mac ocha ("Molua, son of armpit")

diansossad sid saiger már.
Mac lúgna lear ecna ádbuil
mád ghaib talmain trácht nad gó
isin ló illeth fabráth
cenmár[a] cach bus cheli dó.
Búi liadaine[b] inacothad
foradérgud rád nát cil
intan soes agnáis frineam
docer rédlu inagin
IS de genair ingein námra
ciaran sáigre sloinnter lat
7 is de rád cenúaille
atbert luaigne ninba mac.

Liadaine ingen maine chirr mic oengusa
docloind lugdach mic itha máthair chiarain
sáigre 7 is ann rogenair hifindtracht gléri. 7
isaingil rorithoilset iarnagein. gráda immurro
nime rotusbaist ocus is acorco lúigde toisech
rocreited dochroiss fortús inérinn. ocus xxx.
bliadan ria patraic rogab ciaran saigir. ut
dixit patraic

Saig uar[c]
cumdaig cathir forabrú
icind xxx. bliadan band
condricfem and ocus tú
Mac genes itulaig thind
bid idan a óentu frind
mor manach is mainches mall
diaéis dogéba conall.

IS annsin iarum rotharngir ciaran conall 7
fachtna ruiss ailithir. ocus ise ciaran rofácaib
do ri chorco lúigde eneclann rig cuicid dó. ocus
rige 7 oirechus diasil cobráth. ar chretium
crossi occu artús 7 archill chiarain dochostad
occu. Ba ámra tra. intíi noemchiaran sáigre.
uair ba hilarda a indile. ár bátar .x. udorais
forlias abá. ocus .x. crói cechdorais. ocus .x. loig
incech cró. ocus .x. mbai imcech loeg. Nírothomail
tra. ciaran nách hernail mbic dianir-
thoradsin bicén babeo. acht afodail dobochtaib
7 daidilgnechaib inchoimded .l. each riata
laciaran beos fri bar 7 trebad intalman. ocus
bahí aphroindsium cech nóidche díb sin .i.
bóimm bee dobairgin eornai 7 dá mhecon domurátbaig
7 usce firthiprat. Crocni lóeg
nallaid ba he a étuch. ocus cuilche fliuch

To whom great Saigir (is) a station of peace.
Son of Lugna, a sea of vast wisdom,
If he takes laud—a shore that is not false—
In the day at this side of Doom(sday)
Happy everyone who shall be his fellow !
Liadaine was in her sleep
On her bed—a saying not wrong—
When she turned her face to heaven
A star fell into her mouth.
Thereof was born the wondrous birth
Ciaran of Saigir, who is mentioned by thee,
And hence—a saying without pride—
Luaigne said he was not his son.

Liadaine, daughter of Maine Cerr, son of
Oengus of the Children of Lugaid son of Ith,
(was the) mother of Ciaran of Saigir, and it
as there he was born, in Findtracht Gléri,
and angels attended after his birth. Now
Orders of heaven baptized him, and in Corcoluigde
first the Cross was believed in at the
beginning in Ireland. And thirty years before
Patrick Ciaran took Saigir, ut dixit Patrick.

Cold Saig,
Build a city on its brink !
At the end of thirty . . . . years
We shall meet there, (I) and thou.
A child that shall be born in Tulach Tinn,
Pure shall be his unity with us.
Many a monk and gentle nun
After him Conall will take.

It is then that Ciaran foretold Conall, and
Fachtna of Ross Ailithir, and it is Ciaran
who left to the king of Corco-Luigde the
eneclann of a king of a province and kingship
and leadership of his race for ever,
because of the belief in the Cross (being) with
them first, and because Cell Chiarain was
. . . . with them. Wondrous now (was)
that holy Ciaran of Saigir, for numerous were
his cattle. For there were ten doors to the shed
of his kine, and ten stalls at every door, and
ten calves in every stall, and ten cows with
every calf. Now Ciaran consumed not any
little kind of their great produce so long as he
was alive, but distributed it to the poor and to
the needy ones of the Lord. Moreover there
were fifty tame horses with Ciaran for tilling

---

[a] .i. mongenair ("Happily was he born")
[b] .i. máthair ciarain ("Ciaran's mother")
[c] .i. nomen fontis

tairsib immuig. adart cloiche isfair contuiled dogréa.

Cairnech moel . scríbnid ciarain . isiside roscríb inscribenn amra .i. himirche ciarain . conabilgressaib 7 maraid beos inlebarsin isaigir . 7 tabrad cech*oon* légfas bend*ach*tu forainmain chairn*ig* móil.

6. hi feil uictorini .i. nouisimus dies forsambi primesci inite

7. perpetua primdai .i. uxor pétri.

8. Senan ind*se* cathaig .i. dies sepulcri senani híc memoratur. .i. cathach ainm na biast *no* achath hi toil dé

narach .i. goba senain . aduaid iubeist hesium

p. 84, in r. marg.] Senan innsi cathaig .i. rocroch 7 roch*u*imrig senan inmbeist diarboainm cathach isuathi ainmnig[ther] inis cath*aig* 7 isairo roscumrig . uair romarb inngobaind diarbo ainm nárach 7 rothóduisc senán inngobaind abróind nabiasta . 7 robécrati dongobaind inbeist 7 robochrochaire donbeist senan 7 rl.

p. 83.]

Conandil .i. ocess mac neire icon[n]*ach*ta ata conda . ise intainm 7 tuc supra mr. |leg. sua mater] trobáide tuilled sillaibe fris .i. dilem he .i. cona dil .i. inmain . *no* conainde .i. ochill conaind inhu*ib* maine chond*ach*t isogan iutsaindrud 7 ingen m*á*thar hi de senan ind*se* cathaig

espoc beo*æd* .i. episcopus beo æd beo o ard charna icon[n]*uch*taib

9. Das .xl. miled . de capadocia[e] regionia [leg. regione] .xl. comorslog .i. dorig rómani .i. xl. xu.

in marg. inf.] Cethracha míled monuar
tair rocuirit illoch nuar
taitnig doib grian meit brotha
inichtar inmórlocha.

[Thus in the Drummond Missal: Pasio .xl. militum ut quidam ferunt quibus in tenebroso loco positis sol ob signum supernæ claritatis et consolationis emicuit]

10. Constantin cain coindtech .i. filius eclesi*æ*

and ploughing the ground. And this was his dinner every night of (all) those things, to wit, a little bit of barley bread and two roots of *muráthach* and water of a spring. Skins of fawns, this was his raiment and a wet haircloth over them outside. A pillow of stone, thereon he used to sleep always.

Cairnech the bald, Ciaran's scribe, it is he that wrote the wondrous writing, to wit, Ciaran's *imirche*, with its many *gressa* (illuminations ?), and still remains that book in Saigir ; and let every one who shall read it give a blessing on the soul of Cairnech the bald.

6. '*On Victorinus' feast*' i.e. the last day whereon is the first moon of Shrovetide.

i.e. 'Cathach' the monster's name. Or his battle (*cath*) in God's will.

'*Narach*' i.e. Senán's smith. The monster devoured him.

'Senán of Inis Cathaig,' i.e. Senán hanged and fettered the monster whose name was Cathach. From it Inis Cathaig is named ; and this is why he bound it, because it killed the smith, whose name was Narach, and Senán raised up the smith from the monster's belly, and the monster was a foe to the smith, and Senán was hangman to the beast, etc.

'*Conandil*' i.e. at Ess mac nEirc in Connaught he is . Conna, this is the name, and his mother put through lovingness an addition of a syllable to it i.e. Cona *dil* i.e. dear. Or Conainde i.e. of Cell Conainn in Hy-Maine of Connaught, in Sogan especially, and daughter was she of Senán of Inis Cathaig's mother.

'*Bishop Beo-aed*,' i.e. bishop Aed-beo from Ard Carna in Connaught.

9. '*with a great host*,' i.e. of the King of Romans.

Forty soldiers, alas,
In the East were put into a cold lake.
A sun shone to them, much of glowing heat !
At the bottom of the great lake.

11. *oengus itir flathib.* oengus cecinit
Rogad domrig trocar tren
isdigrais acride scél
condomarlaiced cotind
cris*t* cein nobeind icolaind

11. '*Oengus amongst princes.*' Oengus sang:
I asked of my King merciful, mighty—
Excellent (is the) story of his heart—
That Christ may be very yielding to me
While I am in the flesh.

libren .i. abb iæ
constantin rig rathin .i. rig bretan rofacaib arige 7 tanic diaoilithre coraithin inamsir mochuda .i. comorba rathin mochuda indelbna ethra aniarth*ar* mide 7 rig alban he

'*Librén,*' i.e. an abbot of Hí.
'*Constantine King of Rathin,*' i.e. a King of Britons who left his kingdom and came for his pilgrimage to Raithin in Mochuda's time, i.e. the coarb of Rathin Mochuda in Delbna Ethra in the west of Meath, and a King of Scotland was he.

12. *grigoir ruama*
Ua dedad mic sin
grigoir arda mail
abb róma láin letha
incirin*n* atetha æris madáil
ceann nangoedeal nglanmas
síl gel gablas
cid amnas atbcr

12. '*Gregory of Rome.*'
Grandson of Deda, son of Sen,
Gregory of Ard Mail,
Abbot of Rome of full Latium,
Into Ireland came. . . . if it be desired.
Head of the pure, fair Goedil.
A white seed that branches,
Though it be hard, it is said.

13. *mocoemoc* .i. mac beo æda
cuangus .i. mac dall he
o liathmor .i. muman

13. '*My-Coemóc,*' i.e. son of Beo-aed.
'*Cuangus,*' i.e. a blind son (was) he.
'*from Liath-mór,*' i.e. of Munster.

15. *iacop* .i. frater domini
mec nessan .i. monisiu imnesloga .i. dicolla derg

15.
'*sons of Nessan,*' Monisiu with Nesloga, i.e. of Colla Derg.

16. *eugenia* .i. filia pilipi hic sepultus in ierusalem. Eugenia . ingen fir dorómanchuib 7 roéla otustigib imanchuine coroibe iric*h*t manaig innte 7 nifess cumad bean iti*r*. Arái sin búi diatogaidec*h*t cotartad cendus namanach di iarnéc inabad . co*n*ustuc merdrech amus fu*i*rri imoentaid fria. Atbert inmeirdrech condernai oentaid fria. Tanic rig natuaithe iarsin dia aithe fu*i*rrise . 7 baheiside ahathairse . et ipsa aduocauit cum seorsum . et dixit ei habuisti filiam . et ille dixit fuit et ego[a] nescio quo ipsa iuit[b] . illa ait ego sum ipsa . et ita liberata[c] fuit a scelere ipsa et monasterium[d] et meretrix combusta est.

16. Eugenia, a daughter of the Romans, and she fled from her parents into a monastery; and she was therein in guise of a monk, and it was not known that she was a woman. However, it was from her choiceness that, after the abbot's death, the headship of the monks was given to her. And a harlot tempted her (Eugenia) to lie with her. The harlot said that she had lain with her. The king of the district then came to punish her (Eugenia), and he was her father, *et ipsa*, etc.

abban .i. féil etsechta abain mic hui chormaic dolaignib híc.

'*Abbán,*' i.e. feast of the death of Abbán son of Hua Cormaic of Leinster híc.

in marg.] .Uii. mbliadna delbglana .x.
ifuille*d* airme .ccc.
sa*e*gal abbáin delbda duind
inoiret robúi acolaind.

Seventeen fair-shaped years
In addition to the number 300,
(Was the) life of Abbán, shapely lord,
In the time that he was in the body.

[a] MS. euge   [b] MS. fuit   [c] MS. satana   [d] MS. monosterium

17. *Lassar* .i. sinell mac findchada do uib garrchon ise cedduine robaist *patraic inerinn* he . *no* lassair nomen septimæ filiæ branin 7 icill ingine branin ilnigis ata 7 clidna ainm ingine cle dó ota tond clidna.

ocus nessan corenige cum patricio in hoc die.

[In marg. sup.] Cethri cána *erenn* .i. cáin patraic cen clérig domarbad. Ocus cáin adamnan cen mna domarbad. Ocus cáin daríi inchailloch ṡura cen damu dogait. Ocus cáin dómnaig centairmthecht ind *itir*.

18. *tiamda* .i. alumnus pauli apostoli

19. *Molachtoe* .i. lachtain oachad aur *griguir* .i. papa . ordinatio eius in principatum romæ . *no* griguir rontochta *iosep* .i. sponsus mariæ .i. auctus vel adiutus (auditus?) interpretatur
ainm is uaisliu .i. do aite fsu doráḋ fríhiosep .i. quam iosep *no* is uaisle aite ihu. doráḋ ris ina iosep

20. *policroni* .i. episcopus .i. babilonis. vel ut .i. ipse est in britania.
[*noemespuic*] *no* nemepscuip

morsluag . prespiteri diaconi sancti passi sunt cum policrone iubente decio.
Equinoctium hic secundum egiptios et graecos quod melius est propter rationem paschae.

21. *Benidecht* .i. monac[h]orum sum[m]us abbas tot[ac]que coropæ . in monte easion .i. proprium [nomen] ciuitatis quieuit.
enda airderc airne .i. is ní mor énna airne. mac conaill *deirg* airgiallach 7 ingen ainmire rig fer narda am*ath*air
dies epactarum.[a]

22. *failbe* .i. abb iu cholu*im*

23. *ingen* .i. iciannait (leg. ciannait) nomen eius.
feradaig .i. abb iæ beous
ocus espoc mac carthaind oclochar in hoc die

momoedoc .i. mo moedo[c] mac midgna mic meti m. nindneda m. zair m. crimthaind m. cathu*ir* máir

[a] MS. iubenti

17. '*A flame*,' i.e. Sinell son of Findchath of Hui-Garrchon, he is the first person whom Patrick baptized in Ireland. Or *Lassair* the name of the seventh daughter of Branín, and in Cell Ingine Branín in Loix she is, and Clídna the name of his second daughter, from whom is *Tond Clidna* 'Clidna's Wave.'

And Nessan of Cork (is commemorated) with Patrick on this day.

The four rules of Ireland : Patrick's rule, not to slay clerics : And Adamnán's rule, not to slay women : And Darí the marvellous nun's rule, not to steal oxen : And the rule of Sunday, in nowise to transgress upon it.

19. '*My-Lachtóe*,' i.e. Lachtain of Achad Ur.

'*a name that is nobler*,' i.e. 'Jesu's tutor' to say of Joseph *quam* 'Joseph,' or it is nobler to say 'Jesu's tutor' of him than 'Joseph.'

noemespuic or *nemepscuip* ('heaven-bishop') [is the right reading]

'*Enna the conspicuous of Aran*,' i.e. a great thing is Enda of Arran, son of Conall the Red of the Airgiallaich, and his mother was a daughter of Ainmire king of Fir Arda.

22. '*Failbe*,' i.e. an abbot of Hí of Colum (cille).

23. '*a daughter*,' i.e. Ciannait her name.

'*of Feradach*,' i.e. also an abbot of Hí.
And Bishop Mac Carthainn of Clogher (is celebrated) on this day.
'*My-Maedóc*,' i.e. my Maedóc son of Midgna, son of Mete, son of Nindnid, son of Star, son of Crimthann, son of Cathar the Great.

[b] MS. epaciarum

24. *scire cain* .i. scire ingen cogain mic canannan mic ailella mic fergusa mic echach muidmedoin o chill scire iniarthar mide

mochta credal craiblech .i. illugmad no domangort balce bagach .i. quando exiit domangort mac echach in montem et uiuus adhuc in illo. .ccc. annos

25. *Crochad ocus compert isu crist atcori* .i. atat hicóraid 7 cámin iunse celltra . no iscóir aíss . no rofás mor [leg . cóir] dib dosíl ádaim

IN[n]aza[r]eth galilee anuntiatio dominica per gabrielem archangelum ad mariam uirginem quando dixit ei angelus ecce concipies[a] et paries filium et uocabitur nomen eius iesus,. et eodem die pasus est sub pontio pilato.

for oenlith colleri lapais iacopi [léri].i. soeri no coléri.i. cocrábud. *no* isléir dochach conid forlith incóip atat .i. iacop gláinech mac iosep .i. gláinech .i. filius[e] alpéi in hoc die pasus est . uel filius cleopa uel filius iosep .

26. *Hilletha dorochair mochelloc* .i. hi fid lethan ceiss mor .i. nomen loci in quo mortu[u]s est. uel nomen siluc ubi obi[i]t . uel in roma ut quidam dicunt

Mochelloc .i. ochill dachellóc inúib cairpri amumain . sed uerius est quod cillin mac cáilodráin ochatraig conchaid quae nunc est illotha dicitur hic .i. letha nomen silue magnae indéssib muman et in ea ciuitas illa olim fuit. *Mochelloc* .i. cilline mac tulodran indesib muman .

feil dasinchell suthain

Tri .c. bliadan sássad ngrind
robó sin saegul sinchill
la tri .x. bliadan coglo
cenpecad censadaile

28. *maria ronmora* .i. comad hi féil acomfóite[d] ad fidem christi.

29. *La lith ingen mbaiti* .i. hitig ingen mbaiti itaeb suird colaim cille . no inúib failge .i. ethni 7 sodelb nomina earum et christus uenit in forma infantis esse in sinu earum et osculabantur cum et ille bauptizáuit eas.[e] otsi apostoli praedicauerunt illis tamen plus ab ipso acceperunt fidem quam ab illis.

---

24. '*fair Scire,*' i.e. Scire daughter of Eogan son of Canannan, son of Ailill, son of Fergus, son of Eochaid Muidmedon, of Cell Scire in the west of Meath.

'*Mochta trustful, pious,*' i.e. in Louth. Or '*Domangort balcc bágach*' (is the right reading), i.e. *quando* etc.

25. '*The crucifixion and conception of Jesu Christ thou shouldst link together*' (atcóri), i.e. they are in a yoke (*córaid*) with Cámin of Inis Celtra. Or it is proper (*cóir*) to know them. Or from them grew justice (*cóir*) unto Adam's seed.

'*Upon one festival with devotion with James' passion.*' *léri* i.e. freedom or co *léri* i.e. with piety, or it is evident (*léir*) to everyone that they are on the festival of James [the Less] i.e. James the Kneed, son of Joseph i.e. the Kneed [see Euseb. Hist. Eccles. II. 23, cited by dr. Reeves. *Codex Maelbrigte*, 12.]

26. '*In Letha fell my Cellóc,*' i.e. in Fid Lethan at Lismore.

'*My-Cellóc*' i.e. of Cellda Chellóc in Ui Cairpri in Munster . *sed verius est quod* Cillín son of Cael Odrán of Cathair Conchaid *quae nunc est* in Letha *dicitur hic.* i.e. *Letha* the name of a great forest in the Desies of Munster and therein that city was formerly. '*My-Cellóc*' i.e. Cilline son of Tulodrán in the Desies of Munster.

'*The feast of two perennial Sinchells.*'

Three hundred years—fine satisfaction !—
That was (the elder) Sinchell's lifetime,
And thrice ten years brightly,
Without sin, without sloth.

28. '*may Mary magnify us!*' i.e. maybe this is the festival of her, Mary Magdalen's, conversion to Christ's faith.

29. '*At the festival of Baite's daughters*' i.e. in Tech Ingen mBaiti beside Swords of Colum Cille. Or in Offaly. Ethne and Sodelb were their names, etc.

---

[a] MS. consipiet 7 pariet.   [b] MS. ihm.   [c] MS. filia.   [d] Facs. acomfoite   [e] MS. éos.

grigoir nazareni .i. hitír armenia ata.

30. *balla* .i. quasi *bulla* .i. naboilg usci rucad óbendchor co balla hi cera.

colman olaind ligaich .i. ólaind mic luachán amide . no ólaind dacholmóc allic chassain line inulltaib . olaind no olind .i. uacháill .i. nomen demonis icassan linne qui nocebat multis ante colmán.

tola .i. odísiurt tola inuachtar dálcaiss.

31. *Croch ninach anissi* [in lower marg.] Ninach .i. glacach . ut dicitur nin garmna .i. ginol .i. ol ginach nagarmna. [no ninach brecht] ut dixit [poeta]

 Congair infuissi eolach
 téit neach iumnach diafégad
 conaccar angin ginach
 [suas] forneam uinach nélach

 Gebutsa mošalmu
 arneam uóemdai ninach[b]
 domditen cen[an]ad
 arglanad mochinad.

anissi .i. martir. Anesus[d] martir optimus fuit .i. óenach dairen inuib foilge.

'*Gregory of Nazianzum*' i.e. in the country of Armenia he is.

30. '*Balla*' quasi *bulla* i.e. the bags of water that were brought from Bennchor to Balla in Cera (in Connaught).

'*Colman of beautiful Lann*' i.e. of Lann Mic Luachán in Meath. Or of Lann dá Cholmóc in the Lec of Cassán Linne in Ulster. 'From Lann' or 'from Linn' i.e. of Uachall i.e. the name of a demon in Cassan Linne *qui* etc.

'*Tola*' i.e. of Disert Tola in the upper part of Dál Caiss (in Thomond).

31. '*Anesus' forked cross.*' *Ninach* i.e. forked . ut dicitur *nin garmna*,[a] i.e. great mouth i.e. the yawning *ol* (l) of the weaver's beam [. Or *ninach* means 'speckled'] *ut &c.*

 The skilful lark sings,
 One goes out to behold her,—
 So that the gaping mouth is seen
 Up in heaven *ninach*, cloudy.

 I will chaunt my psalms
 For heaven holy, *ninach*,[c]
 To protect me without delay
 For cleansing my sins.

'*of Anesus*': of Enach Daireu in Offaly.

---

[a] "the fork on the head of a weaver's beam."—*O'Curry*.   [b] .i. taitnemach
[c] i.e. bright   [d] MS. nesius

RAWL. 505, fo. 213 b.	LAUD 610, fo. 64.	LEBAR BRECC, p. 85.
1. So[e]rait kl. april ambrois comeit glaine congaib as mo suba feil de feili[b] maire	1. Soerait kl. apreil ambrois comeit nglaine congeib as mosube feil dofeilib maire	1. Soerait kl. apreil ambrois comeit nglaine congaib ismó suba feil dofelib maire
2. Morsluag amphiani diambu domun dubach drebraing iar cath cha- lad issin síth soer subach	2. Morsluag ambiaine diarbu domun dubach dreblaing iar cath calad isinsid sóer subach	2. Morsluag ambifani diamba demun dubach drebraing iarcath calad isinsid soer subach
3. Sluag euagair huasail asrola asreth setaib cothracha derigaib ardib cainib cetaib	3. Sluag euagair uasail asrala seth sétaib sechtmoga derignib ar dib cainib cétaib	3. Sluag euagair uasail asrala seth setaib .lxx. dorigaib ardib cainib cetaib
4. Cain tigernach credal arcrist cechmbais bre- uis asinbruchta sruam sois cluana alle heuis	4. Cain tigernach credal arcristcechmbaism bruais asambrucht sruaim sonis chluana aille eois	4. Cau tigernach credal arcrist cechmbais bruis asambrucht sruaim sonis cluana aille conis
5. H[i]feil mair meicecula beccain combuaid lere bathess phatraice prim- da adrannad inhere	5. Hi feil mair mc. cula beccain combuaid léire bathes patraic primda adrandad in hére	5. Hiféil moir maic cula beccan combuaid leri baithes patraic primda atrannad incri
6. Erenius intepscop ata mor a mile bacain doss conuaig[i] hifiadit find fine	6. Herenius inteps[c]op atamor amile bacaindos connagi adfiadat findfine	6. Hereuius intescop atamora mile bacain doss conuaige hifiadait find fini
7. Finan camm cinn etich imnaib :: mar n[d]elma bagerait crist chainde osleib bledach bledma	7. Finan cam cind eitig imambi mor delma bagerait crist cainni osleib bleidig bladma	7. Finan camm chind etig imbambi mor ndelma bagerait crist cainde osleib bledech bladma

1. He ennobles April's calend, Ambrose guard of purity; he takes—it is an exceed- ing happiness—a feast of Mary's feasts.

2. Amphianus' great host, for which the demon[a] was sorrowful, passed after a hard battle into the noble happy peace.

3. Noble Evagrius' host went from paths of tribulatious, seventy[b] kings with two fair hundreds.

4. Sing pious Tigernach—for Christ he vanquished all folly—out of whom burst a stream of knowledge, (Tigernach) of beauti- ful Clunin Eoais.

5. On the great feast of Beccan mac Cula with a victory of piety, excellent Patrick's baptism was kindled in Ireland.

6. Herenius the bishop,—great is his thousand—was a beautiful bush with vir- ginity, a fair vine in God.

7. Finan the squinting of Cenn Etig, round whom was much noise : a champion of Christ was Cainde, from wolf-haunted Sliab Bladma.

[a] B and D ' world.'   [b] D ' forty."

RAWL. 505.	LAUD, 610.	LEBAR BRECC, p. 85.
8. Bas cnair inmartir bamor tuire tempuil nirærad riamuntir cenn failad abb benn- choir	'. Bas cnair inmairtir bamor tuir a tempuil nirærad la mvintir cennfælad abb benn- chair	8. Bas cnair inmartir bamor tuir athempuil nirbærad lamuntuir ceudfælad abb bend- chair
9. Buaid secht noebuag nennacc incechthreib asrati asafuil nadibdai lafeil cain quadrati	9. Buaid .uii. noemuag nendac incach treib israti asa fuil nadibdai ifeil cain cadraiti	9. Buaid .uii. noemuag nendag incuch treib israite asafuil nadibdai ifeil cain quadrati
10. Croch appolloin cruim- thir arcrist coemtar folaid oross co ainm subaid cuanda rig[d]a romaid	10. Croch apoluair cruim- thir arcrist coemtar folaid orus do ainm subaid cuana rigda romaith	10. Croch apolloin cruim- thir arcrist coemthar folaith oross eo ainm subaich cuanna rigda romaith
11. Ronain moedoc main- ech aris brathair bagach hua acht ronoebad do duulang derb da- lach	11. Rommain mædoc mai- nech or is brathair bagach hua acht ronoemad dodunlang derb dalach	11. Ronain moedoc mai- nech ol isbrathair bagach ua acht ronoemad dodunlang derb dalach
12. Dalais ansa opair crist fri crucha cretair iuil epscop abb popuil sab soer suide phetair	12. Dalais andsa opair crist fri cruiche cretair iuil epscop abb popail sab soer suide petair	12. Dalais andsa opair crist fricruiche cretair iuil escop abb popuil sab sær suide petair
13. Conaprimluag sona argabeoil cech g[e]na gerait cristcain dechoid pol dechoin donrema^a	13. Conaprimsluag sona argabæil cach gena gerait crist cain deo- chaid pol deochain donrema	13. Conaprimsluag sona argobeil cechgena gerait crist cain deo- chnir pol deochain donrema
14. INrigepscop tassach dobert odonanaicc corp crist indrig fir- bailee lacommain dophatricc	14. In rigepscop tasach dobert odonanaic corp crist inrig firbaile lacommain dopatraic	14. INrigescop tassach dobert odonanic corp crist inrig firbaile lacommainn dopatraic

8. The death of Januarius the martyr, he was his temple's great tower. Not reproached by his family was Cennfaelad abbot of Bangor.

9. Seven innocent holy virgins' victory—in every household it is to be told—whose blood perishes not, on Quadratus' fair feast.

10. Priest Apollonius' cross, for Christ treasures are bartered. From Ross Eó, delightful name, Cuanna royal, excellent.

11. May treasurous Maedóc protect us,^b for he is a warlike kinsman, a grandson, but he was sanctified, of Dunlang (the) firm, multitudinous.

12. A difficult work Christ allotted to the consecrated of the Cross, bishop Julius, abbot of (the) people, noble chief of Peter's see.

13. With his chief host, happy for the biting of every mouth, well went Christ's champion: may deacon Paul shelter us!

14. The royal bishop Tassach gave, when he came, (the) body of Christ the truly-strong king, with communion, to Patrick.

^a MS. donrema.   ^b D. 'me

APRIL.

Rawl. 505.

15. Primda breo nad aithbi
arfig tola tothlai
ba cain lia luagmar
ruadan locharn lothrai
16. La carissa rigda
asaruamda relicc
doreith duit forsidit
feil indechoin felicc
17. Lafeil petair deochoin
drebraing martra mbu-
ade
conachleir cain dine
donnan ega huare
18. Arfeit hifeil septim
soerdechoin dodiduad
laisren lassar buadach
abb leithglinne ligach
19. Luid ermogin airdirc
iarforbu agliad
cohissu an soad
asuacht chorpan chriad
20. Lacesad eradi
cruimther crochtha
tuile
feil hiruaim ran mbale
noeb na[c]orpa huile
21. INalbain conglaine
iarlecu cechs[u]bai
luid huan conamathair
armbrathair maelru-
bai[a]

Laud, 610.

15. Primda breo nadathbi
arfig tola tothlai
bucain altia logmar
ruadan locharnn lothrai
16. Lacarissem rigda
assaruamda reilic
dorreith duit forsidit
feil iudeochain felic
17. La feil petair deochain
drebraing martra bu-
ade
conacleir caindine
dondan ega huare
18. Atfed ifeil septim
soerdeochain do did-
nad
laisren lassar buadach
abb leithglindi ligach
19. Luid ermogin urdraice
iarforba agliad
cohisu án soad
assuacht corpan criad
20. Lacessad heradi
cruimthir crochda tuili
feil hiruaim ranbaile
noeb eorapa uili
21. Inalbain conglaine
inrlecud cachsubai
luid uan cunamathair
armbrathair maelrubai

Lebar Brecc, pp. 85, 86.

15. Primda breo nadaithbe
arfich tola tothla
bacain inlia luagmar
ruadan locharn lothra
16. La carisim rigda
asaruamda relic
doreth duit forsidit
feil indeochaiu felic
17. Lafeil petair deochain
drebraing martra mbu-
adi
conacleir cain dine
donnan eca uari
18. Arfet ifeil septim
sœrdeochain dodidnad
laisren lassar buadach
abb lethglinde ligach
19. Luid ermogin erdairc
iarforbu agliad
co ihu. án soad
asuacht chorpain chriad
20. Lacesad herodi
cruimthir crochda tuile
feil iruaim ran baile
noem neorapa uile
21. INalpain conglaine
iarlecud cechsuba
luid uainn conamathair
armbrathair moelruba

---

15. An excellent flame that wanes not: he vanquished urgent desires: fair was the precious stone, Ruadán lamp of Lothra.

16. With royal Carissima, whose graveyard is roomy (?), runs to thee quickly the feast of the deacon Felix.

17. With the feast of deacon Peter who sprang to victorious martyrdom, with his clergy a fair assemblage (?), Donnán of chilly Eca.

18. On (the) feast of Septimus, a noble deacon, Laisrén, a victorious flame *(lassar)*, gentle abbot of Lethglenn, was declared to have been solaced.

19. Conspicuous Hermogenes went, after achieving his fights, to Jesus,—a splendid change!—out of (the) coldness of his poor body of clay.

20. With (the) suffering of Herodius a priest who crucified desire, (the) feast in Rome,—right noble town!—of all Europe's saints.

21. In Scotland with purity, after leaving every happiness, went from us with his mother our brother Maelrubai.

[a] MS. merubai

RAWL. 503.	LAUD, 610.	LEBAR BRECC, p. 86.
22. Ronain pilip apstal asaidbliu cechthredan diannainm arruinatbar gin locharn[n] lethan	22. Ronnain pilip apstal as aidbli cach trethan dianainm arruin athar gein locharnne lethan	22. Romain pilip asp*al* asaidbliu cech trethan dianainm iruin athar gin locharna lethan
23. Lochet epscop ibair asrort cenn cech hernis an breo huas tuinn trilis inherinn bicc bebais	23. Lochet epsc*uip* hibuir asort cend cechciris anbreo huas tuind trilis in herind bic bebais	23. Loichet escu*ip* ibair asort cend cech cris an breo uastuind trilis inch*ri*nn bic bebais
24. Buaid na tri macc nennacc hisurn sochla dine pais giurgi grian buada cotricha[i]t mor mile	24. Buaid na tri mac nennae asurn sochla dine pais geurgi grian buada cotrichait mor mili	24. Buaid na tri macc nendac assurn sochla diue pais giurgi grian buada co xxxait mor mile
25. Marc huasal inegept nadlig foccul faille flesc oir adbul tinne epscop mor macc caille	25. Marc uassal inegept nidlig focul faille flesc oir adbultinne escop mor maccaille	25. Marc uasal ineigipt nidlig focal faille flesc oir adbul tinde escop mor mac caille
26. Cirillus cain cimmid cessais roi rinne dochri*st* cachaind*aille cosluag adbul imbe	26. Cirillus caincimid cessais aroe rinde docri*st* canait aille cosluag adbal imbi	26. Cirillus cain cimbid cesais roi rindi docri*st* canaid aille cosluag adbul imbi
27. IMmacurtis angil acarcraib euatesed alaxander huasal abb roma incresen	27. IMacuirdis aingil accarcraib ciatheset alaxandir huassal abb rom*a* incresen	27. Himocuirtis aingil hicarcraib ciatheised alaxa*n*dir uasal abb rom*a* incresen
28. Cristofor la c[r]onan rois chree cotalci inafcil cen sotlai luid mor miled martrai	28. Cristifer lacronan roiss cree cutailcci innafcil censotlai luid mor miled martra	28. Cristif*er* lacronan ruis*s* chre cotalci inafeil censotla luid mor miled martra
29. Martra germain chruimthir cri*st* bamor atiachra	29. Martra germain crumthi*r* cri*st* bamor athiachra	29. Martra germain cruimthi*r* cri*st* bamor atiachra

22. May apostle Philip protect us, who is vaster than every sea, a vehement name in the Father's mystery, wide mouth of a lamp.

23. (The) light of bishop Ibar, who struck down every heresy's head, a splendid flame over a sparkling wave, in Becc-Eriu he died.

24. The victory of the three innocent children, in a furnace, a famous number. (The) passion of George, a sun of victory, with thirty great thousands.

25. Noble Marc in Egypt deserves not a word of neglect. A rod of gold, a vast bar, great bishop Mac-Caille.

26. Cyrillus a fair captive suffered full sharp spearpoints: to Christ he sings praise with a vast host around him.

27. Angels used to carry him out, though he went in dungeons, noble Alexander, abbot of Rome, the pious one.

28. Christopher with Cronan of Roscrea with starkness. On their feast without vain-glory went many soldiers of martyrdom.

29. Priest German's martyrdom, for

* leg. cachain (= cecinit)   b Facs. incipt

[April 2-20.]

Rawl. 505.	Laud, 610.	Lebar Brecc, p. 86.
coningen cain huaitne	conaiñgen cainuatne	coningen cain uaitne
forocnlith lafiachra	foroenlith lafiachna	foroenlith lafiachna
30. Forcennat cleir napril	30. Forcennat cleir napreil	30. Forcendait cleir napre il
olisleir dorrimi	olisleir dourime	olisleir dourimi
ronan lethrois huamni	ronan liath roiss uaine	ronan liath ruiss uainni
hirroim croch cirini	hiroim croch cirine	irruaim croch cirini

Christ great was his affliction. Coningen, a fair pillar, on one festival with Fiachua. 30. They end April's clergy, and it is industriously I recount them, Ronan (the) gray of Ross Uainni, in Rome Quirinus' cross.

Gloss from the Lebar Brecc, pp. 85, 86.

2. (2) *dubach* .i. toirsech (3) *drebraing* .i. rothrebarling *no* rotrebardring. *calad* .i. cruaid *no* coit

3. (2) *asrala sueth* .i. roéla asnasæthaib

4. (1) *can* .i. cauta (2) *bruis* .i. brisis

5. (3) *primda* .i. airegda (4) *atrannad* .i. rohadandad .i. rotindsenad

6. (2) *moramile* .i. mor achethern (4) .i. inncich fil narfiaduaise .i. hifínemain fiada find .i. in ecclesiam. (leg. ecclesiá) vel in fine iustorum i.e. christi.

7. (2) .i. morni mor inc. *no* morni mora incelebebartha (*sic*) .i. mor mac imalechtan imacuairt. *no* mor nalma *no* mor nalua .i. cassal oifrind *no* mor ndolma .i. reta mora oipne. et ignota res (3) *bayerait crist* .i. hagerait hi crist .i. mac báglic hier*ist* he. *cainde* .i. cáiuní .i. canditis (leg. candidus) .i. alaind he (4) *bledech* .i. bladach. *no* ifilet bleda .i. aige alta. *no* búiredach nanallta imbi. *no* nambled .i. ignotorum animalium .i. magnarum uocum hominum.

8. (2) *ba mortuir* .i. ba tuir mor he. *athempuil* .i. eclesia (3) .i. maith atheist lamúutir achille .i. sái. *no* nirhærad caium

9. (3) .i. uaherchranand *acht* maraid beos afuil inbaile inróches .i. desmirecht sin amartra donchách rosmarb

10. (1) *cruimthir* .i. sacerdotis. *no* craibdig aristechta dochraibdech corob cróm (2) *coemthar folaith* .i. rocoemchlóithea feil aud .i. praemium penda .i. menma. *no* cem (cein ?) afolta (3) *subaich* .i. subeo .i. suaibsech

12. (1) *Dalais andsa opair* .i. teach[t] amartra. *andsa* .i. doilig (2) *cretair* .i. coisecartha (3) *abb* .i. forus

13. (2) .i. argoin mbeoil .i. ardrocherlabra gena. *no* argabáil mbél naráidis so espa *no* pudar. [between vv. 11 and 12] *no* arimrád *no* arecnach. *no* argabail mbel naráidis easpa *no* pudar (3) *gerait* .i. glicc (4) *donrema* .i. ronairume .i. rongaba .i. inamuinterus *no* romæma

14. (3), (4) .i. ise corp erist ba conuáinn dó

15. (1) *primda* .i. ergna. *breo* .i. lassar. *nadaithbe* .i. naderchranann *no* nadíbdann (2) *arfich* .i. robriss *no* rogni anisi *no* toil dé *no* rodluthaigthea æuta ló fria imthoil dé (3) *luagmar* .i. logmar

16. (1) *rigda* .i. reges [leg. regalis] .i. nobilis et carne et spiritu (2) .i. is catharda relic *no* uasal (3) *foreidit* .i. cito.

17. (2) *drebraing* .i. rodring *no* rodirgestar (4) *cea* .i. fons.

18. (1) *arfet* [in marg.] .i. indister (4) *ligach* .i. cendais

19. (3) *án soad* .i. solan. *no* alan sossad *no* sónmige

20. (2) *cruimthir* .i. sacerdos. *crochda tuile* .i. rochroch athola pro deo.

lxxii   THE CALENDAR OF OENGUS.   [APRIL 1-4.

22. (2) .i. aeona 7 arata nasochaide. *cech trethan* .i. *cech* muir   (3) *athar* .i. nemda   (4) *gin locharna* .i. ós lampadis.
23. (1) *loichet* .i. sutrall *no lassar no lochrann*   (2) .i. romarb cen*n* cech heris .i. ilbuaid iarstair .i. deman iarsians quo*d* demon.
25. (2) .i. nidlig faill for*ach*duimniugu*d*
26. (2) .i. roches triarinne roaithe nangæ *forconair. no* roe .i. icath romarbad conarmaib bite icath   (3) *aille* .i. laud*ate* (leg. laudem) .i. m*o*la*d*.
27. (1) .i. ro imarchuirsit aingil leo he cid bicarcraib dochuaid[a]   (4) *incresen* .i. inti isseancró .i. incráibdlech
28. (2) *cotalci* .i. cotangnai   (3) *censotla* .i. cen sobcha .i. só tolach .i. cen uaill .i. cendim*us*. unde dictus est cernach sotal
29. (1) *cruimthir* .i. sacerdos.   (2) .i. bamor duilge amartra ingort*a*
30. (1) *forcendait* .i. forbanat .i. ismithig forcend .i. forbu fo*rr*u   (3) *isleir donrimi* .i. isléir rothuirmes ismithig inforcend

NOTES FROM THE LEBAR BRECC, p. 85.

1. *Ambrois comsit nglaine* .i. cimnorum [leg. hymuorum] et opiscopus medolaniæ .i. ciuitas in italia.
feil do felib maire. cumtach tabarnacla inant*uaip*.

'*a feast of Mary's feasts.*' the building of a tabernacle in Antioch.

p. 86, after the quatrain for 30 April] Maria[e] natiuitas est ut alii putant sed uerius est ut alii sentiunt quod in hoc die fecit magnificat in domu[b] [elizabeth] quae in octauis kl. aprilis[c] ante concepit et postmodum uenit ad domum[d] elizabeth ut lucas refert et remansit ibi[e] per tres menses i.e. usque ad natiuitatem[f] [iohannis baptistae].
sluag cuagair. ccxl.

'*Evagrius' host,*' 240.

4. *can tigernach credal no core tigernach* 7 rl. in cc. .i. cruimther core ochill moir .h. niallain .i. Tigernach cluan*a* coais m*a*c coirpri mic fergus*a* m. enna m. laebain m. briuin m. echach m. daire barraig m. cathair m*á*ir. 7 mac rig h. mbairrche esi*um*

'*Sing pious Tigernach*' or (read) '*Core, Tigernach* etc. i.e. Priest Core from Coll Mór Hua Nialláin. *Tigernach* i.e. Tigernach of Cluain Eoais, son of Coirpre, son of Fergus. son of Enna, son of Laeban, son of Briun, son of Echaid, son of Daire Barrach, son of Cathair Mór, and a son of the king of the Uí-Bairrchi was he.

in r. marg] Can tigernach credal 7 rl. Coirpre mac fergus*a* dolaignib. i. dolaigis athair tigernaig. no is doh*ui*b barrchi dó. Derbfraich im*m*orro ingean echach mic crimthain*n* rig airgiall oraith moir úas clochar am*á*thair. Ruc diu. coirpr*e* lais fochoim he cocill dara. tóit isinteach nóiged. Atchí brigit tórr*um*a aingel oscind [in tige]. ocus iarfaigis cia roboi ann. Oen oclach ann olintimthirig. Feg lat fós olbrigit. Fegaid iar*um*. Ata tra olsé nóide bec anucht inóclæich. Ismaith innóide olbrigit. Tic brigit isinteach

'*Sing pious Tigernach*' etc. Coirpre son of Fergus of Leinster, i.e. of Leix, was Tigernach's father. Or he is of the Uí-Bairrchi. Derbfraich however, daughter of Echaid son of Crimthann king of Oriel of Raith Mór over Clochar (was) his mother. Now Coirpre bore him under cover to Kildare. He came into the guest-house. Brigit beheld a watch of angels over the head of the house, and she asked who was there. "One young man (is) there" quoth the servant. "Look thou still," quoth Brigit. Then he

[a] Facs. dochraid   [b] MS. magnis in domino   [c] MS. april   [d] MS. domine
[e] MS. ibi lecrabast qm.   [f] MS. natiuitas

[APRIL 5-7.] NOTES FROM THE LEBAR BRECC, p. 85.

nóiged ocus baistid inlenub. 7 gebid brigit he fria baithis.

Derbfraich máthair thigernaig. is fria asbert cóochdamair droma dubáin inso iarfémind incroind do dluigi eci oedenum alerrthige

A derbfraich
amáthair thigernaig nocim
toet dochobair nárbomall
dluig incrand bifail intsaeir.

5. *Ili feil moir maic cula* .i. nomen matris eius 7 murchad nomen patris eius 7 inimliuch fia iferaib cúl ata. fia nomen montis (leg. fontis ?)
baithes patraic primda .i. sincll mac findchada dohúib garrchou. ise cétduine robaist patraic inherinn he

6. Nouisimus dies forsambi primesci chasc

7. *Finan canm chindletig* .i. clœn arose 7 dochoree dáilme dó. ceand etig .i. etech mume nafiann roort aud. *no coall eti* .i. oeti impota próchan rofáid brenaind roime atuaid ochluain ferta brenaind

[in r. marg.] Eigne dergoir tarlustar
lais tiar iarfuined gréni
rabroind beenaite* baine
comba hosium aeeli
.i. dia roibe ocafothruead illoch léin. ut dicitur

Nisfil athair talmanta lat
inspirut noem rotsær rotalt
inde alius dixit.
Beenait ingen fdgna adbail
inlia lógmar nárbo gand
fochosmailius mce nahóige
gonair unithe finan cam.
IMbrú beenati robui reré
orateoimpred tria brethir dé
nisfil athair talmanta [lat]
inspirut nœm rotsær rotnalt

looked. "There is in sooth," quoth he, "a little babe in the young man's bosom." "Good is the babe," quoth Brigit. Brigit comes into the guest-house, and baptizes the child, and Brigit holds him at his baptism.

Derbfraich (was) Tigernach's mother. It was to her that Cóochdamair of Druim Dubáin said this after being unable to split the tree while building her oratory :—

O Derbfraich!
O mother of holy Tigernach!
Let come thy aid, that was not slow,
Split the tree anigh the wright!

5. '*On Mac Cula's great feast*' i.e. (Cula was) his mother's name and Murchad his father's name, and in Inliuch Fia in Fir Cúla Breg he is. Fia is the name of a mountain (leg. fountain?)
'*Excellent Patrick's baptism*' .i. Sinell son of Findchad of the Ui-Garrchon ; he is the first person whom Patrick baptized in Ireland.

6. The latest day whereon is the first moon of Easter.

7. *Finan the Squinting of Cennetig* i.e. his eye was crooked, and of the Corco-Dúibne was he. *Ceann Etig* i.e. Etoch the nurse of the Fiann was slain there. Or *Cell-Eti* (is the right reading), i.e. from the flying (*eti*) of the pet scallcrow which Brenainn sent before him from the north from Cluain Ferta Brenainn.

A salmon of red gold came,
After sunset he went behind,
Against fair Beenat's vulva,
So that he was her husband.

i.e. when she was bathing in Loch Léin, ut dicitur :—

An earthly father thou hast not,
The Holy Spirit has saved thee and reared thee.

Inde alius dixit :—
Beenait daughter of a vast . . . . . ,
The precious stone that was not niggardly.
Like the Virgin's Son
Finan Cam was born of her.
In Beenat's womb thou wast for a while,
For thou wast conceived through God's word.
An earthly father thou hast not,
The Holy Spirit hath saved thee (and) reared thee.

* .i. mathair finain 'Finan's mother'

Fínan canu chind etig 7rl. .i. dohíb luchtai dochiarraige luachra amáthair 7 do choreo dúibne aathair. in oculis" eius ista obli[qui]tas fuit[b] .i. cosæb roilerce fornaite intan bói occuinchid neich hospitibus .i. iscead duitt beith amlaidsin semper ariutaide .i. brenaind mac findloga

10. *ross eo* .i. amuig locha ambregaib *cuanna rigda* .i. cuana mac miduirn m. duibratha m. en[u]a m. neill .ix. giullai[c]y .i. uirgo nobilis corpore" et spiritu.

11. *moedoc m:inech* .i. bicluain mor main

olisbrathair .i. dolaiguib doib andís

na acht ronoema l doduulang .i. robidbrad na dodúnlaing moedoc. *acht ronoemad móedoc sech ddúlaing*

12. *tuiI escop* .i. papa rómre qui contra arianam[d] cresim resistit.

13. *pol deochain* .i. nomen pauli apostoli.[e]

14. *tassach* .i. irálth cholpa ileith cathail inulltaib .i. cerd 7 escop patraic. tassach *ocus* féil aetsechta so

15. *ruadan* .i. deoganacht chaissil dó

16. *la cairisim rigda* .i. la féil cairisim uirginis

in r. marg.] Arciepiscopus hiberniæ .i. senoir mac maildalua hi tertid apreil in pace quieuit. ut quidam dixit

Mac maildalua inlegind léir
abás deirinn isaicbeil
ilog achirt gním do cheiu
fuair nem itertid apreil

17. *feil petair deochain* .i. in antiochia pasus est. in r. marg.] Lá féil petair deochain 7rl.

Dondan ega .i. ega ainm oilein íl inalpain 7 isannside ata donnan so icattaib et ibi donnan sanctus cum sua familia obiit .i. ld.

Ishe imlondánsa dochóid foramus choluim cille diagabail dammcharnit. *condebart colam cille friss*, nibam anmcharasa olse do lucht dergmartra. uair ragasa indergmartra 7 domdínter lat .7 issed ón rocomailled. Toit iarum donnan

'Fínan the squinting of Cenn Etig,' &c., i.e. of the Uí-Luchtai of Ciarraige Luachra (was) his mother, and of the Corco-Dúibne his father. *In oculis* etc. i.e. crookedly he looked at his tutor when he was asking something for the guests. "Thou hast leave to be thus *semper*," quoth the tutor, i.e. Brenaind, son of Findlug.

10. '*Ross Eo*' i.e. in Mag Locha in Bregia. '*royal Cuanna*' .i. Cuana, son of Midorn, son of Dubratha, son of Enna, son of Niall the Nine-hostaged.

'*Maedoc the treasurous*' i.e. in Cluain Mór Main [leg. Maedóic?].

'*for he is a kinsman*' i.e. of Leinster both of them were.

'*a descendant, but he was sainted, of Dunlang,*' i.e. Maedoc was given as a grandson to Dunlaing but Maedoc was sainted and not Dunlaing.

14. '*Tassach*' i.e. in Raholp in Leth Catbail in Ulster, i.e. Patrick's artisan and bishop (was) Tassach, and this is the feast of his obit.

15. '*Ruadan*' i.e. of the Eoganacht of Caisel was he.

16. '*With royal Carissima*' i.e. at the feast of Carissima a virgin.

Archbishop of Ireland, i.e. a senior. Mac Mail-da-lua on the fourth before the ides of April *in pace*, &c.

Mac Maildalua of the pious reading,
His death to Ireland is terrible:
In reward of his righteous deeds which he wrought'
He found heaven on the fourth before the ides of April.

17. '*feast of Deacon Peter.*'
'With the feast of Deacon Peter.'

'Donnán of Ega' i.e. Ega the name of an island which is in Scotland, and there Donnán is, or in Caithness. And there Saint Donnán died with his family, i.e. 54 (in number).

It is this Donnán that went to visit Colum Cille to get him for his soulfriend. And Colum Cille said to him, "I will not be soulfriend," quoth he. " to folk of red martyrdom, for thou wilt suffer red martyrdom and thy family with

[a] MS. in hoc aliis   [b] MS. post   [c] MS. corpire   [d] MS. arrianam
[e] MS. apl.s   [f] a mere guess: cf. O'Clery's *cachain* .i. *dorighne*.

[April 18–22.] NOTES FROM THE LEBAR BRECC, p. 86.

conamúinutir ingallgædelaib 7 gebid aittreb indbail ambitis cwerig rígna intíre. indister sin don rigaiu. Amarbad uile olsise. Nicreitmech sin olcách. Tecar chuca iarum diamarbad. ISandsin bui inclérech ocaoifrend. Lécid cairde dún cotáir inoifrend oldonnan. Lécfider olsint. ocus marbthar iarum iarsin inlín bátar uile

cona cleir .i. .l.iiii.
18. arfet ifeil septim .i. hifeil septim .i. diaconorum[a] bonorum .i. ciarain [in marg.] no athath ifeil .uii. særdeochain molaisi lethglinde dochomdidnad .i. dotecht fornem. no arfet .uii. særdeochaine atbathutar and. proprium nomen [sept]imus. lugaid mac mænaig mic fachtnai mc. rossa mic eire mc. threna mc. duach mc. maieniad mc. maiccon mc. luigdech. bi sunt .uii. germani es. .i. escop hrauduib. cusan fachtna. lugna. molua. lochan innúib echach. cailchine .manchine cúla caiss.

Laisrén .i. dul fornеam do molaisse lethglinde

19. ermogin .i. indrúi doroine cuimleng fri hiacop mac zepedei et postea credidit.

20. feil iruaim .i. inanóir mártain
in r. marg.] Lacésad heródi 7rl. comune solemne sanctorum hiberniæ et britaniæ et totius coropæ et specialiter martini.
Crand mor búi isindoman tair 7 noadradis nageunti he corothroiseset nacristaige frianoemaib corpa uile cotrethsad inerand. et statim eecidit.
21. cona mathair .i. subtan ingen sétnai. siur chomgaill máthair mwilrubai .i. dochenél eógain dó 7 inalpain ata .i. inapur[b] crossan 7 feil netsechta so

in r. marg.] INalpain conglaine 7rl. .i. Moelrubai. dochenél eogain dó. ocus inalpain ata achell 7 feil aetsechta so. Subtan din. ingen setnai siur chómgaill bendebuir amáthair .7 inabur chresen ata achell.

22. pilip aspal .i. in frigia sepultus .i. os lampadis[d] cum esset pilipus annorum .lxxxuii. in hierapole[e] gallorum ciuitate phrygiae[f] lapidatus est.

[a] MS. dia oncorum [b] MS. inapur
[d] MS. hós lampidis [e] MS. erapole [f] MS. frigia

thee," and this was fulfilled. Thereafter came Donnán with his family into (the country of the) Gallgaedil and abode in a place wherein the sheep of the queen of the country used to be. This is told to the queen. "Let them all be slain" quoth she. "That is not pious," said every one. Then people go to kill them. The cleric was then at mass. "Give truce to us till the mass ends," saith Donnán. "It shall be given," say they, and thereafter all that were there were killed.
'*with his clergy*' i.e. fifty-four.
'*Was declared on Septimus' feast*' i.e. on the feast of seven i.e. good deacons i.e. of Ciaran's. Or on the feast of seven noble deacons died Molaisi of Lethglenn: '*to have been solaced*' i.e. to have gone to heaven. Or it was related that seven noble deacons died then. [Or] Septimus is a proper name. Lugaid, son of Maenach, son of Fachtnae, son of Rossa, son of Erc, son of Tren, son of Duach (l), son of Mac Niad, son of Mac-Con, son of Lugaid. bi sunt uii. germani eius (l). bishop Brandub, Cusan Fachtna, Lugna, Molua, Lochan in Ui-Echach, Cailchine, Manchine of Cúl Caiss.
'*Laisrén*' i.e. the going to heaven of Molaisse of Lethglenn.
19. '*Hermogenes*' i.e. the wizard who contended with James, son of Zebedee, and thereafter believed.
20. '*A feast in Rome*' i.e. in honour of Martin.

A great tree was in the world in the east, and the heathen used to adore it, and the Christians fasted against all the saints of Europe that the tree might fall, and forthwith it fell.
21. '*with his mother*' i.e. Subthan, daughter of Sétna, Comgall's sister, was Maelrubai's mother i.e. of Cenél Eogain was he and in Scotland he is, i.e. in Aporcrossan,[c] and this is the feast of his obit.
'In Scotland with purity' &c., i.e. Maelrubai of Cenél Eogain (was) he, and in Scotland is his church, and this is the feast of his obit. Subthan daughter of Setna, sister of Comgall of Bennchor, was his mother, and in Aporcrossan[c] is his church.

[c] now Applecross in the isle of Skye.

23. *escuip ibair*. IN istoria cola[i]nu *cille* est ista genealogia. iubar mac cuchuirb mic coirpri mc. meill mc. echach. a quo hui echach ulad indsin. ocus tri bliadna .xxx. ar .xx.it ar. ccc. asægul escuip ibair

in r. marg.] Loichet escuip ibair 7rl. IShe intescop ibaiusi dorigne inconbhlicht mor fripatraic 7 ise foracaib uasligeda lana 7 nacuileda fása inarl macha. Fergaigther iarum intí patraic friss .7 issed atbert. Nibiasu inerinn olpatraic. Bid éri ainm aniuaid ambfusa olescop ibair. Unde bec-éri nominatus est .i. inis fil andib cendsclaig 7 forinmuir amuig ataside.

24. *Buaid natri mac nendac* .i. sedrach. misac. abdinago caldea nomina. [*in r. marg.*] Buaid natri mac nendac 7rl. .i. sédrech 7 misac 7 abdinago auanmunda lacaildib. Ananias .Acarias. Misabel anannuunda lahébraigib. 7 .xxx. m. 7 .dccxxix. icnabeudon duo. Dorata tra itriur lanabeudon isornd tened forlassad iat. acht arai voaer 7 rothesnirg dia athar iat conarirchoitig inteine ni doib

cotrichait mor mile .i. nahi tuc ad christum

25. *Marc uasal incigipt* .i. euangelista acheand in alexandria.

escop mor mac caille .i. icruachan brig eli inuib failge ata achell 7 ise rosuidig caille forcind mbrigte 7 ise rogab lám mochuda araithin.

in l. marg.] nithicsén cocenn .u. bliadan xxx. ar .cccc.
26. *Cirillus* .i. episcopus ierusalem
28. *Cristifer* .i. decim milia .cccc. iii. cum cristifiro [in l. marg.] .i. conchend creitmech hé et sub decio pasus est.

in r. marg.] Cristifer 7rl. .i. conchend sin 7 ladoc rocésair 7 reperibus nomen eius.

Rocleroch conglaine
robe incraibdech cristaige
regairm cendfuues darler
nainm diles cristifer.

in r. marg.] cristifer lacronan. .i. christum ferens 7 conchend creitmech he .i. et sub decio pasus est.

23. '*of bishop Ibar*.' In the history of Columb cille is this genealogy: Iubar son of Cucorb son of Coirpre son of Niall son of Echaid, from whom (descend the) Ui-Echach of Ulster. And 353 years was the age of bishop Ibar.

'The flame of bishop Ibar, &c.' This is the bishop Ibair who had the great conflict with Patrick, and it is he that left the roads full and the kitchens empty in Armagh. Patrick is enraged with him, and this is what he said, "Thou shalt not be in Ireland," quoth Patrick. "Ireland (*éri*) shall be the name of the place wherein I am," quoth bishop Ibair. Whence Bec-éri ('little Ireland') was so called, i.e. an island which is in Ui-Ceunnsclaig and out on the sea it is.

'The victory of the three innocent children' &c. i.e. Sedrech and Misac and Abdinago their names with the Chaldeans. Ananias, Acarias Misabel their names with the Hebrews; and 30,729 with Nebuchadnezzar moreover. The three were cast by Nebuchadnezzar into a furnace of fire aflame, but nevertheless God the Father freed and rescued them, so that the fire hurt them not.

'*with thirty great thousands*' i.e. those whom he brought to Christ.

25. '*Noble Mark of Egypt*' i.e. the evangelist. His passion was in Alexandria.

'*great bishop Mac-Caille*' i.e. in Cruachan Brig Eli in Ui-Failge is his church, and it is he that set the veil on Brigit's head, and it is he that took Mochuda's hand out of Rathin.[a]

He comes not till the end of 435 years.

28. *Christopher* i.e. 10,403 with Christopher i.e. a pious doghead [or wolfhead] was he.[b]

'Christopher' etc. i.e. a doghead was he and under Decius he suffered.

He was a cleric with purity:
He was the pious Christian:
Before the call without reproach over sea
His proper name was Christopher.

---

[a] Some mistake here, for Mac-Caille died A.D. 489, and Mochuda of Rathin died in 636.
[b] See Jameson, *Sacred and Legendary Art*, 449.

cronan .i. crouan quibus mochua dictus mc. h. æla .i. cronan [in l. marg.] .i. othuaim find-lacha ituadmumain
[In r. marg. at 30 April are the following various readings of the quatrain for 28th April:]
    Cristifer lacronan^a
    luchdaigern cotalcai
    inafeil censotla^b
    luid mor miled martra

    Cristifer la cronan
    daig derg combuaid dalta
    inteo oir uastire
    lasluid mile martrai

29. *martra germain cruimthir* .hic de generatione derca .lx. xx.
coningen cain uaitne .i. inga mor bui fairri amal ingin chon .i. iugen rig laigen sed unguem^c canis quodam casu accepit.
in r. marg.] Martra germain cruimthir 7rl. Coningen .i. coniingen siu doraduntir mochuda liss moir 7 indessib mumau ata 7 do choning-nechaib dó .i. tuath fil fri sliab cua atuaid 7 oc ard finain ata . sed uerius est hoc .i. coningen .i. ingen robúi accoin allaid quodam casu sugens lac^d ex uberibus eius cum catulis suis et ista est .i. conach cille finnmaige hindib onechlais ifortuathaib laigeu issí atberair sund 7 issí sin robodalta do mac thail cille cuilind 7 istrithe roccnaigseat clerig laigen mactail

Noe iterum in[i]uit in arcam in postremo die mensis
fiachna .i. manach la mochuda.
30. *ronan liath ruiss uainni* .i. ross uainne .i. cell fil iconaillib . no uainne aheirinn dó

in r. marg.] Forcendait cleir napreil 7rl. .i. Ronan liath ruiss uainne .i. ocsenbuaile iconallib [muirthemne atá uel] in alio loco. no ronan liathroiss .i. unum nomen'. no rónan lethroiss uainne .i. uainne aheirinn do.

irruaim croch cirini .i. papæ romæ

 ^a .i. othuaim findlocha ituadmumain
 ^b .i. censobchai no cendiumus unde dictus est cernach sotal

  ^c MS. tn.   ^d MS. quidam causa uiuens lax

Cronan .i. from Tuaim Findlocha in North Munster.

  Christopher with Cronan^a,
  Lugtigern (?) with starkness,
  On his feast without vainglory^b
  Went many soldiers of martyrdom.

  Christopher with Cronan,
  Daig Derg with gift of fosterlings,
  The yew of gold over lands,
  With whom went a thousand martyrs.

'*Coningen a fair pillar*' i.e. a great nail there was upon her like a wolf's nail, i.e. she was daughter of a king of Leinster, *sed &c.*
'Martyrdom of priest Gernau &c.' Coningen i.e. Coniingen was he, of the family of Mochuda of Lismore, and in the Desies of Munster he is, and he was of the Coningnig i.e. a tribe that is to the north of Sliab Cua, and at Ard Finain he is; but this is truer, namely, Coningen a girl which was by some chance with a wolf, sucking with its cubs the milk from its dugs, and she is Conach of Cell Finnmaige in Ui-Enechlais in Forthuatha of Leinster is she that is mentioned here ; and it is she that was pupil to Mac Tail of Cell Cuilind, and on account of her the clergy of Leinster reviled Mac Tail.

'*Fiachna*' i.e. a monk with Mochuda.
30. '*Ronan the Gray of Ross Uainni*' i.e. Ross Uainne i.e. a church that is in Conailli; or from us (*dainni*) out of Ireland he (went)
'They end the clergy of April' etc. i.e. Ronan the gray of Ross Uainnei.e. at Senbuaile in Conailli Muirthemne he is, or in another place. Or 'Ronan of Liath-ross' i.e. one name. Or 'Ronan of Lethross from us' i.e. from us out of Ireland he (went).

 ^a i.e. of Tuaim Findlocha in North Munster.
 ^b i.e. without haughtiness or without pride whence 'Cernach the haughty' (*sotal*) was so called.

  ^e MS. uii. m. non

RAWL. 505, fo. 214, a.	LAUD, 610, fo. 64, b.	LEBAR BRECC, p. 87.
1. Kl. mai nethchoimi gein pilipp asdixu and tinscan as huaisliu praicept alaind issu	1. Kl. mai mochoimi gein pilip asdixu autinscan as uaisliu precept alaind issu	1. Kl. mái mochoemi gein pilip asdixu and tindscan isuaisliu procept alaind ihu.
2. Escomlud saturnin cocri*st* immeranice la etsecht iarsirchnet nechtain daltai patraice	2. Escomlud saturni cocri*st* imaránic la heitsecht iarsirchneit nechtain dalta patraic	2. Escomlad saturni cocri*st* imarnnic lahetsecht iarsirchneit nechtain dalta patraic
3. Primairece craind cruiche cri*st* conilur buada bas conlaid cain age feil mar maire huaga	3. Primairee craind chroiche cri*st* conilar bu[a]de bas condlaid cainaighe feil mar maire nage	3. Primairec chraind cruiche cri*st* conilur buaide bas coudlaid cainnaige feil mar muire uaige
4. Hipais an[a]tciri mochua cain deochoid macc cuimneni^a chlothaig bifeil siluain dechoin	4. Hipais anathcri mochuæ caindeochaid mac cummaine clothaig ifeil sillain deocha*in*	4. Hipais anterini mochua cain dechoid mac cumine clothaig ifeil sillain deochain
5. INdechoin eutimus bahelair sechphiana lotar laithi litha frisrocaib arfiada	5. Indeochain iustinus lahelair sechpianu lotar laithi litha frisroeaib arfiada	5. INdeochain iustinus lahelair sechpianu lotar laithe litha fris rocaib arfiadu
6. Fer roscrib centercai cainscela cri*st* crochthai admuint*er* laflaithi gein mor matha mochtai	6. Fer roscrib centerca cáinscela cri*st* crochtha atmuinter laflaithe^b gein mor maithi mochtha	6. Fer roscrib centercai cain scela cri*st* crochdai armuinter laflaithe gein mor matha mochta
7. Mochiaroc labreccan digernit atglainiu car[s]at cri*st* as diliu in echdromma dairiu	7. Mochuaroc labreccan dagerait at glainiu carsat cri*st* asdiliu inechdroma dairiu	7. Mochuaroc labreccan digerait atglainiu carsat cri*st* asdiliu indeach droma dairiu

1. On May's kalend my Cóemi. (The) birth of Philip who is noblest. Then began what is highest, Jesu's delightful preaching.

2. Saturninus' departure, unto Christ nigh whom he went, with (the) death, after a long sigh, of Nechtán Patrick's pupil.

3. The first finding of the wood of the Christ's Cross with many virtues. (The) death of Condlad, a fair pillar. Mary (the) Virgin's great feast.

4. On Anatherius' passion, went fair Mochua, son of famous Cumíne, on deacon Silvanus' feast.

5. The deacon Justiuus with Hilary beyond pains: they went on (the) day of festival (whereon) our God arose.

6. A man who wrote without stint fair stories of Christ crucified: commemorated by princes is (the) great birth of Matthew (the) magnified.

7. My-Cuaróc with Breccán, two champions who are purest, loved Christ who is dearest, in Daire Echdroma.

^a leg. cuimnéni.   ^b MS. la flatihe

RAWL. 505.	LAUD, 610.	LEBAR BRECC, p. 87.
8. Uictor ocus maxim imcr*ist*[a] cotaruicset arsere rig rocarsat inafuil fotruicset	8. Uictor 7 maeximo arcr*ist* cotarruicset arseire rig rocharsat inafuil fotruicset	8. Uictor 7 maxim umcr*ist* cotaruicset arseirce rig rotearsat inafuil fotruicset
9. Failsigud mor micheil donbith bascel promtha pais cirill cain cartha epscop santan sochla	9. Failhsiged mor michil donbith bascel promtha pais chairill caincartha escop sanctain sochla	9. Faillsingud mor michil donbith bascel promtha pais cirill cain cartha escop sanctain sochla
10. Hi sichlaith indaltair imbi torm cechtempuil	10. Isithflaith indalltair imbi toirm cach thempuil	10. Hisidflaith inalltair imbi tairm cech tempuil
ronsnada insluagach comgall buadach bennchuir	ronsnada insluagach comgall buadach bennch*u*ir	ronsnaidea insluagach comgall buadach bendchuir
11. Buaid nioib cendermat dorig nel bafordorce mochritoc cain munter ocus cruimther cormacc	11. Buaid inioib cendermat dorig nel ba fordare mochritoc cáinmuinter 7 cruimther cormcc	11. Buaid iob cendermat dorig nel bafordare mochritoc cain muinter 7 cruimther cormac
12. Cyriacus crochtha trichetaib donascnai ailitheir ainm coemda la heirc noebda nascai	12. Ciriacus crochta tricetaib donascnai ailithir ainm coemda la here noemda nascai	12. Ciriac*us* crochda .ccc. aib donascnai oilithi*r* ainm coemdai laherce noemdai nascai
13. Noebm*uinter* teraci probique iarsetaib iarserbchrochaib siraib sesiur ar se cetaib	13. Noem*m*uinter ciraci ispropi iarsetaib iarserberochaib sfraib seisir ar se c*et*aib	13. Noebmuinter teraci propaci iarsetaib iarserbchrochaib siraib .ui.er ar .ui. c. aib
14. Corona is uictor conacleir cenmathim foroenlith ler suthain feil cain carthaig raithin	14. Coroua 7 uictor cona chleir cenmaithem foroenlith ler suthain feil cáin carthaig rothain	14. Coroua 7 uictor conacleir cenmathim for oenlith leir suthain feil chain charthaig rathin

---

8. Victor and Maximus, for Christ they gave themselves: for affection towards the king whom they loved they bathed in their blood.

9. Michael's great manifestation, to the world it was a proven story. The passion of Cyril, fair, beloved. Famous bishop Sanctain.

10. Into the peace-kingdom of the other world, wherein is every temple's noise, may the hostful, victorious Comgall of Bangor convoy us!

11. (The) victory of Job without oblivion, to (the) King of Clouds he was manifest. My-Critóc, a fair servant, and Priest Cormac.

12. Crucified Cyriacus with three hundred who accompanied him. Ailithir a lovable name, with sainted Erc Nascai.

13. The holy family of Teracus and Probus after paths (of this world). After long bitter crosses, six persons and six hundred.

14. Corona and Victor with their[b] train, without abatement, on one festival pious, perennial, the fair feast of Carthach of Rathin.

[a] *no ar* [b] B 'his'

RAWL. 505.	LAUD, 610.	LEBAR BRECC, p. 87-88.
15. Rath in spirta sechtai senaig forcleir ngelbain tiamda saran saidbir feil duiblitir dermair	15. Rath in spirata sechta senaig for cleir ngelbain tiamda saran saidbir feil dublitrech dermair	15. Rath inspirtu .uii.a sennich forcleir ngelmair tiamda saran saidbir feil duiblitrech dermair
16. Togairm brenainn chluana isin mbithlaith mbuadig	16. Togairm brenaind cluana issimhbithlaith mbuadigh	16. Togairm brenaind cluana isinmbithlaith mbuadaig
bas caid carnig firbaile	bas caid chairnig erci-b[d]ig	bas caid charnig firbaile
la feil áin hui suannaig	la feil ain h. suannaig	feil an .h. suannaig
17. Sluagad adrionis uictoris bassillo scorsit cenchuit fainne fordinn flatha finne	17. Sluaiged adrionis uictoiris basilli scuirset cencuit fainde for dind flatha finde	17. Sloiged adrionis uictoris basille scorsit cenchuit fainde fordind flatha nime
18. Feil maire maith rorigad momedoc mór mainech modomnoc mind mbuadach feil brain bicc ochlocnad	18. Feil maire maith rorigad momóedoemindmainech modomnóc mind buadach feil brain bic ó chlamad	18. Feil maire maith rorigad momoedoc mor mainech modomnoc mind buadach feil brain bic ochlænad
19. Cliara urbain glana nisgignetar tola ananmann itgela trebroenan afola	19. Cliar urbain atglana nisgegnatar tola annanmand atgela tria bróenan nafola	19. Cleir urbain itglana nisgignetar tola ananmund itgela tria bróenan afola
20. Fuil mór marcellossro luid fothalmain tassi foroenlith itgessi gerbassi 7 protassi	20. Fuil mor marchellosi luid fothalmain taisse for oenlith itfeisi gerbaissi protaissi	20. Fuil mor marcellossi luid fothalmain tassi forrenlith itfissi gerbassi protassi
21. Tiamda martir mirbuil mordrem* dedo thurinn colman lobur rolainn barrinn dromma culinn	21. Tiamda mairtir mirbuil mordrem do de tuirend colmau lobor roloind barrind droma cuilind	21. Tiamda martir mirbuil mordrem dedi tuirind colman lobor rolaind barrfind droma cuilind

15. The grace of the septenary Spirit dropt on a fair great[b] clergy. Timothy: wealthy Sarán: the feast of vast Duibliter.

16. The calling of Brenann of Cluain into the eternal, victorious kingdom: the holy death of Carnech the mighty[c]: the splendid feast of Suanach's descendant.

17. The hosting of Adrio, of Victor, of Basil: they unyoked without a whit of weakness on a height of heaven's kingdom.[d]

18. The feast of good Mark who was crowned: my Macdóc great, treasurous: my Domnóc, a victorious diadem: the feast of Bran the Little from Claenad.

19. Urban's clergy who are pure, lusts wounded them not: their souls are white through (the) rain of their blood.

20. Marcellosus' great blood went under earth a relic; on one festival they are to be known,[e] Gervase, Protasius.

21. Timothy a marvellous martyr: a great company of divine wheat[f]: zealous Colman a leper: Barrfind of Druimm Cuilinn.

[a] MS. morderin [b] B. and D. 'white' [c] B. 'pious' [d] B. and D. 'of a white kingdom'
[e] D. 'besought' [f] quia sancti triticum Dei snut, Rawl. 505.

RAWL. 505, fo. 214, b.	LAUD. 610, fo. 65, b.	LEBAR BRECC, p. 88.
22. Cechaing anuimm ronain find forriched rinnach lasinfer cain clannach baitheni mac finnach	22. Cechaing anim ronain find forriched rinnach lassin fear cain clannach baithine mac findach	22. Cechaing ainim ronain find for riched rindach lasinfer cain clandach boethine mac findach
23. Fin[d]sluag epecthiti as danu as daingniu iarcesad lahingru frisindled lahaingliu	23. Findsluag epectini asdanu as daingniu iarcessad lahingru frisindlith coaingliu	23. Findsluag epectini isdanu isdaingniu iarcesad lahingru frisindled coaingliu
24. Augustin intepscop ermes abb mor mile colman inmain age aidbe tuathach tire	24. Augustin intepscop ermes abb mor mile colman inmain aige aidbe tuathach tire	24. Augustin intescop ermis abb mor mile colman inmain aige aidbe tuathach tire
25. Totice feil iohannis inmain age huage dionis derb dana dunchad ia huare	25. Totic feil iohannis inmain aighe huage dionis derb dana dunchad hiu huare	25. Dotie feil iohannis inmain aige huage dionis derb dana dunchad ic huare
26. Aritiu choir cholmain stellain* sluind cenladna beccan carais figle hicluain aird nadba	26. Airitiu coir colmain stellain sloind cenledna becan carais figli icluain aird aadhba	26. Airitiu [choir] colmain stellain sluind cenladnai beccan carais figle icluain aird [a]adbai
27. Acolius cruimther conachleir as noebu afuil fiad coch diniu dorortad forocnu	27. Aculius cruinthir conacleir asnoemdu afuil find cechdiniu rofortad forroenu	27. Aculius incruimther conachleir asnoendai afuil fiad cechdiniu dorortad foroenu
28. Ronsnada cohaingliu inmain sonmech sathe german grian arsruithi nite phatraic mache	28. Ronsnade cohaingliu inmain soinmech sathi german grian arsruithe aidde patraic machae	28. Ronsnadea cohaingliu inmain soinmech saithe german grian arsruithe aide patrice machae
29. Morsluag pullionis ronsnada dondrindnim[b] lacummain conglanbail ingen allen inmain	29. Morsluag palionis ronsnadet don rind[n]im lacumain conglanbail iugen allen inmain	29. Morsluag polionis ronsnadat donrindnim lacumain conglanbail ingen aillen inmain

22. Ronán (the) Fair's soul went to starry heaven, with the man bright, prolific, Baethíne mac Findach.

23. Epectinus' fair host that is boldest, that is strongest, after suffering with torments, was escorted by angels.[c]

24. Augustine the bishop, Ermes abbot of great thousands. Colmán a beloved pillar. Aidbe the northern of Tír (dá-glas).

25. To thee comes the feast of Johannes, a lovable pillar of virginity. Dionysius (the) sure, (the) bold : Dunchad of chilly Hí.

26. The meet reception of Colmán and Stellán declare without dumbness. Beccán who loved vigils, in Cluain Ard (was) his house.

27. Aculius the priest, with his clergy which is most sanctified[d]: their blood before every number was poured forth on roads.

28. May he convoy us to (the) angels, a lovable prosperous troop, German sun of our seniors, tutor of Patrick of Armagh.

29. May Pollio's great host convoy us to the star-heaven, with Cummain the pure and good, daughter of lovable Aillén.

[a] MS. stellam [b] MS. dondrind nibm [c] 'unto angels,' A, B. [d] 'holiest' D
[e] literally 'with pure goodness'

Rawl. 505, fo. 214, b.	Laud, 610, fo. 65, b.	Lebar Brecc, p. 88.
30. Noebapstal arfiadat hifudamnaib ecnai gein tomais cenopni hifudamnaib ecnai (sic)	30. Noebapstal arfiadait afodomain ecnai gein tomais cenoibne pais eutaic cenecla	30. Noebas*pal* arfiadat hifudomain ecnai gein tomais cenoipne pais eutaic ceneclai
31. Cesad criosogini lapais paternelle mi mai comeit mile daprimfuil fortnedre	31. Cessad crissogini lapais patroinille mi mái coméit mile daprimfeil fortniadæ	31. Cesad criosogini lapais petronilla mi mái comet mile diaprimfeil fortniadæ

30. A holy apostle of our God in a deep[a] of wisdom, the nativity of Thomas without suddenness: the passion of Eutychius without fear.

31. Chrysogenus' suffering, with Petronilla's passion. May's month, protection of thousands, two chief feasts close it.

Gloss from the Lebar Brecc, pp. 87, 88.

2. (2) .i. roforb abethaid hicr*ist*
4. (2) *dechoid* .i. dochuaid (3) *clothaig* .i. erdaire
5. (4) *rocaib* .i. iter do. namai (sic) *arfiadu* .i. ibu.
6. (3) *armuinter* .i. airmither no adamraigther no bendaigther (4) *mochta* .i. maigthi vel quasi magis[b] aucta a uerbo augeo vel quasi macta a uerbo mucto .i. occido.[c]
8. (2) *cotaruicset* .i. fuarutar ruice 7 indergtha arcr*ist*, *no* arcr*ist* catha ruicset .i. roclathaigset arcr*ist no* doroegsat .i. tanic ruice doib incr*ist*, *no* cotaruibsct .i. arrubartar bith *no* roimchuirset anéri arcr*ist* (4) .i. per martyrium rofothruicset
9. (3) *cartha* .i. carnis cách he
10. (1) *sid* .i. molad no glóir hfc. *alltair* .i. in coelo *no* in eclais .i. in futuro
11. (2) *ba fordare* .i. basolas *no* baréil .i. derc .i. súil
12. (2) *donasenai* .i. roiscnatar dochum nime lais
13. (2) *setoib* [.i.] seculi vel mundi
15. (2) *senaich* .i. snigid
17. (3) *scorsit* .i. roscoirsct *no* roscornigit iarscis saeculi (4) *fordind* .i. forcléthi nime
19. (2) .i. nirogonsat tola colluide (4) *broenan a fola* .i. in martyrio
20. (2) *itfissi* .i. itguito (4) *protassi* .i. tais *no* maith
22. (1) *cechaing* .i. roching (2) *forriched* .i. forrigiath *rindach* .i. for rerand [leg. ferand] inrig hitat renna (3) *elandach* .i. chandmar .i. multitudine discipulorum uel uirtutum
23. (3) *lahingru* .i. la hingoru .i. cumga .i. bahingor frisincorp rochrabud 7 cesad dofulang (4) *jrisindled* .i. rofrithindlend .i. rorithailed .i. tancutar aingil ifrestal anim[a]e suæ.
25. (1) *dotic* .i. tæd (2) *aige huage* .i. ag nag .i. colma 7 og
26. (2) *cenladnai* .i. conlothech *no* cenlaisce *no* cendolma *no* cen guide
27. (1) *cruimther* .i. sacerdos (4) .i. rodoirted forrótu no forconaire intalman .i. foroenchoei
28. .i. ronfuca ad angelum in coelum (2) *saithe* .i. turba angelorum (4) machæ .i. puigne [leg. pugnae, μάχης?]
29. (2) *donrindnim* .i. donim rindaig *no* redlannaig (3) *conglanbail* .i. combail nglain
30. (1) *arfiadat* .i. crist is nafiadnaise ata (2) *hifudomain* ecnai .i. tomas abisus scientie interpretatur (3) *cenoipne* .i. tanic ainbuid. *no* nirbo and he imnach feirg *no* sfibo
31. (3) *comet mile* .i. donoemaib fuirri (4) *fortniadæ* .i. fordúnait *no* foriadait

---

[a] ' in depths' D.   [b] MS. maigis   [c] MS. occiduo

NOTES FROM THE LEBAR BRECC, pp. 87, 88.

1. *mochoemi* .i. abb thíre daglas 7 bráthair do chæmgen he.
gein pilip .i. dormitatio pilipi apostoli hic dicitur et non natiuitas eius secundum carnem. ut in passionibus apostolorum legitur
   in lower marg.] Kl. mai 7rl. gein pilip .i. pilip apostolus domini nostri iesu christi. post ascensionem[a] saluatoris per annos .xx. predicauit gentibus et in anno septuagesimo aetatis in ciuitate[b] hieropoli in regione scitarum *perfecit* ad dominum. non natiuitas eius secundum carnem memoratur hic sed dormitatio eius hic est. ut in passionibus apostolorum legitur. iacobus frater domini et mathias apostolus hic. Iste apostolus tres filias habuit et virgines[c] et sepulta[e] sunt cum eo una a dextris et altera a sinistris[d] qui in Hieropoli[e] ciuitate sepultus' est. Pilipus hautem diaconus[f] .uii. filias profetantes habuit non pilipus apostolus.

2. *Nechtan dalta patraic* .i. filius liamna sethar patraic 7 a findabair ata.
   in lower marg.] Escomlad 7rl. .i. nechtan dalta patraic .i. ochill funchi i *conaillib.* 7 mac lemnai nominatur hic .i. mac liamna im*morro* essium .i. liamain ingen chalpraind am*áthair*. 7 ic findabair aba fil forbrú bóinne imbregaib ata nechtan dalta patraic. INtan din. bói nechtan fribas 7 patraic fria*ndacht* rochuiunig dig aritchonnairc patraic ifochraib dosum 7 aglóir anim resiu atbath

3. *Primairec chraind cruiche* .i. fágbail croiche *crist* inamsir chonsatin mac elena iarnabeth .u. bliadna dóc ar. xx. ar. cc. fodfchleth
   [in lower marg.] Primairec 7rl. prima inuentio crucis xpi. icatat buada imdai .i. intan frith inamsir chonstantin mic elena post .ccxxx. duos annos et non inuenta est crux [quando] romani cum tito et uespasiáno succenderunt[g] ierusalem et tunc absconditu est crux. et in xl° anno post passionem domini.
bas condlaid. Ronchend din ainm chondlaid art*ús* 7 is fris atberair mochonda daire
   condlaed .i. cunnail æd. .i. æd cunnail nomen eius 7 escop cille dara he 7 coin allta adúatar he ic s[c]echaib condlaid itæb liamna amuig laigen .i.

1. '*Mo-choemi*' i.e. abbot of Tír-dá-glas and Caemgen's brother was he.

2. '*Nechtan Patrick's pupil,*' i.e. a son of Liamain Patrick's sister, and in Findabair he is.
'The departure' &c. i.e. Nechtan Patrick's pupil i.e. of Cell Funchi in Couailli, and he is called Mac Lemnai i.e. he was a son of Liamain i.e. Liamain daughter of Calpurn was his mother and at Findabair Aba which is on the brink of the Boyne in Bregia is Nechtan Patrick's pupil. Now when Nechtan was dying and Patrick (present) while he was making his testament he asked for a drink, for Patrick saw . . . . . near him and his glory in heaven before he died.

3. '*The first finding of the wood of the Cross*' i.e. the finding of Christ's cross in the time of Constantine son of Helena, after having been 235 years concealed.
The first finding &c. prima inventio crucis Christi with which are many virtues i.e. when it was found in the time of Constantine son of Helena post &c.

'*Death of Condlaed.*' Ronchend was Condlaed's name at first, and he is called My-Conda of Daire.
Condlaed .i. *cunnail Aed* i.e. 'friendly Aed' was his name, and bishop of Kildare was he, and wolves devoured him at Sciaich Condlaid

[a] MS. ascention*em* [b] MS. scientium [c] MS. uirginis [d] MS. alta nasinistris [e] MS. croliss [f] MS. sepulsuss [g] MS. diac*orum* [h] uespi*siánó* sucenderetur

condlæd mac cormaic mic ængusa mic echach mic setna m. fothaid m. echach laimdeirg m. mesincorb

Primcherd brigde din connlæd 7 isaire fuair bás lasnaconaib .i. triall doroiu daroine dar sarugud mbrigde conidhi brigit roghuid dosara bás oband dísgbail forsligid 7 issed on rocomaillead.

[in lower marg.] feil mar muire 7rl .i. hacc inceptio eius ut alii putant sed in februo mense[a] uel in martio facta est illa quia post .uii. menses nata est ut innarratur uel quaelibet alia feria eius.

4. *hi pais anterini* .i. papa[e] et martiris. *mac cumine* .i. mochua mac cuind he osléib éblinne amumain
feil sillain deochain .i. hic siluain deochain.

5. *indeochain iustinus* .i. deochain iust ofidarta amuig hæi 7 ise robais[t] ciaran cluana 7 dofrangcaib do ut quidam putant .i. sanctus eustinus diaconus apud al[a]xandriam pasus est. et in gallia sancti hilari episcopi et martiris[b]
lotar laithe litha .i. laithe mís gréni na cétfresgabala
6. *fer roscrib centercai* .i. sancti iohannis apostoli ante [portam latinam] ab imperio cesaris domitiani[a] in feruentis olei[c] doleum misus est et incolumis[f] euassit.
gein mor matha mochta .i. féil ageni uel in hoc die occidit christo [leg. occisus est pro christo ?]
[In lower marg.] Fer roscrib 7rl. Matha mochta .i. machta .i. ab eo quod est mochta [leg. macto] .i. occido uel magis aucta ab eo quod est augeó. mathéus ad credendum.
7. *la breccan* .i. o echdruim brecain icocrich dail araide 7 dail riatai
indeach droma dairiu .i. ituaiscert dal naraide icocrich dal naraide 7 dal riatai ata. no is a mucraime aniarthar connacht ata daire echdroma 7 atcither bile nacille donmuig 7 intan tiagar forabiarraid isindoire nifagubar hí 7 atchuinter guth inchluig 7 insailmchedul indsin 7 nifagubar inchell fessin

8. *Victor 7 maxim* .i. in med[i]olano passi sunt.

[a] MS. indsi   [b] MS. indsis   [c] MS. martirum   [d] MS. cesari 7 dormtiano
[e] MS. olefí   [f] MS. incolonis

beside Liamain in Mag Laigen i.e. Condlaed son of Cormac, son of Oengus, son of Echaid, son of Setna, son of Fothad, son of Echaid Red-hand, son of Mesencorb.

Now Condlaed was Brigit's chief artist, and for this he found death with the wolves, to wit, he tried (to go) to Rome in violation (of an order) of Brigit's. So Brigit prayed that he might get a sudden death on his road, and this was fulfilled.

'*Son of Cumine*' i.e. Mochua son of Conn was he, from Sliab Ebllinne in Munster.
'*feast of Deacon Sillan*' i.e. he was Silvanus the deacon.

5. '*the deacon Justinus*' i.e. deacon Just of Fidarta in Mag Aei, and it is he that baptized Ciaran of Cluain, and of France was he, ut quidam &c.

'*They went on the day of festival*' i.e. the day of the solar month of the first resurrection.

'*the great birth of Mathew, the magnified*' i.e. the feast of his nativity, vel etc.

7. '*With Breccán*' i.e. of Echdruim Breccáin on the confine of Dalaradia and Dalriada.
'*In Daire Echdroma*' i.e. in the north of Dalaradia on the confine of Dalaradia and Dalriada he is. Or it is in Mucraime in the west of Connaught that Daire Echdroma is, and the tree of the church is seen from the plain, and when one goes to seek it in the oakwood it is not found, and the voice of the bell is heard, and the psalmody there, and the church itself is not found.

9. *Faillsiugud mor michil* .i. isléib gargan.
co[m]memoratio michaelis in martirio
[in lower marg.] faillsiugug*ud* (sic!) mor michil 7 rl. inne scel gargain fornithmentar sund .i. quando quaesiuit aliquis suum taurum et quando misit* sagitam in taurum et sua sagita ad semet ipsum rediuit et per hoc signum manifestatus est micahel occidenti.

escop sanctain .i. ochill duless do ut ængus dicit et nescio [ub]i est cell da less 7 is leis druim láigille itrad*r*aige .i. espoc sanctan mac do samuel chendisel. Dectir ingen muiredaig muind*eir*g mater cius in futuro. ut dixit

    Escop sanctain is mochean
    mac samúel chendisel
    dectir am*átha*ir cenmeirg
    ingen m*u*iredaig mund*eir*g

10. *Comgall buadach bendchuir* .i. cæmgell. Maelgemrid dixit

    Bendchor alaind idhan
    loc dilguda cinad
    biaid uair dobrug nanabbad

    bud ádba maddad mbirach

[in r. marg.] comgall cecinit
    Ainmne aine figell airc
    narub saithech narub goirt
    foss is fethamla conbáis
    mesrugud cr*ái*s coimet cuirp.

11. *Buaid iob* .i. do demon
cen dermat .i. dé
INtan robriss cath fordemon .i. liberatio iob de martirio liberatio iob dolentis de martirio suo qui pasus est per .xxx. annos sed temptatus est in .lxx. ix. anno ætatis suæ et postea uixit .cxl. annis.

mochritoc .i. forbrú dothra inúib dunchada aniarthar
cruimther cormac .i. sacerdos 7 innchad finniche ata. *no conmac* .i. mac con .i. sad chon alltai rodusnaltraim

[in lower marg.] Buaid iop 7rl. Cormac .i. coemserce .i. a me [tibi] et a te mihi. uel *cormac* .i. mac rucad hicarput. nunc dixit. prius dicebatur. uel *cormac* .i. filius cordis interpretatur.

i.e. in the mountain of Garganus.

'Michael's great manifestation,' &c. The sense of the story of Garganus is related here i.e. quando &c.

'*Bishop Sanctain*'.i.e. of Cell dá less is he, as Oengus says, and I know not where is Cell dá less, and he has Druim Laigille in Tradraige i.e. Bishop Sanctain son of Samuel the Lowheaded. Dectir daughter of Muiredach Redneck his mother in futuro. ut dixit :

    Bishop Sanctan and welcome,
    Son of Samuel the lowheaded,
    Dectir his mother without rust,
    Daughter of Muiredach Redneck.

10. '*Comgall of Bennchor*' .i. caem-gell 'fair hostage.' Maelgemrid said

    Bangor delightful, pure,
    A place of forgiveness of crimes.
    There will be a time for the burgh of the abbots
    It will be a dwelling of snarling dogs.

Comgall sang :
    Patience of fasting, watching the ark,
    Let him not be sated ; let him not be sour.
    Rest and stillness without folly,
    Moderation of appetite, protection of the body.

11. '*Job's victory*' i.e. over the devil.
'*without forgetfulness*' i.e. of God.
'When he won a battle over the Devil,' i.e. &c.

My-Critóc .i.e. on the brink of the Dodder in Hui-Donnchada in the west of Leinster
'*Priest Cormac* .i. sacerdos, and in Achad Finniche he is. Or Conmac i.e. son of a hound i.e. a shewolf nurtured him.
'Job's victory', &c. Cormac i.e. mutual (?) love from me to thee and from thee to me. Or *Cormac* i.e. a child (*mac*) that was born in a chariot.

---

* MS. qn. qu. uitabuit suam tarum 7 qu. nissit

Féil conaill inse cail hic .i. o inis cail aniarthar tíre conaill.

12. *Ciriacus crochda* . qui inuenit crucem^a domini et iudas nomen eius prius.

13. *noebmuinter teraci* .i. in alexandria pasi sunt.

iarserbchrochaib siraib seiser ar sé cétaib. uel sic

   Tigernach rofesiur
   sesiur ar .ui. cétaib
   .i. tigernach bairche.

14. *corona* .i. rocreid dodia . uxor alicuius militis et erat .xui. annorum quando pasa est cum uictore sancto . et sub antoni[n]o imperatore in alexandria pasi sunt.

uictor .i. milid do rig róman

conacleir cen mathim .i. ni robi iedemon ni domnaithem orru .

in lower marg.] corona 7 uictor .i. sub imperatúre antoni[n]o et sub sebastiano^b [qui in] urbe al[e]xandria a romanis constitu[tu]s est. et sub quibus isti pasi sunt.

feil chain charthaig rathin .i. mochuda liss moir. uel finall nomen fratris eius. Mochuda cecinit

   Cech manach cech esmanach
   forsaraga múr
   nibá hifernach iarmbrath
   nibarad irrún.

15. *Rath in spirtu .uii.a*. .i. ishíseo incingigis .i. quando venit spiritus sanctus super .cxx.

senaich .i. snigid .i. rosnig. nofernid in cenaculo in die penticostes in ierusalem.

tiamda saran saidbir .i. nomen disciplini (leg. discipuli?) .i. saran. mac airchuir oinis moir auil mo. caille no anib liathan amumain.

feil duiblitrech dermair .i. abb findglassi caindig itaeb atha cliath.

16. *Togairm brenaind cluana* .i. togairm brenaind cluana ferta iflaith de. id est hua allta do chiarruige luachra .i. braen find mac findlogai mic .h. allta. id est brandan. ut dixit.

   O gabais mac .h. alltai
   brenaind colín aeltai
   acht mas ferr nis mesaide
   ósin cose cluaiu fertai

^a MS. curcem

The feast of Conall of Inis Cael here i.e. from Inis Cael in the west of Tyrconnell.

'*Cyriacus the crucified*'. qui etc.

'*after long bitter crosses, six on six hundreds.*' Or thus

 'Tigernach thou shouldst know,
 six on six hundreds.'
 i.e. Tigernach of Bairche.

Corona i.e. who believed in God: uxor etc.

'*Victor*' .i. a soldier of the king of the Romans.

'*With his clergy without abatement*' i.e. the Devil had nothing to abate from them.

'*fair feast of Carthach of Rathin*' i.e. Mochuda of Les Mór, vel &c.

 Every monk, every non-monk,
 On whom my mould shall go,
 Will not be a hell-haver after Doom.
 This is not a saying in mystery.

15. '*The grace of the septenary Spirit*' i.e. this is the quinquagesima i.e. &c.

'*it showered*' i.e. it dropped or it showered *in coenaculo*, &c.

'*Timothy, Saran the wealthy,*' i.e. name of a disciple i.e. Saran son of Airchor from Iuis Mór in Hui-maie Caille or in Hui-Liathain in Munster.

'*Feast of vast Duibliter*' .i. abbot of Findglas Cainnig beside Dublin.

16. '*The calling of Brennan of Cluain*' i.e. calling of Brennan of Clonfert into God's kingdom: i.e. Hua Allta of Ciarraige Luachra i.e. Braen the Fair, son of Findlug, son of Hua Allta i.e. Brandan, ut dixit [poeta]

 Since the son of Hua Alltai took it,
 Brenann with the multitude of his flocks,
 If it is not better, it is not the worse,
 Clonfert, from that to this.

^b MS. salutio

in lower marg.] Togairm brenaind cluana 7rl. .i. brenaind mac findloga micolchon* m. ogamain m. fidchuri m. delbna m. coin m. usalic m. astomain m. moga tooth qui uocatur ciar m. fergusa m. rossa. no brenaind mac findloga m. olchon m. findchada m. gossa m. gaible m. ecni m. æltai.

Aentu choinnig is barrai
ocus brénaind dibliuaib
cipé sairniges nech díb
fertai in trír ocadígail . ,

16. *bas caid charnig firbaile* .i. cairnech othuilén ifail chenandsa 7 dobretnaib corn do.

feil an .h. suanaig .i. fidmuine ainm. fidairle 7 figus no[me]n fratris suus [leg. sui]. suanach ainm [a sonathar . forbla ainm] amathar.

[p. 90 lower marg.]
A chenel fiachach aeso barnessi

fiachu mac fiachach mic moilebressi.

Rand don æir darónsat na caiuti romarbait forcomairce hui shuanaig . Hirruss corr [dorónad] inrandsa. uair atberait cenél fiachach corub o fiachu mac neill nóigiallaig attatt fessin . ocus nihed amal atbeir inraunsa *acht* o fiachu mac [fiachach mic] moilebressi . et nescio postea . ocus inhicc intsáraigtho sin tucad ross corr do hu suanaig 7 tucad nadáine doronsat inécht beos .i. hui gille shuanaig iraitbin.

Moolbresail mac flaind léna boi forfogail . Ocus oen diasoglaib sarugud crossi hui shuanaig 7 afirchomairce hi fid ela imchleir in oesa cerdi . is de ata cross na cáinte . Hí flaith domnaill mic murchada insaruguilsin . Dórimart domnall mac murchada hui chailchin uile . Ocus foremdid breth 7 éric armet intsaraigthe corolaad forcubas hui shuanaig fessin . ISbí breth hui shuanaig indsin .i. tir inéchta dothuitim indilse domochuda 7 do hu shuanaig .i. ross corr 7 nadoine doronsat nahechta .i. hui gille suanaig 7 hui chernaig 7 hui chonín cen impód doib frifine codé brátha brúd . ,

Here B inserts 'm . alta'

The calling of Brennan of Cluain, &c. i.e. Brenann son of Findlug son of Olchu son of Ogaman son of Fidchure son of Delbna son of John son of Usaloc son of Estamon son of Mugh Tooth who is called Ciar, son of Fergus son of Rossa. Or Brenaind son of Findlug son of Olchu son of Findchath son of Gossa (?) son of Gaible son of Ecne son of Aeltae.

The unity of Cainnech and Barrae
And of Brenand, both one and other:
Whoever outrages any one of them
The miracles of the three (will be) avenging him.

16. '*Chaste death of Carnech the strong*' i.e. Cairnech of Tuilén near Kells, and of the Britons of Cornwall was he.
'*Splendid feast of Hua Suanaig*' i.e. Fidmuine his name, Fidairle and Figus his brother's name. Suanach [his grandfather's name: Forbla] his mother's name.

' O race of Fiacha, Here is your ancestry (lit. ' trace') :
Fiachu son of Fiacha Son of Mael-bressi.'

A quatrain from the satire which had been made by the satirists who were slain while under Hua Suanaig's protection. In Ross Corr this quatrain was made . For the race of Fiacha say that they themselves come from Fiacha son of Niall the Nine-Hostaged, and this is not so, as this quatrain says, but (they come) from Fiacha son of Fiacha son of Mael-bressi, *et nescio postea*. And in compensation for that outrage Ross Corr was given to Hua Suanaig and the men who committed the crime were also given i.e. the descendants of Gille Suanaig in Rathin.

Mael-bresail son of Fland Léna was a-spoiling. And one of his spoils was the outraging of Hua-Suanaig's cross and of his safe-conduct in Fid Ela, of the retinue of the artists . Hence is (the name) 'The Cross of the Satirists.' In the princedom of Domnall son of Murchad was that outrage . Domnall son of Murchad descendant of Cailchin arrested them all. And he was unable (to award) judgment and mulct because of the greatness of the outrage. So it was left to the conscience of Hua Suanaig himself. This is Hua Suanaig's judgment, to wit, the land of the crime, namely Ross Corr,

18. *Feil maire* .i. euangelista et michælis feria in alia .i. anoir apstail do i[s]naccnclaib iarscarthain fri petar.

momoedoc mor maineeh .i. momóedoc foda duin in osraigib .i. momoedoc mac midgnai m. meti m. nindedai m. nazair m. crimthain m. echach m. oengusa m. crim*th*ainn m. cath*air* máir . 7 colam mac nindeda ru. nazair m. crim*th*ainn m. echach m. oengusa m. crim*th*annáin m. cath*air* máir.

modomnoc mind buadach .i. octibrait fachtnai inosraigib

feil brain bic oehlænad .i. inúib fælan amuig laigen. alia feria michelis.

19. *cleir urbain itglana* .i. urbanus papa et martir. in roma pasus est.

20. *fuil mor marcellossi.* passio sancti marcellosi et sanctæ marcello [leg. marcellae?] suæ uirginis .i. uirgo et martir.

21. *tiamdu martir* .i. non discipulus pauli[a] sed alius.

mordrem dedi tuirind .i. dethuir[ind dé] .i. decruithnecht dé .i. quia sancti dei [triticum] sunt. no dethorim .i. tuirmim. unde dixit quidam

    Amuilind
    e[ia]romeilt moir [leg. mór] de thuirind
    niba comeilt for serblind [leg. serbaind]
    romeilt for úib cerbaill
    INgrán meiles inmuilend
    nicorea *acht* iadergthuirend
    isdo thorad inchroind máir
    fotha muilind moelodrain

.i. damac blathmaic mic æda slaine. dunchad 7 cathal qui jugulati[b] sunt a marcano laigin-ensi in quidam preterio (*sic*). isfrisin in damac sin blathmaic athernir indergeruithnecht.

21. *colman lobar* .i. omuig eo indál cais.

barrfind droma cuilind .i. barrfind mac muiredaig mic echach m. conaill m. neill .ix. giallaig 7 itir cheall ata . *no* barrfind mac

[a] MS. paullí

to fall in ownership to S. Mochuda and to Hua Suanaig and (also) the persons who committed the crime (namely) the descendants of Gille Suanaig and Hui Chernaig and the Hui Chonín without reversion to them or their families till the day of Doom.

18. '*Feast of Mark*' i.e. the evangelist, etc. i.e. the honour of an apostle (was paid) to him in his tribes after parting with Peter.

'*My Maedóc great, treasurous*' i.e. My-Maedoc of Fid Duin in Ossory i.e. My-Maedóc son of Midgnae son of Nindid, son of Nazar, son of Crimthann, son of Eochaid, son of Oengus, son of Crimthann, son of Cathair Mór and Colam, son of Nindid, son of Nazar, son of Crimthan, son of Eochaid, son of Oengus, son of Crimthannán, son of Cathair Mór.

'*My-Domnóc a victorious diadem*' i.e. at Tipra Fachtnai in Ossory.

'*Feast of Bran the Little from Claenad*' i.e. in Hui-Faelan in Mag-Laigen.

'*A great company of God's wheat*' i.e. of God's *tuirenn* i.e. of God's wheat, because the saints are *Dei triticum*. Or *dethorim* i.e. I enumerate, *unde dixit quidam*:—

    O mill!
    Though thou hast ground much of wheat,
    (This) was not a grinding of oats:
    Thou groundest on Cerball's grandsons.
    The grain the mill grindeth
    Is not oats, but it is red wheat:
    Of the fruit of the great tree is
    The feed of Mael-odrain's mill.

i.e. two sons of Blathmac, son of Aed Slaine, Dunchad and Cathal, qui etc.

It is of those two sons of Blathmac 'the red wheat' is said.

21. '*Colman the leper*,' i.e. of Mag Eo in Dál Cais.

'*Barrfind of Druim Cuilind*,' i.e. Barrfind, son of Muiredach, son of Echaid, son of Conall, son of Niall the Nine-hostaged, and in Tír Cell

[b] MS. uigilati

muiredaig m. fiach*ach* m. neill .ix. giall*aig*

22. *cechaing ainim ronain .i. olaind ronain find inuib cchach ulad.*
[in marg. at 26 May.] Cechaing ainim ronain 7 rl .i. Ronán find *mac* saráin m*ic* colgan [colcon B] m*ic* thuathail cruindbeoil a quo .h. cruiudbeoil m*ic* fédlim*t*hi m. fiach*ach* cassan m. collai dáchrich m. ech[ach] doimplen.

Boethine mac findach .i. oinis boethine aniarth*ar* laigen 7 créd ingen ronain rig laigen m*átha*ir boethine . 7 ind*ál* mesincorb beos dó *iarum*
[in marg. at 27 May.] Boethine mac findaig. óinis boethine iniarth*ar* laigen. oc*us* créd ingen ronain rig laigen m*átha*ir boethine m*ic* findaig. oc*us* is*a*ml*aid* rogenair boethín. .i. Findach foglaid domla ambarr sciach osintibraid fort*ii* m*er*li f*or*sincill la nand. Cotánic cred diadm*a*d alám dontip*ra*it. Otchounaire finnach hi. sanntaigis inóg coruthuitt toil achuirp uad forsiungas mbiroir boi inatiadnaise. Ithid iarum aningeu ingass forsamboi inchoimp*er*t . conid desin rogenair boethín . ut dixit [poeta]

> Cred robo maith in ben
> ingen ronain rig laigen
> cona coemchill gnathaig glain
> m*átha*ir boethín m*ic* findaig
> Finnach fóglaid robui aggait
> isinsciaich osintip*ra*it
> diandechu*id* dinnm*a*d alam
> créd rindbalc ingen ronán .
> Orosáill infoglaid féig
> for ingin ronáin roréid
> snigis ní do thoil a chuirp
> forsin ugas mbiroir mblathguirt
> Ithid aningen ingass
> forsambí inchoimp*er*t choimdess
> conid desin saer in gleo
> rogénair boethin bithbeo .

23. *epectini* .i. [nomen] p*ro*prium martiris.

24. *Augustin intescop* .i. librorum .i. dalta grigoir róma 7 espoc saxan he .i. librorum. Augustinus migrauit ad dominum in septuagesimo anno ætatis suæ in episcopatu* vero .xl. anno ætatis suæ .

---

he is. Or Barrfind, son of Muiredach, son of Fiacha, son of Niall the Nine-hostaged.

22. '*Ronan's soul went*,' i.e. from Lann Ronain Find, in Hui-Echach of Ulster.
Ronau's soul went, &c., i.e. Ronan the Fair, son of Saráu, son of Colgan, [Colcu?] son of Tuathal [son of] Cruindbel (a quo Hui-Cruindbeoil), son of Feillimid son of Fiacha Cassan, son of Colla dá Chrich son of Echaid Doimplen.

'*Boethine son of Finda*,' i.e. of Inis Boethine in the west of Leinster, and Créd, daughter of Ronan, King of Leinster, and in Dál Mesincorb, moreover, he was afterwards.
Boethine, son of Findach of Inis Boethine in the west of Leinster, and Créd, daughter of Ronan, King of Leinster, was mother of Boethine son of Findach ; and thus was Boethine born, to wit—Findach, a robber, chanced to be at the top of a thorntree over the well designing (?) a robbery on the church one day, and Créd came to the well to wash her hands. When Findach beheld her, virginem avide expetivit, et cecidit semeu eius super nasturtii surculum coram eam. Tune edit puella surculum super quem fuit semen, and thence was Boethine born. *ut dixit poeta* :—

> Cred, good was the woman,
> Daughter of Ronán, King of Leinster,
> With her lovable church, constant, pure,
> Mother of Boethín son of Findach.
> Findach, a robber, was stealing
> In the thorntree over the well,
> When to wash her hands went
> Créd, the starstrong daughter of Ronán.
> When the keen robber looked
> On the daughter of Ronán the smooth,
> Aliquid seminis ejus stillavit
> Super surculum nasturtii amari.
> Comedit puella surculum
> Super quem fuit semen,
> And thence, noble the decision,
> Was born Boethín the Everliving.

'*Augustine the bishop*,' i.e. of the books, i.e. a pupil of Gregory of Rome, and bishop of the Saxons was he.

* MS. episcopata

ermis abb .i. papa.
colman inmain aige . nescio ubi est.
[in lower marg.] Augustin intescop 7 rl. Colman nescio ubi est hic sed a[lii] dicunt conid he intress colmau mor mide .i. colman comraire 7 colman mac luachain olaiud mic luachau 7 colman ela olaind ela itir chell.
aidbe tuathach tire .i. abb tire da glas 7 isand ata achell fri himlech aneass. no ambrechmuig hicérn hiniarthar chonnacht. no is áidben ainm innócib fessin.

in lower marg.] Aidbe .i. æd beo [ab] eo quod ui[u]us est in mirabilibus .i. bituathaib for tir iconnachtaib ata. brechmag no[me]n ciuitatis. uel erber nomeu illi[u]s iarsanni uair berbaid (leg. airberid?) cech ni imanguidther.

25. *feil iohannis* .i. euangilista .i. dormitatio inéfis ['in Epheso'] in Asia minore ut* alii putant . vel alia feria.
[in lower marg.] Lx. xi°. anno scribsit iohannes euangilium et a domitiano[b] in dolium feruentis* olei proiectus liber abscessit[d] postea de[me] anno ætatis suæ dormiuit.
dionis derb dana. ciculi
[in lower marg.] Díonis .i. episcopus med[i]olauensis. uel landan nomen proprium .i. ochluain aird naliatan iciarraig hái et ideo dicebatur litana quia letanias canebant .i. hymnos* et psalmos et ferunt eos .iiii.[f] germanos et episcopos fuisse[g].i. colman landan ciaran garban et de familia comgall fuerunt.
dunchad iæ huare .i. dúuchad mac ciunfælad mic maelchaba mic æda m. ainmirech m. setna m. fergusa ceudfota m. conaill gulban m. ueill .ix. giallaig

26. *airitiu colmain stellain* .i. othir daglas stellan[e] [in marg.] Hace est series[b] abbatum tire daglas 7 cluana eidnech .i. colum nateæim finntan colman stelle . ut est de caeli arce colmani nomine stellarum sacri fulgentis . ut rubique (*sic*) fintan moeldub nateæim
beccán carais figle .i. ochluain mobecóc amuscraige breogain himmmain no ictig .h. conaill inúib briuin chualann

'Augustine the bishop' &c. i.e. Colman : nescio ubi est hic, but some say that he is the third Colman Mór of Meath i.e. Colman of the coffer and Colman son of Luachan of Land Mic Luachain and Colman Ela of Land Ela in Tir Cell.
'*Aidbe the lordly of Tir*' i.e. abbot of Tír-dá-glass, and there is his church to the south of Imlech. Or it is in Brechmag in Céra in the west of Connaught. Or Aidben is the name of the saint himself.
Aidbe i.e. a live fire, *ab eo quod viuus est in mirabilibus* i.e. in the tribes of Fir tíre in Connaught he is. Brechmag ['Wolf-field'] nomen civitatis. Vel *.Erber* is his name because he grants everything for which he is supplicated.

'Dionysius' i.e. a bishop of Milan. Or Landan a proper name i.e. from Cluain na Liatan in Ciarraige Ai *et ideo* &c.

'*Dunchad of chilly Ui.*' i.e. Dunchad son of Ceunfaelad, son of Maelcaba, son of Aed, son of Ainmire, son of Setna, son of Fergus Longhead, son of Conall Gulban, son of Niall the ninehostaged.
26. '*Reception of Colman Stellan* :' of Tír dá glas (was) Stellan. This is the line of abbots of Tír-dá-glas and Cluain eidnech, i.e. Colum etc.

'*Beccán who loved vigils*' i.e. of Cluain Mobecóc in Muscraige Breogain in Munster or at Tech hui Conaill in Hui-Briuin Chualann.

* MS. aissia inut   b MS. dominatio   c MS. fereuentis   d MS. abscetit
e MS. canebantur .i. omnes   f MS. ferteros .uii.   g MS. germanus 7 episcopus fuise
h MS. sires

in left marg.] Becan mac luigdech m. thuathan m. æda m. fergusa m. cogain mc. noill .ix. giallaig
27. aculius ... conachleir .i. proponsi(?)
28. german .i. maigistir patraic
29. lacumain .i. ben .i. uirgo indail mbuinde ata din . cell ingen aillen auíb dróna beos

Cumain ingen aillen mic bredan mic ochach mic briain m. enna m. cathbad m. ochach gunnat m. feic. do dal fiatach iudsin

ingen aillen inmain .i. ben ele odaire ingen aillen inaird ulad
30. noebaspal arfiadat .i. crist isna fiaduaise ata
gein tomais cenoipne. tanic ainbuid no nirbo (f)and he innach foirg no sáibe
pais eutaic . Entaic .i. papa
31. lupais petronille .i. filia petri apostoli 7 isí inpetronilla sin fuair cend poil apstail iarnabeth .xl. bliadna a nerone fodichleith

in lower marg.] Cosad crisogoni 7 rl. petronillae[a] .i. petronilla filia petri apostoli uirgo fuit quae grigorio atestante absque ferri incisione[b] in pace quieuit . Petronilla[c] filia petri apostoli uirgo fuit quae post multa miracula ieiunis et orationibus necnon eleemosynario caetorisquo[d] sanctis actibus dedita cum saucta uirgine felicula collactanea sua[e] post sacramentum corporis et sanguinis christi susceptum so reclinans in lectulo[f] emisit spiritum et sic flaccum coniugem[g] eius potentem cuasit .

Becán son of Lugaid, son of Tuathan, son of Aed, son of Fergus, son of Eogan, son of Niall the Nine-hostaged.

28. 'German' i.e. Patrick's master.
29. 'With Cumain' i.e. a woman i.e. virgo: in Dal Buinde she is. There is a Cell Ingen Aillén in Hui-Drona, besides.

Cumain, daughter of Aillen son of Baedan, son of Echaid, son of Brian, son of Enna, son of Cathbu, son of Echaid Gunnat, son of Fiacc, of Dal Fiatach.

'Daughter of lovable Aillén' i.e. another woman from Daire Ingen Aillén in Ard Ulad.
30. 'Our Lord's holy apostle' i.e. Christ, it is in his prescnce he is.
'The nativity of Thomas without suddenness.' His proper time had come. Or he was not weak as regards any anger or falschood.
31. 'With Petronilla's passion' i.e. a daughter of Apostle Peter, and it is that Petronilla who found the head of Paul the apostle after its having been forty years concealed from Nero.

[a] MS. petronialae [b] MS. ferro incipione [c] MS. Petronillai [d] MS. elimoysi narum coterique
[e] MS. felocula collectien suo [f] MS. lectula [g] MS. placcum coniugium

RAWL. 505, fo. 213, a.	LAUD, 610, fo. 65.	LEBAR BRECC, p. 89.
1. Oid menman feil tecla ardlig din achetal cosluag adbul huasal hikl. iuin etan	1. Oid menman feil tecla ardlig din achetal cosluag adbul uassal hikl. iuin etan	1. Oid menman feil teclai ardlig dun acetul coslog adbul uasal ikl. iuin etan
2. Erasmus intepscop anbreo combruth brige bert cocri*st* cleir mbuada trichet*ᵃ* molbtach mile	2. Herosmus intepscop anbreo combruth mbrigi bert cocri*st* cleir mbuada tri chet molbtach mili	2. Erasmus intescop anbreo combruth brige bert cocrist cleir mbuada ,ccc. molbtach mile
3. Mil cri*st* hicrich nerend ard nainm tartuinn tredan	3. Mil cri*st* icrich neirenn ardainm tar tuind trethan	3. Mil *crist* icrich nerenn ard ainm dar tuind trethan
coemgen caid cain cathar oglind dalind lethan	cremgein caid cáin caitheir inglind dalind lethain	coemgen caid cain caithfer anglind dalind lethan
4. Luid apollinaris doflaith de fordirgi connchleir conuagi latarmrith martini	4. Luid appollináris doflaith de fordirge comorslúag conáni latarmrith martini	4. Luid apollonaris do flaith dé fordirge comor cleir conuaige latarmbreith martine
5. Martra marciani morsus ilar mbuada aill feir moir maith dine	5 Martra marciani morsus ilar mbuada aill fir moir maithdine	5. Martra marciani morsus hilar mbuadai aill fir moir maith dine
aill ingena huaga	aill ingeine huaga	aill ingena uaga
6. Huagcesad amanti morgnim mafolugai mœl aithehen conglanboil luid fothalmain tugai	6. Ogcessad amanti morgnim cia foluga muelaithgin coglanbail luid fothalma*i*n tugai	6. Huag cesad amanti morgnim mad fodluga moelaithgen conglanbail luid fothalmain tuba

1. Music of the mind is Thecla's feast; it behoves us to sing of her with a host vast and noble in the front of June's calends.

2. Erasmus the bishop, a splendid flame with ardour of might!— took unto Christ a victorious traiu—three hundred praiseworthy thousands.

3. A soldier of Christ into Ireland's border: a high name over the sea's wave: Coemgen, chaste, fair warrior, inᵇ the glen of the two broad linns.

4. Apollinaris went to God's kingdom straightway, with a great train with virginity,ᶜ at Martin's translation.

5. Marcianus' martyrdom: a multitude of gifted onesᵈ greatened it: some mighty men, a goodly number, others virginal maidens.

6. Amantius' perfect suffering, an overgreat deed if thou conceal it: Moelnithgen with pure goodness went under ground to a shelter.

ᵃ l. trichait   ᵇ D 'of'
ᶜ B. "with a great host with splendour." D. "with his train with virginity."
ᵈ literally 'a multitude of prize'   ᵉ *mór* here (as sometimes μέγας) has a bad sense attached to it.

[JUNE 7-12.]

RAWL. 505, fo. 215, a.	LAUD, 610, fo. 65.	LEBAR BRECC, p. 89.
7. Togairm poil inmartir iarmorgnim cotalcai feil coluim cenšotlai inmormeicc huiartai	7. Togairm poil inmartir iarmorgnim cotailci feil cholmain cenelccai inmair meicc hui airti	7. Togairm poil inmartir iarmorgnim cotalccai feil colaim cenelcca inmoir maic hui artai
8. Airitiu indnocib ioib iarmbuaid ocus lauchad feil medran mor ndidnad feil murchon comarath	8. Airitin inn nóib ióib iarnbuaid 7 banchad feil medhrain mor ndidhnadh feil murchon comorrath	8. Airitiu innoem ioib iarmbuaid 7 banchath feil medrain mor ndidnad feil murchon comorrath
9. Ronsnadat don bithlaith imbithbi les lainrech boethene ard ainglech columcille caindlech [a]	9. Ronsnaidet donbithlaith imbithbi les laindrech baithini ard aingleach colum cilli caindlech	9. Ronsnadut donbithlaith imbithbi less laindrech baethine ard ainglech colam cille caindlech
10. Condrecat forenchoi cenmair dodafarnaic primfeil maire mind nardirce lafeil mbuada[i]ch barnaibb	10. Condrecat foroenchói ceinmair dodonfairnic primfeil maire mind ordraic lafeil buadaig barnaibb	10. Condrecat forœnchœ cein mair dotofarnaic primfeil mairce mind erdaire lafeil buadaig barnaip
11. Basilla inbuadach bretha huan hifailti feil meicc thail indnoebdai lapais furtunati	11. Basilla inbuadach [b] bretha huaind hifailti feil maic thail indnoemdai lafeil furtunaiti	11. Basilla inbuadach bretha nainn hifailte feil maic thail innoebdai lapais furtunati
12. Feil incredail chæmain diansantlethan slonnad torannan [c] buan bannach darlcir lethan longach	12. Feil incredail choemain diansantlethan slonnad torannan buan bandach darler lethan longach	12. Feil inchredail choemain diansanctlethan slondud torandan buan bannach darler lethan longach

7. The Martyr Paul's calling, after a great deed with starkness. The feast of Colomb without evil,[d] the great descendant of Artae.

8. The reception of the holy Job after victory and white battle : the feast of Medrán a great solace, the feast of Murchú with great grace.

9. May they protect us to the eternal kingdom, wherein is ever a lucid light, Bacthíne high, angelic, Colomb Cille the lustrous !

10. They met on one road : happily they ended : the chief feast of Mark a conspicuous diadem, with the triumphant feast of Barnabas.

11. Basilla the victorious was borne from us into bliss : the feast of Mac Táil the sainted at Fortunatus' passion.

12. The feast of the pious Coemán, who was named vehement Sanct-lethan. Torannán lasting, deedful, over a wide, shipful sea.

[a] MS. caindlecl [b] MS. mbuadach [c] MS. torocnnan [d] D. 'vainglory'.

Rawl. 503, fo. 215.	Laud, 610, fo. 65.	Lebar Brecc, p. 89.
13. Labartholoin primda itmeirb manichuala cechaing huan coriga	13. Laparrtalon mbresta atmeirb manichnala cechaing huaind corriga	13. Laparthalon mbresta atmer mane chuala cechaing uainn corigda
mac nissi caid cluana	mac nissi cáid cluana	mac nissi caid cluana
14. Condrecat diblinaib foroenlith ler sluagach nem mac huibirn brigach labenedicht mbuadach	14. Condrecat diblinib foroenlith ler sluagach noemmac hui birn brigach labenedicht mbuadach	14. Condrecat diblinaib foroenlith ler sluagach nem mac hui birn brigach labenidacht mbuadach
15. Bendacht forsingerait carais crist cofírbuil lasluid slog commorgail uictus maccan mirbuil	15. Bendacht forsinngerait carais crist cofírbail lasluid sluag comorgail uictus maccan mirbail	15. Bennacht forsungerait carais crist cofírbail lasluid sluag comorbailᵃ uitus maccan mirbail
16. Mogerait ingiric immaslecht sluag sobail nifrith set na samail [dó] domaccaib domain	16. Mogerait ingiric immoslecht sluagh sobail nifrith set nasamail dó domaccaib domain	16. Mogerait ingiric imaslecht sluag sobail nifrith set nasamail do domaccaib domain
17. INdoss oir oschrichaib ingrian án huastuathaib congreit rig balec brathair cain mil moling luachair	17. INdos oir huas crichaibᵇ ingrian an uastuathaib congreit righ balc brathair cain mil moling luachair	17. INdoss oir uas crichaib ingrian an uastuathaib congreit rig balc brathair cain mil moling luachair
18. Laboethan finn fechtnach furutbran cofegi meice moenain conuagi o lainn ligaig leri	18. Labáithin find fechtnach furudran coféigi meice moenain conani olaind lighaid lére	18. Laboethin find fechtnach furodrau cofegi mec moinan conuaige olaind ligaig leri

13. With Bartholomew the activeᶜ—thou art weak if thou hear not,—from us to the Kings (of heaven)ᵈ went Mac Nissi the chaste of Cluain.

14. They both meet on one festival, a hostful sea—Nem the vigorous descendant of Bern, with Benedict the victorious.

15. A blessing on the champion, who loved Christ with true goodness! along with whom went a host with great valour, Vitus the marvellous child.

16. My champion, the Quiricus, round whom was slain a holy host: the equal or like of him was not found of the world's sons.

17. The bush of gold over borders! the splendid sun over territories ! white champion of the King, strong brother, fair soldier, Moling of Luachair !

18. With fair, happy Boethín, Furodrán with keenness, Moenán's sons with virginity,ᵉ of beautiful Lann Lére.

ᵃ l. comorgail   ᵇ MS. críhcaib   ᶜ D. 'preëminent'   ᵈ A 'royally'   ᵉ D. 'splendour'

RAWL. 505, fo. 215.	LAUD, 610, fo. 65.	LEBAR BRECC, p. 90.
19. Luid afuil forocnu fiadsluagaib combrnissi dorig batir huissi gerbassi protassi	19. Luid afuil fórócnu fiadsluagaib combrnissi doudrig batarussi gerbaissi protaissi	19. Luid afuil forocnu fiadsluagaib combrassi donrig batar uissi geruassi protassi
20. Pais poil ciriaci cosindunud marsin fielan cosinbuaidsin intamlabar ansin	20. Pais poil ciriaci cosindunad mársin fielan cosinbuaidsin intamlobar ansain	20. Pais poil ciriaci cosindunad marsin foelan cosin mbuaidsin intamlabor ansin
21. Ainle sochla sluagach frismbrucht ammuir inlach (sic) cormacc bacain clerech hua lithan inligach	21. Ainle sochla sluagach frismbruchta muir milach cormacc bacain cleirech hua liathain inligach	21. Ainle sochla sluagach frismbruchta muir milach cormacc bacnin clerech .h. liathain inligach
22. Laiacob nalphei danocht cet chiar ngelda feil fir nadchar corplen cronan fortren ferna[a]	22. Laiacob nalphei danocht cet cleir ngelda feil fir nadchar corplen cronan fortren ferna	22. Lahincop nalpeii danocht .c. cleir geldai féil fir natear corplen cronan fortren fernai
23. Foraithmet mochoe nifail ardonsela insab socla sona ona[e]ndruim donrema	23. Foraithmet mochuc nifil ardonsela insab sochla sona onoeindruim donrema	23. Fornithmet mochoe nifuil ardonsela insab sochla sona onoendruim donrema
24. Riggein iohain babtaist masuleir ronfeithiss latathchor cenaithis iohain meicc do effeiss	24. Riggein ioin babtaist masoleir ronfethis latathchor cenaithis eoin maicc doeflis	24. Riggein ioin bauptaist masaleir ronfethis latachor cenaithis ioin mec doeflis
25. Feil sinchill feil telle batir crend arda lamluoe glangelda grian liss[b] moir dealba	25. Feil sinchill feil teille batar crind arda lamluoe anorba grian lis moir de alba	25. Feil sinchill feil telli batar erind arda lamluoe glau geldai grian liss moir dealbai
26. ISadabal (sic) acesad apais olrostaurus	26. ISadbul acessad apais olrusturus	26. ISadbul achesad apáis ol rostuirius

19. Their blood went throughout (the earth's) roads before hosts with readiness: unto the King (of heaven) Gervasius and Protasius were obedient.

20. The passion of Paul and Cyriac with that great host. Foelán with that victory, that splendid mute.

21. Ainle famous, host-having, against whom burst the monster-abounding sea. Cormac was a fair cleric, the beautiful descendant of Liathan.

22. With James son of Alpheus, twice eight hundreds, a fair train, the feast of a man who loved not bodily ease, mighty Cronan of Ferns.

23. Mochoe's commemoration is not what escapes us. May the champion famous, happy, of Noendruim, protect us!

24. John Baptist's royal birth, if thou art pious thou hast kept it, at the removal without disgrace of John the child to Ephesus.

25. Sinchell's feast, Telle's feast: they were heights in Ireland,[c] with Moluóc pure, fair,[d] sun of Lismore of Alba.

26. Vast is their suffering,[A] their passion,

[a] MS. feran   [b] MS. liis   [c] D. "of Ireland"   [d] B, "a splendid heritage"   [A] "his suffering"

RAWL. 505, fo. 215.	LAUD, 610, fo. 65.	LEBAR BRECC, p. 90.
caingrian gallicanus iohannis is paulus	caingrian gallicanus iohandis 7 paulus	cain grian gallicanus iohannis 7 paulus
27. Ropromtha tremartra ata morthruim threthain	27. Rofromtha triamartrai ata mortrom trethan	27. Ropromtha tremartra atamorthruim trethain
secht ṅderbrathir caithir	secht ṅderbratha[i]r cathir	.uii. nderbrathair cathir
hiruaim^b letha lethain	irroim letha lethain	iruaim letha lethain
28. Hillecoin moir mide cruimmene conani forcenlith colleire paiss find fabiani	28. Ileccain moir mide crumini conáni forcenlith colleire pais find faluiani	28. Hilleccuin moir mide crumine conani forcenlith coleri páis find ḋouiani
29. Feil poil ocus phetair conaidbli angretha nistarcai deilm catha feil fo[r]bruinnib betha	29. Feil poil ocus petair conaidbli aṅgretha niterca deilm catha feil for bruindib betha	29. Feil poil 7 petair conaidble angretha nistarca deilm catha feil for bruindib betha
30. Buaid soli istiamdai tamtiu ioib inmain benait glass find fothmein forsluagad iuin ilmain	30. Buaid zoili 7 tiamdai taimthiu ioib ilmain benait glas find foidmin forsluaiged iuin inmain	30. Buaid stoli 7 tiamda taimthiu ioib inmain benait glas find fodmin forsluaiged iuin ilmain

for I have searched into it, Gallicanus, a fair sun, Johannes and Paulus.

27. They were proven by martyrdom : they are great heavy seas : seven brothers, champions, in Rome of broad Latium.

28. In great Leccan of Meath, Crumíne with splendour, on one festival with piety, Flavianus' (leg . Fabianus' ?) fair passion.

29. The feast of Paul and Peter with the vastness of crying unto them : the noise of battle which is on the world's breasts surpasseth it not.

30. The victory of Zoilus and Timothy (and) the bed-death of lovable Job strike a fair fetter at the end on the hosting of opulent^b June.

GLOSS FROM THE LEBAR BRECC, pp. 89, 90.

1. (1) *oid* .i. ceol *no* airfitiud *no* bindius [in r. marg.] Oid menman 7rl. .i. uigid. bid din. oid .i. ughud *no* aithiugud menman . *no* oid .i. indethmig .i. tabair dotaire. *no* oid . bindig. bid din. oda [ψἰή, Lat. *ode, oda*] .i. adbond . et unde dicitur od .i. binnes . et melodia . ut dicitur

Æs dana inrig corinnib
conacliaraib ceol binde
cid bind lacach dib a od
ni choistfemne anairfiteod

The artists of the king with melodies,
With their trains music-sweet,
Though his (own) song is sweet to each of them,
We will not hear their playing.

.i. tabrad domenma dia hoid . *no* oid dotmenmain . arbid oid .i. ugud menman *no* bindes menman 7 comad oid quasi od ab oda focside^c . *no* oid .i. nanaig dotmenmain .i. tabair dotaire .i. arisni mor libertas et natiuitas cius [h]odie uel in hoc die. (2) *acetul* .i. anisnes *no* acetchantain (4) .i. in fronte huius mensis

^a MS. hiruann   ^b B. ' dear '   ^c MS. asin od hab oda foense

2. (3) *bert* .i. rug
3. (1) *mil crist* .i. milid *crist* he (2) .i. isard aainm cur*ó* achlú tartúind 7 tarfairrge trethnaig .i. ainbthenaig (3) *coemgen* .i. coem ingein *no* coem agin .i. abriathra *no* agnúis *caid* .i. sanctus *caithfer* .i. fer catha *no* cathárdai
4. (3) *comuaige* .i. cocómlaine
5. (2) .i. romorustar imad mbuada marcianum (3) *aill* .i. araill dib (4) .i. aliæ uirgines
6. (1) *huag* .i. cómlan (2) *mad foilluga* .i. cid adluige dogué *no* mafoilgi iat isinraud *no* diaceli *no* diasena *no* diatoingit doine he (4) *tuba* (leg. *tuga*?) .i. hitig *no* foiliten
7. (1) *inmartir* .i. relicionis (2) *cotalceai* .i. cotrcisi *no* cocalmatus *no* cotcindius (3) *cencleca* .i. cenoleni
8. (2) *banchath* .i. nidergmartra[a]
9. (2) *laindrech* .i. taitnemach
10. (1) *forcnchæ* .i. focul albanach (2) *ceinmair* .i. mogenair ut dicitur

  Céin mair[b] naluing indfota Happy in his long vessel is he
  ocambiat alennada With whom are his comrades (?),
  ocimram ard allata Rowing a high . . . . (?)
  iarningnais amennata[c] After absence from his home.

dotofarnaic .i. tarnic *no* tarraid iat
11. (2) *brethu* .i. rucad
12. (3) *bannach* .i. gnimach in bono bannach .i. senex fit bannach .i. a bono band leis sair 7 bann ele les anair
13. (1) *bresta* .i. primda *no* irgna (2) *atmer* .i. atmeta *no* atmeirb (3) *cechaing* .i. roching *corigda* [leg. *corriga*] .i. cennuintir nime
14. (1) *conttrccat* .i. tribus nominibus[d] uocatur
15. (3) *luid* .i. roescumlai (4) *mirbail* .i. fertach he
16. (3) *gerait* .i. inglic *no* intanrud *girie* .i. dimitium (sic) (2) *imaslecht* .i. rosliged *no* imasloiten *sobail* .i. sobeoil .i. beoil maithe occa .i. maith auirlabra .i. confitentes dominum in tempore passionis sue . *no* sobalaid .i. maith ambolad intan rotoebad staise abroind talman
17. (3) *congreit* [.i.] anroth .i. retæb congreit *rig bale brathair* .i. tren inrig is brathair dúinne (4) *mil* .i. milid
18. (2) *cofegi* .i. focchair friademon (4) *ligaig* .i. alaind *no* cendais
19. (1) *forocnu* .i. foroencho[n]aire (2) *combrassi* .i. coslatra *no* cosolam (3) *batar uissi* .i. batar uiss *no* umla *no* innraice *no* comadais
20. (1) *poil ciriaci* propria (nomina) uel duo nomina unius personae[e] (2) *cosindunad* .i. cosinsluagud .i. frecra menman hic .i. úimradud himenmain prius (4) *amlabor* .i. nemlabar *an* .i. fir
22. (3) *corplen* .i. corp sleman *no* laxu *no* sadaile
23. (2) .i. aranéla uainn cenaisnes . *no* nisfil ocula cenachuimniugud
24. (2) *ronfethis* .i. rothaiscis *no* rochuimnigis *no* rochometais .i. adáine legfas inlebar vel ratione[f] dicit ad mentem
25. (2) roptar uaisle ineirinn iat (3) *geldai* .i. taitnemach
26. (2) .i. arrothuiress apáis .i. ga*ll*icanus iohannis 7 paulus
27. (1) *ropromtha* .i. derbtha (2) .i. istromfairrgi mor int (3) *cathir* .i. catharda *no* cathfir .i. fir cathacha fri génntib .i. fridemnaib 7 dualchib *no* sainred ainm[g] ['proprium nomen'] .i. cclas for leith fil oculaid[h] [*no*] chathalacdai cat (4) *letha* .i. a nomine latium .i. leatha

---

[a] MS. indergmartra : cf. Rawl. 505 : *ni tre dergmartra romarbad*. [b] .i. mogénair
[c] .i. úit inamianach lais beith [d] MS. inomnibus : the gloss seems misplaced.
[e] MS. proprium [f] MS. rōa [g] MS. saū nō [h] 'a church apart which Ulstermen have.'

28. (4) *find* .i. taitnemebi
29. (2) .i. sochaide ocanatach .i. grith caich chuca .i. angaire (3) .i. ni derscaig noch frecra di dar deilm inchatha sin arimat naslóg tocait don félsin. *no ni derscaid tre fogur sloig ric athaisse* (4) *forbruindib betha* .i. forbruindiud betha hominum *uel* uita
30. (2) *taimthiu* .i. nóe fri badart (3) *benait* .i. doberat *glas find* .i. adat solus *fodmin* .i. foderiud .i. ut dicitur fodeime *no oband no solam no glic no foger* .i. iter imdia [*in lower marg.*] Fodmin din. .i. fod[e]min . [amal] asbert in fili

> INgoeth targuaire mucais
> tairberfe donach[a] airrged
> isfotmin rchathloechaib
> imdib tǫthaib inaidchib

.i. imespartain 7 imiairmergi 7 octecht doneclais hinglind dalachai [*in top marg.*] unde quidam dixit

> INgoeth tar guaire mucais   The wind over roughness of . . .
> tairb*ir* fidu nacaircheid   Casts down woods . . . . .
> isfodmin friabathlǫchu   Somewhat bitter is it to whilom-heroes
> indib trathaib inaidchib   At two hours in the nights.

.i. isfoger imespartain 7 imiarmergi octecht   i.e. it is somewhat sharp at vespers and at
donecla*is* hinglind dalacho   nocturn, when going to the church iu Glenda-
                                                 lough.

NOTES FROM THE LEBAR BRECC, pp. 89, 90.

1. *tculai* .i. uirgo fuit et martyrio coronata est.
2. *Erasmus* .i. antioch[i]ae a dioclitiano imperatore passus est.
3. *coemgen* . Coemlog nomen patris eius . Cocmell nomen matris eius . Coemau 7 Natcoemi nomina duorum fratrum[b] eius . Aibind sororcula[c] eorum.

> Coeman coemgin mochoemi   Coemán, Coemgin, Mo-choeme,
> tri mic choema choemille   Three lovable sons of Coemell.
> bamaith intriar bᵣnthar   Good was the triad of brothers,
> tri mic máthar aibinne   Three sons of a delightful mother.

.i. áibend anderbsiur   Aibenn was their sister.
glind dalind lethan .i. díloch filet and 7 isatlethan iat   '*ylen of two broad linns*' i.e. two lakes are therein, and broad are they.

4. *apollonaris* .i. discipulus petri apostoli et episcopus [hi]erapolis ciuitatis in asia[d].
morcleir .i. xxx . lutri mile   '*a great train*' i.e. thirty with three thousand .

tarmbreith martine .i. abreith in episcopatum   '*Martin's translation*' i.e. the carrying of him

---

[a] Read *tairber fedo nach*   [b] MS. fratrem   [c] MS. soror clui   [d] ciuitas in aissia

[uel translatio corporis eius de sepulchro in alium locum—Fr.] .i. athaissi alloc hilloc .i. tuctha athaissi asinmainistir inerbail dochum nacathrach

5. *marciani* .i. in egipto.
ingena uaga .i. agatha cum ali[i]s uirginibus.
6. *amanti* .i. nescio ubi ᵃ est .
moelaithgen .i. othig moelaithgin icairpri hua ciardai . *no* amuig locha aniarthar breag

7. *colaim* .i. mocholmog droma moir in huib echach ulad
8. *airitiu* .i. ad caelum in hoc die exiit.ᵇ
medrain .i. medran 7 murchu filii ᶜ hui mic toni et nescio ubi sunt isti .i. medran odaire mic marga
murchon .i. ciuitas cius inuib foelan .i. mac hui mathcene
9. *bæthine* . . . *colam cille* .i. boethine mac brenaind mic fergusa mic conaill gulban mic neill .ix. giallaig . 7 colam cille mac fedlimithe mic fergusa . crimthan ainm coluim cille prius .

Eithne din . ingen dima mic noe mic etine mic coirpri filead mic oilella mair mic brecain mic feic mic daire barraig mic cathair mair máthair coluim cille . Cumine din . 7 minchlot᾽i 7 sinech . tri seathra choluim chille

in lower marg.]

Colum pro simplicitate eius dictus est . cille .i. arthinchtain comenice onchill inroleg asalmu liecómdail nalenab cornocus . bahead adhertissen etarru intanic arcolum becni onchill .i. othelaig dubglaissi hitir lugdach icinel conaill . Crimthau tra. ainm bunaid coluim cille

Ocus ise incolum cille sin dorat grád dermair docrist asanite . Ticed din . aingel donim adochum fecht and .i. axal ainm insingil ticed cocolum cille . quasi auxil .i. ab auxilio 7 issed roraid intaingel friss . Acholuim cille goib umat oigo . Nigeb olcolum cille cotucthar alog dam . Cia log connaige ol intaingel. Adgillim nihenlog ol colum cille acht acethair. Abair

into a bishopric, or the removal of his body from the sepulchre to another place i.e. his relics from place to place i.e. his relics were carried out of the monastery wherein he died to the city.

'Aglabo' in *Ob. and Mart.*

'*Moelaithgen*' i.e. of Tech Moelaithgin in Cairpre Hua-Ciardai. Or in Mag Locha in the west of Brogia.
7. '*of Colomb*' i.e. My-Colmóc of Druim-Mór in Ui-Echach of Ulster.

'*of Medran*' i.e. Medrán and Murchú sons of the grandson of MacToni, and I know not where these are, i.e. Medrán of Daire Mic Marga.
'*of Murchú*' i.e. his city is in Ui-Faelain i.e. son of Ua-Mathcene.
9. '*Baethine—Colomb Cille*' i.e. Boethine son of Brenann, son of Fergus, son of Conall Gulban, son of Niall the nine-hostaged, and Colomb Cille son of Fedlimid, son of Fergus. Crimthann was the name of Colomb Cille previously.

Now Eithne daughter of Dima, son of Noe, son of Etine, son of Coirpre the Poet, son of Ailill the Great, son of Brecán, son of Fiace, son of Daire Barrach, son of Cathair the Great, was the mother of Colomb Cille. And Cumine, Minchloth, and Sinech were Colomb Cille's three sisters.

Colomb 'dove' he was named for his simplicity, *cille* 'of the church' because of his coming often from the church wherein he read his psalms into the company of the neighbouring children. And this is what they used to say amongst them : "Has our little Colomb come from the church?" i.e. from Telach Dubglaisse in Tír Lugdach in Cinél Conaill. Now Crimthann was Colomb Cille's original name.

And it is Colomb Cille that from his youth gave very great love to Christ. Yea an angel once upon a time came from heaven (and Axal was the angel's name that used to come to Colomb Cille,—quasi Auxil i.e. from *auxilium*), and this is what the angel said to him : "Ó Colomb Cille, take virginity around thee !" "I will not take it," says Colomb Cille, "till a

---

ᵃ MS. uir . This gloss is over *mad fodluga*   ᵇ MS. exio   ᶜ Facs. ixli.

iat olintaingel . Atber olcolum cille . i. bás aithrige 7 bás gortai 7 éc indíte . arisgranua nacuirp triasin sontai . bunde cuacte⁰ . Doberthar deit cid tuilled rissin olintaingel .i. bidat primfhaid nime 7 talman .

Rocomailtea din . insin . dochoidsium inoilithri . 7 bahóc intan bamarb 7 dogorta atbath . acht bagorta tholtanach cheua.

ocus issed fodera ingortasin dosum .i. fecht doralai he timchell relci inhii cofaccad incaillig oebein néuntai dochum braisce di . Cid imfuilngessin athróg olcolum cille . abaid athair olsi cenbo fil ocum 7 nirnc loeg beos . atúsa ocahernaide 7 issed so fognus dum iscian uad . Cinnid colum cille anusin comad braissech nentai ismo nofoigenad dó othasin hinuach cobrath. dicens . INtan isarsailechtu nahoenbo anirdaltai atathar isinmorgortasa . Roba deithbir ddinne comad mor ingortai himbemis ocernaide dé. arisferr ocus isdeimin inni sailmit . regnum perenne . ocus atbert fria athimthirig . braissech néuntai unitsin damsa cech noidche olse cen imm cen loimm loe . Dogentar olincoic . ocus tollaidside crand suati nabraisce comba fedán condoirted inloimm[b] isinfhedausin . 7 nochomsuaithed triasin braissig . Rathaigit iarum ineclaissin .i. deigfbéth inclerig 7 inruaidit cturru fessin. Faillsigter docolum cille sin conid and asbert . Fodord oclucht barninaid dogréss .

Maith olsessium frissintimthirid cred doberidsi damsa isinmbraissig cechdin . At fiadnaise fessin olingillai acht minathised asinchrund diamesethar immbraissig nátfetursa ní aile ind acht braissech uama . Faillsigther tra . don clereeh

reward therefor be given to me." "What reward seekest thou ?" says the angel. "I declare (it is) not one reward," says Colomb Cille, "but four." "Say them," says the angel. "I will say," quoth Colomb Cille, "namely, a death in repentance, and death of hunger, and death in youth (for hideous are the bodies through old age) . . . . (?)" "Even more will be given thee along with that" says the angel, "namely, thou wilt be a chief prophet of heaven and earth."

And that was fulfilled. He went into pilgrimage: and he was young when he died, and of hunger he perished: it was, however, wilful hunger.

And this is the cause of that hunger of his. Once it came to pass, as he was going round the graveyard in Iona, that he saw an old woman cutting nettles to make pottage thereof. "Why art thou doing that, thou poor woman?" says Colomb Cille. "O dear Father," quoth she, "I have one cow, and she has not yet borne a calf, and I am expecting it, and this is what has served me a long time back." Colomb Cille then determines that pottage of nettles should serve him more thenceforth for ever, saying "Since it is because of her expecting the one uncertain cow that she is in this great hunger, most were it for us though great be the hunger wherein we should abide expecting God. For better and certain is what we expect, the eternal Kingdom." And he said to his servant "Pottage of nettles give thou to me every night, without butter, without a sip therewith." "It shall be done," quoth the cook. And he bores the mixing-stick of the pottage so that it became a pipe, and he used to pour the milk into that pipe and mix it all through the pottage. Then those churchfolk notice the cleric's goodly shape, and they talk of it among themselves. This is made known to Colomb Cille, and then he said, "May they who take your place be always murmuring!"

"Well," quoth he to the servant, "what do you put for me into in the pottage every day?" "Thou thyself art witness," quoth the gillie; "but unless it comes out of the stick with which the pottage is mixed, I know of nothing else therein save pottage only." Then (the

---

* This corrupt and (to me) unintelligible passage stands thus in Laud 610 (Mr. Hennessy's copy): triasin sendataig sentuinde cunaicdhe.
[b] The facsimile has inloimim. Perhaps we should read inloim 7 im.

7 atbert . sonas 7 deggnim triabithu dfir thinaid olse . 7 iss*ed* ón chomaillter

ISandsin din. roindis boethine do inaislinge naurdairce .i. teora catháire doaicsin do hinim .i. cath*áir* oir 7 cath*áir* argait 7 cath*áir* gloine. ISfollas sin ol [*in r. marg. at the quatrain for 4th June*] col*um* cille. INcath*áir* oir ciar*an* ma*c* intsair araencch 7 arnoigedchaire. INchath*áir* argait tussa fen aboethinc argloine 7 artaitncmchi dochrabuid. INcath*áir* gloino din. misi fen arcid alaind mochrabud isamcollaide 7 isamaibbrisc comenic . ut quidam dixit

> Colam cáincruth cumachtach*
> drech derg lethan lainderda
> corp geal clú cen imarba
> folt cass suil glas chaindelta
>
> Son a gotha col*uim cille*
> lor[b] abinde uas cech cléir
> cocend .u. c. déc coimend
> aidble rémend cad barcill.

11. *basilla* .i. uirgo.
maic thail .i. ochill chuilind amuig laigen. Eogan ser mac dergain *no* eogan mac ængus*a immurro* athair mi*c* tháil. ocus arabeth namac [sacir] atbernir ma*c* tail friss. *no* comad he eochaid mac bair*r* rig laigsi athair mic thail

[p. 91, lower marg.]

> Mac táil chille cuilind cóir
> mac cchach mic dairchin dein
> ocus isaire iamac tail
> arthal intsair dogabail
> Oengus aainm baisto art*us*
> nocorgab inbó bánus
> mac táil he osin amach
> cerbochaid robochlerech

12. *choemain* .i. indsi airrthir sanct lethan .i. sanctus lethan.
[*in r. marg.*] Foil inchredail 7rl. .i. coeman

secret) is revealed to the cleric, and he said "Prosperity and good deed for ever to thy successor !" quoth he, and this is fulfilled.

It is then that Boethine related to him the remarkable vision i.e. three chairs seen by him in heaven, to wit, a chair of gold, and a chair of silver, and a chair of glass. "That is manifest," says Colomb Cille : "the chair of gold is Ciarán son of the wright, for his generosity and hospitality. The chair of silver is thou thyself, O Boethíne, because of the purity and lustre of thy devotion. The chair of glass is I myself, for, though my devotion be delightful, I am fleshly and I am often frail," as a certain poet said :—

> Colomb fair-formed, powerful :
> Face red, broad, radiant :
> Body white : fame without deceit :
> Hair curling : eye grey, luminous.
>
> The sound of Colomb's Cille's voice
> Great its sweetness above every (bard's) train !
> To the end of fifteen hundred paces
> (Vastness of courses !) it was clear.

'*of Mac Táil*' i.e. of Cell Cuilinn in Mag Laigen. Eogan the wright, son of Dergán, or Eogan son of Oengus, was the father of Mac Táil ; and because of his being the son of a wright he is called *mac táil* 'son of adze.' Or Eochaid son of Darr king of Leix may be Mac Táil's father.

Mac Táil of Cell Cuilinn Cóir
Son of Eochaid, son of vehement Dairchen.
And this is why he is Mac Táil
Because he took the wright's *tál* (adze).
Oengus was his baptismal name at first
Until he took the . . . (?)
'Son of Adze' he (was called) thenceforward,
Though he was chaste (and) was a cleric.

12. '*of Coemdu*' i.e. of Inis Airther.

'The feast of the pious' etc., i.e. Coeman

---

* MS. Colam cille cain crothach cumachtach, which is three syllables too much. Laud 610 has, rightly, *Colam cain cruth cumachtach*.
[b] leg . mór?

sanctléthan . orabi [airne] coeman inuib cendsclaig *forbru* locha carmau. Sanctléthan .i. rigan rig laigsi .i. coch*aid* mac bairr isaice boi coeman indoeri inagilla bee et ab eo [leg. eá *l*] nominatur uel *ut* dixit [leg. ideo dicitur] sanctléthan de .i. triachuimling moir trn. ruc escop ibair coeman onrigain .i. oshanctlethain condebairt sanctlothan abainm dó beith forsinugilla 7 dob*ert* sanctlethan briatha*i*r ind comad ho coeman nob*er*ad ambanchú uadsu*m* . oescop ibair ciaroboi icamoriarraid. 7 isse*d* on rocomailled iarsin

Sanctlethan, from whom was Airne Coemáin in Ui-Ceanselaig on the brink of Loch Carman. Sanctléthan i.e. the queen of a king of Leix i.e. Eoclaid son of Barr. With her was Coemán in bondage as a little gillie, and from her is he named. Or for this reason was he named Sanctlethan, namely, through a great contest did bishop Ibair bear Coemán from the queen i.e. from Sanctlethan, and Sanctlethan said that her name should be on the gillie, and Sanctlethan gave her word for this that Coemán would carry away Bishop Ibair's monks from him, though he (the bishop) was much entreating for them; and this was fulfilled thereafter.

*toran*dan .i. palladius rocartad o chomorba petair ineri*nn* riapatr*aic* dforcetul doib . ni ragbad inori*nn* com*d*echaid in albain hic sepultus est in liconio . *no* mothoren tulcha fortchirn anib felmeda 7 odruim clia*b* hicairp*ri*

'*T*o*rannán*' i.e. Palladius was sent (?) by Peter's successor into Ireland before Patrick to teach them. He was not received in Ireland, so he went into Scotland. He was buried in Liconium (?). Or My-Toren of Tulach Fortchirn in Ui-Felmeda and of Druim Cliab in Cairpre.

13. *partha*lon .i. apostolus
14. *nem* .i. pupa[a] airne .i. do dal mbirn do osraigib dó .i. brathair do ciaran saigre 7 comorba énni airne 7 isesin inpapa dicitur dobid in áraind arba orcim doriacht pupa cor*us*tog aad*n*ocul inaraind

13. '*Bartholomew*' i.e. an Apostle.
14. '*Nem*' i.e. Papa of Aran i.e. of Dál Birn of Ossory who he i.e. a brother of Ciarán of Saiger and successor of Enne of Aran; and he is called the Papa who used to be in Aran, for it was from Rome that papa came, and he chose his sepulchre in Aran.

15. *gerait* .i. calbe calbeo eo quod omnes mirarentur . . . pro macio uiuere[b]
uitus .i. proprium [sub ualeriano iudice passus est.—Rawl. 505]

'Qui beatus Uitus in puerili etate uirtutibus maturus, primum a patre suo sacrilego ut a cultura dei recederet, temptatus est, deinde a Ualeriano iudice cathomis [' with scourges of rods,' *cathamus* ain gaisell von roten gemacht, Dief. Supp.] cesus, in confessione permanens, martirio ad extremum coronatus est," *Ob. and Mart.*

16. *in giric* .i. xi. mile .cccc. cum eo in uno die sub alexandro praesid*e*[c] pasus est ciricius. [in r. marg.] Ciricius qui pasus est in antiochia cum matre [sua] iulita sub alexandro praeside et parvus[d] trium annorum erat quando pasus est, tribus mensibus de tribus annis demptis[e]

[a] leg. papa ?
[c] MS. ropraeside
[b] This unintelligible note very likely is misplaced.
[d] M.S. pasu*us*
[e] MS. mensis diebus de *est*.

Diangabad in demun dur
imuud ciric nanilrún
diudás isnuessa fonim
dologfaitis achimaid

[p. 90, in r. marg.] Mogerait inciric 7rl.
cum matre sun[a] iulita pasus est sub alexandro
anno 1° m° praeside decollatus est gladio in
tarsa ciuitate ciliciae[b] erat de genere iconiarum[c]
et infans .iii. annorum sed tamen tres menses
de tribus annis deerant.

17. *Mo-ling luachair* .i. ocleim do dar aroile
escai i luachair dedad bimumain isand roráid
quaedam[d] mulier . is cain moling inscolaige
inluachair conid de ata moling luachair.
7 dairchell ainim prius.

in lower marg.] INdoss oir uas crichaib 7rl.
.i. Moling aluachair. dairchell ainm prius.
Faillén soer *immurro* ainm aathar

Moling cecinit

    Tan bim it*ir* mosruithe
    amteis targairthe[e] cluiche
    tan bim it*ir* inoes mear
    domúinet isme asoiscar .

Diamboi moling ocinadech*t* luachra dedad ocus
cailleeh inachoimitech*t* corbaluath lasincaillig
aindechts*um* comlebairt friss ismaith linge in-
luach*air* olsi . Hinc moling luachrai. *no cumad*
dar lathaig chena illuach*air* nolinged intan
roinerech he . 7 dairchell nomen prius 7 colman
mac luachain claind m*i*c luach*áin* amide [in
uno die cum moling.—Laud 610]

Congreit rig balc .i. re tæb conadgreit[f] rig
isbrathair bailec duinne 7 moling arcnur isinrund fessin . uel sic quod uerius est . quasi fil
isintrachtad infelire ata óremes nanoem inard
macha .i. comling[g] is greit rig imaille friss 7
oirechus donrig sic uel ut sic ut episcopus
sapit[h] .

INdoss oir .i. moling *congreit* rig robo bra-

[a] MS. *suæ*   [b] MS. *cilciloe*   [c] MS. *degren iaconiarum*.   [d] MS. *quidam*
[e] am teist ergaire cluithi—Laud 610.   [f] MS. *conadergit*   [g] leg. *moling*   [h] MS. *sabidem*

If the dour Demon sang
The hymn of Quiricus of the many secrets
To Judas, who is worst under heaven,
His sins would be forgiven .

'My champion, the Quiricus' etc.

17. '*Mo-ling of Luachar*' i.e. as he was leap-
ing over a certain water in Luachar Dedad in
Munster, then said a certain woman "Well
has the scholar leaped (*mo-ling*) the rushes!"
And hence is he called Moling Luachair, and
Dairchell was his name before that.

'The bush of gold over borders,' etc., *i.e.*,
Moling from Luachair. Dairchell was his
name formerly. Faillén the wright, however,
was his father's name.

Moling sang :—

    When I am among my seniors
    I am a proof that sport is forbidden,
    When I am among the mad (young) folk
    They think that I am the junior.

Moling was going over Luachair Dedad, and
an old woman was along with him, and his
going was (too) fast for the old woman, so she
said to him "Well thou leapest (*lingi*) the
Luachair!" quoth she. Hence (he was called)
Moling Luachrai. Or may be it was a puddle
in the Luachair that he was leaping when she
reproved him ; and Dairchell was his name
before that, and Colmán son of Luachán of
Land mic Luachain in Meath is celebrated on
the same day as Moling.

'A clear champion of the King, a strong
(brother)' *i.e.* besides being a King's champion
he is a strong brother to us, and Moling alone
is in the quatrain itself. Or thus, which is
truer, as is in the commentary on the Calendar
which has been since the time of the saints
in Armagh *i.e.* Moling and a King's champion
along with him and superiority to the King.
Or thus *ut episcopus sapit*. "The bush of
gold " *i.e.* Moling with a King's champion who

thair do immaille remoling ocus airechus moling diarérsin

[*The following legend is from the notes on the Félire in Laud 610*] Fechtus dosom acirrnaigthi inn celais conacca inóclach chuice issintuch . étach corcarda uime 7 dealb derscaigtheeh[a] lais . Maith sin acleirig arse . Amin armoling. Cid nabennachaisi dámsa olintóclach . Cia tusa armoling . Misi crist mac dé arse . Ni ctarsa ón armoling . iutan dutheiged *crist* doacallaim nacciled ádé níba corcarda narigda notheiged acht arichtaib natrog .i. nalobar 7 naclam nobíd *crist*.

Ind aimiris notgcib dím arintoclach . cia asdoig lat ann . Badóig lium ar moling comnd he diabul domirchoid . Did olc duit intamiris arintóclach . Maith armoling atá suan dochomorba soiscela *crist* . laturgbail intsoiscela .

Naturgaib acleirig orse isdochu asmisi imraide . ismé infer imnedach . Cid dia dutchad armoling . Cotardta dobennachtain form , Nitiber armoling . ornach nairle ní[pa]ferrde cid domaith duit [iarum] armoling.

Mar nothiastasa indabaig meala gurut fothraigthe inti eotedach nobiad abolath fort mina nigthea tédach . Cid diata let ón armoling . Atá lim cincoterna[c] arnill damsa dobendachtsa biaid a sobarthan 7 abail 7 ablath form ancehtair . Ni[t]bia . armoling ar nirusairla .

Maith arse tabair lan mallach/an form . Cid domaith duit armoling . Ninse a clerig arse inbel forsatarga in mallacht fornusa biaid a neim 7 airchoit atbelse . Airg armoling nidligi

[a] MS. derscaigitech
[b] This part of the legend is obviously suggested by the story of the interview between S Martin and the devil. *Sulpicii Severi de Vita B. Mart. Lib.* ed. Hornius, xxv.
[c] *airle* for *airilli*.
[d] leg. derna

was a brother of his along with Moling, and superiority to Moling according to that.

Once as he was praying in his church he saw a youth coming to him into the house. Purple raiment around him and a dignified form had he. "That is well, O cleric," saith he. "Amen" saith Moling. "Why dost thou not bless me?" says the youth. "Who art thou?" quoth Moling. "I am Christ Son of God," says he. "That cannot be," says Moling. "When Christ used to come to converse with the servants of God (*Culdees*) not in purple nor royally did he come, but in the shapes of the wretched, to wit, of the sick and of the lepers used Christ to be."

"Is it unbelief thou hast in me?" asked the youth: "who is it that seems to thee to be here?" "Meseems," says Moling, "that it is the Devil for my hurt." "Ill for thee is the unbelief," says the youth. "Well," says Moling, ["if thou art Christ] here is thy successor, Christ's Gospel," raising the Gospel.

"Raise it not, O cleric!" says he. "Likelier it is I whom thou thinkest. I am the man of tribulation." "Wherefore hast thou come?" says Moling. "That thou mayst give me thy blessing" [says the Devil]. "I will not give it," says Moling: "since thou deservest it not, thou wouldst not be the better thereof. What good, moreover, would it be to thee?" says Moling.

[The Devil answered:] "Just as if thou shouldst go into a tub of honey, and bathe thyself therein with thy raiment ; its odour would abide upon thee unless thy raiment should be washen." "Wherefore is this thy desire?" asked Moling. "Because, although thy blessing do nought else to me, its prosperity and its goodness and its blossom will be on me externally." "Thou shalt not have it," says Moling, "for thou hast not deserved it."

"Well," says he, "give the full of a curse on me." "What good were that to thee?" says Moling. "Not hard to say," quoth he; "the mouth whereon gathers the curse on me, bendachtain. Robad fherr linm arse condlesaind Cindus dosmuilli[u]b. Fognum dodia armoling. Fe amái orsc nirucninsea. Cid brolaind léicid.ᵃ Nimó doleicindseaᵇ 7 nimcobrath[ar]sa.

the venom and harm thereof will be against thee." " Go," says Moling, " thou hast no right to a blessing." " Better were it for me that I had," said he. " How shall I earn it?" "By service unto God." quoth Moling. " Woe is me!" said he ; " I have not chosen it." "Even a little reading " [says Moling]. "Thy reading saveth me not, and helpeth me not."

Aine din armoling. Atósa amthroscad othossach domain. ní ferrdi dam. Slechtain dodénam armoling. Foremtimᶜ tairnim for beolo. siar atait mogluine. Eirg as armoling ni fetnim dothecosce na dothesorcain. Is dé asbert diabal

"Fasting, then," said Moling. " Fasting am I since the world's beginning : not the better am I." " To make genuflection," said Moling. " I cannot bend forward, for backwards are my knees." " Go forth," says Moling ; "I cannot teach thee, nor save thee." Thereof said the Devil—

Is ór glan isnem imgrein
islestar airggit cofín
isaingil iseaena naem
cachaen dogní toil inríg

He is pure gold, he is a heaven round a sun,
He is a vessel of silver with wine,
He is an angel, he is wisdom of saints,
Whosoever doth the King's will.

ISén imaníadanu sás
as noi tholl diancislind guas
islestar fás iscrann crín
nadéine toil inrig thúas

He is a bird round which a trap shuts,
He is a leaky bark in perilous danger,ᶠ
He is an empty vessel, a withered tree,
Whoso doth not the will of the King above.

IScræb chumra conabláth
islestar islán domil
islía lógmor conabail
doguí toil maic dé donim

He is a sweet branch with its blossom,
He is a vessel full of honey,
He is a precious stone with its goodness,
Whoso doth the will of the Son of God of heaven.

ISenú cæch na[d]bí amáin isbrence brén iscrann crín iscraeb fíadabla coubláth cach nadeine toil inrig

He is a blind nut wherein is no profit,
He is a stinking rottenness, a withered tree,
He is a wild-apple-branch without blossom,
Every one who doth not the will of the King.

Doguí toil maic de donim
isgrian etrocht ambí sam
isairithe dé donim
islestar glainide glan

Whoso doth the will of the Son of God of heaven
Is a brilliant sun round which is summer,
Is an image of God of heaven,
Is a vessel glassen, pure.

ISech buada tar mag réid
fer atcosna flaith de máir
iscarpat fegtar forig
dobeir buada allaig náirᵈ

He is a race-horse over a smooth plain
The man that strives for great God's kingdom,
He is a chariot that is driven under a king,
That bears off prizes in the east.ᶠ

ISgrian guresᵉ riched nóeb
for dian buidech inrí mór
istempall sonnide sóer
iscrín nóeb conutaing órᵃ

He is a sun that warms holy heaven,
A man for whom the great King is thankful :
He is a temple prosperous, noble,
He is a holy shrine which gold bedecks.ᵇ

ᵃ leg. léigind ᵇ leg. doléigendsea ᶜ leg. Foremdim ᵈ read allanáir ?
ᵉ MS. gu rois. ᶠ *allanáir*, a mere guess: the Book of Leinster has *a halaib oir*.
ᵍ MS. noir ᵇ *conutaing*, cf. *cota-utaing* (eam protegit) Ml. 36.

p

ISaltoir forsndailt*er* fín
imacanar ilar cór
iscailech glanta colind
istinddrnine find is ór.
     ISór glan is nem.

18. *boethin* . . . . *furodran* .i. boethin
7 furodran . da mac moenain olaind luachain
imbregaib
   19. *geruassi protassi* .i. duo[a] fratres erant
et in elcidic[b] sunt reliquia sua quae[c] ambrossio
per somnium ostensa sunt.
   20. *foelan* .i. foelan mac oengusa mic natfraich . ornith erend inalbain 7 ochill fælan
ilaigis
   21. [*in left marg.*] la ingriantairismi sin [*in
r. marg.*] sol[s]titium secundum græcos et
egiptios . dies horarum .xuii. nox horarum
uii.
   ainle .i. diarmait [odisiurt] diarmata h*ui*
æda róin . quando perigrinationem uoluit[d] ire
mare sur[r]exit contra eum .i. alaind alli .i. mac-
coem he 7 indisiurt diarmata inuib muiredaig
ata ocus ainle indala hainm boi fair *uo* isamail
atb*eir* trachtad inlilair ata etirchert annsa

   cormac . *no cumad* inand indirmaig col*u*im
cil*le* ata
   in right marg.] Cormac .i. do úib linthan dó
7 indermuig amide ata . 7 isfriss atbert colam
cil*le* . Airis olse sund indermuig. Niairissiub
hic*c*in nocofharghasu ní dottaissib ocum.

Daro chucat ní dib ol colu*m* cil*le* . Dialamaind
[leg. Do lám ind?] olcormac . Sinis colum cil*le*
alaim . Neothais cormac alúdain de . ISgoirt
domairliss achorm*aic* olcolum cil*le* . Cid fíl and
olse acht coin dotithe iud 7 issed on rocomailled.
ISe din . incormac sin rotriall tarmuir indegaid
colu*im* cille conemelt inmuir friss conarléic
tairis he onchindiud corocomailltea briath*ar*
colu*im* cille amlaidsin

He is an altar whereon wine is shed,
Round which is sung a multitude of melodies;
He is a cleansed chalice with liquor (therein),
He is white-bronze, he is gold.

18. '*Boethin—Furodran*,' i.e. Boethin and
Furodran, two sons of Moenán of Lann Luachain in Bregia.

20. '*Foelán*,' i.e. Foelan, son of Oengus, son
of Natfraech, of Rath Erenn in Scotland, and
of Cell Foelain in Leix.
   21. The day of the solstice is that.

'*Ainle*,' i.e. Diarmait of Disert Diarmata
Uí Aeda Roin . When he desired to go on a
pilgrimage, the sea rose against him. (*Ain-le*)
'delightful his colour,' i.e. a youngling was
he, and in Disert Diarmata in Uí Muiredaig is
he, and Ainle was the second name that he
had. Or the interpretation of his name is as
the commentary of the book states.

'*Cormac*,' or he may be the same: in Durrow
of Colomb Cille he is.
   '*Cormac*,' i.e. of the Uí-Liathain was he, and
in Durrow in Meath he is, and to him said
Colomb Cille: "Stay here," quoth he, "in
Durrow." "I will not stay" (says Cormac)
"unless thou leavest[e] with me somewhat of thy
relics."
   "Some of them shall go to thee," says Colomb
Cille. "If I durst" [read "Thy hand on
it,"?] says Cormac. Colomb Cille stretched
forth his hand. Cormac lopped his little-finger
off him. "Bitterly hast thou visited me, O
Cormac!" says Colomb Cille. "Howbeit," says
he, "dogs shall devour thee for this." And
that was fulfilled. He is that Cormac who
proceeded over sea after Colomb Cille, and
the sea rose against him, and allowed him
not to pass it, because of the determination
that Colomb Cille's word should be fulfilled
in that wise.

---

[a] MS. duos   [b] Facs. melcidic.   [c] MS. suo qui   [d] MS. ouluit
[e] literally, 'so long as thou leavest not.'

22. *hiacop* .i. sup[p]lantatur interpretatur do tribu inda[e] . in ierusalem sepultus est hic.
da nocht cét .i. x. c. ui.

in lower marg.] La hiacop nalfei 7rl. alii dicunt duos iacopos esse .i. alfei et zebedei . alii uero .iii. quum dms. episcoporum et nescio eum. Item alii .iiii. iacopos .i. iacopum zepedi et incopum alfei et tertium esse dict. primus est. iacopus frater domini qui primus ordinatus est. icurusolimis episcopus quem occiderunt iudei[a] necciem uel ihc. secundus[b] iacopus filius zepedei quem occidit herodes .iii. iacopus est frater iude apostoli . quartus iacopus filius alfei quem marcus iacopum et minorem dicit in comparationem filii zepedei qui l. utrum an falsum.[c]

Cronan .i. comorba moedoc fernai.

23. *mochoe* .i. mochua luachra masue oliss mor mochua.

in sab .i. mochoei noendroma indelbna ethrai. *no* .ix. ndruimne fil isinbaile hita achell . *no* oendruim .i. oentulach aninis uile 7 forloch cuan ata .

Codlad cenerinad colla
contuil mochoo nocudroma
lucht intsámaid imboi intsai
nitharraid acht anindai

Rochachain domochoe chain
intenán donanemdaib
tribádbaind dobarr inchroind
.l. bliadan cech adboind . ,

24. sol(s)titium secundum latinos.
latachor . . . ioin mec do effis .i. recepcio iohannis filii zebedei ad ephesum de exilio per domitianum.[e]

25. Undecimus apud ægiptios episi (leg. Epifi ?).
sinchill .i. ochill achaid sinchill indib failge
telli .i. othig telli hifail daurmuigi
lamluoc .i. moluoc liss moir inalbain .i. cille delga inardgal

26. *gallicanus* .i. legnit dorí róman tanic cotir frange 7 martir he.

iohannes et paulus .i. duo fratres sunt et martires et in róma passi sunt iuliano cesare.

'*twice eight hundreds*' i.e. 1,600.

'*Cronán*,' i.e. successor of Moedóc of Ferns.
23. '*Mochoe*,' i.e. Mochua of Luachair Masue, from Les Mór Mochua.
'*the sage*,' i.e. Mochoei of Noendruim in Delbna of Ethra. Or nine ridges are in the place wherein his church is. Or *oendruim*, 'one-ridge,' i.e. one hill in the whole island, and on Loch Cuan it is.

A sleep without withering of flesh
Mochoe of Noendruim slept.
Of the folk of the congregation wherein
   the sage had been
Nought remained save their skulls.[d]

To Mochoe the beautiful sang
The little bird from the heavens
Three songs from the tree-top,
Fifty years in each song.

'*of Senchell*,' i.e. of Cell Achid Sinchill in Offaly.
'*Telli*,' i.e. of Tech Telli near Durrow.
'*with My-Luóc*,' i.e. Mo-luóc of Lismore in Scotland, i.e. of Coll Delga in Ardgal.
26. '*Gallicanus*,' i.e. a legate of the King of the Romans who came to the land of Franks, and a martyr was he.

[a] ms. iudie   [b] ms. fus   [c] I can make nothing of much this corrupt note.
[d] literally 'heads,' 'ends,' cf. *ota mind gom bond* 'from my head to my sole.' Z². 954.
[e] MS. post dormitatianum addefosum exilio.

27. .uii. nderlrathir .i. uii. filii sancte simp-
[ho]ro[s]æ femenæ. cum sua matre simp[ho]rosa
martirio coronati sunt in hoc die.

28. *Hillecuin* .i. indib moice uaiss mide.

crumine .i. sine tristitia semper ut dicitur

 Tri xx. bliadan cotri
 oes inchredail chrumini
 ceutam cengalar soi dath
 iarnoifriund iarceilebrad.

flouiani .i. papa roma[e].
29. *feil poil 7 petair* .i. Paulus de tribu
beniamin . In tarso ciliciæ natus est . sub pedi-
bus gamalel nutritus est . in uia damasci ad
fidem [conuersus est.] ter naufragium pasus est.
Paulus a potoi pauli [leg. παῦλα φαύλου ?] .i. a
cessatione[a] persecutionis . Romae[b] sanctorum
passio petri et pauli[c] qui sub scelestisimo nerono
pasi sunt.
in lower marg.] Feil poil 7 petair simoin
deponens macrorem.[d] interpretatur [ob] resur-
rectionem christi tristi[ti]am depossuit. uel
aud[i]ens tristi[ti]am [quia] christus dixit ei
cum senueris extendes 7rl. Simon petruss filius
ionae[e] prouincia galliæ [leg. Galileae] de ciuitate bestatta [leg. Bethsaidae ?] frater andreae
apostoli qui et cephas[f] dicitur .i. capitalis
cephas[f] hautem sirice petrus graece et latine.
paulus de tribu beniamin mort[u]us est et in
tarsa ciliciæ natus est.
30. *stoli* .i. póil
ioib .i. mac bost mic nachor mic tara

.in lower marg.] Buaid stoli 7rl. taithmiu
[leg. taimthiu] .i. tómaithium ['threatening']
.i. hic temptatus est iob.

27. '*Seven brothers.*'
"Natale sancte Simphorosæ, beati Getulii
martiris uxoris, cum septem filiis, Crescente,
Iuliano, Nemesio. Primitiuo, Iustino, Stacceo,
Eugenio." *Ob. and Mart.* v. Kal. Julii.
28. '*In Leceun*,' i.e. in Ui-Mace Uais of
Meath.
'*Crumíne*,' without sadness always, as is
said:—

 Thrice three score years
 Was the age of the pious Crumíne.
 Without disease, without sickness, he
  changed colour
 After offering, after celebration.

'The feast of Paul and (Simon) Peter'—
'Simon.'

30. *of Stolus*, i.e. of Paul.[g]
'*of Job*,' .i. son of Boz, son of Nachor, son of
Tara.

'Victory of Stolus' etc.

---

[a] MS. accesatione.   [b] MS. Romai.   [c] Facs. apostoli.   [d] MS. merioren
    [e] M.S. ioh.   [f] MS. coefas.
[g] 'Celebratio iterum sancti Pauli apostoli,' *Ob. and Mart.* ii. Kal. Julij.

RAWL. 505, fo. 216, a.

1. Iuil hikl. mirbuil
mare maras matha
bas naroin seirb sruithe
simon ocus tatha
2. Taimthiu eutaice epscoip
damassi conani
pais processi rigdai
riag mar martiani
3. Martra cirionis
crist nihattach mbelle
tarmbreth tomaiss aille
feil digraiss dartinne
4. Dagordan mór martain
marosellaib soimle
lacet martir namra
finnbarr inse doimle
5. Donmartir agatho
conacleir cain comul
roir crist sid slemon
amorseircc laomun
6. Moninne intsleibe
cuilinn bacain age
gobais buaid geil glaine
siur maire mare
7. Amorsluagad ligmar
parmeni trom toiden
miel ruainadreth richeth
grian án inse goidel
8. Gabais brocan scribnid
soerbuaith cennachtuisel
ladiarmait derb lassar
grian gel glinne huissen

LAUD, 610, fo. 66, b. 1.

1. IVil hikl . mirbuil
mairi mor ismatha
bas aroin sab sruithi
simon 7 tatha
2. Taimthiu eutaig[a] epscop
damassi conaine
pais processi rigdai
riag mar martiani
3. Martra cirionis
crist nihattach mbille
tairmrith tomais ailli
feil digrais tartinde
4. Dagordon mormartain
marosellaib semle
lacet mairtir namra
findbarr indsi temle
5. Donmairtir agatha
conachleir cain comol
rofir crist sid slemon
amorseire laomon
6. Moninni [in]tslebe
cuilind bacain áige
gabais buaid gil glaine
siur maire mare
7. Lamorsluaged ligach
parmeni trom toiden
melruain adreth riched
grian an insi gæidel
8. Gabais brocan scribnig
soerbuaid cennach tusel
ladiarmait derblassar
grian gel gliudi huissen

LEBAR BRECC, p. 91.

1. Hiuil ikl. mirbuil
muire moras matha
bas aroin sab sruitho
simon 7 tatha
2. Taiutiu eutaic espoc
damasi conani
pais processi rigda
riag mor marciaui
3. Martra cirionis
crist nihatach mbille
tarmbreth tomais aille
feil digrnis dartinne
4. Dagordan mor martain
marosellaib seimle
la cét martir namra
findbarr indse teimle
5. Donmartir agatha
conacleir cain comul
ro ir crist [sid] slemun
amorseirce la omau
6. Moninde intslebi
cuilind bacain aigo
gabais buaid gel glaine
siuur muire maire
7. Lamorsluagad ligmar
parmeni troiu toeden
moelruain adreth riched
grian au indsi goedel
8. Gabais brocan scribnid
særbuaid cenach tuisel
ladiarmait derb lassar
grian gel glinde huissen

---

1. On July's marvellous kalend is Mary whom Matthew magnifies: the death of Aaron a mighty man of wisdom : Simon and Thaddaeus.

2. The bed-death of bishop Euticius, of Damasus with splendour: the passion of kingly Processus : the great torture of Martinianus.

3. Cyrious's martyrdom, no paltry prayer to Christ: Thomas' translation hear thou : Dartinne's excellent feast.

4. Martin's good great ordination, you have not seen its like: with a hundred wonderful martyrs, Findbarr of Inis Teimle.

5. To the martyr Agatha, with her followers, a fair assembly, Christ granted perfect[b] peace, great love of Him with awe.

6. Moninne of the mountain of Cuilenn (Slieve Gullion) was a fair pillar: she gained a bright victory of purity : (she was) a sister of great Mary (the Virgin).

7. With a great beautiful host, Parmenius' heavy troop, Moelruain ran to heaven, splendid sun of the isle of the Gael .

8. Brocan the scribe won a noble victory

[a] MS. eutaīg
[b] lit. 'smooth'

RAWL. 505, fo. 216, a.	LAUD, 610, fo. 66, b. 1.	LEBAR BRECC, p. 91.
9. Asslonnud an onchon mostice cach nodnali fricr*ist* caraiss lere garban can cind sali	9. Aslondud án onchon mostic cach nodnale cocr*ist* carais leire garban cain chindtsaile	9. Aslondud an onchon mostic cach notnaile fricr*ist* carais leri garban cain chind tsaile
10. Sluind cesad sechtbrathar diambu croch cr*ist* carcar	10. Sluind cessad .uii. mbrathar diambu croch cr*ist* carcair	10. Sluind cesad .uii. mbraithre diambo croch cr*ist* carcair
cuan marcc mar sostan dase mile martar	cuan marc morsostan dase mili martar	cuan marce morsostan da .ui. mile martar
11. Lamartra narigna eufemia slog[d]a[a] benedicht balce age mace craib[d]ech conlocha	11. Lamartra narigna eufemia slogdai beinedict bale áge m*a*cc craibdech conloga	11. Lamartra narigna eufemia slogdai benedicht balce aige m*a*cc craibdech conlocha
12. Conruala cohaingliu nazair scel cechsenaid felix bamaitulaid conasluag mor melaid	12. Conroloi cohaingliu nazair sccl cech senaid feilix bamadtulaid conasluag mor melaid	12. Conrualaid coaingliu nazair scel cech senaid[a] felix bamatuluid conasluag mor melaid
13. Milis ainm conani euangeli noeludai lamsiloc donrigraid luid hisidlaith soerdai	13. Milis ainm conáni euangeli noemda lamsiloc donrigraid luid hisitlaith soerda	13. Milis ainm conani euangelii noemdai lamsiloc donrigraid luid hisidlaith s*o*erdai
14. Ronsnada intepscop iacob as næbem atneocham nonalem condechenbur noiden	14. Ronsnade intepscop iacob asnoemem ateocham nonalem condeichenbor nóciden	14. Ronsnadea intepsc*o*p iacop isnoemem ateocham nonailem condeichenbor noeiden
15. INda apstal denc dofarcat [c]echnarim fosdail reasluag dirim issu fosil adaim	15. INdaapstal déac doforchet cech narim rosdail riasluag dirim isu fosil adaim	15. INda aspul denc dofarcat cech nairem fosdail resluag dirim ih.u fosil nadaim

without any fall, with Diarmait, a sure flame, bright sun of Glenn Uissen.

9. A splendid declaring of Onchu : well fares everyone who entreats him : he loved diligence as to Christ, Garbán the fair of Cennsaile.

10. Declare the suffering of seven brethren unto whom Christ's cross was a dungeon, Cuan, Mark a great rest : twice six thousand martyrs.

11. With the martyrdom of the queen, Euphemia the hostful, Benedict, a strong pillar, Conlug's pious son.

12. Unto the angels departed Nazarius the story of every synod. Felix, it was well he went, with his great host he was ground.

13. Sweet the name with splendour of Evangelus the sainted, with my Silóc of the kings, he went into the noble realm of peace.

14. May the bishop Jacob, who is most holy, protect us! we besecch, we entreat him, with a decad of infants.

15. The twelve apostles who excel every number, before a countless host Jesus distributed them among Adam's seed.

[a] MS. senad.   [b] MS. maccam.   [c] 'him' A.

RAWL. 505.	LAUD, 610.	LEBAR BRECC, pp. 91, 92.
16. Doticfa cechdia docri*st* acht conetis[a] itge cosluag suabais inmaccain mammetis	16. Doticfa cechdia docri*st* acht conetis itge cosluag suabais inmaccain[b] mametis	16. Doticfa cechdia ochri*st* acht conetis itge cosluag sualais inmacain mametis
17. Ronmorat anitgi horum atque harum cechmartir adrinem forsluag scillitarum	17. Ronmorat anitge horum atque harum cachmairtir atrinem laslóg chillitarum	17. Ronmorat anitge horum atque harum cech martir atrinem lasluag scellitarum
18. Sluagad innarigna snaidsium insith soerda comorfesiur braithre inxp.ina noebda	18. Sloiged inarigna snaidsiund iusidh særda comorseisir brathar incristina noemda	18. Sloiged inarigna snaidsium insid særdai comorfessiur braithre inxp.ina noemdai
19. Noebitge sisiuni itmerb manifrescai tairce eim fritoscai comorbuidin brestai	19. Noemitge sisenne atmeirb manifresca tairic eim fri toiscai comorbuidin bresta	19. Noemitge sisenni atmeirb manitfrescai taric em fritoscai comorbuidin brestai
20. ITbrestai inbainmeice sabina soer ainbech indromula ruamach lacuriphin craibdech	20. ITbresta inbanmaice sabina sær ainbech indromula ruamach lacurphine craibdech	20. Hitbrestai inbanmee sabina sær ainbech inromula ruamach lacurufin craibdech
21. Croch ard heli martir moraid relicc lechtaig coningenraid tuchtaig pais fraxidis fechtnaig	21. Croch ard hele martir moras reilec lechtaid coningenraid tuchtaid pais fraxinis fechtnaig	21. Croch ard helí martir morais relicc lechtnig coningenraid tuchtaig pais fraxitis fechtnaig
22. Fin[d]gein magdalena maire mind cechdunaid pais apolnair huasail mobiu inse cuscraid	22. Findgein magdalena maire mind cech dúnaid pais apolloin uasail mobi indsi cuscraid	22. Findgein magdalena muire mind cech dunaid pais appolloin uasail lambiu indsi causcraid
23. Lacesad uincenti cocri*st* cechaing saithe hiruaim bareim sruithe danoi miled maithe	23. Lacessad uincenti cocri*st* cechaing saithe irroim bareim sruithe da noi mili maithi	23. Lacesad uincenti cocri*st* cechaing saithe iruaim barein sruithe daix miled maithe

16. Every day will go to thee, of Christ if only thou ask it, the prayer, with the gentle host, of the child Mamimes.

17. Magnify us may the prayers *horum atque harum*, every martyr whom we recount, with the host of the Scillitani.

18. May the host of the queen, the sainted Christina, with seven brethren, protect us[a] into the noble peace!

19. Sisinnius' holy prayer, thou art weak unless thou hope it: quickly he comes at thy wish, with a great, alert troop.

20. Alert are the woman-children, Sabina noble, great, (and) city-having Romula, with pious Curufin.

21. The high cross of the martyr Helius magnified a grave-abounding cemetery: with shapely maidens the passion of happy Praxedes.

22. The fair nativity of Mary Magdalen the diadem of every host: the passion of noble Apollonius, with Mo-biu of Inis Cuscraid.

23. At Vincentius' suffering to Christ went a troop: in Rome was a succession of seniors, twice nine goodly thousands.

[a] MS. coentis [b] MS. maccam [c] MS. mainfrescai [d] A and D 'me.'

Rawl. 505.	Laud, 610.	Lebar Brecc, p. 92.
24. Madail duit ahere dotchobair cing bage tathut cenn cheit mile deelan arde mare	24. Mad toich duit aciriu dotchobair cing bāge tathut cend chet mili declan airdi maire	24. Madtoich duit aciro dotchobair cing baige tathut cend .c. mile declan ardi maire
25. Mocholmoc moṡiloc lanessan dialammais iacob cing innis bas brathar iohannis	25. Mocholmoc mosiloc lanessan dialammais iacob cendinnis pais brathair iohainnis	25. Mocholmoc mosiloc lanessan dialammais incop cendindis bas brathar iohannis
26. Hipais iouiani conacleir cain glanoir tarmchruthad iarndedoil issu hisleib thaboir	26. Hipais iouianí conachleir cain ṅglanóir tarmchruthaid iarndedoil isu isleib taboir	26. Hipais iouiani conacleir cain glangloir tarmchruthud iarndedoil ih.u isleib taboir
27. Taimthin semioin mannaig bamorgrian dontalmain lacesad sluaig inmain inantuaig aird adbail	27. Taimthiu semeoin mannaig bamorgrian dontalmain lacesadh slúaig inmain inantuaig aird adbail	27. Taimthiu semeoin mannaig bamor grian dontalmain lacesad sluaig inmain inantuaig ard adbail
28. ISadbul acobair conaṡluagud chaindlech teophil tor óir ainglech pantaleo laindrech	28. ISadbul acobair conadsluagud caindlech teophail tor oir ainglech pantaleo laindrech	28. ISadbul acobair conaṡluagud caindlech teophil tor oir ainglech pantaleo laindrech
29. Lupus ocus simplice epscoip cenchuit ṅdigna prosper cocleir huagda narethanna rigda	29. Lupus 7 semplix epscuip cenchuit dingna prospeir cocleir uaga noll retlannach rigda	29. Lambus 7 simplex epscoip cenchuiddignai prosper cocleir uagdai noll redlainne rigdai
30. Recht cri*st* nodocantais	30. Recht cri*st* nodocandais	30. Recht cri*st* noech nochantais
corunaib attgleintis lasluag uafrith anfot abdon ocus sennis	corunaib adglendis* lasluag uafrith anfot abdon 7 sennis	corunaib adglentis disluag nifrith anfot abdon 7 enuis

24. If thou likest, O Ireland, a champion of battle to aid thee, thou hast the head of a hundred thousand, Declan of Ardmore.

25. My Colmóc, my Sílóc, with Nessan if we dare: Jacob without reproach (?): the death[b] of John's brother.

26. On the passion of Jovianus, with his train of pure gold[c] (was) the transfiguration, at daybreak, of Jesus on Mount Tabor.

27. The beddeath of Simeon the monk: a great sun was he to the earth: with the passion of a lovable host in Antioch high (and) vast.

28. Vast is his aid, with his radiant hosting: Theophilus, angelic tower of gold: Pantaleo the lucid.

29. Lupus and Simplicius, bishops without a whit of reproach: Prosper with a virginal train, great,[d] kingly stars[e]!

30. Christ's law to every one they used to sing, with mysteries which they used to learn: in their host was not found heedlessness, Abdon and Sennis.

[a] MS. adglenais   [b] B 'passion'   [c] A 'pure-gloried'   [d] D 'the'   [e] B 'starry'

RAWL. 505.	LAUD, 610.	LEBAR BRECC, p. 92.
31. Sluag iuil comeit mile fortniada ard age epscop an [a]here colman mac darane	31. Sluag iuil comeit mile fortniada ard áge hepscop án ahere colman mac darane	31. Sluaig iuil comeit mile fortniada ard aige epscop án aheri colman mac daraine

31. July's host,[a] a protection of thousands, a high pillar closes it: a splendid bishop from Ireland, Colman son of Daráine.

GLOSS FROM THE LEBAR BRECC, pp. 91, 92.

1. (2) doni matha morad mair[e] narrans eam .i. oirdned matha
2. (1) *taimtiu* .i. bas *no* tam *no* serb *no* tamthiu .i. tomaithinm *no* tai[m]thiu .i. tam tai .i. éc arenur *no* serg (2) *damasi* .i. maisse deda nadessise sis. *no* damasus papa romæ (3) *processi* .i. proprium [nomen]. *rigla* .i. ergna .i. rorigad iu caelum (4) *riag* .i. cesad
3. (2) *nihatach mbille* .i. nihatach boicht *no* midlaig *no* genaige. ut dicitur da no bill .i. da no ngenaige *no* bille .i. truaig no lobair *no* mbille .i. onni is imbellis[b] .i. enirt. ut dixit

Diatised intruagan truag   "If the poor wretch should have come
chucaib conabillinn mbuan   To you with his lasting pail,
diambeth oeblegan abo   (And) if he were milking his cow
ní contibred coisced do   Correction was not given to him."[c]

[billi .i. bocht. ian .i. lestar.—Laud, 610] (3) hilms .i. hille thncad (1) *digrais* .i. alathair .i. ergnaid
4. (1) [*in lower marg.*] Dag ordan 7l. Dag .i. maith nt est derb dag imbia .i. derb lium bamaith inebeltiu onebilt (2) .i. sellaisee Mat *connareais* amæ samla *no* marosillis .i. ma connareais *seimle* .i. soimlid .i. indis [*in lower marg.*] Marosellaib .i. marosillis .i. marofégais soillsi .i. matchondareais ni iseosmail friss it*i*r isiugnad arametso *no* mogenar atchondaire nsamail *no* marosellaib ut *prius*. Sóimle .i. sóimlid .i. luathaig diaségad 7 día indbsi. ut dicitur in usu scotorum. dochoid cusolam .i. coluath.
5. (2) *comul* .i. nert *no* adbol (3) *roir* .i. rofúirestar *no* rolarrustar (1) *morseirce* .i. amor dei .i. grád de oman .i. timor dei .i. oman dé
7. (1) *ligmar* .i. taitnemach (2) *toeden* .i. tidacht *no* tiachtain *no* taitnemach
9. (1) *aslondud* .i. aisnes (2) .i. maith tic each dia ail .i. dia guide
10. (2) .i. diarbo carthach *no* diarbo carcair eroch erist (3) *sostan* .i. gloir *no* gair *no* utmaille *no* iuncd. Nososten .i. sossad tend .i. cumsanud. ut dixit intalbunach. ni leic sosten dam .i. cumsanud (1) *martar* .i. martrai
11. (2) *slogdai* .i. erdairee (3) *bulcc* .i. calmai
12. (1) *conrualaid* .i. dochnaid inéla (3) *ba matulaid* .i. mongenair *no* ba imalle dolluid *no* bamaith dothuidecht isinbith freenaire (4) .i. romeiled .i. romianaiged per martir[i]um[d] *no* romeiled per martir[i]um l. milis
13. (2) *euangelii* .f. nomen (4) *hi sidflaith særdai* .i. isinflaithes nglan særda *no* sithamail
14. (1) *ronsnadea* .i. ronditnea (3) *ateocham* .i. aitchim *aitem* .i. guidmit
15. (2) .i. doroiscet *no* derseaigiul eech airem doeleolai *no* inda aspal hic misi sunt apostoli[e] ad praedicandum [per] totum mundum quasi quarto anno post pasionem domini. sed adamnánus sollemnitatem illis constituit[f] hoc die apud scotos[g] (3) *fosdail* .i. xii. apostoli

[a] 'A 'hosts'   [b] MS. isimbilicis   [c] i.e. he was allowed, without reproof, to fill his pail.
[d] This is over the word *milis* in the next quatrain.   [e] MS. adpli.   [f] MS. constituti
[g] MS. scotas

16. (1) *doticfa* .i. doraga chucaind   (2) *conetis* .i. co cuindchitis. *no* coroindsaige *no* coro indise .i. coroguide he *no* coronia imalenmain. *no* acht cosetis .i. *acht* corochoimsetaigi fris .i. diambe foroenset fris .i. for *sét* iustitiae. (3) *cosluag suabais* .i. cum turba felici martirum *suabais* .i. sobésach

17. (1) *ronmorat* .i. ronsnaidet .i. frecra donmenmain fuil hic   (2) *horum* .i. sanctos qui sunt in finem .i. filet indeiriud in raind

18. (2) *snaidsium* .i. degné arsnaidud .i. aruditen assunn .i. ab hoc saeculo[a] praesenti

19. (2) *atmeirb* .i. hitrnag [leg. hit truaig] *no* itmeta   *manitfrescai* .i. achobair   (3) *taric* .i. tic em .i. cosolam (1) *brestai* .i. brotla *no* beodai *no* snilbir

20. (1) *brestai* .i. beoda   banmec .i. banmec na hingina .i. fermec .i. namec .i. ingena ferrda (2) *ainbech* .i. mor *no* trom *no* nasal imluadan   (3) *ruamach* .i. catharda

21. (2) *lechtaig* .i. hitat lechta   (3) *coningenraid* .i. cum uirginibus *tuchtaig* .i. cumthachtaig .i. coemda *no* cruthaig *no* togaide .i. ecemtucht

22. (1) *Findgein* .i. gein solusta   (2) *cech dunaid* .i. cech sluaig *no* cech daingin[b] *no* cech popail

23. (2) .i. roching sluag *no* sochaide mor lais co crist   (4) .i. xuiii. milia martirum

24. (1) *madtoich* .i. matiunnas (l) *no* .i. madail   (2) *cing* .i. fortis homo   (3) *tathut* .i. ata duit

25. (2) *dia lammais* .i. auaisle *no* asruithe   (3) *cendindis* .i. INuis .i. dena aindisi *no* cendinsem *no* cendimes

26. *iouiani* .i. eolas   (2) *glanoir* .i. or glantaitnemach eat   (3) *tarmchruthud* .i. toirndelbad *iarndedoil* .i. iarmatain

27. (1) taimthiu .i. éc *no* tomaithium

28. (1) *isadbul* .i. isathlam

29. (2) *cen chuirt diynai* .i. centáire *no* cendímecin   (4) *noll redlainne* .i. oll *no* móra naredlanda

30. (1) .i. ní uochandais legem christi   (2) .i. nofoglandis cosians moir   *adglentis* .i. nothúirdis   (3) *anfot* .i. bét .i. ecóir [*in lower marg.*] Anfót .i. anfaitchius. ut dicitur

vel sic

Bíd cách ac fairesin ac fót
ambelaib atha nauóc
isde ata fót faitech
ocus aufót anfaitech

Every one is spying and watching
Over against the Ford of the Warriors:
Thence is *fót* watchful,
And *anfót* unwatchful.

Bíd cách afaitchius afóit
isbocht cia inthiagut óic
is de ata fót faitech
7 anfót an*faitech*[c]

31. (2) *fortniada* .i. forlámait

[a] MS. scli.   [b] Facs. daigin
[c] See Cormac's glossary s.v. *Fót* for another reading of this quatrain.

NOTES FROM THE LEBAR BRECC, pp. 91, 92.

1. *hiuil* .i. proprium[a] sancti in allain nescio[b] ubi est.

muire .i. mater domini.
matha .i. oirdned matha
aroin .i. aron .i. pri[m]us sacerdos.

frater m[o]rsi .i. or no[me]n montis in quo mortuus [est] aron. [*in lower marg.*] IUil i kl. mirbuil 7rl. Bas aróin .i. primus sacerdos .i. fratris moyse in monte oir *periit*.

simon .i. cannaneus[c].

tatha .i. tatheus qui dicitur et iudas et frater iacobi alfei [*in lower marg.*] tatheus qui iudas dicitur .i. frater iacopi .i. filii alfei.

2. *marciani* .i. martiris [*in lower marg.*] Taimthiu eutaic ep. 7rl. Marciani vel martiani .i. pro marticiani[d] per concisionem medi[ac] sillabae in utroque nomine vel martiniani.

3. *cirionis* .i. circionis .i. per concisionem.

tarmbreth tomais .i. anair thucad athaissi ahindia cohariiip no co[c]déssa .i. cathair isintsiria. Translatio corporis tomae ab' india in edessam' in ciuitatem quin in india pasus est.

dartinne .i. uirgo .i. ochill airnd in huib garrchon ilaignib

4. *dagordan mormartain* .i. aoirdned hitorinis martini in episcopatum [*in lower marg.*] Már martain .i. mártain mór no robomor ordinatio eius et translatio corporis[c] eius de sepulchro[k] et dedicatio eius basilicae, et haec omnia in die' hac facta sunt.

findbarr .i. hi tír bna cendselaig 7 isnadesib atasum

indsi teimle .i. fotheimel boi ininis cotaneutar damac æda .i. findbarr ocus barrfind .i. damac æda atha cliath .i. damac æda mic dallain mic liathain mic briuin mic eogain mic brice mic artchuirb mic fiach[nch] suigte

sund condric ocus brigit

5. *agatha* .i. uirgo [et] martir 7 hillonghardaib bingallia ata .i. hilongbardaib ata sancta agatha. agatus[l] nomen ciuitatis in illa plebe[k] et ab illo nominata est.

---

1. '*Julius*' i.e. the proper name of a saint in Scotland. I know not where he is.

'*Matthew*' i.e. Matthew's ordination.
'*of Aaron*.'

'*Thomas' translation*,' i.e. from the east were his relics brought, from India to Arabia or to Edessa, a town in Syria.

'*of Dartinne*' i.e. a virgin; of Cell Airnd in Ui-Garrchon in Leinster.

4. '*Martin's good great ordination*' .i. his ordination in Tours of Martin into the episcopate. *már martain* i.e. of great Martin; or great was his ordination, &c.

'*Findbarr*' i.e. in the land of Ui Cennselaig and in the Dési is he.

'*of Inis Teimle*' i.e. in darkness (*temel*) was the isle until Aed's two sons came (thither), namely, Findbarr and Barrfind i.e. the two sons of Aed of Ath Cliath i.e. two sons of Aed, son of Dallán, son of Liathán, son of Briun, son of Eogan, son of Brecc, son of Artchorp, son of Fiacha Suigte.

Here he and Brigit meet.

5. '*Agatha*' i.e. a virgin and martyr. And in Lombardy in Gaul is she, i.e. in Lombardy is Saint Agatha.

---

[a] MS. *prius* [b] MS. *necio* [c] *candaneus* [d] MS. *marcitiam* [e] MS. *abb*
[f] MS. *disa* [g] MS. *corpes* [h] MS. *pulcro* [i] MS. *dei*
[j] In the MS. this word commences the note. [k] MS. *plene*

6. *moninde* .i. monindach atbertis na caillech[a] fri[e] 7 do *huib* echach ulad dl. .i. Moninne ingen mochta mic lilaig mic lugdach mic rossa mic imchada mic fedlimthi mic cais mic fiachach aráide mic oengus[a] goibnend. ut dixit [poeta]

Noí .xx. bliadan malle
doreir riaglai contime
cenbocs [cenbet] cenbœgul
bahe socgul moninde

Odegab criss facolaind
isiar[na]táss atchluinim

nochar [cbnith] saith no séri
moninde sleibe cuilind*

in lower marg.]
Moninde 7rl. .i. moninde slóbi cuilind. ocus sárbile ahainm prius. no darercai ahainm fortuus. acht aruile file balb rotroisce aice conid he toisech rolabair ninim [leg. ninidiu?] unde est mouinde frisin caillig. ocus nine écis fair fén .i. monine quasi monanna atbertis nacaillecha fria.

Siur*muro .i. uirgo enim fuit sicut maria.

Noí .xx. bliadan malle
doreir riaglai contime
cenbais conbet cenbœgul
bahe sœgul moninde.
Moninde dorada di
donnéemoig chraitbdig collii
monanna ahainm corath
atbertis in ingenrad.
No isass roraided iutainm
donchaillig imatogairm
onine écess ferrde
rosataig imáitge.
Nonindisiub dúib amach
ahainm [dilis cognathach]
darereni friare roslean
coruegab intagnomen.
ix. fichit.

6. '*Moninne*' i.e. 'My-nindach' the nuns used to call her, and of Ui Echach of Ulster was she i.e. Moninne daughter of Mochta son of Lilaeh son of Lugaid, son of Rossa, son of Imehad, son of Fedlimid, son of Cas, son of Fiacha Araide, son of Oengus Goibniu; as a poet said :—

Nine score years together
According to rule without warmth,[b]
Without folly, without crime, without fault,
Was the age of Moninne.

Since she took a girdle on her body,
It is according to knowledge of her that I hear,
She ate not her fill or food,
Moninne of Slieve Gullion.

'Moninne' etc. i.e. Moninne of Slieve Gullion, and Sárbile was her name previously. Or Darerca was her name at first. But a certain dumb poet fasted with her, and the first thing he said [after being miraculously cured of his dumbness] was *ninnin*. Hence the nun was called Mo-ninde, and the poet himself Nine Ecis. Mo-nine quasi *Mo-nanna* the nuns used to call her.

'A sister of Mary,' for she was a virgin, even as Mary.

Nine score years together
According to rule without warmth,
Without folly, without crime, without fault
Was the age of Moninde,
(The name) 'Mo-ninde' was given to her,
To the holy virgin, pious, with splendour:
'Mo-nanna' (was) her gracious name
Which the maidens used to say.
Or from this the name was said
Of the nun for her appellation—
From Nine the Poet (the better thereof)
Who besought her for her prayer.
I will tell it out to you,
Her own name usually,
'Darerca' for a time adhered to her
Tell she got the *agnomen*.[c]

Nine score.

---

[a] So Fiacc, 32, of Patrick: *ni-leice a-chorp hi-timmi* 'he let not his body (be) in warmth.'
[b] This quatrain is from Cuimen of Conneire's poem.
[c] lit. "till the *agnomen* ('surname,' but here 'nickname') took her."

Aroile gadaige rogat oenboin aistire thamlachtu moelruain. Gabaid intaistire forgressacht inerluma . oeus atbert . nidambuidech donerlam nadigland muboin for inugataige olse. uair atchiamait he eeuesbuid chruid *no* clainde *no* slanti fair. Tic intérlam cusinaistire iarsin 7 atbert fris . Fecht and olse nimarbumne arnaimtiu focétoir *acht* afuirech inaubethaid *oeus* amcath co*n*adént ní doleass acuirp nach ananma . oeus leemait dodiabul cech olce isáil do dfurail forru . oeus ismessa doibsium sin oltas amarb*ad* focétoir . uair istrumaite apiana anifiurn afuirech oedenam uilce . ut dixit moelruain.

Seang hisessam lind fornech
imchian caingen oeus breth
sechmall alessa areech ló
sirifiurn nihimargo.

Oeus cech tan budail doib olse impod ónulec 7 maith dodénam nilécumne doib *acht* fuirgemait eat don lou arachcliu oedenam uilee cocrich asægail 7 tiagut aniferu iarforbu cechuilce iarum . Fi.n.it.

p. 91] Oeus isaias 7 ioel propheta[e] in hoc die.

7. *parmeni* .i. martir .i. parmenius mille uictus est uel iunctus.

moelruain .i. moelruain othamlachtu 7 colman nomen patris eius. broiesech nomen matris eius oeus escop he féin

8. *brocan* .i. omoethail brócan indessib mumau . *no* brocan scribnig patraic hic . 7 imbrechmuig inuib torta ata acheall

diarmait .i. modimoc inúib bairrche . ise roboi prius hinglind huissen recómgan

9. *onchon* .i. prespiter .i. onchu mac blathmaic oraith blathmeic in uachtar dalcais .i. in uno sepulero religionis[b] [eum finano].

A certain thief[a] stole the only cow of the doorkeeper (*ostiarius*) of Tallaght Mailruain. The doorkeeper began inciting the patron saint, (Maelruain, to avenge him), and said : " I am not thankful for the patron that avengeth not my cow on the thief," says he : " for we see him without want of cattle or of children or of health." Thereafter comes the patron to the doorkeeper and said to him : " Time there," says he, " we kill not our foes at once, but let them remain in their life and their decay, so that they do nothing to profit their body or their soul. And we allow the Devil to enjoin upon them every evil that he likes. And worse for them is that than killing them at once. For their punishments in Hell are the heavier from their remaining (here) doing evil . *ut dixit* Maelruain :

Seng t-sessam (l) have we for every one,
A far-off trial and judgment,
Oblivion of their advantage on every day,
Eternal hell, (it is) not a falsehood.

" And every time that they should wish" says he, " to turn from the evil and to do good, we let them not, but we delay them from the one day to the other doing evil till the limit of their life, and then they go into Hell after fulfilling every evil."

And Isaiah and Joel the prophets on this day.

'*Maelruain*' i.e. Maelruain of Tallaght, and Colman was his father's name, Broicsech his mother's name, and he himself was a bishop.

8. '*Broccán*' i.e. of Moethail Broccáin in Dési of Munster. Or Broccán Patrick's scribe is here, and in Brechmag in Ui-Torta is his church.

'*Diarmait*' i.e. My-Dimóc in Ui-Bairrche . He it is that was formerly in Glenn Uissen, before Comgan.

9. '*of Onchú*' i.e. a priest i.e. Onchu son of Blathmac of Raith Blathmaic in the upper part of Dál-cais. In one *sepulchrum religionis* was he with Finan.

---

[a] the thief.   [b] MS. relicionis.

INmain dias fil cofoiss
iconchroiss comembro thess
onchú nadcar doman diss
finan lobor lam na less
Macc inecis echnech fer
file fortren tracta tuath
inbaile hitoitend incrann
ni husa abarr dobreith uad.

Dear the two who are at rest
At the cross with relics in the south,
Onchú who loved not a despicable world,
Finan the Leper, hand of the benefits.
The poet's son, Onchú, a forceful man,
A poet vigorous in quelling tribes.
At the place where the tree falls,
It is not easy to carry off its top.

aratat membro .i. taissi finnin lobair 7 onchon anoenmaigin . hicluain mor

For the *membro* i.e. the relics of Finan the Leper and of Onchú are in one place, i.e. in Cluain Mór.

9. *garban* .i. hitæb suird choluim *cille* . no ochind saile itine gall. no iuiarthar erenn no icind locha scinnne 7 cend saile nomen eclesiæ.

9. '*Garbán*' i.e. beside Swords of Colomb Cille. Or of Kinsaley in Fingal. Or [of Kinsale] in the west (south) of Ireland. Or at the end of Loch Scimne; and Cenn Saile is the church's name.

10. .uii. mbraithre .i. uii. fratres in roma uel alio locco . quorum proprium matris nomen sancta felicitas*. in roma pasi sunt in hoc die.
cuan .i. cuan airbre in huib cendselaig ocus isinandsom 7 cuan mæthla brocain indessib muman
mare .i. quidam euangelista*.
11. *martra na cigna* .i. xu . milia martirum.
eufemia .i. virgo et martir et sub dioclitiano imperatore passa est.
benedicht .i. pater monachorum . mac . . .
conlocha .i. ódisert mcic conlocha aniarthar mide ocus failbe ainm
12. *nazair* .i. escop leith inqblind . no escop leith móir moir mochoemoc
13. *lamsiloc* .i. ochill mosiloc inúib degad inúib cendselaig
14. iacop . ne[s]cio quis iacop.
15. [in lower marg.] INda aspol deac 7rl.
Simon madian ismatha
parrthalon tomas tatha
petur andrias pilip pol
eoin ocus nada iacop
.xii. apostoli hiberniæ.
Datinen dacholum chaid
ciaran coindech comgall cain
dabrenaind ruadan colli
nindcd mobfi mac natfrnich

'*Cuan*' i.e. Cuan Airbre in Ui-Cennselaig; and he is the same as Cuan of Maethail Broccáin in Dési of Munster.

'son of *Conlug*' i.e. of Disert Meic Conlocha in the west of Meath, and Failbe was his name.

12. '*Nazarius*' i.e. bishop of Liath in Ebliu (?). Or bishop of Liath Mór Mochoemóic.
13. 'with my *Silóc*' i.e. of Cell Mo-silóc in Ui-Degad in Ui-Cennselaig.

15. 'The twelve apostles,' &c.
Simon, Matthaeus and Matthew,
Bartholomew, Thomas, Thaddæus,
Peter, Andrew, Philip, Paul,
John and the two Jameses.

The twelve apostles of Ireland.
Two Finnéns, two chaste Colombs,
Ciarán, Caindech, fair Comgall,
Two Brenainns, Ruadan with splendour,
Nindid, Mobfi son of Natfraech.

16. mametis .i. martir .i. xii. annorum erat quando passus* est.

---

* MS. eorum proprium matris .uii. scn. felecitatis. The seven brothers were (according to *Ob.* and *Mart.*) Januarius, Felix, Philippus, Silvanus, Alexander, Vitalis, Marcialis.
b MS. euangelisto
c MS. pasuss.

[*in lower marg.*]
Aitchimsi momotis
itir sruithib sena
cotisat himchomdail
findchua is colman elai
ISaire nosaitchim
dodichur mochinad
gar cian corlam cuman
intriur umal idan
Cotisat domfres[t]al
iuuair ccni ablaid
cofaicciur ataidbsin
inaimsir anainig.

I beseech Mammes,
Among ancient seniors,
Findchua and Colman Ela,
That they come into my company
For this I beseech them
To expel my sins.
Short be the time till they remember me,
The three, humble, pure!
Let them come to attend me
At the hour of death's warning
That I may see their semblance
At the time of their protection (?)

17. *harum* .i. pas[s]ae sunt in cartagine.

scellitarum .i. proprium [nomen] gentis .i. populus magnus qui [in uno die] occi[s]us est proscilita perigri*nis* Scilla nomen ciui*tatis* . scillita vero patronomicum a scilla diriuatum est. in scilla uero populus magnus est . multi uirorum[a] ac feminarum in hoc die decollati sunt.

18. *in xptina* .i. cristina cum .uii. fratribus . m[ór]s[éssiur] brathre .i. brathair cristinæ abeau. [*leg* . ob eandem, *or* ab eadem I] propter sanctitatem fratres eius nominantur et ab eu[b] loch cristina in italia nominatur proprii mul.

in r. mary.] Slóiged inarigna 7rl. snaidsi*um* insiúl . pul (*sic*) incristine . isuaithe ainmnigther loch cristain .i. propo roman*e* .i. spatio itinerum[d] trium distantes[e] uel cristina.

Ishe so senchus romanorum .i. *conid* aice dorónad ocutochar oróin coslóib ngargain . ISamlaid forcocmnacair ón . Aroli fer saidhir dothabairt grada dermair di . condobairtsi nach intaigfed for nach comaid fris acht minas cungnad lee umdenam amórumaloite.

Dognither amlaid comustargaid denum intochair tria furtacht iurig conustanic rath dé fairsium fossin tresin ngnimsin 7 fognait donchoimdiu andís cenchomrac rium .i. cristina oc*us* inrig 7rl.

19. *in lower marg.*]. Noebitche sisendi 7rl. .i. sisendius duriclarus de familia neronis sed a clemente papa baptizatus[f] est cum omni familia sua[g].i. cccliii. nobiles et illustres et amici[h] neronis

'a great-hexad of brothers' i.e. brothers of Christina.

'May the host of the queen, &c., protect us into the peace.'
From her is named Lacus Christinæ near Rome.
This is a story of the Romans, that by her was made one causeway from Rome to Mount Garganus. Thus did that happen. A certain wealthy man gave very great love unto her; but she said that she would not unite with him on any condition save (this) that he would work along with her in doing her great (deed of) lowliness.
Thus it is done, and, through the king's help, she finished the making of the causeway, and God's grace came upon him through that deed, and they both served the Lord without ever coming together, i.e., Christina and the king, &c.

'Sisennius' holy prayer,' &c.

[a] MS. hororum   [b] MS. eo   [c] Facs. romain   [d] MS. iteneris   [e] MS. ostantes
[f] MS. pratizatus   [g] MS. suæ   [h] MS. amice.

per istum deo cre[di]derunt sed per teodor[am] coniugemᵃ prius isto cre[di]dit . nec pas[s]io eius narraturᵇ hic.
Sol in taurum intrat.
20. *romula* .i. iroim robui *curufin* .i. infib fulgenti amumain ata curufin
21. daniel propheta.
22. *magdalena* .i. a magdalo uico in quo nata est vel nutrita.
in lower marg.] Findgein magdalena 7rl. .i. gein find .i. solusta .i. a matre uel infit [leg. in vitam ?] uel in caelum . Magdalena a magdelo uico quodam dicta est in quo nata [est] quae soror lazari fuitᶜ sed .xuiii mulieresᵈ in comitatu christi erant .iiii. ex illis uocantur a nomine quod est maria . Prima maria mater domini nostri iesu christi . Secunda maria mater filiorum zepedei quae fuitᵉ soror matrisᶠ domini . Tertia maria mater filii alfei quae et ipsa soror matrisᵉ domini fuit . Quarta maria magdalena . ISiso rosuidestar fochossaib *crist* et fudit oleum super caput eius et super pedes . ocus rosnig diadéraib ocus rosglan dinfult . cotardsom dilgad di diapecdaib ⁊ rosbean infarrsaid fairsium .i. for *christus* comairlecud meretricis hicomfocus dó.
appolluin .i. discipulus petri apostoli pasus est urbe ravenna vespasianoᵍ imperatore et sub iudic[e] eiusdem urbis id est demosthene.ⁱ
indsi causcraid .i. iferand duin .i. dabiu mac comgaill innte
24. *tathut* . . . *declan* .i. ata duit *no* atbath declan airde moire indésib muman .i. Declan airde moire mac eirc mic mic niad mic briuin mic eogain mic brice mic airtchuirp mic fiachach suigde mic fedlimthe rechtmair .i. dalta moling he

in lower marg.] Mad toich duit aeri 7rl. .i. dalta moling declan airde moire . ocus hitig moling ata *no* hilliss mor . vel sic
  Mac cathbaid bunid leri
  [*a line wanting*]
  colman airir ard aige
  molua molbthach mairge
25. *Mocholmoc mosiloc* .i. duo principes . *Mocholmoc* .i. colman hua liathan olias mor mochuda

20. '*Romula*' i.e. in Rome was she.
'*Curufin*' i.e. in Ui-Fidgente in Munster is Curufin.

She it is who sat by Christ's feet and poured oil over his head and on his feet, and washed them with her tears, and cleansed them with her hair, so that He gave her forgiveness of her sins, and the Pharisees upbraided Him. to wit, Christ, for allowing a harlot to be near Him.

'of *Inis Cuscraid*,' i.e. in Ferann Duin, i.e. Thy-Biu son of Comgall, was therein.
24. '*Thou hast . . Declan*,' i.e. there is to thee or Died Declan of Ardmore in Dési of Munster .i.e. Declan of Ardmore son of Erc, son of Mac Niad, son of Briun, son of Eogan, son of Brcec, son of Artchorp, son of Fiacha Suigde, son of Fedlimid Rechtmar: i.e. Moling's foster-son was he.
'If thou likest, O Ireland,' etc. i.e. a foster-son of Moling was Declan of Ardmore, and in St. Mullen's he is, or in Lismore. Or thus
  Son of Cathbad, victory of piety,
  . . . .
  Colman of Airer, a high pillar,
  Molua the praiseworthy of Mairge.
25. '*My-Colmóc, my-Silóc*' i.e. two leaders. '*My-Colmóc*' i.e. Colman descendant of Liathan, of Less Mór Mochuda.

ᵃ MS. couigen ᵇ MS. narraturus ᶜ MS. post ᵈ MS. mulieris ᵉ MS. post ᶠ MS. mater
ᵍ MS. sed .iii. ʰ MS. reberda uespesiano ⁱ MS. démos dennen.

[July 25-31.] NOTES FROM THE LEBAR BRECC, p. 92.

nessan .i. deochan [n]essán omunghairit
iacop .i. mac zepedei . iacop mac zepedei qui ab herode agrippa occisus[a] est in ierusalem. et qui primus de apostolis pasus est . ut ferunt si uerum[i] est. Sed cum iacopo[b] filio zepedei memoria martiris christifori .i. kandanei celebratur romanis[c].
 26. *a cleir* .i. cccc.
isleib taboir .i. isléib galile .i. treb neptalim. transformatio christi in monte tabor coram .u. testibus[d] moysi scilicet et heliæ petro et iohanni et iacopo
 27. *semeoin* . in antiochia passus[e] est.
 28. *trophil* .i. episcopus antiochiae.
pantaleo .i. martir et in nicomedia passus[f] est.
 29. *lumbus ocus simplex* .i. bi .ii.[g] episcopi sunt. [*in lower marg.*] Recht crist neoch nochandais 7rl. lupus 7 simplex et prosper tres[h] episcopi sunt.
 30. *abdon* 7 [s]*ennis* .i. duo martires et roma[e] pasi sunt gladio.
 31. *colman* .i. colman mac oengusa mic natfraich 7 indaire mor atasom
in lower marg.] Colman mac dairine .i. siur mathar docholman dairine . ocus dulta dissi[i] esium . Sanct im*murro* siur dairine *máthair* cholm*din* . Ambreith im*murro* dairine . Claunmar din. sanct asiur. Cuinchis tra dáirine colman dia altram forasiair iaruabreith foc*ó*toir . Doberar din. dissi indsin . conid hi dairine rosalt conid de rolil colman mac dairine he . ocus iedaire mor amuig airb atasom .i. itir osraigib 7 hélo . ocus mac táil ochill manach iniarthar osraige in uno die cum eo.

Nessán i.e. deacon Nessán of Mungret.
James i.e. son of Zebedee, James son of Zebedee *qui* etc.

'*on Mount Tabor*' i.e. on a mountain of Galilee in the tribe of Nephtalim.

'Christ's law to everyone they used to sing' etc.

31. '*Colman*' i.e. Colmán son of Oengus, son of Natfraech, and in Daire Mór is he.
'Colmán son of Dairine' i.e. a sister of Colmán's mother was Dairine, and he was a fosterson of hers. Now Sanct, Dairine's sister, was Colmán's mother. Now Dairine was childless and Sanct her sister had many children. So Dairine, as soon as he was born, asked her sister for Colmán to foster him. So then he is given to her, and Dairine fostered him, and thus the name 'Colmán son of Dairine' clave to him . In Daire Mór in Mag Airb he is, that is between Ossory and Ele. And Mac Táil of Cell Manach in the west of Ossory is commemorated on the same day with him.

---

[a] MS. herodes agripa occius [b] MS. iacopu [c] MS. romanus
[d] MS. uestibus [e] MS. antiocia pasus [f] MS. inecomedia pasus [g] MS. uii
[h] MS. tris [i] MS. altaside

[August 1-8.

RAWL. 505.	LAUD 610, fo. 67 a—b.	LEBAR BRECC, p. 93.
1. Do kl. inauguist doraraice mór mbrige lafeil macc mochaba ochtmoga mór mile	1. Do kl. indaugaist feil petair combrigi lafeil macc mochaba ochtmoga mormile	1. Do kl. inaugaist doraraice mor mbrige lafeil mac mochabæ .lxxx. mor mile
2. Lasinmathair marsin teothota inbaidsin lotar forsinbuaidsin natri maccain maithsin	2. Lassinmathair moirsin teothota inbaidsin lotar lasinbuaidsin natrimaccan maithsin	2. Lasinmathair moirsin teothota inbuidsin lotar lasinmbuaidsin natri maccain maithsin
3. Metrapoil indeoin derbiled (sic) conani inairecht connoebi corpan soer stefani	3. Metrapoil indeoin inmain feil conáni inairecht conóemi corpan soer stefaine	3. Metrapuil indeoin inmain feil conani inairecht conoemi corpan srer zefani
4. Bid failid iarrichtu frimm ismor adocha indocbgerait rig[d]a molua macc ocha	4. Bid failid iarrichtain rim is mor adoche indnoehgerait rigda molua macc oiche	4. Bidfailid iarrochtain frim ismor adocha in nocmgerait rigdai molua macc ochai
5. Cesad an herenti ardlig comarce coemda la hosualt noeb nailme airdri sachsan soerda	5. Cessad an herenti ardlig comare coemda lasoalt* nóem nailme ardrí saxan soerda	5. Cesad an erenti ardlig cormac coemdai lahosualt noem nailme ardirig saxan særdai
6. Sistún epscop ruamach rucc suas saithe snamach lamchua cli buadach ocluain dolcain dalach	6. Sistan escop ruamach rue suas saithi snamach la mochua cli buadach óchluain dolchain dalach	6. Sistan epscop ruamach rue suas saithe snamach la mochua cli buadach ochluain dolccain dalach
7. Dlom coic arthrib coce-taib bliadan brig ronfeitheiss morfessiur cen aithiss conattail ineffiss	7. Dlom coic artricetaib^b bliadna brig ronfeithis morseisir cennithis conattail^c ineffis	7. Dlom cuic ar .ccc.aib bliadan brig ronfethis morfessiur cennithis conatuil inefhs

1. To the kalends of August came much of vigour^d, at Maccabee's sons' feast, eighty great thousands.

2. With that great mother, Theodota that dear one, went, besides that victory, those three good children.

3. In John's metropolis (Jerusalem) beloved is the feast with splendour, whereon was found with holiness Stephen's noble body.

4. Blithe is he after arriving (in heaven): great is my confidence in him, the holy, kingly champion, Molua mac Ocha.

5. Herentius' splendid suffering deserves a lovable commemoration, with holy Oswald whom we implore, over-King of the free Saxons.

6. Sixtus a Roman bishop bore upwards a buoyant troop: with Mo-Chua a victorious prince, from multitudinous Cluain-Dolcáin.

7. Announce the five and three hundred years—might which thou beheldest—which the seven without disgrace slept in Ephesus.

^a .i. la hosualt B   ^b l. coec[t]aib B   ^c l. contuilset B   ^d 'Peter's feast with vigour' B.

RAWL. 505.	LAUD 610, fo. 67 b.	LEBAR BRECC, p. 93.
8. Feil beoan meicc nessain noll ni hattach mbille colman epscop aille oinis bo finne	8. Feil beonin maic nessain nuill ní hattach mbille colman escop ailli oinis bó finde	8. Feil beonin maic nessain noll ni hatach mbille colman epscop aille o inis bo finde
9. Feith latt pais antoni firmi fortren muinter inachud cain chlaintair nathi credal crumther	9. Feithlet pais antoni firmí fortren muinter innachad chain clanntar nathi credal cruimther	9. Feith lat pais antoni firnii fortren muinter inachud cain clantar nahii credal cruimther
10. Croch lan lurint dechoin diachorpan bacalad lasluag slan socr sodan blaan cain chinngarad	10. Croch lan lurint deochain diachorpan bacalad lasluag saer slan sodath blaan cáin chindgarad	10. Croch lau laurint deochain diachorpan bacalad lasluag slan saer sodath blaan cain chind garad
11. Guid airennan eccnai assaclu nadchelar laualeran nidan tiburtius tren trebair	11. Guid cireran ecna assa clú nateelar laualeran nidhan tiburtius trén trebar	11. Guid aireran indecnai asaclu nateelar laualiran nidan tributius tren trebar
12. Togairm laissren inse muredaig moir mochtni cocleir moir nadaithbi feil segeni sochlai	12. Togairm laisrein iudsi muiridaig moir mochta cocleir cain nataithbi feil segeno sochla	12. Togairm lasren indse muiredaig moir mochtac cocleir nocim nadaithbe feil segeni sochlai
13. Hipolitus martir bamirbuil athoiden cosluag adbul hunsal momedoc mind goidel	13. Hipolitus mairtir bamirbuil athoidhen cosluag adhbal uassal momædóc mind ngocidel	13. Hipolitus martir bamirbuil athoiden cosluag adbul uasal momoedoc mind ngædel
14. Lagairm furtunati darfairce ler longach mac intair cain cinged feil fachtnai macc mongach	14. Lagairm furtunati darfairrge lir longaig mac intsair cain cimbid feil fachtna maicc mongaib	14. Lagairm furtunatii darfairrgi lir lougaig mace intseir cain cimbid fuil fachtnai maice mongaig
15. Himorfeil ahaithmeit⁎ firmathair arnathar	15. IMor feil ahaithmet firmathair⁵ arnathar	15. Himorfeil ahaithmet firmathair arnathar

8. The feast of Beóán son of Nessán, a great—not a prayer to a paltry one, Colmán bishop of praise, of Inis bó finde.

9. Remember thou the passion of Antonius' (and) of Firmus, a mighty family. In Achad Cáin is buried Nathi a pious priest.

10. The full cross of Deacon Laurentius to his poor body was hard. With a host sound, noble, fair, Bláán of beautiful Cenn Garad.

11. Beseech Airerán of the wisdom whose fame is not hidden, with Valerian the pure, Tiburtius the strenuous and prudent.

12. The calling of Laisrén of the Isle of Muredach, the great and magnified: with a holy⁶ train that ebbs not, the feast of famous Segéne.

13. Hippolytus the martyr, marvellous was his troop. With a host vast, noble, My-Maedóc, diadem of the Gael.

14. With the calling of Fortunatus over a sea of shipful ocean, the wright's son (mac int-sáir) a fair captive: the feast of Fachtnae the hairy child.

15. On a great feast is⁴ her commemoration, our Father's true Mother. With a

⁎ MS. abaith meice   ᵇ l. firbráthair 'true brother' B.   ᶜ B 'fair' B, 'great' D.   ᵈ 'of' D.

RAWL. 505.	LAUD, 610.	LEBAR BRECC, pp. 93–94.
cosluag rig ran clochar fer da chrich cain cathar	coslog rig ran clochar fer da crich cain cathar	coslog rig ran clochar fer da chrich cain cathar
16. Lacroich adrionis cocrir nadchar dichmaree feil maire mind nuagbailce noebmathair morigmaice	16. Lacroich adrionis cocleir natcar dichmaire goin' maire mind nuagbaile nóinmathair morímaice	16. Lacroich adrionis cocleir nadchar dichmairce goin muire mind nuagbailce noemmáthair morigmaice
17. Rocess mammes martir morphian hicroich chalaid lacleir cain cenchinaid taimthiu teimnan manaig	17. Rocés mammes mairtir morpeinn icroich calaid lacleir cáin gau chinaid taimthiu temncin manaig	17. Roches mammes martir morpein icroich calaid lacleir cain cen chinaid taimthiu teimnen manaig
18. Macc cresseni mernoc morais fiadait fairinn bafer raith diarturinn daig mor maith macc cairill	18. Macc cresseni mernoc moris fiadaid foireun bafer raith diartuiriud daigh mor maith macc cairill	18. Mac creseni mernoc morais fiadnit fairind bafer raith diartuirind daig mor maith macc cairill
19. Croch inmartir magni cocleir combuaid blaithe mochta mor maith sith be enan dromma raitho	19. Croch inmairtir magne cocleir combuaid blathe mochta mormaith sithbe énan droma rathe	19. Croch inmartir magni cocleir combuaid blaithe mochta mor maith sithbe enan droma raithne
20. Rochess diascorus arcrist cing asferrdu pampil breo asamru commorsluag bageldu	20. Rocés diarscorus arcrist cing asferrda pampil breo asamru comorsluagud gelda	20. Roches mor diarscorus arcrist cing asferdu pampil breo isamru comorsluagud geldu
21. Guid hifeil uincenti dochongnam fritainmain epscop senach sulbair cluana biraird adbail	21. Guid hifeil uinceinte dochongnam fritanmain epscop senach sulbair cluana iraird adbail	21. Guid ifeil uincentli dochungnam fritanmain escop senach suilbir cluana iraird adbail

king's host—right splendid assembly—Fer-dá-chrích ('man of two districts') a fair shield (?)

16. At Adrion's cross, with a train that loved not theft, the birth of Mary, a virginal, strong diadem, holy Mother of my Prince.

17. Mammes the martyr suffered great pain on a hard cross: with a fair, crimeless following Monk Teimnén's bed-death.

18. Creséne's son, my Ernóc, a troop that magnified God. A man of grace for our wheat was Daig, the good and great son of Cairell.

19. The cross of the martyr Magnus, with a train victorious, blooming,[b] Mochta the great good chieftain, Enan of Druim Roithne.

20. Greatly suffered Dioscorus for Christ—a champion who is most manly. Pamphilius, flame that is most marvellous, with a great, fair host.

21. Beseech on Vincentius' feast to help thy soul bishop Senach the eloquent, of vast Clonard.

[a] l. féil 'festival' B [b] lit. 'with victory (or guerdon) of bloom'

RAWL. 505.	LAUD, 610.	LEBAR BRECC, p. 94.
22. Attaig itge tiamdai daltai poil conani guid maccraith conocbi indnoib emiliani	22. Attaig itge timdai daltai poil conáni guid maccraid conoéimi indnoem emuláni	22. Ataig itge thiamdai daltai poil conaui guid maccraid conoemi indoeim emeliani
23. Lapais furtunati immaluid lin catha forocnlith luad mbetha feil cogain aird sratha	23. Lapais furtunati immaluid lin catha foroen lith luad betha feil cogain ardsretha	23. Lapais purtinati imalluid lin catha forenlith luad betha feil cogain aird sratha
24. Lasreith sluaig stenoni ascela roclotha senphatraice cing catha coemaite arsrotha	24. Lasreith sluag zenoti atasceoil roclotha senpatraie cing catha cóemaite arsrotha	24. Lasreith sloig zenatii atasceoil roclotha senpatraic cing catha coemaite arsrotha
25. Rosreth seel achesta cechleth cosal sruamach	25. Rosreth seel achesta cachleth cosal sruamach	25. Rosreth seel achesta cech leath cosal sruamach
iarmorchroich rorigad inbartholom buadach	iarmorchroich rorigad inparrtalon buadach	iarmorchroich rorigad inparrthalon buadach
26. Buaid pais quinti martir	26. Buaid pais quinti mairtir	26. Buaid pais quintii martir
diachelebrad comeir fornem cosluag roreil rorebraing iarndrobeil	iar* coilebrad comeir fornem cosluag roleir rodreblaing iarndrobeil	dia chelebrad comeir for neam coslog roreil rodrebraing iarndrobeil
27. Drong inmartir glandai ruffi cain combinni corig nel noeb ndoe luid tre rore rinni	27. Drong inmairtir glannai rufin cáin cofindi corig nel nóem doe luid trea roe rinni	27. Drong in martir glandai rupbin cain combindo corig nel noem ndoe luid tre roe rinde
28. Ronain ciriacus conachleir cain chathlaice	28. Rornain[b] ciriacus conachleir cain cathlaic	28. Ronau ciriacus conacleir cain cathlaic

22. Pray for the prayers of Timothy the fosterling of Paul with splendour: beseech the youths with holiness of the holy Emelianus.

23. At the passion of Fortunatus, with whom went warriors, on one festival—a world's talk—the feast of Eogan of Ard Sratha.

24. With the heap of Zenobius' (?) host, whose stories were famed, Old-Patrick, champion of battle, lovable tutor of our sage.

25. The story of his suffering was spread out on every side to the streamy sea: after a great cross the victorious Bartholomew was crowned.

26. The victory of martyr Quintus' passion, to celebrate it arise thou: into heaven with a very clear host he sprang after difficulty.

27. The troop of the purified martyr Rufinus, the fair with melodiousness,[c] to the holy rampart of the King of Clouds went through keenest spearpoints.

28. May Quiriacus protect us, with his train fair, catholic. Hermes suffered a

---

[a] l. dia B   [b] l. Ronnain B   [c] 'whiteness' B

RAWL. 503.	LAUD, 610.	LEBAR BRECC, p. 94.
hermes cessais rochneit	hermes cesais rochneit	ermis cesnis rochneid
intairdire ahaffraicc	interdraic ahafraicc	intaurdaire ahafruic
29. Asneid cesad coin	29. Aisneid cessad coin	29. Aisneid cesad iohain
babtaist bith coleri	babdaist bid* coleire	bauptaist bid coleri
lanoicct conhuagi	lanoc chet conoighe	la .ix. cét conuagi
forfresgabail heli	lafresgabail héle	lafresgabail heli
30. Alainn huag agappa	30. Álaind huag agatha	30. Alaind uag agatha
asgrian dofornaebaib	asgrian dabur noemaib	isgrian dabarnoemaib
adreth buaid huastua-	adreth buaid uasbuadaib	adreith buaid uasbua-
daib		daib
conasethraib soeraib	cona sethraib sóeraib	conasethraib sseraib
31. Sernaitt eithre ñaugau-	31. Sernait eithre august	31. Sernait ethri nauguist
ist		
ædan ingrian gelda	ædan ingrian gælda	ædan ingrian geldai
inse medcoit molma	indsi medchoit molmai	indsi medcoit molmai
lapaulin nafedba	lapaulin nafedba	lapaulin nafedbdai

great wound : (Augustine) the conspicuous out of Africa.

29. Announce the passion of John Baptist a flame with piety, with nine hundred with virginity, at Elijah's ascension.

30. A delightful virgin Agatha who is a sun to your saints: to the reward above rewards she ran with her noble sisters.

31. They overspread the end of August, Aedán the pure sun of praised Inis Medcoit (Lindisfarne), with Paulinus of the widow.

GLOSS FROM THE LEBAR BRECC, pp. 93, 94.

2. (1) .i. frecra domenmain lahoengus inso
3. (3) inairecht .i. ifrith
4. (2) adocha .i. adóchus no adúchus
5. (2) ardlig cormac .i. dligid imchomarc .i. cúimniugud no comardud nafilidechtai coemdai .i. alaind   (3) nailme .i. guid[m]e
6. (1) ruamach [.i.] fertach .i. cathardai   (2) suas .i. in caelum.   saithe .i. buiden snamach .i. forsnam   (3) cli .i. cleath no fraig tren   (4) dalach .i. conair sochaide
7. (1) dlom .i. indis no aisneid   ar .ccc. aib .i. a .u. l. ar c.   (2) ronfethis .i. rochuimniges no rochoimetus   (3) morfessiur .i. uii. fratres   (4) conatuil .i. rochotuilset inuaim hifail hefisse ['they slept in a cave near Ephesus']
8. (2) noll .i. mor ni hatach mbille .i. ni hatach boicht no genaige no meta no faigdech no midlaigi.   ut dicitur balan .i. billian .i. ian inbille .i. inboicht .i. bill 7 ian   (3) aille .i. aille .i. la iudes [leg. laudis ?]   (4) oinis no alla thair
9. (1) feith .i. cuimnig no feg   (3) clantar .i. adnaicther ['is buried']   (4) nahii nomen credal .i. craibdech   cruimther .i. sacerdos.
10. (2) calad .i. cruaid   (3) sodath .i. dath maith bui foraib.   ut dixit
[p. 92, lower marg.] Dag 7 fó clu cen brath
so is mo cen cob gnathach
anmannasin domaith mas
derb lium nisæb insenchas

* l. bréo B

['*dag* and *fö*, fame without betrayal : *so* and *mo* (though not usual) those are names for excellent 'good.' I am sure the story is not false']
12. (2) *mochtai* .i. magistir aucta (*sic*) vel magis   (3) *nadaithbe* .i. nifil erchrai foraib
13. (2) *athoiden* .i. [a]thaitnem *no* abuiden *no* athiudrem *no* a shuag no atbeacht
14. (1) *lagairm* .i. lahatach   (2) *lir longaig* .i. lear forambit longai .i. infairrgi   (3) *cimbid* .i. ciug he *no* roching *no* cimid .i. de familia dei
15. (1) *aithmet* .i. aithmid *no* aithbe   (2) *arnathar* .i. iesu christi
16. (2) *co cleir* .i. maith *no* togaide   *nadchar dichmairce* .i. ni concardis gait   (4) *morigmaice* .i. noriarsat na rigmec .i. mec narig eat
17. (2) *caluid* .i. crusid   (4) *taimthiu* .i. tomaithium *no* ec 7 martir he
19. (3) *sithbe* .i. sithbeo .i. fota achlu .i. saegul mochta
20. (4) *geldu* .i. bagile
23. (2) *luid* .i. ad caelum   *lin catha* .i. de martiribus   (3) *luad betha* .i. o thengaid fer mbetha oca imrad
24. (1) *lasreith* .i. lahaisnes *no* rorith aclu fondoman   (2) *roclotha* .i. rocluinte *no* roherdarcaigthea
25. (1) *rosreth* .i. aisnéid *no* rosrethad   (2) *sruamach* .i. srotha imdai ind ocus ass
26. (2) .i. orig iscssom docheilebrad aféilo   (4) *rodrebraing* .i. rodringestar *iarndrobeil* .i. iarndoccumal   *no* iarndrocherlabra chaich ectairmesc amaithiusa immc *no* iarcúnga moir
27. (3) *doc* .i. techtais *no* nirt *no* doos .i. sine stultitia *no* isnoeb indoos doneoch he beith foditen amarttra.   *no* noeb inclad *no* inmur .i. doe he .i. diada *no* isnoeb indoos doneoch foiditiu achésta pro deo *no* isnoeb 7 isdingna indoe .i. iuclad *no* inmur .i. martirum *no* doe odoos .i. sine stultitia.   (4) *tre roe rinde* .i. tre rinnib roaithe
28. (2) *cuthluic* .i. cathalucda
29. (1) *aisneid* .i. sluind   (2) *coleri* .i. acut
30. (1) *alaind* .i. taitnemach   (2) *grian* .i. taitnemchi   *dabarnoemaib* .i. adaine .i. a lucht legaid inletar   (3) *adreith* .i. adroet
31. (1) *sernait* .i. failgit *no* forbanait *no* srethait   *ethri* .i. deriud

NOTES FROM THE LEBAR BRECC, p. 93.

1. *doraraicc mor mbrige* .i. mar .i. clom .i. oruss chorcumruad inclib thuaiscirt

1. '*came much of vigour*' .i. great i.e. a leper (*lclam*) .i. of Ross Corcumruad in Eli of the North.[a]

feil mac mochabœ .i. in dalpin[l] ciuitate armeniae in eo die passi sunt .i. machabeus ab opido macha a graeco mace [μάχη] .i. pugna ab eo quod ibi multi pugnam faciebant

'*Maccabee's sons' feast*' i.e. in Dalphis (?) a city of Armenia, &c.

2. *teothota* .i. in betania [leg. Bithynia] passa est id est misa in ingnem cum tribus filiis suis .

lotar lasin mbuaid sin .i. martiri[um] qua passa [leg. quod passus 1] mochaba cum .uii. filiis suis.

They went, besides that victory.

na tri macain maithsin .i. tri meic theothota

'*Those three good sons*' i.e. three sons of Theodota.

3. *metrapuil ind eoin* .i. in antiocia fuit ciuitas uel roma uel coronatus interpretatur iohannes cum populo sub corpus stefani ad ierusalem tulerunt

[a] The scholiast seems to suppose the verb *doraraicc* to be a man's name.

in lower marg.] Do kl. in auguist 7 rl. Metrapuil indcoin . iohannis .i. in an[ti]ocia fuit metropolis et sic inuentam est (.i. frith) [corpus stephani] .i. lucianus prespiter eclesiœ quae est in uilla carpagn in alii ipsi (*sic*) corpus zefani christianis demonstrauit haud longe ab[a] ierusolimis uilla illa discat (*sic*) sed gamulel scriba[b] legis qui fuit in uno sepulcro cum zefano indecauit per uisionem noctis *hœc* luc[i]ano dicens Ego[c] gamulel et nicodemus nepos[d] meus et abbisus filius meus dilectis[e] imus nos omnes in uno sepulcro cum zefano sumus[f] et manifest[auit] apostolus ut ostensa zefani manifestentur[g] omnibus

inmain feil conani .i. uirgo .i. ochill derbiled iniarthar chond*acht*

4. *molua mac ochai* .i. ochluain fertai molua 7 ósléib bladmai 7 odruim[a] snechtai ifernmuig

in lower marg.] Bid failid 7rl. Molua mac ochai sic nominaturus est iste. Arise insenchus .i. diambui comgall bendebu*ir* ocimdecht aseta conamúinntir . ecmaing tra cocunlutur ni . scredda nanoi*n*den isinpurit lunchrai 7conaccutar timthirecht aingel uasu sist outsligil . Condebairt frifer dia muintir , feg latt cid fil isinpurt luachra ucat tall . dolluid infer 7 atnaig alua frisinmuine luachrai 7 atchii nóidin inamodon cotuc lais inaochsail he . corusfiarfaib cómgall de cid fuarais olse . illo dixit . Fuarus nóide olse . Cid doriguis fris olcomgall , Doratus molua friss olimmanach . Cáit hita olcómgall . Atmochsail olse . Bidhe aninm olcomgall , Molua mac ochai .i. am fadbail isinlunchair . no arinlua dorat inmanach frisinmuine luachrai iroibsium . Mac ochai .i. mac ochsaille arnbeith inochsail inmanaig . *acht* isa[r]chuimre atbernir mac ochai fris . arocha apud ucteres[b] ochsal dicitur prius . 7 roalt iarsin lacomgall combahendug.

MS. .i. frith et sic inuentum est.

leg . iacet?

'*beloved feast with splendour*' i.e. a virgin i.e. of Cell Derbiled in the west of Connaught.

'*Molua mac Ochai*' i.e. of Cluain Fertai Molua and of Slieve Bloom and of Druim Snechta in Fernmag.

'Blithe will he be' etc. Molua mac ochai , *sic nominatus est iste*. For this is the story, namely, when Comgall of Bangor was wending his way with his family, it came to pass that they heard somewhat: the cries of the babe in the bank of rushes, and they saw a service of angels over it, a little way from the road. So he said to a man of his family : "See thou what is in yon bank of rushes there." The man went and gave a kick into the brake of rushes and beholds a babe amidst it, and he took it into his armpit. So Comgall asked him, "What hast thou found?" quoth he. *Ille dixit*, "I have found a babe," quoth he. "What didst thou to it?" says Comgall. "I gave a kick at it," says the monk. "Where is it?" says Comgall. "In my armpit," says he. "This shall be its name," says Comgall, "My-*lua* (kick) son of *ocha* (armpit)" i.e. because of getting it in the rushes, or because of the kick which the monk gave to the brake of rushes wherein it was. *Mac ochai* i.e. son of armpit, because of its being in the monk's armpit ; but for brevity's sake he (Molua) was called *mac ochai*, for by the ancients *armpit* was formerly called *ocha* ; and afterwards he was reared by Comgall, so that he was innocent.

---

[a] MS. an*te* longue . Abb   [b] MS. scribai   [c] MS. Eco   [d] MS. necodimis nepes
[e] MS. manifsumus   [f] MS. manisfestatur   [g] Facs. drúm   [b] MS. uctures

Ecmaing din. intan bascolóe molua. teit comgall ocus essium doneclais. Tadbanar din. dochomgall iulin batar uile ainbeith cenchend for duine dib. Senais din. cómgall aruscasom 7 atchiatsom similiter. Machtnaigit cumor.

ISde ataso arcómgall .i. mannucharasu atbath 7 atusa cencheand 7 atathaisi cenchind. ariscolund cenchend duine ecnanunchamit. ocus caide barcomairle beos. Ata lemsa deit armolua ciarbahóg intansin he .i. tabair soscela crist chucat 7 congbad neeh ecin frit he 7 slecht do cofhadba anmchara ass. Fornchend deit arcómgall aristu issó and. Téit iarum 7 dobeir lais.

Sillis cómgall fair 7 atbert. Arisitlaim dorala insoscela istu busanmchara dausa olso. Conid he adalta .i. molua lalbanmchara dosam. 7 itchess dochomgall iarsin achend forcech noen istig 7 atchess similiter

5. Cesad an crenti .i. apud setiam ciuitatem. osualt .i. fland finn mac osu

6. Sistan .i. escop hiróim. papa* roime et martir.
mochua .i. mac lugdach qui prius cronan dictus est.

7. conatuil in effis
Tainme morfessiur cenéc
lxx bliadan nibreo
dosrat ri gréine folii
tall inuaim sléibe tellii.
Asecht naunmand mardaeloss
maximianus malcos
constantinus martius
marcianus dionisius.
Serápen iohannes oll
ainm dessi díb cenimroll
nicheil cech auctar anall
hite sin asecht nanmand.

in lower marg.]
Dlom .u. ar .ccc.aib 7rl. .i. Morfessiur de christianis dochotar hinuanaid arimgabail

Now it came to pass when Molua was a student, that Comgall and he came to the church. Then unto Comgall it is manifested that all who were (therein) were without a head on any one of them. So Comgall sained their eyes and they see like him. They marvel much.

"Hence is this," says Comgall, "namely, my soulfriend has died and I am without a head and ye are without heads: for a man without a soulfriend is a body without a head. And what are your counsels besides?" "Here is mine for thee," quoth Molua, though he was young then, "namely, take Christ's Gospel to thee, and let some one uplift it before thee, and kneel to it till thou gettest a soulfriend out of it." "(Go) thou for it," says Comgall, "for thou art the youngest there." Then he went and brings it with him.

Comgall looked on him and said, "Since it is in thy hand that the Gospel happens (to be), it is thou that shalt be my soulfriend." So that his fosterling, to wit, Molua, was soulfriend unto him, and Comgall thereafter saw the head on every one inside, and they saw in like wise.

5. '*Herentius*' *splendid suffering.*'
'*Osuald*' .i. Fland Finn ('of the wine') son of Ossa.

6. '*Sixtus*' i.e. a bishop in Rome.
'*Mo-chua*' i.e. son of Lugaid, who was previously called Cronan.

7. '*who slept in Ephesus.*'
The trance of seven without death.
Seventy years—not a lie—
The Sun's King put them under splendour,
There in a cave of Mount Coelius (?).
Their seven names, as hath been heard,
Maximianus, Malchus,
Constantinus Martius,
Marcianus, Dionysius,
Serapion, great Iohannes (was)
The name of two of them without mistake.
Not any author hides from that to this:
Those are their seven names.

"Announce five and three hundred," i.e. A heptad of Christians who went into a cave to

---

* In the ms. *fertach* comes between *roim* and *papa*; but it is obviously a gloss on *ruamach*.

aningrema fo decius 7 ualir[ianus] et cisterna clausa est super eos . uair noconfess andol innte . et dormierunt in ea c.l.u. [annos] donec uenerunt reges christiani in mundum et quaudi (*sic*) ciuitates constructæ sunt^a et alii exierunt ad cisternam illam [ad] quaerendas lapides^b ad renouandas ciuitates et alius ex illis [iuit] foras post somnum ut putauerunt ut emeret cibum illis et ostendit illis suum argentum in ciuitate et mirati sunt omnes de argento . et dixerunt . o homo uetus argentum habes . et nullus a te capiet^c quin tempore deci factum est et ex quo c.l.u. anni sunt et dixerunt modo est rex christianus id est constautinus filius elena[e] et tunc intellexit eos et gratias egit deo et narrauit omnia sua fabola^d . et inuitati sunt fratres eius a cisterna et postea rex ad eos alloquendos uenit . et narrauerunt ei sua omnia fabola et magnificatum^e est nomen dei per eos sic . Tanui morfessiur cenée 7rl. amal ata romaind.

8. *beoain maic nessain* .i. o fid chuillind in *buib* foelan

O inis bo finde .i. obf choluim cil*le* 7 o inis bó finde for muir thiar hi *conmacuib* marn an iarthar chond*acht*

9. *inach*u*l cain* .i. in achad chonaire hi luignib *con*[n]*acht*

10. *croch lan laurint* .i. martir[i]um eius .i. laurentius archidiaconus^f sixti papa[e] romæ fuit et sub decio passus est ba .uii. fuit (*sic*) sub decio pasus est in roma*e*

sluag .i. lxx. milites numero

blaan cain chind garad .i. dun blaan aprimchathair ocus ochind garad do .i. hingallgadelaib

Dachua o druim bó in hoc die

11. *aireran* .i. *a*thig airemin amide 7 fer legind cluana esium no icluain dolcain no abb taml*acht*u maelruain

ualiran .i. uxor eius cicilia conuertit eum ad christum et fratrem eius.

12. *lasren* .i. molaise mac déclain oinis muiredaig isin tuaiscert

seqeni .i. abb i*n* cholu*im* cil*le*

13. *hipolitus* .i. regulus primus et pasus est cum familia sua numero xix. utriusque sexus sub decio pasus fuit qui cre[di]dit deo per

^a ms. sint   ^b ms. q.randas lipides   ^e ms. magnificata   ^c capiat   ^d ms. fabolo   ^f ms. lurent*us* arcadia consu*s*

avoid the persecution under Decius and Valerian, *et cisterna clausa est super eos*, for it was not known that they had entered it, *et dormierunt*, &c.

'A trance of seven without death,' as is above.

8. '*of Beóán, son of Nessán*,' i.e. of Fid Cuillinn in Ui-Foeláin.

'*of Inis bó finde*' i.e. of Colomb Cille's Hí (Iona) and of Inis bó finde on the sea in the west, in Connemara in the west of Counaght.

9. '*In Achad cain*' i.e. in Achad Conaire in Luigni of Connaught

10. '*Laurentius' full cross*' i.e. &c.

'*a host*' i.e. &c.

'*Bláán of fair Cenngarad*' i.e. Dumblane (is) his chief city and of Cenngarad is he i.e. in Galloway.

Dachua of Druim Bó (is commemorated) on this day.

11. '*Aireran*' .i. of Tech Aireráin in Meath, and lector of Cluain was he. Or in Clondalkin. Or (he was) Abbot of Tamlacht Maelruain.

12. '*Lasrén*' i.e. Molaise son of Declán, of Inishmurray in the north.

'*of Segéne* i.e. abbot of Hí of Colomb Cille.

13. '*Hippolytus*,' &c.

laurentium [in l. marg.] sub decio pasus est in roma et cum eo promiscui sexus [xix.]
monoedoc .i. hi fhid dúin indescirt osraige

14. *mac intsair* .i. escop 7 abb dairindsi .i. dairinis maelanfaid .i. escop 7 abb dairindsi in huib ciunselaig 7 sær din. aathair

mongaig .i. mong mor bui fair intan rucad fachtnai . is assin ismac mongach atbered cách fris

15. *morfeil* .i. dormitatio maria[e] hic ut beata dicit 7 gg. [¹] asumptio sancta[e] maria[e] dei genetricis uel mater maelruain dicitur hic quia maelruain doc[t]or cius fuit no siur mælruain
arnathar .i. iesu christi bas nuire allaasin

for dáchrich .i. abb dairindsi. fer dá crich .i. caithfer no catharda
16. *gein muire* .i. co[m]memorationis [in r. marg.] Moelcoisne diu . ochill moelicoisne in huib maine *connacht for* renla *ocus maria mater domini.*
17. *mammes* .i. hifrangcaib ata qui mulsit lac a feris.
[in lower marg.] Roches mammes martir 7rl. qui mulsit lac a ferinis[a] et cui euangelium datum[b] est et pasus est sub [au]riliano imperatore in ciuitate capadociæ prouinciæ et puer erat annorum .xii. quando[c] pasus est. Vel mammes .i. sanctus fil ilongbardaib .i. añi hifrangcaib 7 *nobilis* martir et confesor fuit sicut incolao loci ill[i]us affirmant.
taimthiu teimnen .i. tomnithium no ec 7 martir he .i. olind lunchan *for* bru chassain linde
18. *mernoc* .i. merno[c] .i. ernin .i. mac craibdech he . no cresen nomen patris cius. no ernine mac cresine oraith noci auidib garrchou ifothartaib laigen 7 ochill draignech inuib drónai beos .
diar-tuirind ut œngus ait diarcruithnecht quia sancti dei triticum sunt
daig .i. [o] inis cáin dega hi conaillib muirthemne
in lower marg.]
Mac cressine mernoc 7rl.
Daig mac coirill gaba tra 7 ceard 7 scribnid togaide indaigsea. IShe din. daroine .ccc. clog ocus .ccc. bachall ocus .ccc. soscelai . ocus prim-

'*My-Maedoc*' i.e. in Fid dúin in the south of Ossory.
14. '*The wright's son*' i.e. bishop and abbot of Dairinis i.e. Maelanfaid's Dairinis .i. bishop and abbot of Dairinis in Hui Cinnselaig ; and his father was a wright.
'*hairy*' i.e. when Fachtuae was born much hair was on him. Hence everyone used to say of him '*mac mongach*' (hairy child).
15. '*a great feast.*'

or Maelruain's sister.
'*of our Father*' i.e. of Jesus Christ. Mary's death on that day.
'*For dá chrích*' i.e. abbot of Dairinis. *fer dá chrích* i.e. a champion or enthroned.
16. *Mary's birth* i.e. &c.
Moelcoisne, moreover, of Cell Moelecoisne in Ui-Mauy of Connaught on the same day as Mary the Lord's mother.
17. '*Mammes*' i.e. in France is he who milked milk from wild beasts.
'Mammes the martyr suffered.'

Mammes i.e. a saint who is in Lombardy i.e. . . . . in France.

'*Temnen's bed-death*' i.e. threatening or death, and a martyr was he i.e. of Linn Luachan on the brink of Cassan Linde.
18. '*My Ernóc*' i.e. Ernín i.e. a pious son (was) he. Or Cresin *nomen* patris eius. Or Ernine son of Cresine of Rath Noe in Hui-Garrchon in Fotharta of Leinster and of Cell Draignech in Hui-Dróna besides.
'*to our wheat*' . *ut* Oengus *ait* 'to our wheat,' because the Saints are God's wheat.
'*Daig*' i.e. of Inis Cain Dega in Conaille Muirthemne.

'Son of Cressíne, my Ernóc' etc.
Daig son of Coirell, a smith and an artist and a choice scribe was this Daig. He it is that made 300 bells and 300 croziers and 300

[a] MS. multis loca fermis   [b] MS. dat nō   [c] MS. ante

cherd dochiaran saigro be. Daig mac coirill mic laisren mic dallain mic eogain maic neill ix giallaig mic echach ruidmedoin.

19. *mochta* .i. escop lugbaid

Nirbo bochtai do mochta
lugbaid liss
.ccc. sacart ar cet escop
araen friss.
Ochtmoga særeland salmach
atheaglach aidble remeand
cenar cenbuain centiraul
ceu gnimrad acht mad leigeand

enan droma raithne .i. druim fotai talman 7 iniarthar mide ata .i. Enán mac ernin mic cail mic æda mic artchuirb mic niacorp.

In r. marg.] Samuel prop[h]eta.
20. *Diarscorus* .i. prespitor qui habebat centum monachos in thebaide aegypti*
pampu .i. escop 7 martir

21. *uincentii* .i. escop .i. *no* combad he unniut fil hi tugmad
escop senach .i. nite ailbe 7 comorba finden 7 icluain fota tine iferaib tulach ata escop senach .i. icluain fotai libréin

22. *Ataig itge* .i. ad [d]iscipulum dixit uel escop (sic) ad corpus dixit
macraid .i. uii. filii cum emeliano .i. macrad *no* maccu raith .i. filii .uii. emeliaui cum filiis .uiii.

23. *eogain* .i. mac escuip erc slaine eogan . ut per[i]ti ferunt 7 ise sin mochua ndeochain fil hichuain bihaigis . uclsic ut alii eogan maccaindig mic cuirp mic fergussa mic fothaid mic echach laindeirg mic messincorp

[in r. marg.] Finis anni egiptiorum . residuos .u. dies epogomenas [leg. epigenomenas?] nocant vel interfalares [leg. -calares]
24. . *senpatraic* .i. ingluinestir nangædel isaxsanaib. Senpatraic orus dela annuig locha sed uerius est cumad inglastingibeira nangædel indesciurt saxanata . scoti enim prius in perigrina-

gospels, and chief artist to Ciarán of Saigir was he. Daig son of Coirell, son of Laisrén, son Dallán, son of Eogan, son of Niall the Nine-Hostaged, son of Echaid Muidmedon.
19. '*Mochta*' i.e. bishop of Louth—

No poverty had Mochta
In the burgh of Louth.
300 priests and 100 bishops
Together with him.
Eighty psalmsinging noble youths,
His household, vastest of courses!—
Without plowing, without reaping, without kilndrying.
Without work save only reading.

'*Enan of Druim Raithne*' i.e. Druim Fota Talman, and in the west of Meath is he, to wit, Enán son of Ernín, son of Cael, son of Aed, son of Artchorp, son of Niacorp.

'*Pamphilus*' i.e. a bishop and martyr.

21. '*of Vincentius*' i.e. a bishop : or he may be Unniut who is in Tugmad.
'*Bishop Senach*' i.e. tutor of Ailbe and successor of Findén, and in Cluain Fota Fine in Fir Tulach is bishop Senach i.e. in Cluain Fota Libréin.

22. '*Pray a prayer*' i.e. *ad &c.*

'*youths*' i.e. seven sons with Emelianus . i.e. youths or sons of grace i.e. etc.

23. '*of Eogan*' i.e. son of bishop Erc of Slane, *ut periti ferunt.* And that is the Deacon Mochua who is in Cluain in Leix. *Vel sic ut alii* : Eogan son of Caindech, son of Corp, son of Fergus, son of Fothad, son of Echaid Redhand, son of Messincorp.

24. '*Old Patrick*' i.e. in Glastonbury of the Gael in Saxon-land. Old-Patrick of Ros Dela in Mag Locha, *sed uerius est* that he may be in Glastonbury of the Gael in the south of Saxon-

* MS. monochos in tibaldaici

tione ibi habitabant^a, *acht* atait athaisi inulaid senpatraic inardumacha.

coennite ar srothu .i. aite patraic macha .i. in britania sancti patriti episcopi doctoris patritii.

25. *parrthalon* . apostolus .i. uiuus sepultus et in india passuss . INindia parthalomeus apostolus. Apud^b cartaginem sanctorum martir*um* tricentorum qui beatus exercitus massa candida nuncupatur^c eo quod in clibanum calcis accensi^d dispersi sunt.

in lower marg.] Lasreith sluaig zenati 7rl. Rosreth scél achesta 7rl. Parrtalomeus apostolus et ui(u)ns sepultus post pellem rasam totam de toto corpore . ante.

26. [in lower marg.] . Buaid pais quinti martir 7rl. comeir .i. erigsiu [si] surrexeris in feria huius quanto^e magis in festis apostolorum et martirum et ceterorum .

28. *ciriacus* .i. martír
cmacleir .i. deccciiii.

ermis . in africa .i. praefectus^f urbis romae qui ab auriliano imperatore marterio coronatus.

iataurdaire ahafraic .i. augustinus episcopus in hoc die bod[a] testante in crouica.

in r. marg] Hic incipit primus [mensis] anni secundum egiptios nomine toth computantes suos menses ad cursum solis.

29. *iohain* . hic iohannis sepultus est in sebastia.

in lower marg.] Aisneid césad coin baubtaist^e 7rl .i. iohannes bauptista ideo^h dicitur eo quod ipse^i prius bautisma^j fecit uel quia christum bautizauit unde decollatio cius uere hic fuit sed inuentio capitis cius in secunda uico^k quoniam in a[u]tumno pasus est sed in uere id est ante pascha in edisn ciuitate fenica[e] prouinc[i]ae et [in]sequentepascha^l post annum christi pasus est et eliuatio elere profeta[e] et dormitatio belesi[æ] profeta[e] 7 .dccc. martires cum eo^m

Dichendad coin inmain áin
macirunda (*sic*) inaraib
sebasten isscribtha seal
ainm inflicha arhadnaiced.

---

^a MS. abitabunt   ^b MS. apl.i apud
^d MS. accnsi   ^e MS. quando
^h MS. .i. deo   ^i MS. ipsa
^l MS. et sequente in edisaci pascha

---

land. (For Irishmen formerly used to dwell there in pilgrimage.) But his relics are in Old-Patrick's stone-tomb in Armagh.
'*loveable tutor of our saye*' i.e. tutor of Patrick of Armagh.

25. '*Bartholomew.*'

'With the heap of Zenobius' (?) host,' &c.
'The story of his suffering was spread out,' &c.

26. 'The victory of martyr Quintus' passion.'
'*arise*' i.e. stand thou up : *si* etc.

'*Quiriacus*' i.e. a martyr.
'*with his train*' i.e. 904 (in number).
'*Hermes.*'

'*the conspicuous one from Africa*' i.e. bishop Augustine, &c.

28. '*of John.*'

'Announce the passion of John Baptist' etc.
i.e.

The beheading of John the lovable, splendid,
. . . . . in Arabia
Sebasten,—the course is written—
The name of the village where he was buried.

---

^c MS. excercit*us* masa candida nuncupatur
^f MS. perfectus   ^g MS. buabtaiz
^j MS. bautismai   ^k MS. infauico
^m MS. martirim res cum ei

Marobuailed marobith
marotuagad tend in fath
amac samla suaire iulia
nibia arbruach aura cobrath .

Muá domain *acht* mad bec dib
itenid bráth[a] breoid
labra friu nocotechta
indegaid échta eóin.

ISindígail marbtha cóin baup*taist* din . tic
inscuap afanait do erglanad *erena* friaderind
domain am*al* rothairrngir aireran inccuni 7
col*um* cille .i. hiteirt intsainduud isand ticfa
inscuap afanait . ut dixit col*um* cille .i. amail
geilt da each hicórait bid hi leri glanfus eir*iun*.

Aireran dixit denscoba[d] .i. dí choirntech
beti inoen liss toeb fri treb . infer rag*us* asintig
inaraile nifuigbea nech amchind imbethaid
isintig hi rag*a* . oc*us* nifuigbe iarum nech
imbethaid isintig asi[n]raga bid hi déine insin
rag*us* inscuap afanait.

Riagail dixit . Tri laa 7 teora áidche for
b*liadain* bes inplagsa incir*ium* . intan bus leir
ethar forloch rudraige odorus inproinntige
isand tent inscop afanait.

Mairt ernaig inm*urro* iarcaisc ise laith secht-
maine hiticfa inscop indígail césta coin . ut
dixit moling ocfiugrad nafeile coin.

Hifóil cóin tiefa tress
sirfess cirind anuiuless
draic lond loiscfes each rouice
cen chomaind cen sacarbaic.

Innentio corporis eius hic memoratur non
decollatio eius nere uel decollatio ut in martyr-
ologio[a] est . decolatio sanctissimi iohannis
bauptistae qui primo in samaria sepultus est .
sed nunc in alexandria reliquiae eius absqu*e*[b]
capite reseruantur . caput hautem[c] de ierusso-
limis ad phoeniciae[d] urbem delatum est

There has not been struck, there has not
been slain,
There has not been axe-hewn—hard the
cause—
His like—pleasant the flood—
Nor will there be on (this) marvellous Earth
till Doom(sday).
The world's women, save few of them,
In the fire of Doom shall burn:
Speech with them is unmeet
After the slaughter of John.

In vengeance of the slaying of John Baptist
it is that the Besom comes out of Fánait to
cleanse Ireland at the end of the world, even
as Airerán of the Wisdom prophesied and
Colomb Cille, namely, at terce especially, then
will come the Besom out of Fanait. *Ut dixit*
Colombcille, namely 'Like the grazing of two
horses in a yoke will be the diligence with
which it will cleanse Ireland.'

Airerán said of the sweeping (namely) 'two
alehouses shall be in one burgh side by side:
he that shall go out of one house into the other
will not find anyone before him alive in the house
into which he shall go, and afterwards he will
not find anyone alive in the house out of which
he shall go, such will be the swiftness with
which the Besom shall come out of Fanait.'

Riagail said : 'Three days and three nights
and a year will this plague be in Ireland.
When a boat shall be clearly seen on Loch
Rudraige from the door of the refectory, then
will come the Besom out of Fanait.'

A Tuesday of spring, moreover, after Easter,
is the day of the week on which the Besom
will come in vengeance of John's passion, as
Moling said picturing the festival of John :—

On John's festival will come an onslaught
Which will search Ireland from the south-east:
A fierce Dragon that will burn everyone it
reaches,
Without communion, without sacrifice.

[a] MS. martiri logio   [b] MS. abasque   [c] MS. iñ   [d] MS. poniciæ

Saliusa teand cotraig
rochuindig ceand mic zachair
coin buuptaist dagmac doilia
roadnact^a insebastia

29. *heli* .i. propheta .i. dormitio helesi hic
.i. in hoc die .i. eliuatio eius in paradisum.
30. *agatha* .i. uirgo et martyr^b
31. *indsi medcoit* .i. inis cathaig no iniarthar
tuaisciurt saxan mbec ata inis medcoit 7 aedan
inte .i. aedan mac lugair mic ernin mic cail mic
aeda mic artchuirp mic niacorp

paulin .i. escop nolae ciuitatis in italia . na
fedba quia se ipsum tradidit ciuidam (*sic*).
in lower marg.] Sernait eithri naugaist 7rl.
Nafedbai .i. quia nidua tradidit eum pro filio
suo in seruitium generi regis uandalorum
.i. gens^c in affrica .i. uandali.

Saliusa (Salome), strong with foot,
Asked the head of Zacharias' son:
John Baptist, a good son of God,
Was buried in Sebastia.

29. '*of Elijah.*'

31. '*of Inis Medcoit*' i.e. Inis Cathaig, or in
the north-west of the Little Saxons is Inis
Medcoit, and Aedán (was) therein i.e. Aedán
son of Lugar, son of Ernín, son of Cael, son
of Aed, son of Artchorp, son of Niacorp.
'*Paulinus*' i.e. bishop of Nola a town in
Italy . 'of the widow' *quia*, &c.
'They overspread the end of August' etc.
'of the widow' i.e. *quia* etc.

---

^a MS. roadnace   ^b MS. martirum
^c MS. traditatem profilios inseruitium genero gegis uandalorum 7 gensi

Rawl. 505, fo. 217 b.	Laud, 610.	Lebar Brecc, p. 95.
1. For septimb*er* kl. cicilia condirgi ce[t]hri cet conuagi fiche lateor mile	1. For septimb*ir* kl. cicilia condirgi cethri chet conuagi tricha la teoramili	1. Morseptimber kl. cicilia condirge .cccc. conunige .xxx. lateor mile
2. Molatha teothota lasenan itsoerseom lacr*ist* cain ambuaid- seom conacleir itcoimseom	2. Molotha teototam lasenan itsoersom lacr*ist* cain ambuaid- seom conachleir atcoemsom	2. Molotha teothotam lasenan itsersam lacr*ist* cain ambuaid- sium conachleir itcoemsam
3. Colman dromma ferta longarad [grian *á*laib] mac nissi comilib ochonderib maraib	3. Colman droma ferta longarad grian alaib mac nissi comilib ó choindeirib maraib	3. Colman droma ferta longarad grian alaib mac nisse comilib ochonderib maraib
4. INmarlaith conattail indatblaithe beceain agait mor amaccain imultan aird brecca[i]n	4. Inmorlaith conctail indatblaithi beeain agait mor am*a*ecain imultan aird breccain	4. INmorllaith cenctail indatblaithe beeain agait mor inn m*a*ccain imulltan aird breccain
5. La brecbunid turimi*a* dorograd ahere colach caid cain age achid bo buaid lere	5. Labreccbunaid doriuue dorograd aheiriu colach caid cain áge achaid bó buaid leire	5. Labrecbuaid dorrime dorograd aheri colang caid cain aige achaid bó buaid leri
6. Lusca lamae cuilind caindecheng adrannai feil sceithi slunn*b* liuni coluim roiss gil glannai	6. Lusea lamae cuilind caindecheng adrannai feil sceithe sund linde colum ruir*c* gil glanda	6. Lusceni lam*a*ce cuilind cain decheng atrendai feil seethi sunt liuli colum ruiss gil glandai
7. Glanchesad senoti assasoilsi slechta slung anathais orta conilur a ferta	7. Glancessad zenoti atasoillsi slechta slung annathais orta conilur aferta	7. Glanchesad senotii atasuills*e* slechtai sluaig annathais orta conilur afertai
8. Foraithmentar maire nitmarbda forterefit	8. Foraith[m]inter maire nitmarb*d*a f*or* terefit	8. Foraithmentar muire nitmarbdai forterepit

1. On*d* September's kalends Cecilia with righteousness: four hundred with virginity, thirty*e* and three thousand.

2. Molotha, Theodota (Theotimus?) with Senán—they are noble: with fair Christ is their guerdon: to His train they are dear.

3. Colmán of Druim Ferta: Longarad a delightful sun, Mac Nisse with thou- sands, from great Conderi.

4. The great sinless prince, in whom the little ones are flourishing, greatly play the children round Ultan of Ard Breceain.

5. With Brecbunid, who was called forth from Ireland, I reckon Eolang, holy, fair pillar, of Achad Bó, a victory of piety.

6. With Mac Cuilinn of Lusk a fair pair of champions divides (this day), the feast of Sciath here we have: Colomb of fair Ross Glandae.

7. Sinotus' pure suffering, whose tracks are shining.*f* Anastasius' hosts*g* were slain with the multitude of their virtues.

8. Mary is commemorated (to-day): they

a MS. turini *b* sic. *c* sic. *d* A. 'great' *e* D. 'twenty'
f The scholiast regards *senotii* as = *synodi* and *slechtai* as a verb meaning occisi sunt.
g B. and D. 'host'

Rawl. 505, fo. 217 b.	Laud, 610.	Lebar Brecc, p. 95.
latiamda iarsetaib cotribcetaib martir	latiamda iarsétaib cotrib cétaib mairtir	latiamdai iarsetaib co .ccc.aib martir
9. Mor lith linass cricha crothass loṅga luatha meicc intair tarriga feil cain ciarain chluana	9. Morlith linas cricha crothas longa luatha mac intsair darriga feil cain cinrain chluana	9. Morlith linas cricha crothais longa luatha mac intsœir tarriga feil cain chiarain chluana
10. Clí derggoir coṅglaini correcht tar sal sidi sui dianeriu inmall[a] fiunbarr maige bili	10. Cli dergoir conglaine correcht tarsal side súi dian heir[iu] inmall findbarr maigi bili	10. Clí dergoir conglaine corinclit tarsal side sni dianeriu inmall findbarr muige bile
11. Pais prothi iacinthi ba conimbud galair sillan salm cech lobuir inimbliuch cain canair	11. Pais' prothi iacinthi ba conimbud galair sillan salm cech lobair iu imliuch cain canair	11. Bas prothi iaquinti ba conimud galair sillan salm cech lobair animliuch cain canair
12. Celebair feil nailbi lafleith sorcha snamaich hifeil laissren ligaig odaminis dalaig	12. Ceilebair feil nailbe fri fleid sorche snamaigh lafeil laisren ligaig odaminis dálaig	12. Ceilebair feil nailbe frifleid sorchai snamaig lafeil laisren ligaig odaim inis dalaig
13. Dlom diis arfichet martir comeit noebe lasinciṅgid rhbage dagan inbir doile	13. Dlom dis arfichit mairtir comeit nocimiu lasincingid mbaigi dagan indbir daile	13. Dlom diis arfichit martir comeit noebi lasin cingid baige dagan inber doeli
14. Dolling duit feil coemain brice ladiis rhbollmair pais caid cipriain dermair[b]	14. Doling duit feil coemain brice ladiis molmaire bás caid cipriain dermair	14. Doling deit feil choemain bric la di[i]s mbolmair bas caid cipriain dermair
lacesad cain cornail	lacessad cain cornil	lacesad cain cornil
15. La coissecrad rhbaslicc maire mur cotalcai	15. Lacoisecrad baislic mairi mur cutailci	15. Lacoisecrad mbaislicc maire mur cotalcu

are not dead on a scanty meal: with Timothy after (the world's) ways and three hundred martyrs.

9. A great solemnity that filleth the borders, that shaketh swift ships, the wright's son beyond kings, the fair feast of Ciarán of Cluain.

10. A body of red gold with purity: over a sea came he: a sage for whom Ireland is (was) sad: Findbarr of Magh Bile.

11. The passion[d] of Protus and Hyacinthus which was with abundance of sorrow. Sillan the psalm of every sick man in fair Imbliuch (Cassain) is sung.

12. Celebrate Ailbe's feast, with Fled the luminous, buoyant: with the feast of Laisrén the beautiful, of multitudinous Daim-inis.

13. Declare two and twenty martyrs with much of holiness: with the champion of Lattle, Dagán of Inber Dóele.

14. To thee hath sprung the feast of Coemán Brecc, with a wise (?) pair: vast Ciprian's chaste death with the fair passion of Cornelius.

15. At the consecration of the Basilica Mary a rampart with strength, Cyrinus

[a] MS. dianseriu ninmall   [b] MS. ndermair   [c] l. bas.   [d] 'death' A.

RAWL. 505.	LAUD, 610.	LEBAR BRECC, pp. 95, 96.
cirinus censottlai	cirinus censotlai	cirinus censotla
luid cosluag mormartrai	luid cosluag mor martra	luid cosluag mor martrai
16. Morthregeṅg nad dona moninn nuall cechgena	16. Mortrecheng nach dona moenen n nuall cech gena	16. Mor drecheng nad donai moinend nuall cechgenai
ini laissren sona lalaissren mor mena	in hí laisren sona la laisren mor mena	inhii laisren sonai lalaisren mor menai '
17. Eufemia [cen] digna riaid apaiss cinn bliadna broccan roiss tuirec tuirme	17. Efernia cendigna raid ap[ais] cind bliana broccan ruistuiretuirme	17. Eufemia cendignai raid apais cind bli*adn*a bracan ruiss tuirec tuirme
lafeil romaith riagla	lafeil romaith riagla	lafeil romaith riaglai
18. Rathatar hiriched secet miled mblaithe lagein cain cendigna enan dromma raithe	18. Rathatar hirriched .uii. cet[b] mile mblaithi lagein cain cendigna énán droma rathe	18. Rathutar irricheg .c. uii. miled mblaithe lagein cain cendigna enain droma raithne
19. Raith conilur sochlach cocri*st* coemda taithlech cosluag rig ran remain enair inmain aithmet	19. Raith conilar sochlach cocri*st* cræmda taithlech cosluag rig rain remain énai*n* inmain aithmet	19. Raid conilur sochlach cocri*st* coemdai taitblech conaslog rig remain enair inmain aithnet
20. Atneocham[a] nahuaga donirset arndala indrigan daroma conasluag ronsnada	20. Ateocham nabogha doairset arndala inrigan doroma conasluag rousnada	20. Ateocham nahuaga donirset arndala inrigan doroma conaslog ronsnada
21. Snaidsium insab sluagach issansid nard noiblech ingrinn gel colligdaid matha mur tren taidlech	21. Snaidsiund insab sluagach isinsíd nard naiblech ingrian geal coligdath matha múr tren tocidloch	21. Snaidsium insab sluagach isossad nard noiblech ingrian geal coligdath matha mur tren toidlech
22. Pantaleo muric ammorsluag catcot	22. Pantaleo muric amorsluaig cad*é*at	22. Pantaleo muric amorsluaig catcat

without vainglory went with a great host of martyrdom.

16. A great triad-of-champions that are not wretched. Moinenn the cry of every mouth: in Iona Laisrén the happy, with Laisrén the great, of Men.

17. Euphemia without reproach tell her passion at a year's end. Reckon Broccán of Ros Tuire, with Riagail's excellent feast.

18. They sped into heaven, a hundred and seven thousand blossoms, at the fair birth without reproach of Enán of Druim Raithne.

19. Sped with a famous multitude to Christ's loveable peace, with his host of preëminent Kings, Januarius—a dear commemoration!

20. We beseech the virgins that they guard our assemblies: may the queen Doroma (?) with her host protect us.

21. May the hostful sage protect us[c] into a high, sparkling station![b] the sun white with beauty, Matthaeus a rampart, strong, shining!

22. Pantaleo, Mauricius, their great hosts whosoever they are, a hundred and eight

[a] MS. atneochain   [b] l. sé cét.   [c] A 'me.'   [d] 'the peace,' B and D.

[Sept. 23–29.] SEPTEMBER.

Rawl. 505.	Laud, 610.	Lebar Brecc, p. 96.
secet cainsluag ooc ardib milib deacc	ocht cet cáin sluag oac ardí milib déac	.c. viii. cain sluag ooc for dib milib deac
23. Doadomnau ia assatoidlech toiden roir issu huasal soerad mbuan mban goidel	23. Do adamnan iae assa toeidlech toeiden rofhír isu uasal saerad buan ban goeidel	23. Do adomnan iae asatoidlech toiden rohír ih.u uasal særad buan bau ngoedel
24. Compert iohain huasail babtaist as mo scelaib acht issu dedoinib asamram ni genair	24. Coimpert eoin uassail babtaist as mo scélaib ach ísu dodáinib as amra rogenair	24. Compert iobain uasail bauptaist as mo scelaib acht ih.u dodoinib isamru rogenair
25. Lacleir iosebi soerais cechtleid foreraid do crist indfir sercaig feil barre ochorcaig	25. Lacleir eusebii sa·rais each fleid foreraid la lith indfír sercaig feil barri ó chorceaig	25. Lacleir eusebi sa·ras cech fleid forcraid labith infir sercaig feil bairre ochorcaig
26. Colman olaind alo lahuaigi alt legend combnhe an nuallan iohain mar mace nerenn	26. Colman o laind ela lahoghe alt légend comad lúé a nualann coin mar mace naheirend	26. Colman olaind ela lahuaigi ailt legend conid he au hualann ioin mar mace nerend
27. Arndigerait chride a croch uipu arlius ronsnadat diarúdilius cosma[s] damianus	27. Arndigerait* craide achroch nibu airlius ronsnadut diarudilis cosmus damianus	27. Ard igerait chride acroch nirbo airliuss ronsnadut diarndilius cosmas damianuss
28. Dofinnio gilla itgessi cechcobair char mar marcill humail iunaill lalith labuir	28. Dofindia gelda itgeissi cech cobair char mar marcill umail iunaill la lith lobair	28. INda findia geldni itgesi imeech cobair cleir mor marcill umail iunill labith lobair
29. Lagleo fridraec ndulach domichiel balebuadach arsil nancrist nirach inmil slisgel sluagach	29. Agleo fridraic ndalach domichel baile buadach arslaig aucrist nirach inmil slisgel sluagach	29. Lagleo frin dric ndalach diarmichel bale badach arslig ancrist nirach inmil slisgel sluagnch

—fair host of youths!—and twelve thousand.

23. To Adamnán of Iona whose troop is radiant, noble Jesus granted the lasting liberation of the women of the Gael.

24. The conception of noble John the Baptist, who is greater than can be told. Save Jesus, of men he is the most wonderful[b] that hath been born.

25. With Eusebius' followers, who freed every banquet from excess, with the festival[c] of the loving man, the feast of Barre of Cork.

26. Colmán of Lann Ela, with perfection of high readings, so that he is splendid (and) praiseworthy, the great John of Ireland's sons!

27. Our two heart's-champions, their cross was not deserved: may they protect us to our possession, Cosmas and Damianus!

28. The two fair Findias are to be besought for every aid. Humble Marcellus' great train, with infirm Junell's (Julianus'?) festival.

29. At the fight against the multitudinous Dragon of our Michael stout, victorious, the soldier whitesided, hostful, will slay wrathful Antichrist.

[a] MS. ardiargerait, with a flat stroke over *iar*. [b] 'wonderfullest thing' D.
[c] 'to Christ' D.

RAWL. 505.	LAUD, 610.	LEBAR BRECC, p. 96.
30. Septimber iarsaithib atsaigtis arscithir sui slan soith[n]ge suthain cirine ban bethil	30. Sciptimber iarsaithib arsaigdis ar sethir sui slan sothnge suthain cirine ban beithil	30. Septimper iarsaithib atsaigtis arscthir sui slan sothnge suthain cirine ban bethil

30. After September's troops, (come) our sisters who used to visit a sage, sound, well-tongued, longlived fair Hieronymus of Bethlehem.

GLOSS FROM THE LEBAR BRECC, pp. 95-96.

3. (2) *alaib* .i. alaind *no* uasnelaib inairde nime. *no* alaib .i. dodáinib alaib .i. glicaib *no* coceill do

4. (1) *cenetail* .i. iscinnte atb[i]achtain *no* nibi atail innti *acht* ead *semper no* cenetail .i. cengúdáil *no* conbreig (2) *becain* .i. humiles (3) *agait* .i. oentaigit .i. subaigit

6. (2) *decheng* .i. daching *no* dachend

7. (2) *slechtai* .i. roslaitea eat (3) *orta* .i. marbtha

8. (2) .i. nirocbletar forproind mbic cideari nomeildis *no* for terccuidib .i. forproind bic ar pit proind quasi dixiset ne ieiunes in feria* maria: . *no* tere cuit .i. omni is uita .i. betha thearec . ut dixit [poeta]

Pít bec doróinless inne
amíe muire iugine
isamaithrech aerist cain
domrat sist fadomenmain

['A little bit I ate yesterday, O Son of Virgin Mary! I am repentant, O fair Christ! it cast me for a while into despoudency'] (3) *iarsetaib* .i. post uia[s] sacculi.

9. (3) *tarriga* .i. uasrigaib *no* derseaigid dorigaib *no itir* rigaib atasom

10. (3) .i. eolchaire *no* ilmaine fer nerenn imme . *no* a ilmáinesium imferaib erend.

11. (3) *salm* .i. orntio.

12. (2) *snamaig* .i. cách oc snam chuice

13. (1) *dlom* .i. dluig *no* aisneid *no* indis *no* erfuacair dis ar *fichit* do dainib (3) *lasin cingid* .i. lasin cuindid *no* lasin imtechtaid . *baige* .i. catha

14. (1) *doling deit* .i. tic ebucat nó lingid chucat cohoband (2) *bolmair* .i. fómaise *no* bolad már .i. maith abolad (4) *eain* .i. taitnemach

15. (1) *baislice* .i. eclesia . basilica .i. rigdoe .i. tegdais rig . bassilius [βασιλεύς] .i. rig (2) *cotaleu* .i. cocalmatus mor (3) *censotla* .i. ceumfiidinige *no* eenchuithiud

16. (1) *drecheng* .i. triar .i. tri cingid mora (4) *menai* .i. drochait

17. (2) .i. indis apais cind bliadna (3) *tuirme* .i. aisneid

18. (1) *rathutar* .i. rorethustar *irricheg* .i. hirigiath .i. iferand inrig .i. in caelum (3) *eendigna* .i. condimicin

19. (2) *taithlech* .i. sithugud (3) *remain* .i. maith *no* reid *no* luid cach dib rianacheli . *no* remain .i. rom uam .i. uam cach renacheli dib in caelum . *no* remuind .i. dochuatar ad caelum.

20. (1) *atcocham* .i. aitchimit *na huaga* hae sunt uirgines *doairset arndala* .i. dartorruma cum suis soc[i]is.

21. (1) *snaidsium* .i. dogns arsnadud . ronsnaide asunn .i. a presenti saeculo (4) *toidlech* .i. taitnemach

* MS. feriæ

[Sept. 1–3.] NOTES FROM THE LEBAR BRECC, p. 95.

23. (1) *adomnan* .i. ada[m] .i. homo .i. adam bec (2) *toiden* .i. drem *no* buiden (3) *rohir* .i. rohortastar (4) *buan* semper adamnan permanet.
25. (2) .i. niroscnith forcraid proinde *no* saernid cech duine inamunigin *conaderna* irchoit dó cianoscnithe forcraid
26. (3) *an hualann* .i. nuallán *no* nuall mor fer nerenn ocamolad.
27. (1) *ar*[*n*]*ligerait* .i. arn anrud (2) *nirbo airliuss* .i. ni roairliset per mala*ᵃ* opera *no* nirbo cendais secundum opera mala (3) *ronsnadut* .i. dogniat arnditen *diarndilius* .i. in caelum.
29. (1) *lagleo* .i. lagluid . *friadric* .i. fria drecain .i. ancrist (2) *balc* .i. tren *no* calma (3) *arslig* .i. slaidfid *irach* .i. fergach
30. (1) *Septimper* .i. genitiu *iarsaithib* .i. iarsligedaib *no* iarsluagaib (3) *sothnge* .i. sothenga *no* sogne fair .i. gné ecuai 7 noeime

---

NOTES FROM THE LEBAR BRECC, p. 95.

Decimus mensis apud graecos sgorpeos. Cen kaluc cennona cen idu iegrecaib 7 icegeptacdaib. Soli*s* xxx . lun*ae* xxx . Sextus ebreorum mensis elul.

1. *cicilia* .i. uirgo et martir .i. cccc.xx et ihu. naue.ᵇ

2. *molotha teothotham* .i. is molta vel duac*ᶜ* uirgines molotha 7 teotham.
    la senan .i. o lathrach briuin inúib foelain

3. *droma ferta* .i. cluana ferta mugaine inúib failge
    longarad .i. isléib mairge *no* amuig thuathat huaisciurt [leg. ituaisciurt] osraige
    in lower marg.] Lon garad coisfind amuig thuathat ituaiscirt osraige .i. inuib foirchelláin .i. amuig garad andisiurt garad saindrud 7 icill gabra isleib mairge ales longarad.

Cos find .i. findfad gcal mor trenachossaib. *no* glefhinda achossa.
Súid légind oc*us* senchais oc*us* brethemnais oc*us* filidechtai he . IS chuige dorala colu*m* cil*le* for áigidecht . corcheil aliubra fair . 7 facbais colu*m* cil*le* brethir foralebraibsiub (*sic*) .i. conarbat greunai dotési olse inní imandcnaid drocheneeh . 7 isse*d* on rocomailled armarnit naliubair beos 7 ni légand nach fer eat.

INtan din . bamarb longarad isse*d* innisit eolaig tiaga lcbar eren*n* dothuitim inaidchesin . *no* isiat natiaga irabutar liubair cechdánai isinaracul iraibe colu*m* cil*le* rothuitset and . 7 macht-

With the Greeks the tenth month is Γορπιαῖος. Without kalends, without nones, without ides were the Greeks and the Egyptians.
Ἰησοῦς Ναυή.

2. '*Molotha, Theodota,*' i.e. is praised, *vel* etc.

'*with Senán,*' i.e. of Lathrach Briuin in Ui-Foeláin.

3. '*of Druim Ferta,*' i.e. of Cluain Ferta mugaine in Offaly.

'*Longarad,*' i.e. is Sliab Mairge or in Mag Tuathat in the north of Ossory.
Longarad the Whiteleggod in Mag Tuathat in the north of Ossory, i.e. in Ui-Foirchelláin i.e. in Mag Garad in Disert Garad especially, and in Cell Gabra, in Sliab Mairge, in Les Longarad.

'Whiteleggod,' i.e. great white hair through his legs. Or bright-white were his legs.
A sage of learning and history and jurisprudence and poetry was he. To him Colombcille chanced to come as a guest, and he hid his books from Colomb, and Colombcille left his curse on Longarad's books, to wit, "May that," quoth he, "as to which thou hast shown niggardliness be of no profit after thee !" And this was fulfilled. For the books still remain and no man reads them.

Now when Longarad was dead, men of lore say this, that the book-satchels of Ireland fell down on that night. Or it is the satchels wherein were books of every science in the

---

ᵃ MS. malo.   ᵇ MS. inaue.   ᶜ MS. duo.

naigid col*um* cil*le* 7 cach bui isiutigain 7 sochtait uile fri tairmchrith nalebar . conid and atb*ert* col*um* cil*le* . Longarad olac inosraigib .i. sái c*ach* dánai atbath innossa . Fotai confirenug*ud* siu olbaith*ín* . Amaires ar tir hinaid arcol*um* cil*le* . et dixit col*um* cil*le*.

ISmarb lon
dochill gar*ad* mor indon
derind *con*ilar attreab
itdith légind 7 scol .
Atbath lon .
icill garad mor indon
isdith legind 7 scol
iudsi er*enn* dara hor.

mac nisse .i. Cnes ingen chomchaide dodál cethirn am*dthair no* mac cnis patraic he arisoc patraic *no*alta .i. nochodlad. Coem*an* brecc mac nisi mic nemnindir mic eirc mic echach mundremair . ocus fobrecc ainm aathar . Œn- gus din acetainm

o chonderib .i. daire nacon .i. daire ambitis coin allta prius et in eo lupe habitabant.

4. *macain* .i. lenib namban romarb inbuide chonaill is*ed* doguid ulltan sineda nambo dothe- scad 7 loim*n*a dodail inntib *ocus* acur nambe- laib . combitis nauoidin iccluthi imme . *no* isairesin rotoga[d] ulltan inablaine šenmochtai lugbaid 7 docuired fúrsa remi cisti

Biathad adaltan do ulltan
co morbaig bi
rosmudaig rosmill rotr*á*cht
tri .l. bárc coalaha chlí .
Diamad deas doberad friu
ulltan uasal adfu
nitharged gall siu na thall
cobrath inoirer cr*eann* .
Nocodobeim for droich neich
isat derga naclorig
isfoill ni dob*eir* gnúis mbain
mac hui c*on*chobair ulltain

cell where Colombcille was that fell then, and Colombcille and everyone in that house marvel, and all are silent at the noisy shaking of the books. So then said Colombcille, " Lon-garad in Ossory," quoth he, " a sage of every science, has now died." " May it be long till that comes true !" quoth Baithín, " Unfaith on the man in thy pl*a*ce* !" says Colombcille, *et dixit* Colombcille.

Dead is Lon
Of Cell garad—great the evil !
To Erin with her many homesteads
It is ruin of learning and schools.
Died hath Lon
In Cell Garad—great the evil !
It is ruin of the learning and schools
Of Erin's island over her border.

'*Mac nisse*,' i.e. Cnes, daughter of Comchaide, of Dál Cethern was his mother. Or son of Patrick's skin (*cnes*) was he, for with Patrick he was fostered i.e. he used to sleep. Coemán Brecc, son of Nisse, son of Nemainder, son of Erc, son of Eochaid Mundremar; and Fobrecc was his father's name. Oengus moreover his first name.

' *Of Conderi*,' i.e. the oakwood of the wolves, i.e. an oakwood wherein wolves used to be formerly and she-wolves used to dwell therein.

4. ' *children*,' i.e. the babes of the women whom the Yellow Plague slew. This was Ultan went to do : to cut off the cows' teats and to pour milk into them, and to put them into the children's mouths, so that the infants were playing around him. Therefore was Ultan chosen into the abbey of Old-Mochtae of Louth, whence Fursa had been put forth before him.

To feed his fosterlings Ultan,
With great living strength,
Wrecked, destroyed, stranded
Thrice fifty ships with his left hand.[b]
Had it been (his) right that noble Ultan
Raised against them hence,
No foreigner here nor there would come
For ever into Erin's land.
Not for a blow on anyone's face
Are the clerics red (for shame),
It is a little thing, he shows a pale visage,
Ua Conchobar's son, Ultán.

---

* i.e. May thy successor be an infidel.
b See the legend here referred to, Todd's *St. Patrick*, p. 212.

p. 99, lower marg.]
    Cet re lubair c*ét* recrabud
    c*ét* fri foglaim fessa fiud
    cócca cailleeh cocruth cuchtban
    re remes ultain nachill.,

p. 95]
5. *brecbuaid* .i. lucht cech aise tuc cocr*ist no* buaid rue do fiannib examlaib .i. bricín o dísiurt bricin inh*uib* dróna *no* [in left marg.] bricin tuama drecain imbrefni *connacht*

in lower marg.] Labrecbuaid doríme 7rl. bricíne thuamai drecoin imbrefni *connacht* taurime. *no* labrecbuaid .i. buaid brec .i. fir 7 mna ic tabairt buadai do .i. ocdul imartra imaille fris aristnaid dosam sin arise ropritchai doib brethir nde.

eolang .i. inachad bó caindig inosraigib ata.

6. *luscai* .i. tech dolustoic .i. do luafudan .i. tech 7 lus di ustoic arniroibe tech oca prius. Tech doronad dolusrad ann prius et ab eo nominatur lusca quasi lusrad tech quia quod tech hodic uo[ini]natur ca p*rius* dicebatur. Unde ulcha quasi olcha et unde cerdcha. Lusca din .i. ca. talamlusta [leg. -lusca] .i. teach talman

decheng .i. sciath 7 colum rois

atrendai .i. randait hi fhéil scéthi am*u*scrnigi trinnaige am*u*main
*ruiss gil gla*ndai .i. ross glanda ainm inbaile prius .i. glan ainm natibrad fil and 7 dómnach mor ainim indíu orofaid patraic .i. colam croxaire orus giallan inh*uib* liatháin in*u*main *no* col*um* dómnaig muigi imclair it*í*r eogain oc*us* glan ainm tiprait fil isinbaile

7. *glanchesad senotii* .i. senad necœ [leg. Nicœn?] vel zenoti martir .i. in[i]erusalem
8. (1) .i. gein muiro foraithme*n*tar sund

9. (1 and 2.) .i. cách octiachtain ilongaib doféil ciarain .i. anuas donloch 7 anís

chluana .i. mic nois
in lower marg.] Morlith línas cricha 7rl.

A hundred for labour, a hundred for devotion,
A hundred for learning white knowledge,
Fifty nuns with fair-coloured form,
In the time of Ultán, in his church.

5. '*Brecc-buaid*' ('various-reward'), i.e. folk of every age he brought to Christ or be won a victory from divers champions, i.e. Briccín of Disert Briccín, in Ui-Drona, or Briccín of Tuaim-Drecain, in Brefne of Connaught.
'With Brecc-buaid I reckon,' etc. Briccíne of Tuaim Drecoin, in Brefne of Connaught, I reckon. Or 'with Brecc buaid,' i.e. various victory i.e. men and women giving him victory namely in undergoing martyrdom together with him, for *that* is a victory to him, since he it is that preached unto them God's word.
'*Eolang*' i.e. in Achad Bó of Cainnech in Ossory is he.

6. '*of Lusk*' i.e. a house of *lustoc* i.e. of ragweed (?) i.e. a house and weed *diustoic*(?) for he had no house *prius*. A house was made of weeds *prius, et ab eo nominatur* lus-ca *quasi* weed-house, because what is now called *tech* used formerly to be called *ea*. Whence *ulcha* 'beard' quasi *ol-cha* ('cheek-house'), whence also *cerd-cha* ('artisan-house,' 'forge'). *Lusca* then i.e. *ea . talamlusca* i.e. house of earth.
'*a pair of champions*' i.e. Sciath and Colomb of Ross.

'*they divide*' .i. they share in the feast of Sciath in Muscraige Tri-maige in Munster.
'*of fair Ross Glandae* i.e. Ross Glanda was formerly the name of the stead i.e. *Glan* ('pure') the name of the well that is there, and Domnach Mór its name to-day, since Patrick sent Colomb Croxaire of Ross Giallán in Ui-Liatháin in Munster or Colomb of Domnach Maige Imchlair in Tyrone; and Glan (is) the name of a well that is in the stead.

7. '*Sinotus*' pure *suffering*' i.e. a synod of . . .
8. i.e. Mary's nativity is commemorated here.
9. i.e. every one coming in ships to Ciarán's feast .i. from the head of the lake and from below.
'*of Cluain*' i.e. of the son of Nos.
'A great festival that fills territories' etc.

Ciarán mor mac intsaeir rochan inernnigthisea intan rosiacht cocricha bais dó .i. nocim erenn rothroisescet umthimdibe asægail chiarain arba leisium aænor leath erenn. Arai ní dernai dia forrasom sin *no* corothroisc fen leo arnifitir cid immandornad . coroindis intaingel dó . *Conid* and rofacnibsium diananchaib cen ní dogellad cofestais. Odran tra . olettrachaib odrain 7 mac cuilind luscai dochotar dia indisin do inneich imathroiseset .

ISceat duib din . innísin dol dosenad inoir olciaran 7 doborthar dúib inni iarrthai . ut dixit ciaran

an rium arí inrichid 7rí.

Tribl*iadna* .xxx. aræs intan atbath. Teora comairli din . ismessa daronad inerinn triachomairlib noem .i. timdibe sægail ciara*in* . *ocus* col*um* cil*le* do indarbud . ocus mochudai dochur arnithin . 7c.

10. *conglaine* .i. cososcela quod est lex noua arise thuc soscela incirinn artús

in right marg.] findbarr .i. folt find bui fair .i. finden

11. *prothi* (proprium [nomen]) *iaquinti* .i. duo uiri de familia[a] eugenie

sillan .i. isnamalaig[b] boi infinda concim 7 cibe tóisech nosaiced cech dia bamarb statim cotuc molaisi lethglinde ass in findasin conid desin athath molaisi silla . *ocus* animlech cassain hicuailngi ata

in lower marg.] Bás prothi iaquinti 7rí. Sillán .i. óimliuch cassan hicuailngiu . Silan oratio cech lobair 7 cech duine *n*obid hingalar throm . arrobe amiau nile finda malach silan do*f*uicsin corœplitis foc*é*toir Arrobe aiste infindasin cech oen atchid artús é isin matain muich aée focétoir. Ecnuaing din. doleth*g*lind. Tic molaisi matan moch timchell narolei. Tecmaid sílan in finda inaagaid dó . Nibia infindusa armolaisi ocmarbud chaich . nib*us* mou ocatharraing as arccin. Atbail din .

[a] MS. familiæ [b] MS. isnanamalaig

Great Ciarán, the wright's son, sang this prayer when he drew nigh to death, namely Ireland's saints fasted in order to cut short Ciarán's life, for he alone had the half of Ireland. However God did not that for them until he (Ciarán) himself fasted with them, for he knew not why it was being done, till the angel told him. So that then he left to his monks (the injunction) not to promise aught till they should know (what it was). Now Odrán, of Lettracha Odrain and Mac Cuilind of Lusk went to tell him for what they fasted.

"Ye have leave, then," said Ciarán "(to do) that, to go to the synod of the ....., and unto you shall be granted what ye ask," *ut dixit* Ciarán:

'Stay for me, O King of the Heaven' etc.

Three and thirty years was his age when he died. Now the three worst counsels that have been acted on in Ireland through the counsels of saints (are these) namely: the cutting short of Ciarán's life: and the banishing of Colombcille; and the expulsion of Mochuda from Raithin, &c.

10. '*with purity*' i.e. with the gospel which is the new law; for it is he that first brought the gospel into Ireland.

Findbarr .i. white hair was on him i.e. Finden.

Sillán i.e. in his eyebrow was the poisonous hair, and every day whoever was the first to see it was dead *statim* till Molaise of Leighlin took out that hair, and thereof Molaisi died *silla* (?), and in Imlech Cassain in Cualnge is he.

'Death of Protus and Hyacinthus,' etc. Sillan of Imliuch Cassain in Cualnge. Silan the *oratio* of every wretched man and of every one who was in heavy disease. For the desire of them all was to see a (certain) hair of Silán's eyebrow so that they might die at once. For the peculiarity of that hair was that whoever was first to see it in the morning early died at once. Now he happened to come to Leighlin. Molaise goes early in the morning round the graveyard. He met Silán of the Hair (com-

molaisi foc*t*oir iarfaicsin infinda . et hinc
silan *dictus conid* amlaid sin bui infindai .

12. *ailbe* .i. imlech ibair
fri fleid .i. lafleid .i. ingen ríg laigen othig
fleide in h*uib* garrchon
laisren .i. molaise mac natfraich ódaiminis
forloch erni
Molaise cecinit

    Fofrith ferand fuaramar
    loch lethan asliabachad
    ruaim choitchend dogoedelaib
    domnás diles dé athar.

13. *dagan* .i. indail mescorb laigen atasom

docli .i. dool nomen amnis in nirther laigen

14. *feil choemain bric* .i. hic ross ech amide
ata 7 mac máthar do . mac rustaing ocus isand
roadnacht he
 p. 96 after 30 Sept.] Doling deit feil coeman
7rl. Coeman brecc mac nisse .i. oross ech
hicaille fallamain himide ataside *ocus* mac
rustaing maroen fris 7 eland ocum*áthar* eat
andís *no* hiross liac ata coeman brecc . ut
oeng*us* dicit* sed nescio ubi est ross liacc .
Adnocul din . mic rustaing iross ech himide .
Níchumaing nach ben atégad cennaidm adelm
esti *no* cen anlgaire boeth iarum . ut dixit

    Lige m*i*c rustaing ráide
    hi ross each cen imnaire
    matchí cech ben báigid
    braigid 7 bán gáirid
    Critan ainm m*i*c rustaing ráin
    garb daire ainm mic samáin
    aindiairr armac conglinde
    mor dolaidib dorinde.

cipriain .i. episcopus cartagenis in africa
uel episcopus romae.
cornil .i. episcopus romae .i. in dominico die
passi sunt cornelius et ciprianus intelligens
circumcisionem interpretatur.
p.96, in lower marg.] Ciprianus after primum
gloriosam rethoricam docuit doinde christianus
factus cicilio (leg. Caecilio) suadente omnem
substantiam suam erogauit et postea episcopus

ing) towards him. "This hair," said Molaise,
"shall not be killing everyone: it shall be no
more," plucking it out by force. Then Molaise
died at once after seeing the hair, and hence
Silán was called . . And thus was the hair.
   12. '*of Ailbe*,' i.e. of Imloch Ibair.
  '*with Fled*,'i.e. daughter of a king of Leinster,
of Tech Fleide in Ui-Garrchon.
  '*Laisren*,' i.e. Molaise, son of Natfraech of
Dam-inis on Lough Erne.
  Molaise sang:—

    Well found was the land we found—
    A broad lough (was) its mountain-field,
    A common cemetery for Irishmen,
    God the Father's own domain.

   13. '*Dagan*,' i.e. in Dál Mescorb of Leinster
he is.
  '*of Docl*,' i.e. Docl the name of a river in
the east of Leinster.
   14. '*the feast of Coemán Brecc*,' i.e. at Ross
Ech in Meath is he, and a son of his mother
was Mac Rustaing, and there was he buried.
  'Sprang to thee Coemán's feast,' etc., Coemán
Brecc mac Nisse i.e. of Ross Ech in Caille
Fallamain in Meath is he, and Mac Rustaing
along with him, and the children of the same
mother are they two. Or in Ross Liac is
Coeman Brecc, as Oengus says: but I know
not where Ross Liac is. Now Mac Rustaing's
grave is in Ross Ech in Meath. No woman can
see it sine crepitu ventris eius or without a
loud foolish laugh afterwards, *ut dixit* [poeta :]

    Mac Rustaing's grave I say
    In Ross Ech without shame,
    If she sees it every woman talks,
    Pedit and laughs aloud.
    Critán was noble Mac Rustaing's name,
    Garb-daire was Mac Samain's name,
    Aindiairr was Mac Conglinde's—
    Many lays he made.

---

* MS. dnt.

cartaginis constitutus[a] est sed huius ingenium
superfluum est dicere cum sole clarior sit inter[b]
opera eius . pasus est sub ualeriano et galliano
principibus persecutione[c] octauo die quorum.
Cornilius pasus est in eodem anno.
15. *cirinus* .i. escop 7 martir.
16. *moinend* .i. moinend cluana conaire
tomain hi tuaisciurt hua foelain . ocus laisren abb
iæ coluim cille . ocus laisren mac huí lugaire .
men nomen amnis ata itir daluaraid 7 cenel
neogain ut *ferunt* . 7 molaise forabru . *no* molaise
mena droichichit (*sic*) .i. men nomen amnis 7
hilnigis ata *no* mena droichit .i. is min droichet
[.i. quaedam congregatio multorum sanctorum
ad illam ciuitatem fuit aliquando propter ali-
quam causam et quidam latro de habitatoribus
dixit is min doroichet][d] ad nos omnes isti et
quidam[e] dixit [de aduenientibus][f] bid he ainm
in baile mindroichet.

17. *Eufemia* .i. femme ingen chairill uirgo et
martir.
ruiss tuirce .i. immuig raigne inosraigib .
idem .i. cluain imorchuir .i. flannan mac toirr-
delbaig tanic donbaile aliquando 'coraibe for
imorchar . inde dicitur cluain imorchuir

riaglai.i. riagail fil bi tig riagla hileth cathail .
no amuic inis forloch deirgdeirce

18. *enain* .i. iniarthar mide [ata] enan

20. *doroma* .i. uirgo nomen.
conasloy .i. cum uirginibus .u. suis.
21. *matha* .i. euangelista qui apud etiopiam
marterio coronatus est.
22. *Pantaleo* .i. legait do romanchuib .i.
tuisech .ui. mile
sluag ooc .i. dochuatar amartrai lamaxin
imper .i. de . ar dib m. dec.

23. *adomnan* .i. ab iæ coluim cille

in lower marg.] Do adomnan iæ 7rl. .i. adamnan doralai inarolle lou oc imdecht muige breng
ocus amathair foramuin conacatar nadachath
icomthuarcain acheliu. Ecmaing din . ronait
mathair adamnain comuscaid inmudi 7 corrdu
iaraind inalaim ocussi octarraing namnd eli asin

15. '*Cyrinus*,' i.e. bishop and martyr.
16. '*Moinend*.' i.e. Moinend of Cluain Conaire
Tomain in the north of Ui-Foelain, and Laisrén,
abbot of Iona and Laisrén son of Ua-Loegairi.
Men the name of a river which is in Daluaraid
and Cenél Eogain ut ferunt, and Molaise on its
brink. Or Molaise of Men-Droichet, i.e. Men
the name of a river in Leix. Or Mena-droichit
i.e. it is a smooth bridge, to wit, a certain
congregation of many saints were once at that
town for some cause, and a certain robber, one
of the inhabitants, said, 'smoothly (*min*) have
all those come (*doroichet*) to us;' and one of the
visitors said 'this shall be the name of the
stead, Smoothbridge' (*Mindroichet*.)

17. '*Euphemia*,' i.e. Femme, daughter of
Cairell, virgin and martyr.
'*of Ross Tuire*,' i.e. in Mag Raigne in
Ossory, idem in Cluain Imorchuir, i.e. Flandán,
son of Toirdelbach, came once to the stead that
he might be carried. Thence is it called *Cluain
Imorchuir* (' meadow of carrying').
'*of Riagail*,' i.e. Riagail who is in Tech
Riagla in Leth Cathail. Or in Muc-inis (' pig-
island') on Lough Derg.
18. '*of Eudn*,' i.e. in the west of Meath is
Euan.

22. '*Pantaleo*,' i.e. a legate of the Romans,
i.e. a leader of six thousand.
'*a host of youths*,' i.e. they underwent martyrdom at the hands of the Emperor Maximinian, i.e. 12,600.
23. '*Adamnán*' i.e. abbot of Colomb Cille's
Hí.
'*To Adamnán of Iona*,' etc., i.e. Adamnán
chanced on a certain day to be journeying
through Mag Breg, with his mother on his back,
and they saw two battalions smiting each
other. It happened, moreover, that Ronait,
Adamnán's mother, saw a woman with an iron

---

[a] MS. constitatus [b] MS. super flumen est dexere cum sole clariore siter [c] MS. perecutione
[d] The passages in brackets are from the Franciscan copy. [e] MS. iste et qui.

chath chotarsnai 7 hileumain acichside boi incorman. Arcuma nobitis fir *ocus* mnái octabairt chathai isinaimsirsiu. Suidis ronait *iarum* 7 atbert nimberusa lat asininadsa corasorthar mná triabithu ariungné ucut 7 arfocht 7 sluagud. gollaid iar*um* adaunain innison. Ecmaing tra iar*um* mordail incrind. Ocus teit adamnan coforglai clerech erend isindailsin 7 særais namná ind.

ITiatso din. iiii. cána erend .i. Cáin patruic cen clérchiu domarbad. Cain dari chailleeh cenbú domarbad. Cain adamnain cennamná domarbad. Cáin domnaig centairmthecht and

25. *eusebi* .i. escop
bairre .i. do síl briain *mic* echach *mu*id*me*doin do barri 7 inachad cille clochair *no* drochait inaird ulad in hoc die cum bairre

26. *Colman.* Colman ela *mac* beoguai *mic* mochta *mic* cuinnedai. o laind ela .i. ela nomen mulieris quae ibi ante colman habitabat et ab ea nominatur ciuitas .i. land ola *uel* ola pro[prium nomen] a[m]nis proximantis celesi.e. Colman ela dixit ex[s]urgam diluculo, confitebor domino, quia non est iname[a] sperare in domino.
ela .i. nomen mulieris [uel nomen] amnis fil hitæb lainde ela
ioin. coin he .i. is cosmail he *fria* heoin ar ecna 7 aróige

27. *cosmas damianuss* .i. duos martires .i. duo filii mulieris .i. teothota.

28. *inda findia* .i. duo sancti ocus in nraind ataut uel unum nomen uel findia gillda .i. findia eluana hiraird memoratur hic nel gillæ nomen sancti uel dofindia. Alii dicunt comad he doboth in fnterna[b] isnarendaibsi uerum[c] est. findia .i. nech dofhind diu. 7c.

cleir mor .i. sine labore seruili.
marcill .i. papa .i. marcialis.
iunill .i. hicorco baiscind ata.

sickle in her hand, dragging another woman from the opposing battalion, and the sickle fastened to her breast. For at that time men and women alike used to be giving battle. Then Ronait sat down and said, "thou shalt not bear me with thee out of this place until women are freed for ever from (things of) that kind, and from fighting and hosting." Then Adamnán promised that. Now a great convention chanced (to be held) in Ireland, and Adamnán with the choice of Ireland's clerics went to that convention, and therein he freed the women.

Now these are the four laws of Ireland:—Patrick's law, not to kill clerics. Darí the Nun's law, not to kill kine. Adamnán's law, not to kill the women. The law of Sunday, not to transgress thereon.

25. '*of Eusebius*' i.e. a bishop.
'*Bairre*' i.e. of the seed of Brian son of Echaid Muidmedon was Barri, and in Achad Cille Clochair, or Drochait in Aird Ulad on this day with Bairre.
26. '*Colman.*' Colmán Ela son of Beógnae son of Mochtae, son of Cuinnid, of Land Ela i.e. Ela etc.

'*Ela*' i.e. the name of a woman, or the name of a river which is beside Land Ela.
'*John,*' a John was he i.e. like is he unto John for wisdom and virginity.

28. '*the two Findias*' i.e. two saints, and in Aran are they. Or it is one name. Or Findia Gillda i.e. Findia of Clonard, is commemorated here. Or Gillae is the name of a saint. Or 'two Findias.' Others say that it is he who used to be in Fnterua [Whithorne, Whithorne, in Galloway, perhaps] that is (mentioned) in these lines. verum est. Findia i.e. one that knows God etc.

'*Iunill*' .i. in Corco-Baiscinn is he.

[a] MS. mane   [b] MS. fut.ra.   [c] MS. unum

lobair no labair .i. indis .i. iunaill lobar .i. dari chaillech.
29. *michel* .i. princeps angelorum.
inmil .i. in milid qui sicut deus interpretatur in monte gargain.
hoc die factum (*sic*) est dedicatio basilicæ michaelis.
Ordo dominicae diei[a] et uestes albæ super altaria ut sine labore seruili communicatio[b] corporis et sanguinis christi et elimosinárum in pauperes[c] et praedicatio michel[is] turbis.
atnaigtis arsethir .i. nosechdis no tegdis ad hi[e]ronimum .i. uidua paula et filia eius eustochium[d] [et cetere quibus poscentibus uetus testamentum transtulit hieronimus — Rawl. 505] .i. socem (*sic*) cirine
bethil .i. obethii iuda

lobair, or *labair* 'say' i.e. infirm Junill, i.e. Dari the Nun.

'*the soldier*' i.e. the champion whose name is explained by *sicut deus:* in Mount Garganus.

'*our sisters used to seek*' i.e. they used to seek or go to Jerome i.e. the widow Paula and her daughter Eustochium, and others, at whose request Jerome translated the Old Testament.

Bethel i.e. of Bethlehem Judaeae.

[a] MS. ord dni . zediei.   [b] MS. scruule communitatio   [c] MS. papes
[d] MS. uidua eius .i. filia paula et eustochium.

Rawl. 505, fo. 218 b.	Laud 610, fo. 68, b. 2.	Lebar Brecc, p. 97.
1. Buaid prisci pais lucœ lith germain grian cetal feil nochreilce nuasal inochtimbir etan	1. Buaid priscil paiss lucais lith germain grian cetal feil nóem reilge uasail inochtimbir etan	1. Buaid prisci pais lucais lith germain grian cetal feil nocmrelci uasal inoctimpir etan
2. Eleuther inmartir admuinter afeili oinne foroenlini lapaiss ioscbi	2. Iuliter in martir atmuinter afeile omne foroenlíne lapais eusebi	2. Iuliter inmartir admuinter afeli oinme foroenline lapais eusebi
3. Soergein maire inœgept asslonnud cech geno candida grian sona gein cain colmain clo	3. Soergein maire inegept asslonnud cech gena candida grian sona gein cain colman ela	3. Soergein marec inegept aslondud cech gena candida grian sona gein cain colmain ela
4. Ail marcellum nepscop conaidbli abriga laccsad nahuage inballgel baluiua	4. Ail marcellum nepscop conaidble abríge la cessad na hoighe inbaillgel ballíne	4. Ail marcellum nescop conaidble abrige laccsad nahuage inbaillgel balline
5. Blog donnliic logmair laslóg martir namra sinech ingen fergnai cruachan maige abna	5. Blog don líc lógmair lacét mairtir namra sinech ingen ergna cruachain maige abna	5. Blog donlíic logmair la cét martir namræ sinech ingen fergnæ cruachan muige abnæ
6. Abb cluana inlucell laboithene mbrigach fer dachrich cli buadach epscop lungach ligach	6. Abb cluana inlucell la baithine mbrígach ferdacrich cli buadach escop lugdach ligach	6. Abb cluana inlucell labœthine mbrigach fer da crich cli buadach epscop lugdach ligach
7. La matha marc nepscop asrort sluag congaiuni lacleir cain cofinni feil cellaig collainni	7. Lamatha marc nepscop asort gnim congaindi lacleir cain combinde feil cellaich collainde	7. Lamatha marc nescop asort sluag congainde lacleir cain combinde feil cellaig collainde
8. Leicset luth conani arbrith (sic) aitrib rigi tret ingen conuagi lapais find faustini	8. Léicset luth conáni arbithaittreb rigi tret ingen conoighe [la] pais fiud faustini	8. Lecsit luth conaine arbithaittreb rige tret ingen conuage lapais find faustine

1. Priscus' victory, Lucas' passion, the festival of German, a sun of songs! the feast of the noble holy relics in October's forefront.

2. Eleutherius the martyr, thou admirest his feast. Oinme on one line with Eusebius' suffering.

3. Mark's noble nativity in Egypt—the declaration of every mouth! Candida a happy sun: the fair birth of Colman Ela.

4. Beseech bishop Marcellus, with the vastness of his vigour, with the suffering of the virgin, the white-limbed Balbina.

5. A fragment of the precious stone, with a hundred*marvellous martyrs, Sínech Fergna's daughter, of Cruacha Maige Abnae.

6. The Lucell, abbot of Cluain, with vigorous Baethine: (Aed) a man of two districts, a victorious prince, Bishop Lugduch the gentle.

7. With Matthew (and) bishop Marcus was slain a host with hardship: with a fair melodious train, the feast of Cellach with sharpness.

8. They left (fading) joy with splendour for eternal possession of the Kingdom, a flock of virginal girls at Faustinus' fair passion.

* 'host' D.

RAWL. 505.	LAUD, 610.	LEBAR BRECC, p. 97.
9. Hifeil iosebi cechaing suas iarsetaib slaug dermar derigaib adeich artrib cetaib	9. Hifeil eusebii cechaing suas iarsetaib sluag dermair derigaib coica ar trib cétaib	9. Hifeil cosebi cechaing suas iarsetaib slog dermair dorigaib .l. ar .ccc. aib
10. Trichet arthrib dechib lafer cain centade fintan find fres fine dromua ingard age	10. Trichét ar .uii. adeichib lafer cáin centáide fintan find frenfine droma ingaird áge	10. Tri .c. for .uii. ndechib la fer cain centaide fintan find frem fine droma ingard aige
11. Itana andirmann intrir immarndamni fortcenn (sic) lomman lainnech cainnech mac huidalann	11. ITana andirmand intrir imeraidem fortchernn loman laindech caindech macc hua dalann	11. Hitana andirmand intriir imradem fortchern loman laindech caindech macc hui daland
12. Dlom fiac ocus fiachraig omni mor inmain sein mobi balc inbuaid sein inclarainech cain sein	12. Dlom fiacc ocus fiachraig omne mor inmainsem* mobí balce abuaidsin inclarinech cainsin	12. Dlom fiacc 7 fiachrai omne mor inmain sin mobii balce inbuaidsin inclarainech cainsin
13. comgan ocus marcill collethet alinne indogrigan glanna feil findsige finne	13. Comgan 7 marcill colleithat allinne indócrigan glanna feil findside finde	13. Comgan 7 marcill collethet allinde inocrigan glanna feil findsiche finde
14. Feil calisti epscop asneid for oenlini lacesad conuagi indepscoip paulini	14. Feil calisti epscoip aisneid for oenline lacessad conoighi indepscoip pauline	14. Feil celesti epscoip aisneid foræn line lacesad conuage inepscoip pauline
15. Primchesad murorum roclos fonmbith mbuidnech damdatar mor dadlach iarserbcharcra cuimrech	15. Primchessad mururum roclos fo[u]mbith mbuidnech damdatar mortaidlech laserbcharcraib cuimrech	15. Primchesad murorum rocloss fonmbith mbuidnech damdatar mor tadlach laserbcharcru cuimrech

9. On Eusebius' feast went upwards after (this world's) ways a vast host of Kings, fifty and three hundred[b].

10. Three hundred and seven[c] tens, with a man fair, unstealthy, Fintan the fair, a vine's root, pillar of Druim Ingard.

11. Splendid are the numbers of the triad whom we commemorate, Fortchern, Lomman the scaly: Caindech descendant of Dálann[d].

12. Declare Fiacc and Fiachra of Omin, great is that treasure!—Mobi (strong is that victory!) that fair flatfaced one.

13. Comgan and Marcellus, with their wisdom's breadth, the young queen Glauna, fair Findsech's feast.

14. Bishop Calistus' feast declare thou on one line with suffering of the virginal bishop Paulinus.

15. The foremost suffering of the Mauri was heard throughout the troopful world: they endured great affliction (?) with 'bitter dungeons of fetters.

[a] MS. minainsem.   [b] '310'—D.   [c] D 'three.'   [d] Read *maccu dálann*.   [e] 'after' D.

	RAWL. 505.	LAUD, 610.	LEBAR BRECC, pp. 97, 98.
16.	Ciar tribeetaib cainib lahocht deich donbuaidsein riaguil raith arreimsein colman oneill ruaidsein	Cliar trib cétaib cáinib ceithri deich donbuaidsin riagail raith arcimsin colman ónchill ruaidsin	Ciar .ccc. aib cainib .iiii. x. donbuaidsin riaguil raith arremsin colman onchill ruaidsin
17.	Roches mór inmartir uecodimus nemda conachleir cain tuidme sab innarbha démna	Rochess mor in nairtir nicodimus nemda conacleir cain tuidme sab indarba demna	Roces mor inmartir necodimus nemdai conacleir cain tuidme saph indarbu demnai
18.	Demin lapais pilipp primmartir donformaig trotima dontrednaig dobert crist cain cobraid	Demin lapais pilip primmartir donformaig trifoniæ triuin trednaig dobert crist cain cobraig	Demin lapais pilip primmartir donformaig treofonia dontrednaig dobert crist cain cobraid
19.	Ropcobair dun auster aschomart treriagu ronsnada ronsoera sluag sussi sechpiana	Rob cobair dun auster ascomart tria ri[a]ga ronsnade ronsiera sluag sussiti sech piana	Ropcobair dun auster ascomart triariagu ronsæra ronsnaide sluag sussi sechpiana
20.	Pais eutaice lafintan mæ ldub mor ingairsin caingrian ocontleibsin dennoog[a]nacht ansin	Pais entaic lafintan mældub mor ingairsin caingrian ocintsleibsin doncoganacht mairsin	Pais eutaic lafintan moeldub mor ingairsin caingrian ocuntslebsiu donooganacht aiusin
21.	Anbreo combruth aithri fintan fírór promtha mac telchan tren trednach cathmil credlach croch[d]a	Anbreo combruth athra fintan fíror promthae mac telchain tren trédnach cathmilcredlachcrochda	Anbreo combruth aithre fintan firor promthai macetaulchain tren trednach cathmil credlach crochdai
22.	Croch pilipp indepscoip lasrort sluag colleri matha mind cechrigo lapais eusebi	Croch pilip indepscoip lasnort sluag coleiri matha miud cachrigi lapais eusebi	Croch pilip inepscoip lasort sluag colleri matha mind cechrige lapais eusebi
23.	Escomlud longini	Escomlud longuini	Escomlad longine

16. Ceicra with three fair hundreds and four[a] tens (went) to that victory. Riaguil ran that course: Colmán of that Cell Ruad.

17. Much suffered the martyr, heavenly Nicodemus, with his train, a fair union, the strong expeller of demons.

18. Verily at the passion of Philip a chief martyr, we increase: to the abstinent[b] Tryphonia fair Christ gave aid.

19. May Eusterius be an aid to us, who was slain through torments: may Sosins' host free us (and) protect us beyond pains!

20. Eutychius' passion with Fintan Macldub—great that shout!—a fair sun at that mountain of those splendid[c] children of Eogan.

21. A splendid flame with the Fathers' fervor, Fintan, true gold proven! Tulchán's son, strenuous, abstinent, a battle-soldier, trustful, crucified.

22. The cross of Philippus the bishop, with whom was slain a pious host. Matthew, diadem of every kingdom, with Eusebius' passion.

23. Longinus' departure to the Kingdom

[a] D 'eight.'   [b] 'to strenuous, abstinent' B.   [c] '.great' B.

RAWL. 505.	LAUD, 610.	LEBAR BRECC, p. 98.
dondriglaith as dixu gegna gnim as huaislin tocban alainn issu	don riglaith as dixin geguiu gnim as uaisliu tocban alaind isu	donrigflaith asdixu geguiu gnim isuaisliu toeb án alaind ih.u
24. Asslonnud soer séuir isferr duit dianaesser frisrocaib nem nuasal cocethrachait chresen	24. Aslondud soer souir isferr duit cofoissir frisrócaib nem nuassal cocethrachat crésen	24. Aslondad sær scuir isferr duit dianfesser frisrocaib neam nuasal co .xlat cresen
25. Condadeich dacoica lamaxim donascnai crist lafeil fir thuicsi laisren mór mac nascai	25. Ceithri deich dachocca lamaxim donascnai crist lafeil fir tuicsi laisren mor mac nascai	25. Cethri .x. da .l.at lamaxim donascnai crist lafeil fir tuicsi laisren mor macc nascai
26. Nasad becan mellan nachmod ataniam innain cethrur coir feil ingen mcicc inair	26. Nassan becan mellan nachmolad dothicm inmain cethrar coir feil ingen maic iair	26. Nasad becain mellain nachmod atatiam inmain cethror coir feil ingen mcc iair
27. Erc domnaig moir mainich abban abb caineliarach odran sab soer snamach colma hua fiachrach	27. Erc domnaig moir mainig aban ab caid eliarach odran sab soer snamach lacolman hua fiachrach	27. Erce domnaig moir mainech abban abb cain eliarach odran abb sær snamach colman hóue fiachrach
28. ISfairsiung andalsom babilon aruamsom tatha ocus simon isdimor asluagsom	28. Isfairsiung andalsom babiloin arruamsom tatha 7 simon isdimor asluagsom	28. ISfairsiung andálsom babiloin arruamsom tatha ocus simon isdimor asluagsom
29. Sluag quinti commorbruth ronnain arcechngabud gabais buaid iarndilgud lataimthene talgud	29. Sluagquinti comorbruth ronnain ar cach ngabad gabsat buaid iarndilgud lataemtheine talgad	29. Sluagquinti comorbruth romain arcech ngabud gabsat buaid iarndilgud latamthine talgud
30. Dacét sescat slane forcenlith connacbi bernach hung ardage colman mace huigaili	30. Dachet sescca slane fornenlith ler buada ernach oc ardaghe colman mac huaguala	30. Da .c. lxat slaine forenlith ler mbuadæ ernach uag ardaige colman macc hui gualæ

that is noblest: he wounded (deed that is highest!) Jesu's delightful side.

24. The noble announcement of Severus: it is better for thee if thou shalt know it —he ascended to high heaven with forty pious ones.

25. Four tens, two fifties, who ascended with Maximus, at the feast of the man who understood Christ, Laisrén, Nascae's great son.

26. The fame of Becán (and) Mellán every way* declare(?) it! The feast of the (four) daughters of Mac Iair—loveable is the just tetrad!

27. Erc of Domnach Mór Mainech: Abbán an abbot, fair,[b] train-having: Odrán, an abbot noble, buoyant, Colmán, Finchrae's grandson.

28. Ample is their assembly. Babylon is their burial-ground: Thaddæus and Simon—huge is their host.

29. May the host of Quintus with great fervor protect us[c] against every danger: they won victory after forgiveness, at death's quieting.

30. Two hundred and sixty in full, on one festival, a sea of victories[d]! Ernach a

[a] 'praise' B.   [b] 'chaste' B.   [c] 'me' A.   [d] 'with holiness' D.

RAWL. 505.	LAUD, 610.	LEBAR BRECC, p. 98.
31. Quintinus cain crochtha faelan comeit meithle sernait cosluag aithre ochtimbir ardethre	31. Quintinus cain crochtha faelan comeit meithle sernait coslóg aithre ochtimbir ardeithre	31. Quintinus cain crochdai foelan comet methli sernait cosluag aithre octimpir ardethri

virgin,* a high pillar: Colmán descendant of Guale.

31. Quintinus, fair, crucified: Foelán protection of reapers; they overspread, with a host of fathers, October's lofty end.

Gloss from the Lebar Brecc, pp. 97, 98.

2. (2) *admuinter* .i. adamraigther .i. bendaicher   (3) *for oen line* .i. imallo doib andís
3. (3) *grian sona* .i. arthaitnemchi
4. (1) *ail* .i. atach
6. (4) *ligach* .i. min no cendais
7. (2) *congainte* .i. condoceumlai
9. (2) *cechaing* .i. rochiug
10. (2) *cen taide* .i. cendicleith   (3) *fine* .i. finemna reclesic
12. (1) *dlom* .i. aisnoid   (4) *clarainech* .i. ceusróin lais itir
13. (2) *allinde* .i. asægail no anecnai
15. (3) .i. forodmatar tuilled uilce beos .i. ammus no tadall fliuch .i. aiuru doáscad dobernir for cochall inscaig . sic rofáiseit isti.   Ocus bamor dodoceumal fuarutar inéemais charerach interp. carnem b. post carnem
16. (3) *raith* .i. rorith
17. (3) *tuidme* .i. acomail isinrand *no* maith auoenta
18. (2) *donformaig* .i. dogni artormach   (3) *treduaig* .i. hitredan róches   (4) *cobraid* .i. dorat cobair *no* cobrait .i. cubair ait .i. glic
19. (2) *ascomirt* .i. rosort *no* romarbad
21. (1) *breo* .i. teine
22. (1) *lasort* .i. lasromarbtha   *sluag* .i. cum eo occisi sunt   (4) *eusebi* .i. bonus dei interpretatur
23. (2) *asdixu* .i. isairde
24. (4) *cresen* .i. cresen impu .i. seniores .i. æntech
25. (2) *donascnai* .i. roascnatar .i. dochuatar cum eo ad caelum (3) .i. lafcil fir thuicsen crist .i. tucsi .i. togaide *no* clu *no* sosad
26. (1) *nasad* .i. gnathugud   (2) atatiam *in right marg.* [.i.] aisnéidi *no* atafiaid .i. atafiadar *no* ata úain .i. isúain dúind anindisi *no* nach mod ata fiadat .i. cepit mod on indisit
29. (1) *bruth* .i. caritatis   (3) *romain* .i. ronditue   *gabud* .i. inferni   (4) .i. latám óca doib *no* tathlugud .i. crithuugud *no* cendsugud
30. (3) *ard* .i. uasal
31. (1) *crochdai* .i. rocrochad   (3) *sernait* .i. srethait   *aithre* .i. sruithe *no* athar   (4) *ard* .i. uasal   *ethri* .i. deriud.

---

* 'youth' B.

NOTES FROM THE LEBAR BRECC, p. 97.

1. *prisci* .i. martir.
lucais .i. euangelista.
germain .i. escop 7 maigistir patraic

feil noemrelci .i. taissi muire óige 7 nanaspal 7 nanuile martir 7 noem cre*nn* archena rotinolta hitamlachtu isinrésin

[in lower marg.] Buaid prisci 7rl. Aduentus reliquarum iesu christi et maria[e] uirginis et profetarum et apostolorum . 7 poil cofolt muire 7 nanuile nóg 7 martir 7 nanoem archena. Ocus intan dorochtatar taisi petair 7 póil cofolt muire 7 namarttra moire fil ocróim lasechnall cohard machai . nó isand sen roforbanad relic mælruain hitamla*ch*tai . *no* din . is*ú*lomuintir thamla*ch*ta tuctha nataisi 7 isaccu attatt . ut dicunt alii. Atberat araile is*an*ardmacha attatt istæ reliquie .i. scrín petair 7 poil . ocus ise sechnall tuc eat anall ad hiberniam et in hoc die uenerunt.

2. Iuliter inmartir 7rl. Oimne .i. mac rig laigen 7 hicill giallán in h*ui*b muiredaig ata 7 inetirecht *no* ingiallacht dorig lethi cúind domtad . cotarut rig lethi cúind bo illáim brigte tarcend ariara oanshair condebrutar nacaillecha isálaind ingiallán becsa olsiat. Bid he nainm olbrigit giallán 7 oimne achetainm . unde giallan dicitur.

Eusebi .i. episcopus et martir.
3. *soergei*n *ma*[*i*]*rcc in egept* .i. catu dó inegipt *no* dochum nime.
astondud cech gena .i. euangelista* in hoc die peruenit ad illos.
candida .i. uirgo.
colmain ela .i. olaind ela hi tir chell
4. *balline* .i. uirgo et martir . *no* comad hí ballína .i. bicsech ochill bicsige indib mic uais mide sed non uerum.
5. *sinech ingen fergnæ* .i. maith *no* fergnai nomen patris eius.
cruachan muige abnæ .i. hicruachan muigi habna ineoganacht chaisil
6. *cluana* .i. mic nois
in lucell .i. pro nomine* eius *no* cluain luicell

'*of German*' i.e. a bishop and Patrick's master.
'*the feast of the holy relics*' i.e. the relics of Mary the Virgin and of the apostles and of all the martyrs and saints of Ireland besides, were gathered together in Tallaght at that time.
Priscus' victory &c.—The arrival of the relics of Jesus Christ and the Virgin Mary and the prophets and apostles and of Paul with hair of Mary and of all the virgins and martyrs and of the saints besides. And when Peter's and Paul's relics with Mary's hair and .... of the great shrine (!) which is at Rome came with Sechnall to Armagh . Or it is at that same time that Maelruain's reliquary at Tallaght was completed . Or it is to the Family of Tallaght that the relics were given and with them they are *ut dicunt alii* . Others say that in Armagh are *istae reliquiae* i.e. the shrine of Peter and Paul: and it is Sechnall that brought them hither to Ireland *et &c.*

2. '*Eleutherius the martyr*' &c. Oimne i.e. son of a king of Leinster, and in Cell Giallán, in Ui-Muredaig he is, and in pledge or in hostageship to a king of Conn's Half[b] he was given, and the king of Conn's Half gave him into Brigit's hands to secure his father's obedience to her, and the nuns said "delightful is this little pledgeling!" said they . "This shall be his name," quoth Brigit, *gialldn* (pledgeling), and Oiune was his first name . *unde &c.*

3. '*Mark's noble nativity in Egypt*' i.e. honour to him in Egypt or .... to heaven.

'*of Colman Ela*' i.e. of Lann Ela in Tir Cell.
4. '*Balbina*' i.e. a virgin and martyr. Or she may be Ballína i.e. Bicsech of Cell Bicsige in Ui-Mic-Uais in Meath *sed non uerum*.
5. '*Sinéch Fergnae's daughter* i.e. good, or Fergnae is her father's name.
'*of Cruacha Maige Abnæ*' i.e. in Cruachan Maige Abna in Eoganacht Caisil .
6. '*of Cluain*' i.e. of mac Nois .
'*the bright one* (!)' (here used) for his name .

ᵃ MS. euangeliza   ᵇ the northern half of Ireland.   ᶜ MS. pro nom*en*

.i. cluain cain .i. abb cluanai luicell din .i. colman mac cuile mic midgnai mic meti mic ninnedai mic stair mic crimthainn mic echach mic crimthainn mic cathair máir

baethine .i. mac alla sed nescio ubi* est.
fer da crich .i. o daire éidnech
[in lower marg.]

 Aed (.i. mac carthaind) babó nainm iarfír
 hic aithmit bamaith agníu
 firbrathair iarnbuaid combinid
 domoelruain diarforcetlaid.
 For da crich nainmm artus
 indisfet dúib aimthus
 nainmm hiclochar babínd
 iarsin escop mac carthaind.,

lugdach .i. odaire nafland incogannacht chaisil .i. lugdach escop icluain aithchein ilaigis no icúil bendchair inuib failge et quod uerum est 7 dana ata intescop lugdach cétna hicúilbendchor ilurg for brú locha erni 7 ata hiraith muige tuniscirt hiciarraige luachrai .i. oc daire mochua for brú féile.

7. cellaig .i. cellach sanctus oglind dalacha in huib mail 7 deochain he.
8. leesit luth conaine .i. féil dabid mic iese hic. unde quidem dicitur. no

 rogní maith conaine
 dabid inarige.

7 féil abraim forreic ha.
Ocus otsecht corcrain illaasin

tret ingen .i. uii. filiæ .i. hi crich aird macha hitermond aird macha atat sancta[e] uirgines.ᵇ

9. l. ar tri cétaib .i. donoemaib nama
10. tri cét for secht ndechib no lxxx. ar tri cétaib . no ax. ar .cccc. aib ar xxx.
droma ingard .i. inuib ségain
11. hitana an dirmand .i. féil áboil mic adaim
intriúr imradem .i. dofein amáthair 7 dulltaib
fortchern .i. fortchern mac lœgaire mic neill 7 inathtruim ilægaire ata . no fortchern icill fortchirn in huib drona laigen.

* MS. uir

Or Cluain Luicell i.e. Cluain Cáin . i.e. Abbot of Cluain . Luicell i.e. Colman, son of Cuil, son of Midgnae son of Mete, son of Ninnid, son of Star, son of Crimthann, son of Echaid, son of Crimthann, son of Cathair Mór.
Baethine i.e. son of Alla (?), sed &c.
'Man of two districts' i.e. of Daire Eidnech.

Aed (i.e. son of Carthann) was his name of a truth:
In commemorating, good was his work:
A true brother, after splendid victory,
To Moelruain, to our teacher.
'Man of two districts' was his name at first,
I will tell you his story,
His name in Clochar was Bind (melodious)
Thereafter (it was) bishop Mac Carthainn.

'Lugduch' i.e. of Daire na Fland in Foganacht Chaisil i.e. Lugdach bishop in Cluain Aithchein in Leix, or in Cúil Bennchair in Offaly, et quod uerum est, and moreover the same bishop Lugdach is in Cúil-Bennchoir in Lurg on the brink of Lough Erne, and he is in Rath Maige Tuiscirt in Ciarraige Luachrai i.e. at Daire Mochua on the brink of the Féilo.

7. 'of Celluch' i.e. Collach a saint of Glenn Dálacha in Ui-Mail, and a deacon was he.
8. 'They left joy with splendour' i.e. David son of Jesse's feast here, unde, etc.
or [this is the right reading:—]

 He did good, with splendour,
 David in his kingdom.

and Abraham's Feast . . . . . ?
And Corcrán's obit on this day.

'a flock of daughters' i.e. seven i.e. in the district of Armagh in the sanctuary of Armagh are holy virgins.

9. 'fifty and three hundred' i.e. of saints only.
10. 'three hundred and seven tens' or 80+ 300 or 10+400+30.
'of Druim Ingard' i.e. in Ui Segain.
11. 'Splendid are their numbers' i.e. the feast of Abel son of Adam.
'of the triad whom we commemorate' i.e.
. . . . . their mother and of Ulster.
'Fortchern' i.e. Fortchern son of Loegaire, son of Niall, and in Athtruim Ui-Loegairi he is. Or Fortchern in Cell Fortchirn in Ui-Drona of Leinster.

ᵇ MS. uirgenis.

loman .i. discipulus patricii 7 inathtruim ata beos
lainlech .i. land achlaime fair.
caindech mac hui daland [*in right margin*] .i. Caindech mac hui daland .i. mac dæd aluind he 7 achad bó aprimchell 7 ata recles do hicill rigmouaig inalbain

Diandechaid caindech cofindia coriarr fair inad ambiad . ní nicim and innossai arfindia uair rogab cách romat . INad fás and areaindech

12. *fiace* 7 *fiachrai* .i. fiachra mac dfiacc he et cum co est.
onme .i. omin .i. cell bec fil it*ir* cluain mor moedoc 7 achad naball isandside ata fiacc 7 islebtib iluiguib *no* in huib drona ata fiacc beos
inclarainech .i. censróin lais it*ir* . Mobí clarainech mac beoain mic bresail mic ailgil mic idnai mic athrai mic lúgnai trínog mic bregduilb mic airtch[u]irp . Hinc mobíí 7 fintan unam geneologiam habent et reliqua . Mobíí clar*ainech* oghis náiden hingaillaib 7 berchan ainm mobíí . 7 beoan ainm aathar . 7 uainind ingen fiudhairr ainm amathar . 7 bicill mic thaidg rocoimpred 7 rucad 7 dochorcorfirtrí doluignib conn*acht* dó . Ocus friamnái mairb docomp*red* he . Clarainech din . he uair rothairind inúir angaid corbahæuchlar vli hí 7rl.

13. *comgan* .i. hicluain condaid hi cuirene.

marcill . marcill .i. episcopus
glanna .i. in africa .uii. milium nongentorum et septuaginti .uii.
findsiche .i. uirgo 7 ernaide nomen ciuitatis eius hisleib guaire hingailengaib . *no* induil arnide ata ceall fhindsiche . *no* amuig reichent illaigis
14. *celesti* .i. papa roma*
15. *murorum* .i. nomen plebis maurri in gallia pasi sunt
16. *riaguil* .i. riagail muicindse forlochd*erg* derc.
colman .i. colman escop mac cathbuid ochill ruaid forbrú locha láig inulltaib

'*Loman*' i.e. a disciple of Patrick, and in Athtruim he is still.
'*Sealy*' i.e. the scale of his leprosy on him.
'*Cainnech* descendant of *Dálann*' i.e. Cainnech descendant of Dálann, i.e. a son of Aed Alaind was he, and Achad Bó is his chief church, and he has a cell in Cell Rigmonaig (St. Andrew's) in Scotland.
When Cainnech went to Findia he asked of him a place wherein he might abide. "I see none there now," says Findia, "for every one has taken before thee." "There is an empty place there," said Cainnech.
12. '*Fiace and Fiachrae*' i.e. Fiachra was a son of Fiachrae's et etc.
'*of Omin*' i.e. Omin i.e. a little church between Cluain Mór Maedoc and Achad Aball. Fiacc is there and in Slebti in Leinster or in Ui-Drona is Fiacc also.
'*the Flatfaced*' i.e. he had no nose at all. Mobí the Flatfaced son of Beóán, son of Bresal, son of Ailgel, son of Idnae, son of Athrae, son of Lugnae Trí n-og, son of Bregdolb, son of Artchorp. Hence Mobí and Fintan have the same pedigree etc. Mobí the Flatfaced of Glasnevin in (Fin)gal, and Berchan was Mobí's name, and Beóán was his father's name, and Uininn daughter of Findbarr was his mother's name . And in Cell Mic Thaidg was he conceived and born, and of Corcofirtri of the Luigne of Connaught was he . And of a dead woman was he conceived. Flatfaced, now, was he, for the mould pressed down his face, so that it was all one flat, etc.

13. '*Comgan*' i.e. in Cluain Condaid in Cuirene.
'*of Marcellus*' Marcill i.e. a bishop.

'*of Findsech*' i.e. a virgin, and Ernaide is the name of her town in Sliab Guairi in Gailenga. Or in Dál Arnide is Findsech's church. Or in Mag Rechet in Leix.

16. '*Riaguil*' i.e. Riagail of Muc-Iuis on Lough Derg.
'*Colman*' i.e. bishop Colman, son of Cathbad of Cell Ruaid, on the brink of Lough Láig in Ulster.

in lower marg.] Tres pueri in fornace ignis*
ardentis hoc canticum[b] fecerunt . Himmaig
senair im*murro* dorónad 7 himmaig díraim
spetialiter . INamsir din . nábcudón nasor
dardnad diaserad arthenid derousat he . unir
naroadairset inteilb nordai dorónad lanábeudou
nasor . isairo rolaitea in fornaceu . Deus tamen
illos cautando hoc canticum[c] de fornace liber-
auit[d] . Annaias Assarias Misahel ananmunda
hebraice . Sodrach . Misac . Abdinago ananmunda kalita.
christe lux eis . ✠

Magnificat anima . Maria mater domini fecit
hunc hymnum[e] . IN tempore din . octauin
auguist fecit . in quadragesimo euim secundo
anno imperii[f] cius christus natus est . in
ierusalem dorónad . no isinamile chathraig
sliabdai hifail ierusalem . O*cus* isiside dileas
zachair . ibi[g] iohannes bauptista natus est .
O*cus* isdonchathraig sin tanic muire d[i]ss
helizabeth intau itchuala alachtai bi . O*cus*
isiudte thucad hirrlabra dozach*ar* . isiunte beos
doroine zach*ar* benedictus . ISho din . infoch-
and .i. muire thanic dofhiss helizaboth setchi
zach*air* . aritchuala aboth alach*ta* post longis-
simam sterilitatem . omnes enim cognati eius
ad eam nisitabant . INtrans ergo maria
ostium[h] domus suae elizabeth' dixit . cum motа-
tione infantis in ueutre suo eu mater domini
uenit ad me et ob id[j] dicunt iohannim profetasse
antequam natus esse[t] et tunc maria dixit .
Magnificat etc. in hoc tempore filium suum
maria concepit.,

Gloria in excelsis deo . aingil dorónsat infers
toisech donimanso óidche nageine . hictur ader
immurro dorousat .i. mile ohierusalem sair.
dia foillsiugud *conid* mac dé intí rogenair and
dorousat he . INamsir hoctaffu vero dorónad
he . Ambróiss din . doróine intuilled .i. a
secundo uersu[k] usque . INfinem laudis etc .

Ambrosius sui escop ise doroine hunc imnum
domolad ih.u . o*cus* inoiche asd[i]r acantain .
tria rithim din . dorónad .uii. cáptil ind o*cus*
.uii. line inecech cáptil o*cus* .uii. sillaeba cech*a*
line .

*Tres pu*e*ri* etc. In the plain of Shinar, now, it
was made and in the plain of Dura *specialiter*.
In the time of Nebuchadnezzar it was made. To
save themselves from the fire they nade it.
For they worshipped not the golden image that
was made by Nebuchadnezzar and therefore
were they flung into the furnace. *Deus* etc.

Their names in Hebrew : Shadrach, Me-
shach, and Abednego their names in Chaldee.

Magnificat anima. Mary mother of the
Lord made this hymn. In the time of Octavian
Augustus she made it, for in the forty-second
year of his reign Christ was born . In Jerusalem it was made. Or in a certain mountain-
city near Jerusalem. And this is Zacharias'
own city. There John the Baptist was born.
And it is to that city that Mary came to visit
Elizabeth when she heard that she was
pregnant . And it is therein that speech was
given to Zacharias, and therein, moreover,
Zacharias made the *Benedictus*.
This then is the cause, namely, Mary came
to visit Elizabeth Zacharias' wife, for she heard
that she was pregnant after a very long bar-
renness, *omnes* etc.

Gloria in excelsis deo. Angels made the
first verse of this hymn on the night of the
Nativity. At the tower of Ader, now, they
made it, namely, a mile from Jerusalem, eastward. To manifest that he who was then born
was God's Son they made it. In the time of
Octavian it was made. Ambrose then made
the supplement i.e. from the second verse to
the end of the praise, etc.

Ambrosius, a sage (and) bishop, he made
this hymn to praise Jesus, and at night it is
proper to sing it. In rhythm, moreover, it
was made. Seven chapters in it, and four
lines in each chapter, and seven syllables in
each line.

[a] MS. hignis   [b] MS. canticam   [c] MS. hic canticumm   [d] MS. liberabit
[e] MS. himnum   [f] MS. immperi   [g] MS. hibi   [h] MS. hostium
[i] MS. helzabeth   [j] MS. hobid   [k] MS. uersa

17. *saph indarpu demnai* .i. achad deo in iarthar erenn
18. *pilip* .i. euangelista.
treofonia .i. rigina rig róman
20. *eutaic* .i. martir
fintan moeldub .i. fintan mældub inúib duach inosraigib 7 deoganacht chaisil dó .i. ocdermuig hua nduachituaiscert osraige ata . uel duo sancti sunt fintan 7 mældub 7 icluain immorroiss inhuib failge ata mældub et quod uerius et germanus cóugan glindo buissean
[in lower marg.] P[ais] eutaic 7rl. Mældub *immurro* . atbernit araile comad deoganacht caisil dó . 1 Arfirinde *immurro* senchusa fer nerenn isdosíl briain mic echach muidmedoin domældub . *Conall glún macbriain . enmæclais.i.* fothad . Damac lafothad .i. amalgaid 7 andud . Damac lahaudud .i. cuanna 7 dubdumach a quibus múinter chuanna 7 *hui* duib dumach dicuntur . Oenmac lahamalgaid .i. mældub a quo muinter mælduib . Mældub mac amalgaid mic fotluid mic conaill glún mic briain mic echach muidmedoin .

Ocus isc inmældubsin rosfuc fechin fabair lais indaltus coroscuir dochum légindhe. Fásaid iarum aecnai coudernai fechin celloir do inachomthinol . conid dinsil muinter mælduib iarum . Ocus isiaruaác atbert fechin

Mældub
bidbai nandeman ndærdub
acht achuilche sa blai lin
nochar thec*ht* ni dontsægul .

Teist tuc michel armældub
maith inti forsatarut
odochuaid hierabud uais
nithard achluais fríhadart .

Teist [tuc] michel armældub
mor inteist ar mac nduine
acht rig narend mac muire
uifuil bud ferr reguide .

Ciatbera¹ asteind modruim
nochoniarmbreith eri thruim
ni bud toirsech inchuil chámm
dia ndernai dulce na dimrall

Dobérsa teist armældub

¹ leg. ci-atberad.

17. '*a strong expeller of demons*' i.e. (of) Achad Deo in the west of Ireland.
18. '*Philip*' i.e. an evangelist. '*Tryphonia*' i.e. queen of a king of the Romans.
20. '*Eutychius*' i.e. a martyr.
'*Fintan Moeldub*' i.e. Fintan Moeldub in Ui-Duach in Ossory, and of the Eoganacht Chaisil is he . and at Dermag Hua-nDuach in the north of Ossory he is. *Vel duo sancti sunt* Fintan and Maeldub, and in Cluain Immorroiss in Offaly is Maeldub, *et etc*.
'*Eutychius' passion*' etc. Now as to Maeldub some say that he was of the Eoganacht Chaisil . However, according to the truth of the history of the men of Ireland, he is of the seed of Brian son of Echaid Muidmedon, is Maeldub. Conall glún son of Brian had one son, namely, Fothad . Two sons had Fothad, namely, Amalgaid and Andud. Two sons had Andud, namely, Cuanna and Dubdumach, from whom the Muinter Chuanna and the Hui Duib Dumach take their names . One son had Amalgaid i.e. Maeldub, *a quo* are the 'Muinter Maelduib'. Maeldub son of Amalgaid, son of Fothad, son of Conall glún, son of Brian, son of Echaid Muidmedon.
And it is that Maeldub that took Fechin of Fore into fosterage with him and sent him to learning . His wisdom waxeth afterwards so that Fechin made a *cellóir* of him in his congregation . And of his seed is the Muinter Maelduib, and after his death Fechin said:—

Maeldub,
The foe of the base black demons :
Save his quilt and his shirt (*l*) of linen
He had nothing of the world .

The witness which Michael bore as to Maeldub
(Good was he for whom he gave it)
Since he entered noble religion
He set not his ear to a pillow.

The witness which Michael bore as to Maeldub
(Great the witness as to a son of man)
Save the King of the Stars, Mary's Son,
There is none better for praying to .

Though it should say that 'my back is sore,'
It is not after carrying a heavy load :
The crooked midge would not be weary
For the evil or error that he (Maeldub) wrought.
I will bear witness as to Maeldub

nocoteist fir combægul
comberad cúil inacrub
andernai dochul maeldub . M .

21. *fintan* .i. nomen artus .i. mundu mufindu .i. fintan
    taulchain .i. drúth artus he
in r. marg.] An breo 7rl. .i. munda mac taulchán druad ideo dicitur fintan fris .i. aentu doroine 7 fintan cl*uan*a béidnech cotardsat ainm cech*t*air de foramile icomartha æntad ut . dixit colum *cille*

Aclerchin cháid chu*mach*taig
a mic thulchain abachláig
ruc m*ac* nandsa do mu*n*tir
inmathair rotuc afintain
        .i. a munna

crochdai .i. cl*a*ime boi fair . corusice mochua mac lonan he donclaimo . ut dixit munda

Buaid dana 7 buaid tige
uaimsi dú lonain mide
buaid mic dia mbai ere lán
luag aérgi dothulchan

23. *geguin* .i. rogon longinus latus christi

in lower marg] Escomlad longine 7rl. [longinus] et eogitianus nom*ina* militum robatar hicerochad cri*st* . eogitianus i*nmur*ro dorat inneim docri*st* . longinus din . rotgon inathæb ndess. 7 longinus praedicauit christum post sua[m] linguam abscisam uidens signa quae fuerunt in illa die id est solem obscuratum et petras[a] scisas credidit in dominum iesum[b] et habitabat in cesarea ciuitate capadocie prouincie quae est in asia[c] minore habens[d] quietam uitam monachorum[e] annis .xxuiii. et sub præside octauiano pasus est.

25. *Laisren* .i. laisren mac nascai oard mic nascai for brú locha láig inulltaib

26. *nasad beoain mellain* .i. tres sancti dobretnaib in una eclesia sunt .i. hitamlachta menand hic loch bricrend inúib echach ulad

cethror .i. darmil 7 darbilín 7 coel 7 coimgell icill naningen hitamlachtai atatt .*no* hicill ingen iaráin hicor corcodúibne (*sic*) atat ingenai

(Not the witness of a faultful man)
That a midge would carry in its claw
What of evil Maeldub wrought. M.

21. Fintan i.e. his name at first .i. *Mundu*, My-Findu i.e. Fintan.
' *of Tulchain*' i.e. an evildoer at first was he.
'A splendid flame' etc. i.e. Munda son of Taulchán the wizard . for this reason is he called Fintan i.e. an union which he and Fintan of Cluain Eidnech made, and they set the name of each of them on the other in token of union. As Colomb Cille said :—

O chaste, mighty little cleric !
O son of Tulchán, O croziered one !
She bore a son hard to (her) family
The mother that bore thee, O Fintan !
        i.e. O Munna !

'*crucified*' .i. there was leprosy on him till Mochua son of Lonan healed him of the leprosy, as Munda said :—

Gift of knowledge and gift of house
From me to Lonan of Meath's descendant.
The gift of a son of whom Ireland was full,
The meed of his rising to Tulcháu !

23. '*wounded*' i.e. Longinus wounded Christ's side.
'Longinus' departure' etc.
Longinus and Eugitianus were the names of the soldiers at Christ's crucifixion. Now Eugitianus gave the poison to Christ, and then Longinus wounded him in his right side, and Longinus preached Christ after his tongue was cut out, *videns* etc.

25. '*Laisrén*' .i. Laisrén son of Nascae of Ard mic Nascai on the brink of Lough Láig in Ulster.

26. '*The fame of Beóán and Mellán*' i.e. three[f] saints of the Britons : in one church are they, namely, in Tamlachta Menann at Loch Bricrenn in Ui-Echach of Ulster

'*tetrad*' i.e. Darmil and Darbilín and Coel and Coimgell : in Cell nan-ingen they are. Or in Cell Ingen Iaráin and in Corcaguiny are

---

[a] MS. solum abscuratum 7 petr*us*   [b] MS. incni. ilim.   [c] MS. asiæ
[d] MS. hi   [e] MS. montorum   [f] The scholiast regards *nasad* as a proper name.

mic iair [in r. marg.] .iiii. filiae iair .i. darmil
7 darbilin 7 coel 7 coimgell ochill naningen
hitamlachtu .ix. intres indib dúnchada . no
ataeg nambretan hitermand chenannsa ut quidam dicunt.

27. *erce domnaig moir* .i. immuig luadat
hituaiscert *hua faelan*
abban .i. ochill abbain inuib muiredaig . 7
omuig arnaide induib cendselaig .i. induib buide
. *no* iuelib thuaisciurt ata acheall . 7 mac bui
chormaic he fesin 7 feil agcine hic .i. abban
mac laignig mic caindig mic imchada mic cormaic mic concorb

Secht mbliadna delbglana déc
hifuilliud airme .ccc.
ssegal abbain delbda dúind
inairet robui hicolaind .

odran abb ser snamach .i. for snam dochuaid
igair mic moga .i. indsi fil icorcoduibne [*in
left marg.*] odran sacerdos othig airernn amide
no oletrachaib odraiu amuscraige thire 7 obi
coluim cille .i. relic odrain inhii . *no* igair mic
moga ata .i. indsi lacorco duibne 7 forsnam[b]
dochuaid innte ut ferunt[b]

in lower marg.] Erce domnaig moir 7rl.
Colman hua fiachrach .i. hi senbothaib fola
induib cendselaig is nachill ataut ualachain 7 ni
lamair eat . arcia focertar iniauroll áidche inusce
fortenid ciaroloisethea feda indomain foncoire
niftheig inusce cotartar iatsam ass isinlind
cétnai

28. *babiloin arruamsom* .i. in eadem[c] prouincia passi sunt
tatha ocus simon. tatha qui et iudas a nomine dicitur . frater iacopi alphei ut luca [in]
euangelio et in actibus apostolorum narrat sed
non proditor christi . simon can[a]naeus frater
iudae apostoli
29. *tamthine* .i. uirgo et ne[s]cio ubi est
30. *slaine* .i. cennf doesbuid dib 7 hislaine
ambregaib atat isti[d] omnes ut ferunt . ocus

the daughters of Iar's son. Four daughters of
Iar i.e. Darmil and Darbilin and Coel and
Coimgell of Cell nan-ingen ('the church of the
maidens') in Tamlachta . . . . in Ui-Dún-
chada . Or in Teg nam-Bretan ('the house
of the Britons') in the Sanctuary of Kells, as
some say.

27. '*Erc of Domnach Mór*' i.e. in Mag
Luadat in the north of Ui-Faelain.
'*Abbán*' i.e. of Cell Abbain in Ui-Muredaig,
and of Mag Arnaide in Ui-Cennselaig i.e. in
Ui-Buide . Or in Northern Eli is his church;
and son of Ua-Cormaic is he himself; and the
feast of his nativity is here i.e. Abbán, son of
Laignech, son of Cainnech, son of Imchath,
son of Cormac, son of Cúchorb.

Seventeen pure-shaped years
In addition to the number 300
Was the age of shapely, brown Abban
While he was in the body.

'*Odran an abbot noble, buoyant*' i.e. by
swimming he went into Gair (?) mic Moga i.e.
an island in Corcoduibne. Odrán a priest of
Tech Airerain in Meath, or of Letraich Odrain
in Muscraige Tire, and of Colomb-Cille's Hi,
namely Relic Odrain ('Oran's graveyard') in
Iona. Or in Gair (?) Mic Moga he is i.e. an
isle in Corcoduibne, and by swimming he went
into it, *ut ferunt*.

'Erc of Domnach Mór' etc. Colman descendant of Fiachrae i.e. in Senbotha Fola in Ui-
Cennselaig. It is in his church that the ducks
are, and no one dares (to touch) them. For if,
by mistake at night, they be put into water on
a fire, though (all) the woods of the world were
burnt under the caldron the water getteth not
warm until they (the ducks) are put thereout
into the same pool (in which they were before).

28. '*Babylon their grave-yard*' i.e. *in etc.*

29. '*Thaddaeus and Simon*'. Thaddaeus qui
etc.

30. '*in full*' i.e. with nothing wanting to
them; and in Slaine in Bregia are those all,

[a] MS. fuchtnam [b] MS. fuerunt [c] MS. eodem [d] MS. isto

anair thancotar dianoilithre Sed in uno die quadam causa*a* mortui sunt.

ernach .i. mac iairnd sainm *acht* uí rothaille isinrund 7 indún døn hi fidbaid dáil araide atasom.

colman .i. dognailfine dó .i. tuath do ulltaib 7 ilaind mochohnog ata *no* hi cam*mus* chomgail fur brú bandai 7 mac máthar do mocholmóg nalainde he

31. *Quintinus* .i. de romanis[b]
in lower marg.] Quintinus et reliqua .i. filius zenonis (proprium*c* nomen) senatoris urbis roma[e] pasus est sub ricia uaro (?) præfecto[d] in regione gallorum iuxta flumen somnæ ubi ciuitas cui*f* nomen est ambiantium[g] et in flumine somnae[e] corpus eius fuit annus[h] .l.u.

foelan .i. brathair fursa 7 martir he

as they say. And from the east they came on their pilgrimage. *Sed* etc.

'*Érnach*' i.e. Mac Iairnd (son of Iron) is his name; but it fitted not in the quatrain; and in Dún Dáén ['Fortress of Two Birds'] in the wood of Dál Araide is he.

'*Colman*' i.e. he was of the Gailfine, a people of Ulster, and in Lann Mo-Cholmóc is he, or in Cammus Comgaill on the Bann's brink, and he was a son of the mother of Mocholmóc of the Lann.

'*Foelan*' i.e. Fursae's brother, and a martyr was he.

---

[a] MS. quidam cassassa [b] MS. romanius [c] MS. gein peir [d] MS. perfecto
[e] MS. ibi ciuitate qui [f] i.e. Ambiani, Amiens [g] i.e. the Samara, Somme [h] MS. annis

RAWL. 505, fo. 219 a.
1. Lonan colman cronan
conacleir gil grianaich
sluaig helair derbdalaich
soerait samain sianaig
2. Sruth apstal artire
patraice primda age
dobert bendacht mbuada
forerce arda slane
3. Sluim clair darromuir
murdebur mind senaid
lith cain corcunutain
lafeil cocmain cnaig
4. Inmain grian ceropni
commorchleir ceneclai
perpetua gen digra
coniunx primda petrai
5. Pais domini airdirc
inmaslechta fermaice
derath de bahorlan
colman glinni delmaice
6. Cedol[e]gsad doine
tremartra conani
adreth riched ruanach
dunad adriani
7. Droṅg adbul eusebi
cerbogur aslige
fofuair fortren toga
tir mór himaig nime
8. Fornem nual claudini
luid cleir cain cenæra

LAUD, 610, fo. 69 b, 1.
1. Lonan colman cronan
conacleir ngil ṅgrianaich
sluag clair derb dalaig
soeraid samain sinaid
2. Sruith epstal artire
patraic primda áge
dobert bendacht inbuada
forerce arda slane
3. Sluind clair darromuir
murdebar mind senaig
lith cáin corcanuthain
laféil chaemain cnaig
4. Inmain grian cenoipni
comorchleir cenecla
perpetua cendigna
coniunx primda petri
5. Paiss domini irdraic
inmaslechta fermaice
dorath dé baforlan
colman glinde delmaic
6. Cia dolégsat dóine
tré martra conáine
adreith riched runach
dunad adriáine
7. Drong adbul eusebi
cinpugur asligi
fofuair fortren táge
tír mór inmaig nime
8. Fornem nuall cechlína[a]
luid cleir cáin ganéra

LEBAR BRECC, p. 99.
1. Lonan colman cronan
conacleir gil grianaig
sluaig clair derb dalaig
sœrait samuin sianaig
2. Sruith asptul artire
patraic primda aige
dobert bendacht mbuada
for escop cre slaine
3. Sluind clair tarromuir
muirdebair mind senaid
laḟith cain corcnutan
lafeil cocmain cnaig
4. INmain grian cenoipne
comorcleir ceneclai
perpetua cendigna
coniux primda petrai
5. Pais domini indaurdaire
imaslechta fermaic
dorath de bahorlan
colman glinde delmaic
6. Ce dolegsat doine
tremartra conani
atreith riched runach
dunad adreani
7. Drong adbul eusebi
ceabugur aslige
fosfuair fortren togæ
tír mor formuig nime
8. Fornem nuall cech dine
luid cleir cain cen æra

1. Lonán, Colmán, Cronán, with their fair, sunny following: the hosts of (pope) Hilarius surely-multitudinous, ennoble stormy All-Saints-Day.

2. The senior of our land's apostles, Patrick, a chief pillar, bestowed a blessing of victory on Bishop Erc of Slane.[b]

3. Announce (bishop) Hilarius over a great sea. Murdebair a synod's diadem: Corcunutan's fair festival at Coemán of Enach's feast.

4. Dear the sun without suddenness, with a great fearless following, Perpetua without reproach, Peter's excellent conjux.

5. The passion of conspicuous Domninus round whom were slain man-children; very full of God's grace was Colmán of Glenn Delmaic.

6. Though men had dissolved them through martyrdom with splendour, Adrian's host ran to mysterious heaven.

7. Eusebius' vast troop, though grievous was their road, they found—mighty choice!—a great land on[c] Heaven's plain.

8. In Heaven (was) Claudinus[d] shout, (for thither) went a fair train without

[a] l. cludini [b] B and D, 'on Erc of Ard Sláne' [c] B and D 'in' [d] A and B 'every number's'

RAWL. 505, fo. 219 a.	LAUD, 610, fo. 69 b, 1.	LEBAR BRECC, p. 99.
lalith linas tuatha	lalith linas tuatha	lalith linas tuatha
barrinn mormaic æda	barrfind mor m. aeda	barrfind mor maic æda
9. Donait ocus daman	9. Donaid 7 daimian	9. Donait 7 daman
niptar ecnaid anbli	nipdar ecnaid aiuble	niptar ecnaig ainble
foroenlith cosuilgi	foroenlith cosuilge	forœnlith cofuilge
feil sinchi cosaidbri	feil sinchi cosaidbri	feil sinche cosaidbre
10. Aed mac bricc dendri-	10. Aed m. bric donrigraid	10. Æd mac bricc donrigraid
graid		
bece nabumo ecaib	bec nabumó ecaib	bec nabumo ecaib
isard isinmorlaith	isard issin morlaith	isard isinmorlaith
insab sil chuind chetaig	insabb sil chnind chetaig	insab sil chuind cetaig
11. Corpbri cula raithin	11. Cairpre chula rathain	11. Can comainm can me-
		dair
rath rig[d]a corromuir	rath rigda coromuir	sair siar cotaromuir*
sanctmartain soer sa-	sanct martain saersa-	sanct martain sœr sa-
muil	mail	mail
sliab oir iarthuir domuin	sliab óir iarthair domain	sliab oir iarthair domain
12. Doridnacht lasuithi	12. Donrignacht lasuithe	12. Doridnacht lasuithe
soas comeit tiachrai	soas comét tiachra	soas comét tiachrai
domchunmain cain	do chumáin cain milti	domchumain cain milte
milte		
mac find fota fiachnai	mac find fota fiachna	mac find fota fiachnai
13. For id eitsecht eutaicc	13. Forrith eitsecht eutaic	13 Forid etsecht eutaic
martir mainmordaiss	martir mamordais	martir ba imrordais
renotlaice ard ergnuiss	renotlaic aird irguis	renodlaig aird aurgais
asneid init corgaiss	dogné init corgais	dogne init chorgais
14. Clemeint ocus colman	14. Clemint 7 colman	14. Clemint 7 colman
celebair afeile	ceilebair afeile	celebair afeli
frigein crist conuagi	friagein crist conoighe	frigein crist conuage
tinscan lechsa leire	tindscain lexa léiri	tindscan lexu leri

reproaches,[a] on the festival that fills territories of Barrfind the great son of Aed.

9. Doñatus and Damanus were not sordid (?) revilers; on one festival with virtues (?) the feast of wealthy Sinech.

10. Aed, son of Brecc of the kings: little —it was not more—(was) death (to him): high in the great realm is the champion of the seed of hundred-battled Conn.

11. Cairpre of Cuil Raithin, royal grace as far as the great sea[b] ! Saint Martin— noble simile ! the mount of gold of the west of the world !

12. There was given, with wisdom, science, with much prudence, to my Cumain of beautiful warfare, the fair tall son of Fiachna.

13. On the ides (of November was) Eutex' death, a martyr if thou hast commemorated: before Christmas a high supplication make[c] at the beginning of (Moses') lent.

14. Clement and Colman, celebrate thou their feasts: at the birth of Christ with perfection begin thou pious chants.

[a] B 'refusal'
[b] A 'chant the surname, chant eloquence, east, west, even over a great sea' [c] D 'utter'

RAWL. 505, fo. 219 a, b.	LAUD, 610, fo. 69 b, 2.	LEBAR BRECC, pp. 99, 100.
15. Lacesad secundi cosluagud cechdatha corgus mafutbotha tinscan greim dochatha	15. Lacessad secundi cosluagud cachdatha corgus mafotbotha tinnscain *gréim* docatha	15. Lacesad secundi coslogud cechdatha corgus mafutbotha tindscan greim achatha
16. Cliar augustin epscoip dóig nochartais tredan troethais mór ngur ngalair cethrach[ai]t cain credal	16. Cleir augustin epscoip dáig nochardais tredan troethsus mor ngur ngalur cethracha cáin credal	16. Cleir augustin escuip dech nochardais tredan troethais mor ngur ngalur .xl. cain credal
17. Celebair feil tecla isiarmbunaid d[o]rochair buaid beo buan balc athair laduilech cain clochair	17. Ceilebair feil tecla isiarmbuaid dorochair buaid beo buan balccathair laduilech cáin clochair	17. Celebair feil teclai isiarmbunaid dorochair buaid beo buan balcc athair laduilech cain clochair
18. Cain coscerad eclass petair isphoil primdai meicc beraich conuagi feil reil ronain rigdai	18. Lacoiscerad neclas petair is poil primdai mac beraig conoghi feil réid ronain rigda	18. Lacoiscerad neclas petair ispoil primdai mac beraig conuage feil reil ronain rigdai
19. Raid coiscerad mbaslicc iohain meicc cenmelacht luid cethracha ndillacht lamaxim mor ngerat	19. Raid cofssecrad baslic coin mac can melacht luid sechtmoga dilecht^a lamaxim mor ngerat	19. Raid coisecrad mbaislic coin mcc cenmelacht luid .lxx. dillacht lamaxim mor ngerat
20. Guid escon lafroechan arbledma balc thbelaib lacesad corunaib sluag bassi hisnelaib	20. Guid escon lafroechan ardbladma bailebelaib lacessad corrunaib sluag bassi uasnclaib	20. Guid escon lafroechan arbledma balc belaib lacesad corunaib sluag sussi hisnelaib
21. Noebdecheng conrualai coc*rist* lagein clemeint macc commain aharainn macc congraid ahereind	21. Noemdechcng co*n*ruala coc*rist* lagein chlemint mac comain aharaind mac chonchraid ahéirind	21. Noeb decheng conrualai coc*rist* lagein clemint macc comain aharaind macc congraid aherind

15. At Secundinus' suffering with a host of every colour, Lent if thou fear it, begin a part of its battle.

16. Bishop Augustinus' following, very well they used to love a three days' fast: great, heavy grief overwhelmed them, forty fair pious-ones.

17. Celebrate Thecla's feast: it is after victory she fell: Buaid-béo a lasting, strong father, with Duilech the fair of Clochar.

18. At the consecration of the churches of Peter and excellent Paul (are) Bernach's son with virginity (and) the clear^b feast of royal Ronan.

19. Relate the consecration of the basilica of John, a son without reproach: seventy^c sinless ones went with Maximus the great champion.

20. Beseech Esconn with Froechán before strong (Slieve) Bloom at the passion with mysteries of Sosius' hosts below^d the clouds.

21. A holy pair of champions departed to Christ at Clement's birth, (Colmán) son of Commán out of Aran, and (Aedán) son of Congrad out of Ireland.

^a .i. dilochta l. dilocht .i. nemlochtuidi .i. sine pecatto   ^b B 'smooth'
^c D 'forty'   ^d B 'of Bassus' hosts above'

RAWL. 505, fo. 219 b.	LAUD, 610, fo. 69 b, 2.	LEBAR BRECC, p. 100.
22. IArcesad himartrai mare loichet laindrech raith corigu*acc* uainglech cicilia cáin caindlech	22. Iarcessad lamartra maire lochet laindrech luid coarig nard nainglech cicilia cáin caindlech	22. IAr cesad himartra muire loichet loindrech luid corigu*acc* nainglech cicilia cain coindlech
23. Cesad cain clementis etertonnaib trethain adorthair achathir fotonnuib lir letha[i]n	23. Cessad cáin clementis eti*r* tonnaib trethain adorthair acathair fotondaib lir lethain	23. Cesad cain clementis itir thondaib trethain adorthar achathair fothondaib lir lethain
24. Lacianan doim liacc caindias diarturinn meee leneni rolainn la colman duib chuilinn	24. Lacianan daimliac cain dias diartuirind mac leincine rolaind lacolman duibchuilind	24. Lacianan doiuliac cain dias diartuirind mvice lenine rolaind lacolman duibchuilind
25. Lasinncoin cascon assaherchoin chorann luid achroich cainferann finchu obri gobann	25. Lasinneoni (*sic*) cassion asasaerchain corann luid acroich cainferann findchú obri gabann	25. Lasineoin cassion asaerchain corand luid hieroich cainferand findchu obri goband
26. Guid decheng^a úderb ńdalach copopul banbuadach banbau bruth oir oiblech epscop siricc sruamach	26. Guid décheng derbdalach copopul bán buadach banbau bruth oir oiblech escop siric sruamach	26. Guid decheng derb dalach copopul ban buadach banbau bruth oir oiblech escop siric sruamach
27. Sruaim ecnai conani sechnall mind arflatha rogab ceol soer sodad molad patraic macha	27. Sruaim ecua conaine sechnall mind arflatha rochan ceol soer sodath molad patraic macha	27. Sruaim ecnai conani sechnall mind arflathi rogab ceol saer solad molad patraic mache
28. Primtrecheng nachduthain trofini cenmaithim meicc bochrai buaid suthain oachud reid raitin	28. Mordecheng nachduthain latrophin cen maithim mac bochra buaid suthain oachud réid rathain	28. Prim drecheng nadduthain latrofin cenmathim mec bochrai buaid suthain oachud reid rathin

22. After suffering in martyrdom—O Mary, (she was) a shining light!—to the angelic, royal Son went^b Cecilia the fair (and) radiant.

23. Clement's fair suffering among the waves of the sea: in his city there is adoring under the waves of the broad main.

24. With Cianan of Doimliac a fair car to our wheat, (Colmán) son of Lenínc the vehement, with Colmán Duib-Chuilinn.

25. With John Cassion, whose crown is very fair, into Croch, a fair country, went Findchu of Bri Gobann.

26. Beseech a pair of champions sure, multitudinous, with a people white, gifted, Banbán a sparkling glowing-mass of gold: bishop Syricus the streamy.^c

27. A stream of wisdom with splendour, Sechnall, diadem of our realm, chanted a song, a noble solace, a praise of Patrick of Armagh.

28. A chief^d champion triad that is not transitory: with Trophimus without abatement: the sons of Bochra, lasting victory! —from smooth Achad Rathin.

^a MS. dechecong   ^b D 'ran'   ^c i.e. with streams of disciples.   ^d B 'great'

RAWL. 505, fo. 219 b.	LAUD, 610.	LEBAR BRECC, p. 100.
29. Rigfeil brenainn birra frismbruchta ler lebenn bacain mind mar fualang* ceun find faithe nerend	29. Rigfeil brenaind birra frismbruchta leir lébenn bacáin mind mor nualann cend find fatha heirenn	29. Rigfeil brenaind biroir frismbruchtai ler lebend bacain mind mar nualand coand find fátha nerenn
30. Andreas asdanu fricroich ceim asuagu dobeir barr nodbagu nouimb*ir* forsluagu	30. Aindrias asdana fricroich ceim asuaga dobeir barr nóbágu nouimb*ir* forslungu	30. Andrias ainm isdanu fricroich ccim isuagu dobeir barr nobagu no[u]imb*ir* forslungu

29. The royal feast of Brenann of Birr, against whom burst the sea-level, fair diadem, great, praiseworthy, white head of Ireland's prophets.

30. Andrew, name that is boldest, against a cross—step that is most perfect—puts a top, I engage, on November's hosts.

GLOSS FROM THE LEBAR BRECC, pp. 99, 100.

1. (2) *grianaig* .i. taitnemaig *no* solusta (4) *samuin* [.i.] samfuin .i. bas intsamraid .i. namaeraide *sianaig* .i.[b] sinaig *no* gloraig

3. (1) *sluind* .i. aisnéid *tarromuir* .i. tarmuir moir dó *no* asinégipt dó .i. tarmuir ruaid aness

4. (1) *cen oipne* .i. confeirg *no* fridenam peccaid . *no* friudiultad dó (2) *cen eclai* .i. friacésad

5. (2) *imaslechta* .i. imaroslaitea *no* romarbtha

6. (1) *ce dolegsat* .i. cia rolegsat acuirp in terra per martir[i]um *no* ciarolegtha .i. ciaroloisethea acuirp per martir[i]um (3) *atreith* .i. roreith *riched* .i. rigiath iath inrig .i. caelum (4) *dunad* .i. sloigend

7. (2) *ceabugur* .i. ciarbo leir *no* ciarbo chalma *aslige* .i. amarbad

8. (1) .i. isuime búi annall .i. agal coroissed caelum

9. (1) *donait* .i. proprium *damau* .i. proprium (2) .i. nibtar ecundaig *no* nidéntais écnach *no* nibtar ecnaide ainble . acht ecnaide fetta *no* forustai (3) *forunlith* .i. forumlaithe *cofuilge* [leg. *cosuilge*] .i. cosuailchib (4) *saidbre* .i. uirtutibus

10. (2) .i. nirodlecht bás *no* arismó æcuai firen [*leg.* éc na firén] ut apostolus dicit ['uolo disolui et esse cum christo"—Rawl. 505] *no* ismo aéc 7 dul fornem dó inas abetha abus isintsægul (3) *ard* .i. uasal *isinmorlaith* .i. in caelum (4) *sub* .i. so abb vel propter firmitatem in fide christi sabb dicitur

11. (1) *can* .i. canta *medair* .i. erlabra (2) .i. comair siar 7 sair *no* dardámuir *no* cusinmuir romoir (3) *saer samail* .i. issær dosam asamail *frihor* propter uicinitatem[d] auri et uirtutum eius (4) *sliab oir* .i. d regis

12. (1) *suithe* .i. legind *no* airchetul comamsa (2) *tiachrai* .i. glicusa (3) *milte* .i. miltnecht

13. (1) *forid* .i. forsd laithe mis gréne isid (2) *ba imrordais* .i. ma roimraides (3) *aird* .i. uasal *aurgais* .i. airguide *no* ergnai denam inchorgais *no* guide uasal (4) *chorgais* .i. moysi

14. (3) *frigein crist* .i. nodlaic . *conuage* .i. cocomlaine itir chorp 7 ainim 7 flathus (4) *lexu leri* i. nanotlac

* .i. romor he hic fulang treblaite ocus fochaido *no* hic fulang pauperum et egenorum pro deo ('very great was he in enduring tribulations and troubles or in supporting the poor and needy for God's sake')

[b] MS. l.   [c] ad Philippenses i. 23   [d] MS. cliritatem

15. (2) .i. bisuailchib .i. brechtrad^a (3) *corgus* .i. coir gus .i. gus coir *mafutbotha* .i. manotfubtand *no* mathomaithid (4) .i. madoroeht chugut
16. (2) *tredan* .i. tredenus .i. trés dies (3) *troethais* .i. rotræth in semet ipso vel malis (4) *credal* .i. craibdech
17. (1) *celebair* .i. frisin fer nolegfad inlebar aderarso
19. (1) *raid* .i. indis *baislic* .i. eclesiæ (3) *luid* .i. ad caelum *dillacht* .i. dilechta *no* dilocht .i. cenlocht (4) *gerat* .i. anrud
20. (4) *hinnelaib* .i. fo nelaib
21. (1) *nueb desheng* .i. di noem forsinænlo *conrualai* .i. dochuaid *no* cain rolló
22. (1) .i. mor amartra *no* adamra (2) *loichet* .i. lasar *loindrech* .i. taitnemach Muire loichet .i. quasi dixisset^b mirabilis est hic exercitus lucidus.
23. (3) .i. adarthar dia inachathair
24. (2) *dairtuirind* .i. diaeruithnecht
25. (2) *erchain* .i. orthaitnemach *corand* .i. coroim [leg. coroinn ?]
26. (1) *guid* .i. ataig *decheng* .i. daching (4) *sruamach* .i. sluagach pro multitudine discipulorum.^c
27. (1) *sruaim ecnai* .i. sruth *no* solam he iuecna
28. (1) *prim* .i. mor *drecheng* .i. tricind *nad duthain* .i. in caelo vel sed manet semper in bono
29. (1) *rigfeil* .i. feil rigda *biroir* .i. bir usce 7 ræ .i. mag (3) *cain* .i. alaind he *nualand* .i. nuall caich icamolad (4) *find* .i. taitnemach
30. *isdanu* .i. islánu friacroich andrías uel uirilis interpretatur ander [ἀνήρ] enim graece [uir] latine (2) *isuagu* .i. iscómlainiu (3) *barr* .i. crich *nobagu* .i. gellaim (4) .i. for sluaiged nouimbir

Notes from the Lebar Brecc, pp. 99, 100.

1. *Lonan* .i. icluain erc . [*in r. marg. at* 13° *Nov.*] Lonan mac talmuig . othreoit imbregaib *no* louan mac telchain ochluain fotai ilaigis

Colman mac dimma óthig *mic* dimmai inúib cellaig chualand 7 ódaire mic dimmai hifail clumai hélnech . *no* colman mac findchada .i. ochluain bruices ifail flesci amumain 7 ise bái artus hindún flesci riasin .

cronan .i. mac hui chuind othuaim greni [hituaig muman, Laud 610]
elair .i. episcopus et papa romæ

2. *in r. marg. opposite Nov.* 15° *and* 16°] Sruith aspal 7 rl. Dobert bendacht ifertai fer féic hi tæb sídai truinm aniar . 7 dobert patraic bennachtain do carce sláine . in prima pascha.^d Escop carce sláine . mac doside escop eogain arda sratha
patraic .i. patricius

1. '*Lonan*' i.e. in Cluain Erc . . ? Lonan son of Talmach, of Tréfot ['Threesod'] in Bregia . Or Louan son of Telchán, of Cluain Fota in Leix.

Colman son of Dimma, son of Tech-mic-Dimmai ('Mac-Dimmai's house') in Ui-Cellaig Chualann and of Daire-mic-Dimmai ('Mac-Dimmai's oakwood') near Cluain Édnech. Or Colman son of Findchad i.e. of Cluain Bruices near Flesc in Munster, and he it is that was at first in Dún Flesce before that.

'*Cronan*' i.e. son of Conn's descendant, of Tuaim Gréne in North Munster.

'Senior of the apostles' etc. He gave his blessing in Ferta-fer-Féice beside Síd Truimm in the west. And Patrick gave (his) blessing to Erc of Slane in the first Easter. Bishop Erc of Slane, a son of his was Bishop Eogain of Ard Sratha.

^a MS. brecthtrad   ^b MS. dix sit
^c MS. pro multa ; but in Laud 610 we have *arimat adeiscipul*   ^d MS. inprimai ipascha

3. *elair* .i. episcopus pictauis
   muirdebar .i. odisiurt muirdebair anib conaill gabrai
   corc[o]nutan .i. indaire ednech ineoganacht caisil .i. daire uaßand alanainm

   coemain .i. coeman enaig thruimm ilaichis laigen frater coemgin glinde da lacha he 7 coemlog nomen patris [eorum 7 coemgel nomen matris eorum. — Laud 610] 7 nateaim tire daglas frater eorum amal ata romaind

4. *coniux* [.i.] ante* apostulatum *petrui* [.i.] pro christo
5. *domini* .i. domangein uel episcopus alexandria[e]
   colman glinde delmaic .i. indísiurt amuig raígne inosrnigib .i. deleug muice frith and . *no* deil muice .i. muc dabliadan . *no* dealba muc allta at*rácht* reime 7 icill matia doucrder amuig hitha ata

8. *barrfind* .i. inachad challten inúib dróna fria berbai aniar .i. inúib breti [reithe.—Laud 610] frialethglind an[d]es 7 brathair findbarr iudsi temli
9. *sinche* .i. ochluain lethtengad .i. nomen ecclesiæ[b]
10. *Aed mac brice* .i. ochill áir himide 7 osleib liac 7 docenél fiachach mic neill dó

11. [*in l. marg.*] no
    Carpre chulai raithin
    raith rigdai darremuir
    sanct martain 7 rl.
    .i. ituaiscert dál naruide ata cul raithin 7 for*e*nla ata 7 martain .
    sanct martain .i. næmmartain escop torindsi ifrangeaib 7 do gallia lugdunensis* do .i. fraingc

    in *l. marg.*]
    Mártain milid mod nach dís
    dogallia lugdanensis
    gormac gradsuairee dosíl rig
    mac manuailt is abrasín

12. *dom chumain* .i. cumin fota mac fiachnai. comorba brenaind cluanai fertai 7 deoganacht

3. '*Hilarius*'
'*Muirdebair*' i.e. of Dísert-Muirdebair in Ui-Conaill Gabrai.
'*Corcunutan*' .i. in Daire Ednech in Eoganacht of Cashel i.e. Daire na-Flann is its full name.
'*of Coeman*' i.e. Coeman of Enach Truimm in Leix of Leinster, brother of Coemgen of Glendalough was he and Coemlog was their father's name and Coemgel their mother's and Nateaim of Tír-dá-glas their brother as is aforesaid.

'*Colman of Glenn Delmaic*' i.e. in Disert in Mag Ráigne in Ossory, i.e. a sucking-pig was found there . Or *deil muice* i.e. a two-year-old pig . Or forms of wild pigs arose before him, and in Cell Matia Douerder (?) in Mag Itha he is.

8. '*Barrfind*' i.e. in Achad Callten in Ui-Dróna to the west of the Barrow i.e. Ui-Breti [leg. Reithe?] to the south of Lethglinn, and he was a brother of Findbarr of Inis Temli.
9. '*Of Sinech*' i.e. of Cluain Lethtengad.

10. '*Aed son of Brecc*' i.e. of Cell Áir in Meath and of Sliab Liac; and he was of the race of Fiacha son of Niall.

11. Or [this is the right reading]
    Carpre of Cul Raithin,
    royal grace over a great sea.
    Saint Martin, &c.

    i.e. in the north of Dalaridia is Cúl Raithin and [Carpre] is on the same day as Martin.
    '*Saint Martin*' i.e. holy Martin bishop of Tours in France, and of Gallia Lugdunensis was he i.e. France.

    Martin a soldier, a man not puny,
    Of Gallia Lugdunensis,
    A loving-gentle adopted-son of royal seed
    Son of Manualt and Abrasín.

12. '*to my Cumain* i.e. Cumen the Tall son of Fiachna, successor of Brenann of Cluain

---

[a] MS. petri   [b] MS. eclecie   [c] MS. luganensi

lacha leín dó . ℞d diu . ainm diles chumin 7 druim daliter ainm abaile 7 hi cumfu frith hicill íte inúib conaill gabra . Cnimín fotai .i. mor e et cum eo ernín mac findchain abb lethglinde 7 metau cael inaird

[P. 98, at foot]

Mugain ingen fiachach find máthair cumine cheolbind sisi mugain amáthair sesium disi derbrathair.

Damac déc rogensit omumain [leg. mugain] .i. uí. escuip ocus .ui. rig . cumin 7 comgall., 14. Clemint . non papa sed alius.

colman .i. ó inis mocholmoc in háib fenechlais iniarthar [in airter—Laud 610] laigen 7 lobar he

16. augustin .i. non librorum[a] sed alius auctor[b]

17. teclai .i. teclai .i. uirgo et martir

buaidbeo .i. buaidbeo mac lugdach mic liathcon mic araide a quo dail naraide .i. ochill moir airthair fine .i. hicind muige heltai [atá] no forloch cuan

duilech .i. o clochar duilig fria feldruim andess [a fíne gall.—Laud 610] .i. itæb suird colaim cille

18. ronain .i. ronan mac bernig mic crimthainn mic e[i]rcloga mic ernaide mic muireni mic sechnasaig mic colmain chúile mic muiredaig mic lægaire mic neill nóigiallaig . oedruim enesclainde iconaillib muirtheimnib atasom

20. Guid escon lafrœchan .i. ataig escop fraechan himb[ó]chluain ilaigis ocluain éidnech sair no escon [leg. episcop froechan] bis and . ut alii putant

in lower marg.] Guid escon lafroechan 7rl. Escon .i. xxx . bliadan boi cenbaistiud . et ideo dicitur escon sed non uerum . acht guid episcop lafrœchan .i. frœchan ainm 7 escop he 7 imbóchluain ata .i. iláigis 7 indruim dáganda indáilaraide . 7 docoll 7 mochonna 7 miochumma craibdech . rel sic. Escon proprium nomen sancti . tanic lais atuaid . vel sic . guid escon lafroechan .i. guid froechan escop . vel sic . guid escon la froechan . escon dicitur ideo

Ferta and of the Eoganacht of Loch Léin was he. Now 'Aed' was Cumin's proper name and Druim Daliter the name of his stead, and in a basket (cumin) was he found in Cell I'te in Uí Conaill Gabra. Cuimín the Tall i.e. big (was) he, et cum eo are commemorated Ernín son of Findchan, abbot of Leighlin, and Metau the slender in Ard.

Mugain, daughter of Fiacha the Fair, Mother of Cumine the sweetsonged. She, Mugain, was his mother: He unto her was brother.

Twelve sons were born of Mugain i.e. six bishops and six kings. Cumin and Comgall 14. 'Clement.'

'Colman' i.e. of Inis Mocholmóc in Ui-Fenechlais in the west [leg. east] of Leinster, and he was a leper.

16. Augustine.

17. 'Buaid-beo' .i. Buaid-beo son of Lugaid, son of Liathcú, son of Araide, a quo Dail n-Araide (Dalaradia) i.e. of Cell Mór Airthir Fine i.e. at the end of Mag Elta he is, or on Loch Cuan.

'Duilech' i.e. of Clochar Duilig, to the south of Feltrim in Fingal i.e. beside Swords of Colomb Cille.

18. 'of Ronan' i.e. Ronan son of Berach, son of Crimthann, son of Erc-loga son of Ernaide, son of Muirene, son of Sechnasach, son of Colman Cúile, son of Muiredach, son of Loegaire, son of Niall the Nine-Hostaged : at Druim Enesclainne in Conailli Muirthemni is he.

20. 'Beseech Escon with Froechán' i.e. pray bishop Fraechán in Bó-chluain in Leix, to the east of Cluain Eidnech, or (it is) 'episcop Froechan' that is here, ut alii putant.

'Beseech Escon with Froechan'. etc. escon ('impure') i.e. thirty years was he without baptism, et ideo dicitur escon 'impure,' sed non verum (est). But Guid episcop Froechan [is the true reading] i.e. Froechan was his name, and a bishop was he, and in Bóchluain he is i.e. in Leix, and in Druim Dáganda in Dalaradia. And Do-Coll and Mo-Chonna and Mo-Chumma the Pious . . . . . Vel sic. Escon is the proper name of a saint that came with

---

[a] MS. liberorum   [b] MS. aug. He was an African martyr, Beda, iv., 154

quia regem laginensium occidit .i. dintomad (leg. tomaidm?) tuc fair dinluirec 7ssé ic bóchuain 7 inrig indabaig fothraicc ocnás . hic est escan .i. escra tond usqri⁴ .i. esca ideo dicitur quia aquam bap*tismatis* infu*lit* .

21. *clemint* .i. episcopus et papa roma[e]
    mac comain aharaind .i. colman aninm .i. aharnind airth*i*r . no áru 7 eri indathclaig toeb fritoeb

p. 100, *top marg.*]
Angelus dixit in iusola [quac] dicitur áru

    Colman mac comáin
    mairg duine nachacia
    escop samlaid dinmunna
    sech niraba nibia.,

mac congraid .i. aedan mac conchraid aainm . *no* icluain cidnech ata ædan oilit*her* mac conchraid . *no* ædan mac iacoip ut alii dicunt.

22. *cicilia* .i. uirgo
23. *clementis* .i. dalta petair 7 papa roma[e]

itir thondaib trethain .i. fonfairge ata cathair oiregdai doclémint and fommuir isininad inrobaided he 7 traigid inmuir eechablia*d*na hifeil clemint . combit cach ocahoilithir itir thondgar in mormara [co fargaib arnili banscal amae fecht ann andernart 7 bahog feind blia*d*na araciud—Laud 610]

24. *cianan doimliac* . imbregaib
    in lower marg.] 1Samlaid din. ata corp cianain [een lobad] conlegal isinmembrai frisin damliac anair 7 issed foderasin .i. Cairncch tuilen tanic fech*t* do damliac cianain . cortriallad fothrucad dó. ni frith din. domain⁴ isindabaig. Pudar sin ar cianan. Créd ar

him from the north. *Vel sic Guid episcop Froechán* i.e. Beseech Bishop Froechan. *Vel sic* 'Beseech Escon with Froechan.' He is called 'Escon' because he slew a king of Leinster i.e. by the dipping (leg. threatening?) with his staff which he made at him while he (the saint) was at Bó-chluain and the king in a bathing-tub at Naas.

21. '*Of Clement*'
'*son of Commán of Aran*' i.e. Colmán was his name, to wit, of the eastern isle of Aran. Or Aru and Eriu are the two hills side by side.

Colmán son of Comnán,
Woe the man that weeps him not!
A bishop like him, from Munster
Never was (and) never will be.

'*son of Congrad*' i.e. Aedán son of Couchrad was his name. Or in Clonenagh is Aedán the pilgrim, son of Conchrad. Or Aedán son of Jacob as others say.

22. '*Cecilia.*'
23. '*of Clement*' i.e. a fosterling of Peter and pope of Rome.

'*among a sea's waves*' i.e. under the sea is a splendid city for Clement: under the sea in the place wherein he was drowned", and the sea ebbs every year on Clement's feast, so that every one is performing his pilgrimage amid the wave-roar of the great sea. And a certain woman once left her child there in forgetfulness, and it was whole at the end of the year (and came) to meet her.

24. '*Cianan of Duleek*' i.e. in Bregia.
In this wise is Cianan's body, without corrupting, without dissolving, in the tomb to the east of the *damliac*, and the cause thereof is this: Cairnech of Tuilen came once to Duleek of Cianan and a bath was proposed for him. No bottom then was found in the tub. "That

---

ᵃ This is corrupt : but the meaning obviously is that *escomn* is a vessel used for distributing water (Corm. Gl. Trans., p. 65), and that the saint was so called because he baptized many.

ᵇ ' Romae natale S. Clementis episcopí, qui jubente Trajano missus est in exilium trans Pontum maris . Ubi multis ad fidem vocatis per miracula ad doctrinam ejus, praecipitatus est in mare, alligata ad collum ejus anchorá. Sed recessit mare orantibus discipulis ejus per tria millia ; et invenerunt corpus ejus in arca saxea in templo marmoreo, et anchoram juxta. Beda, ed. Giles, iv., 156–7. 'Every year at the anniversary of his martyrdom the sea retired during seven days, leaving a dry path for those who went to honour the relics of the Saint.' Jameson *Sacred and Legendary Art*, 627.   ᶜ Cf. *Domain* .i. *más*, O'Dav. 76, and so in Laud 610.

cairnech . Cennas isindabaig ar cianan . Tabar intusce isindabaig ol cairnech 7 dentar indíunach . Atnagar innti 7 nidochaid banda esti . Eirg isindabaig achairnig ol cianan . Tiagam arsen olcairnech . Tiagait iarum . ISalaind incorp aclerig olcairnech . Isamlaid ata din . ol cianan . Ailimsea dia din . ol cairnech corub amlaid ata hes tria bithu cenlegad cotora crist domordail bratha ocus issed on chomailter

Notesetha afolt 7 aingne cecha dardain chaplaite cecha bliadne cohaimsir adomnain . Teit adomnan isinmbemrai diadecsain 7 dolamachtad inchuirp . Bentair arose fair focétoir . Troiseid iarum uime cotardad arose do indsin . Nilám din . noch dol ind osin ille .

Patraic tra roscrib cáin chianain . 7 cianan roscrib cain patraic Archechlod daronsat sin . 7 patraic rochuindig sin arrob ferr scribend cianain

ISamlaid din doronad æntu chianain 7 coluim cille .i. lam coluim cille triasliss innmbemrai riadeiscert* anund coleth innmbemrai . 7 lam chianain annach coleth intlessa 7 dogniat anócentaid amailsin

Cianan mac sesnan mic drónai mic thigernaig mic findchaim mic féic mic imchada uallaig mic condlai mic taidg mic cein mic oilillai audaim.,

mac lenine .i. colman mac lenín ocluain uamai in háib liathain amumain

colman duibchuilind .i. ismarendaib .i. hindún reichet . no colman duib cuilind .i. cuilend sliab til ic belach conglais ilaiguib et aliisb locis. Luid comgall bendchuir do thig athar cholmain duib cuilind . Ben amrit ocai . Cuinchid din . inclorech dub scribind don mnái amrit . Atnagar . ocus comperthar colman de . unde colman mac duib chuilind dictus est.

is a shame," says Cianan. "What?" says Cairnech. "Not to have a bottom in the tub," says Cianan. "Put the water into the tub," says Cairnech "and let the washing be done." (Water) is poured into it and not a drop went thereout. "Get thee into the tub, O Cairnech," says Cianan. "Let us go together," say-Cairnech. Then they both go. "Comely is the body, O cleric!" says Cairnech. "So it is then," says Cianan. "I beseech God then," says Cairnech, "that it may be thus for ever without dissolving till Christ shall come to the great assembly of Doom!" And this is fulfilled.

His hair and his nails used to be cut every Maunday Thursday in every year down to Adamnán's time. Adamnán went into the tomb to behold him and to touch the body. His eye is struck out forthwith. So he fasted to him (Cairnech), and his eye was given (back) to him then. Thenceforward no one durst enter (the tomb).

Now Patrick wrote Cianan's law and Cianan wrote Patrick's law. For an interchange they did that, and Patrick asked it since Cianan's writing was the better.

Thus then was made the union of Cianán and Colomb-cille, namely, Colomb-cille's hand through the side of the tomb on the south even to half (the middle?) of the tomb and Cianan's hand out even to half the side. And they make their union in that wise.

Cianán son of Sesnán, son of Dróna, son of Tigernach, son of Findchaem, son of Fiace, son of Imchath the Proud, son of Condla, son of Tadg, son of Cian, son of Ailill Aulum.

'son of Lenine' .i. Colmán son of Lenín of Cluain Uamai in Ui-Liathain in Munster.

'Colman Duib-Chuilind' i.e. in the Renda(?) i.e. in Dún Reichet. Or Colman of Cuilenn's ink i.e. Cuilenn is a mountain which is at Belach Conglais in Leinster et aliis locis. Comgall of Bangor went to the house of Colmán Duib-Chuilinn's father. A barren wife had he (the father). So the cleric (Comgall) asks writing-ink of the barren wife. It is given, and thereof is Colman conceived. Whence he was called Colman son of Cuilenn's ink.

---

[a] Facsimile: inadeiscert. Laud 610 has *triaslis deiscertach inmembra inánn*. [b] MS. ablis

25. *coin cassion* .i. episcopus constantinopolis[a]
hicroich .i. hicroich nomen amnis[b] amugdornaib .
findchu .i. mochua find iseraib muige féne .i. cluain crucha coirpre ainm naeille asandechaid.

in lower marg.] Findchú .i. obrí goband tra . bahe din . bes findchon cech marb doberthea donchill laige lais incétaidche conid he log rochuindig airesin . cech duine noguidfed he fribás conarobuadaiged demun de 7 conaroissed ifern .

Ocus isí carcar inroshuid .i. leacc cloiche uasachind 7 corrau iarnind cechtar adfochsail conabenad achend suas frisincloich . nach achossa frialar . Cotarlai comgall bendchuir chuice condebairt friss . Tair annas olse .
Inde dixit finden

  ISbi oenitge notguidim
  armoscarad frissin sás
  narub ifernach cechduine
  acht comumguide fribás .

dixit comgall . rotfia sin odia.
Find mac cumaill dodechaid feis áidche dothig máil mic iachtadon mic mornai cocuil muiltt frisinabar brí goband indiu corchausam inrithaireesa octairngire findchon .

  Ticfa sund oilithreach
  bus tren taburtach
  bus cend cosmuna
  bus breo arbidbadaib
  ih.u thirchanus
  amen admolas
  mairg atreuturcu
  bus rig remthechtach
  cia acht crist comfoclach
  bus eutrumai frisinaig narduasal .
  Findchua fermnail fortren forranach
  sochaide laslog sœrchrothach
  dobráth buiden glas
  fosnim treu tabartach
  mairg athrentuatha

25. 'John Cassion.'

'*into Croch*' i.e. Hicroich [leg. Croch] the name of a river in Mugduirn.
'*Findchú*' i.e. Mochua the Fair in Fir Maige Féne i.e. Cluain Crucha Coirpre was the name of the church out of [leg. into ?] which he went.
Findchú i.e. of Brí Gobann. Now this was Findchú's custom ; every corpse that was brought to the church to lie with it the first night. And this was the guerdon that he asked therefor : that the Devil should not vanquish any person who should beseech him at death, and that such person should not go to hell.

And this is the prison wherein he sat, namely (there was) a flagstone over his head and a sickle of iron in each of his two armpits[c], so that his head did not strike against the stone above nor his feet the floor. And Comgall of Bangor chanced to visit him, and he said to him 'come down' quoth he. Then said Findchú:

  This is the one prayer that I pray
  On my parting from the trap[d]—
  That no one be hell-doomed
  Provided that he beseech me at death.

Comgall said "That shalt thou have from God."
Find son of Cumall went for a night's feast to the house of Mael son of Iachtad, son of Morna, to Cuil Muilt, which is to-day called Brí Gobann, and he sang this *rhetoric* while prophesying of Findchú:—

  Here shall come a pilgrim
  Who will be valiant, bountiful,
  Who will be a head of conflict,
  Who will be a flame against guilty men,
  Who declares Jesus,
  Who lauds *Amen*.
  Alas, O valiant princes,
  That he will be a leading king !
  Who save Christ of like name
  Is equal to the high-noble hero[e] ?
  Findchua, manly, mighty, destructive,
  A multitude with a nobly formed host,
  Vigorous for judgment of troops,
  Under grief strenuous, bountiful.
  Alas, O valiant tribes,

---

[a] MS. *constantino apolis*   [b] facs. non animis
[c] i.e. he was suspended by two iron hooks.
[d] i.e. the body, regarded as a source of danger to the soul.   [e] a mere guess

dithfaid ruirecha
aithne fiusrothach
recrist comrunuach
mochin airichles
sunn iarscis chothaiges
gar cian coticfa .   Ticfa

Findchu din . obri gobann mac setnai mic
abrai mic branain mic oenguss mic erca deirg
mic briain mic echach muidmedoin

26. banban .i. escop lethglinde 7 dochorco
duibne dó
    escop siric .i. ómuig bolg hiferaib cúl breg

27. sechnall .i. sechnall filius restituti secun-
dini et de longobardis aduentus[b] erat et secundinus nomen eius erat ibi .i. odómnach sechnaill 7 mac sethar patraic he .i. mac dolianain
    ceol .i. audite omnes admantes etc .i. nadmait
.i. audite omnes admantes

28. trofin .i. a nomine trofinus
    mec bochrai .i. bochra nomen matris eorum
.i. tria capita .i. tres fratres oachad raithin
laideend 7 cainrec [cuindech.—Laud 510] 7
æd cobran nomina ipsorum[c]

o achud reid rathin .i. in huib maic caille
indesib mumau

29. [Birra .i. acoerich eile 7 fera cell ata
birra.—Laud 610]
    frismbruchtai ler lebend .i. inbrosnachai .i.
ler inmara atrácht fris intan ratriall furri cor-
asgab brenaind mac findlogai dialaim he

[.i. foernib doler .i. forbru uisci ata acholl—
Laud 610]
30. andrias . .i. apostolus frater Petri[d] hic
sepultus est in Achaia in Patris[e]

He will destroy chieftains,[a]

Here after weariness which he sustains
Short the time till he shall come.

Findchú, then, of Brí Gobann, son of Setnae,
son of Abra, son of Branán, son of Oengus, son
of Erc the Red, son of Brian, son of Echaid
Muidmedon.
26. 'Bunbán' i.e. bishop of Leighlin, and of
Corco-Duibne was he.
    'bishop Siric' i.e. of Mag Bolg in Fir Cúl
Breg.
27. 'Sechnall' i.e. Sechnall son of Restitutus
Secundinus, and from Lombardy had he come,
and Secundinus was his name there: i.e. of
Domnach Sechnaill, and a son of Patrick's
sister was he, i.e. a son of Liamain's.

28. 'Trophimus'
    'sons of Bochra,' i.e. Bochra was their
mother's name. [drecheng] i.e. three heads
(chiefs?) i.e. three brothers of Achad Raithin:
Laideenn, and Cainrec (? Cuindech) and Aed
Cobran their names.
    'from smooth Achad Raithin' i.e. in Ui
Maic Caille in the Desies of Munster.
29. Birra i.e. in the border of Eile and Fir
Cell is Birra.
    'against whom burst the sea-level' i.e. the
Brosnachae .i. the surge of the sea rose against
him when he went thereon, and Brenainn son
of Findloga caught him by the hand.
    near to sea i.e. on the brink of the water
is his church.

[a] I can make nothing of the next three lines of this obscure poem
[b] MS. de longa bardiadentus   [c] Facs. nosorum   [d] MS. petrií   [e] MS. iachia ipartimus

Rawl. 505, fo. 219, b.	Laud, 610.	Lebar Brecc, p. 101.
1. Sluinn deciinbir kl. candida cain ciwach pais pancrati calad feil noib nesain ulad	1. Sluind decimbir kl. candida cain curach pais panchrati calad feil nócm nessain ulad	1. Sluind decinbir kl. candida cain curach pais panchrati calad feil nocb nessain ulad
2. Ollchesad pomeni iarserbgaibthib gorta gessi lalin martra maelodran mor mochta	2. Ollcessad parmeni iarserbgaibthib gorta geisi lalin martra maolodran mor mochta	2. Ollcesad pameni iarserbgaibthib gortai gessi lalin martra maelodrau mor mochtai
3. Martra ard crach[li] conachleir indirdruin macc oigi conuagboil luaim liss moir mirbuil	3. Martra ard cracli conacleir indíirdruin mac oighi conuagbail luam lis moir mirbail	3. Martra ard craclii conachleir indfirdruin macc oige conligbail luam lis moir mirbuil
4. Merobus cludicus conaidbli asreithe bahoen a[r]soer sruithi infial fer daleithe	4. Meropus claudicus conaidble asreithi bahóe[n]a[r]soer sruithe infial ferdaleithe	4. Morepus claudicus conaidble asrethi babæn arsær sruithe infial fer dalethi
5. Foraithmet iustini indepscoip conani amanti crispine umbani filadi	5. Foraithmet iustini indepscoip conáni amanti crispini umbani filadi	5. Foraithmet iustini inepscoip conani amantii crispanæ umbani filadi
6. Feil gobbain gair mile cocleir martra mare mur ainglech abb huagi macc hui laindrech laine	6. Feil gobbain gair mili cocleir martra maire mur ainglech abb oighe mac ui laindrech lane	6. Feil gobbain gair mile cocleir martra mare mur ainglech abb uage mac h. laindrech lane
7. Lapais policarpi conacleir soer sruamnach omainistir mainich feil bain buti bundaig	7. Lapais poilicarpi conachleir saersruamaig omainistir mainig feil búide maic bronaich	7. Lapais policarpi conacleir sær sruamaig omainistir mainig feil bain búide buadaig
8. Buaid hichtbrichtain humail donarlaid darromuir	8. Buaid ichtbrichtain humail donralad darromuir	8. Buaid ichtbrictain umail donarlaid tarromuir

1. Declare on December's kalend Candida a fair boat! The hard passion of Panchratus, Nessán of Ulster's holy feast.

2. Parmenius' great suffering after bitter dangers of famine: beseech him with (his) martyrs: Maelodráin great, magnified.

3. Heraclius' high martyrdom with his train the truly-strong: Mac-óige with perfect goodness, pilot of marvellous Lismore.

4. Merobius, Claudicus, with vastness of their heaps: one of our sages was the modest Fer-dá-leithe ('man of two parts').

5. The commemoration of Justinus the bishop with splendour, of Amantius, of Crispinus, of Humanus, of Filadus (?)

6. Gobbán's feast, a shout of thousands, with a train of great martyrdom, angelic wall, abbot of virginity, lucid descendant of Láne.[a]

7. At Polycarp's passion, with his train noble, streamy, the feast of white, victorious Buite[b] of treasurous Monaster(boice).

8. The victory of humble Egbert who came

---

[a] or perhaps 'the lucid (one) of the Maccu-Láne'   [b] B 'the feast of Buite son of Brónach.'

RAWL. 505, fo. 220, a.	LAUD, 610.	LEBAR BRECC, p. 101.
docrist cachain[a] figil hicurchan cenchodail	docri*st* cachain figil ścurchan cen chodail	docri*st* cachain figil hicurchán cenchodail
9. Cadlai indúngein[b] aillela nadchlithi iscaiu sluag allaithi digrein airthir liphi	9. ITcadlai daingin[c] ailella nadclithe bacninsluag allaithi digreim airthair liphi	9. ITcadlai diingen oililla nateletthi iscain slung allaithe digróin oirthir liffe
10. Ladacoicat ogda cethracha[d] colani lalith capitolini feil modímoc dani	10. Latri chocca[t] uaga ceirtricha coláni lith caipitolini feil modimoc dani	10. La .lll. uagai cert .xxx. torlani lith capitolini feil modimoc danai
11. Damassus lamśenoc mugnai tuathmaig leth-an feil meltoc cain cathair coslung tren dartrethain	11. Damassus lamsenoc mugnai tuathmaig leth-ain feil moelteoc cain cathair lasluag trón dartrethan	11. Damasus lasenoc mugnai tuathmuig leth-an feil moilteoc cain cathir coslog tren [tar] treathan
12. Tor oir huas cech lermaig gebaid coir frimanmain finnian finn frem inmain cluana hiraird adbail	12. Tor óir uas cachlermuir geibid coir frimanmain finden find frem inm..in chluana hiraird adbail	12. Tor oir uas cech lermuir gebaid coir frimanmain findia find frém inmain cluana iraird adbail
13. Arlaithi fidil ádalach tairset comeit mile boethan cluana credlach	13. Arlaithi dil dala tairset coméit mile baethan chluana credlach	13. Arlaithe dil dala tairset co cét mile boetan cluana credlach
colum trednach tire	colum trednach tíre	colam trednach tire
14. Dourogra dondriglaith rig rouce arsiur saph caid cloithi caor drursus conathriur	14. Dorogra donbithlaith rí rusfue arsiur sab cáid cloithit cóir trursus conathriur	14. Donrogra biriglaith rig ronuc arsiur sab cáid cloithe corad trursus conathriur
15. Togairm fausti fechtnaig	15. Togairm fausti fechtnaig	15. Togairm fausti fechtnaig

over the great sea: unto Christ he sang a vigil in a coracle without a hide (around it.)

9. Beautiful are the two daughters of Ailill who is not to be concealed: fair is the host of their day: two suns of the east of Liffey.

10. With three virginal fifties, a right thirty in fulness[e]· Capitolinus' festival: my bold Dimóc's feast.

11. Damasus with my Senoc of (Belach) Mugnai in a broad northern plain: the feast of my-Eilteoc, a fair city, with a valiant host over sea.

12. A tower of gold over every ocean-sea: he will give a hand to my soul.[f] Findia the fair, loveable root, of vast Clonard.

13. On the dear day of assembly may they come with a hundred[g] thousands, pious Boethan of Cluain [-dá-annabar], abstinent Colomb of Tír (dá-glais).

14. May he call us into the royal kingdom of the King[h] whom our Sister[i] brought forth: a champion firm, chaste, subdued, Drusus with his three (fellow-martyrs)!

15. The calling of happy Faustinus with

[a] MS. cachaing [b] MS. indungein [c] L cadla indi*ingin*. [d] L certricha.
[e] D. 'With two perfected fifties forty with fulness'
[f] *Sic glossographi*: rather perhaps 'he will take sin from my soul.' [g] B. and D. with many.
[h] Christ [i] the Virgin Mary

Rawl. 505, fo. 220, a.	Laud, 610.	Lebar Brecc, pp. 101, 102.
cosluagud atempuir lafeil ñaiun fial impir comarba buain bennchuir	cosluagad atempail lafeil ḋaind féil impir comarba buan bennchair	cocleir cain athempuil lafeil floind féil impir comorbai [buan] bendchuir
16. Buaid finn ualentini cocleir cain atroeroiss feil mophioc* digraiss oard chainnlech camroiss	16. Buaid find ualentini cocleir cain atroiruis feil mobeoóc* digrais oard cainlech cáinrois*	16. Buaid find ualentini cocleir cain atroris feil mobeoc digrais oard choindlech chamroiss
17. Ronsnada sluag uictoir iarmbuaid gnima gaile corisamu ánsuba issu mór mœce maire	17. Ronsnade sluag uictoir iarmbuaid gnima gaili corisam ánsuba isu mor mœce maire	17. Ronsnade sluag uictoir iarmbuaid gnimu gaile corisam ansuba ih.u mar mœce muire
18. Mórgrian innaclannsa^d maguiu^e maith ammiunsa diucaill dian anammsa ropat failte frimsa	18. Morgrian inaclannsa maignend maith inmindsn dichuill dian anamsa corbat ficilti frimsa	18. Flandan flaith nacendsa maignend maith inmindsa dicuill moelruain raite ropatfailte frimsa
19. Frimanmain ropfailid conimmud aslogaid cain glanmainn de dulig samdanu cluana bronaig	19. Frimanmain ropfavilid conaidbli aslogaid cain glanbann dé duilig samthann cluana bronaig	19. Frimanmain ropfailid conaidble aslogaid cain glanmand de duilig samthand cluanabronaig
20. Dabrigach biarleri sluag uar immerali reta' huan forceti hicoemthecht ignáti	20. Babrigach allóchet sluag mor immarádi lotar* uain forchete ieáemhtecht icnati	20. Babrigach illeri sluag mor imeradi lotar uainn forceti icoimtecht ignati

the fair train of his temple, at the feast of Fland, modest ruler, abiding heir of Bangor.

16. Valentine's fair victory, with a bright train thou shouldst join(?): the feast of my excellent Beóc from lustrous Ard Cáinroiss.

17. May Victor's host protect us after victory of a deed of valour, that we may reach the splendid bliss, Jesus, Mary's great Son!

18. The great sun of these clans,^h Maignenn—good is this diadem!—Dichuill'—swift this band!—may they be blithe to me!

19. Blithe unto my soul, with the vastness of her host, be the fair, pure manna of elemental God, Samthann of Cluain Brónaig!

20. Mighty after piety^k was the great host whom thou commemoratest: they went from us to (heaven's) assembly in Ignatius' company.

^a l. mobeodoc   ^b l. mopioc   ^c l. claenrois
^d l. flannan flaith nacensa   ^e l. maguenn   ^f leg. rertha, as in O'Dav. 66.
^g MS. lothar   ^h A. 'Flandán prince of these chiefs.'
ⁱ A. 'Dicuill, Moelruain of Ráth'   ^k A. 'in piety;' B. 'their brightness.'

RAWL. 505, fo. 220.	LAUD, 610.	LEBAR BRECC, p. 102.
21. ITge indnoib thomais atneochain[a] reabannaib abas bascel niúgir inindie hiarrannaib	21. Itge innáim tomais atteocham rebannaib abas bascel ingair inindia irrandaib	21. ITge innoeb tomais atneocham riambandaib abas bascel ingir hinindia iarrandaib
22. Ronnain itge tuæ itharnaise uadlabrai lahemene ngelda debrú berba balbai	22. Ronnain itge tuæ itarnaise notlabra lahemene ngelda debrú berba balbai	22. Romain itge thuæ itharnaise natlabrai bui lahémin ngeldæ debrú berua balbai
23. Pais ochtcet cain martra	23. Paiss ocht cét cáinmartra	23. Bas ocht cet cain martrai
cosescait soer slechta lamthemnioc denrigraid cluana firmaith ferta	cosescait sóer slechta lamtemneoc don rigraid cluana firmaith ferta	lascacait sœr slechtai lamtheinneoc don rigraid cluana firmaith fertai
24. Fresdal luciani lamchua cain coclait macc lonain doudeicemaice indadaig renotlaice	24. Frestal luciani la mochua cain cocraid macc lonain donecmaice indadaig re notlaic	24. Frestal luciani lamchua cain cocrait macc lonain dondecmaic inadaig renodlaig
25. INnotlaice múr mirbuil crist omaire bagaig genair ladith ndorea ri sorcha sil adaim	25. Innotlaic mormirbuil crist ó mairi bángil[b] genair ladith ndorcha rí sorcha síl ádaim	25. INnodlaic moir mirbuil crist omuire bángil genair ladith ndorchæ rig sorchæ síl adaim
26. Atneocham[a] diarudigde mochommóc conani caingrian guires mile ainm sorcha stefani	26. Ateocham iarnitge mochomóc conáine cáin grian goires mili ainm sorcha stefaine	26. Ateocham diarndigdi mochomoc conani cain grian goires mile ainm sorchæ zefani
27. Slanchotlu iohannis inetis án bortgal abrathair asarddam laiacob[d] nordan	27. Slanchotlad iohannis inetis án bordgal abrathair isardam la iacop nordan	27. Slánchodlad iohannis inetis[e] án bordgal abrathair isardam lahiacop nordan

21. The prayer of the holy Thomas we beseech it before deeds (?): his death was a sad story, in India, according to (historic) verses.

22. May (Ultan) the Silent's prayer protect us[f]! Itharnaise who spoke not, who was with pure Emin from the brink of the dumb Barrow.

23. The passion[f] of eight hundred fair martyrs with sixty noble slain ones: with my-Temneóc of the kings, of excellent Clonfert.

24. A waiting on Lucianus with my-Cua a fair couple. Lonán's son chances (to come) to us on the night before Christmas.

25. At great, marvellous Christmas Christ of white-fair Mary was born with ruin of Darkness,—(Christ) the luminous King of Adam's seed!

26. Let us pray to bless us[e] my-Commóc with splendour: a fair sun that warms thousands: Stephen's luminous name.

27. The sound sleep of John in Ephesus —splendid bordgal—his brother who is highest with James of the sovranties.

[a] MS. atneochain [b] l. glain [c] Facs. inetif [d] MS. lacacob [e] 'me' A.
[f] 'death' A. [g] 'after beseeching' B.

RAWL. 505.	LAUD. 610.	LEBAR BRECC, p. 102.
28. Airdirc annuall suthain sech[e]ach coemda methil cantais duais dianathair inmacain^a obethil^b 29. Bidemid acobair inceehuair donneerai uictor cosluag sochla laheierau nocnai 30. Ecen charcra crochais cliar mar mansueti labelbi conuaigi arricefamm^c afeli 31. Lochan ocus enna siluester soer sallann diafeil ni leim nimfann asenam seith for kl.	28. Erdraic an nuall suthain sech each caemda methil canta duais dianathair inmaccain ambeithil 29. Uas demit acobair ineaehuair donncena uictor cosluag sochla la airer inneena 30. Eicen charera crochais cleir mor mansueti lahailbe conoighe ariefam afeile 31. Lochan 7 enda siluester soer talland dia feil nileim inmall asenam seeith for kl.	28. Aurdeire annall suthain sech each coemda methil cantai tuas diarnathair inmacain obethil 29. Bid émid acobair inceehuair dondeerai uictor coslog sochlai labaireráu indeenai 30. Eeen charera crochais sluag mor mansueti labailbe conuage arriefie afeli 31. Lochan 7 endai siluestar soer talland diafeil nileim nimand asenam eeim for ka<i>ll</i>and

28. Conspicuous is the eternal acclamation which the little children from Bethlehem, beyond every (other) loveable band, sing unto their^d Father.
29. Swift is their aid at every hour that .... to us, Victor with a famous host, and Airerán of the wisdom.
30. A dungeon's compulsion tortured the great host of Mansuetus: with "virginal Ailbe we shall^e attain their feasts.
31. Lochán and Endae, Silvester a noble talent: from their feast—not a feeble leap—(is) a fair passage to the calend (of January).

GLOSS FROM LEBAR BRECC, p. 101.

1. (2) *cain* .i. iedin chaich *curach* .i. curach oeimarchor naich tarmuir intsægail . *no* curach achuirp fon oeimarchor nanma   (3) *calad* .i. cruaid *no* catholiem.
2. (3) *gessi* .i. guid [.i. guais .i. guide—*Laud*, 610] (4) mochtai .i. tarmochta.
3. (2) *infirdruin* .i. hitoil de *no* infirglie iarfir.
6. (1) *yair mile* .i. oentach *no* mile manach batar [occai] (2) *martra mare* .i. martire iumda aice beos (4) *laindrech* .i. lainderda

GLOSSES FROM RAWL. 505, fo. 220, and LAUD, 610,
With a few from the Franciscan copy.

7. (4) *buti* .i. beo *no* tene (Ra.)
8. (2) *donralad* .i. donaraill .i. doroacht tar romuir .i. tarinmuir moir (La.)7 in ullt*u* tainic dana (Fr.) (3) *cachain* .i. rochain (La.) (4) *c*n *chodail* .i. censeeed inmo (La.)
9. (1) *cadlai* .i. cathalaedai (Ra.) .i. cotailei (La.)
10. (1) *ogda* .i. ogi (Ra.) *uaga* .i. anoighe (La.) *colani* .i. forcomlani (Ra.) (4) *dani* .i. dana (Ra.)
11. (2) *tuathmaig lethan* .i. forsinmaig lethain atuaid .i. frinmaig nailbe atuaid (Ra.) . *tuathmaig lethain* .i. forsinmaig lethain atuaid .i. mag afuilet tuatha imda .i. mag life (3) *cathair* .i. catharda (La.) (4) *dar trethan* .i. trans mare^f (La.)

^aMS. inmacradain   ^bMS. oib . . .   ^cMS. arricefamin   ^d 'our' A   ^eA. 'thou wilt.'   ^fMS. trasnwara.

12. (1) *lermaig* .i. mag letan (Ra.)   (2) *coir* .i. cocóir (La.) .i. laim Fr.
13. (1) *urlaithe* .i. dies iudicii et mortisarisfris ata dail caich.—Fr.   (2) *tairset* .i. doroiset Fr.   (3) *credlach* .i. credulus Fr.   (4) *trednach* .i. troisetheeh Fr.
14. (3) *cuor* .i. carad (Ra.) *cloithit cóir* .i. demna (La.)
16. (2) *atroiruis* .i. atchius .i. tairisi *no* roiraemais (La.) *adroeris* .i. tarrais (Fr.)
17. (2) *iarmbuaid* .i. mórgnimaib (Ra.)
18. (1) *morgrian* .i. nitór .i. morgriau code (*sic*) (La.) iustorum morgriau eadem (Fr.)
19. (3) *glanmainu* .i. glanniain [leg. glan in main l] vel cibus celestis (Ra.) *glanbann* .i. glanmain (La.)
20. (3) *for chete* .i. for conair *no* for sét[a] (La.)
21. (2) *attrorham* .i. aitchimit (La.)
22. (4) *balbai* .i. bec a foghur (La.)
24. (1) *fresdal* .i. frithailem (Ita.) *frestal* .i. fritháilem (La.)
26. (1) *atrocham* .i. diarcomdignad (La.)   (3) *goires* .i. coteges (La.)
27. (1) *slanchotlad* .i. dormiuit sine dolore[b]   (2) *bortgal* .i. angal iohannis in efflis (Ra.) *bortgal* .i. robo gal angal iohain in eifis[c] .i. gal condechaid tar bord annach (La.)
28. (1) .i. isaindraic 7 issuthain nuall na mac romarbad ambeithil la hirnath (La.)   (2) *coemda methil* .i. crem immethcl (*sic*) eat .i. propter innocentiam (Ra.) *caemda* methil .i. is mcithol chaem iat (La.)   (3) *cantais* .i. infantes qui occisi sunt ab herode in bethlem duo milia c . . . . (Ra.)
29. (1) *bid emid* .i. bid lu[a]th (Ra.) *nas demit* .i. bid deimin *no* bid luath (La.)   (2) *donnecrai* .i. donnoa (Ra.)

NOTES FROM THE LEBAR BRECC, p. 101.

Rawl. 505, f. 219 b, 220 a ; Laud 610, ff. 69 b 1, 70 a 1, and the Franciscan MS.

1. *candida* .i. in roma (Ra.) .i. uirgo in roma passa vel cainneda .i. espoc mac caiu[ne] oath da loarg ittaeb cenannsa ut illi ferunt . (Fr.)

panchrati .i. sub dioclctiano[d] passus est (La.) *nessain ulad* .i. innib condselaig .i. icinis ulad . Nesan .i. indse ulad .i. ulaid aitrebsat iunte odain inis ulad 7 inis teimle 7 nesan corcaige in hoc die (L.B.)

2. pa(r)meni .i. martiris (LB.)
maelodran .i. othuaim indbir *no* druim indbir aniarthar mide (LB.) 7 oinis angin forloch (Ra.)

3. *mac oige* .i. abb lis moir mochuda (LB.) 7 is fris adbertea infunscrec[h] *no* infunsnadaeh *no* iu funiscroch 7 issed fodera sen intan bói ina maccéem bec seisrecha in domain intan atcidis hé notheichdis ascén 7 afuascur reime 7 cach ernail indile archena notoghnatais dodáinib issed rotuiced assin iu mor foghnam ambeitis uile dósom iarsin (La.)

1. 'Candida' i.e. Rome i.e. a virgin who suffered in Rome . Or (the true reading is *cainneda* i.e. a bishop, son of Cainne, of Áth-dá-loarg beside Kells *ut alii ferunt*.

'*of Nessan of Ulster*' i.e. in Ui-Connselaig i.e. at Inis Ulad . Nesan i.e. of Inis Ulad i.e. therein dwelt Ulstermen from Duiminis Ulad and Inis Teimle ; and Nesan of Cork (is celebrated) on this day.

'*Maelodran*' i.e. of Tuaim Inber or Druim Inbir in the west of Meath and of Inis Angin on Lough . . .

3. '*Mac-Oige*' i.e. abbot of Lis Mór Mochuta, and he it is that used to be called the Frightener or the Disturber ; and this is the cause : when he was a little child (all) the plough-teams of the world on seeing him used to flee in affright and in terror before him, and every kind of cattle besides which used to serve human beings. By this was understood the great servitude to him wherein they all were to be thereafter.

---

[a] The words *for sét* are written after *epscop*: the gloss on *tomais* in the next line.
[b] MS. dormuitsine doloni.   [c] MS. eisis.   [d] MS. decioclitiano

4. *Merobus eludicus* .i. in laodicia hi ambo passi sunt (Ra.)
conaidble asrethi .i. ix.l.c. (LB.)
fer da lethi .i. berchan chluana sosta in *huib* failge (LB.) . *no* fer da lethe itaid treóit innalbain sacerdos[a] hé . Fer da leithe .i. leth a tsaegail dó andoman 7 aleth aili in ailithre ut ferunt (La.) .i. leth a sægail in alpain 7 a leth aile in *erinn* (Fr.)

5. *amanti* .i. episcopus (La.)
crispanæ .i. crispiaine uirgo (LB.) crispini martir in affrica (Fr.)

6. *gobbain* .i. chille lamraige inuib caitrend aniarthar osraige hicluain eidneach 7bi *cluain* eidnech atat taisi gobain (LB.) .i. ochill lamraige iniarthur osraige (Ra.) *no* comad he *for* bru nabanna hitigh da ghoban inuib echaech ulad (Fr.)
mur ninglech .i. aingil rochlaidset mur achille do (LB.)
lane .i. laine .i. sentuath sin fil indeiscert [herenn] 7 isdibsin dogoban (LB.)

7. *policarpi* .i. episcopus effesorum (Ra.)
conacleir .i. martyres cum ipso in antiochia passi (Ra.)
mainistir .i. mainistir buan buan bunata ata achaide mac bronaig Ailbe uassal ulta rosoum is roscornaig[b] (La.)
báite .i. báide mac brónaig mic balair mic cais mic níad mic airmedaig mic fergusa mic isinchain(?) mic feic (La.)
buiti .i. buiti .i. beo dé[c] no buiti .i. tene ut in prouerbio dicitur .i. bot fobrega . unde dicitur hodie butelach .i. ubi fit magnus ignis . buti *dana* quasi beti ab eo quod est beatus . Beatus autem dicitur quasi bene auctus (vel aptus) arbacain intormach dosamh retlu ocfoillsiugud acoinperta *amal* roboi ocfoillsiugud comperta *crist* . no bute quasi beo de arba dodin ba beosom sicut scriptum est qui uiuunt iam non sibi uiuunt sed ei qui pro ipsis[d] mortuus est et resurrexit [2 Cor. v. 15] non suam seculi in hoc mundo [facientes] uoluntatem sed eius qui pro ipsis passus est (Fr.)

8. *ichtbrichtain* .i. ic dungeimin i cianachta

'*with vastness of their heaps*' i.e. 159 (?)
'*man of two parts*' i.e. Berchan of Clonsost in Offaly. Or '*man of two parts*' in Laid Treoit in Scotland : a priest was he. 'Man of two parts.' i.e. half of his life in the world and the other half in pilgrimage, *ut ferunt* (*periti*). Half his life in Ireland and the other half in Scotland.

6. '*of Gobban*' .i. of Cell Lamraige in Ui-Caitrenn in the west of Ossory in Clonenagh, and in Clonenagh are Gobban's relics i.e. of Cell Lamraige in the west of Ossory. Or he may be on the brink of the Bann in Tech-dágobann in Ui-Echach of Ulster.
'*angelic wall*' i.e. angels founded the wall of his church for him.
'*Láne*' i.e. *Laine* i.e. an old tribe that which is in the south of Ireland, and of them is Gobban.

'*Monasterboice*' i.e. a monastery lasting, lasting, settled has Buide son of Bronach . Ailbe . . . . and arranged it
Báite i.e. Búite son of Bronach son of Balar, son of Cas, son of Nía, son of Airmedach, son of Fergus, son of . . . (?) son of Fiacc.
'*of Buite*' i.e. *Buiti* i.e. 'living-to-God,' or *buiti* i.e. 'fire,' *ut in prouerbio dicitur* i.e. 'fire (bot) throughout Bregia,' unde dicitur hodie *butelach* i.e. where there is a great fire. Or *Buti*, moreover, as if *beti*, from *beatus*. *Beatus autem dicitur quasi bene auctus* (*vel aptus*), for fair was his aggrandizement, a star making manifest his conception, as happened at the manifestation of the conception of Christ. Or *Bute quasi beo dé* 'living unto God,' for it was unto God that he was alive, as hath been written "they which live should not henceforth live unto themselves, but unto Him which died for them, and rose again," doing in this world not their own will, but His who suffered for them.

8. '*of Egbert*' i.e. at Dungiven in Cinnachta

---

[a] MS. sacardus   [b] This seems a quatrain.   [c] MS. dr.   [d] MS. ibsis

[DEC. 9-11.] NOTES FROM RAWL. 505 AND LAUD, 610.

glind[e] geimin *no* iconnachta ata .i. amaig eó nasaxan icera (La.) .i. odun gemin hiefannacht glinue [geimin] *no* himaig éo nasachsan iniarthur chonnacht *no* hitalaig leis nasachsan inluib conaill gabra (Ra.) uel in alio loco diuersi diuerse sentiunt[a] . *no* othulaig leis nasaxan amumain . 7 bercert aainu *no* icht ber 7rl. .i. icht brict ñl itig saxan inuib cachach muman 7 brathair-sidhe dobendict tailcha leis uasaxau 7 brathair doibh cuitbrict 7 tair tarasarsen (Fr.)

of Glen Geimin. Or in Connaught he is .i. in Mayo of the Saxons in Cera .i. i.e. of Dungiven in Ciannacht of Glenn-Geimin, or in Mayo of the Saxons in the west of Connaught, or in Tulach-leis of the Saxons in Ui-Conaill Gabra . *uel* etc.
Or of Tulach-leis of the Saxons in Munster and Bercert was his name of Ichtber etc. .i. Ichtbrict who is in Tech-Saxan in Ui-Echach of Munster ; and brother was he to Benedict of Tulach-leis of the Saxons, and a brother of theirs Cuitbrict and . . . . . .

9. *indi ingein* .i. mugna 7 fedelm due filiæ allela meice dunglaing rig laigen iceill ingen aillela iniarthur maige liphi (Ra.) .i. mumain 7 feidlimid icill ingen naililla ntáib liamna aniarthar [maige] liphi atait (La.)

9. *'the two daughters'* i.e. Mugna and Fedelm *duae filiae* of Ailill son of Dunlang king of Leinster in Cell Ingen Ailella in the west of the Plain of Liffey i.e. Mumain and Feidlimid in Cell Ingen Ailella beside Liamain in the west of the Plain of Liffey are they.

ailella .i. mac dunlaing rí laigen .i. liamain. nicóir acleith[b] 7 acill ingen aililla inairter maigi lift sunt simul . Mugain 7 feidelem nomina (La.)

'of Ailill' i.e. son of Dunlang king of Leinster i.e. "Liamain (not right to conceal her)" and in Cell-Iugen-Ailella in the east of the plain of Liffey *sunt simul*. Mugain and Feidelm are their names.

10. *capitolini* .i. martyr (La.)
modimoe .i. felúain cáin árad isinmumain (La.) .i. ruis conaill .i. isinmumain ata .i. icluain cain arad (Fr.)
11. *Damassus* .i. papa romae (Ra.) .i. abb romae (La.) .i. episcopus [et] papa romae (Fr.)
senoe .i. omugna iniarthur laigen forbrú berba (Ra.) .i. mosenóe imbelach mughna .i. aniarthar laigen forbrú berba (La.)

10. *'of Capitolinus'* i.e. a martyr.
'My-Dimóc' i.e. in Cluain Cáin Arad in Munster, i.e. of Ross Conaill i.e. in Munster he is, i.e. in Cluain Cáin Arad.

'Senoc' .i. of Mugna in the west of Leinster on the brink of Barrow .i. My-Senóc in Belach Mughna .i. in the east of Leinster on the brink of Barrow

Mosenoc mugna dana .i. mugna darbile mor 7 ba coimlethan abarr frisinnagh uile . Tritoraid gacha bliadna fair 7 romairestar ouimsir dilenn fodichleth gusanoidee inrogenair conn cét cathach 7 isiarom rofoillsiged. Tric[h]a edh remhet incrainnsin 7 .ccc. eadh anirde . Niunine eicis immurro rotrascair incrainnsin ut dixit

My-Senóc of Mugna, moreover, i.e. Mugna (was) a vast tree, the top whereof was as broad as the whole plain. Thrice a year did it bear fruit, and it remained hidden from the time of the deluge until the night on which Hundred-battled Conn was born, and then was it made manifest. Thirty cubits was the girth of that tree and its height was three hundred cubits. Ninnine the poet, however, laid low that tree. *ut dixit (poeta)* :—

Eo mugna bamor incrann
.xxx. edh athimthacmang
fodiamair re hedh dobi
.ccc. edh ina airdi 7rl. (Fr.)

The yew Mugna, great was the tree,
Thirty cubits was its girth;
Hidden for a time was it :
Three hundred cubits in height.

tuathmaig lethain .i. forsinmaig lethain atuaid

'On the broad north plain' i.e. on the broad

[a] MS. sensiunt [b] This interpolation—*Liamain, ní cóir a cleith*—seems a line of some poem.

[.i. fri mag nallain atuaid *no* tuathach—Fr.] .i. mag afuilet tuatha imda .i. mag life (La.) .i. forsinmaig lethan atuaid .i. fri maig nailbe atuaid (Ra.)

moelleoc .i. eiltene chind tsaile andeiseirt ereand (La.)
12. *finden* .i. mac hui thelduib abb chl*uana* nirair*d* (La.) .i. Finnian mac fintain mic con*-*craid mic daircella mic senaigh mic diarmata mic æda mic fergusa mic ai*l*ella tellduibh mic celtcair mic uitecair (Fr.)

13. *baethan chluana* .i. baethan chluana hannabar inh*u*i*b* muiredaig .i. mobí mac huí alta 7rl. (La,) ochluain abannabair in uib *muire*daigh (Fr.)
colum trednach tire .i. colum mac crimthain ótir daglas isinmumain (La.)

Colum *dana* mac nindeda mac naxair (leg. nazair?) mac crimth*ainn* mic echech mic œngusa mic cremthannain m*i*c cathair moir. Do uib corm*aic immurro* amathair .i. mincloth ingen cainnig mic coisi mic lugd*ach* mic labra*d*ha mic corm*aic* mic concorp (Fr.)

[*In* Fr. *on the last line of a poem ending* reilgi mic hui crimtannain . *bérthar co* ninis coltra *occurs the following gloss :—*]
.i. reliquio .i. taise coluim mic crimthainn ructha la mochoemhe tire da ghlas 7 la hodran maigister for fon tar esge fodhes co hinis coltra co camini iunsi coltra

14. *ríg no mac* .i. crist (Fr.)
arsiur .i. maria (La.) .i. muire (Fr.)
drursus conathriur .i. martyres* in autiochia teste grigorio . . . (Ra.) *trursus* .i. martir (La.) cum .iii. sociis suis (Fr.)
15. *fausti* .i. faustinus in affrica passus est (Ra.)
16. *ualentini* i.e. episcopus (La.). i. in rauenna (Ra.)
mobeoóc .i. o loch garman (La.) . *no* mobioc .i. oard coimruis for bru loca garman *no* camrois .i. ros cain icl*uain* fergaile .i. indelbna tire daloch *no* mobeoc loca gerg isintuaiscert in aquilone (Fr.)

plain in the north i.e. to the north of Mag n-Allain (?) or (*'tuath'* *means*) populous i.e. a plain wherein are many peoples i.e. the plain of Liffey i.e. on the broad plain in the north i.e. to the north of Mag nAilbe.
'*My Elteóc*' i.e. Eilténe of Kinsale in the south of Ireland.
12. '*Findín*' i.e. son of Teldub's descendant, abbot of Clonard, i.e. Finnian, son of Fintan, son of Concrad, son of Daircill, son of Senach, son of Diarmait, son of Aed, son of Fergus, son of Ailill Telldub, son of Celtcar, son of Uitcar.
13. '*Baethan of Cluain*' i.e. Baethan of Cluain [dá] n-Annabar in Ui-Muiredaig, i.e. Mo-bí, son of Ua-Alta, etc., of Cluain Abannabair [leg. dá-hanabar ?] in Ui-Muiredaig
'*Colomb the abstinent of Tir(dá)glas*' i.e. Colomb, son of Crimthan, of Tír-dá-glas in Munster.
Colomb, now, son of Nindid, son of Nazar, son of Crimthann, son of Eochaid, son of Oengus, son of Cremthannán, son of Cuthair the Great : of the Uí Cormaic, however, was his mother, namely Minchloth daughter of Cainnech son of Ceise, son of Lugaid, son of Labraid, son of Cormac, son of Cúcorp.
The relics of the son of Crimthannan's descendant will be taken to Inis Celtra.

The relics of Colomb son of Crimthann were taken by my-Coemhe of Tír dá glas and by Odran the Master on a wain over Esge (?) southwards to Inis Celtra to Camine of Inis Celtra.
14. '*The King*,' or Son, i.e. Christ.
'*our sister*' i.e. (the Virgin) Mary.
'*Drusus with his three.*' i.e. martyrs etc.

'*My Beóóc*' i.e. of Lough Garmau, or My-Bíoc of Ard Camruis on the brink of Loch Garman, or of Cain-ross i.e. Ross-cáin in Cluain Fergaile i.e. in Delbna Tíre dá Loch. Or my-Beoc of Loch Gerg in the North.

* MS. martiris

[Dec. 17-24.]

17. *uictoir* .i. in affrica (Ra.) martir 7 senchaid duib aedha imbregaibh (Fr.)

18. *magniu* no magnend ó chill maignenn itocb atha cliath ata (Ra.) 7 tarcairtend .i. ouachtar aird (La.)
dichuill .i. do mugdornaib maigeu dó .i. modíchú ilgaig* inuaib faelain (La.) Diucaill duo .i. do mughoruaibh maigheu do 7 moditiu lilcaigh in uib faelan 7 in araib *immurro* ata diucaill iarfir (Fr.)

19. *samthann cluana bronaig* .i. icrich choirpri 7 itefa (La.) .i. icrich cairpri 7 tebta .i. samthan *ingen* dianarnin mic ferdomnaigh mic dic[h]on mic tricim mic feie mic imchada (Fr.)

20. *ba brigach* .i. iguaithe .i. epscop (La.) .i. episcopus sed post petrum episcopatum tenuit sed sub trainuo imperatore passus est ignatius et leonibus datus est et aliis bestiis (Fr.)

21. *thomais* .i. tomas apostolus in india passus est, sed corpus eius ad edisam ciuitatem siriae aportatum est sub alaxandro imperatore rege romanorum .... (Ra.) .i. epscop (La.) .i. episcopus et apostolus in india passus est. sed corpus eius ductus est ad edisam et ibi expectat resur[r]ectionem iustorum (Fr.)

22. *tua* .i. othigh thuae ind huaib faelain 7 ultan tigi dia . ideo tua (La.) dicitur quia lapis in labiis eius per omne tempus quadragesimae fiebat ut non posset loqui et inde tua dictus est. Itge tua *dana* .i. tothainci dogui ardin .i. cloc tua nabclaib fut inchorg*us* narolab*radh* . unde ultan tua . *no* connadh ambclaib tua fesin nobidh incloch dogr*és* unde tua dicitur (Fr.)

itharnaisc .i. óchlocnad inbuib faelan immolle forbran (Ra.) .i. felocnad (La.) in uib faelain (Fr.)
emene .i. orus glaisse namumnech forbrú berba (Ra.) .i. fross glaissi (La.)

23. *lamthemnioc* .i. mothemnoce coice cluain ferta molua (Ra.) .i. ochluain ferta molua (La.)

24. *luciani* .i. martir (Ra.) .i. coic molua cluana ferta (Fr.)

17. '*of Victor*' i.e. in Africa : a martyr ; and Seuchaid of Dub-Aeda in Bregia (is celebrated on the same day).

18. '*Magniu*' or Magnend of Kilmainham beside Dublin he is. And Tarcnirtenn of Uachtar-aird (is celebrated with him).
'*Dichuill*' i.e. of Mugduirn Maigen was he i.e. My-Díchú of Lilgach in Ui-Faelain. Diucaill, now, of Mugduirn Maigen was he, and my-Ditiu (?) of Lileach in Ui-Faelain, and in Arabia is Diucaill of a truth.

19. '*Samthann of Cluain Brónaig*' i.e. in Crích Coirpri and in Teffia .i. Samthan, daughter of Dianarnn, son of Ferdomnach, son of Díchú, son of Trichem, son of Fiacc, son of Imchath.

20. '*Mighty was*' i.e. of Ignatius i.e. a bishop.

22. ('*Ultan*) *the Silent*' i.e. of Tech Tuae in Ui Faelain and Ultan of Tech Dia i.e. Tua. He is called *tua* 'silent,' because a stone used to be in his mouth during the whole of Lent so that he could not speak, and hence he was called *Tua*. "(Ultan) the silent's prayer," i.e. he kept silence for God's sake, i.e. a silent stone (was) in his mouth during Lent so that he used not to speak. Whence (he was called) Ultán the silent. Or it may be in the mouth of Tua himself the stone used to be always, whence he is called *Tua*.

'*Itharnaisc*' i.e. of Clocnad in Ui-Faelan together with Forbran (?) i.e. in Clocnad in Ui-Faelain.
'*Emene*' i.e. of Ross Glaisse of the Munstermen on the brink of Barrow, i.e. in Ross Glaisse.

23. '*with my Temnebc*' i.e. My-Temneóc, cook in Cluain Ferta Molua i.e. of Cluain Ferta Molua i.e. cook of Molua of Clonfert.

24. '*with My-Cua*' .i. Mo-chua, son of Lonán of Tech Mochua in Leix of Leinster, and of

---

* leg. modichú lilgaig ?

clxxxiv THE CALENDAR OF OENGUS. [DEC. 25-31.

lamchua .i. mochua macc Ionain otaig mochua illaichis laigen 7 odaire nis (nuis, Fr.) isleib fuait (Ra.) .i. óthig mochua alaigis .i. Mochua mac lonain mic senaig mic aengusa mic lugna mic breg duilb mic airt chirb [cuirp.—Fr.] (La.) mic fiachach .i. mic foidllin*the* rechtmair (Fr.)

25. *innotlaic* .i. isanotlaic moir facta est natiuitas christi (La.)

26. *mochommoc* .i. commai orus comman iconnachtaib 7 iarla de tuama dagualann in eodem die cum comman (Ra.) .i. coman mac faelcon orus comain amaig áe (La.)

stefani .i. clocha*d* in cét*mairtir* .i. stefain in ierusalem imbliada*in* desgabala cri*st* (Fr.)

27. *Iohannis*. Iohannes apostolus et euangelista apud effesum . lx . viii° post passionem domini anno etatis sue xc . ix obiit atque iuxta eundem sepultus est (Fr.)

28. *inmacain ambeithil*
Cethracha arcét comall ńgle
domaccaib is damile
roort ambeithil combuaid*
lasinimpir lahiruaith.
Tricha maigi sochla suaire
immau inbeithil immacuaird
cét cach maigi marbtha ann
domaccaib suareca sacrclann .
Cothra[cha] iscét* truag indal
ambeithil nahaenuran (La.)

alii dicunt quod duo milia .c.xx, occisi sunt. Alii idem duo milia .cc.xl. (Fr.)

29. *uictor* .i. martir 7 papa rome (Ra.)
aireran .i. fer leiginn cluana imird (Fr.)

30. *Mansueti* . martir qui pasus est cum uiris in alaxandria ciuitate (Fr.)
elbi .i. imlecha ibair (Ra.) imlech ibair (La.)

31. *Lochan 7 enda* .i. lochan 7 enda ochill manach inhuaib dúnchada atát duo isti 7 acill mic cathail ind huaib bairrche .i. imbelach gabran 7c. (La.)
siluester .i. papa romae et confessor (Ra.) .i. episcopus et papa roma[e] (La.)

Daire Mis[i] in Sliab Fuait: i.e. of Tech Mochua in Leix i.e. Mochua, son of Lonán, son of Senach, son of Oengus, son of Lugna, son of Breg-dolb, son of Art-chorb, son of Fiacha i.e. son of Feidlimid Rechtmar.

25. '*at Christmas*' i.e. it is on the great Christmas that Christ's Nativity took place.

26. '*My Commóc*' .i. Commai of Ross Commáin in Connaught, and Iarlaithe of Tuaim-dagualann (is celebrated) on the same day with Commán i.e. Commán son of Faelchú of Ross Commáin in Magh Ae.

'*Stephen's*' i.e. the stoning of the protomartyr, namely Stephen, in Jerusalem in the year of Christ's ascension.

28. ' *the children in Bethlehem.*'
Forty and a hundred—bright fulfilment—
Children, and two thousand
Were slain in Bethlehem with victory
By the leader, by Herod,
Thirty fields famous, pleasant,
Round about Bethlehem
In every field were slain there a hundred
Children pleasant, of noble race,
Forty and a hundred—piteous the lot—
In Bethlehem alone.

29. ' *Victor* ' i.e. a martyr and pope of Rome.
'*Airerán*' i.e. lector of Clonard.

30. '*of Ailbe*' i.e. of Imliuch Ibair.

31. '*Lochán and Enda*' i.e. Lochan and Enda of Cell Manach in Ui-Dunchada are these two and of Cell Mic Cathail in Ui-Bairrche i.e. in Belach-Gabráin etc.

[The notes on the Lebar Brecc copy of the Félire cease, as we have seen, at December 6. The margins of pp. 101, 102 thus left vacant are partially filled by miscellaneous notes in Irish, or Latin, or both, in the hand of the scribe. Of these the following are specimens:]—

p. 101, r. marg.] Diamba clerech . Nibahirach . Nirba roard doguth. Nirba sanntach.

If thou be a cleric, be not wrathful. Let not thy voice be overloud. Be not greedy.

* nembuadh Fr.   b ar cét Fr.

Nirbasatach.[a] Nirbaneoit. Nirbat breccach. Nirbatærerach *fri* sere.

    Dothoeb lethfas. Doligo lethfuar.
    lacr*ist* mac ńdé rothia aluag.

Abb anfine fort. INgnáis dochenéoil duit collaa becca. Uir aniuil tarut hiforcend dosota. Fiss. foss. feidle. Tói. Uimle. Ilidna. Ainmne. Nirgaba doman abachlaig.

Be not sated. Be not niggardly. Be not false. Take no delight in food.

    Thy side half bare: thy bed half-cold,
    With Christ, God's Son, thou shalt have the reward thereof.

A stranger abbot over thee. Thy family absent from thee till the day of thy death. Foreign mould over thee at the end of thy way. Knowledge. Steadfastness. Permanence. Silence. Humility. Purity. Patience. Take not the world, O Shepherd!

p. 101, r. marg.]
Moelisu hua brolchan cecinit.

    Deus meus adiuua mé
    tuce dam doshere ama*i*c modé
    tuc dam doshere ama*i*c modé
    deus meus adiuua mé.
    INmeum cor ut sanum sit
    tuc[b] arí rán. dogr*ad* cogribb
    tuc arí rán dogr*ad* cogribb.
    in meum cor ut sanuum sitt.
    Domine da quod peto a té[c]
    tuc tuc codian agrian glan glé
    tuc tuc codian agrian glan glé.
    domine da quod peto a té[c]
    Hanc spero remm. et quaero *quam*
    dosherec dam sund doserec dam tall
    [doserec dam sund doserec dam tall]
    hanc spero remm. et quaero *quam*.
    Tuum amorenm *sicut*[d] uis
    tuc dam cotren atber doris
    tuc dam cotren atber doris.
    tuum amorem *sicut* uis.
    Quaero postulo petto a té
    mobeith anim ama*i*c dil dé
    mobeith anim ama*i*c dil dó
    quaero postulo petto a to.
    Domine domine exaudi mé
    manimm roplan dotgr*ad* adé
    manimm roplan dotgr*ad* adé
    [domine domine exaudi mé.]
    deus meus a[d]iuua me
    deus meus adiuua mé.

Mael-ísu, grandson of Brolchán sang:—

    My God, help thou me!
    Give me thy love, O Son of my God!
    Give me thy love, O, Son of my God!
    Deus meus adjuva me!
    Into my heart, that it be whole,
    Put, O glorious King, thy love quickly,
    Put, O glorious King, thy love quickly
    In meum cor ut sanum sit.
    Lord, grant thou what I entreat of thee,
    Give, give swiftly, O pure, bright Sun!
    Give, give swiftly, O pure, bright Sun!
    Domine, da quod peto a te!
    This thing I hope and seek
    Thy love to me here, thy love to me there.
    Thy love to me here, thy love to me there.
    Hanc spero rem et quaero quam.
    Thy love, even as thou wilt,
    Give me strongly I will say again.
    Give me strongly I will say again.
    Tuum amorem sicut vis.
    I seek, I demand, I entreat of thee
    That I may be in heaven, O dear Son of God.
    That I may be in heaven, O dear Son of God.
    Quaero, postulo, peto a te.
    Lord, Lord, hearken unto me!
    Let my soul be full of thy love, O God.
    Let my soul be full of thy love, O God!
    Domine, domine, exaudi me!
    My God, help thou me!
    Deus meus adjuva me!

p. 101, r. marg.]
Dice mihi quis primus accepit decimamm. ninse. abraham dochrud loith' fratris. *no* dischrud fén. Cid comad dechnad sech cethrumad

Tell me who first took tithe? Not hard to say. Abraham, of the cattle of his brother Lot, or of his own cattle. Why is it a tenth

---

[a] leg. sáthach.   [b] MS. tuc dam.   [c] MS. petto adé.   [d] MS. s.   [e] Facs. loich

no cuiced *no sésed no nomad* . *ninse* . arisdecti dia 7 duine .i. tredattu natrínóite 7 eethardattu cuirp .i. sér 7 talam . tene 7 usque .7 tri shianse anmma .i. irascibilis et concupiscibilis[a] et rationabilis .i. [leg. l.] u. cetfaide cuirp 7 .u. sianns(a) anmma . uisus . auditus . odoratus .[b] gustus . tactus . la corp sin . Cúic siansa anmına .i. timmor . amor . oidiumm . gaudiumm . tristitia . No arrobé indechınad fer roseerad ardilind noei .i. abuumm suumm [leg. seruum?] Abraam . cubaid ciamad dechmad nogabad . uair robi treb leui dechmad mac nisrael . robad cubaid ciamad dechmad nogabad abrnam . Cid eumad domeleesedech noberad . nach daron tuee. *ninse* quia obtulit melcesedech panem et uinumm et aquam in figuram christi . Aron autem buice 7 tairb 7 ocdaim nohidpradsum . *conidairesin* nach daron tuee . quia obtulit *haec* .

rather than a fourth, or a fifth, or a sixth, or a ninth? Not hard to say. Because God and man are a decad i.e. the threeness of the Trinity and the fourness of the body (i.e. air and earth, fire and water) and three senses of the mind i.e. irascible and concupiscible and rationable. Or five senses of the body and five senses of the mind, sight, hearing, smell, taste, touch: with the body are those. Five senses of the mind i.e. fear, love, hate, joy, sadness. Or because the tenth man was saved from Noah's flood i.e. . . . . It is meet that Abraham should take a tenth, for the tribe of Levi was the tenth of the children of Israel. It were meet that Abraham should take a tenth. But why was it given to Melchisidech and not to Aaron. Not hard to say. Because Melchisidech offered bread and wine and water, as a figure of Christ. But Aaron, goats and bulls and oxen *he* used to offer, wherefore it was not given to Aaron because he offered these.

De baculo[e]
Pars baculi doc[e]o designat curua coronam .
Atque bonos mores demonstrat robore recto .
Pungere[d] terrenos intus pars infima[e] praefert
Prespiter alme uide . qualem te uirgula format
Praesul iura scies . baculum si cernere cures
Curua trahit[f] mites . pars pungit acuta rebelles[g] .

ISand basfoillsiu intréblait intan bias inmairtir ifoiditin 7 inriagaire océnann uafert . arbid doig lacách bid he bias forcoir inriagairi.

Then is the tribulation most manifest when the martyr shall be in suffering and the executioner making the graves, for it is clear to every one that he will be in the executioner's power.

p. 102 in upper marg.]
    Codlud ocus sadaile
    longad cipe tan tairo
    ifern conailphinaaib
    issed doberair aire .

Sleep and ease,
Eating at whatsoever time thou reachest,
Hell with its many punishments
This is what is given for those.

p. 102 in lower marg.]
    Maire ingen iachimm aird
    dosíl dabíd indirbaird
    anna ingen samuel sund
    ainm amathar cenfordull.

Mary daughter of high Iachem,
Of the seed of David the great bard,
Anna daughter of Samuel here
(Was the) name of her mother without error.

[a] MS. irascipulis 7 *concopiscipulis* [b] MS. adoratus [c] MS. bachula [d] MS. Purgere
    [e] MS. inifimma [f] MS. trabtit
[g] This line is cited by Hugo a S. Victore in Speculo Eccles. cap. 6, Ducange s.v. *Baculus pastoralis*.

[Dec. 31.] NOTES FROM LEBAR BRECC, P. 102.

Melchas (.i. rí saba). Casper (.i. ri tairsi) Arifaxat (.i. ri arabi)

Hua annoc 7 hua chellchin chillo mori hua shluasti ochuil osluaisti hua glesain. ISiatsin roghadsat eich 7 muil 7 assain in charilnail tanic óroim cotír nerenn diaforcedul. inamsir domnaill moir hui briain rig muman. coniddesin rorecustar comorba petair cis 7 dliged erenn frisaxanaib. Conid he sin cert 7 dliged lenait saxain forgoedelu indiu. Arba co comorba petair curoim teged cis 7 dliged erenn cosin 7rl.

Cuig adbair forsambatar cach ocádrad crist isinfasach. Morbus .i. oes galair diaslanugud. Signa .i. oes noingantaiged he aramirboldacht. Cibus .i. dremm diasasad obiadaib. Blasfemia .i. dremm diaaithisiugud. Dogma .i. oes forcetail.

Melchas i.e. king of Sabaca. Caspar i.e. king of Tarsus (?). Arifaxat i.e. king of Arabia.

O'Annoc and O'Cellchin of Cell Mór, O'Sluasti of Cuil O'-Sluaisti O'Glesain: these are they that stole the steeds and mules and asses of the cardinal who came from Rome to the land of Ireland to teach it, in the time of Domnall Mór O'Briain, king of Munster.[a] Wherefore Peter's successor sold the tribute and due of Ireland to the Saxons. Wherefore right over and due from the Gael cleave to the Saxons today. For unto Peter's successor, (and) to Rome Ireland's tribute and due used to go till then, &c.

Five causes (were there) why every one was worshipping Christ iu the wilderness. *Morbus* i.e. sick persons for their healing: *Signa* i.e. persons who wondered at him for his miracles. *Cibus* i.e. persons for satisfying themselves with foods: *Blasphemia* i.e. persons for reviling him. *Dogma* i.e. teachers.

Petrus apostolus dixit. Credo in deum patrem.
Andreas apostolus. Et in ihesum christum.
Hiohannes apostolus. Qui conceptus est.
Hiacopus maior. Passus sub pontio.
Tomas apostolus. Dé[s]cendit ad inferos[b]
Hiacopus minor alfei. A[s]cendit in caelum
Pilipus apostolus. INde ueuturus est.
Partholomeus. Credo in spiritum sanctum
Matheus apostolus. Sanctam sanctamque (sic) eclesiam
Simon candaneus apostolus. Sanctorum comunionem
Tatheus apostolus. Carnis resur[r]ectionem
Matheus[c] apostolus. Et uitam eternam. amen.

[a] ob. A.D. 1194.   [b] MS. adniferos.   [c] leg. Matthias.

THE CALENDAR OF OENGUS. [1-28.

Epilogue.

Rawl. B. 512, fo. 54ª.	Laud, 610, fo. 70, b. 2.	Lebar Brecc, p. 103.
1 [O]nkl. coaraili rofersam arniarraid aih.u cofirbuil dosealba dobliadain	1. Onkl. co araile rofersam arniarair aih.u cofirbail asselba dobliadain	1. Onkl. co araile rofersam arniarair aih.u cofirbail fortselba dobliadain
5 Buiden ceacha laithea dosrimemar renmain concnecmaingseam urain arceanu friceanu eanair	5. Buiden cachoen laithi dosruimdemar remain conecmaingsem aurain arcend forcend enair	5. Buiden cechalaithe dosrimemar remain conecmaingsem aurain arcend fricend enair
9 Bahenirt arcumang hichorpán isisli acht ronscart isuaisli searc ard arbuir ih.v	9. Bahenairt arcumunung arcorpán asisliu acht rosert asuaisliu serc ard arbair ih.u	9. Bahenirt arcumang hicorpan isisliu *acht* ronsert isuaisliu serce ard árbair ih.u
13. Huasalathraig faithe doxp, ciaptar céli ladoine illaino nifeas[a] aféli	13. Huassalathraig fáithi docri*st* ciaptar ceile ladúini illaini nifessa afeile	13. Huasalathraig faithe docri*st* ciaptar céli ladoine illaine nitfessa afeili
17. Act rofeas nadráinic ardriched inrigsa anim do[n]bith buansa acht in æn nalithsa	17. Acht rofes natrainic ardriched indrigsa anim donbith buansa acht inoen nalithsa	17. Achtrofess nadranic ardricheg inrigsa ainim donbith buansa acht inoen nalithsa
21. (Luchtlach) lán eachlaithe illithlatha leastar iarmbuaid 7 coscur cotisat dia[r]frestal	21. Luchtlach lan eachlaithe alligª latha lestar iarmbuaid 7 coscu*r* dodigsetᵇ diarfrestal	21. Luchtloch lan cechlaithe alliglatha lestur iarmbuaid 7 coscar cotisat diarfrestul
25. (Fornem a)conruala cachlaithe dindire nigó cerobaige asmo mileib mile	25. Fornem aconruale each laithe din dire ní gó cianobágo ismó milib mile	25. Forneam anconrualai cechlaithe dindireᶜ nigo cerobaige ismo milib mile

Translation.

1. From the one calend to the other we have made our search. O Jesu with true goodness take possession of thy year!

5. Of each day the leading troop we have recounted: we have cut off the excess from head to head of January.

9. Weak was our power in aᵈ poor body that is lowliest, but what is noblest strengthened us—the high love of Jesu's cohort.

13. Patriarchs, prophets, though they were comrades of Christ's, unto people in plenty their feasts are unknown.

17. But it *is* known that, save on one of these festivals, not a soul of this enduring world hath reached the high heaven of this King.

21. The full multitude of each day in the beautiful Kingdom's vessel, after victory and triumph, may they come to attend us!

25. (The number) that went to heaven on each day from earth, thou wilt not be wrong if thou engage that it is more than thousands of thousands.

ª l. oslig   ᵇ l. dotiset   ᶜ .i. dontalmain   ᵈ B. 'our.'

Rawl. B. 512, fo. 54ᵃ.	Laud, 610, fo. 70, b. 2.	Lebar Brecc, p. 103.
29. (Demil)ib amorsain ammuir brigach buansain nituesam donlinsain acht riga nasluaghsain	29. Demilib ammorsain amur mbrigach buansin ni thuesam dindlinsin acht riga nasluagsin	29. De milib ammorsain ammuir brigach buansain nituesam donlinsain acht riagail nasluagsain
33. S(luagad) caiu cachlaithe adanaidbli briga dacachleith dartuatha cotisat lariga	33. Sluaged caiu cech laithe ada aidbli briga docach leith dartuatha domnisat lariga	33. Sluaiged cain cechlaithe atanaidble briga docech leith dartuatha cotisat lariga
37. Arí noeb notguide isiarseis doruirmius rombithbeo ipardas lasinslog doruirmes	37. Arí noem notguidiu isiarseis forurmius rombith beó iparrdus lasinsluag dorurmius	37. Ari noeb notguidiu isiarseis foruruirmius* rombithbeo hitpardus lasinslog doruirmius
41. IN(rig)rad doruirmius olisloimm deromuir cechae conachleir credail robet oeamcobuir	41. INrigrad doruirmius olisloim doromuir hicóemtecht crist credail robet ocmochobair	41. INrigrad doruirmius olis loimm deromuir cechai cocleir credail robet acomchobair
45. C(otamr)ocbat uile comrig rimther flaithi romsnaidet mosruithe cach colucht alaithe	45. Cotomrocbat uili comrig rimther flaithe romsnadet cosruithe cach colucht alathe	45. Cotamrocbat uile comrig rimther flaithe romsnaidet mosruithe cach colucht alaithe
49. L(ucht) fris failte feraim cosincach notcarnim rosnaidet comfairind cunu ceil curp comanaim	49. Lucht fris fuilte feraim cosincách nocharnim romsnáidet comfuirind cund ceille curp comainim	49. Lucht fris failte feraim cosincách notcaraim romsnaidet comfairind cund curp ceill comainim
53. Nachanain roainic riched reim asdixa roicfa isunisliu ronbe beannacht ih.u	53. Nach ainim roinic riched reim asdixiu rodicfa bas uaisliu rosmbé bendacht issu	53. Nachainim roanic riched reim asdixu roicfa asuaisliu ronbé bendacht ih.u

29. That greatness of thousands, that Sea mighty, eternal, from that number we have given only the chieftains of those hosts.

33. Each day's fair host, whose vigours are vast, from every side over tribes may they come to me with Kings!

37. O holy King I beseech thee—it is after fatigue I have counted up—may I be above in Thy paradise with the host that I have reckoned!

41. The Kings whom I have reckoned—and it is 'a sip from a great sea'—may each of them with a pious train[b] be aiding me!

45. May they all upraise me to (Thee) my King who numberest princes! may my elders protect me, each with his day's folk.

49. The folk to which I bid welcome, with every one whom I love, may they protect me to my territory (in heaven), sense, body, reason, and soul.

53. Every soul that hath gone to heaven —course that is highest—will attain what is noblest, will have Jesu's blessing.

---

* leg. foruirmius   [b] B, 'in pious Christ's company,' C. 'with his pious train.'

RAWL. B. 512, fo. 54ᵃ·ᵇ.

57. Asobarthan uile
lasinsluag custiagat
ronocbat ronmornt
inairdrig atgiallat
61. Labendacht inírigsa
conasluagaib cainib
robe uasbarndalaib
formoelruain riandoinib
65. Domrairbeʳi maite
la xp. coemthar ndile
diabeandacht conglaine
laduthracht acridhe
69. Acrist cotamroither
tis tuas arecnch mélacht

frimdiubairt ladilacht
arecnaire dogérat
73. INgraffann rofersam
flatha xp. ascolba
arrothuirsium liubra
congaib mór ditorbai
77. IStorba do oscraib
diamba luirech lere
arpeti cechdine
dotoscelad fele
81. Cit suide nodlegat
ataleathna linde
fil and mor nard uaille
frismelat arinde
85. Rig nime conainglib

LAUD. 610, fo. 70, b. 2.

57. Asobarthan uile
cosinrig costiagat
ronócmat romorat
inardrig atgiallat
61. Lanbendacht inrígsin
conasluagaib cáinib
robbó uas forndalaib
formaelruain riaúdóinib
65. Domrairbera maiti
lacrist coemdar ndile
labennacht conglaine
laduthracht achride
69. Acrist cotomroether
tair thiar arcach mel-
acht
frimdubart badillacht
arécnaire dogérnt
73. INgrafand rofearsam
flatha crist iscolbu
oroluaidsim liubra
congeib mor di torba
77. IStorba di oscraib
diamblu lurech leire
arpeite each díne
dothaiscelad feile
81. Citsúide notlégat
attalethna linde
fil mor and ard aille
frismelat arinde
85. Ri nimi conainglib

LEBAR BRECC, p. 103.

57. Asoburthan uile
lasinslog costiagat
ronoebat ronmornt
inardrig atgiallat
61. Labenducht inrigsa
conaslogaib cainib
ronbe uasbarndálaib
formaelruain riandainib
65. Domrairbera maite
lacrist coemthar ndile
diabendacht conglaine
laduthracht achride
69. Acrist cotamroither
tís tuas arecchmelacht

frim dubairt ladilacht
arecnaire dogerat
73. INgrafand rofersam
flatha crist iscolba
arrothuirsium libra
congaib mor dothorba
77. IStorba dooscraib
diambaluirech lere
arphete cechdine
dothoscelad felo
81. Citsúide notlegad
atalethna linde
fil and mor nárd uaille
frismelat arinde
85. Rig nime conainglib

57. The benefit (?) of them all (be) with the host to which they come: may they hallow, may they magnify, the high King whom they serve!

61. May this King's full blessing, with His beautiful hosts, be over your assemblies on Maelruain before (all other) men!

65. Let my tutor grant to me with Christ a . . . of affection, of his pure blessing with his heart's desire.

69. O Christ let me preserved, above, belowᵃ from every reproach, at my earnest prayer with sinlessness, for sake of thy champions' intercession!

73. The race that we have run is .... of Christ's kingdom: for we have searched books that contain much of profit.

77. It is profit to the ignorant unto whom it is a corslet of piety: every number sings it to show forth the feasts.

81. Though they be sages that read it whose wisdoms are greatᵇ (as) there is therein much of high praises, they will extol it for (its) meaning.

85. Kings of heavenᶜ with angels, whose renown we will not hide, (and) every martyr whom we tell of, have come to make it.

ᵃ B. 'in the east, in the west.'   ᵇ lit. 'wide.'   ᶜ B. 'Heaven's King.'

EPILOGUE.

Rawl. B. 512, fo. 54. b.	Laud, 610, fo. 70, b. 2.	Lebar Brecc, pp. 103, 104.
asaclu nadcelam	asachlú nateélam	asaclú nadcelam
cachmartir adrimem	cachmairtir atrimem	cechmartir adrimem
tancatar diadenam	taugadar diadenam	tangatar diadenam
89. Nisoas dorigne	89. Nisoas dorigne	89. Nisoas dorigne
inleabráu léir laindrech	moleabran léir loindrech	inlebran leir laindrech
acht fortacht rig aing-	acht fortacht rig aing-	acht fortacht rigainglech
lech	lech	
isucan cain caiudlech	issucan cáin coiudlech	ih.ucan cain caindlech
93. Cainsenad domainic	93. Cainsenad dommainic	93. Cáin senad domanic
imideuaird motige	immideuairt mothighi	hinidchuairt mothige
diacoicertad fiadaib	diachocertad fiaduib	dia coicertad fiaduib
foriagail rig nime	foriagail rig nime	fori[a]gail rig nime
97. Niaine fodruair	97. Nihane fotruar	97. Niaine fondruair
iscol duin dia foirgleam	iscoll dun dianabram	iscol dun diafoirglem*
cach nocban conidna	cach nóeban conidnai	cechnoeban conidna
dorigne acoipd[el]	dorigne achaibdell	dorigne achoibtell
101. Intord inacaiptel	101. Intord inacaiptel	
	mabeith nech bodussna	mabeth nech foruasna
	atbeir fiad inlinsa	atbiur fiad inlinsa
	isdithár dontsluagsa	isdithair dontsluagsa
105. INsluag conacoicert	105. INsluag conidnaicert	105. INsluag conitcocert
inlebran colléri	inlebran colleire	inlebran coleri
rianctsecht conóige	frianetsecht conoighi	rianctsecht conoige
rocindset afeli	rochindset aféile	rochindset afeli
109. Felere roscrutas	109. Feilire roscrutus	109. Felire roscrutas
iccin 7 acus	iccéin isafoccus	hicén 7 ocus
laduthracht dorignius	fiad ainglib doriguius	laduthracht dorignius
doncemaib doradas	dodainib[b] domtus	donoebaib doratus
113. Doratsat ambendacht	113. Doratsat ambendacht	113. Doratsat ambend*ach*t
forcaclnuen notgeba	forenchóen notgéba	forcechnæn notgeba
doragsat diafrestal	doragat diafrestul	doragut diafrestal
inaimsir atbela	inaimsir atbela	inámsir atbela

89. Not (earthly) science hath wrought the pious lucid booklet, but the angelic aid of the King, Jesukin fair, lustrous.

93. A fair synod came to me in the midcourt of my house that I might correct it[c] before them according to the rule of heaven's King.

97. It is not (earthly) knowledge that hath prepared it—it is a sin to us if we assert it—(but) every saintling with purity hath wrought his chapter.

101. The order of the chapters, if there be any who disturbs, I say before this number it is an outrage to this host.

105. The host hath adjusted the booklet with piety: by their death with perfection they determined their feasts.

109. I have searched out a calendar afar and anear: with desire I have wrought: to the saints I have given (it).

113. They have given their blessing to every one who shall repeat it: they will come to attend him at the time he shall die.

* MS. diaforirglem   [b] l. donoebaib   [c] lit. 'for correcting of it.'

RAWL. B. 512, fo. 54 b.	LAUD, 610.	LEBAR BRECC, p. 104.
117. Labethaid aanmæ iflaith gréne gile iarnabreith sech ingra fordindgna seacht nime	117. Labenthaid aanma hiflaith greine gile iarnabreith sech ingru fordingna .uii. nime	117. Labethaid aanmæ hiflaith greni gile iarnabreith sechingra fordingna .uii. nime
121. Nidichell nadermad incach narotuirmead acht cuimriugud indsce fosons docuibded	121. Nidermat nadichell inchaich narotuirmed[a] acht cumrugud indsci lasoas dochuibded	121. Nadermat nadichell incach narotuirmed acht cuimbrignd indsce fosons docuibded
125. Cebetis secht tengtha amgin soee suilbir cobrath mó each dealmaim isend madoruirmeand	125. Ciabeitis .uii. tengtha imgin sóer suilgind cobrath mó each delmum issed mad doruirmim	125. Cebetis .uii. tengtha amgin soee suilbir cobrath mocech delmaim issed madoruirmind
129. Niroach narudrad anlebran colere acht taithmet conoige[b]	129. Niroach narudrach inlebran co leire taithmet nócm conoighi	129. Ni roach narudrad inlebran coleri acht taithmet noeb nóige
lasoas foreide	lasoas corćide	lasoas forédi
133. Cesareid arlebran coluith[ig]e altæ nisuirge nasotla rocruide mórpartæ	133. Cessu reid inleabran coluathaigi alta ní suiri[c] na sotla rocruidi morparta	133. Cesu réid arlebran coluithige altae nisuirgi nasotlæ rocruide morpartæ
137. Pairt adbul ambroisi seis clair colleire andgraib hironimi martarlaic iosebi	137. Pairt adbul ambrosi seis elair coleiri angraib hirumini martarlaic eusébi	137. Pairt adbul ambrossi seis elair co léri andgraib hironimi martarlaic eusebi
141. Sloiged lebar nerend asatrebar toiden rotúirsim andirmand felere fer ngoidel	141. Slóged lebur neirenn asatrebor tóiden rothúirsem andirmann feilire fer ñgoidel	141. Sloiged lebur[d] nerenn asatrebar toiden[e] rothuirsem andirmand felire fer ngoedeal

117. With life of his soul in the realm of the white Sun, having been borne past miseries, on the hills of the seven heavens.

121. (There has) not (been) forgetfulness nor neglect of every one who was not recounted : but (my book is) an abridgment of speech with[f] science which was harmonized.

125. Though there were seven tongues in my mouth of eloquent wisdom until Doom —greater than any noise[g]—this I should not recount.

129. Not *roach* nor *rudrad* is the pious booklet, but a commemoration of perfect saints, with science and[h] smoothness.

133. Though smooth be our booklet with gladness of verse, neither . . . . nor vainglory hath (here) milked great tomes.

137. The vast tome of Ambrose : Hilary's pious *Sensus*, Jerome's *Antigraph*, Eusebius' Martyrology.

141. Ireland's host of books, whose troop is prudent, we have searched a great number of them, the calendars of the men of the Gael.

[a] MS. narotairmed [b] l. connoebe. [c] L. ni suirgi. [d] Facs. Sloig edlebur [e] Facs. toiten.
[f] lit. ' under ' [g] the poet refers to the 'crack of Doom.' [h] lit. ' under.'

RAWL. 512, fo. 54.	LAUD, 610, fo. 70, b. 2.	LEBAR BRECC, p. 104.
145. Foirtgillim cenruided cerois allechta nifuigbe laluchta feleri bas certa	145. Fortgillim cenrudrad cérosis allechtu nifoigbe laluchtu feilire bas certu	145. Fortgillim cenruidiud cerois allechtu nifuidbe laluchtu felire bas certu
149. IScaitbir dochoimet acetal cen merbæ ismur tren cen dolma fridoine fri demna	149. IScathair dochomét achetul cen merba ismúr tren cen dolmai fri demon fri demna	149. IScathir dochoimet achedul cenmerbai ismúr tren cen dolmai fridóeine fridemnai
153. Fridia isdiubart frí deman isdinert issalm sloindeas mórnert isfeleri fircert	153. Fri dia isdúbart fria deman isdinert issalm sloindes mornert isfeiliri fírchert	153. Fridia isdubart frideman isdinert issalm sloitudes mornert isfeilire firchert
157. Cachæn diamba easnad asærcetal mbuansa imbithfl*aith* inrigsa no*d*ansnaidfi[a] insluagsa	157. Cachócndiamba besenad asho[e]rchetal mbuansa imbithflaith inarigsa snaidfidi insluagsa	157. Cechæn diamba esnad asærchetul mbuansa imbithlaith inrigsa nodosnaidfea insluagsa
161. Sluag romaith indrigsa lasata mobagsa beas comland annuallsa daraceann amrathsa	161. Sluag romaith narigsa lasa atá mobágsa bescomland anuagsa[b] taracend amraithsa	161. Sluag romaith inrigsa lasata mobagsa bescomland anuallsa daracend amrathsa
165. Amráthsa diaraithsim	165. Biamraithsa diaraithsium	165. Amrathsa diaraithsium
notgeba cachdia fortgillim cengua isinbithflaith imbía	nodgeba cachdia fortgillim cengua inbithlaith rodmbia	nodgeba cechdia fortgillim cenguba imbithflaith ronbia
169. Labethaid aannuc laxp. coemda ne*r*tlaith	169. Labethaid aanma lacri*st* cóemda nertlait[h]	169. Labethaid aannm lacri*st* coemdai nertlaith[c]

145. I assert without blushing[d] though thou shouldst repair to their grave, thou wilt not find with (any) folks a calendar that is more correct.

149. It is a city of protection, to sing it without mistake: it is a strong rampart without slowness against human beings,[e] against devils.

153. Towards God it is a vehement prayer: against the Devil it is vast strength: it is a psalm that declares great might: it is an unerring calendar.

157. Every one whose music is this noble continuous song, into this King's eternal kingdom this host (of saints) will convoy.

161. The excellent host of this King along with whom I fight: that this cry will be a conflict (with the Devil) I am surety for them.[f]

165. I am[g] surety for the grace of him who will sing it daily. I assert without falsity that he will abide in the Eternal Kingdom

169. With the Life of his soul, with Christ the loveable, mighty Prince: if he

---

[a] MS. nmodansnaidfi.   [b] MS. *no* anuallsa.   [c] Here is inserted the syllable ro*m*.
[d] B. 'tediousness.'   [e] B. 'against (the) Devil.'
[f] This version must be wrong: but I can make nothing else of the text.   [g] B. 'May I be.'

Rawl. 512, fo. 54.	Laud, 610, fo. 71. a. 2.	Lebar Brecc, p. 104.
diambagnath corocneit	diambu gnath corrochneit	diambagnath corocneit
abeith slan nideacmaing	ní báslan bas dechmaic	abeith slan indecmaicc
173. Madetal not gaba fodéraib conglaine fertai amrai ile dogen[a]tar aire	173. Mádettal notgéba fódéraib conglaine ferta amrai ile dogeinither airi	173. Madetal notgabai fodéraib conglaine ferta amrai ile dogenatair aire
177. ISarra .uii. naifrenn mad noeb aritlega isarra tri .l. dodilmain notgéba	177. ISarra .uii. naiffrend mad noeb aridlegha isarra thri coecat dondilmain nodgeba	177. ISarra .uii. noifrend matuoeb aritlega isarra .lll. dodilmain nodgebai
181.	181. ISarra anerdaig nafeilisea uile isnóemad aanma istroethad athuile	181. ISarra anaurthaig nafelesi uile isnoebad aanmai istraethad athuile
185. ISfirthabairt coibsean isarra tri treadan dicachpurt icanar isurnaigthi cet credal	185. ISfirthabairt choibsen isarra tri tredan docach phurt icanar ernaigthi chet credal	185. ISfirthabairt coibsen isarra .iii. tredan dacechpurt hicanar isaurnaigthe cet credal
189. ISeretair iscumand iscantaic forsalma isdidnad docredlaib isocenaire domarbv	189. ISeretar iscommand iscantaic forsalmaib isdidnad do chredlaib is denaire do marbaib	189. ISeretar iscomand iscantaic forsalmu isdidnad dochredlaib isdenaire domarbu
193. IS(todiu)sead etla cesa durda achride doformaig aanai berthi iflaith nime	193. IStodfuseud etla eid durdu achride sech doformaig ana berthi hiflaith nime	193. Stoduscad etlai cesadurdai achride doformaig aanai berthe hiflaith nime
197. ISluirech imerabud fri[a]slaige demna isdiorad figle isicaid cachtedmai	197. ISlúrech imerabud fria haslaigi demna isdiorad figli isiccaid cech thedma	197. ISluirech imchrabud friaslaigi demna isdiorad figle isíccid cechthedma

were acquainted with sorrow, for him to be saved will not be hard.*

173. If he who sings* it in tears (and) with purity is clean many wondrous miracles will be wrought for him.

177. It is a quittance of seven masses, if he who recites it is holy: for the freeman who shall sing it, it is a quittance of the thrice fifty (psalms).

181. It is a quittance of a splendid festival, all those feasts; it is a sanctifying of his soul: it is an abating of his desire.

185. It is a true giving of confession: it is a quittance of three three-days-fasting: for every place in which it is sung it is a prayer of a hundred believers.

189. It is a reliquary, it is a communion, it is a canticle on psalms: it is a solace to believers: it is a requiem for the dead.

193. It is an awaking of penitence though his heart be hardened: it increases his splendour: it bears him into Heaven's kingdom.

197. It is a corselet round piety against the Devil's seductions: it is a great prayer of vigils: it is a healer of every disease.

* This is very doubtful. Reading and meaning are both obscure. ᵇ B. 'shall sing.'

RAWL. 512, fo. 55, a.	LAUD, 610, fo. 71, a. 2.	LEBAR BRECC, p. 104.
201. IS(écn)aire imbetha frihomun cechbægail isnæbad dognimaib istinbuanad sægail	201. ISécnairee imbethu frihomun cach biégail isnóebad dognimaib istinbuanad sægail	201. ISécnaire imbethu frihomun cechbægail isnoebad dognimaib istinbuanad sægail
205. ISfoillsiugad fertai doformaig ceach mbordgal dobeir grad isardam iscomgabail ordan	205. ISfoillsiugud ferta doformaig eachbrotgail dobeir grád asardam conócaib ahordan	205. ISfoillsiugud fertai doformaig cech mbordgal dobeir grád isardam iscuingabaib ordan
209. ISuromun fiadat issearc deodai daingen isindarbad demun istochuired aingel	209. ISoromon fiadat issere deoda daingen isindarba demna istochuired aingel	209. ISauroman fiadat issere deoda daingen isindarbud demna istocuired aingel
213. ISadamra uile nafertai adfiadam bennacht foreach nduine atalegfa iarain	213. ISadamra uile naferta atūadam bendacht foreach ñduine ardileghfa iarum	213. Hitndamra uile naferta atfiadam bendacht foreech nduine atalegfa iarum
217. Combahed notgeisid donceoimde comaissi mila uire nipromfat nilobfat ataisi	217. Cimbaded nogessed dochomdid comaissi mila húre ní fromat nílobat athaissi	217. Conbahed notgesed donchomdid co maise mila úire nipromsat nilobsat athaisi
221. Aainim cencosnam iriched congile din eis iarnariachtain icfaid drucht alige	221. Annam cenchosnam irriched congili diaeis iarnariachtain icfaid drucht alighi	221. Aainim cencosnam hiriched congile diaéis iar[nar]ichtain icfaid drucht alige
225. Lataithmet afeli romain gress anguide nochansæthar madæ doruirmisium uile	225. Latathmet afeile rommain gres anguide ní consæthar mada dorurmisom huile	225. Lataithmet afeile romain gres anguide nochonsæthar madæ doruirmisium uile

---

201. It is a litany in life against fear in every danger: it is sanctification to deeds: it is making a lifetime lasting.

205. It is a manifestation of miracles: it extends every bordgal (?): it gives grade that is highest: it is an uplifting of dignities.[b]

209. It is dread of God: it is love divine, secure: it is a casting forth of devils: it is an invoking of angels.

213. Wondrous are all the miracles which we declare: a blessing on everyone who shall recite them then.

217. Provided that this be what he shall pray to the Lord with beauty, beasts of the mould (worms) will not prove him: his remains will not decay.

221. His soul (shall be) without conflict in heaven with whiteness: behind him after attaining it, the dew of his grave will heal.

225. At commemoration of their feasts, let urgency in beseeching them protect me:[c] it is not a vain labour that we have recounted all.

[a] leg. niphromfat ni lobfat?   [b] B. 'it upraises its dignity.'   [c] C. 'us.'

RAWL. 512, fo. 55, a.	LAUD, 610, fo. 71, a. 2.	LEBAR BRECC, p. 104.
229. Inrigr*ad* doruirmius isocus arcundu iartuire*m* afele dorime andrunga.	229. INrigrad doruirmis iso*cus* acundu iartuirim afeile dorimfem andrungu	229. INrigraid doruirmius isocus arcun*n*u iartuirem afeile dorimiub andrungu
233. Drong archaingeal nime lamichel soer sobail lanái ngrad rig rathmair	233. Drong árchaingel nime lamichel sáer sobail la nóe ngrád rig rath- mair	233. Drong archaingel nime lamichel sœr sobail laix ngr*ad* rig rathmair
cathrach inrig romair	catrach inrig romair	cathrach inrig romair
237. Drong reraich imnoe tarsalnuire sretha celi indrig flaithgil lahed aithgin inbetha	237. Drong rerach[a] imnóe tarsalmuir[e] sretha ceile indrig flaithgil bahed aithgin mbetha	237. Drong reraig imnoe tar salmuire sretha ceile inrig flaithgil bahed aithgin inbetha
241. Drong faithe iesaœ profetœ cain canmœ uasalathr*aig* guidine lahabraham namrœ	241. Drong fáithe imesnie profeta cáin can*m*a uassalathraig guidine la habraam namra	241. Dr*ong* faithe esaie pr*ofetœ* cain canmœ uasalathraig guidme lahabraham namr*a*
245. Drong apstal uimpetar condeisciplaib ih.u pól primda cen caclai ceann ecnai isdixu	245. Drong apst*al* uimpetar condeisciplaib issu pol primda cen ecla cend ecna asdixiu	245. Dr*ong* asp*ol* impetur condesciplib ihu. pol primdai ceneclai ccim ecnai asdixu
249. Drong martir la stefan dos ordu conglaine ancarrait imseanpol drong noebuag immuire	249. Drong mairtir imsteffan dos orta[b] conglaini áncharait imsenphol droug naemúng immaire	249. Dr*ong* martir lazefan doss ordni conglaine ancharaid imsenpol dr*ong* nœbuag immuire
253. Drong noehepscop romœ	253. Drong noeb epscop ro- mœ	253. Dr*ong* noebescop roma
impetar[c] anbordgal epscuip ier[u]salem laiacop nordan	impetar ánbrotgal epscoip iarusalem la iacop norrdan	impetar anbordgal escuip ierus*al*em laiacop nordan

229. The Kings whom I have recounted close is our friendship: after reckoning their feasts, I will[d] number their troops.

233. A troop of heaven's Archangels, with noble, holy Michael: with the nine ranks of the gracious Kings of the City of the exceeding great King.

237. A troop of ancestors with Noah over ranks of mainseas: servants of the white-realmed King—this was the restitution of the world.

241. A troop of prophets with Isaiah prophets, we sing beautifully: patriarchs we beseech with wondrous Abraham.

245. A troop of apostles around Peter with Jesu's disciples: Paul excellent, fearless: wisdom's highest step!

249. A troop of martyrs with Stephen the golden bush with purity: anchorites around Old-Paul: a troop of holy virgins around Mary.

253. A troop of the holy bishops of Rome around Peter—a splendid *bordgal* (?) bishops of Jerusalem, with James of sovranties.

[a] l. riarach   [b] MS. dosorta   [c] MS. imeps.   [d] B. 'we will number.'   . C, 'I number.'

RAWL. 512, fo. 55, b.	LAUD, 610, fo. 71, b. 1.	LEBAR BRECC, p. 105.
257. Drong epscop aantuaig lapetar pleo primdai epscoip alaxandri lamare ruadgorm rigda	257. Drong epscop ónantuaig lapetar breu primda epscoip alaxandriu lamaire romaith rigda	257. *Drong* escop inantuaig lapetur pleo primdai esc*uip* al*e*xandria lamare ruadgorm rigdai
261. Drong noeb onoráti cathmil sochla sluagach drong cenai rorigad labeinidecht mbuadach	261. Drong noeb honorati cathmil sochla sluagach drong cena romorad lab*en*dicat mbuadach	261. *Drong* noeb onoráti cathmil sochlai sluagach *drong* cenai rorigad labenidecht mbuadach
265. Drong airdi*re* giuirgi ni dedbul rafethim nachmac dochuaid martra la irvath imbethil [a]	265. Drong irdraic ciricii ní dedbol frifeithem cachmacc dochuaid martra lahiruath imbeithil	265. *Drong* erdaire giurgi nidedbol rafethim nachmac dochuaid martt*ra* lahiruath imbethil
269. Drong sacart rocraite docrist cestai cruichi domchoba*ir* cechlaithe laarón sab sruithe	269. Drong saccart adodpart corp cri*s*t cesta cruithi domchobair cachlaithe la harón sab sruithe	269. D*rong* sacart rocráite docri*st* cesta cruiche domchobair c*e*chlaithe laharón saph sruithe
273. Drong manach imantón	273. Drong manach immanton	273. D*rong* manach imantón
atarundai retha lamartain mil catha drong ard noeb inbetha	ata rúuda retha lamártain mil catha drong ard mém in betha	atarunda retha lamártain mil catha *drong* ardnoeb inbetha
277. Drong uasalnoeb nerenn	277. Drong huassal nóeb néirenn	277. D*rong* uasalnoeb nere*nn*
la*p*atr*aic* asardam col*um* cill*e* congaib condrongaib noebnalban	lapatraic as ardam col*um* chilli congbaid *con*drongaib uóem nalban	lapatraic isardam colum cill*e* congaib condrongaib noeb nalban
281. Drong dedenach dermar forcennai caingebenn	281. Drong dádenach dermair forcenda cáiu géibenn	281. D*rong* dédinach dermar forcenda cain gebend

257. A troop of bishops in Antioch with Peter, primal flame! bishops of Alexandria, with Mark red-fiery, royal.

261. The holy troop of Honoratus a battle-soldier, famous, hostful: a troop of sages who were crowned[b] with victorious Benedict.

265. Georgius' conspicuous troop, not paltry to contemplate: every child that went to martyrdom through Herod in Bethlehem.

269. A troop of priests who were tortured, (priests) of Christ[c] who suffered on a cross, to aid me every day, with Aaron champion of sages.

273. A troop of monks round Antony, whose courses are mysterious: with Martin, soldier of battle, a troop of the high saints of the world.

277. A troop of the high saints of Ireland with Patrick who is highest. Colomb Cille takes up with troops of the saints of Scotland.

281. A final vast troop which ends a

---

[a] In the MS. this quatrain follows the next.   [b] B. 'magnified.'
[c] B. 'who offered the body of Christ.'

RAWL. 512, fo. 55, b.	LAUD, 610, fo. 71, b. 1.	LEBAR BREEC, p. 105.
sancbrigit iarmbuadaib	sanct brigit iarmbuadaib	sanct brigit iarmbuadaib
conuagaib naherenn	conuagaib na heirenn	conuagaib noeb nerenn
285. INnadruingsi uili conardrigaib socraib domchobair cleirgelbain sluag dermar donoebaib	285. Innadruingsea uile conardrigaib socraib docholair cleir ṅgelbain sluagdermairdonóemaib	285. INadruingsea uile conardrigaib socraib domchobair cleir gelban sluag dermar donoebaib
289. Cach noeb bói fil bias cobráth brigach fodail icoimthecht xp. credail	289. Cach nóem búi fil bias cobrath brigach fodail hicoemthech crist credail	289. Cech noeb robui fil bias cobrath brigach fodail hicoimtecht crist credail
robet ocumchobair 293. Robet ocamchobair fornim 7 talmain cotisat nambuidnib dochungnam frimanmain	robet icomchobair 293. Robet icomchobair fornim isfortalmain cotisset nambuidnib dochungnum frianmanmain	robet acomchobair 293. Robet acomchobair fornim 7 talmain cotisat nambuidnib dochungnam frimanmain
297. Mainim mochorp cnedach cein beti frisoethar robet icomdignad inrigrad atrœthech	297. Maniu mochorp cnedach cein beiti frisoethar robet icomdidnad inrigrad adroethech	297. Mainiu mochorp cnedach ceinbeti fri srethar robet icomdidnad inrigrad adroitheach
301. Atrœthech indrigraid forsaraba iarair aisu cofirbail atateoch[sa] iaram	301. Atroethech inrigraid foraraba iarair a ibu. cofirbail atotecsa' iaram	301. Atroithech inrigraid forsaraba iarair aibu cofirbail atateocha iarum
305. Iartuirem nandrougsa anirdrig nad clithe axp. dianda céli misereri mihi	305. Iartuirem nandrongsa aardrí nadclithi acrist diambuchele misserere mihi	305. Hiartuirem nandrongsa aardri nadelithe acrist diandacéli miserere mici
309. Misereri mihi arigflaith fortuili	309. Misserere mihi ariglaith fortuiliu	309. Miserere mici arigflaith fortuiliu

bright chain, Saint Bridget, after victories, with the Virgins of Ireland's saints.[b]

285. All these troops with noble high kings, a fair white following to aid me, a vast host of saints!

289. Every saint who was, who is, who shall be till Doom—a mighty dividing—in company of pious Christ, may they be helping me!

293. May they be helping me in heaven and on earth, may they come in their troops to work along with my soul!

297. My soul, my wounded body, while these shall be in trouble, may they be consoling me, the kings whom I have besought.

301. I have besought the kings, for whom there has been search. O Jesus with true goodness, then I beseech thee.

305. After the recounting of these troops, O high King who art not concealed, O Christ to whom I am servant, *miserere mihi!*

309. *Miserere mihi*, O royal Prince, abund-

[a] l. ateochasa.   [b] B. and C. 'with the virgins of Ireland.'

Rawl. 512, fo. 55, b.	Laud, 610, fo. 71, b. 1.	Lebar Brecc, p. 105.
aihv. notcara	aihu. notcaru	aih.u notcaru
adé móir notguidiu	adé moir notguidiu	adé moir notguidiu
313. Adé moir notguidiv	313. Adé moir notguidiu	313. Ade moir notgúidiu
clvnti mocncit truaigsi	cluinte mochncit truaig-sea	clúinte moncit trunigsiu
robéo iarsinmbaigsi	ronbéosa iarsinmbáigsea	robeo iarsinmbaigse
imbithgnais intsluaigsi	imbithgnais intsluaig-sea	imbithgnais intsluaigsiu
317. Insluag [mór] dorinu	317. INsluag mor dorurmais	317. INsluag mor dorinu
atbath incach besena	atbath incach besenu	atbath incechbesenu
frit axp. isunisli	frith acrist asuaisliu	frit acrist isuaisliu
atsluindiu acestai	asluindiud acesta	atsluindiu acestu
321. Atslundeiu a fuile	321. Asluindiu afuili	321. Atsluindiu afuile
fírendgu forroena	fir endga for rócnu	firendgu forténu
atsluinniu analta	asluindiu analta	adsluindiu analtu
allaigne tria treba	allaigraib triatócba	alaigniu triantæbu
325. Atsluinniu acneta	325. Asluindiu acneta	325. Atsluindiu acnedu
anosnada fégi	anosnada féige	auosnadu fcige
frit acrist comtruaigi	firt acrist cotruaige	frit acrist comthruaige
atsluindiu afeli	asluindiu afeile	atsluindiu afeile
329. Fri tudrach indomuin	329. Fridudrach indomain	329. Fritudrach indomaiu
olismór adinert	olismor forñdinert	olis mor adinert
inutsa combantlacht	inmutsa cutbanlucht	imutsa combantlacht
atsluindiu asirecht	asluindiu asirecht	adsluindiu asirecht
333. Atsluinniu afirtu	333. Assluindiu aspirtu	333. Adsluindiu aspirtu
atrig flaith commassi	itriglaith comaissi	hitrigflaith comaise
duitsi olitfise	ol is dit it fissi	duitsiu olatfisse
atsluinniu atassi	assluindiu ataissi	atsluindiu ataisse
337. Nachitge not guidiu	337. Nach itge nodguidiu	337. Nachitge nodguidiu
duitsiu arnachera	ditsiu arnach nera	duitsiu arnach éra
tarangnuisi bana	tarangnuissi bána	tarærngnuisi bana
atsluindiu andera	asluindiu andéra	atsluindiu andéra

antly, O Jesus I love thee! O great God, I entreat thee!

313. O great God, I entreat Thee, hear my wretched sigh! may I abide after this battle in the everlasting presence of this host!

317. The great host I enumerate died in (the practice of) every rule: to thee O Christ who art noblest, I appeal by their sufferings.

321. I appeal by their blood truly innocent (poured forth) on roads. I appeal by their (severed) limbs, their lances through their sides.

325. I appeal by their groans, their sharp sighs, to thee O Christ with my wretchedness I appeal by their feasts.

329. Against the incitement of the world, for great is its vast strength, I appeal by their longing (as they stand) around thee with white raiment.[a]

333. I appeal by their spirits in thy royal kingdom with beauty: to Thee, for they are to be known, I appeal by their relics.

337. Any prayer that I pray to thee refuse not: I appeal by their tears over their, white faces.

[a] B. 'with thy fair folk.'   [b] A. 'our.'

RAWL. 512, fo. 56, a.	LAUD, 610, fo. 71, b. 2.	LEBAR BRECC, p. 105.
341. Atsluinniu doriched condermaire dai[n]gen omedon coimbel conoemairbrib aingel	341. Ashuindiu doriched anderamra daingen ómedón cohimel conóebairbrib aingel	341. Atsluindiu doriched condermaire ndaingen omedon cohimbel conoebairbrib aingel
345. Atsluinniu cachnidbairt atroidbred fobroenaib docorpan isuélaib foraltóirib nochaib	345. Assluindiu cachnedpairt atedpraid fó broenaib dochorpan isnélaib foraltoraib nóemaib	345. Atsluindiu cechnaudpairt adroipred fobrœnaib dochorpan isuolaib foraltoirib noebaib
349. Atsluinniunuallmbuada cias each mac lere brœnan fola naire triatoeban fodeine	349. Assluindiu nuall mbuada cias each mac leire bróenan fola uaire triathoeban bodéine	349. Atsluindiu nuall mbuada cias cech mac leri bróenan fala uaire trethoeban fodeine
353. Dodoendacht dodiadacht lat noebspirat ndelbda atsluindiu dotuidme lasinathair nemdai	353. Dodoenact dodeacht latnóebspirut ndelbda assluindiu dothuidmi lassin athair nemdai	353. Dodoenacht dodeacht latnoebspirut ndelbda atsluindiu dothuidme lasinathair nemda
357. Atsluinniu lat noebu frit anuall notraidiu condomraib itrigiu nachní arambaigiu	357. Assluindiu latnóebu frit anóg roraidiu conanraib itrígu aní ara[m]báigiu	357. Atsluindiu latnoebu fritanuag noraidiu condomraib itrigiu nachní arambáigiu
361. Nachbag forsa torchar momenma muad medrach labeim domchurp evinnech roguidet doteglach	361. Nach bág forsatorchair momenma muad medrach labeim dom churp cuibrech rogé deit dotheglach	361. Nachbág forsatorchair momenma muad médrach labeim domchurp cuimnech roguidet dotheglach
365. Cluinte lat aihu dodeorudan lobar ferr lium inas aund searad frisin ndoman	365. Cluinte lat aíh.u dodeoradán lobar ferr lim anda anad scarad frisindoman	365. Cluinte lat aih.u dodeorudan lobur ferr lium inasanad scarad frisindoman

341. I appeal by thy heaven, with (its) strong vastness: with holy cohorts of angels from middle to edge.

345. I appeal by every offering, which has been offered up in tears,[a] of thy Body on holy altars under clouds.

349. I appeal by the shout of victory which every son of devotion utters, by the rain of cold blood through his own side.

353. By thy Manhood, thy Godhead with thy beautiful Holy Spirit, I appeal to thy union with the Heavenly Father.

357. I appeal with thy saints to thee by all that I have said, that I may have in thy kingdom everything[b] for which I contend.

361. At every battle in which my proud, elated mind has fallen, at the smiting of my mindful body, thy household prayed.

365. Hear thou, O Jesus, thy feeble exile! severance from the world (seems) better to me than staying (therein).

[a] Lit. 'under showers.' [b] B. 'the thing.'

RAWL. B. 512, fo. 56ª.	LAUD, 610.	LEBAR BRECC, p. 105.
369. Corhicthar mobara lalogad mognide nidiultadach mochara atsluindein frit niliv	369. Coricthar mobara lalogad moguidiu nidiultach mochara assluindiu frit hvile	369. Corhicthar mobara lalogad mognide ní diultach mochara ats*laindiu* frit uile
373. Ailli [a] cliar nime nech naib ardomtuaisi cenbeith inbar ngnaisi ismor fodamgluaisi	373. Aille achleir nime nech naib arimthussa cenbith inforngnáissi ismor fodamgluaisi	373. Aille achliar nime nechuaib ardomtúasi cenbeith inbarngnáisi ismor fodomgluaisi
377. Fomgluaisi mor nguba sund isriched riudmas olismaith farcomgnas istrom form far ningnas	377. Fomgluaissi mor úduba sund irriched riudmas olismaith forcomgnas istrom form farningnas	377. Fomgluaisi mor nduba sund isriched riudmas olis maith forcomgnas istrom form forningnas
381. Conicid mochobair olismor barngaire slánaigid mocride arcenaire mic maire	381. Comiced mochobair olismor farngairi slanugad mochridi arcenaire m*ric* nuaire	381. Conicid mochabair olismor forngaire slanaigid mochride arcenaire m*r*i*c* maire
385. Morcumce itusa icorpan coel coda[i]l at mora mochinaid conice mo chobair	385. Morchumei itussa icorpan chóel chodail olit mora midain bamithig mochobair	385. Mor cúimce hitusa hicorpan choel chodail atmora mochinaid c*o*nicid mochobair
388. Manodtechtaid deseirc conatuiriun techta bui sund duib indisliu boctan frisba dentai	389. Mádonroute deerce inna tuirim" techta bói duib sund anisli bochtan frismā dénta	389. Manodtechtaid deserce conatuirem téchta búi sund duib inisliu bochtan frismbu dentu
393. Maconicsid coisced bamithid fartiachta atasunn isuaisliu deidblen dituaith ihv.	393. Manntechtaid coicsed bamithid far tiachtu atá sund as huatiu dedblen dethuaith issu	393. Maconicsid coisced bamithid fartíchtu atasund isuaisliu dedblén dethuaith ih.u
397. Ceni islind libsi argnuis inrig nellsa olamdeidblen truagsa cencobair modérsa	397. Cannieslin*n* libsi argnuis inrig nélsa olimdedblen truagsa cenchobair modérsa	397. Cenieslind libsi argnúis inrig nelsa olamdedblén truagsa cenchobair modérsa

369. Let my affliction be healed by rewarding my prayer: not given to refusal is my Friend, I appeal to thee by all.

373. Hear, O train of Heaven! let one of you perceive (precede?) me! not to be in your company greatly disquiets me.

377. Much sorrow disquiets me here below heaven beautiful with constellations, since your companionship is good, grievous unto me is your absence.

381. Ye are able to aid me, for great is your piety : heal my heart for sake of the intercession of Mary's Son.

385. Great the straits wherein I am, in a poor body, slender, skinny : great are my sins[b] : ye are able[c] to help me.

389. If ye have[d] charity, with its due attribute, here you have in lowliness a poor wretch to whom it may be shown.

393. If you be able to instruct, timely were your coming: here is he who is loneliest[a], a feeble one of Jesu's people.

397. Though you have no danger before this King of Clouds, yet I am this wretched feeble one, without help (to wipe away) my tears.

[a] l. cona tuirim.   [b] B 'pangs.'   [c] B 'it were timely.'   [d] D 'have wrought.'   [e] A. and C. 'Noblest.'

Rawl. B. 512, fo. 56.ᵃ	Laud, 610.	Lebar Brecc, p. 105.
401. Adrong noeb .uii. nime olismór farngaire slánaigid mochride arecnaire mic maire	401. A drong noebᵃ .uii. nime ól ismor far ṅgaire slanaigid mocride arécnaire naic maireᵇ	401. Adrong noeb .uii. nime olismor forngaire slanaigid mochride arécnaire maice muire
405. Arecnaire inrigsa frisnagar innuallsa farith ísintsnimsa inpauperan truagsa	405. Arecnairce inrigsa frisnagar annuallsa fárith arinsnimsa inpauperáin truagsa	405. Arécnaire inrigsa frisnagar innuallsa farith asintsnimsa inpauperáin truagsa
409. Cid truag lasnabraithri naguidisiu uile deit acrist intrat[h]sa rongadsa moguide	409. Cid truag lasnabraithriu naguidisca uile deict acrist intrathsa rogádsa moguidi	409. Cidtruag lasnabraithre naguidese uile deit acrist intrathsa rogadsa moguide
413. Guide itge naile tar cend fer inbetha acoimdi naflatha arí beres bretha	413. Guidiu itge naile tarcend fer inbetha achoimdiu na flatha arí beiris bretha	413. Guidiu itche naile tarcend fer inbetha achoimdiu naflathu ari berens brétha
417. Bes nipaill dudainib andubartsa uile dianéis arnabbarœ coemcloither inguide	417. Bes nibail doddiuib indubartsa uile diarneis arnab barn cloemchlaiter inguide	417. Bes nipaill dodainib indubartsa uile dia[r]neis arnapbarre cloemcloither inguide
421. Inguide rongadsa ni arule fridoine ferr lim inas anad scarad frisinsoegal	421. INguide rogád[s]a ni arule fri dóine ferr lem anda anad scarad frisinclóine	421. INguide rongadsa ni arule fridoine ferr lium inasanad scarad frisin clócine
425. Cluinte lat aihu. acrist diandacheli roerusi nili guide cach meic leire	425. Cluinte lat aih.u acrist dianam céile roheraso huile guide cach micc leire	425. Cluinte lat aih.u acrist diauda céile roeresiu uile guide cechmoc lére.
429. Guide cach meic leire acoimdi ni hespa roeresi doib madcoir angestai	429. Guide cach mice leire achoimdiu ní hespa rocrisi dóib mád cóir angestaᵈ	429. Guide cechmec lére achoimdiu nihespai roeresiu dóib madcoir angestai

401. O holy troop of seven heavens, since great is your piety, heal ye my heart for sake of the intercession of Mary's Son.

405. For sake of this King's intercession this cry is made, help ye fromᶜ this sadness, this wretched mendicant.

409. Though all these prayers seem wretched to the brethren, to Thee, O Christ, at this time I have prayed my prayer.

413. I pray another prayer on behalf of the men of the world, O Lord of the realm, O King that givest judgments.

417. Though all that I have said be not pleasing to men-folk, that there be not anger after us, the prayer is changed.

421. The prayer that I have prayed is not for evil to men. Severance from unrighteousnessᵈ I prefer to abiding (here).

425. Hear thou, O Jesus, O Christ, whose servant I am, grant thou all the prayer of every son of piety.

429. The prayer of every son of piety, O Lord, is not an idle thing: grant (it) to them if what they shall pray be right.

ᵃ l. soer. ᵇ l. bithomsa moguid[e], guididse maee maire. ᶜ B 'for' ('in').
ᵈ U 'the world' (saeculum).

RAWL. B. 512, fo. 56.[a]	LAUD, 610.	LEBAR BRECC, p. 106.
433. Madcoir angesta arí conic talmain ronsoera [a]curpa ronnæba ananmain	433. Mád cóir angesta arí cónic talmain rosoera acurpu ronoema ananmain	433. Madcoir angesta arí conic talmain ronsœra acurpu ronóebu ananmain
437. Ainim cach meic bethad istriut ronoebad sil nadaim asdixu aihu, rosaerad [a]	437. Anim cach micc lére istritsu ronóemad sil nádaim a[s]dixiu lahissu rosoerad	437. Ainim cechmec bethad istriut ronoebad sil nádaim asdixu aih.u rosœrad
441. Ronsoera aihv mocorp 7 manmain arcachule dochuisin frisioirg forsintalmain	441. Romsoera aissu mochorp 7 manmain arcachule docuissiu frisoirg for[s]intalmain	441. Romsœra aih.u mochorp ocus manmain arcechule docuissin frisoirg forsintalmain
445. Ronsœra aihu, acoimdi cain comul amal soersa heli laenóc dondomun	445. Romsoerasa aisu achoimdi cáincomul amail soersi héli lahénóc don domun	445. Romsœra aih.u achoimdiu cain comul amal sœrsa héli laheuóc dondomun
449. Romsœra aihv, arcachule forire amal soersa noe mac lamiach dondile	449. Romsóera a issu arcach nolc forire amail soersai nóe mac lamiach don dile	449. Romsœra aih.u arcechule forire amal sœrsa nóe mace laimech dondile
453. Romsœra aihu, ari glesi glaudre amal [soersai] abraham delamail nacallæ	453. Romsoera aissu arí gleissi glandæ amail sóersai abraham delámail nacallde	453. Romsœra aih.u ari glesi glandæ amal sœrsa abraam de lámaib nacallda[b]
457. Romsœra aihu, ari runda rathmar amal soersa loth dipeacad nacathrach	457. Romsoera aissu arí runda rathmar amail sóersai loth de phecethaib nacathrach	457. Romsœra aih.u ari runda rathmar amal sœrsa lóth depeccad nacathrach
461. Romsœra aihu, ari uasal amræ amal soeras ionas debrú ceti magnæ	461. Romsoera aissu arí uassal amra amail soersai ionas de brú cetí magní	461. Romsœra aih.u ari uasail amræ amal sœr[s]a ionas dobrú chéite magnæ

433. If what they shall pray be right, O King, who rulest Earth, save thou their bodies, sanctify their souls.

437. The soul of every son of Life through Thee hath been sanctified. Adam's seed that is highest by Jesus[c] hath been freed.

441. Free me, O Jesus, my body and my soul, from every ill which exists, which strikes on the earth.

445. Free me, O Jesus, O Lord of fair assemblies, as thou freëdst Elijah, with Enoch, from the world.

449. Free me, O Jesus, from every ill on earth, as thou freëdst Noah, son of Lamech, from the flood.

453. Free me, O Jesus, O King of pure brightness (?), as thou freëdst Abraham from the hands of the Chaldaeans.

457. Free me, O Jesu, O King mysterious, gracious, as thou freëdst Lot from the sin[d] of the cities.

461. Free me, O Jesu, O King high, wonderful, as thou freëdst Jonah from a great whale's belly.

[a] In the MS., lines 437-440 come before lines 433-436.
[b] MS. sechplagaib . delámaib [Facs. delámdaib] nacallda.
[c] A. and C. 'O Jesus.'

RAWL. B. 512, fo. 56.[b]	LAUD, 610.	LEBAR BRECC, p. 106.
465. Romsoera aihu. atriched [il]rathach am*al* soer*sai* isac dolamaib aath*ar*	465. Romsoera aissu itriched arratach am*ail* soer[s]a issaac delamaib aathar	465. Romsœra aih.u itriched i[l]rathach am*al* sœr[s]a isac delamaib aath*ar*
469. Romso*era* aihu. latnoeba tan tiastæ am*al* soer*sai* teela diginol nabiastæ	469. Romsoera a aissu lat nóebu tan tiastæ am*ai*l sóersai teclum deginol nobiastæ	469. Romsœra aih.u latnoebu tantiastæ am*al* s*oersai* teclam deginol nabiastæ
473. Romsoera aihu. arccnaire domath*ar* am*al* soer*sai* incop[a] dolamaib abrath*ar*	473. Romsoera aissu roherais domaithre am*a*il sóer[s]a iacob de láma[ib] abraithre[b]	473. Romsœra aih.u arécuaire dom*ath*ar am*al* sœrsa iacop delámaib[c] abrath*ar*
477. Romsoera aihu. areach ule nadrachrad am*al* soer*sai* ioain doncim ina uatrach	477. Romsaersa aissu areach nole nadrochrad am*a*il soersai eóin doncim inanatrach	477. Romsœra aih.u arcechnule nadrochrad am*al* sœrsa coin doncim ina nathrach
481. Romso*era* aihu. arife*rn* cotroige am*al* soer*sai* d*a*bid degail claidim golao	481. Romsoera aisu ariffirn cotróige amail soersa d*a*bid de gail chlaidib gólai	481. Romsœra aih.u arifern*d* cotróige am*al* sœrsa d*a*bid degail chlaide*m* góile
485. Romsoer*a* aihu. rosoerais nauile am*al* soersai susanna[d]	485. Romsoera aisu rosoerais nahuile susannam conordun	485. Romsœra aih.u rosœrais nahuile am*al* s*oersai* susadna conordan
iarsinforgol fui*r*re	iarsind forgiul furri	iarsi*n*forgul fuirre
489. Romsoera aihv. arccnaire dobaige am*al* soer*sai* ninuen indaims*ir* naplaige	489. Romsoera aissu arécnairce dobáge amail soersai ninuén inaimsir napláige	489. Romsœra aih.u arécnaire dobaige am*al* sœrsa ninuen inaimsir napláige

465. Free me, O Jesu, in thy many-graced kingdom, as thou freëdst Isaac from his father's hands.

469. Free me, O Jesu, when thou shalt come with thy saints, as thou freëdst Thecla from the monster's maw.

473. Free me, O Jesu, for thy Mother's intercession, as thou freëdst Jacob from his brother's hands.

477. Free me, O Jesu, from every evil that is not . . . . . as thou freëdst John from the serpent's venom.

481. Free me, O Jesu, from hell with (its) misery as thou freëdst David from the valour of Goliah's sword.

485. Free me, O Jesu, who hast freed all —as thou freëdst Susanna with sovranty after the lie concerning her.

489. Free me, O Jesu, because of thy conflict's intercession, as thou freëdst Nineveh in the time of the plague.

[a] MS. adds 'congradaib.' [b] In the MS. lines 473-476 come after lines 477-480.
[c] MS. congradaib . delamaib. [d] B. 'sins.' [e] MS. adds conordan.

RAWL. B. 512, fo. 56.ᵃ	LAUD, 610.	LEBAR BRECC, p. 106.
493. Romsoera aihv. gle lim ata ndidmæ amal soersai popul israel de monte gilbæ	493. Romsoera aissu gle lim atomdidmæ amail soersai popul israel de gilbæ	493. Romsera aih.u gle lim atumdidmæ amal sersa popul israel de monte gilbæ
497. Romsoera aihu. achoimde asdeodam amal soersa dainiel de cuithi nadeoman	497. Romsóera a issu achomdiu asdeodam amail soersai daniel assin cuithi leoman	497. Romsæra aih.u achoimdiu asdeodam amal sersa daniel asin cuithe leoman
501. Romsoera aihu. arig sochla soibis amal soersai moisen do manu faroinis	501. Romsoera aísu arí sochla suabnis amail soersai moysen de manu faraonis	501. Romsera aih.u arí sochlai sobis amal sersa moisoan de manu faronis
505. Romsoera aihu. mórferta dorignis amalsoersaina trimaccu de caimino ignis	505. Romsoera a íssu morferta dorignis amail soersa na maccu de camino ignis	505. Romsera aih.u morfertai dorignis amal sersa na tri maccu de camino ignis
509. Romsoera aihu. arig cecha clainde amal soersai tóbo dotroige nadaille	509. Romsoera a issu atrí cacha clainne amail sóersa tóba dethroige nadaille	509. Romsera aih.u arí cecha clainde amal sersa toba dethroige nadaille
513. Romsoera aihu. arecnaire domartrae amal soersai pol petar fiad rigaib de digail nacarcrai	513. Romsoera a issu aréenaire do martra pol petar fiadrigaib dedigail nacarera	513. Romsera aih.u aréenaire domartrai amal sersa pol petur fiadrigaib dedigail nacarera
517. Romsoera aihu. aracuis each tedmæ amal soersai iob de fochaidib nandemnæ	517. Romsoera aissu araccus cachthedma amail soersa iob de ochaidib demna	517. Romsera aih.u araccuis cechthedma amal sersa iob defochitib domnai
521. Romsoera aihu. acrist niropáilsed amal soersai dabid arsaul diatáinsium	521. Romsoera aissu acrist niropailsed amail sóersa dabid arsaul diatháinsem	521. Romsera aih.u acrist nirobailsed amal sersa dabid arsaul diathainsem
525. Romsoera aihu.	525. Romsoersa aissu	525. Romsera aih.u

493. Free me, O Jesu, I desire that thou wilt protect me, as thou freëdst the people of Israel *de monte Gilboae.*

497. Free me, O Jesu, O Lord who art divinest: as thou freëdst Daniel out of the lions' den.

501. Free me, O Jesu, O King famous, gentle, as thou freëdst Moses *de manu Pharaonis.*

505. Free me, O Jesu, who hast wrought great marvels, as thou freëdst the Three Children *de camino ignis.*

509. Free me, O Jesu, O King of every clan, as thou freëdst Tobit from the misery of blindness.

513. Free me, O Jesu, for sake of thy martyrdom's intercession, as thou freëdst Paul (and) Peter before kings from the vengeance of the prison.

517. Free me, O Jesu, from the anguish of every disease, as thou freëdst Job from the Devil's tribulations.

521. Free me, O Jesu, O Christ let there not be neglect, as thou freëdst David from Saul, from his censure (?)

525. Free me, O Jesu, for thy Mother's

RAWL. B. 512, fo. 56.[b]	LAUD, 610.	LEBAR BRECC, p. 106.
arecnaire domathar	arécnaire domaithre	arecnaire domaithre
am*al* soer*s*ai ioseb	am*ail* sóersa ioseph	am*al* s*æ*r*s*a iosep
dolamaib abrathar	delámaib abraithre	delamaib abraithre
529. Romsoe*ra* aihu.	529. Romsoern aissu	529. Romsæra aih.u
ari benedicti	arí benedicti	arí benedicto
am*al* soer*s*ai isr*ae*l co-noibe	am*ail* sóerasa isr*ae*l	am*al* sær*s*a israel conoime
dodoiri egipti	de ur cigipti	de dóire égipte
533. Romsoe*ra* aihu.	533. Romsoera aissu	533. Romsæra aih.u
olisfrit mocnairde	ol isfrit mocharde	olisfirt[b] mochairde
am*al* suer*s*ai pedar	am*ail* soerso petar	am*al* s*æ*r*s*a petur
dethondaib nafairgi[a]	dothondaib nafairrge	dethonnaib nafairrge[c]
537. Romsoe*ra* aihv.	537. Romsoera aissu	537. Romsæra aih.u
arifern [ngér] ngeinech	ariflirnu ngér goned	arifernd ngér uginach
am*al* soer*sai* ioain	am*ail* soersai eóin	am*al* s*æ*r*s*a eoin
asindabaig thenead	assindabaig thened	asindabaig thei*n*ed
541. Romsoe*ra* aihv.	541. Romsoera aissu	541. Romsæra aih.u
arig uasnaflaithib	arí uasnaflaithib	arí uasnaflaithib
am*al* soer*s*ai snmsón	am*ail* soersai samson	am*al* s*æ*r*s*a sámsou
terno asincaithir	terna asin cathair	ternai asincathir
545. Romsoe*ra* aihu.	545. R*o*msoera a*is*su	545. Romsæra aih.u
mainim areach ndigail	manmain areach*n*digail	manmain areech ndígail
am*al* soersai martain	am*al* soer*s*ai martain	am*al* s*æ*r*s*a mártan
arsacart ind idail	arsacart indigail	arsacart indidail
549. Romsoera aihu.	549. Romsoera a*is*su	549. Romsæra aih.u
arecnaire dothegla*i*g	arécnaire dotheglaig	arécnaire dotheglaig
am*al* soer*s*ai patraic	am*al* soer*s*ai patraic	am*al* s*æ*r*s*a patraic
dethonnagh ateamr*aig*	ditonnad itemra*ig*	de thonnud hitemraig
553. Romsoe*ra* aihu.	553. R*o*msoera a*is*su	553. Romsæra aih.u
olisduit ameéli	olisduit am céle	olisduit ameéli

intercession, as thou freëdst Joseph from the hands of his brethren.

529. Free me, O Jesu, O blessed King, as thou freëdst Israel with holiness from the slavery of Egypt.

533. Free me, O Jesu, for with thee is my covenant, as thou freëdst Peter from the waves of the sea.

537. Free me, O Jesu, from Hell sharp, greedy, as thou freëdst John from the vat of fire.[d]

541. Free me, O Jesu, O King over the princes, as thou freëdst Samson who escaped from the city.

545. Free me, O Jesu, my soul from every vengeance, as thou freëdst Martin from the priest of the idol.[e]

549. Free me, O Jesu, for intercession of thy household, as thou freëdst Patrick from the poisonous drink at Tara.

553. Free me, O Jesu, for I am a thrall

---

[a] In the MS. lines 533–536 come after lines 541–544.   [b] leg. frit.
[c] MS. *nafairge*, with a line across the left down stroke of the *r*.   [d] i.e. boiling oil.
[e] The reference is perhaps to the story told by Sulpicius Severus, *De Vita B. Mart. Lib.* c. xiii. (ed. Hornius).

RAWL. B. 512, fo. 56.b	LAUD, 610.	LEBAR BRECC, p. 106.
amal soersai coomgen decutaim intslebe	amal soersai coemgen dechutum intsleibe	amal sersn coemgin dechutaim intslébi
557. Romsocrn aihu. itbithbuan doferta acoimeli nonailiu frisailiur dothechta	557. Romsocra aissu it bithbuana therta achomdiu nanvili frisailiu dothechta	557. Romsœra nih.u atbithbuan dofertai achoimdiu nonailiu frisailiu dothechta
561. Intan domitecht irguis cid icaisc no icorgus romsnadat ipardus inrigrad imrordus IMrordus.	561. Tan dommitecht hirgais cid icaisc no corgus ronsnaidet diarndidnad indrigrad inrordus IMrordus. Finit. amen Finit.	561. Tan dommitecht hirguis cid hicaisc nocorgus ronsnadat diarndidnad inrigrad imrorduss IMrorduss inrigrad imunrig uns nélaib. 7c. F.INIT. amen

of thine, as thou freedst Coemgin from the falling of the mountain.

557. Free me, O Jesu, everlasting are thy miracles, O Lord whom I entreat, I await thy coming.

561. When I shall ask (?) a great boon of thee, whether in Easter or Lent, may the kings whom I have commemorated protect us to our solace.

565. I have commemorated the kings around the King above clouds.

GLOSS FROM THE LEBAR BRECC, pp. 103, 106.

26. *diulire* .i. dontalmain.
496. here *monte*, a gloss on *gilbœ*, is written in the text.
507. here *na tri* 'the three,' a gloss on *maccu*, is written in the text.

GLOSS FROM LAUD, 610.

1. .i. enair cokl. enair aile. 2. .i. dorónsam inrraid nafeile. 3. *cofirbail* .i. bail fort cofir. 4. .i. áselb bliadain infeilire. 5. buiden .i. uaib. 6. remain .i. remann isin feilire *no* cach dib renncheile. 7. *conecnaingsem* .i. robensam aurain .i. eráibind. 9. bahenirt .i. bafand. 11. *rosert* .i. rosreith *no* ronert. 11. *arbair* .i. sluag. 13. huassalathraig .i. aithri uaisli. 14. *ciaptar ceile* .i. ciapdar carait. 15. *illaini* .i. icombaine. 21. *luchtlach* .i. lucht *lan* .i. comlan. 22. .i. ligi flatha alaind [.i.] de . lestur ifilet da thúailli [leg. datha ailli]. lestur .i. nem. 25. *aconruale*. .i. roclai. 26. *diulire* .i. den talmain. 30. *brigach* .i. fertach. 33. *cain* .i. taitnemach. 34. .i. ismor 7 isadhbul ambrig 7 anert. 35. *dartuatha* .i. darnatúatha itait. 38. *iarscis* .i. iartairachtain infeliri *forurnius* .i. fonruirnuius mé imtast. 42. *loim* .i. bolcum [bolc loim Fr.] *doromuir* .i. domuir mor. 45. *cotomrocbat* .i. romtóebat. 49, 50. .i. nanaim frisaferaim faeilte icamolad nomsnadet cocrist caraim sech cach. 51. *comfuiriud* .i. commuintir 7 comcheill 7 comain[i]m. 54. *asdixiu* .i. isairdiu. 55. *rodicfa* .i. rosua coriched. 60. *atgiallat* .i. dia fognat. 63. *nas forudalaib* .i. inbarnairechtaib uaislib. 65. *dumrairbera* .i. [rom]tairbera. 71. *ba dillacht* .i. corp dilgudach. 72. *arécnaire* .i. arimpide. 73. *ingrafand* .i. dfelire *rofersam* .i. rogniscm. 74. *flatha* .i. nóib. 76. .i. martarlaig[a] 7 paisi nauáeb. 77. .i. istarba 7 isluireeh

* MS. mortarlaig.

crábuid dona hoscraib .i. dolucht cen ecna. 79. *arpeite* .i. airfited. 82. *linde* .i. ecna. 84. *frismelat* .i. molad *arinde* .i. atuiesc. 89. *soas* .i. fis maith. 94. *immideuairt* .i. imedonchuairt 97. *nihane* .i. niforbas *fotruar* .i. fodera adenam. 102. *boduama* .i. cumscaiges nafoili aluc doluc. 103. *atbeir* .i. fri betircert. 119. *sech ingru* .i. sech ingaire. 127. .i. ismo brath ina each delm .i. fogur. 128. *mad doruirmim* .i. mad diannáirbim. 129. .i. fat nimsire nasillab .i. ní rohuathad dorchugud *no* rodfrech *no* ní rochosmaili imrcera tarand. 134. *alta* .i. airchetal. 136. *morparta* .i. lebur. 137. *pairt* .i. libair *angraib hirumini* .i. feilire cirine[a] 143. *andirmann* .i. animmat. 163. *bescomland* .i. bid comlan fri denma. 166. *cachdia* .i. cechdia .i. cec[h]lái. 167. *cengua* .i. cengái. 177. .i. isamlaid is arra [.i. iseraic Fr.] máini fogbaither na haifrinda. 188. *credal* .i. craibdech. 199. *isdiorad* .i. isetarfuarad *no* cumdach. 209. *isoromon* .i. tossach uamain *fiadat* .i. dé. 230. *acuundu* .i. a cairdes. 234. *sobail* .i. bail maith. 242. *cauma* .i. canmait. 247. *cen ecla* .i. inbáis. 248. *asñixiu* .i. asnirdiu. 320. asluindiud .i. aitchim. 321. asluindiu .i. atchim. 322. *feige* .i. cruaide. 327. asluindiu .i. aitchim.. 329. *fridudrach* .i. miscais .i. tromdacht. 330. fornádinert .i. for nadbulnert fri miscais in domain. 369. *coricthar* .i.. icbascairi 7 ic slechtain *mobura* .i. mocemiti. 370. .i. cotardad dia dó ani roguid *no* corndilgad do marbécoir ani rocuindig. 371. *ni diultach* .i. ní diultadach. 372. .i. aithchim frit ar na huilisco anuas. 494. *gle* .i. maith. 538. .i. ger ora genedair iffirn.

[a] This gloss is written over the words *adbul ambrosi* in the preceding quatrain.

GLOSSARIAL INDEX.

-a for -æ or -e (see Z¹. 229), cétna, Prol. 202, andsa, Ap. 12, lobra Prol. 223, locharna Ap. 22.
a for c, by assimilation, Sapaint, Jan. 20, achad, Alaxandria Ep. 259, clochar Nov. 17, Comgall May 10.
a for i, anglind June 3, an imliuch Sep. 11, amgin Ep. 126, ambáithes Jan. 25 : by assimilation, martarlaic Ep. 140, ar-at-roglus Prol. 18.
a for o, fala Ep. 351, cabair Ep. 381, conamraib Prol. 11, tarba 143, prolach 144, deman Mar. 16, dabar Aug. 30, mctrapuil, Aug. 3, cotamrocbat Ep. 45, cotamroither Ep. 69, dénam Ep. 88, acom Ep. 292, 293 : by assimilation ; manach Prol. 97, ancharaid Ep. 251, apstal, Nov. 2.
a for u, nomolar, Prol. 13, libra Ep. 75, doman, March 16, asloudad, Oct. 24, codlad Dec. 27.
a elided, rog'bus, Prol. 18.
1. a, pronoun of the 3rd person. 1. possessive, gen. sg. masc. and neut. a (=Skr. asya) *his, its*, infecting : a thempuil Dec. 15, con- a chleir Sep. 2 : fem. a (= Skr. asyās, not aspirating) *her* : con-a-sethraib Aug. 30. After a *her* b is found : aháine, Prol. 127, and d is once written tt (a ttún daingen), Prol. 130, B. pl. a-n (before vowels, g and d) *their*, Prol. 58, 66, 67, 68, 150, 154, July 17, Oc. 28, a-m (before b and m) Prol. 34, 87, Jan. 13 al (before l) Oc. 13, Ep. 146, a-r (before r) Oc. 28, a before other letters. 2. personal infixed : dat. and acc. sg. masc. a-n, da-n, neut. and pl. a, da (infecting), fem. sg. a, da (not infecting).
2. a for san, neuter article, nom. and acc. sg. see ind.
3. a, prefix to numerals : adódéc *twelve*, acethair fichet *twenty-four* pref. B.
1. á prep. for as = ex, Prol. 126, Jan. 11, a h- Egypt, a héri Aug. 5, a h-Arnind, a h-Erind Nov. 21.
2. á interj. a christ Prol. 1, a crist Ep. 69, 319, 327, 426, a eiriu July 24, a rí Ep. 37. 433, a isu Prol. 303, 365, etc., a ardrí 306, a dé 312, a chliar Ep. 373, a drong 401, a choimdiu 415, 430.
ab (abann?) s. f. *river*, gen. sg. lédsa irricht inich aba *I went into a river salmon's shape*, LU. 16ᵇ, stagno abae fluminis, Reeves, Col. 60, dat. sg. abaind, pref. B. acc. sg. abinn Tir. 13, isinnabaind LU. 16ᵇ ; arrecat abaind LU. 24ᵃ.
abb. s. m. a t-stem, *abbat*, Z². 255, Jan. 2, 13, Feb. 8, 24, Ap. 8, 12, 18, 27, May 24, Oc. 6. 27, Dec. 6, acc. sg. gabs-i cadessin abbaith *he chose himself abbot*, Tirech. 15. W. abad. Corn. abat.
abbair, *dic* (ad-beir) pref. B. abbair a fir frind, LU. 55ᵇ, abrum *dicamus* Ep. 98, B.
Abbán. a man's name, dimin. of abb. Abbán mac h. cormaic, Mar. 16, Oc. 27. Cland maic ind abbáin = The Macnabs.
Abdon, July 30, a Persian prince, martyred at Rome in the time of Decius.
Abraam, Ep. 433. Abraham-n, acc. sg. Ep. 244.
Abundius, Feb. 27, a martyr at Thessalonica in Macedonia.
ac, prep. see oc : ac du guidiu-siu Ml. 22ᵃ. ac-a Prol. B. 227.
acciu, (ad-cesiu or ath-cesiu), *I see*, v. facca. inn-aci (gl. viden, videsne?) Z². 429.
accuis, s. *anguish* Ep. 518, seems the same word as accuis, which O'Dav. 48 explains by imnigh (leg. imnidi) *tribulationis*. If so, it is borrowed from, or cognate with, angustia:

GLOSSARIAL INDEX.

accais is also explained as *satire* or *malediction*, and P. O'C. has acais *rancour, venom, poison*.

achad, achad, s. m. *field*, in cathedra hac ipsa est achad fobuir, Lib. Arm. 13, b 1, gen. s. achid, achaid, Mar. 26, Sep. 5, dat. achud Aug. 9, Nov. 28, du achud fobuir Lib. Arm 13, b 1.

Achad Bó, Sep. 5, *campulus bovis*, now Aghaboe in Queen's county, written Achad-bou, Reeves Col. 121.

Achad Cáin, Aug. 9, now perhaps (acc. to Mr. Hennessy) Aughnakilly (Achadh na Cille), barony of Kilconway, co. Antrim. Proc. R.I.A. MSS. series i. p. 82, n. [Dr. Reeves thinks it is Achonry in the barony of Leyny, co. Sligo, otherwise written Achad cain conaire].

Achad Rathin, Nov. 28, now (according to Mr. Hennessy) Aughrane in co. Roscommon, near Athleague.

acht, *save, but, except* Prol. 194, Z. 703, derived from as *ex*, 3 Beitr. 276.

Acobrán, of Cell Roiss, Jan. 28, a dimin. of accobor *desire* (ad-color) Z². 222.

ac-om, Ep. 44, 292, 293, a combination of prep. oc *apud* and possess. pron. of 1st sg.

Aculius, May 27. Acculus, Aquillus or Aquilinus presbyter, an Alexandrian martyr.

1. acus, *and* Z. 699, generally ocus, q.v.

2. acus, *near* (2 Beitr. 159), hi cén ocus acus, Ep. 110=iccin 7 inocus, Patr. h.

ad-, a prefix Z. 867, which in the MSS. of the Félire is sometimes written at. ad-r-annad Ap. 5, ad-roi-pred Ep. 346, ad-it-cialla Feb. 23, ad-gleutis July 30, ad-muinter Oc. 2, ad-rannai Sep. 6, ad-reth Prol. 120, ad-rimeru Ep. 87. assimilated : accobor, atá.

adaig, s. f. *night*, acc. s. Dec. 24, cognate with aidche. Many fem. i-stems have a twin iā-stem. So sétig and sétche.

Adam, gen. ádaim, Prol. 131, July 15, Dec. 25, Ep. 439 = Adim Z². 223.

adamra, adj. *admirable*, Corm. 2: n. pl. Ep. 213.

adann, s. *rushlight* Corm. 4—Hence

*adannaim, adnaim *accendo*, 3d sg. pret. pass. atrannad (adrandad B, adrannad D) Ap. 5, i. robadnad *was kindled* .i. rotindsenad *was begun* : adhuadh .i. lasadh, O'Cl.

adba (adbai A), s. f. *house*, May 26 (=W. addef f.) : cf. adba othnoe Corm. acc. sg. con adba .i. con tech LU. 8ᵇ.

adbiur, *affero, offero*, an ā-verb : 3d sg. pret. pass. adroipred Ep. 346.

adbul, adj. u-stem, *vast, enormous* Ap. 25, June 1, 26, July 28, etc., gen. sg. m. adbail, Aug. 21, Dec. 12, gen. sg. f. aidble, Mar. 26, dat. sg. m. adbul Mar. 4, Ap. 26, dat. sg. f. adbail, July 27. n. pl. m. aidble Prol. 81, aidbli Prol. 133 B, n. pl. f. ? aidble Ep. 34, Comparative aidbliu Ap. 22 : adv. indadbol *valde* Z. 608. Skr. bala.

adcíu, *video*, see atchiu.

*addam-, atumdidmæ, Ep. 494 = ad-dum-didmæ. This is a reduplicated future active in the 2d. sg. : the meaning seems *thou wilt protect me*.

adfét, v. atfét.

adgiallaim, *I give pledges to anyone*, and hence *I submit, I serve* (see atgialla), 3d sg. pres. indic. act. conneuch ad-it-cialla, Feb. 23, where e is written for g to show the absence of infection after the infixed pronoun. Rawl. 505 has conneoch ad-idū-gialla.

adgliunu, *disco*, cornmaib adglentis, July 30, .i. rotoglandis co sians moir .i. nothuirdis *they used to learn with great sense*, i.e. *they used to search*, glen .i. tuir no foghlainn, O'Dav. 95. 3d sg. pres. indic. atgleinn Ml. 61ᵃ. cf. fogliunn (gl. doceor), Z. 428.

adlégaim, atalegfa *qui ea leget* (ad-da-légfa) Ep. 216 : cf. legenn, arléga

admat, s. m. (n. ?) *timber, material* Prol. 294 (now adbmad) ; isochma dodia corocumtaige cenadbar no de adbar deroil coch n-admat no coch n-aicde bes áil do, *God hath power to form without matter or of a trifling matter every material and every structure that is pleasing to him*, LU. 37ᵇ.

admuiniur Z. 949, admuinter (atmuinter B. O'Dav. 50) Oct. 2, is glossed by

GLOSSARIAL INDEX.

adamraigther no bendaich(th)er *is admired or is blessed* [cf. atmuinemar .i. bennachmaid O'Don. supp. admuinemmair noebpatruicc, Ninine's prayer]. But I would rather take adnuinter as a 2d sg. deponent indicative governing féili in the acc.

adnacim *condo, sepelio,* roadnocht *sepultus est,* pref. nephadnachte *inhumatus* Sg. 20ᵃ : root NANK, NAK, *tradere* (Zimmer).

adnacul, -cal s.n. *sepulcrum,* acc. sg. pref. B. an adnacul n-crsoilcthe *ró sepulchrum apertum* Ml. 22ᵇ.

adnaim, see adannaim.

Adomnán, (a dimin. of Adam), ninth abbot of Hí, ob. A.D. 703. dat. sg. Sep. 23.

adrad, s.m. *adoratio,* Prol. 187, gen. sg. adartha, acc. adrad Prol. 207.

adraim, *adoro* Zᵉ. 434, adorthar (adorthair B,) *is adored,* Nov. 23.

adrannaim, *divido,* 3d sg. impf. indic. act. adrannai (atrendai* A) Sep. 6, where the glossographer has .i. randait *they part :* see rann.

adrethim, *accurro,* adreth *accurrit,* Prol. 120, July 7, adreith Aug. 30 (adreth B), atreith Nov. 6, atarethusa (=ad-da-rethus-sa) *I attacked them,* 1 Proc. R.I.A. (MSS.) 170.

Adrianus, Nov. 6, son of Probus husband of S. Natalia, martyrized in the tenth persecution, Jameson S. and L.Art, 798. In Us. at this day there is a Nicomedian martyr.

adrímim, *numero,* Z. 867, adriquem *numeramus* Ep. 87, atrimem *quem adnumeramus* July 17. adruirim (gl. computaverit) Ml. 28ᵈ : cf. rími, do-rímin.

Adrion, an Alexandrian martyr, gen. sg. Adrionis May 17, Aug. 16.

adsluindiu, see atsluindiu.

ae, 1. diphthong for oe : saer, naem, tracthad, taebu, braenaib, etc. 2. vowel for e.

aed, s.m. n-stem, *αἶθος,* W. aidd. 1. *fire* Corm. 2, LU. 45ᵃ .2. a man's name, Prol. 204, Jan. 31, Glück K.N. 14. gen. Aeda pref. 39, Nov. 8 : compounded : Beo-aed Mar. 8.

Aed mac Bricc, Nov. 10, voc. sg. Aido mec Pricc, Mone's Hymni, iii. 181. Of Ralugh (Rath Aedha) in Westmeath, Joyce, 555. Reeves, Progs. R. I. A. Nov. 8, 1858.

Aed Oirlnigthe, overking of Ireland, pref. : the date of his decree exempting the clergy from military service is A.D. 803. Reeves Col. 389.

Aed mac Setna, first bishop of Ferns, Prol. 204, Jan. 31.

Aedán, (dimin. of Aed) of Lindisfarne (or Farne?), Aug. 31, Reeves Col. 374.

áei, umlaut of the diphthong áe : laeidib Prol. 334, saeir Aug. 14.

aei, pron. cech-aei (leg. cech-ae ?) *quivis* Ep. 43 : cf. cachus Zᵉ. 361.

áen, for óen, q. v. May 20.

Acngoba, (leg. Oengoba ?) gen. Oengobaud, pref. n.

áer, áir s. n. *vituperatio* Zᵉ. 30. acc. pl. aera, Nov. 8.

áeraim, *I reproach, satirize,* 3d sg. pret. pass. nir haerad *non vituperatus est,* Ap. 8, áirid *vituperatis* Zᵉ. 30.

Afraic, s. f. *Africa,* gen. sg. na hafraice, LU. abl. afraic, Aug. 28.

agaim, *ago, ludo,* agait *agunt* Sep. 4 : the gloss is .i. oentaigit, – leg. oenaigit no subaigit. So O'Cl. aghaid .i. aonaighid no bid go subach : 3d sg. pres. pass. agar. *agitur* Ep. 406. So in O'Dav. 53 : athgabail agar a fai(th)che nemid is coir a ditiu *a reprisal that is driven from a noble's green, it is right to protect it.*

agaid, s. *face,* agaid inagaid *vis-à-vis* pref. agad fochoel, LU. 55ᵃ, nom. pl. aigthi, LB. 8ᵃ : root AK, whence oculus, ὄψις.

Agatha, Feb. 5, Aug. 30. A Sicilian virgin, Jameson S. & L. Art, 608.

Agatho, July 5.

áge, v. áige.

Agna, (ἀγνή) her natalis Jan. 21, for Agnes a Roman virgin and martyr, Jameson S. & L. Art, 600.

ai umlaut (epenthesis) of a : manaig, Jan. 17. ái umlaut of á : pláige Ep. 492.

* The rhyming word in A is glandai.

2 e 2

GLOSSARIAL INDEX.

-ai for -a : nodgcbai, Ep. 180.
ai for oi : mainistir Dec. 7. ai for ui : saegail Ep. 204, riagail, Ep. 96, domain, see domun.
ai from i by progressive assimilation : Mártain, Afraic, Patraic, athair : by progressive harmonization, Eutaic.
ái, (diphthong) for ói : laid láidib Prol. 314. 323, taided Jan. 1.
-aib, -ib, suffixed dat. pl. of the pron. a.
aiccept, s. m. *a lesson*, gen. sg. aicceptu pref. B. acc. aiccept ib. Low Lat. accepturium.
aicde, s.m. (u.) *fabric, structure* Corm. B, gen. sg. aicde (leg.-di) Prol. 293, acc. sg. aicde, supra s.v. admat : moiser aicdi ara deimne O'Dav. 80, aicdhe .i. cumhdach, O'Cl.
aicc, *apud eum*, pref. B. a combination of the prep. ac and the pron. e.
aichne (aith-gne) s. : *means of recognition, mark*, pref.
Aidbe, of Tír-dá-glas, May 24.
aidble, s. *vastness*, dat. sg. June 29, Oc. 4, Dec. 4, 19. deriv. from adbul q. v.
aided v. oided.
aige, áge, s. *pillar*, pref. Prol. 119. 243. 339. Feb. 7, 10. Mar. 21, May 24, 25. July 6, 31. Sep. 5, Oc. 10, Nov. 2, gen. sg. áigi (aighi B, aige A) May 3. The word is glossed by calma *brave* (leg. colna *column*?) Prol. 119, by tuir *pillar* Feb. 7, Mar. 21, and by colna *column*, May 25 :
ail, see aill.
Ailbe, Sep. 12, Dec. 30, bishop of Imbliuch Ibair, now Emly, ob. A.D. 534. His Latin life, E. 3. 11. (T.C.D) fo. 133. a. b.
áildi, áilli v. álaind.
aile, pron. =alius, ἄλλος, 2 Beitr. 159, Z². 358, acc. m. Ep. 413 : neutr. aill = ali(u)d.
ailgis, s.m. *a request, a suit*, int-ailges, S. M. i. 300. and Corm. 4, gen. sg. ailgiusa, I.U. 38ª ailgesa S.M. i. 300, acc. sg. ailgis, Jun. 13, where the glossographer explains cen ailgis by ni egean roailges riu *not necessary with them* (is) *importunity*, nilgius (ise doral ailgius for findtan) Dinnsenchas cited in Petrie's Tara 105. rolaisi trá fodcoid algis fairsium, I.U. 39ª. Hence ailgesach *importunate*.
Ailill, son of Dunlang, gen. Ailella, Oililla Dec. 9, (=Ailello Lib. Arm. 11, b. 1, 12, b. 1), acc. Ailill Prol. 178.
Ailithir, of Muccinis May 12, (oilithir A), fourth abbot of Clonmacnois, died A.D. 599. Reeves Col. 24 : cf. ailither *pilgrim*, ailithre *pilgrimage* (dat. ailithri Ml. 154), ailitherde *peregrinus*.
ailiu, -= óro, an ia -verb, no-n-ailiu *whom I beseech* Ep. 559, no-dn-áili (notnaile A, nodnale B), nodnali D. *who beseeches him*, July 9, no n-ailem *we beseech him*, July 14, ailme *we beseech* Jan. 10, Aug. 5, 2d sg. imper. ail *beseech* Oc. 4. 3d sg. s-pret. abs. áliss Tir. 11, fut. part. pass. bed ailti (gl. ad implorandum) Ml. 65.
1. aill, ail s. Ep. 417, *will, pleasure*, mad aill duib *si placeat vobis* Z². 453.
2. aill, pron. v. all.
1. aille, s. n. *praise*, gen. sg. Aug. 8 (.i. laudis B), acc. Ap. 26 (.i. molad) .i. laudem, Three Ir. Gl. 131, gen. pl. aille Ep. 83.
2. aille, *hear* July 3, Ep. 373, 2d sg. conjunctive : cf. aill .i. cluin, O'Cl. Gl. .i. cluinte O'Dav. 47.
Aillen (leg. Aillén ?) gen. sg. May 29, doire inghen aillen, Mart. Don. at May 29.
Ailliu, gen. sg. ailiune Prol. 189 ; a palace of the Kings of Leinster on Cnoc Ailinne near Old Kilcullen, co. Kildare, see O'Curry, Lect. 492, note (67), where another form of the gen., ailend, occurs.
ailsed, (áilsed ?) s. *neglect*, Ep. 522. This word occurs in S.M. i. 58, 60 (where it is rendered by *violation*) and 286, where it is rendered by *neglect*. I have found it glossed by faill : uilbe *negligence* P. O'C.
ailt, adj. (.i. uasal O'Cl.) Sep. 26.

GLOSSARIAL INDEX. ccxiii

aimser, s. f. *time* pref. (W. amser), gen. sg. aimsire Z^2. 242. dat. aimsir, amsir Ep. 116, 492, Z^2. 243, acc. aimsir Z^2. 244, n. pl. aimsera pref., acc. aimsera Z^2. 246.

ain, see anach.

ainbech, adj. .i. imda *abundant*, Mar. 24, .i. mor no trom no uasal *great or heavy or noble*, July 20, dat. s. anbich (ainbig, B. rhymes with chraibdig) Mar. 30. Seems a compound of the neg. prefix an and *bech a by-form of becc *little*.

ainbil, adj. *penurious*, n. pl. m. aiuble, anbli, Nov. 9, *sordid?* The glossographer here, as often, gives three interpretations: ainbhil *stingy, penurious*, P. O'C.

aine, ane, s. Ep. 97, seems to mean *wisdom*, or *knowledge* : cf. O'Cl. aine .i. ái án no aoi án .i. ealadha mhaith no fios maith.

1. áine, s.f. *gladness*, Prol. 67, 127, dat. sg. áni Feb. 6, Oc. 8, is glossed, Prol. 67, 127, by aibnius *gladness* and by airfitiud dat. sg. of airfited *music, rapture*: n'imda febach fuaim n-aine *not abundant is a goodly sound of gladness*, Gl. 868.

2. áine, s. f. *splendour* dat. áni, Jan. 19, 28, Mar. 6, June 4 B, June 28, July 2, 13, Aug. 3, 22, Nov. 6, 27, Dec. 5, 26, acc. sg. anai Ep. 195. deriv. from án.

3. áine, s. *jejunium*, dia áine *Friday* pref. 16, in aine 7 hicetain LU. 25^b, better óine, cf. inti óinus qui abstinet, Z^e. 31, aoinim .i. troisgim O'Cl. ni aened ní nábui irrect ríg Amra Chol.: roainius mo trodau ... roáinius nomaid LU. 16.

ainech, s. *face*, O.W. enep (gl. faciem), ἐν-ωπή : see clár-ainech.

aingel, s. m. *angelus*, n. pl. augil Z^2. 226, gen. pl. aingel-n Prol. 132. Ep. 344, dat. pl. ainglib Ep. 85, acc. pl. ainglin, anglin Prol. 7, 159. Mar. 10, May 23, 28. July 12.

ainglech, adj. *angelic* Mar. 4, 10, 16, June 9, July 28, Nov. 22, Dec. 6, Ep. 91.

ainim, see anim.

ainle, (anle D) adj. 1. *fair, well-featured* P. O'C. Mar. 22: 2. Ainle, a man's name, June 21.

ainm, s.n. *nomen* (W. enw, ὄνομα) Prol. 171. Jan. 31. Mar. 19. Ap. 10. May 12. July 13. Nov. 30. Dec. 26. gen. s. anma Z^2. 268, dat. anmaim, anmaimm 269, acc. sg. Prol. 112, n. pl. perhaps anmand May 19, anmann Z^1. 269, but see anim infra. Compound : noebainm.

Ainmire, a man's name gen. Ainmirech, pref.=Ainmurech, Ainmuireg, Reeves Columba 91, 201. The nom. is latinised Ainmorius ib. 32.

áir, see anáir *anterior, east*.

airethid, s.m. *inventor*, pref. From airec *invention, finding*.

airdae (leg. ardae?) s. f. Jan. 8, seems here to mean *a height*, in apposition with epscop: airde (gl. celsitudo) Ir. Gl.

airdire, airdere, irdraic, adj. i-stem, *conspicuous* (περιδερκής ? Ebel), Mar. 21, compar. irdurcu, irdorcu, airdircu Z^1.276. Hence urdarcaigim (gl. celebro) Corm. celebrad. Root dark, Skr. driç. Lat. larva from *dareva (Siegfried).

aire, s. *care, heed*, doralus ar m'aire *I have put for my care, I have had in mind* Prol. 15 : cf. cid dorala ar barn-aire ! F.D.G. 62, translated *what object occupies your attention?* cf. mairg dobeir seire do duni menes tarda dia airi Sgl. Conc. LU. 49^b. tabrad cách dia airi LU. 34^a. is lathe bratha dorat dia aire LU. 14^a. and the similar phrase co tucsat dia n-uid LU, 51^a :

airec, *to find*, airecar *invenitur* Z^e. 471. 3d sg. pret. pass. airecht Aug. 3=airnecht O'Dav. 50.

airec, s.m. *a finding* Feb. 27, gen. airice pref. secla airice na crochi, Leb. Br. p. 237. see prímairec and ic and cf. fuirec (fu-airec) Z^2. 470.

airenach, s.n. *forefront*, dat. sg. airenach, aerinuch Prol. 118 : in airinuch ind rígthige, LU. 99^b : in airinuch in tige, LU. 101^a. O'Cl. explains airenach by tosach *beginning*, Pl. airinigi (leg.-e) *fronts?* LU. 99^b.

Airer, Dec. 29 B.

Airerán, Dec. 29 A. Eleran D, lector of Clonard.

airi, aire *for him* Ep. 176.

Airie, name of a river, gen. Airgge, Argge, Eirge, Jan. 2.

airitiu, s. a *taking, reception* Z^2. 264. Feb. 2, May 26, June 8, a fem. n-stem (are-EM-tion). gen. sg. airiten Z^2. 265, dat. airitin Z^2. 214, acc. tre airitin (gl. per assumptionem) Z^2. 266. In O'Dav. 50 the phrase forutha airitiu oighedh do cach ina moam seems to mean *a guest's reception is due to everyone according to his service*.
áirle, árle, s. *will, counsel* Prol. 261. airle .i. comairle, O'Cl. Gl.
airliuss, arlius, adj. *deserved ?* Sep. 27 seems a derivative from arilliud *meritum* ; but O'Dav. 50, explains it by cendais *gentle*.
airnecht (air-chon-echt), v. airec.
aisndéid, aisneid, asnéid (as-ind-féid, root VID), *make known, declare* Oct. 14, Aug. 29, cf. aisndis *expositio*, Z . 885.
aiste, s.f. pref. seems to mean *a peculiar kind of verse, style* : isi aisti aran dernad in cennportsa *this is the measure in which he made this preface*. II. 2 16. col. 684.
aite, aidde, s.m. (gl. nutritor) *fosterfather, tutor*, Mar. 19, May 28, Ep. 65, air danimmart greim á aite, *for his tutor little restrained him*, Z. 1066 : cf. Goth. attâ *mother* Gr. ἄττα.
aith, adj. i-stem, *sharp, keen*, aith amhail altaiu *sharp as a razor*, O'Dav. 53 : compar. aithiu (.i. gériu, B) Mar. 31, superl. cia aitheamh éo *what is the sharpest of points ?* O'Dav. 81.
áith, s. fem. i-stem (W. odyn) *kiln*, gen. na hatha pref. B ; acc. inn-aith ib. dat. isin aith pref.
aith- a prefix (in aith-gin, aith-met) 're-'=*iru*, Lat. et. et(iam), at(avus).
aithbi, aithbe, *ebbeth*, Ap. 15 (.i. tragenu, Rawl. 505) Aug. 12, : aithbhe .i. traghadh no laghdughadh mara *ebbing or abatement of sea*, O'Cl.
aithgin, s.n. *restitution, equivalent* (O'Don. suppl.) Ep. 240. In Ep. 240 (A and C) inbetha should be mbetha, as in B.
aithigim, *I visit*, 3d sg. pres. indic. aithigid, athigid, Prol. 224.
aithis, aithiss, s. *opprobrium*, acc. sg. June 24, Aug. 7 : athis maile *disgrace of baldness*, Bruden dá Derga, aithisigther (gl. imputatur) Ml. 22ᵃ.
aithmet, s. *remembrance, commemoration ?* Sep. 19, gen. sg. aithmet, (leg. aithmeit) ? Aug. 15 : cf. taithmet.
aittreb, s. v. bith-aittreb, treb.
al, by assimilation from an : im-al-luid *round whom went*, Aug. 23.
ala, v. dorala.
álaib, adj. *beautiful*, Sep. 3 : O'Dav. 50, glosses by glig no coccill no álainn.
alaile, pron. *another, quidam*, Z^2. 359, acc. sg. Prol. 325, v. aruile.
álaind, adj. *beautiful, pleasant*, Mar. 19, May 1, Aug. 30=álind Z^2. 234 : acc. sg. m. Oc. 23, n. pl. m. aille Prol. 133, aildi, ailli Jan. 9, (for álndi, álindi) it ségdai 7 it áildi na caern, Táin bó Fráich : briathra aildi la cechtar de frialaile 7 meumeo togaisc calleic la cechtar de *verba pulcra apud utrumque in alterum et mens fraudis statim apud utrumque* Z. 564 n. The superl. áildem occurs in Táin bó Fráich and Scirgl. Conc. aldem LU. 129ᵇ. The compar. áille (O. Ir. áildiu Z^2. 275) in Mart. Don. 176. Hence áille *beauty* : in folt do rofáilli *the hair of great beauty*, Táin bó Fráich.
Alaxander, (bishop of Alexandria and confessor, Rawl. 505) Feb. 26, Alexander abbot of Rome Ap. 27 : Alexander II. Pont. Max. is mentioned by Boll. at 22 April. There was also a S. Alexander, the martyr, a soldier of the Theban legion.
Alaxandria, *Alexandria*, Ep. 259.
Alba, s. *Scotland*, gen. sg. Alban Mar. 23, Ep. 280, Z. 264, dat. Albain, Alpain Ap. 21, Alba Jan. 8, albai (alba B) June 25.
1 all, s. n. *cliff, rock or steep cliff* P. O'C. Jan. 6. With all nglaine cf. all togu Goidel. 176.
2. all, pron. ἄλλος, *alius* : n. pl. m. aill . . . . aill (gl. alii . . . . alii, B.) Prol. 23, 24, June 5. This pronoun has hitherto only been found compounded in ull-slige *another way* Z^2. 358. So arall, n.p. m. araill : comérgit ulaid ara ammus. araill dib for less. araill for dorus liss, LU. 60ᵇ. araill do macnrid ulad *certain ones of the children of Ulster*, LU. 72.
altar, (alltair ?) s. m. (n.?) *another place, the other world*, gen. sg. alltair May 10, acc. s. Prol. 283. cf. arphein in alltair Gill. 53.

GLOSSARIAL INDEX.

alt, s. m. a *joint*, *limb* (= artus?), acc. pl. altu, Ep. 323, or is it from álath, aladh, which seems to mean *wound* in Z^2. 949, O'Dav. 120, s.v. tiscail?

altae, Ep. 134, in the phrase co luithigi altae (.i. airchetal B.) seems gen. sg. (or pl. ?) of alt .i. aircetal, O'Dav. 47. gló-alt. i. glain-innsce no innsge glan, O'Cl.

altóir, s. f. (W. allor, Corn. altor), *altóre* Z^2. 249. gen. sg. altora, teacht fa ix. atimcheall na haltorn *to go nine times round the altar*, 10 Proc. R.I.A. acc. sg. Tir. 3. dat. pl. altórib Ep. 248, 43.

1. am, *I am* Prol. 26. Ep. 104, 165, 399, 554, asmi, εἰμί.
2. am, *ro̊*, the neut. article before a labial, Ep. 29, 30.
3. am, *their*, the possessive pronoun 3d pl. before a labial, Prol. 34, 87, Jan. 13, Sep. 2, Ep. 113.
4. am, negative prefix, am-labor June 20, Z^2. 860.
5. am, for im, Jan. 25.

amach, adv. *out* pref. B. Mid. and Mod. Irish for immach, immag : *in*, *into*, mag acc. sg. of mag *field* a neut. s-stem, Ebel, Beitr. v. 225.

amal, prep. *instar*, *like*, as Prol. 208, Z. 657, cognate with samail=similis.

Amantius, mart. Niveduni (Nyon), Boll. June 6, Dec. 5.

Ambifanus, see Amphianus.

Ambonius, see Umbanius.

amlabor, adj.(W. aflavar), *mutus*, June 20 : dat. pl. dunaib anmandib amlabrib *mutis animalibus* Ml. 55^d.

Ambrois, Ap. 1=Ambrosius Ep. 137, born at Treves, A.D. 340, bishop of Milan, 375, died 397.

Amphianus, (corruptly Ambifanus A) an African martyr, April 2.

amlaid, see *thus* pref. B.

amm, (better ámm) s.n.=agmen Dec. 18, Rawl. 505 and Laud 61. ám (gl. manus, hostium), Ml. 36^b : dat. ond-ammaim (gl. manu) Ml. 36^d.

amrae, amra adj. *wondrous*, *wonderful*, gen. sg. f. Feb. 8, acc. m. Ep. 244, voc. m. 462. n. pl. n. Ep. 175, gen. pl. m. July 4, Oc. 5. Compar. amru Aug. 20, amradair Amra Chol. see adamre supra.

amsán, s. m. dimin. of amus *soldier*, (amos Corm.) : n. pl. amsáin Prol. 152.

amus, s. m. (n. ?), *temptation*, acc. sg. amus-n O'D. Gr. 443, gen. pl. amus Jan. 30. Hence aimsigud *a tempting*, LU. 10^a.

1. an, for san, nom. acc. neut. of the article : see ind.
2. an, possess. pron. 3d pl. see a.
3. an, relative pronoun (for san), asan (*e quo*) Ap. 4 : before a labial am : ar-am -báigiu Ep. 360.
4. an, conj. *when*, Jan. 25. Z^2. 709.
5. an, adverbial prefix : see anáir, an-all.
6. an, negative prefix in anfót July 30 : see Curtius, Gr. Et. No. 420. In an-bail it seems to have an intensive meaning.

án, adj.*splendid* Prol. 171. Jan. 11, Feb. 8, 24, Mar. 24, Ap. 19, May 16, June 17, 20, July 7, 31, Aug. 5, Dec. 27, acc. sg. m. Prol. 303, acc. sg. f. áin May 16 B and D, gen. sg. f. áine, dat. sg. f. áin Oc. 20, n. pl. n. ána. It seems to occur in composition with ainm Feb. 16, aurthach, Ep. 181, bree, Ap. 23, June 2, bordgal Ep. 254, cethrur Jan. 20, cing, Feb. 25, croau Prol. 51, eirge (leg. airge?) Jan. 2, epscoip Jan. 29, orba Jan. 8, suba Dec. 17. But in the MSS. the words are often separated.

anach-, *protegere*, anich, aingid *protegit* Z^2. 430, 431. anacht *protexit* 455, menit-ainge ben *unless a woman protect thee* LU. 15^a, 3d sg. s-conjunctive -ain *protegat* Prol. 18 (cf. nit-ain, LU. 116^b), Ap. 11, 22, Aug. 28, Oc. 29, Dec. 22, Ep. 226, ainsium (=ainis + um) Jan. 30, 3d sg. 2dy s-conj. cómnair noda-ansed *happy he who should protect them* LU. 90^a : cf. ainech *protectio* Z^2. 476. The guttural is uninfected in ainced, anacul *protection*, nim-aincend *non me protegit* Corm. s.v. aittenn (=nim-anaice B), roainicfind *protexero* F.D.G. 75.

anad, s. m. *a resting, staying*, Ep. 367, 423 : nibo sirsan int-anaal LU. 44ᵇ: gen. anta S. M. i. 98. acc. rogáid Labraid dó anad dind imguin, LU. 48ᵇ.

anai, see áne.

anáir, adv. *from the east* Feb. 13, fri grecia anfar et fri etail anair *contra Graeciam ab occidente* et *contra Italiam ab oriente* Z². 612 : see Z². 57 n. tanic iarum Manannán anair *then M. came from the east*. Sgl. Conc.

anall, adv. pref. *illinc* Z. 567.

anamchara, s. m. *a spiritual guide* (Skr. kalyâna-mitra), lit. *soulfriend* : is maid mo anamchare (gl. nonne Jesum Christum dominum vidi ?) Z². 255, dat. anmcharait, pref. B dat. pl. anamchairtib, acc. pl. anamchairtea (gl. doctores), Z². 258. Hence anamchairtes *institutio* Z². 254.

anathais, seems gen. sg. of some man's name, Anastasius ? Sep. 7.

anbail, adj. i-stem, *very great, excessive*, íta anbháil *sitis nimia, great thirst*, Martyr. Dom. 2ᵇ, gen. sg. m. (or n. ?) anbail Feb. 17 : anbhal .i. romhór, O'Cl. gl. Skr. bala.

ancharait, s. u. *anachoretae, anchorites* n. pl. Ep. 251, cf. Corn. ancar.

anerist, s. m. (W. annghrist) *Antichrist*, acc. sg. Sep. 29. S. Michael is addressed as a marbad anchrist ainglig in H. 2. 16, col. 336.

and, adv *there, then*, Z². 353, pref. Prol. 164. May 1, annsin pref. annsom Prol. 260.

andach, s. m. (n. ?) *anger*, gen. andaig, annaig, Prol. 237 .i. feirgi. Three Ir. Gl. 126. Query if this be not the same word as annach q. v.

andgnib, s. ἀντίγραφον ? Ep. 139, title of some work said to be by S. Jerome. O'Clery has 'Grailb hieronimi .i. feilire no sgribheann chirinc,' whence it appears that he regarded the *and* as the Irish article. The word occurs in Wb. 26ᵇ commimmis angraib dúilsi do gabaal desinrechta diinn *that we be a copy to you for taking example from us*.

Andreas, Andrias, Feb. 6, Nov. 30, Saint Andrew.

anfót, s. *incaution, heedlessness*, July 30, Corm. 21 s.v. fót. O'Cl. writes anbfhott and explains it by ainbfios, *ignorance*, fod .i. fios.

aní, pron. *that, illud* Ep. B. 360.

anim, s. f. *soul* Z². 264. Corm. Br. enef. May 22, Ep. 19, 53, 221, 437, gen. anma Ep. 169, anmae Ep. 117, anmai Ep. 183, dat. anmain Jan. 24=aumin Z². 265. ainim Ep. 52, acc. anmain Aug. 21, Dec. 12, Ep. 296, 436, 546, n. pl. anmin Z². 267, gen. pl. anman Mar. 27, dat. anmanaib Z². 267, acc. anmana ib. In Middle Irish the pl. is identical with that of ainm *nomen* viz., n. and acc. anmand, gen. anmand-n. dat. anmandaib, and perhaps in May 19 we should translate anmand by *souls*.

Anissus, Mar. 31. leg. Anesus or Anesius, an African martyr.

annach, s. (.i. olc, O'Dav. 50) *evil*, gen. annaig, annaich, Feb. 16, dat. sg. dian anduch Ml. —48 : cf. andgidiu (gl. nequior) Z². 275. indandgid (gl. nequiter) Z². 608.

annsin, annsom v. and

ansa, andsa, adj. *hard* Ap. 12=anse, annse *difficilis* Z². 42, 970 : ris nid andsa .i. ris nad dolig. Sgl. Conc. W. anhawdd.

Anterinus (Anatherius B) May 4, from Anterus, papa et martyr, Boll.

Antón, Ep. 273, gen. Antóin, Jan. 17, Antonius an Egyptian hermit.

Antonius, Aug. 9, for Antoninus 'martyr apud Graecos,' Boll.

Antuach, *Antioch*, dat. antuaig, antoig, Feb. 22, July 27, Ep. 257.

Apolloin, gen. Ap. 10 = Apollonius pr. mart. Alexandriae. Boll.

Appoloin July 22.=Apollonius a Roman martyr, Boll. at July 23.

Apollonaris, A, Appollinaris B, June 4,=Apollinaris D, perhaps the first bishop of Ravenna, martyrized temp. Vespasiani. A martyr of the name is mentioned by Boll. at June 5.

april, apreil, *Aprilis*, s. gen. sg. Mar. 27, Ap. 1, 30.

apstai, s.m. (W. apostol) *apostle*, gen. apstail, epstail, Jan. 18=apstil Z². 223, aspoil Prol. 109.

n. dual, dá apstal July 15. n. pl. apstil Z^2. 226. gen. pl. apstal Nov. 2. dat. apstalib Z^2. 227.
Aquilinus, an African martyr, Jan. 4.
1. ar, (1) prep. *for* (=παρά, Lat. per, Nhg. ver-) Prol. 12, Aug. 20, Oc. 8, Ep. 422, *for sake of* Mar. 12 ; with verbs signifying *to protect, to save*, it must be rendered in English by *against, from*: see Jan. 24, 30, Feb. 3, Oc. 29, Ep. 538, 548 ; cum dat. *in addition to* May 13, Oc. 9 : *before :* argnuis Jan. 9.
    (2) conj. *for, because*, Prol. 18, 55, 263. Z. 679.
2. ar, from an *ro* by assimilation: ar-réim-siu, *that course*, Oc. 16.
3. ar, defective verb, *says*, pref. B.
4. ar, possess. pron. v. aru.
A'ra, see áru.
arachind, pref. B. =arachinum Z^4. 622, *before him*, literally : *ante ejus caput*.
araibe, pref. B. *because of*, lit. *quia fuit*, ar raibe.
araile, pron. (W. arall) *another, other*, gen. sg. aroile pref. 47.
áram, s.f. *number*, acc. sg. árim, July 15, W. eirif : see Curtius G. E⁴. No. 488.
arbar, s.m. *a host, throng, cohort*, gen. arbair Ep. 12=arbir (gl. coortis) Lib. Arm. 188. b. 1. dat. pl. airbrib LU. 17ᵇ, O'Dav. 50 : acc. pl. ránic axalu la airbrim archangliu, LU. 9ᵇ. oll-arbhar .i. sluagh mór, O'Cl.
arbélaib, nom. prep. *before, opposite* O'Don. Gr. 289. nirubi tinfed arbelaib x 7 n. *there was no aspiration before x and* n, Sg. 21ᵇ. ar bledma baile bélaib Nov. 20= arbélaib bledma baile *opposite strong* (Slieve) *Bloom*, a mountain in Queen's county. Maith or inrí frisin forthaigis tinta cia as toisech fodla 7 arandentar bélaib LL. 207 a. 2. anumbélaib *before us* Trip. Life, B. 163ᵃ. arabélaib *before him* ib. 166a. arfarmbelaib *before you* Tain bó Fráich. See bél.
archaingel, s.m. *archangel*, gen. sg. guth ind archaingil, LU. 34ᵃ. gen. pl. Ep. 233.
archena, adv. *besides* pref.
archrinim, *deficio*, 3d sg. redupl. pret. ar-ro-chiuir *defecit*, Prol. 67. 127, 3d pl. arrecoratar Ml. 26⁴, fobithin ar-a-chiurat *quia defecerunt*, Ml. 59ᵇ. cf. erchnae inchrin, arinchrinat, Z^2. 868, 430, 433.
1. ard, adj. *high* (cf. Ardnemna. Lat. arduus), Feb. 6, June 9, July 21, 31, Nov. 10, Dec. 3, Ep. 12. gen. sg. f. airde Jan. 2, dat. sg. f. aird July 27, (ard A) Nov. 13, n. pl. m. aird Prol. B. 155. Compar. ardu Z^2. 275. Superl. ardam Mar. 23, Dec. 27, Ep. 207, 278.
    compounded : with aige Prol. 119, 243, Feb. 7, Oc. 30, ainm June 3, césad Mar. 22, erail Jan. 1, ethre Oc. 31, imel Prol. 131, noeb Ep. 276, rí Aug. 5 (acc. ardrig Ep. 60. vv. ardri Ep. 306, dat. pl. ardrigaib, Ep. 286), riched Ep. 18.
2. ard. s.f. *a height* Prol. 168, gen. sg. arde July 24, but ad aquilonalem plagam airid mache Lib. Armach. 7 a. 2, oblatione airdd macha, ib. 20 a. 2, and aird sratha Aug. 23, abl. ard, Dec. 16, n. pl. arda June 25.
Ard Breccáin, Sep. 4, now Ardbraccan in Meath, gen. sg. familiam aird breccáin Lib. Arm. 15. b.
Ard Camrois, (Cáin-rois?) Dec. 16, now, according to Mr. Hennessy, Camross in co. Wexford.
Ard Macha Prol. 168, and see May 28, Nov. 27, now Armagh.
Ard Már, gen. Arde Máire, July 24, now Ardmore, in the barony of Decies within Drom, co. Waterford.
Ard Sratha gen. sg. aird sratha Aug. 23, familia aird sratha Lib. Arm. 11. b. 2 : now Ardstraw, in co. Tyrone.
ard, s. seems to mean *alliteration*, pref.
ardlig, *decet, convenit*, June 1, Aug. 5. See dligim.
arfét, Mar. 23 (atfet B. adfet D. .i. roairim *he recounted*, 3 Ir. Gl. 130), a contraction of arfeded *narrabat* as arfet Ap. 18 (atfed B. arfeit D.), a contraction of arfiadad, *narratus est*.

2 *f*

arlich, *fregit*, Ap. 15 (ardig B and D). The glossographer explains this by *robriss fregit* and O'Clery by *dobhris*, but is not lich - Lat. vicit?

argnáis, nom. prep. *before* Jan. 9, Ep. 398 : see gnúis.

arlégaim, *perlego, recito*, ar-id-légu *qui id recitat* Ep. 178, airléch (gl. pellige, recita) Z.^{2} 443, conar légidsi (gl. vos legatis) 441, ronírlég in baithis *he read out the baptismal office*, Todd L. II. 29.

árinim, *numero* = áirmim Z.^{2} 435, armaid *numerat*, from áram q.v.

armuiniur, *reueror, honoro*, 3d sg. pres. indic. pass. armuinter (atmuinter B, admuinter D), May 6 ; cf. arsas-muinethar feid *cum honoret* Ml. 36^d, aratnuinfersu feid (gl. te veneratus, egrediar) Ml. 63^d.

ar-n, pron. poss. *our* before vowels, g and d : Z.^{2} 339, Prol. 90, 293, Aug. 15, Sep. 20, Ep. 2. ar- m before b ; Ap. 21, ar before other letters, Prol. 86, 141, May 28, 30, Aug. 24, Sep. 30, Nov. 2, 27. Dec. 14. Ep. 9. suffixed to prepositions : di-arn, q.v.

arná, post. neg. *ne*, Z.^{2} 744, Prol. 297, arná-p *ne sit*, Prol. 323, Ep. 419.

arnabárach, *after the morrow*, Feb. 15, A, better iarnabárach D, intráth nóna arnabárach, Táin bó Fráich : báit and iarum eo arnabárach ib, im-bárach=W. yn fory Z^2. 617.

arnách, part. neg. *ne*, Ep. 338. Z^2. 744.

Arón, the high Priest, gen. Aroin July 1 (deposition in Mount Hor). acc. arón Ep. 272.

arpeti, arpheto, *canit* Ep. 79 : aruspettet (.i. sennit) anés ciuil, LU. 57^b : peiteadh .i. airfideadh, ceol no lánneas, O'Cl. ba binniu cec ceol in chrot arpete hibraid loingsech lore, LU. 9^a.

arrae, s. *value?* Ep. 177. 179, 181, arra 186, glossed by eric *mulet*, O'Dav. 50, arra .i. tuarusdul. ut est séna in arra .i. intuarusduil, H. 3, 18, p. 51^b. also glossed by fiach *debt*, geall *pledge*, and ic *payment*. DC. arreum remissio poenae, permutatio imminutio vox hib. Z^2. xl : 'arra' means the thing itself, or a thing similar to what was injured, stolen or destroyed ; anarra means a different thing, as e.g. a horse, or a cup in place of a cow, laws III. 150 note.

arriefae, *adibis?* arriefam *adibimus?* Dec. 30.

arsaichim, arsaigim, *adeo*, arsaigcis B (atsaigtis A) *adibunt* Sep. 30, v. saichim.

arselaim, *praetereo, effugio*, ardonsela *a nobis digreditur* June 23 : root SAL, SAR *to go*, Skr. srí, Lat. salio ? The same root occurs in con-selai .i. ro-elai, Br.h. 62 and in the noun sel : cachla sel . . . in sel n-aile *modo . . . modo* Z. 500.

arslig, *slays* Sep. 29. tongu . . . arnomsligfitis *I swear that they would slay us* LU. 90^a, root SLAC, Goth. slahan. D has arsil *occidet*, the 3d sg. s- future, which is clearly the right reading.

Artae gen. Artai, June 7, (Airti B) : ἀρταῖοι οἱ δίκαιοι παρά Πέρσαις, Justi 30, 'Αρταῖοι *Persians*, Herod. 7. 61.

artúaisi-, arslom-tuasi, Ep. 374, should be -túaisi to rhyme with -glúaisi. The meaning is obscure to me.

artús, *ad initium, at first* pref.=arthuus Z^2. 610. W. tywys.

:ru, (gl. rien) Z^2. 16 (=W. aren) *kidney* : also a name for an island ' Arran' in Bay of Galway : dat. áraiun, áraind Nov. 21. cf. the Praenestine nefrones, Gr. νεφροί. The gen. áirne, Mar. 21, comes from a different stem.

1. as, (1) *qui* (quae, quod) *est*, Prol. 185, Mar. 20, Sep. 24, Oc. 23, Ep. 55.

2. as, prep. ex, *iž*. in composition with the article and pronouns : assin, asin, *out of* the Ep. 500, 540, 544, uacht Ap. 19 (not *a huacht*) the retention of the s is strange. Can we here have the equivalent of ἔξω ?

asa, assa *whose is* Prol. 50, 98, 330, Ap. 9, 16, Aug. 11, Sep. 23, Nov. 25. Ep. 86, 142, *quorum, quarum* Ap. 9, asa-rsechmaillius (gl. quorum praeterii nomina) Gild. 82. The as- seems the verb subs. in its relative form, and the -a is the possessive pronoun. The form isa occurs in the LB. 121^a, line 44 (inti isa flesc foran-ásfad 7 foran-nicfithi druclit 7 duile 7 torad selb ua sacerdoti dothabairt do, *he on whose rod dew and leafage and fruit should grow and should be seen, to him possession of the priesthood should be given.* ise so intárchangel asa-guth resan erigfe in cined doemna ' *hic est archangelus cuius voce in die iudicii omne humanum genus consurget* ' LB. 73ᵇ, line 50), and Mart. Don. 156. O'Don. Gr. 131, 132, gives this as the gen. sg. of the relative.

ascnam, s. *accessus* Z². 868. *acquisitio, adire, obire,* Prol. 262. Dec. 31. asguam .i. imthecht O'Dav. 50 : inm-us-ascnat (gl. ob(v)iaverunt sibi), oc ascnam tíre tairngire, Z². 234, *visiting* (not *in possessione!*) *the land of promise* : root skand.

ascomore, *cædere*, 3d sg. pret. pass. ascomart *cæsus est*, Oc. 19. 1 sg. pret. act. ascomort (gl. cecidi) Z². 454 cf.: asort, as-r-ort *occidit* Ap. 23, las-r-ort Prol. 106. see asore, ore.

aslach, s. n. *seduction, temptation*, like many nouns in -ach (e.g. étach, airenach, oenach, fásach, erdach) declines in the singular as an a-stem (gen. aslaig Z². 855), acc. aslach Z². 653. dat. asluch, aslug, Z². 855), but in the plural as an s-stem : acc. pl. aslaige Ep. 198. The dat. pl. aslaigthib Patr.h. Rawl. B. 512 is a mistake for aslaigib. The verb occurs in LU. 13᷾ : ní roaslaig heris for nech, and in LU. 51ᵇ: issí roaslaig fair *she solicited him*.

aslondud, asslonnud s. m. *declaratio* (= O'Clery's aslonnadh .i. atach no aisnéis no innisin) July 9. Oc. 3, 24 : see slondim infra.

asore, *occidere*, asoire *cædit* Z². 430, 3d sg. (pret. asort (=asoret) Ap. 23. 3d sg. pret. pass. as-r-ort, asort Oc. 7 : cf. ascomore.

asrala, *evasit* Ap. 3=as-ro-ala.

as-r-indid, Jan. 12, if the true reading be Críst as róma rindid, seems the 3d sg. pret. of aisndedim q.v. asríndid (gl. retulit) Ml. 58ᵃ.

assa, gl. *socens* Sg. 22ᵇ v. lethassa, pl. assai Corn. fual, and cf. W.hosan, Corn. hos, Ohg. hosa. 2 Beitr. 175.

asselba, Ep. 4 (B) seems to mean *thou hast possession* (selb, W. helw). But the three MSS. here differ, and the true reading is therefore doubtful.

1. at for ut, infixed pron. of the 2d sg. nach-at-risad, Prol. 284, at-at-eoch(spa, Ep. 304.

2. at, pron. of 3d sg. occurs suffixed in the forms bath-at *he has*, lit. *apud eum est*, ciat *let him go*, tri-t, tremi-t *through him*. In ar-at-roghus Prol. 18, it seems a corruption of *it*, O. Ir. *id*. In éat Sep. 22 at occurs in composition with é *they*. At is often suffixed to the absolute forms of the 1st pl. in verbs and the first sg. of the b-future: cf. the Latin use of hic for ego.

3. at, a prefix for O. Ir. ad, Z². 867. But in at-chissiu, atíadam, atgiallat, atrinem the t may due to an infixed pronoun.

4. at, *thou art*, July 19.

5. at, *they are*, Prol. 151, Ep. 335, 387, 558, a corruption of it, Z². 488 : cia-t *quinneis sunt* Prol. 153, at-e *qui sunt*, Prol. 34, cat-éat Sep. 22.

ata, ata-n *whose are*, ata cléri cóema *whose trains are lovable*, Mar. 14, ata móru míli *whose thousands are great*, Ap. 6, ata mórthruim trethain *whose seats are very heavy*, June 27, ata n aidble brígn *whose powers are vast* Ep. 34, ata rúnda retha *whose courses are mysterious* Ep. 274. This is the pl. of asa *whose is* q. v. In O. Ir. ata sometimes seems to mean *who are*. So in Ml. 16ᵇ inna hé ata *qui sunt*, itsib ata chomarpi abracham, *it is ye that are A's heirs*, Z². 660.

atá, *est* (= ad-tā *astat*) Prol. 172, Ep. 162, 395, pl. atát *sunt*, pref.

atach, s. n. *a prayer* Aug. 8, attach trócaire, atach faesma O'Dav. 53. See attach infra. atagur oro LU, ataich (gl. obsecro) Z². 652=ataig Aug. 22.

ataim, *confitere* pref. B. ataimet *profiteatur* Z². 432, = addaimet LU. 100ᵇ, at-n-aim *he admits it* O'D. supp.

atatiam, Oc. 26. This obscure form does not rhyme, as it ought, with laair and is obviously corrupt. The MSS. vary greatly : dothiem B, ataniam D, and in marg. ata fiaid [nach mod ata fiaid .i. cipe mod on innisid eat] : atachiam, Three Ir. Gl. The true reading is suggested by O'Dav. 86 and is atafiadaid, i.e. ad-da fiadaid, the 2d pl. imperat. of adfiadaim, with the infixed pronoun da of the 3d plural : adfiadat .i. aisneidit H. 3, 18, col. 520.

2 f 2

athath. *obiit, periit*, Prol. 163, 190, Ep. 318, a t-preterite ; 3 pl. athathatar : cf. πέ-φα-ται, φα-τός.
atbail-. *mori, perire*, atbail (gl. evanescit) Z^2. 430=epil ibid. 3d sg. t-pret. at-ru-balt LU. 17. b 18, 3d sg. reduplicated future atbéla *morietur* Ep. 116: root BAL.=GVAL, whence O. Sax. quelan *to die*. Old Norse quelja, A.S. cwellan, Eng. quell, kill.
atbiur, *dico, id dico?* Ep. 103, generally epiur, adbeir *dicit* Z^2. 430, atbert *dixit* pref.
atchiu, for adciu, *video*, atchissiu *quae vides* Prol. 150, atchi *videt eum* Z. 839 : see -ciu, frescíu.
atcois, Prol. 182 (atchois B), leg. atchóis (a trisyllable). ciatchoiss .i. cia etsi no indisi O'Dav. 65 (Mac F.'s copy), meaning obscure, and glossographer doubtful. If his second thoughts (cia indise : cf. m'atchous .i. dianinnisiur Br. h. 37) are best, we might translate atchóis by *thou shouldst relate* and regard -cóis as an s-future : cf. the verb inchoi .i. no innisfed. Amra Chol.
atcóri, it córi, possibly a verb compounded with at, possibly the verb subst. 3d pl. pres. with an adjective in the nom. pl.
atcoch, *precor*, atatoch[s]a *te precor* Ep. 304, Sanct. 1, adcochasa .i. atgim LU. 67ª, 1st pl. atcocham *precamur* July 14, Sep. 20, Dec. 26, at-n-cocham, Dec. 21, 2d sg. imper. ataig Aug. 22.; 1st sg. redupl. pret. atroitheach atroithech Ep. 300, 301, better atroithach or atroetach (.i. roatchius, Sanct. 20). Windisch connects this verb with O. Sax. thiggian, Ohg. dikkan.
atfiadaim, *narro*, atfiadam, adfiadam *quae narramus* Ep. 214=adfiadamni *proferimus nos* Z^2. 431. atfiadat *narrant* Prol. 247 = adfiadat Z^2 432. atfét, adfét (=adféded) *narrabat* Mar. 23, atafindaid *narrate eos*, Oct. 26, atfét - atfindad *narratus est* Apr. 18. Curtius G.E. No. 282.
atgiallaim *servio*, atgiallat (.i. dia fognat *cui serviunt*, O'Dav. 50), Ep. 60 ; cf. gialluidecht *captivity (slavery?)* 1 SM. 4. The same verb, compounded with ar-, occurs in LU. 120ᵇ argiallsat cóic coicid erend dó *Ireland's five fifths served him*.
athgabaim, *recipio*, ni-r-athgab *non recepit* Prol. 107. Hence athgabáil.
athir, s.m. (=pater, *warήp*) masc. r- stem Z^2. 262, Nov. 17, gen. sg. athar Prol. 215, Ap. 22, Aug. 15, Ep. 468, dat. athair Dec. 28, acc. athair-n, Ep. 356, gen. pl. aithre-n, Oc. 21, 31,=athre Z^2. 262.
athlaech, s. m. a *rehilom layman, an ex-hero*, pref. dat. pl. athloechnib ib. cf. attaoiseach *a deposed chieftain* O'D. supp. and see laech infra.
atvith, v. adrethim.
atrímem; see adrimim.
atroerois, Dec. 16, atroris A, atroiruis B, adroeris, adroeruis .i. tairis *stay* O'Dav. 50, rhymes with cáin-rois. It is the 2d sg. of a reduplicated s- future, from a verb possibly cognate with Lat. arrogo.
atsaigi, atsaigtis v. arsaichim.
atsluindiu, *alloquor* Ep. 320, 321, 325, 328, 332, etc. adsluindiu Ep. 323, atsluinniu .i. aitchim, O'Dav. 50, 3d sg. asluindi (B, atsluine A) Prol. 110.
au for ai see audpairt, aurdaire, bauptaist.
au for u : causeraid, taulchain.
audpairt, s. *offering*, Ep. 345 generally idpairt (indhairt D) or edpairt as in B.
(h) aue, hua Ap. 11, Z^2. 229 *grandson, descendant*, a dissyllable, cognate with παῖς εκ παιδός : gen. hui. h(aui) May 16, dat. pl. auib Z^2. 232, acc. pl. la nnu Tir. 11. In Jan. 22, Feb. 7, June 14, Oc. 11, Dec. 6, for mace hui we should perhaps read maccu.
augaist, august s.m. gen. s.g. auguist, Aug. 1, 31.
Augustín, Aug. 28, third of the doctors of the Church, born A.D. 354, at Tagaste in Numidia, wherefore Oengus calls him int-aurdaire a hAfraic.
Augustín, May 24, gen. sg. Nov. 16. This is the missionary sent by Gregory the Great to the Saxons.
aur-, air-,-er- an intensive prefix.
aurail, (erail, B.) s. Mar. 3, *exhortation, injunction* : cf. erail.

aurain, s. *excess* Ep. 7, aurain *excess, orerplus,* O'D. supp.=urain, which he explains by *portion, remainder, excess*: crain .i. imforcraid, O'Dav. 81.
aurdaire, aurdraic, aurdeirc, erdaire, airdirc, erdraic adj. *conspicuous,* Prol. 171, Aug. 28, Dec. 28, gen. sg. m. aurdaire, irdraic, airdirc, Nov. 5, from the intensive prefix air, aur, er, and the root daire.
aurgnais, (irgnis B) *a great prayer* Nov. 13, root GAD.
aurnaigthe, (ernaigthi B, urnaigthi D, air-chon-ig-the) s. *a prayer,* Ep. 188.
aurőman, oromon, uromun s. *great fear* (omun, W. ofn), Ep. 209.
aurtach, gen. aurthaig, (leg. aurtaig) Ep. 181 (erdaig B), secms=aurtach Corm. s. v. Lugnasad, which O'D. rendered by *festival or feast.* O'D. has an aurthach explained by uasal teastughadh séna *a noble testifying of denial.* O'Clery has eardach .i. fesda no sollamain. aurtach .i. *anniversary assemblies, games, shows, exhibitions in testimony of some event.* P. O'C.
Auster, Austerius Oc. 19 = Eusterius 'Episcopus Salernitanus confessor in Italia,' Boll.
b from g (ben), from bb (ball, blaith, bói), from f (cubus), from v (larr), from p, cáibtel Prol. 295 : infected b for infected m : mebraigther, Mar. 2.
b, a graphic *bezeichnung* of the v-sound, see balb, banb, Berba, (= Berua Dec. 22 A), Cerball, Dabid, deichenbor, delb, Faílbe, fedb, Gerbassi, colba, lar-n, marb, molbtach, nicirb, merbac, serb, sessilbe, and tarb = tarvos.
ba, *fuit,* bad, *esto* Prol. 261 (bud A). see biu.
bá, adj., *good* (bá .i. maith O'Cl. gl. and see Corm. s.v. espa), Nov. 13, where, however, B and R have ma. In O'Dav. 59, it is used as a subst. ni-beir in ben bá on tír dinnad cethra (leg. dinaib cethraib?) *the wife takes not from the husband profit of the cattle.*
Babaill, Jan. 24,=Babylas, bishop, martyrised at Antioch, in the time of Decius. A Babylas martyrised in Sicily is also commemorated on 24th January.
Babiloin, *Babylon,* Oct. 28.
badrae, v. Crum bodrae.
báegal, s.m. (n. ?) *danger,* gen. sg. báegail Ep. 202 : dat. arnachatfagthar imbáegul, LU. 75ᵇ. acc. dusin tairsimmis a baegal, LU. 74ᵇ-75ᵃ, a living word, now written baoghal.
baeth bannach, gn. Baith bannaich, Jan. 12 (baeth gl. hebes Sg. 66ᵃ).
Baethine, June 9, the first cousin and immediate successor of S. Columba, Reeves Col. 182, 372, a diminutive from baith or bóeth : v. Boethine.
bág, s.f. *a fight, battle,* 2 Beitr. 173. Ep. 162, 361, gen. sg. báige, báge July 24, Sep. 13, Ep. 490, acc. fri baig, pref. iarsinm-báig-se Ep. 315 : báigbe .i. catha, O'Cl.
bágaim, nobágu .i. gellaim *I engage* Nov. 30, 2d sg. conj. ce robaige Ep. 27, 1 sg. s- pret. robágus LU. 68ᵇ: cf. bágh .i. briathar, taighim .i. briathraighim, O'Cl.
bágach, adj. *warlike,* (cathach O'Cl.) Mar. 8, Ap. 11, acc. sg. m. Prol. 190, from bág supra.
bágim, *pugno,* aram-báigiu Ep. 360 *pro qua pugno* : O. H. G. págon (págant *pugnant,* Muspilli).
baid, adj. *dear, fond,* Aug. 3.
bail, s. *goodness* [combail .i. co-maithius, O'D. supp.] see fírbail, glanbail, morbail infra, and cf. Skr. bhála, Gr. φαλός.
baile, adj. *great, strong,* Sep. 29, B. n. pl. bailce, Prol. 73, bailci, Three Ir. Gl. 125 : see balc, W. balch *proud.*
baile, bale, s. m. *villa, town, home* pref. Prol. 146, Ap. 20, in bale LU. 49ᵃ, dat.sg. isinbaliu, LU. 48ᵃ.
baillgel, ballgel, adj. *white-limbed,* Oc. 4, from ball *membrum* and gel, q. v.
báine, s. *whiteness* Prol. 307, a deriv. from bán q. v.
Bairre, Barre of Cork, gen. sg. Bairre, Barre (leg. Bairri), Barri, Sep. 25.
bais, baes s. f. *folly,* mór in baes LU. 6ᵇ, gen. sg. inna baise (gl. hebetudinis), acc. sg. bái Ap. 4 : a deriv. from báith (gl. idiota, stultus) Z². 30.
baislec, s. ' basilica,' gen. sg. baislic, baslice Sep. 15, Nov. 19, baislic .i. eclais righ, O'Dav. 58, O.W. Bassalec, Lib. Land. 261.

Baite, Buite, gen. sg. Baiti, Buiti, Mar. 29.
báith, s.m. *fool, idiot,* see bóeth.
baithis, bathes, baithes, bathess, s.m. (n. ?) *baptism* Jan. 6, Apr. 5, gen. sg. baithis Tir. 1, dat. baithius, acc. sg. baithis, Jan. 25, Tir. 13. O.W. betid.
Báithín, Baethin, Boethán, acc. sg. June 18.
Báithíne, (Boithéne, Baethíne) mac Alla acc. sg. Oc. 6.
bal, v. atbal.
balb, adj. *mutus,* gen. sg. f. balbai for balbae=Dec. 22. The final b is written for v, and is regularly vocalized in Manx balloo *dumb;* balv and the Lat. balbus may both come from *gvalvus.
balbda, *mutus* Mar. 5, deriv. from balb.
balc, balce, adj. *strong, stout* (=Lith. smarkùs *gewaltig* ?), Feb. 1, Mar. 21, 2, June 17, July 11, dat. sg. m. Sep. 29, Nov. 17, arbledma balc belaib Nov. 20: compar. balcu Jan. 4, compounds: balc- itge *a strong prayer,* Jan. 13, balc-cathair, *a strong city,* Nov. 17.
ball, s. m. *membrum* Z^2. 210, gen. baill Z^2. 224 (=φαλλός), in baillgel q. v.
Balla, Balda Mar. 30, a village in co. Mayo, about eight miles S.E. of Castlebar, O'Don. Four MM. 1179. The legend referred to in the note pl. xvi is told in Laud. 610, as follows: —in adluiu uisci tuargaibed in topur otá bennchor in-ultaib cori[sed] balla i cérú.
Balnina, Ballíne, Oc. 4, a corruption of Balbina; the Roman saint who discovered S. Peter's chains.
ban, gen. pl. of ben s. f. *female,* q. v. in composition banmaicc, bainmeicc, banmee *female children, girls,* July 20.
bán, adj. (=φανός. cf. Skr. bhānu *lumen* and Lat. Fānu, Corssen, i. 421), *white, fair,* Jan. 15, Feb. 1, Sep. 30, gen. sg. m. báin, Dec. 7, dat. sg. m. bán, Nov. 26, f. báin, Mar. 31, acc. pl. f. bána, Ep. 339.
bán-chath, s. m. *white fight,* June 8 : cf. bán-martre Z^2. 1006.
bán-gel, adj. *white-bright,* dat. sg. f. bán-gil, Dec. 25, gen. sg. m. (n. ?) iar ndinltad baithis bangil L. Br.=gelbán, q. v. bán-lucht *white folk* Ep. 331 B.
bán-tlacht, s. *a white garment,* Ep. 331.
Banba, pref.
banb, s. *pig.* Here, as in balb, the final b is written for v, and is regularly vocalised in W. banw ; hence the diminutives
Banbán, a man's name, Nov. 26 and Banbanátán, Mart. Tall. xxx.
banmac, s. m. *a girl,* n. pl. banmaice, bainmeice,banmee, July 20. Hence banmacán in the verse Diambad messe in banmacan noccchrainn cachfaelmacan *were I the little girl I would love every student,* Book of Ballinote.
bann, s. *a work, a deed,* O'Cl. Gl. dat. pl. bandaib (bannaib B.) Dec. 21, bann is explained by O'Clery as gach cumhsgughadh *every moving or every journeying,* bás *death* and gniomh *deed.* The last of these significations suits here, for S. Thomas is the patron of architects and builders, Jameson, S. and L. Art. i. 247. Hence
bannach, adj. .i. guimach Three Ir. Gl. 132, and O'Cl. Gl.) *deedful,* June 12, gen. sg. m. Jan. 12.
bara, s. *affliction* Ep. 369, bara *anger* Ep. 419, acc. sg. baraind LB. 127ᵃ. 25, W. bar *affliction, fury.*
barn,- form- farm-, for, far, bar, possess. pron. 2d pl. Z^2. 339, Aug. 30, Ep. 63, 375. This seems a gen. pl. The stem occurs infixed as bar, bor, and affixed in verbs in the 2d pl. pret. act. as -bair : the Goth. izvara seems cognate.
Barnabb, Barnap, St. Barnabas, gen. Barnaibb, Barnaip, June 10 (should be June 11 ?), Saint Paul's fellow-labourer.
barr, s. m. gen. bairr *top, end,* from *barsa, *varsa, Skr. varshíyās *higher,* varsh-man *gipfel,* Lat. vere-uen, W. bar, etc., acc. sg. Mar. 31, Nov. 30, Jan. 31. Compound : cath-barr, Jan. 10.
Barrfind, Barrind, Barrinn, of Druim Cuilinn, May 21, of Achad Cailten, Nov. 8.
bart, see dubart.
bás, s. n. *death,* Z^2. 213, 222, Jan. 4, 18, March 9, Apr. 8, May 3, July 1, 25, Sep. 11, 14, Dec. 21, 23, gen. sg. báis Z^2. 223, acc. sg. bás pref.

GLOSSARIAL INDEX.   ccxxiii

Basilla, a Roman martyr (Boll.) June 11. An Alexandrian martyr, May 17.
Bassus, (in Heraclea) Nov. 20, B and D.
bauptaist, s. m.=baiptist, babtaist, *baptista* undeclined, gen. sg. June 24, Aug. 29, Sep. 24, acc. sg. Prol. 102.
bebais, *mortuus est*, Prol. 95. Feb. 18, Ap. 23, O. Ir. bebai Fiacc's h. 23. (Franciscan copy) 3d sg. redupl. pret. of a verb cognate with πέφα-μαι. The -s in bebais seems an instance of the common middle-Irish addition of the endings of the s-preterite to those of the reduplicated and t-preterites.
bece, adj. *little* (W. bach) Nov. 10. gen. sg. m. bice, bic May 18, dat. sg. f. bice, bic. Ap. 23.
Bécc mace Eogain, Prol. 203, gen. sg. Bécce ib. 200.
beccáin, s. m. *parvulus*, n. pl. beccain, becain Sep. 4.
Beccán. son of Lugaid, May 26, (Beccán mac Cula) gen. sg. Beccain Ap. 5, Beccán mac Cula pref. "patron saint of Imleach-Fia, near Kells in Meath," O'Don. Four Masters, A.D. 1119.
bech, s. m. (gl. apes) Z^2. 273: n. pl. beich 2 S.M. 122, gen. pl. bech-n Feb. 13, dat. pl. bechaib, 2 S.M. 120. Perhaps in W. beg-egyr *drone*, (for beg-segur?). As to the Irish bees see Joyce p. 146 and *Lives of the Cambro-British saints*, p. 134.
béim, s. n. *a blow* acc. sg. Ep. 363, n. pl. béimmen Z^2. 270 a stem in men=benmen whence bémnech Br. h. 6, root BHAN, whence φόνος,ἐ-πε-φν-ον, ON. bana *to slay*, Goth. banja *wound*, 2 Beitr. 167.
beith, s. *being* Ep. 172, acc. sg. Ep. 375, so in Fiacc (beith in géilliu meie maire).
bél, s. m. *lip, mouth*, n. pl. beiúil *labia* Z^2. 226, dat. pl. bélaib Nov. 20 (=bélib Z^2. 227) in the nom. pron. arbélaib q. v. acc. béulu Z^2. 20, 227.
Belach mugnae (now Ballaghmoon), Dec. 11.
ben, s. f. *woman, wife* 2 Beitr. 159, gen. sg. mná Z^2. 242, dat. mnái, acc. mnái-n, voc. á ben, n. pl. mná, gen. pl. ban-n Jan. 15, Sep. 23. W. benyw.
bendachim, *benedico*: 3d sg. pres. indic. act. hóre non-bendacha-ni Z^2. 434, 3d sg. pret. ro-s-bendach, ro-s-bennach pref. see 2 Beitr. 141.
bendacht, bennacht s. f. *benedictio* Prol. 275, Jan. 13, June 15, Ep. 56, 215, gen. sg. bendachtae Tur. 85, also bendachtan Z^2. 265, acc.sg. bendacht-n Nov. 2, Ep. 61, 113, Z^2. 244. W. bendith.
Benedicht, (beinidict B) July 11, Benidecht Mar. 21, [S. B. *translatio relata hoc die*, Boll.]. acc. sg. Benedicht-n June 14 (Benidacht A); founder of the Benedictine order 'Casini in Italia,' Boll., ob. 543.
Bennchor, now Bangor (in Down) on the south side of Belfast lough, gen. Bennchuir, Bendchuir, Bennchoir, Bendchair, Bennchair, Feb. 28, Ap. 8, May 10, Dec. 15, see Joyce 352.
benim, *ferio*, Z^2. 429, 3d pl. pres. indic. act. benait Jan. 31, June 30, in the phrases benait barr for, benait glas for : root bhan whence πέφανται, ἐ-πε-φν-ον, see béim.
béo, adj. *quick, living*=(g)vivus, Goth. qvius, W. byw, 2 Beitr. 160 : gen. sg. m. bii pref. n. pl. m. bi Z^2. 226.
Beoáed, Mar. 8, bishop of Ard-carna in Roscommon : ob. A.D. 524.
Beoán, gen. Beoáin, Aug. 8, bishop of Fid Cuillinn now Feigheullen, county Kildare. Beoán, Oc. 26, bishop of Tamlachta Menann, in the county Down.
Beogna, Beóna, gen. sg. Jan. 22, cf. Adamnán's Beognai, Beogni : Reeves' Columba, pp. 29, 124.
beos, adv. *adhuc* pref. Z. 569.
ber-, (1) *ferre*, (2) *dicere*. 3d sg. pres. indic. ni beir *non fert*, Prol. 223, berth-e berth-i, *fert eum*, Ep. 196, rel. sg. beres *qui fert* Ep. 416, 3d sg. pret. bert Jan. 27, June 2, bert ráiriu ingin do thadg *R. bore a daughter to T.* LU. 41ᵇ. 3d sg. pres. pass. berthair Prol. 175, 3d sg. conj. ro-m-berthar Prol. 3, 3d sg. secondary pres. bretha Jan. 25, June 11. Compounds see ad-biur, do-biur.
ber, s. spit, =veru. Hence
Berach, ('*verutus*'?) gen. sg. Beraich, Bernig Nov. 18. See Colgan's expl. of this name, Reeves Col. 48.
Berba, Berua, the river *Barrow* in Leinster, gen. sg. Prol. 222, Dec. 22.

berg, s. acc. pl. berga, berca Prol. 42, O'Cl. explains bearg by dibheargach *brigand*, *laoch champion*. fearg *anger*, and see O'Dav. 58: *a soldier* also a *robber* P. O'C. If not borrowed from the M. Lat. vargus *expulsus*, Goth. vargs, O.N. vargr, A.S. vearg *maleficus homo proscriptus*, it may be cognate with the Romance briga, brigand, etc. Diez. Ét. Wört.

1. bés, s. m. *custom, usage*, pref. n. pl. béssi, bésse Z^2. 240, dat. bésib 461, acc. bésu 438.
2. bés, 3d sg. rel. fut. of biu, in bes comland a nuall-sa Ep. 163.
3. bes, (bés?) seems an adv. or conj. Ep. 417 bes nip-aill : cf., perhaps, bes ni rom LU. 40^a, bes nipádrith lutsu mo lecunsa LU. 49^b, bes ar Emer noconmerr in ben dia lenai Sgl. Conc. bes .i. donrb H. 3, 18, p. 51^b. bess is mise is ole aichne ann ol isáce LB. 113^a-114^a.

besenad, (leg. bésenad?) s. Ep. 157 B.

béscna, s. m. .i. dlighedh *law* O'D. supp. dat. sg. bescnu Ep. 318 (rhymes with céstu), acc. rofitis mo bésgnose frib *ye know my custom as regards you*, Z^2. 458, ar is for tri huidhibh rosuigi (leg. rosuided) besena deirigh (leg. bésena deirid) gach righ *for it is on three terms was based the final law of every king*, O'Dav. 59.

Bethel, *Bethlehem* gon. Bothil, Boithil Sep. 30, dat. Dec. 28, Ep. 268, S. Jerome (Cirine) died in a monastery which he had founded at Bethlehem. Hence the allusion at Sep. 30.

bethu, s. m. *life*, a t-stem =βιότης, gen. s. bothad Ep. 437, Z^2. 255 (=βιότητος), dat. bethu Ep. 201, Z^2. 256, acc. bethaid Ep. 117, 169, Z^2. 257. W. bywyd.

bíae, Mar. 22, seems the gen. sg. of some word=βία.

bíast, s. f. *bestia*, W. bwyst, gen. biastae Ep. 472 (where it is applied to a lioness), dat. pl. biastaib Prol. 41. Now piast. There seems to have also been an i-stem béist, whence n. pl. béssti Z^2. 245. Other forms (biasta, béis) occur in LU. 107^b: frissin mbiasta . . . . intan dosíned in beis abragit.

bid, bith s. m. (n. ?) .i. breo *flame* Aug. 29, dat. sg. cosind biud (gl. cum emphasi) Ml. 23^a.

bidbu, adj. *reus* for bibdu Z^2. 255, n. pl. m. bidbaid Prol. 175 = bibdid, bibdaid Z^2. 258. Cognate are bibdanus LU. 14^a, O.W. bibid (gl. rei), M. Br. bevez 'coulpable.'

bile, s. m. (n. ?) *a tree*, pref. bile Medba LU. 70^a, acc. sg. juxta bile torten, Lib. Arm. 15 b, 1 : dat. sg. don biliu busda LU. 47^a, n. pl. tribile dochorcorglain, LU. 48^a, gen. pl. bile Sep. 10.

bille, adj. *paltry*, *mean* July 3, Aug. 8 .i. gonaide *laughable* .i. ceirt *scanty*, Corm. B, and see Three Ir. Gl. 133.

bind, adj. i-stem, *melodious*, n. pl. f. binde: binne Prol. 181, compar. binnithir Vis. Ad. and bindiu (gl. sonorius) Z^2. 275. Cognate with Lat. fides or fidis *the string of a musical instrument*.

binde, s. f. *melodiousness*, dat. s. binni, binde Aug. 27, Oc. 7.

biror, gen. biroir means *watercress*. W. berwr, but in Nov. 29 A uses it for Birra.

Birra, now Birr or Parsonstown, Reeves Col. 193, 209, gen. sg. Nov. 29. Birra .i. in cell for imad tibrat innti *the church*, [so called] *on account of the abundance of wells therein*. O'Mulc. 191.

bisex, (bisix B), s. Feb. 24, pp. xliv. and liv., bisextus *an intercalary day*.

bith, s. m. *world*, Prol. 115, 157, gen. sg. betho Z^2. 238, betha Prol. 140, 195, June 29, Ep. 240, 276, 414, dat. bith Mar. 21, May 9, Ep. 19 (=biuth Z^2. 239), acc. bith-n Oc. 15 : acc. pl. bithu, Mar. 31, gen. pl. betha Prol. 156. Gaulish bitu, W. byd. Comp. bith-ché Prol. 102.

bith, a prefix meaning *always*, Z^2. 12 ; bith-aittreb Oc. 8, im bith-bí *in quo semper est* June 9, ro-m-bithbeo *semper sim* Ep. 39, bithbuan *everlasting* Ep. 558, bithchoemnc *eternal protection* Mar. 13, bithflaith *eternal Kingdom* Prol. 272, June 9, Dec. 14 B. Ep. 168^a. acc. May 16, Ep. 159, bithguas Ep. 316, bithgolait *semper plorat* Prol. 62, bithmairid *semper manet* Prol. 255, bithmarait *semper manent* Prol. 88, bithmóraid *semper laudat* Prol. 232, biththrógaid Prol. 231.

biu, *I am*. Some of the forms come from the root GVIV (Lat. vivo) ; others from the root BHU. Pres. indic. 2d sg. -bí-siu Prol. 274, 3d sg. bid Aug. 4, Dec. 29, -bi Prol. B. 146,

Feb. 29, Ap. 7, n.p. Preterite 3d sg. absolute form : bói Ep. 289 : búi Dec. 22 A : ba, Jan. 14, Feb. 8, Ap. 7, May 11, June 21, July 6, Aug. 10, Nov. 5, Dec. 20, Ep. 9 : suffixed form : ra-ba Ep. 302, -ba, Prol. 125 (ciarba=cé-ro-ba), diam-ba, diam-bu, diar-bu Ap. 2, na-bu, na-bo Nov. 10, Prol. 114, ciarbo Prol. 214, córbo Prol. 93, nírbo Sep. 27, ciapu, ccabu Nov. 7, ní-bu, ní-bo frisinbu Ep. 392, robni pref. ropu pref. Plural 3, batar June 19, 25, batir June 19 D, cebtar Prol. 74, ciaptar Prol. 133, Ep. 14 (=cé-batar), naptar Mar. 18, niptar Nov. 9. In Prol. 139 A. buaid (ba, B) seems a mistake for bói.
Fut. sg. 3 ro-n-bia Ep. 168, ron-bé, ro-sui-bé Ep. 56 : relative form : bias Mar. 13, Ep. 289 : pl. 2, perhaps bet (leg. béth l) Prol. 188 : pl. 3 biatt Prol. B. 155, biait Prol. 308 : rel. beti Ep. 298.
Conj. sg. .i. robeo Ep. 315, robeo-sa Prol. 271, 273 (robbeosa B), biam Ep. 165 B, sg. 3 ron-bia Jan. 13, con-am-rai-b Prol. 11, con-dom-rai-b Ep. 359, arna-p Prol. 323 : ro-p Jan. 24, Mar. 17, Dec. 19, perhaps na-ba Prol. 294, diam-ba Ep. 78, and the relative bas, bas Ep. 148. pl. 3 robat Jan. 21, robet Ep. 44, 292, 293, 299.
Secondary Present, sg. 3 bad Mar. 31, comad (=combad) Sep. 26. B. cia-ron beth Prol. 141, ma-beth Ep. 102 : pl. 3, betis Ep. 125. Imper. bad esto Prol. 261. bid Prol. 241, ro-m-bith, Prol. 271 B. Ep. 39.
blá (.i. buidhe *yellow*)=flavus. Hence probably
Bláán, Aug. 10, (where it is a dissyllable), the name of the bishop of Ceunugarad now Kingarth in Bute.
Bladma, gen. sg. Ap. 7, Nov. 20 B=bledma, q.v. tarcusal ag breaghaibh for bladhma. Battle of Moylena, p. 76.
bláith, s. *blossom*, n. pl. m. blaithe (blaithi B) Sep. 4, 18, W. blodau *flowers* 2 Beitr. 174 : bláithe Aug. 19, is perhaps, a noun meaning (and cognate with) 'bloom' : cf. Vis. Ad. comblathe 7 boltonugud.
bled, s. seems to have meant originally *belllua*, but is specialised in Irish to mean 1. *a whale*, Z^2. 85 (bleth .i. míl mór O'Dav. 59 : cf. Juvenal, iv. 127, where bellua is applied to a big turbot), 2. *a stay*, note Ap. 7. In the British languages it means *a wolf* (W. blaidd, Corn. bleit, Bret. bleiz), and so in Rawl. 505 bledach bledma .i. na conallta *of the wolves*.
bledech, bledach (from bled q. v.) adj. *monsterful* l *stay-haunted* l dat. sg. n. Ap. 7, f. bledig, Pref.
Bledma, sg. Ap. 7, Nov. 20 (Bladma B) anglicised 'Bloom,' Joyce, p. 159. The nom. sg. is written bladma in the Book of Leinster, fo. 112, a. 2 : Bladma no blod mac con maic cais clothmuin maic únchalla romarb bregmael gobaind cuirchi maic snithi rig hua fuata. Dolluid iarum inanóedin coragaib irruss bladma. Ros náir aninm artús. Dolluid asside issinslinb.
Blese, name of a swineherd, gen. blesce Jan. 3.
bliadain, s. fem. i-stem, *year* Ep. 4, gen. bliadna Sep. 17, dat. bliadain Prol. 281, 292, acc bliadain Feb. 29, n. pl. bliadni Z^2. 251, gen. pl. bliadne Z^2. 252, bliadna, Aug. 7 B. W. blwyddyn, Corn. blidhen, Bret. blizen. There was also an ā stem bliadan, gen. bliadne, Z^2. 250. to which belongs the gen. pl. bliadan Aug. 7. A, D.
blog, s. f. *a piece* Oc. 5, gen. congab rígi blogi do ultaib, LU. 22ᵃ. blog thalman LII. 326. lat. frag(men), fra-n-go, Goth. brikan.
bó, s. f. *cow* (βοῦς, bos Z^2. 56, O.W. bou in boutig), gen. sg. bó, Aug. 8, dat. sg. boin, acc. boin-n (cf. W. bôn), n. pl. bai Z^2. 272, gen. bó, báu (Táin bó Fr. 294), dat. buaib, acc. bú.
Bochrai, gen. sg. Nov. 28.
bocht, adj. *pauper*. Hence bochtán s. m. *pauperculus* Ep. 392, gen. sg. clúnti díncaire in bochtain *hear thou the cry of the poor man*, LB. 74ᵇ. dat. pl. dosbera do bochtánaib *give them to poor men*, LB. 261, a 74.
bóeth, s. m. *fod*, acc. pl. boethu, baethu, Prol. 30. cf. báis.
Boethán, Baethán, Dec. 13.
Boethíne mór, son of Cuana, Feb. 19, Reeves' Columba 318.
Boethíne, Báithéne, Báithíne, mac Findach, May 22.

2 *g*

bol, gen. buil .i. eigsi no eicceas O'Cl.
bolg, s. *a bag* Mar. 30=bulga, Goth. balgs, 2 Beit. 173, Z². 14, Lat. con-flug-es, fluctus Schmidt, *Vocalismus*. 11. 4, bolg bélchi, bolg uisci Corm. W. boly *belly*, bolcan *pouch*.
bolmar, adj. *learned, wise* (deriv. from bol q. v.), acc. s. f. bolmair Sep. 14.
bordgal, s.n. Dec. 27, Ep. 253, gen. sg. ceeba bordgal (brotgail B.) Prol. 275, acc. sg. bordgal Ep. 206, n. pl. bordgala Prol. 71, meaning doubtful. Can the bordgal of our text be a loan from the low Latin bordigolum, burdigalum (Fr. bourdigue) *locus arundinibus seu cannis circumseptus, quo pisces capiuntur et servantur*, Du Cange? Should this conjecture be right, the fishes are believers ('pisces qui hanc enavigant vitam,' S. Ambrose). That the idea was familiar to Irish ecclesiastics appears from S. Patrick's confession (Idcirco oportet quidem bene et diligenter piscari) and from Secundinus' hymn (Dominus illum elegit ut . . . piscaretur per doctrinae retia).
borg, s.m. 'a burgh' Lat. burgus, a small fortified place, Br. bourch, Goth. borg-s, φραιτὸν πόλισμα Aesch. Sept. 63, written broc (with provection of g after c and metathesis) Prol. 189, 193 (brog B.), acc. pl. burcu Prol. 140 (brugu B), n. pl. liss aurslocthi, búirg fánbéla, LU. 107ᵃ.
brage, s. *gullet, neck*, au ant-stem : imma bragait pref. B=W. breuant *windpipe*, and cognate with βρόγχος and gurges.
Bran-Dub, King of Leinster, slain A.D. 601, Prol. 222 : bran *corvus*=Slav. vranū 2 Beitr. 178.
Bran Bece, (of Clane in Kildare), gen. sg. Brain Bice May 18.
bras, adj. *big, great* : nosirfed inm(b)ith mbras, LU 47ᵃ n. pl. f. brasa Prol. 75. bras .i. mor, O'Dav. 58. W. bras.
brasse, s.f. *quickness, readiness*, dat. sg. brassi June 19, braise *quickness, briskness* P. O'C. cf. bras *activity* Táin bó Fráich : braise (gl. lassiun) Ir. Gl. p. 41. W. brysiaw *to hurry*.
bráth. s. an u-stem, *judgment*, gen. sg. brátha Prol. 174, acc. sg. bráth Ep. 127, 290. W. brawd, Gaulish brátu.
bráthir, bráthair, s.m. r-stem *brother* (Z². 262, 2 Beitr. 159) Ap. 11, 21, June 17, Dec. 27, gen. sg. bráthar July 25, gen. pl. bráithre (brathar, B.) July 10, 18, brúthar (braithre B) Ep. 476, braithre Ep. 528 (brathar, D), acc. pl. braithre Ep. 409.
bréc, s.f. *a lie* pref. B. Prol. 145 (brég B), acc. bréic *dolum* Z². 19, 79.
brécad, *deception* : armbrécad *to deceive us*, pref. B.
brecc, adj. *speckled* (W. brech), gen. sg. m. bricc, bric, Sep. 14. From *merga (=Lith. márgas), *mercca, *mrecc.
Brecc -buaid=Bricin, Sep. 5, Brecc father of Aed, gen. Bricc Nov. 10.
Breccán, of Echdruim, acc. sg. May 7.
breith, s. *bearing, carrying*, dat. sg. Ep. 119.
Brenann, of Cluain Ferta=Brendenus Mocu Alti. Reeves' Col. 220, 221, gen. Brenaind May 16. So Marianus Scotus : Feil brenain innoct for dardain. a impede fordia indilgud do muiredach trog, Bibl. Imper. Vind. MS. 1097.
Brenann Biruir (Birra B), gen. Brenainn, Nov. 29 is=Brendenus, Reeves' Col. 193, 209.
bréo, s. *flame* Ap. 15, Aug. 20, compounded ; án-bréo ; Ap. 23, June 2, Oct. 21.
bress, adj. n. pl. m. bressa Prol. 74, breas .i. mór P. O'C. [But B treats bressa here as a substantive and glosses it by bága *pugnae*].
bresta, adj. *lively ? eloquent ?* dat. sg. f. brestai July 19, acc. sg. m. bresta (.i. solam no solabair B) June 13, n. pl. m. brestai July 20. P. O'C. glosses breasda by (1) priomhdha (2) leodha no suilbhir (3) breaghda.
breth, s.f. *decision*, acc. sg. breith pref.=brith Z². 244. n. pl. bretha Z². 244, acc. pl. bretha Ep. 416, Z². 246.
Brí gobann (lit. 'Smith's hill') dat. Nov. 25, now Brigown, co. Cork, Mart. Tall. 38.
bríathar, s. a fem. ā stem (=Ϝρήτρα Z². 166) *word*, gen. bréithre, acc. sg. brethir Z². 244, dat. pl. bríathraib Mar. 22.

bríg, s.f. *vigour, might* Z². 21, Prol. 145, 147, Aug. 7, gen. sg. bríge Feb. 7, June 2, Aug. 1, Oc. 4, n. pl. bríga Ep. 34, Prol. 87 (MS. brigu), dat. pl. brígaib Prol. 34. W. bri Glück KN. 127. Ital. brio, O. Fr. bri, Diez E.W. 87. In Aug. 7 brig seems for dobríg *because*.
Bríg, gen. Bríge, name of a virgin, dat. sg. Jan. 31. St. Ende's mother was called Brig 'id est vigorosa vel virtuosa.' Boll. 21 March.
brígach, adj. *vigorous, mighty*, Jan. 26, Feb. 13, Dec. 20, Ep. 30, gen. sg. m. brigaig Feb. 15, acc. sg. m. brígnach m. Prol. 102, June 14, Oc. 6, Ep. 290. O'Dav. 56 explains brígach by uallach *proud*, in Three Ir. Gl. 126, 128 it is explained by craibdech *pious* and nertmar *vigorous*, and in O'Clery's Glossary by feartach and neartmhar.
Brigit, s. a fem. i-stem, Prol. 101, Feb. 1, Ep. 283, gen. brigtæ, Lib. Arm. 11 a 1. She died A.D. 523 or 525. Her 'city' was Kildare.
broc, see borg.
brocc, s. m. *badger* (W. Corn. Bret. broch). Hence Broc(c)án scríbnid July 8, gen. brocain LU. 41ᵇ. Broccán of Ross Tuirc, Sep. 17.
bróen, s. m. *rain* Z². 31, acc. sg. amal broen nailgen LU. 34ᵃ, dat. pl. broenaib Ep. 346, $\beta\rho\acute{\epsilon}\chi\omega$, $\beta\rho\omicron\chi\epsilon\tau\acute{o}\varsigma$.
bróenán, s. *a little rain, a showerlet*, broenán fota fola fland *a long red drip of blood*, LU. 48ᵇ, acc. sg. May 19, Ep. 351.
brolach, s. m. = *prologus* [as bóc gl. osculum = pac(em), bi=pix and bis *piece* from pitia], dat. sg. broluch. pref.
brón, s. *grief*, gen. bróin (is for etan bit aithgne mbroin no failte, II. 2, 16, col. 93), W. bruyn.
brónach, adj. *mournful*, n. pl. brónaig, Prol. 188.
Brónach, gen. sg. bronaich Dec. 7 B, and v. Cluain Br.
1. bru-, *to forget*, ní bruifem (.i. nidermatfam 3 Ir. Gl. 127) *we will not forget* Prol. 304 [O'Dav. 58 has brudh .i. dermut ut est brudhfe—leg. brudhfidh—in uallsa *he will forget this pride.*]
2. bru-, *to break*, 3d sg. s-pret. bruis *fregit*, breuis .i. robris Rawl. 505, Ap. 4, 3d pl. pret. pass. robruthea B (robruitea A) *fracti sunt* Prol. 35. Cf. W. breuo *to grow brittle*, briwio *to break*.
1. brú, s. *brink, edge*, abl. sg. Dec. 22.
2. brú, s. (W. bru) *womb, belly*, Z². 264, gen. bronn, dat. broinn, abl. brú Mar. 27, Ep. 464. Cf. $\check{\epsilon}\mu\beta\rho\upsilon\omicron\nu$.
bruchtaim, *I burst*, asam-brucht *out of whom burst* Ap. 4 : 3d sg. imperfect (?) frism-bruchta *against whom broke* June 21=frism-bruchtai Nov. 29, as m-bruchta Ap. 4 D. brucht .i. sceith *vomiting*, O'Dav. 58.
bruinne, s. f. *breast* (W. bron), dat. pl. bruinnib : for bruinnib betha June 29, lit. *on the world's breasts*, compare Goth. bru-sts, brunjo.
bruth, s. m. gen. brotha (1) *a glowing mass of metal :* bruth óir Jan. 24, Feb. 10, Nov. 26, acc. pl. bruthu Vis. Ad. (2) *fervor*. dat. sg. bruth June 2, Oc. 21. Compounds see Mórbruth. Compare bruthnaigim (gl. furo) Z². 435 : Lat. furor, Ohg. bru-nst, Corssen, i. 145. Root bhru from bhur.
búadach, adj. *victorious*, Prol. 191, 222, Feb. 13, 19, Mar. 8, Ap. 18, May 10, 18, Aug. 6, 25, Oc. 6, gen. sg. buadaig Dec. 7, dat. sg. m. buadach Sep. 29, Nov. 26, f. buadaig, Prol. 272, acc. sg. m. buadach-n June 14, Ep. 264, f. buadaig-n, May 16, June 10.
búaid, s. neut. i-stem (1) *victory*, (2) *prize, booty* (3 Beitr. 174, Glück K.N. 53) Prol. 3, Feb. 15, Ap. 9, 24, May 11, Aug. 26, Sep. 2, Oc. 1, 12 (where A has in buaidsin but B a(m) buaidsin), Nov. 28, Dec. 8, (where B has buaid n-ictbritain), 16, gen. sg. buada Prol. 183, Jan. 16, Feb. 10, Ap. 24, June 2, 5, Nov. 2, Ep. 349, buade Ap. 17, buadæ Oc. 30, buaide Mar. 21, dat. sg. buaid Ap. 5, June 20, Aug. 19, Oc. 16, Dec. 17, Ep. 23, acc. sg. buaid-n Jan. 28, July 6, Oc. 29, voc. sg. a búaid n-óc n-Ulad, LU. 100ᵃ, gen. pl. buaide May 3, buada Mar. 12, dat. pl. buadaib Jan. 27, Aug. 30, Ep. 283. Compounds see

Brecchuaid, glanbuaid. This word is neuter in Z.'s glosses (niba óin gébas ambuáid busíbse (*non erit unus e vobis qui accipiet palmam*) and so in Fél. D May 11, Fél. B. Oc. 12, and Fél. R. Dec. 8. But in two places in the Félire we find the masc. or fem. article: cosinm-buaid June 20, lasinm-buaid Aug. 2. We must therefore assume that buaid had two genders, or that the text is corrupt in these places, or that when the Félire was composed the neuter article was becoming disused.
Buaid-beo, Nov. 17.
buan, adj. *lasting*, Prol. 123, 302, June 12, Nov. 17, Dec. 15, Ep. 30, 158, dat. sg. m. buan Ep. 19, acc. sg. m. Sep. 23. u. pl. f. buana Prol. 181. Compounds v. bithbuan.
buide, s. f. *gratia*, gen. Prol. 55, acc. pl. buidi Z. 987: cogn. with W. bodd, boddus and Gaulish boduo, Glück KN. 52. Hence adj. buidech *gratus*.
buiden, s f. (W. byddin) *band, troop* (gl. turba Corm. s. v. torb), Ep. 5. dat. sg. buidin Jan. 4, July 19, dat. pl. buidnib Ep. 295, hobuidnib (gl. copiis) Z. 791. O.W. bodin (gl. phalangem). bodiniou (gl. phalanges). Root bhad *to bi-n-d*.
buidnech, adj. *troopful*, acc. sg. m. Oc. 15.
Buite, son of Brónach, of Monasterboice, gen. búiti ' Boetius ' Dec. 7, ob. A.D. 521.

c=Skr. ç (cét, cretim),=Skr. K (cía, cruim), provected from g after r: burcu Prol. 140: after th: freera Feb. 22: for g in loanwords: martarlaic Ep. 140. c for h: mici Ep. 308, 309.
cach, pron. *quivis* with a substantive Prol. 11, Feb. 29. B. gen. sg. f. cacha pref. 8.
cách, pron. *quivis*, placed absolutely, Prol. 57, 248, Feb. 17, July 9, Ep. 48 with the article: cosin-cách Ep. 50. Z². 361. O.W. paup.
cadlai, adj. n. pl. f. *beautiful (comely, graceful* P. O'C) Dec. 9: cadhla .i. cáomh no álainn O'Cl. Gl., cnomes cadla *beautiful nutfruit* note to Sgl.
cádus, s. pref. 5 *nobility, excellence*, deriv. from cáid: cadhos *honour, respect, privilege* P. O'C.
cai, v. oenchai.
cáibtel, see caiptel.
caid, adj. Jan. 4, Feb. 1, 10, 18, Mar. 13, May 16, June 3, Sep. 5, 14. O'Clery explains this by glan *pure* and geanmnaidh *chaste*.
cáid, adj. (.i. uasal *high, noble*, Laud 610), June 13, Dec. 14, cáid cach néemais Sgl. The comparative is cádu, Mar. 20: cf. perhaps κικάζ-μαι, Dor. pf. of καίνυμαι ' I excel.'
caidhe, *what is it*?, ca idb-é, pref. 51.
caille, s. *velum* acc. sg. Tir. 2, borrowed from *pallium*: Hence
caillech, s. f. *a nun*, acc. sg. caillig-n Br. h. 39, u. pl. caillecha Tir. 5, gen. pl. caillech-n, Feb. 1.
cáin, adj. (W. cain) *clear, bright, fair* (ex *skaino, Goth. skein) Prol. 139, 192, 249, Feb. 10, Mar. 10, June 3, Aug. 10, 14, Nov. 22, Dec. 19, 24, acc. sg. m. Jan. 19, Aug. 27, dat. sg. f. Jan. 12, Feb. 12, 21, acc. sg. cáin-n, masc. May 22, fem. July 26, gen. pl. cáin, dat. dual and pl. cáinib Ap. 3, Oc. 16, Ep. 62.
Compounds: cain-áige July 6, Sep. 5, cain-cathar Aug. 15, cáin-ciubhid Ap. 26, Aug. 14, cáin-cing Feb. 14, cáin-clérech June 21, cáin-cocrait Dec. 24, cáin-decheng Sep. 6, cáin-dias Nov. 24, cáin-ésce Jan. 3, cáin-grian Jan. 5, June 26, Oc. 20, Dec. 26, cain-kalland, Prol. 324: cain-mil June 17, cáin-ordan Prol. 179, cáin-popul Prol. 19, cáin-scéla May 6, cáin-uaitne Ap. 29, cáin-canmae Ep. 241, cáin-deochaid Ap. 13, May 4, and perhaps Cainross Dec. 12.
Caindech mac húi Dalenn Oc. 11= Cainnechus mocu dalon, Reeves' Col. 220.
caindel, s. f. = *candela*, W. cannwyll. Hence caindelta, adj. *luminous, flamy*, Feb. 19.
caindlech, coinlech, coindlech adj. *lustrous, shining-white*, Mar. 10, June 9, Nov. 22, Ep. 92, dat. sg. m. caindlech July 28, abl. sg. f. caindlech Mar. 4, Dec. 16. Rosc cainlech glas ina chind, LU.130ᵇ.
Cainne, Ap. 7. A Cainncóc is celebrated at May 15.

caiptel = capitulum *chapter*, cáibtel Prol. 299, acc. sg. coibtell Ep. 100, n. pl. caibtil Prol. 329, gen. pl. caibtel Prol. 295, 332, 333, but caiptel Ep. 101, where the old p has been left untouched by the mediaeval scribe.
cairde, s. f. (gl. pactum, South. 56ᵇ) *covenant* Ep. 534, gen. sg. ní forcraid cairde dau anísin, LU. 107ᵇ. cairdigter (gl. foederari) Ml. 126ᵃ, nocairdnigthea (gl. foederatae sunt) Ml. 37.
Cáirech dergan (coeirech d. A), sister of Endae of Áru, Feb. 9.
Cairell, gen. cairill, father of Bishop Daig, Aug. 18.
caisc, s. dat. sg. Ep. 562, Corm. 10 *paschati*, acc. in caisc *pascham* Z². 253.
caithfer, see cathfer.
calad, adj. (W. caled) *hard* Prol. 42 (.i. cruaid O'Dav. 65) 107, Aug. 10, Dec. 1, dat. sg. m. calad Ap. 2, dat. sg. f. calaid Aug. 17, n. pl. m. calaid Jan. 17. Probably for *scalad : cf. O. Boh. skala *stone*, Goth. skalja *ziegel*.
Calistus, (Celestus A) Oc. 14 = Calixtus, a pope, mart. at Rome temp. Alexander, *Ob. & Mart.* pp. 166–7, spelt by Boll. Callistus seu Callixtus.
callaind, callaut (=kalendae), s. *the calends*, particularly the calends of January, O'Don. Four Masters A.D. 1563 dat. sg. Prol. 325, Jan. 1, Ep. 1, gen. pl. kaluc (kailnc B) Prol. 306 and kalland Prol. 324 : 6 callaind có hinit *from the kalends of January to Shrovetide* S.M. 186, W. calan-ganaf *All Saints' day*. In the St. Gall Priscian the n is assimilated : de chaldigud (gl. de kalendario) 181ᵃ, prídkalde (gl. pridie kalendas) 220ᵃ. So in áildiu compar. of álind.
Callda, Callde, Callae, gen. pl. *Chaldaeorum*, Ep. 456.
callece, adv. *at once, forthwith* Prol. 239, (where A has coleci, B colléce).
camm, adj. *crooked* (= σκαμβός, Gaul. cambo, Glück K.N. 34, W. cam) Ap. 7.
Camross, Dec. 16. Ard Camrois is said to be on the margin of Loch Carman in Uí Cennselaig. But in Dec. 16 Camross is inserted in the text by mistake. The rhyme requires Cáinroiss or Cóenroiss, gen. sg. of Cain-ross = Ross-cáin q. v.
canim, *cano* pres. indic. act. 3d sg. canaid Ap. 26, 1st pl. absolute form, canmae, Ep. 242, 3d pl. rel. cantai (canta B) Dec. 28, 2d sg. imper. can (cain B= cane) Feb. 15, Apl. 4, Nov. 11, 2dy. pres. 3d sg. nochannad *canebat* pref. B. 3d pl. nochantais July 30, cantais Dec. 28 D. pret. 3d sg. rochan Nov. 27 B. reduplicated pret. 3d sg. cachain Ap. 26 D. Dec. 8, 3d sg. pres. indic. passive canar Ep. 187, canair Sep. 11.
Candida, martyred at Rome, Boll. Oct. 3, Dec. 1.
canóin, s. *a canon*, Corm. 11 : (W. canon), gen. sg. (pl. ?) canoine pref.
cantaic, (= canticum, W. canig) s. Ep. 190, gen. pl. ba bind cool inanén ic gabail tsalm 7 cantaci ic moludh incboimhdhidh, *sweet was the song of the birds a-singing psalms and canticles in praise of the Lord*, H. 2, 16, col. 393.
Capitolinus, Dec. 10.
caor, s. m. Dec. 14 D = caur *champion* LU. 114ᵃ (= W. cawr *giant*, Skr. çūra, KAVARA), n. pl. córaid Prol. 65, gen. pl. corud (leg. córad) Prol. 167.
carim, *I love* (W. caru) pres. indic. act. 1st sg.-caru Ep. 311, carim (cairim B) Ep. 50 (carim, cairimse Z². 434), 1st. pl.-caram Prol. B. 134. 3rd pl. 2dy pres. no chartais Nov. 16. 1st pl. imperative, caram Prol. 264 : s- pret. 3rd sg. carais Jan. 15, 27, May 26, June 15, July 9, car Mar. 24, pl. carsat May 7, 8, carsait Mar. 15, pret. part. pass. cartha May 9. Cognate with Lat. carus, Fr. 'cherir, Gaul. Carnutus *amatus*, Glück K. W. 7.
cara, s. m. (gen. carat, dat. carit) an ant-stem, *friend* Ep. 371, Z. 4, 255. W. câr pl. ceraint.
caratrad, s. *friendship* pref. B. P. O'C. also gives the form caradras.
carcair, s. f. (= carcer, W. carchar) July 10. gen. sg. carcra Dec. 30, na carcra Ep. 516 (but carcre Z². 212.), dat. pl. carcraib Prol. 45, Ap. 27.
Carissim, Ap. 16, a virgin. A Corinthian martyr Charicssa is commemorated at this day. A Saint Carissus also.
Carnech, gen. carnig, May 16 : cairneach is said by O'Clery to mean *priest* (sagart).

Carpre (Cairpre, Corpbri) Cúla raithin, *of Coleraine*, Nov. 11. Died circ. A.D. 560.
Carthach the senior, Mar. 5. carthaig (gl. amantes) Z^2 226, carthacha (gl. affecta) Ml.-66, W. Carataue, Z^3. 72. O. Celt. Caratâcos. Carthach the junior, of Rathin, May 14.
Cass, mac Finchrach Araide, pref. B.
cateat, lit. *quicunque sunt illi* (c'at-éat) Sep. 22.
cath, s. masc. u-stem (= Gaul. catu, W. cad, O.H.G. hadu *battle*) Prol. 242. gen. sg. catha Prol. 139, June 29, Aug. 23, 24, Nov. 15, Ep. 275, dat. sg. cath Ap. 2, June 8.
    Compounds: cathbarr, caithfer, cathmíl, ban-chath.
Cathach, gen. enthaig Mar. 8 = W. cadawg.
cathar, Aug. 15, case and meaning doubtful. O'Curry translated '*of cathedrals*.' Can it be an adjective = W. cadarn *firmus, fortis, strenuus*, or the nom. sg. in opposition with Fer dá chrích, meaning *shield* (W. cadar).
cathardu, acc. pl. pref. seems to mean *cathedrals*.
cathbarr, s. m. *helmet* Jan. 10 (lit. '*battle-top*'), gen. sg. oc tar(r)aing in cat(h)bairr orda dia cind, LU. 51ᵃ.
cathfer, caithfer (W. cadwr) s. m. *champion* (lit. *battle-man*) June 3, n. pl. cathfir June 27 : a 'Nemanus filius Cathir' occurs in Reeves' Col. 51.
cathir, cathair s. fem. c-stem, *city*, Z^2. 259. Dec. 11, Ep. 149. gen. sg. cathrach Ep. 236, Z^2. 260, dat. sg. cathir Prol. 180, Ep. 544. acc. cathraig Z^2. 261, n. pl. cathraig Prol. 205, Z^2. 261. gen. pl. cathrach Ep. 460. In Nov. 23 according to the glossographer cathair is the locative singular. Cognate with Lat. castrum, W. caer.
cathlae, adj. = catholicus (Corm. 10, W. cydolig), dat. sg. f. cathlaic Aug. 28.
cathmíl, s. m. *battlesoldier* Oc. 21, Ep. 262, gen. sg. cathmíled, LU. 88ᵇ, 129ᵃ.
cc for c after r and l: sercc Prol. 186, balce Mar. 21, 22, Ercc May 12, talccai, elccn, June 7, Doleenin Aug. 6.
cé, cia, ci, conj. *because, although* Prol. 101, 230, 241, Ap. 27, Nov. 6, Ep. 27. 125, 146, 397, Z. 671 : *if* Prol. 257 : in combination with the verb subst. cit Prol. 245, Ep. 81, ciat *quamvis sunt* Prol. 149 B, 153, cé-r-bo *quamvis fuit* Prol. 93, ciapu Nov. 7 B, cé-btar *quamvis fuerunt* Prol. 74=ciaptar Ep. 14, ce-s-u *quamvis est* Ep. 133, cipé pref.
cé, s. .i. talam *earth* O'Cl. in the phrase for bith-ché Prol. 103 *on earthworld*: omun fíadat for bith- ché Harl. 1802 fo. 36 *the fear of the Lord on the earthworld*, dílnd (.i. indlies) bethath ché (.i. indomuin chentair) *profit of the life of earth* Broce. h. 22. From the root KI to go, as γῆ from root ga *to go*, πέων from root PAD, Curtius No. 291, οὖας and solum from root SAD, Curtius No. 281. From the primary meaning 'go' was developed that of the ground gone upon.
Cebrianus, Jan. 23 for Severianus, q. v.
cech, pron. adj. *every*, Prol. 110, Ep. 289, Z^2. 361, gen. sg. m. cech Sep. 11, cech neut. Prol. 160, 228, Ep. 21, 33, doubtful whether masc. or neut. cech Ap. 13, 23, July 22, Oct. 22, Nov. 8. gen. sg. fem. cecha elainde Ep. 510, neut. cecha bordgail Prol. 275, cecha laithi Ep. 5. dat. sg. n. May 27. Dec. 12. Ep. 35. acc. sg. cech-n Prol. 49, Jan. 24, Ap. 4, July 15, Sep. 28, Oc. 29, Ep. 206, 215, 345, 546, abl. sg. Ap. 22.
cech-ei *quisque* Ep. 43=cachae, Z^2. 361.
cech-óen *unusquisque* Ep. 157=cachóen Z^2. 361, and Ep. 5 B.
cechaing, *ivit* Jan. 25, Mar. 20, May 22, June 13, July 23, Oc. 9, 3d sg. redupl. pret. act. of cingim q. v.
céim, adj. Dec. 31 .i. caoin, O'R.
ceim, Prol. 139A a mistake for géim q. v.
ceim, s. neut. n-stem, *step, grade, degree*, Mar. 20, Nov. 30, Ep. 247, gen. pl. cémenn South. 92ᵃ dat. pl. cémmnaib LU. 27ᵇ. acc pl. cemmen, céimmen inna ccimmen (gl. gressus) Ml. 22ᵃ. W. cam as leim from *lengmen=W. lam. From *cengmen, v. cingim, &c.

cein mair June 10, a phrase used as an interjection *O happy*, lit. (I think) *bene manrat*.
céiu, conj. *while*, pref. B. Ep. 298. Z². 707.
ceithri v. cethri.
1. céle, céile, s. m. *a bondservant* Mar. 3, Ep. 239, 307, 426, 554 : cf. sóir-chele (gl. libertus) Z. 40.
2. céle, s. m. *socius* Z². 365, n. pl. céli Ep. 14. O'Dav. 65 ceile .i. cara, Z². 229. dat. acc. pl. célib, ceiliu ib. 231.
celebrad, s. *celebratio*, dat. sg. Aug. 26, acc. sg. Feb. 15. W. celefrad.
celebraim, *celebro*, 2d sg. imperative celebair Sep. 12, celebair, ceilebair, Nov. 14, 17.
celim, =*celo*, Goth. hila, 3d sg. ni cheil *non celat* Z². 430 : 1 pl. pres. indic. act. celam Prol. 142, 3d pl. nuda chelat (gl. latentes) Ml. 54ᶜ, fut. -célam (rhymes with dénam) Ep. 87. 3d sg. pres. indic. passive -celar Feb. 20, Aug. 11, p. part. pass. clithe Dec. 9, Ep. 306.
cell. s. f=*cella*, gen. sg. cille pref., Mar. 1, 26, dat. sg. cill, Oc. 16.
 Cell Achaid dromfota, Mar. 26, now Killeigh in King's County.
 Cell Muine, Mar. 1 *cella rubi*, the Welsh Hen Meneu ' Vetus rubus ' Haddan & Stubbs i. 121 St. David's in Wales, Mart. Tall. 39.
 Cell Rúaid, Oc. 16, now Kilroot, Co. Antrim.
Cellach, a deacon, gen. Cellaig, Oc. 7 : in dioecesi colgion filii cellaig, Reeves Col. 65.
Cellar, gen. Cellair pref. n.
célliu, céilliu, Prol. 316, seems to mean *guidance*=W. pwyllad, Br. poellat.
Cellóc, Mar. 26.
cen, prep. *sine* (governs the acc. and aspirates) Prol. 42, 63, 207, Jan. 13, 17, 22, Feb. 10, Ap. 28, May 11, 17, 26, 30, July 8, 29, Aug. 7, 17, Sep. 15, 17, Nov. 8, 19, 28, Dec. 8, Ep. 167, 221, 247, cognate with κενεός.
 cen-beith, Ep. 375, *not to be*, lit. *without being*.
 cen-nach (cenach A) *without any* Prol. 291, July 8.
cén, cian, adj. *remotus*, *longinquus*; bicén *afar* Ep. 110, compared by Glück (K.N. 59) with Aeol. κῆνος, Ion. κεῖνος, O.N.hân, hón *ille*.
cengal, s.=*cingulum* (W. tengl), dat. sg. cengul pref. B.
cenn, cend, s. m. (W. penn, Πένθος?) *head*, *chief*, *end*, Feb. 1, 25, July 24, Nov. 29. gen. sg. cind Feb. 27, Ap. 7, July 9, Aug. 10=cinn Z². 223, dat. ciunn Z². 224. acc. sg. cend Ap. 23, loc. sg. cind (cind bliadna *at the year's end*) Sep. 17, gen. pl. cend-n Dec. 18, ar cend fri cend *from end to end*, Ep. 8.
Cenn-etig, Ap. 7 (lit. *Etech's head*) a place in King's County, now Kinnitty, Joyce 148.
Cennfaelad, Abbot of Bennchor, Ap. 8. He died A.D. 704.
Cenngarad, Aug. 10, now Kingarth in the S.E. of Bute, Scotland, gen. Iolan episcopus Cinngarath obiit, Reeves, Col. 377.
Cenn Sáili, July 9. now Kinsaley in Co. Dublin, Mart. Tall. 39.
céol, s.n. *music*, *song*, gen. sg. ceoil, ciuil, acc. sg. cool Nov. 27, cansit céol mbec LU. 43ᵇ : in fogur íarum dorígensat bá céol melduch n-ailgen-som, LU, 24ᵇ.
céolda, adj. .i. binn, 3 Ir. Gl. 128, *musical*, *melodious*, acc. sg. Jan. 22.
Cerball, gen. Cerbaill pref. = Kjarval of the sagas. Adamnán (Reeves Col. 68) latinises the gen. sg. by ' Cerbulis ' : the b here is a v.
cert, s. *a right* pref.
cert. adj. *right*, is hí in riagail chert pref. fír-chert Ep. 156 : comparative certu Ep. 148, ingcert *incertus* Ml. 128.
césaim, *patior* : céssimse Z². 434, 3d sg. pret. rochés Prol. 86, Jan. 17 B, Aug. 17, 20, Oc. 17 : rocés *qui passus est*, Ml. 17ᵃ, 3d sg. s- pret. abs. césais Jan. 17, Feb. 23, Ap. 26 (céssais B), Aug. 28. Lith. kencżù *dulde*, Windisch.
césad, céssad, s. m. *passio* Jan. 23, Feb. 20, May 31, June 26, Aug. 5, Nov. 23, gen. sg. césta Aug. 25, Ep. 270, Z². 239, also césto, dat. sg. césad May 23, Nov. 22, acc. césad Feb. 15, 27, 28, Mar. 4, Ap. 20, July 10, 23, 27, Aug. 29, Sep. 14, Oc. 4, 14, Nov. 15, 20, acc. pl. céstu Ep. 320.

césu, céssu *quamvis est* Ep. 133.
cet, s. *permission* pref. 38 : cet cia théis fri búig : cet (gl. fiat) Tirech. 7 ; now cead O'D. Gr. 429-430. W. ced *favour, gift.*
cet, *hundred, centum,* W. cant, gen. sg. céit, July 24 D. cét Mar. 12, Ep. 188. acc. sg. cét-n July 4, Oc. 5, n. pl. cét, Sep. 1, Oc. 10, n. dual Oc. 30, dat. dual cétaib, Ap. 3, fo cét cét *a hundred hundred times,* Prol. 151. dat. pl. cétaib Prol. 212, 328, May 12, 13, Aug. 7. Sep. 8, Oc. 9 B, Oc. 16. cét mfle ' 100,000,' July 24.
cétach, adj. *centenarius* Z². 307, gen. sg. m. cétaig, Nov. 10, applied to Conn cétchathach *hundred, battled.*
cétáin, s. *first fast* (jejunium), dia cétain *Wednesday* pref. dat. hi cetain LU. 25ᵇ. Here cét is = Gaulish cintu. Glück K.N. 126.
cetal, s.n. *song* June 1, Ep. 150, cetul pref. gen. pl. Oc. 1. v. soér-chétul.
céte, s. *road, way :* for chete .i. for conair Dec. 20. B. But O'Dav. 66 explains ceite by aonach (nine) *heaven's assembly,* and so in the addition to Cormac's glossary : " cete a coitu, vel quia ibi equi cito currunt." O'Clery gives the four meanings, conair, *path,* aonach *assembly,* faithce, *a green,* tulach, *a hill.*
cethair-fichet, *twenty-four* pref. B.
cethardae, s.n. *four things* pref. Z². 313.
cethorcha, *forty* (an ant-stem), used alone, gen. s. cethorchat (cethrachat B) Mar. 9.
cethorchat, *forty* (an a-stem), dat. sg. co cethorcat cresen Oc. 24, literally *with a forty of venerable ones.*
cethramad, *fourth,* Feb. 29.
cethramain, s. *quarter,* dat. pl. cethramnaib pref. B.
cethramthu, s.f. a *fourth part,* Patric, Tara, 176, dat. sg. cethrumthain pref. pl. cethramdin Z². 309.
cethri, ceithri, *four,* with all genders, ceithri deich Oc. 16, cothri deich Oc. 25, cetri chet Sep. 1 B.
cethrur, s.n. *four persons* Jan. 20, Z². 313 == cethror Oc. 26.
cétne, cétna, *same* Z². 229. Prol. 202, 244.
ch, from c between vowels (loch, liche), from g, in the desinence of monosyllables, tech, dí-rinch, tor-mach, im-mach, ro-scáich, prolach, Prol. 144. cht for ct, secht, ocht.
chucut, *unto thee* Prol. 280 : compare for the infection of the first c chucut *ad te* Z². 181, chucunn *ad nos,* Maelísu's hymn : cuc =the reduplicated cu-cth, where cth=ar in sará (Windisch) and ut is the suffixed pers. pron. of the 2d sg.
cia, conj. *quod, quamvis* see cé.
cia, pron. interrog. Z². 355 (W. pwy, Skr. kim, kis, Lat. quis) : cia(ernail) aiste *what kind of metre ?* pref. cia roadnocht isin lige *who was buried in the grave ?* ib. ciamnith, cia rét, ib.
ciall, s.f. *sensus* (W. pwyll, Skr. ći *wahrnehmen,* Beitr. viii. 39), gen. sg. ceille Z². 242, acc. sg. ceill Ep. 52, n. pl. at báetha cialla ban *silly are women's minds* Sgl.
cían, adj. *remotus, longus,* in erchian : see cén supra.
Cianán of Doimliacc (now Dulcek), Nov. 24, a dimin. of cian.
Ciar, a virgin, Jan. 5, Oc. 16, Goth. skeirs ?
Ciarán, Prol. 182, of Saigir, Mar. 5. Ciaran Clúana (maccunois) p. 9 and Reeves Col. 23, 24, latinised Quiarnus Lib. Hymn. fo. 31ᵃ. His father was Beóán the wright, of the Lathairn Molt, his mother Darerca, LB. 16. n. pl. Ciaráin Prol. 235.
cías, *qui ptorat,* Ep. 350, 3d. sg. rel. pres. of cíim (now written caoidhim), root KVAS, whence also Lat. quer-or, ques-tus.
Cicilia, Sep. 1, Nov. 22 = Cecilia virgin and martyr : see her legend, Jameson S. & L. Art, 583.
cid, *cur est,* pref. 3, *quamvis est* Prol. 201.
cimbid, s. *a captive* Ap. 26, Aug. 14, Z². 233, gen. sg. cimmeda Br. h. 2, acc. pl. cimbidi (gl. custodias) Lib. Arm. 189, b. 1, seems a deriv. from cim .i. cuing *a yoke* Gl. 183.
cin, s. *a crime,* acc. sg. cinaid Jan. 17, Aug. 17, n. pl. cinaid Ep. 387, acc. pl. cen chinta friusom (gl. gratis) Ml. 19, conmill cin na cumachtach, ní aibéor bús mó, itir elainn is geinelach cusa nómad n-ó O'Dav. 71.

cing, s.m. a t-stem, *champion, warrior*, Z². 255, July 24, Aug. 20, 24, acc. sg. cingid-n Sep 13, gen. pl. cinged-n Feb. 14 (this is exactly the Gaulish Cinges, gen. Cingetis, Glück K. N. 76, Cingeto-rix, Ver-cingeto-rix). Hence ain-ching .i. anraidh no laoch O'Cl. and cingthecht *championship* in dochingthecht.
cingim, *I go*, cingid dar firu *he surpasses men* LU. 48ᵇ: cengnit .i. tiagait *runt* LU. 29ᵃ. is cumma no cinged dara cholaind 7 no chessed fón dar crínach, LU. 84: redupl. pret. cechaing q.v. cognate perhaps with κωχεύω, Windisch, Kuhn's Zeits. xxi. 432.
cinniu, *I determine* : ní ciunet *non finiunt* Sg. 147ᵃ. 1 sg. s-pret. rocinnius (gl. definivi) Z.² 462, 3d sg. rochind pref. B. 3 pl. rochindset Ep. 108: a deriv. from cenn q.v.
cinniud, s. *determination*, dat. sg. iarsin cindiud, pref. B = cinniuth *definitio* Z². 802.
cipé, *quamvis sit ille*, ci-p-é, pref.
Ciprian, gen. cipriain, Sep. 14, Cyprianus bishop of Carthage and mart. A.D. 258, Boll. and Jameson S. & L. Art, 684.
Ciriacus, May 12, June 20, for Quiriacus Aug. 28. At May 12 the martyr (Roman?) Cyriacus is meant: at June 20 Cyriacus mart. Tomis in Scythia, Boll.
Ciric, Prol. 137 and see Giric = 'S. Quiricus filius' commemorated with S. Julia vidua and martyred at Tarsus in Cilicia, Boll. He is the Welsh Curig. See a paper on his legend (by Mr. H. W. Lloyd), Arch. Cambrensis for April, 1875, pp. 145–164.
Cirill, gen. s. (Cairill B), May 9. Not identified.
Cirillus, Ap. 26 = Cyrillus, 'martyr Axiopoli in Mysia inferiore,' Boll.
Cirine, Sep. 30 (= Hieronymus, as mici for mihi) S. Jerome, first of the four Latin Fathers, ob. A.D. 420. acc. mad la cirine Ml. 74ᵈ.
Cirinus, Sep. 15 = Cyrinus a martyr.
cit, *quamvis sunt* Prol. 245, Ep. 81. See cé.
-cíu, *video* from *cesiu, root cas *to shine, to see* (Windisch). See at-chíu, fres-cíu.
Claenad, Cloenad, May 18, now Clane in Kildare, Mart. Tall. 3, nomen cille fil illaignib .i. in huib faelan, Rawl. 505. Cassan claenta, the Path of Claue, occurs in the Talland Etair, LL.
Clacnros, Dec. 16, B, a variant of Cáinros.
claideb, cloideb, s. m. *gladius* (from cladius, as gloria from closia) Prol. 101, gen. sg. claidib (ms. claidem!) Ep. 484. W. cleddyf m. Corn. cledhe; cf. Gr. ἐλαύω *I. brandish*, Lat. clādes.
cland, s. f. *proles* pref., gen. sg. clainde Ep. 510, Z². 242, dat. sg. claind Tir. 3, Z². 243, gen. pl. clann Dec. 18 Rawl. 505. W. plant *offspring*: borrowed from Lat. planta *scion*: So case, caille, corcur, clúm, cruimther, cuithe, s-cipar from pascha, pallium, purpura, pluma, pre(s)byter, puteus, piper.
clandach, adj. *having children* (W. plantog), dat. sg. f. clandaig, Jan. 12 .i. clann mor propter multitudinem ejus discipulorum, Rawl. 505, acc. sg. m. clandach May 22.
clandaim = *planto* (W. planu, planthonnor, gl. fodientur, Juv.) 3d sg. pres. indic. pass. clanntar Aug. 9, 3d sg. pret. roclandad, roclannad Feb. 14.
clár, *table* (W. clawr *a cover*) dat. sg. hi claar cridi *in tabulá cordis* Z². 230.
clár-ainech, lit. '*table-face*' Oc. 12, a noseless person, O'Cl.
clais, s. f. n. pl. classa Prol. 181 : ' clais .i. claischeadul no cantaireacht' *music, melody, harmony*, especially church musick, P. O'C.
Claudicus, Dec. 4 (= Claudius, Ob. & Mart.) a Nicomedian saint.
Claudinus, Nov. 8, perhaps for Claudianus.
cléir, s. f. *a train, a company*, May 19, June 22, Sep. 28. Nov. 8, 16, Ep. 287, dat. sg. cléir Jan. 3, 12, Mar. 31, May 14, 27, July 5, 26, 29, Aug. 16, 28, Oc. 17, Dec. 7, 15, Ep. 43, acc. sg. cléir-n Feb. 28, B., Ap. 30, May 15, June 2, Oc. 7, voc. sg. a chléir Ep. 373 B, n. pl. cléri, cléire Mar. 14.

2 h

GLOSSARIAL INDEX.

Clemens, bishop of Ancyra and a martyr, Jan. 23 : third bishop of Rome and a martyr temp. Trajan, Nov. 23.

Clemint, Nov. 14, 21. At Nov. 14, the Clemint is Clementius, Clemens, or Clementinus, a saint of Eraclea in Thrace.

clérech, s. m. (=*cléricus*, Corn. cloireg, Bret. cloarec) June 21, n. pl. clerig pref., acc. pl. clérchiu ib.
1. clí, clíi, s. f. *body* Sep. 10 (in chlí Goidil. 38), cf. κρέας ?
2. clí, clíi, March 8, Aug. 6, Oc. 6, Corn. 10 *housepost* or *beam*. Metaphorically *a prince*, cf. 'the kingpost.'

cliar, s. f. *a train, a company*, and in the case of an ecclesiastic '*clergy*' (Br. cloer), May 19, B, Sep. 28, B, voc. sg. a chliar Ep. 373.

cliarach, adj. *having trains* Oc. 27.

clithí, Dec. 9, Ep. 306, part. fut. pass. from celim q. v.

clóim, *muto*: menic rochloi dath a drech *often his face changed colour*, poem after Félire, see coemchlóim.

cloch, s. f. *stone*, acc. sg. cloich Z.² 244, n. pl. clocha Prol. 194, acc. pl. fri clocha LU. 19ᵃ=κρόκη *pebble*. The W. clog is masc. Hence Clochar.

1. clochar, gen. Clochair Nov. 17 *stony land*, name of Clogher in Tyrone : a loco qui clocher uocatur Lib. Arm. 8ᵇ 1 : 'usque ad Clocherum filiorum Daimeni,' Reeves' Columba 111 : cf. κροκάλη.

2. clochar, s. .i. coimhthionol, O'Cl. *an assembly* Aug. 15 (cf. Gael. clachan *village*).

cloemchlód, *mutare*, cloemcloither *mutatur, mutabitur* Ep. 420, rocloimcloiset *mutarunt* Lib. Hymn. p. 204. Seems a corruption of coemchlód.

clóen, adj. *wrong, partial*, a na-participle from the root cli (Corssen Ausspr. i. 536), as ἐπινός from ἐι (Schleicher Comp. 430). Goth. hlains, Lat. in-clinare. Hence

clóine, s. f. *unrighteousness, wrong*, acc. sg. Ep. 424, duairci clóini ndo fadesin inti asagusi etarthotaim acharat *he who greatly desires his friend's ruin causes wrong to himself*, Ml. 128.

cloithe, *victus*, Dec. 14, dat. pl. donaib cloithib (gl. victis) Ml. 45, cloithir (gl. involvitur) Ml. 16ᵇ, clod (gl. prosternere) Gild.

cloor, *audio* 3d sg. pret. pass. rocloss Oc. 15, 3d sg. 2dy pres. pass. roclotha Aug. 24.

clothach, adj. *famous*, gen. sg. m. clothaig, May 4, O.W. Clotuc Glück K.N. 81.

Clothrann, Clothrand, gen. sg. Jan. 10.

clú, s. *fame, renown* (ςravas, κλέος, Gl. K. N. 71, Slav. slovo, slava Z.² 57) Mar. 5, Aug. 11, Ep. 86.

cluain, s. m. (n. ?) *a meadow* Ir. Gl. p. 90, gen. sg. clono Lib. Arm. 9, b. 2. 12, a. 1, cluana Prol. 180, 184, Jan. 15, Feb. 17, Ap. 4, May 16, June 13, Aug. 21, Oc. 6, Dec. 12, 13, 19, 23, dat. cluain May 26, Aug. 6, hi cloin lagen Lib. Arm. 16, b. 1. κατ' ἐξοχήν applied to Chuain maccu Nois, Z². xxiii, the celebrated monastery erected by S. Ciaran A.D. 548.

Clúain Aird, May 26, now Kilpeacon (Cell-Beccáin) barony of Clan William, co. Tipperary.
Clúain Brónaig, Dec. 19, now Clonbrony in co. Longford.
Clúain Credai, Jan. 15, now Killeedy, in co. Limerick, Joyce 141.
Clúain Dolccáin, Aug. 6, now Clondalkin in co. Dublin.
Clúain Eidnech, Feb. 17, and Pref. now Clonenagh in Queen's County.
Clúain Eoais, Ap. 4, now Clones in co. Monaghan : familia clono auiss Lib. Arm. 9, b. 2.
Clúain Fertae, Dec. 23, now Clonfert in co. Galway.
Clúain Iraird, Aug. 21, Dec. 12, now Clonard in co. Meath.

cluinim, *I hear*, 2d sg. imperative cluinte Ep. 314, 365, 425, 2d sg. redupl. pret. cúala June 13, root klus. 3d sg. pres. passive clúinter Prol. 282. Root klu.

clúm, s. f. = *pluma*, gen. sg. clúime Prol. 126, acc. lár gel amal chluim LU. 25ᵇ. W. pluf *plumage*.
cn for gu, Icnati, Dec. 20 (Laud, 610).
cned, s. f. *wound*, acc. sg. ro-chncid Aug. 28 A, dat. pl. cnedaib 1 Proc. R.I.A. (MSS.) 167 : cf. κνίζη, κνίζω, A.S. hnitan *tundere*, or is it from KAN, καίνω ?
cnedach, adj. *having wounds*, Ep. 297. So in O'Dav. 61 s. v. cnocht : ced cnedach achoindsi cucht.
cnet, s. f. *a sigh* Prol. 228, acc. sg. cneit Ep. 314 B. rochuala cneit echach iúil LU. 49ᵃ, and v. rochneit, sir-chnet, acc. pl. cneta Ep. 325 (where, in A, we have, wrongly cnedu). Root KAN *to sound*.
có, co. 1. prep. (= κατά) cum acc. *to*, Jan. 5, 6, 25, Feb. 17, Mar. 10, May 23. Nov. 11, 22 : used after verbs of motion, calling, proclaiming.
  2. prefix forming adverbs from adjectives (cf. κατὰ μικρόν, ὀλίγον, κ.τ.λ.), co-firbail June 15, co-hopunn pref. B. coleir, colléir Prol. 332, co-rígda June 13, cu-menice pref. 48.
  3. prep. for con, Ep. 43.
  4. conj., for con, Prol. 298, Ep. 36.
cobac, see Echaid cobac.
cobair, s. *help, assistance*, July 28, Oc. 19, Dec. 29, Fiacc 15, dat. sg. July 24. Ep. 44, 271, 292, 293, acc. sg. Colm. 5, Sep. 28, Ep. 381, 388, 400. An acc. sg. cobraid (cobraig B) occurs in Oc. 18.
coblu, v. colba.
Cobthach Coeilbreg pref., from cob *victory*, with which Fick (die Griech. Personennamen, lxxvi) compares κύβων and O.N. hap *erfolg*.
coclaid, s. the reading of the Franciscan copy in Dec. 24 for the cocrait of A and B.
cocrait, s. *a brace, a couple*, Dec. 24, shortened from co-corait ? see Cormac s.v. Essem, and cf. amail geilt da each hi corait *like the grazing of two horses in a yoke* O'Curry Lect. 634. For a cognate verb see at cori supra. In Three Ir. Gl. 138 cocrait is explained as a verb = imraidit.
cocrich, s. *a province*, pref.
codail, adj. dat. sg. m. Ep. 386, meaning doubtful, qy. *skinny* ?
coduil, s. *skin, hide* (ms. codail), acc. sg. Dec. 8, rhymes with romuir. Root SKU ? codal a cutilia .i. a pelle, quia cutis cutilia cuticula sit, O'Mulc. 231. As to the hide absent from Ecbyrht's coracle, cf. the description of S. Brendan's boat, cited by Wright, St. Brandan, p. 58 : Sanctus Brendanus et qui cum eo erant, acceptis ferramentis fecerunt naviculam levissimam, costatam et columnatam ex vimine, sicut mos est in illis partibus, *et cooperuerunt eam coriis bovinis* ac rubricatis in cortice roborina linieruntque foris omnes iuncturas navis, et expendia quadraginta dierum et butirum ad pelles præparandas assumpserunt ad cooperimentum navis, etc.
coel, adj. *slender* (W. cul), Ep. 386, coil (gl. exilis), Ml. 18.
Coeil-breg, v. cobthach.
Coelbud, gen. Coel buid pref.
cóem, (cupima ? root KUP) adj. *loveable* (W. cu, Corn. cuf), n. pl. m. coim, coem Sep. 2. fem. coema, Mar. 14, comparative cóimiu, Táin bó Fr., superl. coemem Z². 78. The form cóima cited Z². 236 as an example of the n. pl. m. is probably a mistake for cóimsa *caritatis* : cf. gaibid inumib an etach macc cóimsa *sumite circa vos hanc vestem filiorum caritatis*, Z². 214. cóem-aite s. *loveable tutor*, Aug. 24.
Cóemán, of Ard Coemáin, now Ard Cavau, in Wexford, gen. Coemáin, June 12.
Cocmán Brecc, of Ross-ech, now Russagh, in the north of Westmeath, Sep. 14.
Coemán of Enach Truim, now Annatrim, in Queen's County, Nov. 3.
coemchlóim *I change*, coemchlóither, Ep. 420 C, *mutatur* : coinchláim (gl. cambio) Z². 435, dia coemchlót dath *if they change colour*, LU. 23ᵇ. ro-choinchlóiset L. Hymn. p. 104.
cóemdae, coemda adj. *loveable*, May 12, acc. sg. Aug. 5, Sep. 19, Dec. 28, Ep. 170.

2 h 2

Cóemgen, (Coemgein B.) June 3, acc. sg. Coemgen, Coemgin Ep. 555. The 'falling' here referred to is the falling of the rock which formed the roof of the cave at Glendalough. See Vita S. Coemgeni, Bolland. 3 June.
coemna, s.=caomhna .i. comairce *protection*, O'Cl. Gl. mian lim cella do chaemna, Battle of Moira, 162, don bith-choemnu *to the eternal protection*, Mar. 13.
Cóemóc, dimin. of coem, Mar. 13.
coemthar, la crist coemthar folaith, Ap. 10, la crist coemthar ndile, Ep. 66, meaning obscure
cóemte, see coimti ?
coibse, s. f.=*confessio*, Tir. 3, gen. sg. coibsen, Ep. 185, n. pl. coibsena *confessiones*, Corm. acc. pl. ib. Tur. 58.
coibtell, v. caiptel.
cóic, cuic, *five*, Prol. 327, acc. Aug. 7.
cóica, cúecca, (*cóicechant*) *fifty*, Jan. 30, Oct. 9, coecca ar cét martir, *fifty*+100 *martyrs*, dat. pl. coectaib, Aug. 7 D, coccaib, Aug. 7 B (but coua trib cóectuib srian I.U. 85ª), acc. pl. coeca Dec. 10 B (leg. cóecta ?)
cóicat, n. *fifty*, absolute form, n. dual dá choicat, Oc. 25 : acc. dual in da coicat, Dec. 10 D. n. pl. na tri coicat, Fiacc 25, gen. pl. Ep. 179.
coicertad, Ep. 95, *correction, adjustment*, cen smacht rig oc cocertad acotrebi, I.U. 46ª ; cf. in coceirt (gl. emendationem) Z. 997, cocart *corrige*, cocarti *emendandum*, conaicertus *emendari*, concoiccortar .i. brothocar, O'R.
coich, pron. interr. *who* ! Pref. coich boi coich bia beo *who has been, who will be alive* ? Amra Col. coich thussu. oliat *who art thou ? say they* Scirgl. Conc.
cóim, adj. v. cóem.
coimdiu, comdiu s.m. *lord*. Z.² 255, Prol. 90, 160, 229, gen. sg. coinded Mar. 10, Z.² 256, dat. sg. comdid Ep. 218=coimdid Z². 257, coch cenu nad timmairgg a coimdiu *every chief whom his lord constrains not*, Crith Gablach, 503.
coimét, s. *protection*, dat. sg. Ep. 149=cumét q.v.
cointi, (coemti B.) n. pl. *comrades*, Mar. 11, coimide, *a train or retinue, waiters or attendants*, P. O'C. The nom. sg. must be coimid or coimte, which, however, I have not met.
coimtecht, coemthecht, s. *company*, dat. sg. Dec. 20, Ep. 291.
coindlech, adj. v. caindlech.
coir, s. *sin*, dat. pl. coruib espai, Reeves' Culdees. The acc. sg. perhaps occurs in Dec. 12, but the Franciscan gloss explains it by laim *manum*, and so O'Dav. 66.
coir, adj. *just*, Oc. 26, Ep. 432, 433. It is a dissyllable, like cauir in the Sg. Incant. compar. coru, Z.² 276.
coisced, coicsed, (con-sochedi) s. *correptio, institutio*, acc. sg. Ep. 393.
coisecrad, coissecrad, coscorad, s. m. *consecratio*, gen. sg. cossecartha, pref. B. dat. sg. coisecrad, Tir. 13, acc. sg. Sep.15, Nov. 18, 19.
col, s. m (n. ?) gen. in chuil gl. piaculi, *sin*, Ep. 98, like W. cwl, is ex *culpa : cf. Lat. culpa.
colba, (leg. colbu ?) *love, friendship*, Ep. 74. O'Dav. 65 gives the line as flatha crist is cobla (coblu, MacF.) O'Cl. has colbha .i. condalbha no connailbhe .i. baidh. P. O'C. has colbha .i. baidh no cairdeas, *favour, friendship*, and explains cobla by condalbu= O'Reilly's condalbha, *lore, friendship*.
colinn, s. f. *caro*, Z.² 212, 249 (=W. calon *heart*), gen. sg. colno, colna. Z.² 250, dat. colinn colain Z.² 251, acc. colain, colaind, Mar. 12.
coll, s. *destruction*, Ep. 98 D.
colléce, (coloci A) adv. see calléce.
Colmán, dimin. of Colomb, Feb. 18, May 24, Nov. 1, 14, gen. Colmáin, May 26.
  Colmán Stellán of Tír-dá-glas, May 24.
  Colmán the leper, May 21.
  Colmán of Cell Ruaid, now Kilroot, co. Antrim, Oc. 16.

Colmán of Druimm Ferta, Sep. 3.
Colmán Dub-chuilinn, son of Leníne, of Cluain-uama (Cloyne), Nov. 24.
Colmán Ela, Sep. 26, Oc. 3, Reeves' Columba, 29, 124.
Colmán of Glenn Delmaic, Nov. 5.
Colmán of Inis-bó-finde, now Inishbofin, off the west coast of Mayo, Aug. 8.
Colmán of Inis Mocholmóc, Nov. 14.
Colmán of Land Mocholmoic (now Magheralin in Ulster), Todd, 1 Proc. (MS.) R.I.A. 80, Mar. 30.
Colmán son of Commán, Nov. 21.
Colmán son of Daráine, July 31.
Colmán son of Dímma, Nov. 1.
Colmán maccu Beona, Jan. 22, seems Adamnán's Columbanus filius Beognai.
Colmán maccu Guala, Oc. 30.
Colmán descendant of Finchra, of Senbotha, now Templeshambo, co. Wexford, Oc. 27.
Colmóc, dimin. of Colomb : see Mo-cholmóc.
colomb, s. m. (=W. colomen, Corn. colom, Bret. coulm) gen. coluimb,=Lat. columbus.
Colomb Cille (of the church) June 9, founder and first abbot of Hí. His name is so written in Lib. Arm. 15. b. 2, but Columb in Reeves' Col. 19 : gen. sg. eductio martirum .i. ossuum coluimb cille, Lib. Arm. 16. a. 1.
Colomb of Druim-mór, now Dromore, co. Down, June 7.
Colomb of Ross Glandai Sep. 6. This is Adamnán's Columbanus filius Echudi, vir sanctus, illius monasterii fundator quod scotica uocitatur lingua snamluthir, now Slanore, co. Cavan, Reeves' Col. 171, 173.
Colomb of Tír-dá-glas, now Terryglass, co. Tipperary, Dec 13.
com (1) ex coth-m' *to my*, Jan. 21, Ep. 46, 51.
  (2) ex con-m' *with my* Ep. 327.
  (3) a prefix : com-ainm, com-arbae, com-arc, etc.
  (4) the form assumed by con before a labial, see con.
comainm, s. n. (W. cyfenw *surname*) *cognomen*, Mar. 14, acc. sg. Nov. 11.
Commán, gen. comain, Nov. 21.
comann, s. f. (W. cymun) *communio* (Sacrament of the Lord's supper) Ep. 189, acc. sg. comainn, Ap. 14, but comman, Fiacc, 27.
comarbae, comorba s. m. *heir, successor* Dec. 15, gen. sg. Feb. 27 : cf. Goth. ga-arbja, 2 Beitr. 173.
comarc, s. .i. cuimniugudh *commemoration?* O'Dav. 66, acc. sg. Aug. 5. P. O'C. explains comharc by *demand, request, intreaty*.
combair, s. *aid?* dat. sg. Prol. 243 seems equivalent to cobair.
coinéirgim, *I arise*, 3rd sg. pret. ro choinéirig cách 3 Frag. 172: 2d sg. s- conj. coméir, Aug. 26, imper. comérig LU. 92ᵇ 2d pl. imper. comérgid 97ᵃ ; coineirge laigen *a rising of Leinstermen* 3 Frags. 178, see eséirgim.
comét, s. *a guard*, Mar. 1, Oc. 31, Nov. 12, comet timnae udae (gl. mandatorum custodia, Ml. 45. coméit, s. Ap. 1. May 31. July 31. comét, comeit *servatio* : The transported n in Ap. 1 (comeit n-glaine) shows that this noun is neuter. Root yam?
Comgall, [i.e. Comgell(us) mocu aridi, Reeves' Columba, 220] Abbot of Baugor, May 10. gen. sg. Comgaill Jan. 22=comgill, Reeves' Col. 32. Hence the dimin. comgellan Lib. Arm. 12. b. 1.
Comgan, of Cluain-connaid, Oc. 13.
Comgan, of Glenn-uissen, now Killeshin, near the town of Carlow, gen. comgain Feb. 27.
comgnás, s. seems to mean *companionship? presence?* Ep. 379, where it seems used as the opposite of ingnas.
comiur, better comiuir .i. comdirech O'Dav. 98. adj. *equally just* Prol. 229 : com-iu-ri, root yu *to bind*, whence Lat. jus. O'Cl. writes coindiuir.

comlan, adj. *complete* pref. see Corm. s.v. lanamnas.
comland, s. *a combat, a conflict*, Ep. 163.
comlín, s. *an equal number*, Prol. 295.
Commóc, v. Mochomóc.
comorba, v. comarba.
compert, coimpert, compart, s. f. *conception*, Mar. 25. Sep. 24.
comul, comol s. n. *a gathering, an assembly* (=combal .i. coimlicheangal O'Cl.) July 5. gen. pl. Ep. 446. cethrar ar cét comall ngle do maccaib is da mile, poem cited Dec. 28 B. lll. salm comáll ngle. poem after Félire, l. Br. comull sollamun .i. comtinol bi(id) arcind na sollaman 2 Senchas Már 358, cf. comaltar *jungitur*, accomallte (gl. socius) comaccomol *conjunctio*.
con, adj. *clear, pure*, in con-greit June 17. It occurs uncompounded in the verse A chubus con a anim glan *O clear conscience! O pure soul!* LU. 6ᵃ : cf. καινός from κυρjος and for the change of meaning ἱερός and ishira *fresh*.
1. con, co, cu, prep. cum dat. *with*, Prol. 6, 34, 37, 154, 210, 212, 227. Jan. 19, Feb. 5, 6, 11, 23. July 14 : before b : com Prol. 307, Jan. 27, Aug. 19, 27. before r : cor, Prol. 37 B ; before l : col, Prol. 299, Feb. 21, Oc. 7, 13, 22.

In combination with the possessive pronouns : com *with my* Ep. 52, 327 : cona *with his* Prol. 105, 254, Jan. 24, July 26, Sep. 19, Dec. 3 : *with her* July 5, Aug. 30. Sep. 20 : conan, cona *with their* Jan. 23, July 28 ; before b : conam Prol. 34.

2. con, co, conjunction '*ut*,' con-id Sep. 26, con-om-raib Prol. 11 [cf. conomraib mo riar, LU. 113ᵃ] : com- before b : Ep. 217, com(b)ad Sep. 26, B.
conaicertim *I amend*, con-idn-aicert *eum emendavit*, Ep. 105 B ; conaicertus (gl. emendavi) Z.
conala, v. conrualai.
Conandil, of Es-ruaid (Assaroe) Mar. 8.
concocertim, seems to mean *I adjust*, con-it-cocert *eum concinnavit* Ep. 105 : cf. concoiceccartar (leg. concoiccértar ?) .i. brethocar, O'R.
Cond (Conn?) cétach Nov. 10 = Cond cétchathach LU. 41ᵇ. Four Masters, A.D. 123, gen. cuind Feb. 7.
conda, condu v. cunnu.
condagar, *is required* pref. 1 = coindegar, cuindegar .i. cuingid O'D. supp. condegar Z². 471, condaig *quaerit* Ml. 77.
Conderi, Coinderi : dat. pl. Conderib, Coindeirib, Sep. 3, now 'Connor' a bishop's see in Ulster.
Condlæd, gen. Condlaid, S. Brigit's chief artist, May 3.
condrecaim, *I meet*, 3d sg. pres. indic. act. condrecat, June 10, 14=coindreagaid, O'Don., Supp.
conecmangim, *I cut off*, 1 pl. s-pret. conecmaingsem, Ep. 7, .i. robensam 3 Ir. Gl. 139 : conecmaicsimair sin *we have reaped rushes* O'Dav. 81. cf. iarsin tra dorochair a claideb alluim conculainn conecmoing a láim dói di lugaid, *so then fell his sword out of Cuchulainn's right hand and cut off from Lugaid his right hand*, Ll.
conesta, *quaereretur* pref. 3d sg. s-fut. passive of cuintgim.
conetis, *thou shouldst ask*, 2d sg. sg. s-conj. act. of cuintgim (con-aith-tachim), July 16 : 3d sg. pret. is airi conaitech som a adnacul and *it is therefore he requested his burial there* LU. cited Petrie's Tara, 146, O. Ir. conaitecht : cf. aitchim .i. iarraim no athchuinghim O'Cl. Root TAK.
congabim, *I contain, I take*, 3d sg. pres. indic. act. congaib, congeib Ap. 1, Ep. 76=concipit ; in Ep. 279 it means *sets up*, congabsat gl. continuerunt, aures suas) Lib. Arm. 175, b. 1.

congairiu, Prol. 249, translated by Ebel Z². 249, *voco* (cf. O'R.'s congairim) is possibly not a verb, but merely misspelt for co ngairi *cum pietate*.*
Congrad, gen. Congraid, Conchraid, Nov. 21.
congreit, s. *a fair champion*, June 17.
conicim, *I am able* Z². 429 (con-icim : cf. ἱκανός) pres. indic. 2d. sg. conic Prol. 7. Ep. 434, 3d sg. conic Prol. 159=conicc Z². 431, 2d pl. conicid Ep. 381, 388, 2d. pl. s-conj. conicsid, Ep. 393=Old-Ir. conísid.
Coningen, Conaingen Ap. 29.
Conloch, gen. Conlocha (Conloga B) July 11 (con=cuno, W. cyn).
conn, s. m. *sense, understanding*, dat. sg. cunn, cund Ep. 52, Glück compares κορνέω, but it seems rather from cog-na, cug-na=Goth. hugs.
Connmach of Armagh, ob. A.D. 807, Pref.
conócbaim, *I raise*, 3d. sg. pres. indic. conócaib Ep. 208 B, cotamrochat *may they upraise me!* Ep. 45 (con-tam-ro-ocbat), conocaeba (gl. sublimet) Ml. 20ᵇ. cotaucbat (gl. se attollunt) Z². 433, cotaocbat (gl. exsurgunt) ib., an condamnuclaitisse (gl. me ... efferentes) Ml. 39ᵈ.
conói-, *servare* co-tam-r-oither (cotomroether B) *let me be preserved* Ep. 69, cf. con-n-oi *qui servat* Z². 431 conróeth biu bath *he who protected life has died*, Amra Chol. LU. 8ᵇ. conróiter recht robust ib. LU. 10ᵃ. dobeir dig conói rig dogní echt, *he gives a drink which protects a king who doth a crime*, LU. 98ᵇ. The simplex occurs in the note to June 17 : ni-m-ó do léigendsea 7 nimchobratharsa *thy reading saves me not and helps me not*. The root is AV *to protect*, connáoi .i. coimhédaidh no cumhdaighidh, O'Cl.
con-rualai, Nov. 21, Ep. 25, con-rualaid (cf. con-id-rualaid, Br. h. 49), conroloi B, conruala D, conruaile O'Dav. 66, July 12 (cf. conhualai Fiacc 65), a defective verb meaning *ivit*, from a stem conala : cf. in-ru-alaid *offendit* and the Gr. ἰλάω.
conruidiur, Prol. 277. O'C. rendered this by *may I succeed, may I attain to* : cf. condotrudi sudi nóg *that thou mayst attain the warriors' seat*, Serglige Conc. O'Dav. glosses by corarir and the reading of B is conroether.
consádu, *I set together* Jan. 23—sádu=Skr. sādáyāmi, root SAD.
Constantín, the Emperor Constantinus I., Mar. 10.
Constantín (King of Britain) 'son of Fergus' B, of Rathin, Mar. 11., Died A.D. 820.
Constantinus, Jan. 29, is perhaps Constantius bishop of Perusia (Perugia), martyr.
contulim, *I sleep* : conatuil, *qui dormivit* Aug. 7, contuil *dormivit* Finec 62, contulctsom for *andergodaib they sleep on their beds* LU. 25ᵃ. lánamain contuiled sund, LU. 51ᵇ.
conuagu, conuaigiu, *I stitch together*, Jan. 20, from con- and -uagu, -uaigiu now fuaghaim with prosthetic f.
cor, s. f. *hand*, acc. sg. coir (.i. laim B) Dec. 12. O'Dav. 66, gives the nom. as coir, but cf. the compound ten-chor πυρόλαβις. With gúbaid coir frim anmain cf. ragab láim ara araid arungabad acocho *he enjoined* [lit. '*he took hand on*'] *his charioteer to harness his horses*, Táin cited O'Curry, M. and C. iii. 422, tancutar . . . do gabail alámu ass *they came to enjoin him* (to go) *out of it*, LB. 33ᵃ. Cor is cognate with καρπός and Skr. karu *ductio, missio*, di cor-cruinn *de ductione sortis*, Tur.
cor, s. m. *ponere* .i. urchor, O'Cl. gl. dat. sg. cur pref. B. pres. cuirim.
corach, adj. *having a choir*? gen. sg. m. corrig Feb. 21, from cor .i. ceol O'Cl.
córaid, n. pl. Prol. 65, gen. pl. corud Prol. 167. This may come from caur *champion* LU. 114ᵃ, .i. trenfer .i. daghlaech Amra H. 3, 18, p. 49, dat. don curaid Vis. Cath. Mór, W. cawr pl. cewri *a mighty man, a giant*, Skr. çūra, κοῦρος, κύριος.
corann, s. f.=corona (W. coron, Corn. corun) Nov. 25.
corcach, f. (1) *a marsh*, (2) *Cork*, dat. sg. corcaig Sep. 25.

---

* This conjecture is strengthened by the fact that B has here conglaini *cum puritate*, and cf. aitiu for aitu.

Corcunutan, of Daire na flann, now Derrynavlan, near Killenaule, co. Tipperary. Nov. 3.
corgas, s. *quadragesima* (W. y grawys *the lent*), gen. sg. corgais, corgaissa, corguis Jan. 7, Nov. 13, dat. sg. corgus Nov. 15, Ep. 562.
Cormac, of Armagh, gen. cormaic, Feb. 17. Ob. A.D. 497.
   Cormac hua Liathain abbot of Dermag (Durrow), June 21=Cormacus nepos Lethani. Reeves Col. 30, 166.
   Cruimther Cormac of Achad Finniche, May 11.
Corona, May 14, an Egyptian martyr. Boll.
Cornil, gen. sg. Sep. 14. S. Cornelius pope in A.D. 250, commemorated with Cyprian of Carthage as they were contemporaries and friends. He was martyred at Centumcellæ in Etruria. Boll.
corp, s. m. (Z^2. 210, W. corff, Lat. corpus) Prol. 293, Feb. 5, Ep. 297. gen. sg. coirp Z^2. 231. dat. curp Ep. 52, 363. acc. corp Ap. 14, Ep. 442, n. pl. cuirp Prol. 79. LU. 56ª, acc. curpu Jan. 4. Ep. 435=corpu Z^2. 213.
corpán, s. *little body* Aug. 3, mochorpau ba crethnaigthe, LU. 114ᵇ. gen. corpáin Ap. 19, dat. sg. corpán Jan. 24, Aug. 10, Ep. 10, acc. sg. corpan Ep. 347.
corpdae, adj. *corporeal* pref.
corplén, s. *bodily ease*, acc. sg. June 22, lén .i. sleman no laxa no sadail, Three Ir. Gl. 132.
cos, *to which* Ep. 58, Middle Irish for cosa, cosan.
cosaite, gen. sg. meaning doubtful, pref. cosait .i. cocad *warfare* O'Don. Supp. cf. cosnam. The modern cosáid is explained by *accusation*, *complaint*, *calumny*, *slander*, *detraction*, P. O'C. and this is the meaning in LB. 139ᵇ. line 52 : 7 luid iarum poimp co róim do chosait nan-iudaide fri suil césair *and then went Pompeius to Rome to complain of the Jews to Julius Cæsar:* imchosait *mutual complaint* occurs frequently in the Fled Bricrenn.
coscar, coscor, s. *victory*. gen. sg. cemailte in choscair *insolentia victoriae*. Ml. 33, c. 13, dat. sg. Prol. 63, Ep. 23, sonis go coscear *he returned with victory* O'Don. Supp. coscraim *destruo*.
cosccartha, p. part. p. of cosecraim=consecro, u. pl. n. Pref. B.
cosin (con-sind), *with the*, June 20, Ep. 57 B.
Cosmas and Damianus, Sep. 27, the patron saints of medicine, beheaded in Cilicia by the proconsul Lycias in the time of Diocletian.
cosnam, s. m. *contest* O'Don. Supp. dat. sg. ag cosnam rigi no apdaine *contesting a kingdom or an abbacy* ib. acc. sg. Ep. 221, n. pl. coisnimi Z^2. 240, cosnama ib. cf. cosnaim contendo ro-chosain *contendit* LU. 39ᵇ. 23, cossénat *contendent*, imfresna (imbfrith-sena) Z. 884, root S(T)AN a *weiterbildung* of the root STA ?
cotaruicset, 3d pl. pret. act. May 8. The glossographer would connect the form with ruice .i. náire and translate *contumeliam passi sunt*, Act. Ap. v. 41. But perhaps it should be analysed thus : con-ta-r'-uicset *sese contulerunt*: cf. rouiccius brith *tuli judicium* Z^2. 461, rouic buáid diib *tulit victoriam de iis* ib. 462.
cotlaim, *I sleep*, 2d. sg. imperat. cotail, pref. B. 3d. sg. pres. indic. ní chotlai LU. 89ᵇ. 1 sg. s-pret. dochotlus ib. 3d. sg. 2dy. pres. no chotlud Sgl. cf. contul.
cotlud, s. *sleep* Dec. 27, LU. 43ᵇ. gen. sg. cotulta, LU. 33ᵇ. 89ᵃ.
crabud, s. (W. crefydd) *piety*, Ep. 197, gen. sg. crabaith Z. 993. Root krabh, Skr. çrambh (Windisch), vi-çrabdha *lowlyminded*.
craibdech, adj. *pious*, Mar. 24, July 11, Tir. 3 (where it is written cráibdech), gen. sg. m. craibdig Mar. 30, acc. sg. m. craibdech July 20, acc. sg. f. lam chraibdig Br. h. 29, n. pl. m. craibdig Prol. 79, Jan. 16.
cráidim, *I torment*, 3d pl. pret. pass. ro-cráite Ep. 269. 3d sg. ol rom-chraided *since I have been tormented*, Trip. Fg. 7 a. 1. From the noun crád. cf. do-r-a-cráid (gl. exacerbavit) Ml. 28 a.
crann, crand, s. n. *a tree* (W. prenn, Lat. quercus) Mar. 10, gen. sg. craind May 3, dat. sg. co cruun Tur. u. pl. cam-chrauna Sg. 189 a.

cré, s. f. *clay*, Z^2. 255, gen. críad Ap. 19, Z^2. 256. W. pridd.
credul, adj. *pious, devout* (lit. *trustful, believing ?*) Jan. 15, Feb. 4, Mar. 24, Aug. 9, gen. sg. m. credail June 12, Ep. 291, acc. sg. m. Prol. 111, dat. Ap. 4, sg. f. credail Ep. 43, gen. pl. credal Nov. 16, Ep. 188, dat. pl. credlaib Ep. 191 : cretal .i. craibtheach Leb. Lecain Voc. 137.
credlach, adj. *trustful* Oc. 21, Dec. 13, gen. sg. m. credlaig (.i. creidmig, 3 Ir. Gl. 129) Feb. 25.
crésen, adj. *pious* Feb. 4, Ap. 27 (.i. craibhtech O'Dav. 66, .i. cretmech no craibdech 3 Ir. Gl. 129), gen. pl. m. crésen Oc. 24 : rhymes with féser and tésed : cresen .i. cleirech Gl. 217. Hence créseno : Atri on aircour tol dé .i. *genus* inóide. cressine immidais. ettla frihaes ('three things by which God's will is found: chastity in youth : piety in mid-age : penitence at (old) age') LB. 71, lower margin.
Cresene, Cressene, (leg. Creséne ?), gen. croseni Aug. 18, latinized Craseni, Reeves Col. 25.
cretar, cretair, s., *something consecrated*, Ep. 189, Mart. Don. 176. Applied to a consecrated person, Prol. 114, Ap. 12, and cf. is cretair is comand with ba comman ba cretair, H. 2, 13 col. 393.
cretem, s.f. *belief* (W. cred) Prol. B. 173 (A, corruptly, credium), gen. sg. creitme Z^2. 242, dat. cretim 243, acc. cretim-n 244.
crích, s.f. (1) *boundary, limit, end* : (2) by metonymy, a *district or territory* inclosed within boundaries (cf. the use of Lat. finis) : acc. sg. crích-n Feb. 28, June 3, gen. dual dá crích Aug. 15, Oc. 6, dat. pl. críchaib June 17 (honaib crichaib gl. sulcis Z^2. 245), acc. pl. crícha Sep. 9, crich ua Failge pref.
cride, s.n. *heart, κραδίη*, Ep. 194, gen. sg. Prol. 228 (leg. cridi), Sep. 27, Ep. 68, dat. cridiu Z^2. 230, acc. sg. cride-n Ep. 383. See 2 Beitr. 160.
crinner, s. .i. tuitim *falling*, dat. sg. crinniur Prol. 297 B=arnabe for crinnur O'Dav. 65.
Crisoginus, May 31=Chrysogonus, a Aquileian martyr Boll. and Jameson S. & L. Art, 639.
Crispina, (Crispana A) Dec. 5, beheaded in Africa, temp. Diocletian.
Crist, *Christus*, undeclined, nom. Prol. 244, gen. Nov. 14, acc. Jan. 25, Feb. 8, voc. Prol. 1, Ep. 307.
Cristina, July 18. The Italian lake referred to in the note is perhaps Bolsena. See Jameson S. & L. Art. 666.
Cristofer, Cristifer, Ap. 28. See the legend of St. Christopher, Jameson S. & L. Art. 439. The Irish name for this Saint is Conchenn, *doghead* or *wolfhead*, and "M. Didron tells us that in the Greek churches he found St. Christopher often represented with the head of a dog or wolf, like an Egyptian divinity. He adds that he had never been able to get a satisfactory explanation of this peculiarity." Jameson S. & L. Art, 449.
croán, s. *bravery*, Prol. 51 .i. cronughadh *rebuking* no cródhacht *or valour* O'Cl. *prowess, valour* P. O'C.
croch, s.f. *cross* (W. crog) Jan. 11, Mar. 31, Ap. 10, 30, July 10, 21, Aug. 10, 19, Sep. 27, Oc. 22, gen. sg. croiche Mar. 10, cruiche Ap. 12, May 3, Ep. 270=cruche Z^2. 242, dat. sg. croich Aug. 17, Z^2. 243, acc. sg. croich Aug. 16, Nov. 25, Z^2. 244, dat. pl. crochaib Prol. 46.
crochad, s.m. *crucifixion* Mar. 25, gen. sg. crochda Feb. 24, Ap. 20=crochtho Z^2. 239, dat. crochad ib.
crochaim, *I crucify, I hang* (W. crogi), nudam-chrocha (gl. discruciat me) Z^2. 434, 3d. sg. s- pret. crochais Mar. 8, 12, Dec. 30, 3d. pl. rotus-crochsat Prol. 73, 3d. sg. 2dy. pres. pass. crochta Feb. 5, 3d. sg. pret. pass. rocrochad Prol. 89, pret. part. pass. crochthae, crochta, crochda May 12, Oc. 21, 31, gen. sg. m. crochthai May 6, dat. sg. f. Feb. 12.
Cronán, of Tuaim gréine (now Tomgraney) Nov. 1 of Glas Már (now Clashmore) Feb. 10: of Ross Cree (now Roscrea) Ap. 28 : of Fernæ (now Ferns) June 22 : gen. sg. cronáin Lib. Arm. 16, b, 2, n. pl. cronáin Prol. 236.

crothaim, *I shake*, 3d sg. pres. crothid Sgl. Conc., rel. pres. crothas, crothass, Sep. 9, B, D (A has crothais *shook*). Intan no croithed *eum id quatebat* Proc. R. I. A. (MS.) 161. The verbal noun is crothad LU. 64ᵃ. Hence perhaps ro-cruide, rocruidi, *shook out, rifled?* Ep. 136. In Three Ir. Glosses, rocruidhe is glossed by rocroid .i. tuc ní eisib *he brought somewhat thereout*. ro-tus-croith imman-ór *he plundered (?) them of their gold*, LB. 213ᵃ.

Crúacha, gen. sg. cruachan Prol. 177, Oc. 5, voc. sg. a cruachu, LU. 38a, Cruachu Maige Abnae, Oc. 5, now Crohane near Mowney in the barony of Slieve Ardagh in the E. of the co. of Tipperary, O'D. Supp.

cruimther, s.m. *a priest* May 11, 27, Aug. 9, gen. sg. cruimthir Feb. 24, Ap. 10, 20. This word and O. W. premter are borrowed from *prebiter*, a low-Latin form of *presbyter*.

Crumine, June 28, perhaps a dimin. of cruim.

Crunn Badrae, gen. s. Cruind Badrai pref. n.

cruth, s. m. *form, figure* (cruth .i. gné O'Dav.) Z. 562 n. acc. Jan. 5.

cruthad, s. *formation*, gen. sg. crutai pref. 13.

cu, prep. (1)=có. Dlom tassach [leg. Dlomthus cách] cu hollmuir Feb. 17, L B. 23ᵃ. (2) see con.

cua, v. Mochua.

cuairt, s.f. *a visit, a circuit* (root KUR Curtius No. 81 *sojourn*, acc. sg. Jan. 22, dochoidside for chuairt iconuachtaib . . . tanic fine do chuairt leis, Pref. to Fiacc's hymn.

cúala, *heardest* June 13, 2d sg. redupl. pret. of cluinim, root clu, KRU, Skr. çru.

Cuan of Airbre, July 10.

Cuana, gen. sg. cuanach, Feb. 19.

Cuangus mac dall, Mar. 13.

Cuanna, (cuana B) of Lismore, Feb. 4 : of Ross co. Ap. 10.

Cuar, gen. cuair pref.=Scaurus? κουρεύς.

cuaróc, s. Mochuaróc, dimin. of cuar.

cubus, s.m. *conscience*, dat. sg. is for cubus righ ata on *a King's conscience it is*, O'Dav. 70. acc. sg. cubus-n pref. 33=con-VID-tu.

cucut, *unto thee*, see chucut.

cuibde, s. *concinnitas* LU. 35ᵇ. root bad, bhadh, Curtius. No. 326. Hence

cuibdim, *I harmonize*, 3d. sg. præt. pass. do cuibded *which was harmonized* Ep. 124, cf. cubaid LU. 74ᵇ. compar. as chubaithiu (gl. concinniore) Ml. 7r. in-chobaid (gl. concinnenter) Z. 563, in immchuibdius (gl. armoniam) L.H. 11ᵇ.

cuibrech, s. *bond, fetter*, gen. pl. Ep. 363 B. see cuimrech.

cúil, s. *a corner, recess* (W. cil): Cúil Bennchuir pref. 88, Cúil Raithin gen. cellola cuile raithin in eilniu, Lib. Arm. 15. a. 2 : Carpre cula raithin, Nov. 1.

1. cuilenn, s.=*hollin* (W. celynen), gen. cuilinn May 21, July 6.

2. cuilenn, s. gen. cuilinn Nov. 24, is perhaps a different word. See note.

cuimbrigud, s. *abridgement* Ep. 123, cf. cumbair *brevis, curtus*, cumbre *brevitas*, W. byr *brief* Ir. berr .i. gairit.

cuince, (cumeo B) s.f. *straitness* Ep. 385 (cum-angia). Hence cumcigim (gl. ango) Z².

cuimnech, adj. *mindful*, Ep. 363, or is it a mistake for cuimrech q. v. ?

cuimrech, s.m. n. *chain, bond*, gen. sg. cumrig Feb. 25, dat. sg. cuimriug Z². 238, gen. pl. cuimrech Oc. 15, Ep. 363, dat. pl. cuimregaib, cuimrigib Z². 338, cf. conring (gl. ligo) Z². 428. cuimrechta (gl. alligatus) Z². 479, cuimrechti (gl. ad stringendum) Ml. 37.

cuintgim, *I ask*, v. concsta, conctis.

cuiriur, *pono*, 2d sg. pres. cuirther Jan. 25, 3d pl. cuiretar Z. 1075 3d pl. 2dy pres. imm-a-curtis, im-o-cuirtis *eum vehebant* Ap. 27, Windisch, Beitr. viii. 43, connects W. paraf *faciam* Skr. kar, karoti, Lith. kuriú *baue*.

cúis, s.f.=*causa*, Corm. 11, pref. B.

cuit, s.f.=*quota* acc. sg. July 29.

cuithe, s.(=*puteus*, W pydew) *a den*, abl. sg. Ep. 500. Cognate seems cuithech f. *pitfall*: for clandas cuthigh a tir a ceili cen athcomarc *one who digs a pitfall in his neighbour's land without asking*, O'Dav.
culmen, gen. in chulmin, Note Jan. 31.
cumain, s. *remembrance* pref. 99 (W. cof), root MAN.
cumang, s.n. (m . ?) *power* Ep. 9, dat. cumung Z^2. 224, Curtius G.E. No. 473.
cumce, see cuince.
cumgabail, s. *an uplifting*, Ep. 208.
Cummain, daughter of Aillén, May 29. Cummain Fota Nov. 12: see Todd L. II. 84–93.
Cummine, seventh Abbot of Hí, Feb. 24. Cummeneus Albus, Reeves' Col. 199, 375, cf. cumméne Lib. Arm. 16, b. 2.
Cummine, father of S. Mochua, May 4.
cumrech, s. cuimrech.
cumscaigim, *I move*. *I change*, 3d. pl. s- pret. cumscaigset Feb. 6, 3d. sg. pres. indic. pass. cumscaight(h)er O'Don. Supp. pret. part. pass. cumscaigthe (gl. motus) Ml. 19ᵃ. Ebel, 2 Beitr. 163, connects this with the verb conoscigim *muto*. The words foscochat (gl. concedunt) Sg. 215ᵃ, in foscugud (gl. secessionem) are cognate. Root SKAK, Fick 199. Br. hegaff *quatire*.
cunchid, cuingid, s. *seeking*, dat. sg. Prol. 329.
cungnam, congnam s. *assistance*, *co-operation*, dat. sg. Aug. 21, Ep. 296 : adcochasa (.i. atgim) or cúchulaind inna husci do chongnam frim ' *I beseech*,' *saith Cúchulainn*, ' *the waters to help me!*' LU. 67ᵃ.
cunnu, s. *relationship*, Ep. 230, (=conda O'Dav. 65), glossed by cairdes, Three Ir. Gl. 65, 140, by connailbe no cairdeas, O'Cl.
curach, s.m. *boat* (from curoch, Adamnán's curuca, W. corwg). gen. curaig Dec. 1 (lucht curaig *a boat's crew*, LU. 40ᵇ. dat. curuch LU. 24ᵇ. acc. pl. curchu LU. 85ᵃ.
curchán, s.m. *a little boat* dat. sg. Feb. 13, Dec. 8 : curchan tar sal septais cló *wind blew a skiff over sea*, O'Mulc. 276, in tocéb mo churchan ciar forinn ocian n-uchtlethan nán, LL. 19, a. 2.
Curufin, Curphine, July 20, spelt Cuirbhin in Mart. Don. 196.
cutaim, s. (.i. tuitim O'Dav. 66, 69) *fall*, dat. sg. Ep. 556=W. codwm *a fall*, *a tumble*.
Cyrion, an Alexandrian martyr, July 3.

d (infected) for th, passim : for g (infected). fuidbe Ep. 147 A, mithid Ep. 394.
d for t, nodluig, Nov. 13, Dec. 24, nodlaic Dec. 25, nochardais, Nov. 16, Fíladi, Dec. 5, slanchodlad Dec. 27, creidium Prol. 173, mairde 194, aidiu Mar. 19, cuid July 29, cedul Ep. 150, ancharaid Ep. 251, notlegad, Ep. 81, cedul, Ep. 150, dermad Ep. 121. In proclitics : do *tuus*, dar *trans* : caused by a lost n : dia *duarcaib*, March 9 D.
d infixed pronoun of 3d sg. notlomaim=no-d-dlomaim, Prol. 315, fo-d-luga, June 6, fo-n-d-r'-uair Ep. 97, no-d-géba, Ep. 166, 180.
1. da prep. *to*, pref. 1, and cf. da-bar.
1. da (=d+a ?) infixed pron. of third sg. and pl. Z^2. 331, 332 : cotaruicset, May 8 (=.coth-da-ro-ucset), atatiam Oc. 26 (=ad-da-tiam). See -dan.
dá, *two*, in Sep. 28, Oc. 30, fem. dí Sep. 27, Dec. 9 : dia May 31,=W. dwy,— so in dia loit fina .i. dá bhrat tind, Corm. B. s.v. *cermnas*, dia arainn 2 SM. neut. dan, dá June 22, Oc. 25, gen. dá Prol. 196, and perhaps March 26, dat. díb, Ap. 3, June 14, acc. f. dí Mar. 3, B. dí is wrongly used for dá in Prol. 324.
dabach s.f., *a vat*, Corm. 15, gen. sg. daibche SM. 166, dat. sg. dalmig, Ep. 540, where the poet refers to the caldron of boiling oil, out of which St. John came "as out of a refreshing bath," Jameson *Sacred and Legendary Art*, i. 157.

ccxliv   GLOSSARIAL INDEX.

Dabid, of Menevia, Mar. 1, the King, Ep. 483.
dabar, *to your*, Aug. 30 A, better do for D.
dádaig, adv. *that night* or *at night*, Feb. 15 (rhymes with námait), translated by O'Curry *after the night:* fhaid sind inn aidchisin dadaig 7 tindabair, *ye and F. shall wed there that night*, gaibthir fledugud len dadaig, *feasting is begun with them at night*, imbarach dadaig, *to-morrow at night*, Táin bó Fráich. contuli iarum ndadaig, *then she slept that night*, LU. 128ᵃ, nislibeirg cúchulaind dana dádaig assatháibaill *Cúchulainn did not shoot at them that night out of his sling*, LU. 69ᵇ. B. has lagaig.
dag, adj. *good* (W. da), Gaulish dago in Dago-vassus. Hence—
Dagán (bishop of Inber-dóele, now Ennereilly, co. Wicklow) Sep. 13, dimin. of dag. O.W. Dagan, Lib. Land. 167.
dagordan, s. *a good ordination*, July 4.
Daig mac Cairill, of Inis cáin Dega (now Inishkeen, on the borders of Louth and Monaghan), Aug. 18.
dáig, Nov. 16 B, dóig D.
daille, s. f. *blindness*, gen. sg. Ep. 512, from dall.
daimim *I suffer*, 3d sg. depon. redupl. pret. damair Feb. 9, domair Feb. 16, 3d pl. rodamatar Prol. 53, D. ro-damdatar, Prol. 32, A. B. 53. B. damdatar Oc. 15, perhaps for dadmatar Redupl. fut. in-didma th'anacol. Noco dídem, LU. 63ᵇ. 3d sg. t-pret. rodet. See fodam=W. goddef.
Daiminis, (dam-inis), dam *bos* Sep. 12. Devenish Island in Lough Erne, Fermanagh, gen. familia daminse in doburbur, Lib. Arm., 15 a 2.
1. daingen. adj. (gl. durus, gl. firmus) Z². 25 n. prol. 130, Ep. 210, compar. daingniu, May 23.
2. daingen, s. *a fort* (*dungeon* Z². 25 n.), gen. pl. Ep. 342.
daire, s. m. (n. ?) *oakwood* gen. sg. dairi (in dorso dairi, Lib. Arm., 9. b 2), dat. sg. dairin May 7, and Tir. 1. Daire Echdroma, May 7, (.i. itunáscirt dail araide, Laud 610)= Doire Echdroma Mart. Don. p. 121, now probably (according to Dr. Reeves) the church of Desheart, co. Antrim. Eccl. Ant. Down and Connor pp. 72, 335, 378.
daith, adj. .i. esgaidh no tapaidh no luath, O'Cl. a. compar. daithiu occurs at Mar. 31, if we read ba dathiu. But the glossographer of B obviously read bad aithin.
1. dál, s. f. Z². 17, *an assembly*, Z². 17, Oc. 28 (O'Dav. 75 writes dail), gen. sg. dála Dec. 3, dat. sg. isindail-sin LU. 46ᵃ, acc. cussin mór-dail-sin, ib. dat. pl. dálaib Prol. 35, 211, 315, Ep. 63, acc. pl. dala, Sep. 20, O.W. datl (gl. forum).
2. dál, s.n. *a division*, O.W. daul Z². 27. Dál n Araide pref. B. gen. for naemaib dail araide LU. 41 a. Dal Riada. Hence dálem (gl. campo) Z². 17.
dálach. adj. *multitudinous*, from 1, dál, Prol. 192, 196, dat. sg. m. dálach Ap. 11, Aug. 6, dat. sg. f. dálaig Sep. 12, dat. sg. n. dálach Jan. 1, acc. sg. m. dálach, Sep. 29, Nov. 26.
dálaim, *I allot* (from 2 dál) 3d sg. s-pret. dálais Ap. 12: cf. fodáli *infra*.
Dalann, gen. sg. Oc. 11, the great grandfather of Cainnech, whose father was (according to Dr. Reeves, Columba, p. 221) Lughteach son of Lughaidh.
dall, adj. *blind*, W. dall.
dall-chéillin, Prol. 316, *blind guidance !*
dalte, daltae, dalta, s.m. *alumnus, discipulus*, May 2, Z². 229, gen. sg. daltai, Aug. 22=dalti Z². 229, dat. daltu, ib. 230, acc. sg. daltae-n Tir. 2, dat. pl. daltib Z². 232.
dam, see Addam.
Daman, Feb. 12, either Damianus miles, martyr in Africa, or the Irish Damán of Tidowan, Queen's Co.
Damasus, a Roman martyr, July 2. See Boll. p. 295: a pope Dec. 11.
Damian, Nov. 9, a Spanish saint.
Damianus, Sep. 27. See Cosmas.
-dan-, infixed pron. 3d pers. pl. ro-dan-ort sam *eos occidit* Prol. 57 B.

dána, adj. *audax* May 25, gen. sg. m. dáni, dánai Dec. 10, dat. sg. m. (n. ?) dána Jan. 23. Compar. dánu Mar. 20, May 23, Nov. 30. Hence dánatu (gl. audacia) Z^2. 16.
Daniel, Dainiel, propheta, Ep. 499.
dar, prep. cum acc. for far *trans, super*, Z^2. 653, Feb. 13, Mar. 5, 22, June 3, 12, Aug. 14, Ep. 35.
dar-a-cenn, (=taracend B.) praep. nom. *for them*, lit. *pro capite eorum* Ep. 164.
Dartinne, of Cell Airnn, July 3.
dath, s. (gl. color) Ir. Gl. 125, gen. sg. datha Nov. 15 : for compounds v. lig-dath, so-dath.
1. de, di, praep. cum dat. Jan. 8, June 25, Dec. 22, Ep. 42, 396, 512, 516, 520, 528, 532, 536, 552, 556 : with art. dind, Ep. 26 ; with pron. dím, de, díb, q. v. Compounded, see deseree.
2. de, *ex eo* Prol. 188.
dé, *two* in compounds and derivatives Z^2. 301. See décheng.
dé, déa, *diem*, Prol. 174.
déec, déace, *ten* absol. July 15, Sep. 22, in both of which places it is a dissyllable : cf. the Mid. Br. deace *decima*, deaugaff *decimare*.
déacht, s.f. *godhead* Ep. 353, gen. sg. deachte Z^2. 242, dat. deacht 243, acc. deacht-n 244.
Dece, *Decius*, gen. Deice, Prol. 134 B.
1. dech, adj. *better* (deach .i. fearr, O'Cl.), used as a superl. pref. 31, Nov. 16 : so in láech as dech di ocaib domain LU. 44ᵇ. It seems cognate with Lat. decor and the O. Celtic Decangi, Decanti, Decetia, Glück, Neue Jahrb. 1864, p. 603.
2. dech, *ten*, absol. n. pl. deich Oc. 16, 25, dat. pl. dechib, deichib, Oc. 10, cogn. with decem, δέκα.
dechoid, deochoid, deochaid, (.i. dochunid *ivit*, O'Dav. 75) May 4, see deochaid. In Prol. 201, dechaid, B. deenis : din tuidecht dundechaid crist hitech inna sacard *of the wending which Christ went into the priests' house* Ml. 44. The other persons are sg. 1, dechud-sa, 2. deochad, Pl. 1, dechommar, 3, dechatar.
décheng, s.m. *a pair of champions*, Mar. 7, Sep. 6, acc. sg. Nov. 26, from dé- and cing with progr. assimilation.
dechoin v. deochain.
decimber, s.m. *December*, gen. decimbir, Dec. 1.
Declan, of Ardmore, July 24.
decmaice, Ep. 172, seems to mean *by chance* or *occasionally*. O'Dav. 55 gives the line thus : a beth slan ni decmaic and explains it by ni decmaing bias slainti dó acht do gres *it is not occasionally that safety shall be to him, but always*. At p. 75, he explains it (1) by sist *a while*, (2) by ingna *wonder*, citing decmaic fer cen enech *a man without honour is a wonder*, (3) by doiligh *difficult*, citing ben dofairgeth ar decmaic *a wife that was got* (!) *for a difficult dower*, coibche. In the last sense it seems=decuing *absonum* Z^2. 234. O'Clery glosses deacmaic by docamhlach no doilidh *difficult* and deacmaing by iongnad *a marvel*, so Z. 862 ni decming (gl. non mirum)=ni deacmaing Ep. 172 D. The comparative occurs LU. 89ᵃ : ni fail ní bas decmaicci.
dedblén, s.m. Ep. 396, 399, gen. pl. Jan. 24, *a puny person, a weakling*, gen. sg. deidhleoin LB. 74ᵇ, a dimin. from dedbol. The three weaklings mentioned at Jan. 24, were Urbanus, Prilidianus and Epolonius. A similar word déblén=deiblen, Jan. 24 C. (acc. pl. déblénu LB. 244ᵃ), is perhaps borrowed from debilis.
dedbol, dedbul (=de-adbul) *petty*, dereoil O'Dav. 75, Jan. 25, Ep. 266.
déde, adj. *divine* (generally díade) gen. sg. m. déli (leg. déodi?) May 21.
dédenach, dédinach, didenach, adj. *latter, last* Pref. 49, Ep. 281, cond rainn dídenig, *ex parte posteriore* Z^2. 243, isan dedenach (gl. in posterum) Ml. 59, from deud, q. v.
dedol, Corm. 15, v. iarndedol.
deich-n, *ten*, the conjunct form : deich nóebuaga Feb. 28, dat. deich n-uagaib Jan. 27.
deichenbor, s. *ten persons*, gen. sg. deichenboir inscr., dat. sg. deichenbor, dechenbur, July 14.

deilm, delm, s.n. *noise*, Prol. 163, June 29, gen. sg. delma Ap. 7, dat. sg. delmnim Prol. 154. Ep. 127 : deilm .i. torann, L. L. Voc. 63, Root dhar, dhran l
deit, deitt, det, (better duit) *to thee*, Sep. 14. Ep. 364, 411.
deithbir, dethbir, Prol. 114, *reasonable*, or perhaps *lawful* (deitbbhir .i. dlightheach O'Cl.) : *indubius, necessarius,* Z². 73, compar. deidbiriu ib.
delb, s. f. *forma, idolum* (W. delw), gen. delbe Z². 242, Hence
delbdæ, adj. (dealbhdha gl. formosus) acc. sg. m. Ep. 354, n. pl. f. delbdai, Feb. 28.
delmac, gen. sg. delmaic, delmaice, Nov. 5, is glossed in Laud 610, by deil muicci .i. mucc dabliadan *a two-year-old pig.*
1. **demin,** see fodmin.
2. **demin,** adv. *certainly*? Oc. 18, demin (gl. immunis) Z². 231, comp. demnithir *certius* Z². 274.
demon, *demon* Feb. 16, declined in the sg. as a masc. a-stem, in the pl. as an i-stem : gen. sg. demain, demuin, Prol. 253, Z². 466, acc. sg. deman, demon, demun Prol. 242, Mar. 16, Ep. 154, gen. pl. demnae, demna Feb. 24, Oc. 17, Ep. 198, 211, 526.
dénam, s.m. *a making*, dat. sg. Ep. 88.
dénim, *I make*, Z². 435, 1 pl. imper. dénam Prol. 317. pret. part. pass. used as a part. of necessity : dénta Ep. 392. Root DHĀ whence τιθημι, Ohg. tó-m *I do* etc.
denn, v. gledenn.
deochaid, [=deuchuid,] dechoid, deochoid '*ivit*' pref. 22, Ap. B, May 4, pl. dechutar pref. 23, 24, a reduplicated pret. : the root seems KAD, Skr. çad, Lat. cadere.
deochain, dechoin, s.m. *a deacon,* Ap. 13, May 5, gen. sg. deocbain, dechoin, deochoin, Jan. 14, Ap. 16, 17, May 4, Aug. 10, Fiacc 4, n. pl. ban-dechuin *diaconissae* Z². 226.
deoda, adj. *godly, holy* Jan. 9, Mar. 7, Ep. 210, dioda Feb. 9, superl. deodam Ep. 498.
deorad, s. m. *an exile* (gl. advena) Ir. Gl. No. 303. Corn. diures (gl. exul). Hence
deoradán, deorudán, s. m. *a little exile,* acc. sg. Ep. 366.
dér, s. f. *a tear,* (W. dagr, δάκρυ, dacrima), gen. sg. fand iarom ainm na dére dothart tairis, LU 45 a. gen. pl. dér-n Ep. 400, dat. pl. dérait Prol. 24, Ep. 174.
derb, adj. (now dearbh) *sure, true,* Jan. 3, May 25, dat. sg. m. derb, Feb. 2, Ap. 11, acc. sg. m. Nov. 26, if it is not here compounded with dálach. The b here is a v. The sister form, dervh, may represent an Old-Celtic dergvo which would be=Goth. triggva.
der(b)-bráthair *own brother,* voc. sg. derbráthir (gl. germane) Z². 263, n. pl. June 27. The omission of one of the b's is regular. So himbroind talman taebuaine *in the womb of the lasting-sided earth,* taeb-buan, poem after Félire, L. B. sreabhborb *stream-violent* (sreabh-bhorb), braitirim *mantle-dry* (brat-tirim), see MacCurtin's Dictionary, Paris, 1732, p. 677, where this phenomenon is called báthadh consoineadha *drowning,* or *extinction, of consonants.*
derb-dálach, adj. gen. sg. m. derb-dálaig, derb-dalaich, Nov. 1, acc. sg. derb-dalach, Nov. 26.
derb-lassar, s. f. *a sure flame,* July 8.
derg, adj. *red*. Hence
Dergán, Feb. 9, an epithet for Cairech.
derg-ór, s. m. *red gold,* gen. sg. derg-óir, derggóir, Sep. 10, rond dercóir LU. 43ᵇ.
dermair, adj. *vast, huge* Oc. 9.
dermaire, s. n. *vastness* Ep. 342, where B has andermmra. The true reading is perhaps andermaire, an being the neut. article.
dermár, adj. Mar. 27, Ep. 281, 288, gen. sg. m. dermair May 15, Sep. 14, dat. sg. m. Mar. 23, W. dirfawr.
dermat, s. n. *forgetfulness* Ep. 121,=dermet Z². 223, gen. dermait ib. deoga dermait *drinks of forgetfulness* Sgl. acc. sg. May 11, root MAN : niu dia dermen *God has not forgotten me* O'Dav. 79, condermanammai ni *ut obliviscamur,* Z². 228.

dernaim, *I make*, dernai *fecit* (*faciebat?*), dernad *factus est* Pref. Cognate with ἔρδω.
des, *right-hand, south* (dextralis pars in Adamnán's latinity), andess *a meridie* Z.² 612, v. desmag, W. deheu, Goth. taihsva, ὰεξιός, Skr. daksha, dakshina, 2 Beitr. 161.
descipul, s. m. *discipulus*, n. pl. descipuil, Z². 226, dat. pl. desciplib, deisciplaib,Ep. 246.
deserce (de-serc), s. f. *charity*, Ep. 389, gen. sg. desercce Z. 242, dat. deseirce 243.
désillabach, adj. *dissyllabic* pref. 54.
desmag. s. n. *southern plain*, loc. desmaig, desmuig Prol. 226. So in des-muma *Desmond*; cf. tuathmuig Dec. 11.
détla, adj. .i. dána *bold*, acc. sg. m. Prol. 242.
déud, s. *end*, (a dissyllable, W. diwedd) Prol. 220, the case is doubtful: diaid in B. Hence fo-diud *postremo*, Ml. 29ª. in-dead *post*, Z². 660. Cognate with Goth. divan *to die*.
di, prep. cum dat. *from*, Ep. 552 B.
1. dí, *two* see dá.
2. dí, an intensive prefix, see dímór, dínert, díthair, díorad, and cf. didil .i. adhbhaldil no gradh mór O'Cl. dímeas .i. meas mór no mhoirmheas, ib.
1. dia, *two* see da.
2. dia, s. m. *god*, 2 Beitr. 161, gen. sg. dé Prol. 104, 215, Feb. 11, 15, Nov. 5, Dec. 19, dat. dia Z². 224, acc. dia-n Ep. 153. Voc. sg. dé Ep. 312, 313, n. pl. de Z². 226, gen. dea-n. ib. dat. déib Z². 227, acc. deu, deo. ib.
3. dia, s. *day*, 2 Beitr. 161, gen. sg. cach dia, cech dia *daily*, July 16, Ep. 166, where it is a dissyllable, dat. in-diu Prol. 220 ; acc. déi, dé. dia mairt, dia cetain, dia haine, dia sathairn, pref.
4. dia, (=du + a), *to his, to its*, Feb. 11, Aug. 10, 26, Ep. 95, 115.
1. dia-n. *cui, quibus* (=du+san) Mar. 9, July 10, diam-bo *quibus fuit*, Sep. 10, diam-dá *cui sum* Ep. 307, 426, dian-it, diam-bí *cui est* Prol. 146, diam ba (*cui fuit*) Ap. 2, diarbu ib. B=dian-ro-bu.
2. dia-n (=du + an) *to their*, dian-éis *after them* Prol. 79, 252.
3. dia-n, conj. *if* Prol. 143, (where dianpromam=dian-u-promam) 219 (where dian medair =dian-n-medair) ; July 25, Oc. 24 (where dian-fesser=dian-u-fesser), Ep. 98, diam-ba *si fuit* Ep. 171, *when* : dian-dechutar Pref.
dian, adj. *vehement, swift* (in form=ὰεινός, is glossed Z². 18, by creber, celer, praepes, pernix, cf. Skr. dyámi *I hasten, I fly*, ἵεσθαι), Dec. 18, B. and D, dat. pl. dianaib Prol. 24. Compounds : dian-ainm Ap. 22, dian-medar Prol. 219, dian-sauct-lethan, June 12.
Diarmit, Lib. Arm. 19, a, 1, gen. diarmata Pref. acc. diarmait July 8.
Diarmait of Inis-clothrann, Jan. 10.
Diarmait of Glenn Uissen, July 8.
Diarmait Mac Cerbaill, Pref.=Diormitius filius Cerbulis, Reeves' Col. 67, 68.
diar-n (=do-arn) *to our* Prol. 243, 323, Jan. 14, 29, Mar. 7, Sep. 27, 29, Nov. 24, Dec. 26, 28, Ep. 24, 563, diarnéis Ep. 419, B.
Diarscorus, Aug. 20, a mistake for Dioscorus, q. v.
1. dias, s. f. (gl. spica) *an ear* Nov. 24 (a dissyllable)=W.twys as druim=W.trwm.
2. dias, s. f. *duitas, two persons*, Mar. 13 (a dissyllable), gen. sg. désse Z². 311, acc. sg. dís Sep. 13, 14, dat. pl. déssib, déissib,Prol. 210.
dib (O. Ir. diib), *of them*, pref.
dibad, s. *extinction, perishing*, Corm., W. difa *extermination*, difâd *extermination*. Hence dibdaim 1. *I perish*, 2. *to extinguish*, 3d. sg. pres. indic. na dibdai Ap. 9, (cf. indi ardibdai gl. extinguentis, Ml. 48ᶜ), 3d. sg. pret. act. dorodbath, dorodbad Prol. 96, is perhaps= do-ro-dibath. The verbal noun is dibdud : do dibdud a brotha *to quench his ardour*, LU. 48ᵇ, ba líach dibdud na flatha sin, LU. 91ᵇ.
diblinaib adv. *e duabus partibus, utrimque*, June 14, Z². 367.
dichell, s. f. (dicell *neglect*, 2 Senchas Mór 2), Ep. 121, acc. sg. dichel (dichil B.) Prol. 291.

The phrase cen dichill occurs in the Book of Dimma. So in LU. dognìat trócaire cen-dichill, 30ᵇ, a forcetul ceu dichill, 103–104.

dichmaire, (di-comairc *without asking*), a common Brehon law-term, meaning apparently any unpermitted, and therefore illegal, act, see Corm. 61, acc. sg. Aug. 16.

dichra, adj. *fervent, earnest*, Jan. 10, isiat sede doguiat ifus aithrige udichru tria chongain cride, LU. 32ᵃ, tabrad each óen dib fóleith amenmain 7 a innithim codic(h)ra fri scélaib lái brátha *let every single one of them give his mind and his attention earnestly to the tidings of Doomsday*, LU. 31ᵇ. Hence dichrato *ferrour*, Reeves' *Culdees*, 83.

dicsu, see dixu.

Dichuill, Diucaill, Dec. 18.

dídnad, s. m. *solace* June 8, Ep. 191, gen. dithnatha Z². 239, dat. sg. Ep. 299, 563.

dídonaim, dodonaium Z². 434 *I solace*, 3d sg. pret. pass. dodidnad Ap. 18.

dígal, s. f. (W. dial, di-gal) *vengeance*, dat. sg. dígail, Ep. 516, acc. dígnil Ep. 546.

didge, s. *a blessing* (dighdbe .i. beannachd, O'Cl.), dat. sg. digdi Dec. 26.

dignae, digna, s. *reproach*, (.i. tairi uo troige uo dimicin 3 Ir. Gl. 128), acc. sg. Jan. 22, Feb. 9, 10, Mar. 7, Sep. 18, Nov. 4, gen. sg. dignai July 29, where it rhymes with rígdai.

dignae, dígua adj. *reproachful*, dat. sg. m. Prol. 254. O'Dav. 75, explains the adj. dighnae by dimicin (leg. dimicnech), and the substantive by drochgne. In H. 5, 18, between pp. 70 and 71, dignu is glossed by sárugadh.

dígraiss, dígrais, adj. *excellent*, Jan. 9, July 3, gen. sg. m. Dec. 16, acc. sg. f. Feb. 2, digrais cloth Br. 69, oenmac dígrais dechtere, LU. 18ᵃ.

dii, (=du+si) *ad eum, ei, de eo*, pref. 28.

dil, adj. *dear* Ir. Gl. p. 129, dat. sg. neut. Dec. 13, compar. diliu Prol. 185, May 7, Z². 275, superl. dilem Z². 278.

dilacht, Ep. 71 A and D, seems O'Clery's diolacht .i. di-lochd .i. gan locht *without fault*. But it is written dilucht by O'Dav. 75, and explained by dilgudach *forgiving*: see dilgud, so B. glosses dillacht by corp *dilgadach*.

dile, s. *dearness, affection*, (.i. grudh no annsa, O'Cl. gl.), gen. sg. dile (leg. dili, to rhyme with cridi?) Ep. 66.

diles, s. *proprium, property, possession*, dat. sg. dílius Jan. 29, Sep. 27, where it is applied to heaven. W. dil *dus, debt, right*.

dili, s. f. *a deluge*, gen. dilenn (fochoud na dilend LU. 2ᵇ), dat. dile Ep. 452, iarn (d)ilind, LU. 2ᵇ.

dilgud, s. m. *forgiveness*, gen. dilgotho Z². 239, dat. sg. Oc. 29, see dilacht, dilucht.

dilis, adj. *proprius*, and hence *carus, fidelis*, ; comparative dilsiu Prol. 262, Jan. 7.

dillacht, adj. *sinless* Nov. 19, Ep. 71 B, dat. sg. m. dillucht Sanct. h.

dilmain, s. *a freeman* pref. 36, Jan. 29, dat. sg. Ep. 180, adj. dilmain .i. dilis O'Dav. 73, 79, *licitus* Z². 250, dilmainiu (gl. liberius) Ml. is dilmain (gl. licet) Sg. 137ᵇ.—ni dilmain damsa dul in egept, LB. 117ᵃ.

dilucht, adj. (.i. dilgudach *forgiving*, O'Dav. 75) Ep. 71.

dim, *from me*, Prol. 223.

dimais, dimis, seems an adj. Feb. 2, *inestimable*? The meaning is doubtful.

dimór, adj. *enormous*, Oc. 28.

din, s. *protection* (ba din do nochtaib, Amra Chol.), gen. sg. cathair dina, note Jan. 4.

din, conj. *then*, pref. The 'dim,' in Z². 699, is a mistake for din.

1. dind, (leg. dinn?) s. m. *a height, a hill, a fort*, gen. sg. indred in denna *the destruction of the fort*, LL. 175, a. 2, dat. sg. Prol. 155, May 17, where O'Dav. gives the line thus: for dinn flatha finne *on a fair kingdom's height* .i. for cleithe neime.

2. dind, (=di + sind) *from the*, Ep. 26.

dindis, (dinnis .i. tarcaisne *reproach* O'Cl. Gl.), acc. sg. s. cen dindis, *without reproach*, Feb. 27, July 25.

díne, s. m. (n?) Ap. 17, 24, June 5, gen. sg. dine (leg. díni) Nov. 8, Ep. 79, dat. sg. díniu May 27, acc. sg. secheuch ńdine, St. Paul codex, dat. pl. do dinibh Petrie's Tara, 169, where it is glossed by airem *number*. So at Nov. 8 in B. the gloss lína, gen. sg. of lín *a number of persons* has got into the text. O'Curry, however, rendered the word by *generation*, and O'Clery by líne no saoghal, and P. O'C. and Lhuyd have o dhine go dine *from generation to generation*.
dínert, s. *vast strength*, Ep. 154, 330, is dínert .i. is adluil-nert, Three Ir. Gl. 140.
dingna, (leg. dindgna?) s. *a hill, a fort*, dat. sg. bása iaronn o dingnu do dingnu I.U. 15ᵇ: acc. pl. Ep. 120, dat. pl. dindguaib, St. Paul.
dioda, (deoda B.) adj. *godly* Feb. 9, cf. deo-chratechu (gl. sacrilegos) Z². 227.
Dionis, Mar. 14, May 25, = Dionysius. The bishop D. celebrated at Mar. 14, was martyred at Thessalonica, Boll.
diorad, (a trisyllable, di-oradh .i. oradh mor, O'Cl.) *a great prayer* Ep. 199. But B. glosses by etarfuarad no enuidach *refreshment or covering*.
Dioscorus, Aug. 20, an Alexandrian martyr, Boll.
dír, adj. *due* Pref. 34, Z². 21. In Ll. 176, a. 2, it occurs as a subst. doneoch ba dír udbarta.
dírge, s. f. *directness* or perhaps *righteousness*, dat. sg. con dírgi Jan. 28, Sep. 1, for dírgi *straightway, directly* Mar. 9, June 4 : derived from díriug, díriuch, q. v.
1. dírim, adj. *countless, innumerable*, dat. sg. m. July 15.
2. dírim, s. n. (.i. inad, O'Dav. 75) *a multitude*, dirimm atchiusa, Táin bó Fráich, gen. sg. ard in dirma, LU. 82ᵃ, acc. sg. dul fo dírinm inua mna, ib. 299, n. pl. dírmann, dirmand Oc. 11, acc. pl. dirmann, dirmand Ep. 143.
díriuch (di-rigu), adj. *right*, compar. dírgiu, dírgu Mar. 20 : cach ńdíriuch (cech díriuch, A.) adv. *quite right* Prol. 292, cachúdiruch Z². 612, superl. dírgimem (gl. equissima) Ml. 49ᵈ.
disert, s. n. Corm. 16, *a hermitage*, from *desertum* a monastic term, Reeves, Col. 366. Disert Oengusa Pref. B.
dith, s. *destruction*, acc. sg. dith-n Dec. 25, co deora domain dith *till the world's destruction come* O'Dav. 79, where it is glossed by crích *end*.
díthair, (dithár B.) Ep. 104, meaning obscure : If *dí* is the intensive prefix and *tair* means *insult* dithair may be *outrage*.
dithrub, s. *a desert, a hermitage*, dat. sg. Prol. 98, Z². 224 : Corm. 16, writes dithreb.
dítin, s. f. *protection* (gl. teges, gl. velari, Z². 264) Mar. 17, gen. sg. díten Z². 265.
diultach, adj. *denying*. The cognate subst. is diultad *a negative* Corm. s. vv. au-, duilbir.
dixu, *higher, nobler*, a comparative (glossed by airdi *higher, nobler*, O'Dav. 59) Jan. 18, 21, Mar. 19, May 1, Oc. 23, Ep. 54, 248, 439, where it always rhymes with I'su. I do not know the positive. O'Davoren's dixsa .i. ard no uasal is founded on an erroneous reading of Ep. 54. The cognate noun dixsa *height* occurs in I.U. 23ᵃ : cf. airdixa *productus* Z². 801, 980.
dligim (gl. mereo) Z². 429, 3d sg. pres. indic. ni dlig Jan. 6, Ap. 25, Z². 430 = nadlig Mar. 7. Goth. dulgs.
dlomaim, *narro, annuncio*, Prol. 315, = dlomhaim .i. foillsighim O'Cl. 3d sg. pres. indic. act. dlomaid I.U. 39ᵃ. with suffixed pron. dlomth-us *annunciat eam*, Feb. 17, 2d sg. imperat. dlom Aug. 7, Sep. 13, Oc. 12 : dlom .i. abair no indis no raid, LL. Voc. 120, dlomad .i. funera ib. 560.
-dn-, infixed pronoun of the 3d person sg. no-dn-áili *eum orat*, July 9, etsecht maire (leg. mairi) martha conjugum noduali D. Jan. 19. In Middle Irish this pronoun becomes -tu-.
1. do, du pron. poss. *thy*, Prol. 13, 16 A, 267, 269, 278, Ep. 4.
2. do, du prep. = *to*, Goth. du, Lat. do in endo-, indu, Gr. ἐς in οἰκόν-δε, Mar. 6, Ap. 26, Ep. 14 :

2 k

of, Prol. 52, see 2 Beitr. 171. Used as a verbal prefix Z^2. 417, do-chúaid Ep. 267, dolégsat Nov. 6, do-lluid, d-rebraing, do-rreith. In composition it sometimes becomes t, see tabairt, táiuic, tarla, torchair.
3. do-, du, a particle of quality = ἐυς, Goth. tuz-, NHG. zer-, dochingthecht (where the vocalic infection of e is due to the false analogy of so-, su-), dóire, donae, dolmae.
1. dó, *ei*, June 16, also dán=do aru.
2. dó, *two*, in dó déc q. v. do Finnio, Sep. 28, D. do Findia ib. B.
doairbiur, tairbiur *annuo, concedo*, 3d sg. a-conj. do-m- r-airbera Ep. 65, 3d sg. pres. indic. tairbirid illatu pian necsamail dona maccaíb báis *he bestows a many divers torments on the sons of death*, Vis. Adamn.
doairis, *consists?* (do-air-sistit) Pref. donairissid *quod perstatis*, Z^2. 437.
doairset Sep. 20, dofairset in the Franciscan copy, is=tairset Dec. 13. See tairic.
doasenaim, tasenaim *aideo*, 3d sg. pret. (impf. ?) do-u-asenai May 12, Oc. 25, 3d. pl. s-pret. do-da-ascansat Br. h. 53.
dobiur, dubiur *affero*, (gl. do) Z^2. 248, 3d. sg. pres. indic. act. dobeir Mar. 31, Nov. 30, Ep. 207, 1 pl. dobernu Prol. 144, 3d sg. t- pret. dobert Ap. 14, Oc. 18, 3d sg. pret. pass. dobreth Feb. 13.
doche, s. *confidence*, Aug. 4, doiche .i. duchas *trust, confidence* P. O'C. .i. dochus no duthchas O'Dav. 75.
dochingthecht, s. f. *a bad combating*, Prol. 241, see cing supra.
dochóid, dochúaid *ivit, adiit* Ep. 267.=duchooid Tir. 11, pl. dochúatar Prol. 279, a reduplicated pret. (root SKUD, Fick 208, Skr. codayāmi W.) with the reduplication lost and enhancement of the rootvowel.
dochrinim, *I fall*, 3d sg. redupl. pret. act. do-ro-chair *cecidit* Mar. 26, Nov. 17, Tur. 10, torchair Ep. 361, docer (ex do-ce-cer) *cecidit* Tur. pl. dociuchratar, dorochratar, torchratar.
docoemnactar, they *washed*, Jan. 4=do-com-ne-nachtar, root NAG, of which the Skr. nij is a weakened form.
docuissin, ('*which exists*' O'D. supp.), dochuisiu Ep. 443.
dó déc, *twelve?*=2+10, Pref. B.
dóe, s. *agger, mound, rampart*, Mar. 2, Aug. 27, where it is a dissyllable: dáe no dúa .i. cloidhe ard no múr ard O'Cl., dar doe .i. dar clad na fairge Rawl. 505.
doecmae, (=tecmae), tecmang (gl. fors) *evenire, accidere*, do-n-ecmaicc *qui evenit*, Dec. 24 B= donecmaing Z. 852. 3d sg. s- fut. tecma, Jan. 10; 3d sg. conditional docemoised *accidisset* Z^2. 469; see tecmang.
doecrai, do-nn-ecrai, Dec. 29, reading and meaning obscure: B has do-nn-ecna, R. condremai.
Doel, gen. doele, Sep. 13, the old name of the Penny-come-quick river, Co. Wicklow.
doemim *protego* do-n-r-ema *nos protegat?* Ap. 13, June 23, pl. don-ro-emat *nos protegant?* Feb. 3. The glossographer here explains donroemat by ron-airinet *nos recipiant*. But I would rather render it by *nos protegant*: cf. coluemn (gl. tuctur) Ml. 53ᵃ., duema sóu (gl. uindicabit) Ml. 67ᵃ. duemsa *protegam* 37ᶜ. duemar *protegitur* 39ᵃ=do dormar Corm. s. v. elf: codo-b-emtharsi *defendamini* Ml. 53ᵇ. amal dumemat étin a suthu *ut protegunt aves pullos suos* 39ᶜ, duemtis (gl. uelabant) 79ᵃ. dorét (=do-ro-emt) gl. velavit 16ᶜ.
doenacht, s. f. *humanity* Ep. 353: cf. dóini *homines*.
dófairci, *fences, guards:* cf. ἔρχατο σάκεσι Il. 17, 354. do-do-t-fairci Jan. 26, do-don-fairchi B, *who guards us:* fairci .i. forcomed no derrscaigh no doroua O'Dav. 87, root VARG, εἴργνυμι.
dofarnic, (=táirnic .i. do criochnaigheadh O'Cl.) *finivit:* do-to-farnaic *finierunt illi*, June 10; but O'Cl. explains fáirnic by fuair *invenit*.
doforcat, dofarcat, *antecellunt* July 15. .i. doroiscet no derrscaighit O'Dav. 75, see tarea infra.

doformaig, (=tórmaig) *auget* Ep. 195, 206, Ml. 117. do-n-formaig *we increase* Oc. 18. do-fortagat *augent*, Z^2. 433. dofoirmsed (gl. adderet) Ml. 35ª.
dofosat, *constituere, condere*, 3d sg. t-pret. dorosat Prol. 91 =dorósat (do-ro-fo-statuit) Z^2. 413. doforsat do-fo-ro-*statuit*, ib.
dogar, adj. *sad* Feb. 20 .i. toirsich O'Dav. 116, toirrsech Three Ir. Gl. 129. Hence dogra (dat. dogru Sgl.) and dograch.
dogaur, *advoco, appello*, 3d sg. pres. indic. act. dogair Z^2. 430, 3d sg. a- conj. act. dogara, do-ro-gra, Prol. 112, do-n-ro-gra *nos appellet* Mar. 28, Dec. 14, 3d sg. pret. pass. do-ro-grad Mar. 10, Sept. 5. dogairemmi *vocamus*, Ml. 80. darogart som noib *sanctum se appellavit*, Ml. 20ᵇ.
dogniu, *facio*, see guiu : 2d sg. conj. dogné *facias* Nov. 13, 3d sg. 2dy. pres. dognid, dogneth *faciebat*, Pref. s-pret. 1st sg. dorignius *feci* Ep. 112, 2d sg. dorignis Ep. 506, 3d sg. dorigne (leg. -gni) Ep. 89,100. Pl. dorigénsam, dorigénsid, dorigensat. Conjunctive forms hitherto unexplained are doróusa *fecero* Prol. 268, 269, (cf. do-nd-rón Z^2. 447., do-r-ronai *feceris*, donad *faceret* Z^2. 447, doronaid *feceritis*, Prol. 186, do-n-ronte, doróutae-si *fecissetis* Ep. 389 B, Z^2. 447. passive : doronad *factum est*, doronta *facti sunt* Prol. 239, 3d pl. reduplicated future :. dogénatar Ep. 176. A Middle Irish daronsat *fecerunt* Pref. shows a mixture of s-forms.
dogrés, adv. *continuo, semper*, Feb. 3. see grés.
doib, *to them* Prol. 17, but O'Cl. explains by uaidhibh *from them*, doibside Pref.
doig, Nov. 16. D.
doim-liac, (daimliac B) Nov. 24, has been explained as *domus vitulorum* [line=Corn. loch gl. vitulus] liassa liag .i. ait a ndearnadh cróoithe for líoghaibh *a place in which were made huts for calves* O'Cl. and this seems its meaning in a story (Leb. Brecc,) about a bishop committing adultery with a king's wife in the royal damliacc (for repeating the Félire he was miraculously transported to his bed in his own church). But O'Clery explains daimhliag by englas *church*, a glossographer in H. 2. 16, col. 101, explains daimliacc by tegduis cloch *a house of stones*. So in H. 3. 18, p. 635, col. 2 ; Doimliac .i. tegais clach, and it probably means *domus lapidum* : lia gen. liac, gen. pl. liace-n. Saint Cianán's daimliac is now Duleek in the Co. of Meath.
dóire, s. f. *captivity*, abl. sg. Ep. 532, opposite of sóire : cotabucabarsi .i. biid ersoilethi archiunn for rig dothét cona popul a doiri *be ye lifted up, i.e. be ye opened before your king who comes with his people out of bondage* Ml. 98.
dolá, *apponere, to put, to set*, doralus *posui*, Prol. 15. (=do-ro-láus), rola .i. rochuir O'R. rálsid, rolasid *posuistis* Z. 613. ralsat Chron. Scot. 150. haidh .i. cuiridh *ponit*, O'Cl. Gl. see lá.
Dolecán, Aug. 6, gen. Dolecáin.
dolmae, s. n. *slowness, delay*, acc. sg. dolmai Ep. 151, opposite of solmae (diarsuadud co solma, Mael-ísu) : uoco techtand in spirut noeb dolma no doos in a gnimaib LB. 53ᵇ, dolma naithise ar fear th' inaid dogres ar colum cille *slowness of answer on thy successor continually*, says C. C., II. 2. 16, col. 683.
dolluid, see luid.
dom, *to my*, Prol. 25. Jan. 21, 24, Nov. 12, Ep. 271.
dom, -dam-, infixed pron. *me, to me* : cotomroebat, cotamroebat (=con-dam-ro-ad-gabat) Ep. 45.
domidiur, *judico* 3d pl. pres. indic. pass. domiditer Pref.
Dominus, Nov. 5, a mistake for Domninus q. v.
domnitecht, Ep. 561, see titecht.
domnach, s.m. (n. ?) *a church* (from dominicum, ecclesia, aedes sacra Domino seu Deo, Du Cange), gen. sg. domnaig Feb. 15, Oc. 27. Domnach mór mainech Oc. 27.
Domnall, gen. Domnaill, Pref. (=Domuaill, Domnill, Reeves *Col.* 135, 201), n. pl. domnaill Prol. 234.
Domninus, Nov. 5, a martyr (Us.) 'In Cesaria Capadocie ; natalis sanctorum Domnini, Epiphanii, Antonini' Ob. & Mart. Chr. Ch. p. 175 (Non. Novembris).

2 *k* 2

Domnóe, of Tibra Fachtna, Feb. 13.
domuinim, Pref. 70 seems=O. Ir. domoiniur *puto?*
domun, s. m. *world* Z². 220, 222, gen. sg. domain Prol. 83, 93. 145, 149, 220. June 16, Ep. 329, better domuin Nov. 11 (where it rhymes with romuir), Z². 223. dat. sg. domun Ep. 448. doman, dumun, Mar. 16. acc. sg. doman Ep. 368. cognate with Skr. dhâman 4 Beitr. 217.
-don- infixed pron. 1st pl. ar-don-sela June 23.
donae, donai adj. *wretched*, Sep. 16, Corm. 16, the opposite of sonae.
Donait, Nov. 9, Donatus a Spanish saint. ' In Hispannia ; natalis sanctorum Fausti et Marcialis. Et eodem die [v. id. Nov.] Ursicini episcopi et sanctorum Donati et Damiani,' Ob. & Mart. p. 176.
dond, don *to the*, Prol. 31, 292. Jan. 23, Feb. 16. B., Mar. 21, May 29, D., June 19, B. Before s (h) the d becomes t : dont-šluag-sa Ep. 104.
donecmaicc (.i. tic *comes*, Three Ir. Gl. p. 138) Dec. 24 B.=donecmaing *accidit* Z. 852 : do-nd-ecmaic A, seems for donnecmaic *nobis accidit*.
doneoch, pron. *who*, Pref. 98, lit *'to whom*,' neoch (for neach) being the dat. sg. of nech.
donn, adj. *fuscus*=W. dwn (cf. Gaulish Dunnius?). Hence
Donnan, of Eig, Ap. 17, Reeves Col., 304, 305.
Donnchad, Prol. 221, gen. Donchada (leg. Donchada) Pref. 20, Donchad mac Donnaill, Pref. 20, overking of Ireland A.D. 770.
dont, v. dond.
doragat, *advenient* Ep. 115, O. Ir. doregat, a future from the root REG.
doráhi, *adiit*, do-m-r-ala *iri* pref. B.
doráhis, Prol. 15, *posui*=do-ro-láus : cf. dorabsat 6enclár catha foraib dia tobart, LU. 19ᵇ. ralsid *posuistis*, rolá .i. rochuir O'R.
doratus, *dedi* Ep. 112, doratsat *dederunt* Ep. 113. 3d sg. perf. pass. doratad, a defective verb.
1. dorchae, s. *darkness* (do-riche, opposite to sorchae, so-riche), gen. sg. dorchae (leg. dorchai) Dec. 25. n. pl. fritataibret na dorche, Sg. 183ᵇ.
2. dorchae, adj. *dork*. dat. sg. m. dorchu Mar. 9.
dorige, (dorige?) *adveniet?* Prol. 258.
dorimin, dorimm *adnumero (adnumecori?)* Ep. 317. do-n-rími, do-r-ríme, *quem adnumeras*, Ap. 30, Sep. 5, 1 sg. 2dy. pres. dornirmind Ep. 128. 1 sg. pret. dornirmins Ep. 40, 41, 229, 1 pl. doruirmisium (leg. doruirmisem) Ep. 228, do-s-rimemar Ep. 6, do-s-ruimdemar B. 1 sg. b. fut. doriminiub Ep. 232, 1 pl. dorimfem, Ep. 232 B.
Dorn, gen. Duirn Feb. 2.
dorochair, torchair, v. dochriuim.
dorodbad, (dorodbath B) *periit* Prol. 96, either=do-ro-adbath or do-ro-dibad.
dorósat, see dofosat.
Doroma, Sep. 20. 1 know not whether this is intended for the name of some virgin or whether it should be read do-Roma, de Roma *of Rome*.
dorreith, doreith, doreth, *accurrit*, Ap. 16. 3d pl. dorertatar, v. rethim.
dórtaim, *I shed* : dorortad (rofortad B.) .i. doloirteadh O'Cl. *effusus est*, May 27, defortad (gl. effunderet) Ml. 36ᵃ.
dorus, s. n. (W. drws 2 Beitr. 161) *door*, Jan. 30, andorus (gl. limen) Ml.—56. nom. pl. dorsi, LU. 32ᵃ, acc. pl. frisnatorus Ml. 98, dat. doirsib (gl. portis) Z. 801. voc. pl. a doirsea Ml. 98.
-dos- infixed pron. *them* Prol. B. 73. dus Prol. A 57.
doselba, Ep. 4 D. seems to mean *thou possessest* : see asselba.
doss, s. m. *bush* Mar. 16, Ap. 6, June 17, Ep. 250, cognate with Lat. dusmus, densus, Gr. ἴασύς,

čúσης. Doss 'a poet of the third order' which Cormac fancifully refers to doss *bush*, is perhaps connected with Skr. dāsas, Zend daṅhaṅh *wisdom*.
1. dot, *to thy* Prol. 12, *for thy* July 24.
2. -dot- infixed pron. 2d sg. do-dot-fairci *who guards thee*, Jan. 26.
dotic, *tibi venit*. May 25, dot-ic (totic B.), the verb tic with the pron. of the 2d sg. infixed.
draic, s. m. *draco* (W. draig), gen. sg. cride n dracon LU. 106ᵃ. acc. sg. draic-n (dric-n A) Sep. 29, gen. pl. combruth dracon conanáil nathrach combeim leoman, LU. 66ᵃ. drac Corm. 15, dracondae ib. s. v. base.
drebraing, *saliit* Ap. 2, 17, Aug. 26 (.i. rodhring no rodirgestar) 3 Ir. Gl. 131. = do-vrevrangi, a reduplicated preterite. The root is VRANG a nasalised form of the root which appears in Skr. as vraj.
drecheng, s. m. *three champions*, see prim-drecheng and cf. decheng. O'Cl. however, explained it by caoin triar.
drem, s. f. *a company*: see mór-drem. gen. sg. datrian na dreme dorochair do nim *two thirds of the company fell from heaven*, O'Dav. 77, dat. con-dreim aile do mathib ulad, LU. 38ᵇ.
dric, adj. (.i. feargach, O'Cl. Gl.) *angry* Prol. 221, gen. sg. m. dric Prol. 134.
drobél, s. f. *difficulty* dat. sg. drobéil Aug. 26, dat. pl. indoilgib in drobelaib hicailtib hi cocrichaib LU. 104ᵇ. drobhel .i. docamhail *difficult* O'Cl. Gl. droibheil .i. ainnridteach no docamlach amail coillte *like woods*, O'D. supp.
drochraud, s.f. *an ill lot* (.i. mala pars apud inferos, Rawl. 505), Jan. 10, droch=W. drwg, rand=W. rhan.
dron, adj. (.i. daingean O'Cl. Gl.) *strong*, v. firdron : saor dron durtaigh O'Dav. 79. dron .i. drochte no direach, LL. Voc.
drong, s. m. *a troop* (=Lat. drungus 2 Beitr. 170-1) Prol. 199, Aug. 27, Nov. 7, Ep. 233, 237, 241, 245, 249, 253, 257, 261, 265, 269, 273, 277, 281, voc. sg. drong (leg. druing) Ep. 401, n. pl. druing Ep. 285, gen. pl. droug Ep. 305, dat. pl. drougaib Ep. 289, acc. pl. drungu Ep. 232.
drúcht, s. *dew* Ep. 224, gen. sg. ni taudchaid banua drúchta di féor comedón lái, LU. 86ᵇ. n. pl. druchta Corm. Perhaps from drupta, drub-ta, root DHRUB, whence O. N. drjúpa, A.S. dreópan.
druimm, s. n. (W. trum) *dorsum, ridge*, gen. sg. dromma May 21, Aug. 19, Sep. 3, 18, Oc. 10 = drommo Z². 269, acc. pl. dromand (gl. terga) Gild. 171 : druimm ex drosmen is cognate with Lat. dorsu-s, dorsu-m, Gr. τεpψ, Aeol. τέρρα. v. Noendruim, Echdruim.
    Druim Cuilinn, May 21, Drumcullen, barony of Eglish, King's co.
    Druim Ferta, (Mugaine in Uib Failge), Sep. 3.
    Druim Ingard, Oc. 10, in north of co. Meath.
    Druim Raithue, Aug. 19, Sep. 18, in West Meath.
Drusus, Dec. 11, martyred at Antioch with three companions, Zosimus, Theodorus and a virgin Lucia (Us.).
1. du- a prefix (=δυς, Nhg. zer-), see duba, duthain.
2. du, prep. see do.
dúan, s. f. *a song*, gen. dúaine, dat. sg. dúain Mar. 7, acc. sg. dúain LU. 6ᵃ, n. pl. gailbir dúana St. P. duan molta *song of praise* L.U. 5ᵇ. cf. Zend du *denken, sprechen*, Justi, 156.
duas, (D. duais) Dec. 28, seems a corruption of tuas q.v.
1. dub, adj. (a-stem?) *dark, black*, dat. sg. m. dub Mar. 9 : cognate with O.N. dökkr *dunkel*.
2. dub, s. n. *ink*, nom. sg. is taua an-dub-so *thin is this ink*, Z². xii. gen. sg. duib Nov. 24.
duba, s. *grief*, gen. sg. Ep. 377, opposite of suba, q.v.
dubach, adj. *mournful* Ap. 2, dat. sg. m. Prol. 98, opposite of subach, q.v.
dúbart, s. *an urgent, vehement prayer*, Ep. 153, 418, acc. sg. dubairt Ep. 71, dubairt .i. diprecoit

.i. adbulguide O'Dav. (Mac F.), dúbairt .i. dibeargoid (=diprecoit) no guidl..
dhuthrachdach O'Cl.
Dublitir, gen. duiblitrech A. dublitrech B, May 15, abbot of Finglass, near Dublin : ob. A.D. 796.
dubsluag, s. m. *a black host*, dat. sg. Prol. 254.
duib, *to you*, Ep. 391.
Duibréa, gen. Jan. 5.
dúil, s. f. *an element, a creature*, Z^2. 249, gen. sg. dúlo 250, acc. sg. dúil Prol. 91, gen. pl. dúile
Prol. 337, Z^2. 252, acc. pl. dúile Pref. 17=duli, dvli Z^2. 252. Cogn. with Skr. dhátu as
gnúis *facies* Z^2. 25, with jnátu.
dúilech, adj. *elemental*, gen. sg. m. dúilig, dúlig. Dec. 19.
Duilech, acc. sg. Nov. 17, of Clochar Duilig near Swords.
Duinlesce, Jan. 3, better Dún-Bléscc q. v.
duine, s. m. *homo*, Z^2. 229, gen. sg. duini Z^2. 230, dat. duiniu ib. acc. sg. duine, Ep. 215, nom.
pl. doine, leg. dóini Nov. 6, gen. pl. dóine-n, dáine, Prol. 8, 9, 340, Jan. 1, dat. pl.
dóinib, Prol. 316, Sep. 24, dáinib Prol. 153, Ep. 64, 417, acc. pl. dóine (leg. dóiniu) Ep.
15, dóeine Ep. 152.
duinn, duin, *to us* Ep. 98, duindne Pref. B. see dun, dunn.
dúire, s. f. *durities*, gen. sg. Prol. 66.
duit, *to thee*, Ap. 16, July 24, Oc. 24, Ep. 554, duitsiu Ep. 335.
dun, *to us*, June 1, Oc. 19, Ep. 98, Z^2. 24, 270, dunn, Prol. 164.
dún, s. n. au s-stem, *stronghold, fortress* Prol. 130, gen. sg. dúine 1 S.M. 246, dat. in duin
sebuirgi, Lib. Arm. 15 a, 2, n. pl. lúine Prol. 68, 150: W. din A.S. tún, Eng. town,
Ohg. zûn, 2 Beitr. 175, O.N. tún. Root du in Lat. du-rus and Gr. ξύ-ραμαι.
Dún Cuair Pref. now Rathcore in co. Meath. See O'Don. 4 Mast. 799, 800, 815.
Dún-Blésce, (now Doon, co. Limerick), Jan. 3.
dúnad, s. m. (n.?) *a host*, Nov. 6 gen. dúnaid July 22, i each thaurchómraic dunaid móir,
LU. 55ᵇ, isé lín arndúnaid, LU. 57ª.
Dunchad, eleventh abbot of Hí, May 25, ob. A.D. 717, Reeves' Columba 379, Beda H. E. v. 22.
Dunlang, Ap. 11.
dúr, =durus (W. dir, Z^2. 25 u.). Hence dúire s. supra and
dárdae, adj. *hardened*, Ep. 194.
-dus-, *them* an infixed pronoun, Prol. 57 A, O.Ir. das.
duthain, adj. *transitory, short-lived* (opposite of suthain q. v.) Prol. 158, Nov. 28, bid
airdairc . . . . acht bid duthain LU. 61ᵇ, acc. pl. m. eter marbu duthainai, LU. 120ª.
dúthracht, s. *desire*, (do-fu-thract) acc. sg. Ep. 68, 111 ; dúthracht *votivus* Z^2. 225 : duthracair
voluit. Root trac, Skr. tark *to suppose* (W.)

e for ä : berim, celim, ech : for i: atsluinne Prol. 110 A, semplex, July 29, benidecht March 21,
cuimne May 4.
-e for -eu, coinnle, Prol. 288, for -eo, inse Feb. 7=O. Ir. inseo, for -iu, notguide Prol. 265 A,
achoimde Prol. 2 A, cumaige Jan. 20 A.
e a breaking of i : for Feb. 8, neodemus Oct. 17, pelait Prol. 85A, lebrán, Ep. 90.
e umlaut of a : mec June 24, Oc. 26.
é (ia) from ai : ad-féded : é by compensation : dér, én, féu, cenél, éccu, cét, ergim.
1. é, hé, háe, *he*, Prol. 293, 335, Sep 26 : as a suffixed pronoun e in roscaich-e Prol. 177, 193.
2. é, *they*, hit-e, Pref. 48.
3. é, =es *(ev)*, a negative prefix, v. énirt.
ea tor o, Senupól Prol. 97, gleand ib. 196 A, neam ib. 216, 280 A, Oc. 24 A, Ep. 25 A, leacht
Prol. 227, eneat ib. 228 A, caibteal ib. 319 A, taitneam ib. 330 A, beach Jan. 13 A.
ea for ia : adreani Nov. 6, cea Nov. 7.

éat, *they* (é+at) Sep. 22, e-at-éat rhymes with déne, no taidled eat cotaprad a phennait cóir for each *he used to visit them that he might impose on every one his proper penance*, LU. 13ª, cf. iat. The form seat (leg. séat?) also occurs : ol-scat-som LU. 21ᵇ, 24ᵇ.
ec, s. *compulsion*, acc. sg. (rhymes with bece) Pref. 43.
écaib, s.(cf. W. angen) *death* Nov. 10. dat. sg. décaib (=doécaib) Corm. s. v. Gaimred. With the phrase bece na bu mó écaib *he was almost greater than Death*, cf. in the Four Masters, A.D., 876. ba moo Aodh Oiligh égaibh *Aed of Ailech was greater than Death*. Root ANK=NAK whence Skr. root nay, Gr. νέκ-υς, νεκ-ρός, Lat. nec-are.
ecemaing, *it happened?* Pref. 13. see ecmaic, tecmac.
écen, écen, s. f. *necessity, force, compulsion*, Dec. 30, (gl. violentia) Sg. 51ᵃ, arecin *per necessitatem*=W. angen, Corn. anken, M. Br. anquen, cognate with ἀνάγκη, necesse, ἀγκώνη.
éces, s. m. *a sage*, gen. sg. écis, éciss, éiccis, Feb. 8.
ech, m.=equus 2 Beitr. 161, acc. sg. ech-n Z². 225.
Echdruimm, *horse-ridge* (anglicised Aughrim), gen. sg. Echdromma May 7.
Ecimonius, see Egimonius.
ecla, s. f. *fear*, acc. eclai, May 30, Nov. 4, Ep. 247.
eclas, s. f.=ecclesia Z². 249, Pref. 28, gen. sg. ecailse Jan. 2, recaillse, *ecilse* Z². 250, dat. sg. eclais, Pref., n. pl. eculsa Pref., gen. pl. eclas, eclass, Nov. 18, acc. pl. eculsa Pref. but also eclaisi, Pref. 4, which comes from the fem. i-stem eclais, gen. ecolso, accalsa, acolsa Z². 250.
ecmaic, *happening, chance*, dat. sg. d'ecmaicc, d'ecmaing, Ep. 172. see tecmung O'Dav. 55, gives Ep. 172 thus : a beth slan ni decmaic, and explains it by ní decmaing bias slainti dó acht do gres *it is not by chance* (ecmaing, better, perhaps, *occasionally*) *that safety shall be to him, but always*.
écnach, s. m. *reviler*, better écndach q. v.
ecnae, s. n. *wisdom, knowledge*, gen. sg. ind ecnai Feb. 9, Aug. 11, ecnai May 30, Nov. 27, Ep. 248, 263, acc. sg. ecuai (leg. ecnae to rhyme with Toelne) Feb. 22 : from aith-gnae : cf. etar- gnae n.
écnaire, s. *a prayer, intercession* (ess-con-do-ARG-i) Ep. 192, 201, acc. sg. ar ecnaire. Prol. 266, Ep. 72, 384, 404, 405, 474, 490, 514, 526, 550. The word écnaire signifies *litany, intercession* for the absent, and is more general than *requiem*, as it extended to the living as well as the dead, Reeves, Culdees 88.
. écndach, s. m. *reviter*, nom. pl. éen(d)aig Nov. 9 : cf. éiendag connessim *detrectator proximi* Z². 45, amal non-avic(n)dichtherni (gl. sicut blasphemamur) ib.
écra, *an enemy* (éss-cara), acc. sg. ecrait Mar. 8. Hence éccradach (leg. écratach) *hostility*, *hostility*, O'Cl. Gl. and écraide (leg. ecraite) *hostility*, ib.
ectoir, (echtair B.) Pref. 82. Hector!
ed, hed, pron. *it*, Ep. 217, 240.
édenn, s. *ivy*, eden Corm. 18. Hence
édnech, adj. *having ivy*, gen. sg. édnich, éidnig, édhnig, Feb. 17.
Efis, Effis, Effeiss, Elliss, *Ephesus*, dat. sg. June 24, Aug. 7, Dec. 27 : so in Lib. Hymn. 14ª in effis dana doronad, where dr. Todd has, wrongly, in efesis dana doronad.
Egemonius, Jan. 8, bishop of Augustodunum (Autun).
Egipt, Éigipt, Égept, Aegept, dat. sg. Jan. 11, Ap. 25, Oc. 3, gen. sg. égipte Ep. 532.
ei, umlaut of a : meice=O. Ir. maicc June 24, Oct. 26, of e : teined Prol. 44 : éi umlaut of é : roféiser, éigipt, téiscal, féilire.
Eic, (now Eig), gen. eca, ega Ap. 17, Egea insula, Reeves' Col. 223. an island which with Muck and Rum constitutes the parish of Kildonain. The word eca is glossed by 'fons' and in Lib. Arm. 13b 2. enga is written over 'ueuiebat aqua supra petram': cf. πηγή ?
éim, ém, adj. *swift* July 19, where it is used as an adverb : cf. anéim *slow* Corm. s. v. An.

ciuech, s. m. (n. *l*) *mercy, bounty*, acc. sg. Prol. 42. P. O'C. also gives the form cineachas.
eipistil, s. f.=epistola, Pref. B.
Eirge, Jan. 2, perhaps for Eirce, Airce gen. of Airic.
éirgim-, *I arise* (ess-rigim), 3d sg. s-pret. virgis *surrexit* Pref. B. see érgu, 3d sg. t-pret. nochan éracht noch amchind istaig *no one arose before him within*, Trip. Life B. 163ᵃ.
eirlech, Pref. 62, meaning obscure.
éis, eiss, s. *track* (.i. lorg O'Cl. Gl. but in Fiacc 8 the nom. sg. is és) used in the nominal prep. diéis (gl. retro) Z. 565, dianéis, dianéiss, *after them* Prol. 79. The acc. found in the forms tar-ési-n, dar-ési-n seems to come from a cognate in-stem.
elaim *evado*, 3d. sg. t-pret. elaid *erasit* Pref. B. Beitr. viii. 2.
Ela, Elo, Oc. 3, a stream near Tullamore in the King's Co. Reeves' Col. 124 n.
Elair, =Hilarius episcopus Pictaviensis Jan. 13, Nov. 3; pope, Nov. 1, gen. Elair Ep. 138, see Hilarius.
elatha, s. f. *science* gen. sg. elathan Pref. 8, dat. sg. elathain Pref. 1. acc. sg. elathain Pref. 17.
elc, adj. *bad*, cognate with ἕλκος as olc with ulcus. Hence
elcu, s. f. *badness*, acc. sg. elccai June 7.
ém, a particle, *indeed* Pref. 48, 51, *autem* Z.
EM=Lat. em- in emere v. airitiu, EM=Skr. yam (with carma), v. doemim.
Emain (Macha), gen. Emna Prol. 193, now the Navan fort about two miles W. of Armagh, was the palace of the Kings of Ulster till A.D. 332, when it was destroyed by the three Collas.
Emelianus, Aug. 22. I cannot find him in Boll. or elsewhere.
émid, adj. *swift*, Dec. 29, where in the Franciscan MS. bid emidh is glossed by bideim no bidluath.
Emin, Emene, acc. sg. Dec. 22.
enach, s.m. *a marsh* (used for Enach truim in Laoighis, now Annatrim, Queen's Co., in the W. of Leinster, Mart. Don. 288), gen. sg. enaig, Nov. 3.
1. Enair =Januarius, a bishop martyred at Puteoli in Campania Felice. Boll. Sep. 19. Enair an African martyr, Ap. 8, where it is in the gen. sg.
2. Enair, *January*, gen. sg. Jan. 1, 31, Ep. 8.
Enan, (gen. Enain) of Ros-mór (in Ui-deagha in Ui-Ceinnselaigh) Jan. 30 : of Druim-Raithne in Westmeath, Aug. 19, Sep. 18.
Enda, Endae, Enna, of Aran, Mar. 21 : of Cell na manach (or Cellmac Cathail *l*) Dec. 31.
énirt, adj. *weak* (gl. imbecillis 3 Ir. Gl. 133) Ep. 9, from nert. q. v.
ennac, endac, adj. (=innocuus *l*) *blameless*, gen. pl. Ap. 9, 24, acc. pl. f. endga (leg. ennea) Ep. 322.
eo for ia : deoda, Jan. 9, deochan Jan. 14. for io : Eoin.
eo from ó by progressive assimilation : méiltede, temneóc.
eo from eu : neort Prol. 163, B. do-neoch Prol. 146, and see Eognin, Eornip, Eosebius.
eo, s. 1. =*yew* (W. yw, Br. ivin=nn (gl. taxus) Ohg. iwa), gen. pl. Ap. 10.
2. *wood*, Mar. 10,=eu (gl. stipes) Z². 35.
eoais, (in cluain eonis, eois, euis, Ap. 4), is said in Laud 610 to be the name of Conchobar's swineherd : "nomen muccada concobair nognathaiged aud *who used to frequent there*."
eobail, Prol. 198, meaning doubtful, perhaps a compound of eo *good* (Corm. s. v. iubar) and bail *great*, see anbail.
Eochaid Cobai, Pref.
Eogan, gen. Eogain, Prol. 200, 203, Aug. 23, a man's name, from εὐγενής *?* or avigenus *?* Eogan of Ard Sratha Aug. 23.
Eoganacht, s. f. dat. sg. Oc. 20, descendants of Eogan.
Eoin, =Iohannes, gen. sg. Aug. 3, Nov. 19, acc. sg. Nov. 25, Ep. 479, 539, always a dissyllable.
Eoin Cassion, Nov. 25, "The celebrated John Cassian, who was ordained deacon by S. Chrysostom (c. A.D. 404), and whose works on the monastic life and institutes were so widely read during the middle ages." Todd, *Lib. Hymn.* 258.

Eolang (Eolach B and D) of Achad Bó, Sep. 5.
eolas, s. m. *knowledge*, gen. sg. eolais Prol. 317, eolus .i. tuicsi iar foglaim. O'Dav. 81.
Eoraip, s. f. *Europe*, gen. sg. Eorapa, Ap. 20.
Eosebius, Oc. 9=Eusebius. This is probably the Pope and confessor commemorated at Oct. 2 in Ob. and Mart.
Epectitus, May 23, seu Epitacius, mart. in Hispania, Boll.
epscop, s.m.=episcopus (W. esgob), Jan. 2, 8, Feb. 9, 11, Mar. 8, Ap. 6, 12, May 24, June 2, July 14, Oc. 4, gen. sg. epscoip Mar. 4, Oc. 14, 22, Dec. 5, epscuip Tir. 11, Z^2. 230, dat. sg. epscop Nov. 2, acc. sg. epscop-u Feb. 12, Oc. 4, n. pl. epscoip, epscuip, July 29. Often written contractedly eps., esp. In A sometimes escop.
er-, an intensive prefix (see er-chiau, erdaire) = περί, Lat. per.
éraim, *recuso*, 2d sg. a-conj. éra Ep. 338.
éru, Nov. 8, B. for dern.
Eraclius, Dec. 3, a corruption of Herculeus or Ἡράκλειος ?
erail, aurail, s. *an injunction, exhortation, bidding*? Jan. 1, Mar. 3, cf. do erail creitme for ríg nereud, L U. 113ª. do erail ringla 7 sobhesa for cach, O'Don. supp. cid aru n-emilend isu foirn sund ernaigthi etir do dénum? ib. s.v. ceasnaigther. This seems the same as iráil, which Ebel (Z^2. 999, 1,000) renders by *confirmatio*.
Erasmus, June 2. a bishop martyred, temp. Diocletian, at Formiae, in Campania, between Rome and Naples.
erbim, *committo*, nom-érpimm *confido* Z^2. 60, 434, ni-t-erpi *non committis te*, ib. erbaid (gl. credit). 3d pl. earbait *they order*, O'D. Supp. na berat anerpther doib ae *auferant quod committitur eis* Z^2. 444, ruairptha *commissi sunt* 478, verb *he charged* Pref. B.
Erc, Ercc, gen. circ, a man's name. Erc i telsig lis, May 12. Erc of Domnach mór maige Luadat, Oc. 27. Erc of Sláine, Nov. 2, "Ercc filius dego cuius reliquie adorantur in illa ciuitate quae uocatur slane, Lib. Arm. 4ª. 2, gen. fide eirc filii dego ib. 20, a. 2. In LB. 23, lower margin, occurs the following quatrain :—

Escop erce (.i. britheṁ patraic)   Bishop Erc (i.e. Patrick's brehon),
cechni concertad bacert   Everything that he adjudged was just,
cechoen beress [coicert] cert   Everyone who passes a just judgment,
fodreith bendacht escuip eircᵃ   Bishop Erc's blessing succours him.

erchian, aerchian, adj. *very far*, Prol. 122.
Ercnait, Jan. 8, a fem. dimin. of Erc. O'Curry (Manners and Customs of the Ancient Irish, III. 123) gives the following translation of a note, which he states to be "to the Felire Aenghuis : Ercnat, the virgin nun, was cook and robemaker to St. Columb Cille, and her Church is Cille (*sic*) Chocu [or Kilcock] in Cairbre ua Ciardha [now Carbury in the County of Kildare.] Ercnat was her true name, which means an Embroideress because Ercadh, in the ancient Gaedhelic, was the same as drawing and embroidering now ; for it was that virgin who was the embroideress, cutter, and sewer of clothes to St. Columb Cille and his disciples."
erdairc, adj. *conspicuous*, gl. celebre Z^2. 234, Ap. 19, June 10, Ep. 265, nom. pl. m. erdarcni (gl. honore conspicui) Z^2. 236 : ardirce, airdirc, aurdairc, erdraic, irdraic, urdraice are other spellings of the same word.
Erentius, Herentius, Aug. 5, seems a corruption of Hirencus mart. at Axiopolis.
éres, s.=haeresis, gen. Ap. 23, éiris .i. michreideamh *misbelief*, O'Cl.
érge, s. *a rising up*, erigere Pref. 99 = ess-rigia : cf. rig infra.
ergna, s. *intellect* (eargna .i. inntleachd O'Cl. gl.), gen. sg. Feb. 24, cf. co-remiergnaitis (gl. praenoscerent) Ml. 19ᵇ. Root gnā, Lat. gno, Gr. γνω, Skr. jñā.
Ériu, Éiriu s.f. *Ireland* (Iverio, W. Iwerddon) Sep. 10, gen. sg. érenn, éirenn, (= Iverionos)

ᵃ The scribe adds 'Iair' *on him*, spoiling sense and metre.

Feb. 1, 13. Mar. 17, June 3, Sep. 26, Nov. 29. Ep. 277, 284, dat. sg. érinn, éirinn, Ap.
23, Nov. 21, abl. éri Ap. 5, Sep. 5, voc. éiriu, éire July 24, locative érinn, June 25.
erlam. Pref. B.
Ermes, (Ermis, A.) leg. Hermes, a martyr, May 24, Aug. 28. The Hermes at Aug. 28 was
  an Alexandrian martyr, Boll.
Ermogin, Ap. 19.=Hermogenes q. v. See the legend of his conflict with S. James, Jameson
  S. & L. Art. 232.
ermór, s. *the bulk, the greater part*, Pref.
Ernach, of Dún dá én. Oc. 30.
ernail, s. *a kind, a species*, ernail aiste *a kind of metre*, Pref. Laud 610. frisin crnail airigthi ib.
Érnóc, see Mérnóc.
Esaias, gen. sg. Esaie. Ep. 241.
ésca, ésce s.n. *moon* Pref. 15 : compound : cáin-ésce Jan. 3, gen. éscai, ésci.
escomlud, s. *a going forth, a passing away, emigration* (escomlad, A), May 2, Oc. 23.
Escon, Esconn, Nov. 20.
escor, s. *a fall* l (eascar O'Don. Supp.) acc. sg. Prol. 63. If O'Dav. 81 (esgair .i. osger .i. leim)
  be right, for cen-escor we should read án escair *a noble leap*, the án-asccur of B.
eséirgim, (as-as-rgim) *surgo*; 3d sg. t-pret. as-r-eracht Prol. 92, Mar. 27, Tur. 19 : cf. do-r-
  eracht *surrexit*.
eslind, eslinn Ep. 397=eislinn .i. esinnill no édaingen *unsafe or infirm* O'Cl. Gl.
esnad, s. *music, song, melody*, Ep. 157, (easnadh .i. ceol, .i. amhran no binneas, O'Cl. Gl.)
Esodir, Essodir, Jan. 2, Isidorus, bishop and martyr at Antioch.
espac, adj. *idle, vain*, Ep. 430=espa Corm. 18. Hence espach *otiosus*.
etal, ettal, adj. (=eatal *a pure person* O'Don. Supp.) Ep. 173 : gen. sg. etail Ir. Gl. p. 151 ;
  n. pl. aircindig etail, O'Don. Supp. ainetal *an impure person*, ibid.
etail, s. acc. sg. Sep. 4, O'Curry '*falsehood*,' but it seems=etoil .i. cen toil .i. sine peccato,
  O'Mulc. 461.
étan, s. *front, forehead*, dat. sg. June 1, Oc. 1 : cf. Lat. ante, antiae.
Ethecn, Etchen, bishop of Cluain Fota Boetain Aba. Feb. 11.
ethre, eithre s.m. *end*, acc. ethre-n Aug. 31, Oc. 31, eithre .i. deiredh no forbera no err, Three
  Ir. Gl. 136 .i. err no deireadh no crìochnúghadh, O'Cl.
etla, s. f. *repentance, regret, penitence* Mar. 24, (eatla .i. ciamaire, congain croidhe. aithrighe
  no dera O'Cl.), gen. sg. etla Jan. 8, Ep. 193, tormach n-etla LB. 259ᵇ. dat. sg. etlai Ir. Gl.
  p. 142, iarsin caiset cohetla unhethnide oirrderca, poem after Félire : acc. sg. dorigensat
  . . . . etla [leg. etlai] fridia fair, LU. 115ᵇ.
étrocht, adj. *bright*, Feb. 10.
étsecht, éitsecht, estecht, s. *death* Jan. 19, 22. Mar. 20, Nov. 13, acc. sg. May 2, Ep. 107,
  (renetsecht .i. rian éc, 3 Ir. Gl. 139).
Eufemia, July 11, Sep. 17=Euphemia of Chalcedonia, Virgin and Martyr, Jameson, S. & L.
  Art. 561. Note that Oengus agrees with the Greek Church in celebrating S. Euphemia
  at 11 July. In the Roman martyrology, her day is 16 Sept. 'quo die Graeci quoque
  eam repetunt,' Boll.
Eugenia, Mar. 16, martyred at Nicomedia temp. Severus.
Eusebius, Sep. 25. Oct. 2, 9, 22. Nov. 7. Ep. 140. The Eusebius at Oc. 2, was a pope.
Eutaic, gen. sg. S. Eutichius, 'mart. Aquiliciae in Italia,' Boll. May 30, Euticius a Roman martyr,
  July 2, Eutychius a Nicomedian martyr Boll. Oc. 20, a corruption of Eutyches (εὐτυχής).
  In Nov. 13, eutaic is=Euticis, gen. sg. of Eutex (?) a Thracian martyr, Bede iv. 153.
Evagair, gen. sg. Ap. 3,=Euagrius, martyr 'Tomis in Scythia,' Boll.
Evangelus, an Alexandrian martyr, July 13.

f. in anlaut from v (fáith, fedb, fiche, fluith) : a graphic *bezeichnung* of the v- sound, see farn.

GLOSSARIAL INDEX.   cclix

f infected dropt ; bithlaith Prol. 272, Ep. 159, morlaith, Nov. 10, imand, Dec. 31. ingen ergna Oc. 5, B. tór- = do-for, tó- = do-fo.
fa, = foan, *under whom* Prol. 86, and see foirithim.
Fabianus, an African martyr, June 28.
fácbaim, *I leave* (=fo-ad-gab-) 3d sg. pret. act. fácab, Tir. 2. 3d pl. s-pret. forfácsat (=fo-ro-ad-gab-sat) Pref.
Fachtnae, Aug. 14, gen. Fachtni (de Gallano filio Fachtni, Reeves' Col. 65.)
fáel, s. *wolf* (faol .i. cú allaidh no mac tire, O'Cl.) Hence the diminutive Fáelán, Fóelán, Jan. 9, June 20, Oct. 31 : failán, gen. failáin Lib. Arm. 16, b, 2.
Failbe, Mar. 22, eighth abbot of Iona, son of Pipán (faillbhe is explained by beodha, O'Cl. Gl.), Adamnán's Failbeus, Reeves' Columba, 16, 26, 376.
fáilid, failid, adj. i- stem, *blithe* Aug. 4, Dec. 19, n. pl. fáilte, faeilte, failti, Prol. 64, Dec. 18.
faille, Ap. 25 (.i. dermait Rawl. 505) seems to be the gen. sg. of faille *neglect*, cognate with faill *negligence, failure*, O'Don. Supp.
faillsigim, *I manifest*, 3d sg. pret. rofaillsig, Pref. 17, Z². 212, 224. See foillsigim.
fáilte, faelte, s. f. *joy, bliss, welcome*, Prol. 49, acc. sg. fáilti-n June 11. Z². 248, Ep. 49, dat. sg. huand failti (gl. hilaritate) Ml. deriv. from fáilid.
fainne, s. f. *weakness*, gen. sg. May 17, deriv. from fann q. v.
fairinn, s. f. (=O. W. guerin) *a company of persons, a troop*, Aug. 18, acc. sg. Ep. 51, better foirinn which glosses factio in Z.
fairge, s. f. *sea*, gen. sg. fairge, fairrge, Ep. 536, acc. sg. fairrgi, Aug. 14.
fairsing, fairsiung, adj. (gl. amplus Ir. Gl.), Oc. 28.
fáith, s. m. (vātes) *prophet* Z². 230, n. pl. fáithi, fáithe, Ep. 13, gen. pl. fáithe-n Ep. 241, fátha-n, Nov. 29.
falaig ł imfalaig (imfalaid B) : falach or folach is explained by *reil, cover, screen*, P. O'C.
fann, adj. *weak* (=W. gwan) in imfann, Dec. 31.
far-n, *your*, Z². 339, Ep. 394, also for-n.
farith, see foirithim.
fás, adj. *waste*, n. pl. f. fása, fássa, Prol. 207, n. pl. n. fása, Prol. 68. Hence rofásiged *evacuatus est*, Z². 477, and fásach *wilderness*.
fásaim, *I wax*, rofas crevit, Pref. B. Mid. Ir. for ásaim, ro-ás : roásaiset drissi *creverunt spinae*, Z². 464, Skr. vaksh *to grow*.
fáth, s. m. *cause*, Pref. 2, 3, acc. sg. roinniscmar tra in fath arnách and roadnacht cormac *we have declared the cause for which C. was not buried there*, LU. 51ª.
Faustinus, Oc. 8, martyred at Antioch, Boll.
Faustus, Dec. 15, a metrical license for Faustinus, an African martyr.
febda, (felba A) .i. aesmar *longlived, aged*, Feb. 24, a deriv. from feib *life, age*, q. v.
febrae, s. m. *February*, gen. sg. febrai Feb. 1, 28.
1. fecht, s. m. *fight*, Pref. 22. (.i. cath, P. O'C.) originally *work* (W. gwaith).
2. fecht, s. f. *a time* (=W. gwaith *course, turn*) Pref. 92, fecht and (=W. gweithan *now*), fecht n-oen, ib. B. fectso *nunc*, Z². 212.
fechtnach, adj. Jan. 14, acc. sg. m. June 18, gen. sg. m. fechtnaig Dec. 15, is explained by firenta *righteous*, in O'Cl. Gl. but it generally means *lucky, happy, prosperous*, and its derivative fechtnige *happiness*.
fedb, s. f. (=vidua 2 Beitr. 166), gen. sg. fedbae Aug. 31.
fége, s. f. *sharpness*, gen. sg. feige Prol. 331 B. (fégi A), dat. sg. fégi, féigi, June 18, a deriv. from feig q. v.
1. feib (.i. amhail *as*, O'Cl. Gl.), Pref. 31, feib *sicut* Sg. 14 b. 210ᵇ. Goth. sva.
2. feib, s. *life, age* (feibh .i. snoghal fada *long life* O'Cl. Gl.), dat. sg. Jan. 3. Lat. vegeo, vigeo.
Feidlimid, gen. sg. feidlimthe pref. B. This name seems a corruption of the O. Ir. Fedelmid

2 l 2

Lib. Arm. 16. b 1, gen. sg. feidilmedo, fedelmedo, fedelmtheo, ib. 16. a. 2. 16. b. 2. latinized Fedilmithus, Reeves' Col. 8.

feidm, s. n. *effort, exertion,* O'Don. Supp., Jan. 21.

féig, adj. i-stem, *sharp* i.e. gér, O'Cl. Gl. : corop féig rose forn anme *ut sit acutus oculus animae vestrae,* Z. 994. acc. pl. m. fégi, féige Ep. 326 : fegb .i. amnas no feochuir, O'Dav. 86.

féige, see fége.

féil, fail, *est* (generally fil) Mar. 3, June 29.

féil, s. f. (=W. gwyl) *festival,* Feb. 27, Ap. 20. May 14, 15, 23. June 22, 25, 29, Aug. 3, 8, 23, Oc. 7, 14, Nov. 9, 18, Dec. 1, gen. sg. féle, féile Ep. 225, 231, tene féile coin, L. H. 14 a. dat. sg. féil Jan. 16, Feb. 21. 25, 28, Mar. 6, 29, Ap 5, 28. Aug. 21, acc. sg. féil·n Prol. 300, Jan. 19, June 10, Sep. 12. Oc. 23, Nov. 3 (but féili, Oc. 2, Dec. 30), nom. dual féil, May 31, nom. pl. féli, féili, féle, Ep. 16, 182. gen. pl. féle-n, féile n Prol. 329, Ep. 80. dat. pl. félib, féilib, Prol. 312, 336, Ap. 1, hi felib mártir I.U. 25ᵇ. acc. pl. féli Mar. 2, Nov. 14, Ep. 108, féile Ep. 328. See Prim-féil, Ríg-féil.

feith, (.i. fég B), *behold,* Aug. 9. Erig nan-díaid a mic olse 7 feith coglic iat, LB. 138ᵃ. see fethem infra. The root seems VAT, whence fáith, Lat. vātes, Zend apa-VAT-aiti *he understands,* &c.

féle, s. f. *verecundia,* dat. sg. féli, féili, Feb. 3, Mar. 29, a deriv. from fial q.v.

Felic =felix, Jan. 14, 22, gen. sg. Ap. 16. Two saints named Felix are commemorated on Ap. 16, one martyred at Caesaraugusta (Saragossa).

Felicitas, Mar. 7, the African slave and companion of S. Perpetua (Jameson S. & L. Art, 565 : ' Martyres Carthagine aut Tuburbi in Africa.'

félire, féilire s.m. (n.?) ἑορτολογιον, *fasti* (barbarously latinised festilogium). Ep. 109, 156. gen. sg. felire Pref. (leg. félire), acc. sg. félire ib. and Ep. 148, gen. pl. felire Ep. 144. a deriv. from féil. Ebel Z². 247, citing the gloss félire (gl. codice i.e. fastorum) Cr. 32ᵃ, regards this word as feminine. But the gen. sg. rutha in felire, Pref. shows that it must be either masc. or neut.

Felix, an African martyr Jan. 9, Felix of Nola, Jan. 14, Felix of Saragossa Jan. 22. Felix an African martyr Feb. 3, a martyr July 12.

fellsam, s. m. = philosophus, gen. pl. Pref. 9, O. Ir. fellsub.

femdim, *I deny, I refuse* ; femdit tra ulaid 7 concobar 7 fergus an ctergleod LU. 105ᵃ. 3d sg. b-fut. pass. (conjunct form) ni femdibther, Prol. 260 : for femmedus cach rét nogniind remi do denam, LU. 16ᵇ. 3d sg. pret. pass. is uad rofémded bith do rer dé, Reeves Culdees 96. The verbal noun is feimdheadh .i. diultadh, O'Clery Gl. but we also find femeth : iar femeth naduaisi *after refusing the reward* (to the poet) B. Ballim. 160 b. 1.

fennad, s. *tearing the flesh to pieces,* Prol. 48. fennaim (gl. excarnifico, gl. carnifico) Z². 434. P. O'C. explains feannadh by *flaying.*

fer, s. m. (=vir, W. gwr, 2 Beitr. 166) Feb. 8, May 6, Aug. 18, gen. sg. fir Feb. 25, Mar. 29, June 22, Sep. 25, Oc. 25, Z². 223. dat. fiur Z². 224. acc. fer-n May 22. voc. sg. á-fir Z². 225, n. pl. fir June 5, Z². 226. gen. fer-n Ep. 144, 414. Z². 226. dat. fernib Z. 227. acc. firu ib. fer na hatha *kiln-man,* Pref. B. fer dá chrich *man of two districts,* Aug. 15, Oc. 6. fer dá leithe *man of two halves,* Dec. 4. i.e. Berchan son of Muredach, patron saint of Kilbarchan in Renfrewshire (Reeves' Columba, p. 315), so called because half his life was spent in Scotland and half in Ireland. For compounds, see caithfer, tréafer.

Feradach, gen. feradaig Lib. Arm. 16. b. 2 = feradig Lib. Arm. 16. b. 2.

fermim, *I do, I make* Ep. 49, 1 pl. s-pret. rofersam Ep. 2, 73. Root VAR, Skr. vrata *werk, heiliges werk* ?

ferann, ferand (gl. ager, W. grwn?) s. m. (n. ?) *a territory,* Nov. 25. gen. sg. feraim, fernind, Mar. 12, ociarraid feraind LU. 41ᵇ, acc. ferenn (gl. agrum) Lib. Arm. 5, a. 2.

ferdae, ferrda adj. *manly* Feb. 8, gen. sg. m. ferdai Feb. 28 ; compar. ferdu, ferrdu Aug. 20. As to the double r see rr.

Fergna, gen. Fergnai Mar. 2, fourth abbot of Hí, Reeves' Columba, 224, 372 = Adamnán's Virgnous, where gno (gnó ?) is perhaps=Lat. gnāvus. Fergna, Sinech's father, Oc. 5.
fermacc. s. m. *manchild*, n. pl. fermaicc, Nov. 5.
Ferna, *Ferns* Prol. 198. gen. sg. Jan. 31, June 22, about five miles north of Enniscorthy, co. Wexford. St. Maedóc (A.D. 624) erected a monastery there. In LB. 80 lower margin are the lines :—

    Mag ferna   The Plain of Ferns.
    May imbia moedoc fédba   The plain wherein will be Maedóc the aged.
    May itat coin is cuana   The plain wherein are wolves and dogs.
    May imbiat nualla némdai   The plain wherein will be heavenly shouts.

ferr, *better* (= Skr. varyas 2 Beitr. 78, Glück KN. 165) Oc. 24, Ep. 367. 423. Z². 277.
ferrda, see ferdae.
fess, see fetar.
féssin, *self* Pref. 19. Z². 367.
fetar, *scio* Pref. B. ni fetor-sa Tir. 11=vid-ta-r, a praeterito-present like oĩda. 2d sg. s-conj. rofeiser Feb. 4, fésser Oc. 24, 3d sg. pret. pass. rofess (=ro-vid-ta) Ep. 17, fess Prol. 113. 135, p. part. pass. n. pl. n. fessa Prol. 76, but inn-a-fess (gl. scita) Z². 228. part. of necessity fissi (leg. fisst) *sciendum* May 20, Ep. 335.
fethem, s. f. *observation, contemplation*, (root VAT *to know, to mark*) acc. sg. fethim, Ep. 266: see feith supra. In LU. 53ª, fethim seems to mean '*waiting*': ferr lé a fethim cenclaind cirt inda cethir do choumpert *she would rather wait without proper offspring than conceive a quadruped*. P. O'C. writes feitheamh *a viewing, gazing, observing: a waiting, hoping, expecting:* ni dú damsa fethium no findigecht forru LB. 138ᵃ, line 17. So in F. D. G. 72, the queen sees a youth's palm and hand, ocus bui 'g feithem cofada *and was contemplating for a long time*.
fethis, feithiss, a 2d sg. s.-pret. keptest, preservedst (?), June 24, Aug. 7: according to the gloss *preservedst* (.i. do thaisgis no dochoimhedais O'Cl.): fetheadh *a holding in care or trust*, P. O'C.
Fiacc Oc. 12=feec qui postea mirabilis episcopus fuit, cuius reliquiae adorantur hi sleibti, Lib. Arm. 4. b. 2. gen. féicc, ib. 10. a. 1.
Fiachna, gen. sg. Fiachnai, Nov. 12, acc. sg. Fiachna, Ap. 29, latinised Fechnaus Reeves, Col. 59.
Fiachra, Feb. 8, a c-stem, gen. fiachrach Oct. 27, fechrach Lib. Arm. 10, b. 1, ficchrach, 17 a 1, fiachrach 18 b. 2 (=fechureg, fechreg, Reeves Col. 45, 225), acc. sg. fiachruig, Oc. 12.
fiad, prep. cum dat. *before* Prol. 33, 36, 81, Jan. 27, May 27, June 19, Ep. 103. The d is dropt before d: fia dálaib Prol. 315, fiadainib 153. W. gwydd *presence*.
fiada, feda s. m. (an ant-stem, vedant : cf. Skr. Vidhan a name for Iudra, Windisch) a name for God, Prol. 86, Jan. 27 (moeda, moida=mo — fiada) May 5, gen. sg. fiadat Mar. 11, May 30, Ep. 209=fedot, Cambray MS. dat. fiadnit, Jan. 14, Ap. 6, acc. fiadnit-n, Aug. 18.
fiaduib, *before them*, Ep. 95.
fial, adj. (= W. gwyl) *modest*, Dec. 4, gen. sg. m. féil Dec. 15.
flam, adj. (.i. granna no adhuathmhar O'Cl.) *foul, horrible*, Prol. 50, a dissyllable (from visama ?) cognate with fí *virus*, Skr. visha.
fich, see arfich.
fiche, *viginti, twenty* (an ent-stem) used alone : fiche miled, Mar. 18, dat. for fichit mor mile, Jan. 16, Sep. 13, n. pl. tri fichit fer Tir. 11, acc. pl. trichtea bliadne Tir. 2.
fichet, *twenty*, viginti (a neuter a-stem) used with other numbers : ceithri sillaeba fichet *twenty-four syllables*, Pref. B., Ebel would regard fichet here as a gen. sg. See cóica, cethorcha, tricha.
Fidrui, gen. sg. pref. n.
figil, s. = vigilia is explained by O'Cl. (who writes fighill) as *a prayer which one makes on one's knees*: acc. sg. Dec. 8, gen. pl. figlo-u Ep. 199, acc. pl. figli, figle, May 26, figell a vigilia .i. frithaire, Gl. 399, figlis *vigilavit*, L U. 9ᵃ.

figlech, adj. *prayerful*, gen. sg. m. figlich, figlig, Feb. 17.
fil, *is*, a defective verb, Prol. 164, 180, 314. Ep. 289, also written feil q. v. 3d sg. rel. file *quod est*, Prol. 336.
Filadus, Dec. 5 = Filadus, a Roman saint, Ob. & Mart. Dec. 1.
fili, s. m. *poet*, gen. filed, dat. pl. filedaib Pref.
filidecht, s. f. (gl. poema, gl. carmen) acc. sg. Pref. 100.
Finan, the leper, Mar. 16. Reeves, Col. 95, 96. Finan cam*m the crooked* ('obliquitas fuit in oculis ejus,' Mart. Don. 97, n.) Ap. 4. His pedigree L.B. 18d.
find, finn, adj. (= W. gwyn) *white, fair*, Jan. 9, 14, Feb. 3, 24, Mar. 2, Nov. 29. Dec. 12, 16, gen. sg. m. find May 22, gen. sg. f. finde, finne, Aug. 8, Oc. 13, dat. sg. m. find Nov. 12, acc. sg. m. find, finn, June 18, 30, Oc. 8.
Finda, a c-stem, gen. Findach May 22. In the Mart. Don. the gen. is fionnaigh, which comes from a nom. Fionnach.
Findbarr, *pulcher vertex* ('propter candorem capillorum,' Colgan cited Reeves, Col. 103) of Inis Toimle July 4. Findbarr (also called Finnian) of Magh Bile, Sep. 10, Reeves, Col. 103 n.
Findchú, of Brí Gobann, Nov. 25.
finde, s.f. *whiteness, fairness*, dat. sg. findi Aug. 27, B.
findgem, s. *a fair offspring*, July 22.
Findia, latinised Finnio, acc. Finnionem, Reeves, Col. 195, F. of Chuain Irairi Dec. 12, ob. A.D. 550. In the Mart. Don. this name is written Finnén, in B. finden, in R. finnian, nom. dual in dá findia, do finnio, Sep. 28.
Findsech, gen. findsiche, findsige, Oc. 13, a fem. diminutive from the adj. find *fair* : so Biesech L.B. 21ᵃ, 22ᵃ, Coirsech, Córsech, 21ᵃ, Cruimsech 22ᵃ. The ending sech is still used in geirsech = girl : cf. ciursech (gl. merula), a hen blackbird.
findslúag, v. m. *a fair host*, May 23.
fine, s. f. *vine*, Ap. 6, gen. sg. fine Oc. 10. Borrowed from vinea.
Findig, Finnich, acc. sg. Feb. 2. This man's name seems a c-stem and to come from a nom. = Lat. vindex. In Mart. Don. the noun is Findeach an a-stem.
Findlug, Finnlug, gen. Finnloga, Jan. 3.
Fintan, Jan. 3, Oc. 10, 21, gen. sg. Finntain Feb. 17, 21, fintain LU. 41ᵇ, acc. sg. fintan Oc. 20. The F. celebrated at Oc. 20 is the abbot called Fintenus filius Tailchani by Adamnan, Reeves Col. 18.
fir, adj. = W. gwir, Lat. verus, occurs in the Félire only in compounds.
firbaile, (-baile) adj. *truly strong*, gen. sg. m. firbailc Ap. 14, May 16.
firbail, s. *true goodness*, dat. sg. June 15, Ep. 3. 303, see bail supra.
firchert, adj. *truly correct*, Ep. 156.
firdron, adj. *truly strong*, dat. sg. f. firdruin Dec. 3.
fire, s.f. *truth*, dat. sg. fire (leg. fíri), Prol. 306.
firennac, adj. *truly innocent*, acc. pl. f. fireudga (leg. firennca) Ep. 322.
firian, adj. *righteous*, voc. sg. m. Prol. 10, voc. pl. m. á fírianu Zᵃ. 228 ; compar. fírianu Zᵃ. 276.
firmaith, adj. *truly good*, gen. sg. m. (n.?) Dec. 23, voc. sg. m. Prol. 10.
firmanach, s.m. *a true monk*, Pref. 32.
firmáthair, s.f. *a true mother*, Aug. 15.
Firmus, Aug. 9, martyred at Verona, in Italy, Boll.
firór, s.n. *true gold*, Oc. 21.
firt, s. (a neuter u-stem) *miracle*, gen. ferto, n. pl. ferta, fertai Ep, 175, 214, 558 ; gen. pl. fertai Sep. 7, Ep. 205 ; dat. pl. fertaib Br. h. 23. acc. fertu Zᵃ. 452. Borrowed from Lat. virtus (Marc. VI. 5), whence also W. gwyrth, Bret. berzut and Corn. marthus.
-firscuich, *vere finem habuit*, Prol. 84, see scuchaim infra.
firthabairt, s.f. *a true giving*, Ep. 185.

firthuillem, s.m. (n.?) *true enhancement, recompense*, acc. sg. Prol. 55. cf. niderna tuillium buidhi, B. of Moira, 56.

fisid, adj. Pref. 2, 50, seems to mean *worth knowing*, but qy. is it not, like fisig, a medieval corruption of fissi, q.v.

fissi, *sciendum*, part. of necessity from root VID. ba fisse .i. as coir a fhios O'Cl. Gl. see fetar.

fiu, adj. *worthy*, Prol. 111=W. gwiw, Z²=56. cia fiu todlaigersu (gl. quam justa postolem) Ml. 38ᶜ. Skr. adv. vishu *aque*, Gr. ἴσος, fiu .i. cosmhail O'Cl.

1. flaith. s.f. *kingdom*, (=W. gwlad, 2 Beit. 172-3). Prol. 215. gen. sg. flatha Prol. 155, 166, May 17, Ep. 74=flatho Z². 226. 250. dat. sg. flaith Prol. 104, Feb. 14, Mar. 6, June 4, Ep. 118, acc. sg. flaith-n Ep. 196. dat. pl. flaithib Prol. 179.

2. flaith, s.f. *prince*, Dec. 18, gen. sg. flatha Z¹. 250. gen. pl. flaithi, flatha (leg. flathe) Nov. 27, dat. pl. flaithib Mar. 11, Ep. 542. acc. pl. flaithe flaithi Prol. 286. May 6, Ep. 46.

flaithem, s. *socrau*, Prol. 337, also in Colm. h. 31. gen. flaitheman.

flaithgel, adj. *princely-bright*. gen. sg. m. flaithgil Ep. 239.

Fland, Pref. 69. gen. flaind, flainn, floind Dec. 15. Fland find (of Cuillinn) Jan. 14. Fland o, Benuchor Dec. 15 : flann .i. gach ruadh O'Cl.

Flandán, of Cell da lua Dec. 18.

fled, s. f. *banquet, feast* (=W. gwledd), dat. sg. flid Z². 243. loc. sg. cech fleid foreraid *excess in every feast*, Sep. 25, dat. pl. fledaib Z¹ 245.

Fled, a virgin, acc. sg. fleid, fleith, Sep. 12.

flesc, s.f. *rod*, Ap. 25, Z¹. 53. acc. pl. annail flesca óir, LU 47ᵇ. W. llysg *virgula, bacillus*.

Florianus, Mar. 3, an African martyr, Boll.

Flouianus. Faluianus, June 28, mistakes for Fabianus q. v.

fo, prep. (W. guo, go) cum dat. *under* Prol. 24 B. Jan. 1, May 20, Ep. 174. In the phrases fo-chet-óir, fo lige 7 fo érge, Pref. 99, it means *at*. In July 15 and Oc. 15, (fo sil n Adaim, fonm) bith mbuidnech- it means *throughout* and governs the acc.: cf. oca hiarraid fo eirinn *seeking her throughout Ireland*, Corm. s.v. prull. Prefixed to numerals it forms adverbs : fo-chét cét *a hundred, hundred times* (deciens milliens) Prol. 151. In composition : fodail, fogníu, etc. It is = Gr. ὑπό, Skr. upa, the p having been ejected and the initial u (v) then becoming f in Irish, gu in Welsh.

foa, *under his*, Prol. 257.

fobith, adv. *because*, Jan. 17. Z². 619. fo-barm-bid-si *restra causa* Z². 54. Corn. govys.

fochétóir, adv. *prima hora, statim*, v. fo.

fochand, Pref. B. is obscure to me : fochan is *corn-blades*.

fochith, s.f. *tribulation*, Z². 249. gen., sg. fochodo, fochedu, fochatho Z². 250 : n. pl. fochaidi, 251. gen. pl. fochide 252. dat. pl. fochit(h)ib, fochaidib, Ep. 520.

fochunn, fochund v. *cause*, Pref. 92. = fochonn Z². 213.

focul, foceul, focal, s. =vocula, acc. sg. Ap. 25.

fodail, s. *a dividing*, (.i. rainn no sgaoiledh, O'Cl. gl.), acc. sg. Ep. 290.

fodálim *distribuo, divido* : fundali (gl. quae impertit) Ml. 20ᶜ. 3d sg. pret. fo-s-dail *eos distribuit*, July 15, an fo-nd-ro-dil Z². 230. fodlid *dividite*, Táin bó fráich : cf. Goth. dailjan 2 Beitr. 170.

fodaimim, *I suffer, I endure*, fodaim *patitur* Z². 430, 3d pl. 2dy. pres. fodamtis Prol. 51. forodamar, *passus sum*, fodéma *patietur*. W. gwoddaf Z². 27.

fodéine, pron. *self*. Ep. 352, cf. fadéin (gl. ipse) Z²., 367, rothuissim dia in duini fo imáigin foden, B. of Ballimote cited O'D. Gr. 357. The forms bodéine and uodein also occur. Hence we see that the first element of the word cannot be, as Ebel asserts, the root of the verb subst. bhu. It is rather the reflexive SVA.

fodera, Pref. 16 (efficit Z²., 434) seems a blunder for fodered *sub fine* : see dered.

fodmin, foidmin, fothmein (.i. fodered, Three Ir. Gl. 132) June 30, O'C. translated this by *final*, as if it were an adj. It seems rather=fodemin, where demin is cognate with deimhe

darkness of night, O'Cl. The meaning would thus be *at the close of day, at the end,* (fo-deriud).
oebar, s.m. *edge of a sword or tool,* dat. pl. foebraib Prol. 48. Siegfried equated this with the W. gwaew *lance,* pl. gweywyr.
fóeruim, *I prepare, cause, make,* 3d pl. ni fóiret (non efficient) Z². 432. r-oeresiu, roberaso, Ep. 427, 431. dófor *efficit* Z². 430. fo-nd-ru-air *that has caused it,* Ep. 97. inmé fodrúar *is it I that have caused it* I.U. 69ᵃ. fo-d-ru-air, *has caused it,* Chron. Scot. 34. foruar *effecit, præparavit* Z². 22. foruar *effecit* Z². 22. roerad Prol. 206.
fofuair, *invēnit,* Nov. 7, fofuair iasc ann, Egerton 93, 2 b. 1. fo-s-fuair Nov. 7, and 3d sg. pret. pass. fofrith, fofrid, Feb. 25. The simplex occurs in Jan. 22, and Egerton 93, 2 b, 1 : ní fuair iasc ann. ní frith ní dó ann.
fogbaim (fo-gabim) *suscipio, obtineo, assequor,* 2d sg. a-conj. fuigbe, foigbe Ep. 147. 3d pl. pres. indic. act. ni faigbet dig na biad, LU. 33ᵃ.
fogluaisim, *I disturb, disquiet,* 3d sg. pres. indic. act. fo-dom-gluaisi, fo-m-gluaisi Ep. 376, 377 : cf. fogluasacht, 1 S. M. 76, *removal of hairs,* toghluasacht (do-fogluas.) *motio* O'D. Gram. togluasset *morent,* Berne.
fognam, s.m. *service,* (W. gweinif?) : cóir in fognam *iustum est seruire* Z². 233 gen. fognuma Pref. B. (=fognamo, fognama Z². 238), dat. fognam ib. and Fince 5.
fogniu, *I serve,* (W. gweini l) 3d sg. imperative active fognad Pref. 42, 3d sg. 2dy pres. act.: batar ile cothraige cethartrebe diafognad *multi erant, quibus serviebat Cothrigius quatuor vicorum,* scil. Patricius, Fince 6.
foillsigim, *I manifest,* foillsiged, Pref. B. deriv. from follus *manifest,* root SVAR.
foillsigud, foillsiugud, faillsiugud, s.m. *manifestation,* May 9, Ep. 205, gen. foilsichtho, foilsigthe Z². 239.
foirgim, fuirigim *I delay,* ar-id-fuirig *detinet,* Z². 430, 3d sg. s-fut. -foer, faeir, foir Prol. 322, 326, nim-foirse a sallanu .i. ní fhuirgheann me a radh O'Cl. s.v. Sallanu.
foirithim, *I succour,* 2d sg. imper. farith (fo-a-rith) Ep. 407 : 3d sg. redupl. pret. foraith, foraid (.i. rofortachtaig B), better forraith, *succoured,* Jan. 15, O. W. gnoraut : so in Br. h. 32 : fororaid in ri blegon, *the king aided (increased) the milk,* and in Tir. 11, is disin diu furraith fiace find dubthach, *so thereby it is that F.F. aided D.* 3d sg. s-fut. fu-m-ré-se *mihi succurret,* Tir. See rithim.
folad, s.n. *substantia,* (W. golud *wealth, riches),* vis, Z². 213, folad naill Z². 446, nom. pl. folaith, folaid Ap. 10, isinnunn fúad folid leu *est eadem figura substantiae apud eos,* Z². 223–4, indfolid (gl. significationis) Z². 214. O'Dav. 87, cites the line in Ap. 10, as ar crist caomtar fola and glosses fola by meunma *mind.*
folt (gl. coma=W. gwallt) *hair of the head,* Pref. B. dat. folt Z². 224, fult, LU. 48ᵃ.
folngaim, *I conceal,* fullugainm (gl. abdo) Z². 874, 2d sg. conj. fo-d-luga *id celes,* June 6. part. pass. follaigthe M. W. golo.
fonn, *throughout the,* fonn-bith mbuidnech *throughout the troopful world,* Oc. 15.
for, prep. ὑπέρ: upari, s-uper : cum dat. *upon, over,* Prol. 46, 103, 136, Jan. 20, 31, Feb. 26, Mar. 16, 31, June 10, 30, Nov. 2, 13, for biastaib *before beasts* Prol. 41, for forbairt *a growing,* Prol. 172 : cum accus. for cech ndúil Prol. 91, for róenu Ep. 322. With numerals : trimile for fichit mór mile *3,000 on a score of great thousands,* i.e. 23,000 Jan. 16. cet ocht for dib milib déac (12,800) Sep. 22, tri chét for secht ndechib *three hundreds on seven tens,* i.e. 370, Oc. 10. cum acc. after a verb of motion : for nem rodrebraing, Aug. 26, for nem luid, Nov. 8, for nem an conrualai, Ep. 25. ecchaing for riched, May 22. dochuatar for nem, Prol. 280, senaich for cleir ngelmair, May 15, dobeir barr for slúagu, Nov. 30, rolaithe for biasta Prol. 41 (where A has biastaib). With possessive pronouns : forth, forh, *on thy,* Prol. 276, forar-n *on our,* Prol. 314, foran *on their,* Prol. 290 : with the article : for-sin-talmain, Ep. 444, for-sin-ngcrait, June 15, for-sna-felib, Prol. 336.
for, *your,* see forn.

foraithminiur, *I commemorate*, 3d sg. pres. indic. pass. foraithmentar, Sep. 8. .i. docuimnighedar Three Ir. Gl. 136, 3d pl. s-pret. : foruraithminset (gl. meminisse) Ml. 47.
foraithmet, s. n., *commemoration*, June 23, Dec. 5=fornidmet Z. 614, gen. foraithmit Ml. 44 r.
forbenim, *I complete, I perfect*, 3d sg. pres. indic. pass. forfenar, Tur. 45, pret. pass. roforbad Pref. 104, Skr. root van.
forbe, forba, s. *completion*, Pref. B. dat. sg. forbu, Ap. 19, Ml. 55ᶜ. Z². 230.
forbart, s.f. *growth*, dat. sg. for forbairt, Prol. 172. But perhaps this is the pret. of forbiur.
forbiur, *cresco, augeo* (gl. redoleo) Z². 428, 3d sg. pres. indic. act. ant. formbeir et foirthigedar indilsi, *as it grows and fructifies in you*, Z². 439, 3d sg. t-pret. fororbairt (by metathesis from for-ro-bairt) Prol. 173.
forcenn, s.m. *finis*, Z. 875=W. gorphen. Hence
forceunaim, *I end*, 3d sg. pres. indic. forcenda, forcennai, Ep. 282, 3d pl. forcennat, Feb. 28, B., Ap. 30, B. where A has the Mid. Ir. furcendait, 3d pl. pret. pass. forcennta Prol. 87 A, where the MS. has forforcennta and Laud 610 has fororcnait.
forcraid, s. (forcraidh .i. iomarcaidh, O'Cl.) *excess*, abl. (?) sg. Sep. 25. So forcruidh duaisi *excess of reward*, duas. 1 S. M. 58, or it may be forcraidh .i. cirghe *arising*, O'Cl. forcraidh maidne .i. eirghe maidne, O'Cl.
fordarc, adj. *manifest*, May 11, fordharc .i. solas no réil, O'Cl. Gl.
forgal, s.m. *a lie* (.i. bróg, O'Cl. gl.), dat. sg. forgul, forgol, forgiul, Ep. 488.
forgillim, *I assert, I testify*, =forgellim (gl. perhibeo) Sg. 21ᵇ. forgilim LU. 123ᵇ. 1st pl. pres. indic. foirglem Ep. 98. 3d sg. (conj. form) fuirgli 1 S. M. 84, 3d pl. 2dy. pres. foirglidis (leg. fuirglitis) .i. do uhionnaighdis *they used to swear*, O'Cl. Gl. foirgheallaidh, *an attesting, proving*, P. O'C.
foriadaim, *I close up*, 3d sg. pres. indic. for-tn-iada *closes it*, July 31, but for-tn-iadae, May 31, to rhyme with Petronillae (so in Ep. 470, tinstae for tiasta, to rhyme with biastae). For the simplex iadaim, see infra.
forlán, adj. (W. gorlawn) *very full, abundant*, Jan. 24, Nov. 5.
forleth, adv. *apart*, Pref. 30.
form, *on me*, Ep. 380.
forn, far-n, *your*, forn-ingnas, forn-gaire, Ep. 380, 382, for, far, Ep. 64. 379.
forosnaim, *I illumine, I manifest*, 2d sg. pres. indic. for-n-osna (for-n-osnai B.) *who illuminest*, Prol. 5, 3d pl. forosnat O'Dav. 91, where forosna is glossed by forsunna na faillsiugaidh. 3 pl. pres. ind. pass. forosnaiter and o soillse oeus o etrochta lnac logmar, Fis. Ad. By metathesis for forsonna ? cf. Goth. sunna, Eng. sun.
forsan, *on whom, on which*, Ep. 302. 361. forsambf. forsm-bi *on which is*, Feb. 24.
fort, a prefix (= W. gwrth) found apparently in fort-gillim, fort-sclba and foirt-be .i. gearrfaidh, O'Cl. Gl.
fort, *on thy*, Prol. 273, 307. for(t)h-, Prol. 276.
fortacht, s. f. *aid*, Prol. 213 B, Ep. 91, gen. fortachtan Z². 265, acc. sg. fortacht-n Z². 244, fortachtain-n 267 : cf. fortiag (gl. conniveo) Z². 428. furtacht (gl. suffragium) Ir. Gl. W. gwrtaeth.
Fortchern, Fortchernn, Oc. 11. 'Foirtgirni nomine' Reeves Col. 126, ex ver-tigernu ?
fortgillim, Ep. 145, 167. *I testify*: so in the quatrain Maccan umal atbeir cet. deus ei indulget. fortgella nu ocus fet. imbethaid suthain surget *a humble youth who says 'fiat', d. e. i., who declares the new and the old testament, in eternal life will arise*, LU. 12ª. fortgillim com buidnib bind nidat cuibule a comanmand, Leb. Br. p. 219, Pattmig foirtgbealla gach rí .i. do ni fiadhnaisi ar gach rí, O'Cl. fortgellaim dia 7 barre, LB. 214ᵇ.
fortrén, adj. *mighty*, Prol. 198, 330, June 22, Aug. 9, Nov. 7, acc. sg. m. Jan. 31.
fortsclba, Ep. 4, seems to mean *thou possessest*.
Fortunatus, Furtunatus, Purtinatus, June 11, brother of Felix, mart. at Aquileia, Boll. Aug. 14, a Syrian martyr, Boll. Aug. 23, mart. at Aquileia, Boll.

formasnaim *I disturb*, 3d. sg. pres. indic. forúasna Ep. 102, (boduasna, B) is glossed by cumscaiges, and see O'Dav. 87.
1. fót, s. *a sod*, Pref. B.
2. fót, s. *caution*, v. anfot.
fota, adj. *long, tall*, Nov. 12.
Fothud na canoine, Pref. 26. dat. sg. ib. 21. See Reeves' Col. p. 255.
Fotla, a name for Ireland, gen. sg. Pref. 70.
fothrucim, *I bathe*, 3d pl. s-pret. fot(h)ruicset May 8, 3d sg. pres. indic. pass. fothruicther, Goidil. 44. The verbal noun is fothrucud, Corm. 20 (gen. pl. fothairethe Z². 240)=M. Br. gouzronequet.
frassach, see frossach.
frecre, frecra (frith+gaire) s. *answer*, (Corm. 20) Feb. 22 (lán frecra).
frém, s. m. *root*, Oc. 10. Dec. 12. From vred-ma, W. gwraidd.
fresciu, *I look for, I hope*, Chron. Scot. 66, 2d sg. conj. frescai July 19, 3 pl. s-pret. ro(f)rescesset, Ml. 34ᵇ. See ciu: cognate is frescsiu *spes*, Z². 264.
fresgabail, s. f. *ascension*, acc. sg. Aug. 29. See frisgabaim.
frestal, s. m. (n.l)*attendance*, Dec. 24 (.i. friothaileamh, O'Cl. Gl.), frestal na hátha Pref. B. dat. sg. frestul Ep. 24, frestal Ep. 115, gen. sg. setig a chom(f)restail. LU. 121ᵇ.
fri, prep. cum acc. has almost all the meanings of πρός (with gen. dat. and acc.), but is cognate with Lat. versus, W. gwrth.
  (1.) *from*, scarad frisin ndoman Ep. 368, sc. frisinclóene, Ep. 424. firthuillem buide fri ísu, Prol. 55. fria nochainm séntai cech slóg, Prol. 99, gébaid coir frim anmain, Dec. 12.
  (2.) *near, at*: coin beti fri saethar, Ep. 298, taric ciu fri toscai, July 19, fri gein crist tindscan lexu leire, Nov. 14. nit morda fri-an guide, Mar. 1. friu is mor a doche, Aug. 4. is frit mo chairle, Ep. 534.
  (3.) *towards, to, against*, fri croich Nov. 30, dalais fri cruiche cretair Ap. 12, frit a cr. atsluindiu Ep. 319, 327, atsluindiu frit Ep. 372. fri tudrach in domain Ep. 329, múr fri dócine, fri demnai Ep. 152. fri dia is dubart, fri deman is dínert, Ep. 153, 154, cath fri demon Prol. 242, do chungnam frim anmain Ep. 296, d. c. frit anmain Aug. 21, frit anoug noraidiu Ep. 358, lucht fris failte feraim Ep. 49, ropat failte frimsa Dec. 18, frim anmain rop sáilid Dec. 19, frism-bruchta muir June 21. bochtán frismba dénta Ep. 392. In the phrases fri crist carsait sanais, Mar. 15 (which O'Curry rendered *of Christ they loved full knowledge*), and fri crist carnis léri, July 9, it seems to mean *unto*.
1. fria, *from &c. his*, Prol. 99. In Prol. 242, A, fria seems a mistake for fri.
2. fria, Mid. Ir. for frie, *with her*, Pref. B.
fria-n, *at &c. their*, Mar. 1.
1. frim, *to &c. me*, Aug. 4, frimsa, Dec. 18.
2. frim, *to &c. my*, Dec. 12, 19. Ep. 296.
fris, fres, forms which the preposition fri preserves in composition, Z². 875.
friscuirtur *revolvo*, 2d sg. pres. indic. friscuirther, Jan. 25 (better perhaps 3d pl. friscuirter '*revoluntur*,' as in Rawl. 505), friscoirter ceill (gl. incoli, loca ab his), Ml. 21ᵈ.
frisgabaim, *ascendo*, hence perhaps 3d pl. s-pret. frisrogabsat (.i rorescaibset Rawl. 505) *ascenderunt*, Jan. 16. But these forms seem corruptions of fris-r-ócabsat.
frisin, *from the*, Ep. 368, 424.
frisindlim *I attend on*, 3d sg. pret. pass. frisindled.
frismelaim, *I grind against, I sharpen*, 3d pl. pres. indic. act. frismelat, Ep. 84. cf. airnem frisa melaiter crna *a whetstone against which irons are ground*, Corm. B. s. v. cotud.
fris-n, *to which, at which*, June 21, Prol. 302, Ep. 49, 392, 406.
frisnigim *I wash*, 3d sg. pret. frisnaig Mar. 24, perhaps for fris-snaig *washed it or them*, root NIG. O'Curry translates '*who shed*,' root SNIG.

frisócbaim, (fris-ud-gabaim) *ascendo*, 3d pl. pres. indic. frisóchat, LU. 29ª. 3d sg. pret. frisrócaib, May 5, Oc. 24. 3d pl. frisrocobsat, frisrogabsat, Jan. 16.
frisorcaim, *laedo, offendo*, 3d sg. pres. indic. act. frisoirg Ep. 444, pass. frissorcar (gl. offenditur) Z. 845 : frisuorgar (gl. afficitur) Ml. 77ᵈ. donaib hi frissidnoircetis (gl. laedentibus) Ml. 39ª, frisoirctis (gl. qui adversabantur) Ml. 67.ᵇ
frisriuth, *incurro*, 3d sg. pres. indic. frisreith, Prol. 302.
frissailiur, frissailiu Ep. 560 = *I await*: frissailemmarni (gl. praestulamur) Ml. 63ᵈ. frisailifarsa (gl. praestulabar, leg. -bor ?) Ml. 38 : cf. the mod. saoilim *I think*.
1. frit, *to thee*, Ep. 319, 327, 358, 372, 534.
2. frit, *to thy*, Aug. 21.
frith, see fuair.
frithgnam, s.m. *diligence*, acc. sg. Prol. 331, gen. sg. frithgnama, Corm. s. v. Lethech.
friu, *to them*, friu-side Pref. 15.
Froechán, Nov. 20.
Fronius, Feb. 4, perh. a corruption of Philoromus ' tribunus militum,' mart. Alexandriæ.
fross, s.f. *shower*, Feb. 1, dat. sg. is banna ria frais, LU. 106ᵇ. acc. sg. sreidis forro frais do clochaib, H. 2. 16, col. 374, u. pl. frassa derga tentide, Fis Ad. fross argait, fross tuirinne 7 fross do mil, Four MM. A.D. 759, etym. doubtful. Windisch regards it as = vrastā and compares Skr. varsha *rain*, Gr. ἔρση *dew*. Rhys compares W. gwreichion *sparks*, from the root VRASK Fick², 182. This may be the modern. Scotch Gaelic fras m. gen. frois *seed*.
frossach, *showery*, gen. sg. m. frassaig, Pref. Niall was so called from three showers which fell at his birth.
fuair, *invēnit*, Jan. 22, 1st pl. fuarammar, 3d pl. fuaratar, 3d sg. pret. pass. frith, Mar. 10, June 16, July 30, pl. foritha. See fofuair supra.
fubothaim = fobothaim (gl. consternor,-aris) Z. 1037. 3d sg. pres. conj. fu-t-botha Nov. 15, where the pron. of the 2d sg. is infixed.
fudomain, adj. i-stem, *deep* (gl. altum, mare) Z². 234, isin goithbluch fudumain (gl. in profunda palude) Z². 235. dat. sg., used as a noun, May 30, acc. pl. n. fudumne (gl. profunda) Z². 237. The domain is = W. dwfn, Glück K.N. 72, and cf. perhaps Lith. dubù-s *hollow, deep*.
fuil, s. f. an i-stem, *blood*, Ap. 9, May 20, 27, June 19, gen. fola May 19, Ep. 351=folo, Z². 250, dat. sg. fuil, Jan. 4, May 8, dat. pl. fuilib, Prol. 82. acc. pl. fuili, fuile, Ep. 321. gen. pl. fuile, Z². 252.
fuil, *est*, June 23, see fil.
fuilge, Nov. 9, dat. sg. glossed by suailchib.
Fuinche, Jan. 21.
fuirmim (fo-remim) *pono, repono*, 1st sg. s-pret. fo-m-ruirmius *I have laid me down, rested myself*, Ep. 38. foruirmius *positi*, foruirmiset *posuerunt*, LU. 114ᵇ, 182ᵈ. Lith. rémiu *stutze*.
fuirre, (for-si) *on her*, Ep. 488, fuirri side, Pref. B.
Furodran, June 18.
Fursa, gen. sg. Jan. 16.
Furtunatus, see Fortunatus.

g for original G: gáir, genim, gudin, for GN: gin, gó, gonaim: g for c: tangatar Ep. 88, og-ri Prol. 92, eudag Ap. 9, endga Ep. 322, nodlaig Nov. 13, Dec. 24, saegail (=saeculi) Ep. 204, frisoirg Ep. 444.
g for ch after i : craibdig, uelaig, búadaig, cathraig: for d: ardricheg Ep. 18, óedig Prol. 49.
1. gabaim *I take*, gaib *cupit* Z² 430, 3d sg. 2dy. pret. corraghad *ut caperet* Pref. 3d sg. redupl. fut. gébaid Dec. 12, 2dy fut. gébad Pref. B 3d sg. gabais July 6. 8, rogab *cepit* Pref. 19, 3d pl. gabsat Jan. 28, Oc. 29, 3 pl. pret. pass. rogabtha Prol. 209.
2. gabaim *I sing*, 3d sg. pr. indic. act. geibid Pref. 2d. sg. imperat. geib Pref. B. 3d. sg. redupl.

fut. géba Ep. 114, 166, 173, 180, 2dy. fut.-gébad Pref. 48, pret. 1st sg. rogbus Prol. 18, 3d sg. rogab Nov. 27.

gabáil s. f., *a taking* Pref. B.=W. gafael *praehensio, arreptio* (Davies) from gabagla ; see Fick³ II. 731, s. v. zabenkla.

gábud, s. m. (n. ?) *danger*, acc. sg. Oc. 29, dat. iar mórgábud, LU. 26ª, dat. pl. gaibthib [cf. loiscthib from loscud] Dec. 2, where it is translated '*sufferings*' by O'Curry, a ngabhadh aibneadh '*in danger of rivers*,' P. O'C.

gainde, gainne, s. f. slung congaindi, Oc. 7,=gainne *scarcity, scantiness, hunger*, P. O'C. O'Curry translates *cruelty*, but is it not rather *with hardship* (gainne .i. docamla, O'Cl.) or *with fewness*: cf. the phrase gainne sluaig *paucitas hominum*, Highland Soc. Dic. From gand .i. cumang, 3 Ir. Gl. 136.

gair, adj. *short*, Prol. B. 59.

gáir, s. m. (or f. ?) *shout*, Oc. 20, Dec. 6, was neut. in O. Ir. angair roboi *vox quae fuit* Z. 234. W. gawr, γῆρυς, Skr. gír, root GAR, whence dognur supra.

gaire, s. f. *pious service, maintenance*, Ep. 382, 402, where it rhymes with Maire. dat. sg. gaire (leg. gairi) Prol. 225, and see infra s. v. gur. This is always goire in Zeuss: fedb as nisse do goiri, 619, denad si goiri doibsem 1049, arnap éicen angóire, 1050; so in Tirech. is már a goire. A comparative goirin (gl. magis pius) occurs in Z.

gairm, s. n. *a call*, dat. sg. garmaim, Feb. 11, acc. sg. gairm, Aug. 14, gen. sg. garma Fiacc h. 16. root GAR, see gair supra.

Gaius, a bishop, Feb. 20.

gal, s. f. *valour*, gen. sg. gaile. Prol. 54, Jan. 11, Dec. 17. dat. gail Ep. 484. comor-gail June 15, B. n. pl. gala mathgamna LU. 89ᵇ.

galar, s. n. *disease* (W. galar *grief*) Nov. 16, ang-galar *the disease* Camb. gen. sg. galair Sep. 11, =galir Z². 223, acc. sg. galar-n Jan. 15, acc. pl. galra Maelísu 8.

Gallicanus, June 26, a martyr, vii. Kal. June, Obits and Mart.

garb, adj. *rough* =W. garw, Zend zaurva 'greisenalter,' Lat. (h)ravus, 'gray.' Hence Garbán of Ceunsaile, July 9.

gat, s. m. *a withe*, Pref. B. now gad.

gébend, (gébenn, géibenn) s. acc. sg. Ep. 282, may be =geibend '*gyre*' S.M.i. 110=W. gefyn.

géim, s. *a shout*, Prol. 139. B. gen. sg. géime, Three Fragments 42; with géim catha cf. deilm catha June 29.

gein, s. f. *a birth, offspring*, Jan. 27, Feb. 10, 22, Mar. 2, May. 1, 6, 30, Aug. 16, Oc. 3, gen. sg. tarcend na geni *over the head of the foetus*, Reeves Culdees 92, but do iugabail in mór-geine, LU. 27ᵇ. acc. sg. gein-n Prol. 178. Sep. 18, Nov. 14, 21. farsin ngein Reeves Culdees 93. comp. see rig-gein, soer-gein, and cf. Glück KN. 169.

geinech v. ginach.

gel, adj. (gl. albus) *white, bright*, Feb. 10, July 8, Sep. 21, gen. sg. m. gil Sep. 6, gen. sg. f. gile Prol. 4, Ep. 118, dat. sg. f. gil Nov. 1. acc. sg. f. gil, geil July 6, n. pl. n. gela May 19. Compounds: see baillgel, slisgel, gel-bán, gel-grian: root GHAR (glänzen), GHAL, whence χάλις (Fick), χαλκός, Curtius No. 182.

Gelaisse=Gelasius, Feb. 4, pope, celebrated in the Ob. and Mart. at Nov. 18. Three saints named Gelasius are mentioned by the Bollandists at 4th Feb.

gelbán, adj. *bright-white*, Ep. 287. acc. sg. f. gelbáin, May 15.

geldae, adj. *fair*, June 22. Aug. 31. dat. sg. m. geldu Aug. 20. acc. sg. m. geldae June 25, Dec. 22. n. dual m. geldai Sep. 28.

gelgrian, s. f. *white sun*, voc. sg. Prol. 5.

gelmár, adj. *bright-great*, acc. sg. f. gelmair, May 15.

genim *gigno*, 3d sg. redupl. perf. deponent génair *natus est*, Dec. 25, rogénair Sep. 24: see mad gonair, and for cognate words 2 Kuhn's Beitr. 161.

gene, s. *birth*, Feb. 26 = γενεά.

GLOSSARIAL INDEX.   cclxix

genti, gennti=gentes, Prol. 175, Z². 236. gen. pl. gente-n, gointe-n Prol. 61, B. 205, B, Z². 237, dat. geintib, ib. voc. pl. geinti Z². 228.

geintlecht, s. f. *heathenism*, Prol. 213 B. (A, mendosè, genntliucht), gen. sg. geintlecte Z² 1040.

ger, adj. *sharp*, acc. sg. ger-n, Ep. 538.

gérait, s. m. (f. ?) *champion* Feb. 5. Ap. 7, 13. June 16, acc. sg. gérait June 15. acc. pl. gérta Prol. 232. nom. dual gérait May 7, Sep. 27, where the fem. numeral dí is used. See grádgreit infra, gerait .i. glic no anroth no beoda, Lebar Lecain. Voc. 116.

gérat, s. m. *champion*, Prol. 20, acc. sg. Nov. 19, gen. pl. Ep. 72.

Gerbassi, see Gervassi.

German, May 28. gen. sg. germain, Ap. 29. Oct. 1.

   German cruimther, Ap. 29.='S. Germanus Presb. mart. Alexandriæ,' Boll.

   German martir. Feb. 4.

   German aite Pátricc, bishop of Auxerre, May 28, Oc. 1. Fíace h. Reeves Col. 149.

Gervassi. June 19, Gerbassi, May 20=Gervasius, who, with Protasius his twin brother, was martyrised temp. Nero.

gesim *rogo*, Z². 429. 2d sg. pres. indic.-geiss ib. 3d pl. rel. pres. gestai (leg. gestae) Ep. 432. 433. 2d sg. imperative with suffixed pron. gessi Dec. 2. 3d sg. 2dy. pres. gesed, gessed, Ep. 217. fut. part. pass. gessi, gesi, geissi, Sep. 28: gigsesa (gl. supplicabo) Ml. 47ᵈ. gessid (gl. precator) Ml. 74ᵈ.

Geurgus, Giurgus (of Cappadocia) martyred at Pinarolium, Ap. 24, Ep. 265.

giall, s. m. *a hostage*, (W. gwystl, Corn. guistel, Ohg. gisal) : n. pl. géill Jan. 9, gell *pignus* is neuter Z¹. 223. dat. sg. do giull domanmain, Tain bó Fráich.

gíle, s.f. *whiteness*, dat. sg. gíli, Feb. 5. Ep. 222.

Gillas, Jan. 29=Gildas, abbot in Brittany.

gin, s. *mouth* (=*ginu : W. genau=*genava) Ap. 22, an u-stem, gen. sg. geno, gena, Ap. 13, Sep. 16, Oc. 3, dat. sg. gin Ep. 126=giun Z. 986, cogn. with Lat. hi-o, χα-ίνω, O.N. gin *I yawn*.

ginach, acc. sg. m. Ep. 538 *greedy, craving*,=gionach P. O'C. but qy. if the text is right here, for Rawl. B. 512 has goinech and ginach rhymes ill with teinel.

ginol, s. dat. sg. Ep. 472, must mean *mouth* or *jaw* or *gullet* : to me it is ἀπ. λεγ.

Giric, mart. June 16 ; a corruption of Ciric (q.v.), Ciricus in Ob. and Mart.=Quiricus.

glaine, s.f. *purity*, Z². 212. gen. sg. glaine Jan. 6, Ap. 1, July 6, dat. sg. glaini (ms. glaine) Prol. 227, 249, B. Jan. 9, Feb. 5, Ap. 21, Sep. 10, Ep. 67, 174, 250.

glan, adj. (gl. purus, W. glân, A.S. clæne, OHG. chleini, γλῆνος, γλήνη), dat. sg. n. glon Pref. B. *pure*, acc. sg. m. June 25. n. pl. f. glana May 19, compar. glainiu Prol. 246, May 7. Hence glanaim *purifico*, whence, perhaps, glanna, q.v.

glanbail, glanboil, s. *pure goodness*, dat. sg. Feb. 11, 17, May 29, June 6, see bail supra. But in Rawl. 505, at Feb. 11, glanbail is glossed by lí .i. dath *colour*.

glanbúaid, s.f. *a pure victory*, acc. sg. Jan. 27.

glanchésad, s.m. *a pure passion*, Sep. 7.

glanlae, adj. *pure*, gen. sg. m. glandai, glannai, Aug. 27, gen. sg. f. glandae, Ep. 434.

glanmann, glanmainn, s.m. *pure manna*, Dec. 19.

glanna, Oc. 13, can hardly be a corruption of Chalidonia, ' virgo apud Sublacum in Latio,' mentioned by Boll. at this day. Is it an epithet for ócrgan ? If so, it is a participle passive, a *weiterbildung* of -na, as the participles in -tae are of -ta.

glanór, s.n. *pure gold*, gen. sg. glanóir July 26.

glas, s.m. (n. ?) *lock, bolt, fetter*, acc. sg., June 30, v. Corm. Langfiter : dat. sg. huan glas fritobarthu l. diamir (gl. a sera obdita) Sg. 183ᵇ.

Glas Már, gen. Glaise Máire Feb. 10.

glé, adj. *clear, good*, Ep. 494, Z². 57, O'Cl. gives three meanings : follus *manifest*, glan *clean*, maith *good* ; cf. MHG. glizan : glé lim, like maith lim, is=*I desire*.

ro-glea, (ro-gléal) *mundavit, purificavit* Jan. 5.
gléclenn, glédend adj. Feb. 1, 13, .i. dathglan *pure-coloured*, Rawl. 505, from glé and denn (cf. O'Clery's deann .i. li no dath).
glenn, glend s. (an s-stem ?) *a glen*, Prol. 196. gen. sg. glinne. glinde July 8, Nov. 5. dat. sg. glind June 3, acc. glend (darsinn glend, tarsinn-glend), isin nglend ugaibthech, Fis Adamn. dat. pl. glinnib, glindib, Prol. 240.
Glenn dá locha, Glenn dá linn, Prol. 196, June 3, now Glendalough, county Wicklow, where S. Coemgin (ob. A.D. 618) founded a monastery.
Glenn Delmaic, Nov. 5.
Glenn Ussen, July 8, Killeshin, Queen's County, 43, barony of Slieve Margy.
gleo, *a fight*, acc. sg., Sep. 29.
glesi, gleissi (glese ?) gen. sg. Ep. 454, cf. rombi csuin dar héissi nemthech ngleisi nglanóll, .i. Trip. Eg. 2, b, 2, or a derivative from gleith .i. glé no glan P. O'C.
gliad, s. *a fight*, gen. pl. Ap. 19, where it is a dissyllable.
glún, s. (a neuter s-stem, Z^2. 270), *knee*, acc. sg. for moglún Pref. B. n. pl. glúne Goid. 180, gen. pl. glunæ M1. 36. W. glin, Ohg. chniwu *ball*, cláwu, Eng. claw.
Glycerius, Jan. 14, where the gen. sg. is written glucori, luceri.
gnáis, s.f. *presence*, maith les águaisi (leg. a guás-si) gl. consentit habitari cum illa Z. 31 ; dat. sg. in barn gnáis-(si) Ep. 375, im bith-gnais Ep. 316 cf. inagnais *in his company*, 1 S.M. 20, na scarad frisin fer dús inrictar tria-gnáis-si (*ne secedat a viro ut forsan salvetur* ro-ictar—*per praesentiam ejus*) Z. 708 ; bith iugnais *perpetuam absentiam*, Goidil. 18.
gnáith, adj. *usitatus*, Ep. 171, compar. gnathiu Z^2. 17, gnaithiu 275. W. gnawd.
gné, s. (a neuter s-stem Z^2. 270,=genus, γένος Goth. kuni) *kind, species, form*, n. pl. gnee Pref. B. dat. pl. gneib Pref. 55.
gním, s.m. *a deed*, Oc. 23, gen. sg. guímo, gnima Z^2. 238, Dec. 17, acc. sg. gn'm-u Prol. 54, dat. pl. gnímaib Ep. 203, acc. pl. gnimu Z^2. 237. W. gnif *toil*.
gníu, *I make, I do*, 3d. sg. imperat, act. guid Pref. 35. a denominative from gné, as genero is a denominative from genus, see doguiu, fognin.
gno, v. Fergna.
gnúis, s.f. *face*, Z^2. 250, gen. sg. gnúso, gnúsa ib. dat. sg. in the nominal preposition argnúis *before* Jan. 9. Ep. 398. ógnúis (gl. a facie) Z^2. 25, n. pl. gnuissi (gl. ora) 251, acc. pl. gnúisi, gnúissi, Ep. 339.
gó, adj. *false*, s. *falsehood* (W. gau, cf. χάος, χαῦνος), Ep. 27, acc. pl. gua Ep. 167 B and D. O'Clery gives gó the further meanings of muir, *sea*, and ga, *spear*.
goba, s.m. *smith*, gen. sg. gobann, goband, Nov. 23, O.W. gob now gof : cf. O. Celtic Gobannium, Gobannitio, Glück KN. 108.
Goblán, better Gobán, gen. Gobbain Dec. 6, a dimin. of gop q. v.
gobeil, (gabaeil B, gabeoil D) Ap. 13, acc. sg. of some word meaning *morsus* and cognate with gob *bill*. In ar gobeil coch gena *ob morsum cujusvis oris*, the poet seems to refer to the mordacia dicta, *the biting words*, of the enemies of Paul's faith : goballach *a morsel, a mouthful*, P. O'C.
Golmait, Gobnat, better Gopnat (as in Rawl. 505) *little mouth*, Feb. 11, a virgin.
góidel, góedel, goeidel, gaedel, gacidel s.m. *an Irishman*, (W. gwyddel), gen. pl. July 7, Aug. 13. Sep. 23. Ep. 144. Cognate, according to Siegfried, with haedus, goat etc. root GHID, whence χαδ, χαιζάτω, pre-hendo, Goth. gitan, Eng. get.
Goile, Gólae, Goliah gen. sg. góile, (leg. Goili), gólai, Ep. 484.
gorim, *I warm*, (root ghar, whence Skr. gharma, W. gwres) 3d sg. rel. pres. goires, guires, Dec. 26.
golaim, *I wail, weep*, 3d pl. pres. indic. act. golait, Prol. 62. In Corm. 23 and O'Dav. 94 the subst. gol is explained by dér *tear*.
gonaim, *I wound*, 3d sg. pres. indic. act. -goin 1 S.M. 242. 3d sg. redupl. pret. geguin Oc. 23.

(gegna! D), 3d pl. -gignetar, gegnatar May 19. O. Bactr. jan *to slay*, Skr. han-ti, O.H.G. gund, A.S. gúdh *fight*.
gop, whence Gopnat Feb. 11. (D.) *mouth*=Skr. jambha, Gr. γαμφή.
gor, adj. (.i. gairit O'Dav. 95 .i. gairid O'Cl.) *short*, acc. sg. n. Prol. 59.
gorm, adj. (in ruad-gorm Ep. 260 and gorm-ríg Prol. 233) .i. dearg *red*, O'Clery, who cites ga gormruadh .i. ga deargruadh. If gorm be, as I suppose, from the root ghar, it probably meant *fiery red*.
gorte, gorta, s.f. *famine*, Z². 247. gen. sg. Dec. 2. dat. sg. gorti Jan. 26. Z². 248.
grád, *a grade*, Z². 223. gen. sg. gráid Z². 364. acc. sg. grád Ep. 207. Z². 225. acc. pl. grád Ep. 235, W. gradd, cognate with gradus. Corm. 23.
grádgreit, s.m. *a champion of rank* (grád-gérait) Mar. 19 : see greit.
grafand, graffann, s.f. *a race*, Ep. 73, is explained by tromaige, II. 2. 16, col. 113. Hence graifne Corm. B. s.v. Magh. iar cor graphand doib in oenach na cruachua, LU. 108ᵇ. ferniset grafaind, II. 2. 16, col. 373. agait grafaind, ib.
greim, s. *a bit, morsel*, acc. sg. Nov. 15.
greit, s.m. *a champion* (.i. gaisgeadhach, O'Cl. Gl.) Jan. 5, June 17. See congreit, gradgreit. grod .i. gaisceadach, Leb. Lecain Voc. 559.
gres, gress s. Feb. 11. Ep. 226. *fervor?* or if we read grés, *continuance*, dat. sg. dó grés, do gress *semper* Z. 565. Hence gresach (gl. continuus) .i. gnathach O'Cl. gresgugud *continuatio*.
gresche, (grescha B) s.f. in gresche (gl. instantia) Z². 809. acc. sg. greschi Prol. 16. If the penult is short this word would mean *urgency*; if long, *constancy*.
greth, s. *a shout*, greath .i. gair O'Cl. Gl. root GAR. Hence perhaps n. pl. gretha Jan. 25. But this may come from grith q.v.
grían, s.f. *sun*, Prol. 302. Jan. 15, Feb. 10, Mar. 9, Ap. 24, May 28, June 17. 25. 26, July 7. 8. Aug. 30. 31. Sep. 3. 61. Oc. 1. 3. Nov. 4. gen. sg. gréne, gréine Prol. 4. 321. Mar. 17. Ep. 118. dat. sg. gréin Z². 243, nom. dual. di gréin Dec. 9.
grianach, adj. *sunny*, dat. sg. f. grianaich, grianaig Nov. 1.
Grigoir, Grigair Mar. 12. 29. acc. sg. Mar. 19. Grigoir Ruama (the fourth doctor of the Latin Church. doctor et apostolus Anglorum, ob. A.D. 604) Mar. 12. The scholiast in Laud 610 says that this Gregory bequeathed his body to be put into a coffer on the Tiber, with an ounce of gold on his breast. God sent the body to Arran, and the strand (*tracht*) on which it floated is called after Gregory, and his relics are there.
Grigoir Nazareni (o thir armenie, Rawl. 505.) Mar. 29. 'S. Gregorij' Magni memoria inscripta est additionibus Greueni ad Vsuardum' Boll. xxix Mart.
grith s. (W. gryd, Z. 791) *shout, cry*, gen. sg. gretha June 29. gen. pl. gretha (leg. grethe) Prol. 154.
Gualae, gen. sg. Oc. 30.
guba, s. acc. Ep. 167, prob. a mistake for gna *lies*. O'Clery explains guba by cath *battle* and caoineadh *wailing, lamentation*. See also Corm. B. s.v. guba, and cf. cladar a fert sátir alia scribthair a ainm nogaim agair a gubae *his grave is dug, his stone is set, his ogmic name is written, his lamentation is performed*, LU. 69ᵃ.
guide, s.f. *a prayer*, Ep. 420. 421. 429. Z². 247. 252. gen. sg. guide Ep. 370. dat. sg. guide (leg. guidi) Prol. 16. acc. sg. guidi-n, guide-n Mar. 1. Ep. 412, gen. pl. guide-n Ep. 226. There was also a neut. (or masc.?) form Z². 252.
guidiu, guidim, *I pray* (for gaidiu) Z². 429. Prol. 17. 265. Ep. 37. 313. 337. 413. 3d sg. ni guid *non petit* Ml. 42ᵃ. 1st pl. pres. indic. guidme Ep. 243. 3d pl. pres. (imperf.?) roguidet Ep. 364. 2d. sg. imperat. guid Aug. 11. 21. 22. Nov. 20. 26. 3d sg. s-conj. rogé Ep. 364 B. 1st sg. redupl. pret. ro-gád-sa (=Skr. jagāda) Ep. 412. ro-n-gád-sa Ep. 421. The root is GAD, whence Skr. gadati, gada-s.
guin, *killing by wounding, slaughter*, Prol. 58. Z². 233. gen. sg. gae gona éisc (gl. fuscina) Sg. 37ᵇ. see gon. O'Dav. explains guin by sarughudh.

gúr, adj. is explained by O'Dav. 95, and in Three Ir. Gl. 138, by léir *pious* and calma *brave*: and by O'Clery as calma *brave* and gér *keen, sharp*, all which but the last seems guesswork. It occurs thrice in the Félire, viz. as an epithet for galar *disease*, Jan. 15. Nov. 16, and as an epithet for slige *road*, Nov. 7. I conjecture that it is = gravis, βαρύς, guru. It occurs as an epithet for gaire *pietas*, in a quatrain attributed to Fothud-na-Canoine, Harl. 1802. fol. 36. Ecena intliuct comarle. Is nert gaire gúr. omun fiadat for lith chó . secht dana dé dún, which (as Dr. Reeves has remarked) is borrowed from Isaias xi., 2, 3, spiritus sapientiæ (*eccna*) et intellectus (*intliuct*) spiritus consilii (*comarle*) et fortitudinis (*nert*) spiritus scientiæ (*fis*) et pietatis (*gaire*). Et replebit cum spiritus timoris domini (*omun fiadat*). So in the complet inti charas crabad gúr is didnad lais nisce púr *he that loves severe asceticism, unto him pure water is a solace*. A derivative gúre occurs in the Táin bó Fráich: la gúri nauidan *with the soreness of the pangs*.

h occurs in the Ogham alphabet, and with great frequency in certain words, such as háue, hoa, *grandson* (= ηαυια παΐς), *hériu Ireland* (= Iverio), Hí (= Iova). gen. híne where a vowel-flanked v appears to have been first changed to h and then transposed to the beginning of the word. So in híaru gen. híairn Z². 949 = W. haiarn, where a vowel-flanked s, changed to h, may have undergone metathesis. In hires, hilar, hetho it may possibly represent a lost p, see Kuhn's Beitr. III., 90°, 281. But there is no doubt that h is, as a rule, not a radical letter. In the Middle-Irish codices of the Félire it occurs regularly *in hiatu*—

1. After the article na. 2. After nouns ending in a vowel. 3. After the possessive pron. a *her*. 4. After the verb subst. ba. 5. After certain prepositions (a, co, fri, la), ending in a vowel. 6. After the negative ni. 7. After the particle ro. Examples follow.

1. gen . na huage Oc. 4. acc. na huaga Sep. 20. na huile Ep. 486. inna hirise Z². 181. So in Patrick's hymn na huile nert-so.

2. grían gel glinde huissen July 8, mila húre Ep. 219 B. aige huage, Dunchad hiæ huare May 25. cf. mac mailae humai O'D. Gr. 43. sluag sussi h-is nelaib Nov. 20.

3. a háine Prol. 127. a haithmet Aug. 15. a haeged Broc. 26. inna himthechtaib ib. 63, a hathig, ib. 87, ahérlam ib. 100. tarahésisi *after her* Z². 340. So in Welsh y h-enw *her name* = a h-ainm.

4. ba hilmain Feb. 11. ba horlau Nov. 5. ba haen Dec. 4 (= ba hoen Br. h. 43), ba henirt Ep. 9. But this has no warrant in O. Ir. cf. ba ingnad Milan poem, ba amru = ba amra Br. 59. Fiacc 9. ba oenmathair, Br. 63. ba óg. ib. 76.

5. la huaigi Sep. 26. la hémin Dec. 22. la hiacop Dec. 27 (but la iacop Ep. 256), la habraham Ep. 244, la harón Ep. 272, la hairerán Dec. 29, la hailbe Dec. 30, la hosualt Aug. 5, la hetsecht May 2, la hisu Feb. 5. B, la herce May 12. la hiugru May 23. la haililI Prol. 178, a hegipt Jan. 11, a héri July 31, Sep. 5, a hafraic Aug. 28, co himbel Feb. 16, Ep. 343, a herind a harniud Nov. 21, co hollmuir Feb. 17, fri hilchu Mar. 9, fri honuan Ep. 202, co haingliu Mar. 10, May 28, co hissu Ap. 19, but co aingliu May 23, July 12 A, có iadomdu, co ammondu M. and Z. 586, o ard Dec. 16, ho epscop, Tur. 49, o adrad, Fiacc gl. 30, do alba June 25, o aimsir Z. 589.
do oscraib Ep. 77.

6. ni hatach July 3, Aug. 8, ni hespai Ep. 430. This has no warrant in O. Irish: cf. ni etercerta Goid. 45. ni insa, Goid. 38, ni esgaibter Goid. 33.

7. ro-hir, Sep. 23, nir-haerad Ap. 8, cor-hicthar Ep. 369. This has no warrant in O. Irish: cf. ro asaiset, Goid. 33, ruoirtned Tirech. 11, ro airptha Z². 4. In other cases h occurs unnecessarily: h-in india Dec. 21, h-il-lecuin June 28, h-illoscud Prol. 62, h-illetha Mar. 26, hi Feb. 13, 14, Mar. 6, 27, Ap. 5, 27 May 10, June 11, Aug. 15, Nov. 25, Dec. 14, Ep. 10, 187, 222, 291, 562, hit *in thy* Ep. 334, hitúsa Ep. 385, hitaimne Prol. 157, 161,

himocuirtis Ap. 27, himou Feb. 12, his nclaib Nov. 20, h-it *sunt* Prol. 81, March 10, Oct. 11, hiar, Ep. 305, humsalathraig Ep. 13, hirguis, Ep. 561, hile Mar. 18. In for h-ordan, Prol. 276, and nahii, Aug. 9, h stands for th.
Helius, July 21, Mart. Caesenae in Italia. Boll.
Herenaeus, (MSS. Herenius, Erenius) Ap. 6, ep. et mart. Nicomediae in Bithynia, Boll.
Hermogenes, Ap. 19, mart. at Melitina in Armenia Boll. Another Hermogenes, an African martyr, is commemorated on the same day.
Herodius, (Heradius, Eradus) Ap. 20. No such saint is in Boll. at this day. Can Oengus have meant Oratus, an African martyr?
Hippolytus, Jan. 29, bishop, drowned in the sea, sub Claudio, Aug. 13, a Roman martyr, B.
Hilarius, (Helair) May 5, bishop of Arles.
    Nov. 1, bishop of Poiton and confessor.
    Nov. 3, deacon and mart. (sub Maximiano), Usuard.
Honoratus, Ep. 261, see Onoratus.
Hyacinthus, see Iacinthus.

i for original i: biad, fid: i changed by breaking to e: fer, fetar, pelait Prol. 85, necodimus Oc. 17.
i for original a: mid *medius* (in mid-chuairt), dligim: from a by umlaut: bethid: from e by assimilation: nifid, dligid.
i for -iu: unaissi, Ep. 218, 334: i for -e: gréni Prol. 4, noemi 6, gennti 61, rédi 120, slébi 237.
  i for o: icom, Ep. 299.
  -i suffixed pron. of 3d sg. gess-i Dec. 2, snaidfid-i Ep. 160, B. air-i Ep. 176, imb-i Ap. 26.
i for original á: rí, fír: for Latin í: lí: for diphthongal ó: di=Skr. dve.
1. i, hí *ea*, Pref. 18, 40.
2. i, locative of the pron. é? Z². 351, intí *celui*, forint-ii Pref. 48=O. Ir. forsinni Goid. 20.
Hí, s.f. *Iova* (commonly called Iona), gen. sg. hia, hiae, ie, iae, ia, Feb. 24, Mar. 2, 22, May 25, Sep. 23, dat. sg. hii, hi, í, Sep. 16.
Iacinthus, Iaquintus, a corruption of Hyacinthus (Boll.) Sep. 11. He and Protus were eunuchs of S. Eugenia, and were beheaded at Rome, temp. Gallieni, Ob. and Mart. p. 156.
Iacóp, Iacob, July 25, Ep. 475, gen. sg. Iacoib (Iacóp A), Mar. 15, acc. sg. Iacop-n, Iacop-u, June 22, Dec. 27, Ep. 253. The Latin gen. sg. Iacobi occurs as a quadrisyllable, Mar. 25.
Iacop Alpeii, June 22.
Iacop, Eps., July 14, a 'Iacobus episcopus Fesulanus' and a 'Iacobus episcopus Tullensis' are mentioned by Boll. in July, Vol. III, pp. 332, 211.
iadaim=πιάζω, see forindaim: eu immo n-iada sás *a bird round which a trap closes*, St. P. ubull oir ocá iadud, I.U. 48ᵃ. Bugge compares Skr. pîdayâmi.
Iair, Inair, gen. sg. Oc. 26, a dissyllabic r-stem: O'Cl. has iar .i. dubh.
iar, *posterior*, *occidens*, Z². 57: see s-iar.
iarair, (iar-ar-i, see iarraim), s. *search*, Ep. 302, dat. iarair, Prol. 290, acc. iarair-n, Ep. 2, Dec. 2.
iarum, see iarum.
iarfaigim, *I ask*, 3d sg. pret. ro-iarfaig-sium Pref. 94, 3d sg. s-pret. iarfoigis Pref. B., now fiafraighim, with prosthetic f and metathesis of r, 3 Beitr. 279, iarfaigid *inquisitio*, *quaestio* Z². 9: root VAK.
iar-n, prep. cum dat. *post, secundum*, Prol. 27, 64, 247, 311, Jan. 26, Mar. 6, 26, Ap. 19, 21, May 23, June 8, Aug. 4, 26, Sep. 30, Oc. 9, 29, Nov. 17, 22, Dec. 2, 17, Ep. 23, 305, see Z². 57. In iar-sinm-baig-se Ep. 315. it governs the acc. which is never found with this preposition in Old Irish.
iaru-a, *after his*, (*her*, *its*) Prel. 225, Ep. 119, 223, iarn a-n *after their*, Prol. 48, 69.
iarnabárach, s. *the day after to-morrow*, Feb. 15 (Rawl. 505).
iarndedól, s.m. (n. ?) *daybreak*, gen. sg. iarndedoil July 26: cf. remdedoklae, remdedólte, *antelucanus* Z. 731, 821, luan cetnu dedol ind laithi (gl. a primo crepusculo) Ml.

iarraim, (iar ARaim) *I seek*. 2d pl. imper. iarraid, Feb. 24.
iarsin, adv. *after that, thereafter*, Pref. 36.
iarsind, iarsiun, iarsiu, *after the*, Prol. 279, B. Ep. 315, 488.
iartain, adv. *afterwards*, Pref. B.
iarthar, s. *occidens*, gen. sg. iarthair, iarthuir, Prol. 195, Nov. 11.
iarum, iarain, adv. *postea*, Pref. B. Ep. 216, 304, Z². 57, Z. 568.
Ibor, a bishop, gen. sg. ibair, hibuir, Ap. 23.
1. ic, *to come* (=ᴀɴᴋ, Skr. añch), 3d sg. pres. indic. tic (=do-ic) July 9, dotic, totic (do-t-ic) May 25, 3d sg. redupl. pret. ro-ánic Ep. 53, ránic May 2, ránic Ep. 17, 3d sg. b-future ro-icfa, ro-d-icfa Ep. 55, do-t-icfa July 16, 3d sg. 2dy s-conj. nach-at-r-issed, -isad Prol. 284. Compounded with (*a*) do : 3d sg. redupl. pret. t-anic, ó do-n-anic, dom-anic Pref. 102, Jan. 11, Ap. 14, Ep. 93, 3d pl. tancatar Ep. 88, (*b*) tar (=do+ar) see taric : (*c*) av : airec : ire Táin bó Fr. 267, creid *ite* LU. 33ᵃ.
2. ic, prep. *apud*, for O. Ir. oc, icom, Ep. 299.
icc, s.f. *salus* gen. icce Z². 49, 225, W. inch, from isaccá or isaneá (cf. ἰάομαι from ἰσαομαι, see Fick, i. 30.) Hence
iccaim *I heal* (W. iachau) 2d sg. b-fut. act. icefe (gl. salvum facies) Z². 459, 3d sg. icfaid Ep. 224, 3d sg. pres. indic. pass. icthar Prol. 228, 3d. sg. imperative passive co-r-hicthar Ep. 369, p. part. p. icethe Z². 49, co-nu-m-ictha *ut salvatus essem* Ml. 74ᵃ.
iccid s.m. *healer*, Ep. 200.
Ichtbrictan, gen. sg. -brictain, Dec. 8. In the Franciscan copy this is ictbritain, and in the Mart. Don. at Dec. 8, there is an entry in a later hand : ' Ecbrit no Ictbrit. Marian. Videtur Anglus.' He was clearly not an Irish saint, for Oengus says ' he came over (the) great sea', and his name is probably (with the Irish -án added) Akipreht, Eggibraht, Ekpreht (Förstemann, *Deutsches Namenbuch*, 13), of which the A.S. form was Egberht or Ecbyrht. Bede writes Ecgberet, Reeves Col. 378. An ' Eichericht Christi miles' is mentioned *ibid.*, p. 383.
icom = O. Ir. ocom, Ep. 299.
id, s.f. *idus*, dat. sg. id, Nov. 13, n. pl. idae, ida, Prol. 305.
1. id, infixed pron. of 3d person sg. : ar-id-legha Ep. 178 B. so in Fiacc's hymn con-id-fargaib, ar-id-ralastar, before vowels. g and d idn : con-idn-aiccert Ep. 105 B. ad-idn-gialna, O'Curry, Manners and Customs, III. 497.
2. id *est vel sit* : con-id, Sep. 26, so in Z². 33 : con-id gau dóilsem *ut id sit falsum eis*, dianid O'Don. Gr. 442, dianid-id cui est Z. 598, in id *ubi est*, ond-id, *ex quo est*, id-ón est -hoc, written .i. Pref. 1, but idón in Tir. 11, edon in Corm. B. Plural it, hit Prol. 47, 68, 207, Mar. 11, July 20, Sep. 28, Dec. 9, it-e, Prol. 69. These plural forms may, however, belong to the root ms.
In combination with ma, si, cia, etsi, quamvis, cia, quis, mani, nu : Sg. mad, *si id est*, pl. mat, cid *quamvis id sit*, ced *quis est*) [ced a athair ba fissi, Fiacc], pl. cit. manid *si ce d'est pas*, na-n-d, *quod non est*, Z². 276. The root seems i *to go*, and id (non aspirating) would then=Lat. it + is, it (aspirating, it chethir chet Z²., 303)=cunt+ii.
idain, Ep. 387 B. seems to mean *pangs*.
idan, adj.=*idoneus* Corm. 25. acc. sg. m. Aug. 11, n. pl. m. idain (gl. bonam fidem ostendentes) Z. 787. O'Cl. explains it by glan *pure*, and the verbal noun idnad means *to purify* (topor. . . . do glanad occus d'idnad annamd inna firén, *a well to cleanse and to purify the souls of the righteous*), LU. 29ᵃ. Hence also
idna, s. *purity*, dat. sg. Ep. 99. con idhna O'Dav. 97 : cf. cisidhna *impurity*, O'Dav. 83, esconna.
idol, s.m. *idolum*, Corm. 25 Z.ª 210 (W. eiddawl), gen. sg. idail Ep. 548=idil Z.ª 210. n. pl. idail Ml. 31 r. gen. pl. idul, Trip. Life Eg. 18a. 2. and cf. idul-taiga (gl. fani), Z². 180.
idón, *hoc (ón) est* (id)=edon, Corm B. is usually written ' i.'
Ierusalem, Iarusalem, gen. sg. Ep. 255.

GLOSSARIAL INDEX.

Ignatius Theophorus, bishop and martyr, Dec. 20.
ifernn, s.m. *hell* (inferna, eufer, Corn. yfFarn, W. ufferu), acc. sg. ifernd-n, ifern, iffirn, iffirnn, Ep. 482, 538.
il, adj., an u-stem (=Goth. filu, πολύς, Skr. puru), *many*, nom. pl. ile, ili, Prol. 133, March 18, Ep. 175, gen. pl. ile Z^2. dat. ilib Z^2. 227. The penult is marked long (híli) in Z. 611, and in Maelisu's hymn *il-ulee*, rhymes with *spirut*. Comparative lia.
ilach, s.m. gl. pæan, Z. 777, n. subhachas no luthgair no luthgair O'Cl. (cf. W. ioli *to praise*), gen. pl. ilach, Prol. 106 (but in Three Ir. Gl. 126, this is explained as an adj. by sulai), acc. pl. ilchu, Mar. 9. Hence ilchugud (gl. inbilatio) Ml. 109.
ilar, s. (iolar .i. iomad, O'Cl. Gl.), *a multitude*, dat. sg. ilur, ilar, May 3, Sep. 7. 19, Z^2. 224.
ille, adv. *huc.*, Pref. B.=in leth *in*, *ad latus*. In illei Z. 568 the ei is for e.
ilmain, adj. i-stem, *opulent?* Feb. 11. gen. sg. m. ilmain, June 30. B. In Rawl. 505, at Feb. 11, ilmain is glossed by colchair, *and*, but this is inmall? P. O'C. writes iolmhaoin, *wealth and riches in abundance*.
ilrathach, adj., *having many graces*, ratha, acc. sg. m. Ep. 466.
im, *in my*, Ep. B. 126.
im-, (for in- before a labial) *in quo*, Prol. 274, locative sg. of au-.
imann, v. imufand.
imb', imm', im, prep. cum acc.=ἀμφι, Lat. amb-, W. am-, Prol. 182, Feb. 8, 11, 12, Sep. 1, 28. Ep. 197, 245. 251. As an intensive prefix it occurs in imfann Dec. 31. As a reflexive perhaps in imorádim.
imba, imma, *around his*, Pref. B.
imba-n, imma-n, *around whom*, imbam-bi, Ap. 7, inna-ránic, May 2, imal-luid, imma-luid, Aug. 23, inma-rocrad, Prol. 206, imma-slecht Feb. 20, June 16, imma-slechta Nov. 5.
imbed, *abundance*, gl. ops, imad (gl. multitudo), dat. sg. imbud, immud, Prol. 66, Sep. 11.
imbel, imel, s., *a border*, Prol. 131, acc. sg. Feb. 16, Ep. 343, dat. pl. ahimilib nahEgipte, L.B., 115^a.
imbi, imbe, *circa eum*, Ap. 26=imme Pref. 5.
imbliuch, s., *land verging on a lake*, (O'D. Corm. 25), gen. imblecha, dat. sg. imbliuch, imliuch (cassáin), Sep. 11, ad imbliuch hornou, Lib. Arm. 11 b. 1. in imbliuch equorum ib. 16 b. 1, a deriv. from imbel *edge*.
Imchath, mac Feidlimthe, gen. sg. imchatho, Pref. B.
immchuirim, *veho*, 3d pl. 2dy. pres. act. imma-curtis, hinocuirtis *eum rehebant*, Ap. 27, 3d pl. s-pret. roim-chuirset anćri ar christ, *they bore their burden for Christ*, note on May 8, 3d sg. pres. pass. tuarn imchuirther do chein in domuach, Reeves' Culdees, 93, cf. commimarchoirther (gl. vehar), Gild. 268, imarchor auptha, *carrying love-charms*, I S.M. 176. See cuir.
imnde, immda, adj. (gl. multus), *abundans*, Mid. Ir. acc. pl. imda, Pref. 48. Compar. imdu, Z^2. 276, indiammdae (gl. examussim), Z. 563, deriv. from imbed, q. v.
immach, adv. *forth*, lit. *in campum* (mag), now amach ósin immach, *thenceforth*, Pref. chuaidh só amach, *he went forth*.
immalle, (=imm-an-leith *circa eorum latus*, Ebel, 4 Beitr. 9), adv. *una*, *simul*, Pref. B., Z. 569.
immfann, imand, imfann, *very weak*, Dec. 31.
immon, himon, imun, uman, *around the*, Prol. 22, Feb. 12, Ep. 566. Here the article is suffixed, not to imm, but to the compound prep. immu (=abhy-ava?), which occurs in immu an eclis, Tir.
immurro, imorro, adv., *vero*, Pref. 7, 22.
immut, *around thee*, with suffix immutsa, imutsa, Ep. 331.
imper, s. m., *imperator*, Ir. Nenn. 66, gen. sg. impir, Dec. 15.
imrádim, immerádim *I think of, meditate, commemorate* (gl. tracto), Z^2. 435, Goth. ga-redan auf etwas bedacht sein, und-redan 'besorgen,' Ohg. rátau, rathen Beitr. VIII. 11, 2d sg. pres.

2 n 2

indic. imm-e-rádi, *whom thou commemoratest*. Dec. 20, 3d sg. imradi, Ml. 35ᵃ, 1st pl. imrádem, Oc. 11.. 1 sg. s-pret. imrorduss, imrordus (=im-ro-radus), Prol. 20, 21, Jan. 7. Ep. 564, 565. (So in L U. 40 a.: diambá fo lind locha láin imrordus ríg richid ráin). 2d sg. imrordaiss imrordais, Nov. 13, 3d sg. 2dy. pres. am. imme-radad (gl. quasi deliberans), Ml. 68ᶜ, 3d sg. perf. pass. imrordad. Verbal noun: oc imradud chloine nobith *in meditatione iniquitatis erat*, Ml. 55ᶜ.

imthig, *go thou*, Pref. R.
in for an before g, d, n, p, b, m, (cingim, ingor, ind, arimp, imbliu).
1. in, *the*, see ind.
2. in, im-, ir-, il-, prep. *in, into*.
   (*a*) cum dat. Prol. 35, 45, 62. Jan. 16. Feb. 22. Mar. 3. 9. Oct. 1. Dec. 21. Ep. 10, 15, 29.
   (*b*) cum acc. May 10. Sep. 10. Ep. 159.
   Compounded with the article: isind, isinn: with the possess. pronouns: im, it, ina. inarn, inbarn, iná-n.
   Before cech the n is kept: in cech nair Dec. 29. in cech bescnu Ep. 318 : so in cach cethrumthain Pref. 51. in cach rand ib. 105. So before sid (in sid saerdai July 18) and the v-sound (in barn, in forn, Ep. 375.) In one instance the unaccented i is dropt: nam buidnib Ep. 295, an aphaeresis never found in Old Irish.
3. in, (im-, i-) loc. sg. of the relative (s)an : in airecht Aug. 3, l im-bi Sep. 10, hi-tú-sa, Ep. 385, hi-táimne Prol. 157, 161.
4. in, a privative particle Z². 860, see inbalbdac, ingir.

ina-n *in their*, Ap. 28.
inás, see inda.
inbalbdae adj. (adv.) *unsilent* Mar. 5, A : the other MSS. have ni-balbdae.
inbarn (i.e. invarn) *in your*, Ep. 375.
ind *the*, for sind = SANDA. The Old Irish paradigm is as follows :—

		Masc.		SINGULAR. Fem.		Neut.	
nom.		int,	iu	ind',	in	an,	a
gen.		ind',	int'. iu'	inna,	na	ind', in', int'	
dat.		{-sind, sint', -sin' -nd -nt', -n}		{-sind, -sint, -sin -nd, -nt -n}		{-sind', sint', -sin' -nd, -nt, -n}	
acc.		-sinn, iun	-sin iu	-sinn, inn	sin in	san, an,	-sa a
				PLURAL.			
nom.		ind', int,'	in'	inna,	na	inna	na
gen.		inna-n	na-n				
dat.		-snab -sna,	-snaib -snai, na	For all genders.			
acc.		-sna, inna,	na				
				DUAL.			
nom.	gen.	dat.	acc.	in		For all genders.	

Sg. masc. nom. int Prol. 333. Jan. 2. Feb. 20. 23. Mar. 12. 14. Ap. 6. May 24. June 2. 20. July 14. Aug. 28. Ep. 101. in Prol. 28. 144. 199. 229. 244. Jan. 1. Feb. 18. May 5. 27. June 17. 23. Aug. 4. 25. Sep. 21. Oct. 6. 17. 20. Dec. 4. Ep. 90. 105. 106. 130. 160. 317. 406. gen. ind Prol. 27. B, Feb. 8. 25. Mar. 4. Ap. 14. May 10. June 11. Aug. 1. 3. 22. Sep. 25. Oc. 14. 22. Nov. 5. Dec. 5. 21. Ep. 548. int Aug. 14. Sep. 9. Ep. 316. iu Prol. 145. 149. 187. 202. Jan. 11. Mar. 10. Ap. 8. 16. June 7. 8. 11. 12. Aug. 27. Ep. 61. 159. 161. 240. 329. 398. 405. 414. dat. iar-sind Prol. 279. ó-n 325. do-nd June 19.

co-sin 20. do-n Ep. 19. 448, do-nt Ep. 104, as-sin Ep. 500. asint Ep. 407. acc. la sin May 22. for-sinn June 15. fo-nm Oc. 15. la-sinn Nov. 25. Ep. 40. 58. 60. 356. fri-sinn 368. 408. 411. Fem. nom. Prol. inn, in 20. 173. 213. Jan. 15. June 11. 17. July 18. 20. Sep. 4. 21. Oc. 4. 12. Ep. 41. 390. 420. 421. geu inna, ina, na July 11. 18. Ep. 415. 472. 492. 512. 516. 536. dat. ind Dec. 3. v-sind, i-sin Prol. 272. 274. 281. dou June 9. July 5. 13. 27. ón Oc. 16. dond Oc. 23. asin Ep. 544, acc. in Prol. 21. la-sin Jan. 19. issinm May 16. co-sin June 20. iar-sinm Ep. 315. fri-sin Ep. 424.

Neut. nom. an, al- Prol. 130. 268. Jan. 25. Sep. 26. Dec. 28. Ep. 163 gen. ind, Feb. 9. Aug. 11. in, int July 6. dat. dou Oc. 16. oc-int, ocont, oennt, Oc. 20.

acc. an, ar Oc. 16 (where ar-réim-sin is from an-réim-sin Ep. 342 (where con, in A and D, seems a mistake for an) Ep. 358.

Pl. nom. masc. Prol. int 47 B. ind 209. 233. in 234. 235. 236. July 20. Sep. 4 (in mmacain), Dec. 28. Fem. Ep. ua 182. 410. Neut. Prol. na 161. 237. Ep. 214. geu. inua-n ina-n Prol. 61. 333. nan Prol. 205. ua 266. 301. 321. 329. 332. 357. Ap. 24. Dec. 18. Ep. 20. 32. 101. 305. 456. 460. 480. dat. dona, for-sna, uasna Prol. 240. 336. Ep. 512. acc. tria-sna, Prol. 44. na Sep. 20. la-sna, Prol. 409. 486.

Dual nom. in, July 15. Sep. 28.

Besides these, there are some examples, of whose gender I am doubtful—issind-alltar Prol. 283, dond-richiud Feb. 23. iarsiud forgiul, Ep. 488. asintsninn-sa, Ep. 407. in mind-sa Dec. 18. [mind is neuter in the Turin ms.] isin-sid, Ap. 2. don rigiu Prol. 31. don bithchoemnu, Mar. 13. ingrafand Ep. 73.

Middle-Irish influence is perceptible in the use in two places of na, in(n)a in the nom. pl. masc. na tri maccain, Aug. 2, inna druing-sea, ina druing-sea, Ep. 285.

ind, inn (=Gaul. ande-), see indber, indsaigim, intslincht.

ind, inn prep. (=Lat. indu-), ind echdroma dairiu May 7. A. inn insib mara, Fiacc 11, forneeaib Lomman ind inber Boinne, Trip. B. 166, col. 1.

inda *than*, Z. 681.=inna Pref. B. anda Ep. 367 B. inda as, indás (inas Ep. 367. 423) *than is*, Z. 681. pl. indat: bahairde he indat tige in baile *it was higher than are the houses of the town*, Lib. Brecc. 108 a. 1 cited Petrie's R.T. 369. mod. Ir. ionáid, O'Don. Gr. 322.

indarbu, indarpu, inudarbba, s.m. *an expeller* Oc. 17. With saph indarpu demnai cf. sab indarba cloeni, Fiacc h. 23. The gen. sg. is prob. indarban: cf. ro-indar-panta na dorchai *expulsae sunt tenebrae* Trip. Life. Eg. 3. b. 2. indairben *expelle eos* Goidil. 45. redupl. pret. sg. 3d r-indarpai, pl. inar-patar indarbanar *subjicitur*. The root is BHA, BHAN, φα. φιr.

indarbud, s. *expulsion*, Ep. 211. cf. indarpi *rejectionis* Z². 230. isanindarbae (gl. in repulsam) and other forms, Ir. Gl. p. 93.

indat, *ia quo sunt*, Sep. 4, seems the pl. of inid *in quo est*.

indber, s. (W. ynfer) *estuary*, gen. sg. indbir, Sep. 13. Indber Doele now *Ennereilly*. near Arklow, County Wicklow. Hence the Gaelic inbhir, wrongly explained in Z². 905.

indeemaice, Ep. 172, seems a mistake for ni decmaic.

indel, s. *a yoke*, .i. congal, Three Ir. Gl.129. i. cumrech, Rawl. 550, acc. sg. Feb. 16.

India, s. f. Dec. 21.

indiaid, adv. *after*, Pref.

indisim, *I relate*, 3d sg. pres. indic. act. indissid (ms.-ig) pass. indister Pref. B. cf. nisndis and indinth .i. indisin ut est nis-féidigh [leg. féitid] mo rose indiudh ni fedam mo rose a indisin cofrinde, H. 3.18. p. 51ᵇ: in Feb. 27 D, innis is perhaps the 2d sg. imperative active.

indiu, adv. *today*, Prol. 220, W. he-ddyw.

indsaigim, *I approach. I visit*, 3d sg. pret. act. roindsnaig Pref. B.

i idsin, adv. *there*, Pref.

ingen, s. f. *daughter, maiden, virgin*, Prol. 129, Jan. 5, 21, Mar. 23, May 29, Oc. 5, gen. sg, ingine Z². 242, dat. ingin 243, nom. dual ingin Dec. 9 B (ingeu A, ingein D), n.pl. ingena (ingeine, B) June 5, geu. pl.ingen-n, Jan. 22, Mar. 29.

ingenrad, s. f. *a number of maidens*, dat. sg. ingenraid-n July 21, gen. sg. milliud an-ingenraidi LU. 121.
ingir, Dec. 21 (ingair B, an-gir) seems an adj. meaning *tristis*, cf. is *ingir* lem cen chretim duib (gl. tristitia est mihi magna) Z. 614. O'Dav. 98, writes ingar and explains it by dainim no goirt no tinchair, and glosses the word in Dec. 21, by teinn.
ingor, s.m. (=an-gor?) *sorrow, misery*, dat. sg. do ingor maic cecht LU. 98ᵇ. acc. pl. ingru May 23, ingra Ep. 119. As to the change to i of a before ng, see Z². 5, ingar (gl. enigma) Ir. gl.
inis, s. f. *island* (W. ynys, *anusti*, Lat. insula ex ansula, anasula?) gen. sg. inseo, Tir. 11. inse July 7, Tir. 11. indso Jan. 10, Feb. 7, Mar. 8, dat. sg. inis Mar. 15, Aug. 8.
  Inis bó finde, *insula vaccae albae*, Aug. 8. Inis boffin or Bophin, island off the coast of co. Mayo, Joyce p. 161, inis bó finne forsind (f)airge, LU. 9ᵇ.
  Inis cathaig, Mar. 8, Scattery Island in the Shannon, co. Clare.
  Inis Clothrann, Jan. 10,Iniscloghran or Quaker's Island in Lough Ree, co. Longford.
  Inis Cúscraid, July 22, 'Inishcourcey,' co. Down, written Inis Cumhscraigh by the Four MM. Canmscridh Mart. Tall. xxx., see Joyce 67.
  Inis mac Nessain, Mar. 15, 'Ireland's Eye.' co. Dublin.
  Inis maic bui Chuinn, Feb. 7, now Inchiquin island in Lough Corrib.
  Inis Medcoit, Aug. 31, prob. the British name of the Island of Lindisfarne, O'Don. Four Masters, A.D. 627, and see Reeves' Columba 374, n. (r).
  Inis Mór (*big island*), Pref. 58.
  Inis Muiredaig, Aug. 12, now Inishmurray, co. Sligo.
  Inis Teimle, (Temle, Doimle) July 4, the Little Island, near Waterford.
init, s. f. *initium*, Nov. 13. W. ynyd *shrovetide*.
inmain, adj. i-stem, *dear, loveable*, Prol. 130, 339, Feb. 11, Mar. 7, 16, May 24, 25, 28, Aug. 3, Sep. 19, Oc. 26, Dec. 12, gen. sg. m. inmain May 29, June 30, July 27, superl. inmainem, LU. 129ᵇ.
inmall, s. *weariness, sadness* (inmall .i. colchaire O'Dav. 98, (ionnmall .i colchaire no toirse O'Cl.) Prol. 323. In Sep. 10 it seems an adj. So in B Dec. 31. In LU. 33ᵃ. acht bidhesin inmall nithrigo cen gnim fuirri.
1. inna, *than*, see inda.
2. inna, art. nom. pl. (fem. and n.), gen. pl., acc. pl. see ind.
inne, s. f. *sense, meaning*: acc. sg. indi, inni occurs, according to the scholiast in the Franciscan copy, in Ep. 84, where he glosses it by tuicsin. But the true reading is a rinni, see rind.
insce, s. f. (=in-scciá) *sermo*, gen. sg. indsce, Ep. 123.
inso, *here*, Pref. 48, 68.
int, see ind.
intan, adv. *when* (lit. 'at the time', tan) Pref. 101.
intsliucht, intliucht, inntliucht s. m. u-stem, *intellect, meaning* Z². 210. dat. sg. Prol. 298, 318, acc. pl. do thintud in suin ebraidi sluindes ilsésu 7 ili intliuchtu la chreu *to interpret the Hebrew word which expresses many senses and many meanings with the Hebrews*, Ml. 37ᵃ.
io, for ia : dioda Feb. 9 A.
Iób, gen. icíb, May 11, June 8, 30.
Iocundus, Iucundus Feb. 21. A martyr who suffered at Adrumetum in Africa.
Iohannis, Ioandis, Iohannis, June 26, gen. sg. iohannis Feb. 27, May 25, July 25, Dec. 27, ioandeis Feb. 24, B iohainnis, July 25, B. The Iohannes et Paulus mentioned at June 26, were brothers ' quorum primus prepositus, secundus primicerius Constantie uirginis filie Constantini.' They were beheaded by order of Julian, Ob. & Mart. p. 129, Jameson S. and L. Art. 629. The Ioannes and Dionysius commemorated at May 25, were two priests martyred at Rome.
Iohen, gen. sg. iohain, Aug. 29, Sep. 24, acc. sg. iohen, Prol. 102.
Ioin, (Eoin, Iohain) Sep. 26, gen. sg. ioin (eoin, iohain) June 24.

Ionas, acc. sg. Ep. 463.
Iosep, Ioseph, Ioseb, Mar. 19, acc. sg. Ep. 527.
Iovianus, July 26, mart. at Laodicea in Phrygia, Boll
Ipolitus, Jan. 29. See Hippolytus.
1. ir, *dedit*, ro-ir, rofír, July 5, robír, rofhír Sep. 23, róir dún (gl. regula quam mensus est nobis deus) Z².462.
2. ír, .i. ferg, *anger*, Corm. B. s. v. mer. la demon confr, LU. 114ᵇ. ren aibnib ir .i. risna haibnibh fergacha, O'Curry, Lect. 617, cesfaid in ifpiana(ib) in ifernn ír, O'Dav. 98. Hence irach, adj. *ireful* acc. sg. m. Sep. 29, diamba cleirech nirbat irach, Mart. Tall. p. xxiv.
irarda, (ilarda B) Feb. 8, abb irarda amra O'C. translated by '*the illustrious abbot of Irard*', but Fiachra was abbot of Congbail Glinne Suilighe (Mart. Don. p. 42), now Conwal in Tirconnell. I suspect irarda or ilarda to be an adjective, meaning perhaps '*eagle-like.*'
hiriu, s. *land* 1 S.M. 258, gen. irenn, dat. hirind oc collud an hirend, LU. 128ᵃ. 1 S.M. 258, íre, Ep. 450, abl. ire Ep. 26, íriu .i. ferann O'Dav. 97, irionn .i. fearann O'Cl. Gl. cf. perhaps Goth. fēra, Ohg. fiara.
irguis, hirgais, s. *a prayer* (iorghuis, .i. firgheis, .i. guidhe, O'Cl. gl.), acc. sg. Ep. 561. See aurguis supra.
1. is, =*est*, Aug. 4, 30, Sep. 24, Oc. 24, 28, Nov. 10, Ep. 28, 554, used impersonally: is-tú *thou art*, Prol. 14.
2. is, conj. *and*, Prol. 210, June 26, Nov. 18, Ep. 294, B. is nad dixnigedar nach técue (gl. sie non est inter vos sapiens quisquam) Z. 781. Another form is es: bennach ultu es con(n)achtu, Z. 944.
ís, his (W. is), prep. cum dat. *below*, is nélaib Nov. 20, Ep. 378.
Isác, Issaac, son of Abraham, Ep. 467.
ísel, (W. isel) adj. *lowly* dat. sg. n. isul Z. 1081, n. pl. m. ísil Prol. 152, dat. donaib íslib (gl. ad inferna) Z². 237. Compar. isliu Prol. 153 (isle, A), Ep. 10, Z². 275.
isin, *in the*, Prol. 272, 274, Nov. 10, isinn- '*into the*,' May 16.
ísle, s. m. (n. ?) *lowliness*, dat. sg. isliu, Ep. 391.
Israel, Ep. 495.
I'su, I'ssu, (W. Iesu), generally written contractedly Ih.u, not declined, nom. Prol. 56, July 15, Sep. 23, 24, Dec. 17, gen. Prol. 63, Jan. 21, March 19, July 26, Oc. 23, Ep. 12, 56, acc. Feb. 5, Ap. 19, voc. Ep. 3, 303, 311.
I'sucán, dimin. of I'su, Ep. 92. So eúcán L.U. 77ᵇ is a dimin. of eú (canis).
1. it, hit, *sunt*, see id.
2. it, *est*, Prol. 146, a Middle-Irish form of id, mat *si est*, Ep. 178 A. (B and D have the Old Irish mad.)
3. it, hit, *in thy*, Prol. 310, Ep. 39, 334.
4. it, *eum*, ar-it-rogbus, Prol. 18, ar-it-léga, Ep. 178, con-it-cocert, Ep. 105. Middle Irish for id. q. v.
I'te, of Cluain Credal, Jan. 15, Joyce 140, 141. The story of Ite and the *dóel* p. xxxiv reminds one of a mode of torture sometimes practised in India. Half a cocoa-nut shell with a large stagbeetle inside is fastened on the victim's body. The beetle struggles to escape, and at last endeavours to burrow through the flesh.
iter, eter, prep.=Lat. inter Pref. 94, itir flaithib March 11, A, itir thondaib Nov. 23. In Old Irish eter always governs the acc.
itge, itche, s. m. *prayer*, July 16, Dec. 21, Ep. 337, acc. sg. itge-n, itche-n Prol. 17, Jan. 10, Ep. 413, at coted-æ inn itge *impetravit ille precem*, Tir. 8.
Itharnaise, Dec. 22.
1. itir' prep. See iter.
2. itir, adv. *omnino*, Pref. 97, Z. 568.
iu for e: aidiu, Mar. 19, A.
for ea, unimtiu, Prol. 231.

for i, isliu. fairsiung Oc. 28. gairiu Prol. 249 A. In iulaut creidium, Prol. 173, A, genn-
thnecht 213, A, rotluirsinu, Eq. 75, so failtiugit (gl. exultent), Lib. H.
for eu: niurt Prol. 219, iuliter Oc. 2. giurgi, Ep. 265.
Iucundus, see Jocundus.
Iuil, Ap. 12=Julius A. Julius Romanus Pontifex is mentioned at this day by Boll.
Iulian, Jan. 6, Julianus, a martyr.
Iuliana, Feb. 16, a virgin martyr, beheaded under Maximinian. Infer niger nomen demonis
qui temptauit euam et adam et cain et christum et item iulianam, ... cuncta eius
scelera ligatu narrauit uirgini, Rawl. 505. See the Acta S. Julianae in the Bollandists
at Feb. 16, cap. 2, 'ego multorum hominum oculos extinxi, aliorum pedes confregi, alios
in iguem misi, alios appendi, alios autem sanguinem uomere feci, alios in pontum sub-
mersi, alios vitam finire feci violenter, alios autem in suo furore manibus suis cruciari
feci: et ut breuiter dicam Omnia mala, quae in isto mundo sunt, meo consilio peraguntur,
et ego ipse perficio, et alios quos inueni non habentes signaculum Christi, interfeci.'
Iuliter, Oc. 2, a corruption of Eleutherius, mart. at Nicomedia in Bithynia, Boll. Rawl. 505
has here Eleuther.
iún, *June*, gen. sg. iúin June 1, 30.
Iunill, Iunnill, Sep. 28.
Iustinus, a deacon, May 5, Dec. 5. At May 5 Justinus may perhaps be a corruption of Justus,
bishop of Jerusalem and martyr, who is mentioned at this day by Boll.

Kallaind written Kl. See callaind.

l corresponds with l in Greek, Latin, and Gothic: lige λέχος, Goth. ligan: elú ελέος : at-luchur
loquor, lán plenus, leth latus.
la, le prep. cum. acc. *apud, penes, cum* (=prati προς) Prol. 30. 111. 132. 166. 178. 216.
Jan. 28. Feb. 19. Mar. 16. 18. July. 4. 5. le bás Donchada Pref. 21. with the article las
inu—q. v. with the relative lasn—q. v.
with the suffixed personal pronouns :—
sg. limm, lium, lemm   1. pl. linn
lat   2.   lib
lais, less, f. lae.   3. lethu, leu, leo.
with suffixed possessive pronouns: lam,' lat, lia (la in Prol. 93).
lá, s. n. *day*, Feb. 24. (where the masc. art. is used) láe, lae, laithe, Z². 229. dat. sg. láo, lau,
lóu, Z². 231.
láaim *I cast, I put*, roláe side menmain forn macsom I.U. 39ª. 3d pl. pret. pass. roláithe
(rolatha B) Prol. 41. barntrum .i. loc illáiter senori, *a place into which old people are
cast*, Lib. Hymn. ed. Todd, p. 230. cf. rolaesat *they cast* O'D. Gr. 259. 326, but laaid
(leg. laait) .i. cuirid *ponunt* : in conflicht rolasat (leg. rolósat?) O'Cl. Gl. lanidh .i. cuiridh.
ib. O'D. Gr. 314. rolsat ár mór for tionn-gallaib, Chron. Scot. 150. rolasat gáir mesca.
Longes mac uisnig *they uttered a shout of drunkenness*. The primary meaning seems to
set in motion : ἰλάω (ΑΛΑΛΑ) is perhaps cognate. See do lá supra.
labra, s. m. *loquela, sermo, oratio* (W. llaferydd) Feb. 8. dat. sg. oc nuall 7 oc labra mór,
LU. 25ª. acc. sg. labra Prol. 1. Glück K. N. 50 compares Gaulish Labarus, Labara, but
these names may be cognate with λάβρος.
labraim *loquor* (W. llafaru, 2 llcitr. 176) 3d. sg. pret. (impf. 1) -labrai, Dec. 22 = W. llafarodd.
In Zeuss' glosses, it is a deponent. Cognate perhaps with Lat. labrum : cf. a summis labris
venire *to be lightly spoken*, see amlabar.
Lachtoc. Mar. 19.
ladnae, s. acc. sg. ladnai May 26 : meaning doubtful. The glossographer gives four different
meanings, and O'Clery a fifth, viz. bailbhe *dumbness*, so in Rawl. 505 ladna is glossed
by lothi *dumbness*. O'Curry rendered it by *debility*.

láech, (in athláech pref.) s.m. acc. pl. laeochu LU. 45ᵇ = borrowed from Lat. laicus, whence also W. lleyg, Corn. leic.
laid, laith see lóid.
Laidcend, Laidgenn Jan. 12.
laige, acc. (O. Ir. laice) *languor, weakness*, acc. sg. Pref. 60.
Laigen, s.m. *Leinsterman*, gen. pl. Pref. 24.
laigen, s.m. *lancea*, λαγκια, acc. pl. laigniu, laigne, Ep. 324.
Laimech, Lamiach, Ep. 452.
láine, see líne.
lainnech, laindech adj. *scaly*, Oc. 11. from lann.
lainne, lainde, *sharpness* (gl. acrimonia, gl. acredo) Z. 726. dat. sg. laindi Feb. 21. Oc. 7. laind, adj. (gl. acer) Corm. s.v. aicher. See rolaind tichair laiun (gl. hic acer) Sg. 41ᵇ.
lainnrech, laindrech, loinnrech, loindrech adj. *lucid* Prol. 197. Mar. 4. 16. June 9. July 28. Nov. 22. Dec. 6. Ep. 90.
lais, leiss, leis *apud eum, secum*, Feb. 11. Pref. 24. 99.
Laissrén, Laisrén, Lasrén Ap. 18. Sep. 12. 16. Oc. 25. gen. sg. Lasrein laisren, Aug. 12. Sep. 12. 'The L. whose obit is celebrated at Sep. 16. was third abbot of IIí. Reeves' Columba, 372. The following verses relating to him on the margin of p. 96 of LB. were accidentally omitted :

La patraic la giric	Patrick's day, Quiriac's day,
la laisren con-áine	Laisren's day with splendour,
la beoe ceu urchra	Boëc's day without waning ;
leo drumchla cech raithe.	They have the ridge of each quarter (of the year).

Nollaic bee is feil patraic	Little Christmas and Patrick's feast.
feil adomnan *feil* martain	Adamnán's feast, Martin's feast,
feil ciaran *feil* molassi	Ciaran's feast, Mo-Lasse's feast,
aderim rib cenbrassi	I say to you without . . . .
melnraigther lib immalle	Let it be remembered by you together,
forcenlathi *sechtm*aine	(Are) on the same day of the week.

Laisranus filius Feradachi, Reeves, Col. 40. 57. There is a hymnus lasriani .i. molasse daiminnse in Lib. Hymn. 31ᵇ, where macculasrius, gen. macculasri, is used as the equivalent of Lasrianus.

laithe, lathe, s. n. *day* Prol. 283. Jan. 25. Z². 229. 2 Beitr. 130. gen. sg. laithi (ms. often laithe), Prol. 288. May 5. Dec. 9. Ep. 5. 26. 33. 48. 271. dat. sg. laithi, laithe (leg. laithiu as in Z². 231) Dec. 13. n. pl. laithi, laithe Prol. 301. 321. gen. pl. laithe-n Prol. 296. dat. pl. laithib lathib, Prol. 23. 309. Mar. 26. Contracted lae, la q. v.

lam' *apud meum*, June 25. July 13. 22 A, Dec. 23. 24.
lám, s.f. *hand* (W. llaw) gen. sg. láime, dat. sg. láim, Prol. 273. dat. pl. lámaib Ep. 456. 468 : for *plâma, cf. παλάμη, palma, Beitr. VIII. 8.
lamiur, *I dare*, rolamuir, rulaimur, rolomur *audeo* Z². 438. laimemmar *audemus*, 3d sg. redupl. pret. rolamair Prol. 58. 1 pl. 2dy. pres. lammais, July 25.
lán, adj. (W. llawn = plenus, 2 Beitr. 162 Pref. 94. Feb. 26. Aug. 10. Ep. 21. dat. sg. m. lán Jan. 11. Compounds : lan-bendacht Ep. 61 B, lan-frecra Feb. 22.
lann, s. f. *area* (W. llan, Goth. land 2 Beitr. 176), dat. sg. laind Mar. 30, June 18, Sep. 26, O'Cl. explains lann by eaglas *church*, O'Dav. 101, by ithlann no ferann. In his edition of the Irish charters in the Book of Kells) Miscellany Ir. Arch. Soc. i. 1846, p. 140,

where it is declined as a t-stem: gen. lainded p. 140, dat. pl. lanntaib p. 132) O'Donovan renders land by *house*, and this is its meaning in the following quatrain (LB. 93, t.m) :—

Mabeth aige lat it laind	If thou hast a guest in thy house,
Mád concela praind aire	And if thou hidest dinner from him,
Nihe int-áige bís cenní	It is not the guest who is without anything,
Acht und isu mac maire.	But Jesus, Mary's Son.

Land Ela, Sep. 26, now Lynally near Tullamore, Joyce 310, ela ainm mna boi isin baile prius. is uaithe ainmnichther land ela, L B. 21ᵃ.
Land Léri, June 18, now Dunleer co. Louth.
Land Modomnóc, Mar. 30.

1. láne, láine, s. f. *fulness*, Z². 247, dat. sg. láni, Feb. 3, Dec. 10, Z². 242, láini, Ep. 15.
2. láne, láine, gen. sg. the tribe to which Gobban belonged, Dec. 6.
1. lann, s. *gridiron*, (.i. greideal no róistin, O'Cl. Gl.), dat. pl. lannaib, landaib, Prol. 40.
2. lann, s. f. *a scale* (squama) acc. pl. *amal* lanna (gl. tamquam seamae) Lib. Armach. 176. b. 2. Hence lainnech q. v.
lanomain, s. *a pair, couple*, generally *a married couple* (fer 7 ben, O'Dav. 102) Mar. 24. acc. sg. couaccai in lanamain ina cotlud *he saw the pair*. Deirdriu and Nóisi, *in their sleep*, Longes mac nUsnig. n. pl. doluid for longais cethcora lanamna lichet, *four and twenty couples went into exile*, Scél Tuain, LU. Hence lánamnas *wedlock*.
lár, s. m. (n. ?) = *floor, ground*, gen. láir, dat. lár (gl. solo) Z². 16. acc. sg Pref. 94, where neam 7 lar = W. nef a llawr, lar srotha *alveus fluminis*, Tur. For plár = flur, A8. flór, 2 Beitr. 176.
lasa-n, lassa-n, lasn-, las. *with whom*. Prol. 65. 106. Mar. 10, Oc. 22. June 15. Ep. 162 (where one would have expected lasnatá'. In Feb. 16, lascrith stands for las scrith *apud quam ronuit*.
lasinn, lasin, lassin, *at the, with the*, Jan. 18, 19, May 22, Aug. 2, Sep. 13, Nov. 25. Ep. 40, 356 (where we should have lassinnathair).
lasna, *at the, with the* (pl.), Ep. 409.
Lasren, gen. sg. Aug. 10, see Laisren.
lassar, lassair, lasair (W. llachar) *flame*, Mar. 17, Ap. 18, July 8, Z². 259, 260. Root RAK, ARK. 21 Kuhn's Zeits. 426.
1. lat, latt, let, lett. *with thee*, Feb. 19, Aug. 9, Ep. 365, 425.
2. lat, *with thy*, Prol. 271, Ep. 354. 357, 470.
lathe, see laithe.
láthruch, s. m. (n ?) *a house-site*, dat. sg. du láthruch da arad, Tir. 8, acc. sg. Prol. 208, Joyce Ir. Names. 41, 298, Lathrach Lugdach Prol. 208. Another form of the nom. was láthrech cf. Lathreg-inden Reeves' Col. 50. Laithreach Briuin, Four MM.
Laurent, gen. laurint, lurint, Feb. 22. Aug. 10, deacon of Sixtus II. and martyred at Rome. When roasted on his gridiron he said, Assatus est, jam versa et manduca.
le, =la, q. v.
lebenn, lebend s. *a platform*: lerlebenn seems a compound meaning *the sea-level* or *the sea-side* Nov. 29, lebend inmurro 7 fond inichtarnch na cathrach., Vis. Ad. dat. pl. lebennib in tige coitchenn *tabulis domus communis*, Pertz 5, 481. P. O'C. writes leibheann *the deck of a ship*, also a *scaffold* or *gallery*. The glossographer on A seems to regard lebend as a gen. sg. (nom. lebiu ?) meaning 'maris.' If so, cf. λείβω, libo.
leblaing, *saliit*, a redupl. pret. for le-l'baing, of lingim q. v. and see the forms do-eir-bling, do-air-blaing, Tur. 59, 60, and fo-roi-blang, Ml. 43ᵃ.
lebor, lebar, s. m. *liber, a book*, gen. sg. libuir Z². 428. dat. libur, gen. pl. lebur-n. lebar-n (leg. lebor-n) Ep. 141, acc. pl. libra (libra A, liubra B, D) Ep. 75.

GLOSSARIAL INDEX. cclxxxiii

lebrán, s. m. *libellus* Ep. 90. 106, 130, 133, n. pl. lebráin Prol. 289, dat. pl. lebránaib Prol. 310.
lécim = linquo, λείπω, 2d sg. impernt. léic *sine* Pref. 29, ralléic (gl. dimisit eum) Ml. 53ᵇ.
  3d pl. s-pret. léesit, léicset Oc. 8. see lécud : leicsi *dimisit eum* Ml. léictidir *concedetur*, Z.
  469, noléicthe *dimittebatur* Tur.
Leccain, (leccuin A, lecoin D) dat. sg. f. June 28, Leckin, barony of Corkaree, co. Westmeath.
lecht, s. m. *a grave* Corm. 27. dat. sg. lecht Prol. 227, acc. pl. lechtu Ep. 146, originally,
  perhaps, the bier : cf. flebis et arsuro positum me, Delia, *lecto*, Tibull.
lechtán, s. m. dimin. of lecht, acc. sg. Prol. 116.
léce, in the adverbial phrase colléce, Prol. 239. See calléice, and cf. perhaps W.llwyg *taru*.
lécud, s. *leaving*, dat. sg. Ap. 21.
1. légaim, *I dissolve, I destroy*, 3d pl. s-pret. do legsat (leg. dalégsat i. e. do-a-légsat ?) Nov. 6,
   cf. il-lobad et legad (gl. in corruptione) Z. 580.
2. légaim, *I read :* no-d-légat not legat (ms. legad) *id legunt* Ep. 81, ar-id-légha, ar-it léga *id
   recitat* Ep. 178, airlech (*recita*).
légend, s. *reading*. dat. sg. leigiund Pref. B. gen. pl. la huaigi ailt-légend *with perfection of high
   readings*, Sep. 26. W. dar-llen.
léim, s. n., *a leap* (from leugmen, W. lam, as céim from ceugmen, W. cam), Dec. 31, acc. pl.
  lémenn (andlémend, deslémend, Sergl. Conc.).
léir, adj. i-stem, *industrious, pious*, Z². 233, 274, Ap. 30, June 24, acc. sg. m. Ep. 90, dat. pl.
  lérib, léirib Prol. 310, 334, acc. pl. m. léri, léiri, Nov. 14. adv. colléir, Prol. 312, Z².
  235. compar. lériu, léirithir. Hence lére q. v.
léu, see corpleu.
léu, s. m. (n l) *woe*, acc. sg. Jan. 24, cormac ceu lén, LU. 51ᵇ.
lenaim, *I follow, I adhere*, (Skr. lináṁi, Lat. lino) 3d sg. pres. indic. lenaid Z. 1022, 3d pl. lenit,
  Z. 1051, where it takes the prep. di, 3d pl. s-pret. lensat O'D. Gr. 176. 2d sg. redupl. s-
  future lilessai, lilessa Prol. 309, 311, gur lil .i. gurlean O'Cl. gl., ní fes in lil citir in
  t-ainm. *it is not known whether the name has stuck at all,* 1 S.M. 192 (where both text and
  translation are wrong) : nilil *non cohaesit*, rolil *adhaesit*, Z². 449.
lénaim, *vulnero*, 3d sg. pret. pass. roléuad Prol. 253.
Lenine, gen. Lenini, Nov. 24.
leoman, s. m., *a lion*, (W. llew), gen. leomain, gen. pl. Ep. 500, brotha léoman LU. 89ᵇ. The
  diphthong eo reminds one of the OHG. lewo (n), O. Slav. livŭ.
ler, s. n. (W. llŷr), *the ocean, a great sea*, O'Dav., 100, for oenlith ler sluagda Mar. 21, for
  oenlith ler suthain May 14, for oenlith ler siuagach June 14, for aenlith ler mbuadae
  Oc. 30, gen. sg. lir March 15, 22, D, Aug. 14, Nov. 23, acc. sg. leru June 12.
  Compounds : ler-lebend Nov. 29, ler-mair, lermaig, Dec. 12.
lére, léiro, s. f., *industria, piety, devotion*, gen. sg. buaid lére Prol. 3, Ap. 5, Sep. 5, luirech lére
  Ep. 78, mac lére Ep. 350, gen. nuec lére Ep. 428, 429, dat. léri, Mar. 6, 25, June 28,
  Aug. 29, Oc. 22, Dec. 20 (but O'Dav. 101, here reads la brigach a lere), Ep. 106, 130,
  138, acc. sg. léri-n, July 9.
lermuir, s. n. *main sea*, dat. sg., Dec. 12.
les, less, s. m. (n. l) *a fort*, gen. sg. lis, liss, June 25, Dec. 3. gen. pl. ad fontem loig-les in scotica
  nobiscum, uitulus ciuitatum, Lib. Armach. 10 b. Less Mór in Ross-shire June 25, in
  Co. Waterford, Dec. 3. Less obaig Pref. W. llŷs.
lés, léss, s., *light*, March 4, 22, June 9=leos Corm. and O'Dav. 101.
lestar, s. n. (W. llestr) *a vessel*, lestar n arggit *vas argenti* StP. dat. sg. lestur Ep. 22, Z². 224,
  252. There was also a fem. form : lester chorthón (gl. effutilis) Z². 252.
1. leth, s. (neut. s-stem Z². 270) =*latus*, dat. sg. leith Ep. 33, fo leith Prol. 230 B. acc.
  sg. ille (th) q. v. gen. dual fer da lethe Dec. 4.
2. leth, s. (n. a-stem) : *half*, Z². 223, dat. leuth, in composition with nouns often *one of two*,
  O'Don. Gr. 338.

2 o 2

leth-assa, *one shoe*, Pref. D. cf. mo leth-rosc-sa, *one of my two eyes*, F. D. G. 34, i lenmain dia leathchois, ib. 80.

Letha, s. m. (n. f), *Italy*, gen. sg. June 27, dat. sg. March 26. The W. cognate Llydaw (Letavia) denotes Armorica, and so Letha, O'C. 503, O.W. litau. Dieser name scheint . . . mit lit. Lëtuva Litauen verwandt zu sein und ein küstenland zu bezeichnen wenn mann nämlich an lat. litus erinnern darf, Windisch, Beitr. viii. 15.

lethan, adj., *broad*, πλατύς, Prol. 214, 2 Beitr. 163. gen. sg. m. (n. ?) lethain, June 27, gen. sg. n. Nov. 23, loc. sg. lethan Dec. 11, n. pl. f. lethna Ep. 82. This is the W. llydan, Gaulish litanos, Glück. K. N. 85.

lethet, s., *breadth*, dat. sg. Oc. 13, but lethit, *latitudinem*, Z. 770.

Lethglenn, now Leighlin, gen. sg. Lethglinde, leithglinne Ap. 18. Joyce, Irish Names, 416.

lethrunn, s. gen. lethrainn, *a half quatrain*, Pref. 52.

lex, *a cry, noise, a chant*: acc. pl. lexu, lexa, lechsa, Nov. 14. This obscure word occurs twice in I.U. 25ᵃ. cocualatar anairtuáid gáir moir 7 lex amal bid occetol salm nobethe and *they heard from the north-east a great cry and chant as if some one was there a-singing psalms*: co festais cia gair no cia lex rochualatar *(that they might know what cry or what chant they heard)*. A later form seems to occur in H. 2, 16, col. 393, osbarr an crainn coinsit lessa.

1. lia, s.m. (stem in nc) *a stone*, Ap. 15 (where it is a monosyllable), gen. sg. liacc, nom. dual inda liic LU. 59ᵇ. In Laud 610 al-lia is neuter. In I.C. 65ᵃ. lia, acc. liic is fem. (gabais liic moir, ib). Seems cognate with λᾶας, λᾶϊγξ.

2. lia, *with his*, Prol. 190, Ap. 8. See la supra.

liacc, s. f. *stone, flag*, gen. sg. licce (in aecclesia magna aird licce, Lib. Arm. 9. b. 2), dat. sg. liic Oc. 5 (where it is a dissyll.), foaid for léicc luim, *he used to sleep on a bare flag*. Fiacc h. 31, gen. pl. doim-liac q. v. gen. dual oc beluch da liac, LU. 39ᵃ. (or is this from lia ?).

liath, adj. (W. llwyd), *grey*, Ap. 30 (from pléta=palita, acc. to Rhys).

Liath Mór, Mar. 13, gen. leith moir Mart. Tam. xviii., now Leemokeevoge, barony of Eliogarty, near Thurles.

Liathán, gen. sg. liathain, June 21.

lib, lib-si, *with you*, Ep. 397.

Liba (Liba ?). See Moliba.

Libren (Librén ?), of Cluain Fada, Mar. 11, latinised Libranus, Reeves' Col. 156. A dimin. from Liber (gen. libir ib. 203).

Liffe, Liphe, the river Liffey, Liphe lígda Goidil. 38, gen. sg. in campo liphi, Lib. Arm. 10 a 1. liphi Dec. 9, B. where A has wrongly liffe.

lig, s., *colour*, O'Dav. 103, acc. pl. liga (h. lig .i. maisi, LL. Voc. 66.

ligach, adj. alaind no ceulais *beautiful or gentle*, Prol. 197, 214 B. Mar. 24 B. Ap. 18 (.i. uain O'Dav. 101) June 21, gen. sg. m. lígaig Sep. 12, dat. sg. fem. lígnich Mar. 30, lígaig June 18.

ligbail, Dec. 3, A, seems a mistake for uagbail.

lígda, adj. *beautiful*, Prol. 214 (where O'Dav. 101 explains by láitir *strong*), dat. pl. n. lig-daib, Prol. 23, diandathoig Liphe lígda, Goedil 38.

ligdach, adj., Mar. 24, perh. a mistake for lígach, which is the reading in B.

lígdath, s. *a beautiful colour ?* dat. sg. Prol. 19, Sep. 21. I know not whether this is a compound (lig-dath, cf. lig-flaith) or a derivative from lígda.

lige, s. n. *bed, grave*, Prol. 113 (gl. torus, gl. lectus) Z². 37, gen. sg. ligi, Ep. 224, acc. sg. lige Pref. 93, n. pl. lige Prol. 76. Cognate with λέχος, lectus, Goth. liga, Eng. lie.

ligflaith, s. f. *a beautiful kingdom*, gen. sg. liglatha, Ep. 22.

lígmar, adj. = lígach, July 7.

linm, lim, *with me*, Ep. 494 = lium. Ep. 367, see la.

lín, s.n. *number* (collective) Z². 238 (where it is confounded with línn q. v.) lín catha Aug. 23, gen. líno, lína, Z². 238, dat. sg. lín Prol. 106, 115, 167, fo lín Prol. 296, fiad in lín-sa,

GLOSSARIAL INDEX.   cclxxxv

Ep. 103. don lín Ep. 31, acc. ar lín Jan. 30. la liu Dec. 2, dat. dual diblínaib, comp. comlin.

línaim, *I fill*, 3d sg. rel. pres. línas, línass *qui implet* Sep. 9, Nov. 8, pret. rolín *implevit* Prol. 140, 215.

líne, s.f. = linea, dat. sg. líni Oct. 2, 14, nom. pl. líni Prol. 308, dat. pl. línib Prol. 311, 335.

lingim, *salio*, 3d sg. pres. indic. lingid Z. 1074, mo-ling June 17, is explained as a third sg. pres. and Fick 391 refers lingim to the root LANGH. But the O.Ir. pret. -leblaing is a reduplication from a nasalised form of VALG, Skr. vavalga.

linu, lind s. (W. llyn) *a pool*, dat. sg. baidfider airiu 7 comaing sin lind lethain, LU. 39ᵇ, but ata labraid for lind glan, LU. 47ᵇ, gen. dual dá lind June 3, dat. pl. linnib, Fiacc hymn 27.

linn, linni, lindi, *with us*, Sep. 6.

línn, s.f. (.i. saoghal O'Cl.) *age, wisdom*, gen. sg. linne, linde (.i. saegail no ecne, Three Ir. Gl. 136) Oc. 13, nom. pl. linde Ep. 82, millun .i. drochsaoghal O'Cl., bá maith iarom bái inderiu rialind, *well, then was Ireland biding at his time*, LU. 50ᵇ, nocho-berad orm ria-linn cluchi crail ar-fidchill, LU. 50ᵃ, ream linu *in my time* P. O'C. relinn an líne se *during this age or generation*: ib. In Zeuss' glosses línn, like áes, is used as a pronominal substantive: in línn rofitir a peccad *aetas quae scit ejus peccatum* (i.e. *ii qui sciunt eorum p.*) Z². 364, in linn rodchluinethar *ii qui id audierunt*, ib. arna dergaba linn cretmech *ne deficiunt credentes*, Z. 705.

líth, s. m. u-stem, *festival* (Bret. lid), Jan. 25, Oc. 1, Dec. 10, gen. sg. lítha, May 5, indlíthæ ueteris, Lib. Arm. 176ᵇ. dat. sg. líth (in the phrase for óen líth), Jan. 20, Feb. 26, Mar. 21, Ap. 29, May 14, June 28, Aug. 23, Oc. 30, acc. sg. líth-n, Jan. 18, Mar. 29, (when one would have expected la líth n-ingen), Sep. 25, 28, Nov. 3, 8, gen. pl. líth Ep. 20 (which either is a Mid. Ir. form, or shews that líth was declinable as an a-stem), acc. pl. líthu Z. 1041. Hence líthtai (gl. festivi) Ml.131ᵃ.

lium, *with me*, Ep. 367. See la.

ll, for l: callda Ep. 456, fellsam Pref. (cf. fellsube Z.), colluo Z². 250.

lobaim, *I rot*, 3d pl. pres. indic. lobat Ep. 220 B. 3d pl. b. future -lobfat Ep. 220, Rawl. 512: cf. illobad et legad (gl. in corruptione) Z. 580, rolegai 7 rolobai *he melted away and rotted*, LU. 116ᵇ.

lobar, lobor adj. *sick, infirm*. dat. sg. m. lobur Z². 225, acc. sg. lobar, lobur, Ep. 366, n. pl. m. lobuir (gl. imbecilles), Z². 226, compar. lobru Z². 276. W. llwfr.

lobre, s.f. *infirmity* Z. 987, gen. sg. lobre (mss. lobra, lobrai), Prol. 223, dat. lobrai (slántu du thindnaccul du neuch bis hi lobrai), Ml. 61ᵇ. acc. sg. lobri Tiroch. 14, acc. pl. lobri Z². 249.

loc, locc, m. a-stem borrowed from locus (W.lle, Br. lech) pref. 1, 2, 4, dat. sg. luc, lucc, Mar. 9. luce Pref. 3, Z². 224, n.pl. luicc Pref. 5, = luic Z². 226.

locán, s. m. dimin. of loc, n. pl. locáin, Prol. 209.

loch, s. n. u-stem, *lacus* (the gender is shewn by Loch n-Erlsen, Loch n-Echach LU. 98ᵃ, now Lough Corrib, Lough Neagh), gen. sg. locha, Feb. 7, gen. dual dá locha Prol. 196. Loch Uair (Uar?) Feb. 7, Lough Owel, Westmeath, Mart. Tall. 19.

Lochan, Dec. 31.

lócharn, luacharn s. f. *lucerna* (Corn. lugarn, W. llygorn), Feb. 7, Ap. 15, Corm. 28, gen. s. lócharnne B (locharna A), Ap. 22, acc. sg. lochairnn-u Z². 244.

lóchet, lóichet, lochat s. *lustre, brightness*, Prol. 197, Jan. 26, Ap. 23, Nov. 22, Dec. 20 D.

locht, s. *fault, defect*: ar is locht dosom mad olec a muntar *for it is a fault of his if his family be evil*. Z. 1059, gen. sg. is amlaid bói mairend cen folt cosid mind rígna nobid ocfoloch a lochta, *it is thus was M., without hair, so that a queen's diadem used to be hiding her defect*, LU. 52ᵃ. n.pl. lochta Mar. 18. Hence the verb lochtaigim *crimino*, lasse nollochtaigtis *quum criminabant*, Ml. 74ᶜ.

Lóeguire, Prol. 170, (son of Niall of the nine hostages) 'non potuit credere dicens nam Nél pater meus non siniuit mihi credere sed ut sepeliar inconcuminibus temro quasi uiris consistentibus inbello quia utuntur gentiles insepulcris armati prumptis armis facie adfaciem usque addiem erdathe apud magos .i. est iudicii diem domini, Lib. Arm. 10ᵃ. 2. Erat caput scotorum loiguire ib. 2. a. 2. gen. filias loiguiri ethno alba fedelm rufa, ib. 11. b. 1.

lóg, luag, s. n. (Z². 270.) *a reward, price*. Pref. 101, gen. ind lóge Z. 577, dat. il lóg farn irnigde *in reward* of *your prayers*, Z. 1043, il-luag mo saethir, Book of Dimma (luaig *l*), acc. lóg, luach, cogn. with lú-crum, lo-ta, loot.

lógad, s. *rewarding*, Ep. 370.

lógmar, lúagmar adj. *precious*, Ap. 15, dat. sg. lógmair Oc. 5.

loid, láid, s. *a lay*, lóid loin luad *a blackbird's swift lay*, Z. 928, acc. sg. laith, laid Prol. 323, dat. pl. láidib, laeidib Prol. 314. 334, Feb. 27. Goth. liutha, NHG. lied.

loimm, s. n. *a sup, a draught* (W. llymaid, Corn. lemyk) Ep. 42. So in Cormac, s. v. coire-Breccain: scéid iterum in loimm sin suas *it vomits up again that draught*, loim for saith *a draught over in addition to a surfeit*, Sergl. Conc. loimm n-aiss *a draught of milk*, Reeves' Culdees 84, dorat din intí lucat mael loimm do uim isinn-ardig robói for laim patrice, *then L. put a sup of poison into the cup that was biding by P.'s hand*, Rawl. 505, p. 163 a. n. pl. lommaud LB. 11ᵃ (loimm gen. lomma '*milk*' seems the same word) conda-sloic-side lasa-loim galais asind lestur, *so that she swallowed her with the draught which she took out of the vessel*, LU. 129ᵃ.

loindrech, see laimrech.

Lommau, Feb. 7, Oc. 11.

Lonán, Nov. 1. (dimin of lon *merulus*?) gen. sg. lonain Dec. 24.

long, s. f. *a vessel* (W. llong) acc. sg. loing (gl. nas) Lib. Arm. 177, b. 1. *a ship*, acc. pl. longa Sep. 9 : cf. Lat. langula.

longach, adj. *shipful*, gen. sg. n. longaig Aug. 14, acc. s. n. longach, June 12.

Longarad, Sep. 3.

Longinus, Oc. 23, the centurion who pierced Christ's side.

loscim, *I burn*, 3d sg. pres. indic. act. loscid Vis. Ad. loise (gl. ure) Ml. 47ᵃ. 3d pl. pret. pass. roloiscthe, roloisethea Prol. 39. W. llosgi. From locscim, root RAK.

loscud, losceud s. *burning* (W. llosg), dat. sg. Prol. 62.

lotar, see luid.

lothe, luithe s. f. *dumbness*, acc. sg. loti (loithi 3 Ir. Gl. 127) .i. bailbe Prol. B. 287, loithi ib. 319, gen. luithi .i. gen bailbe O'Dav. 65.

Líth. Ep. 459.

Lothra, now Lorha, a village six miles N. of Borrisokane, barony of Lower Ormond, co. Tipperary, gen. sg. lothra, lothrai Ap. 15.

lua, (in the name of Mo-lua) .i. preab *kick*, O'Cl. ni bá mó no ó mir no ó dúrnu no o lua mairfes cach fer héo, *it will not be from more than from a finger, a fist or a kick that every man shall die through them*, LU. 90ᵃ.

Luachán mac Cuilinn, Sep. 6.

Luachar, gen. Luachair, June 17, according to Mr. Hennessy, Luachar-bairnig, a district about the river Barren, co. Carlow.

luachté, adj. *white-hot*, dat. pl. luachtétib Prol. 40. Of luach (= λευκός, Gaulish Leuci =λευκοί Glück) the root seems RUK : as to té see infra.

luad, s.n. *rumour, mention* (P. O'C.), luad mbetha *the talk of the world*, Aug. 23, acc. sg., urdarcaigimm luad anma dé, Corm. s.v. celebrad. W. llod *a forcible utterance* may be cognate.

luam, s. m. (= W. llyw) 1. *ruler, rudder, pilot* Corm. s.v. manannan mac lir, 2. *abbot*, Dec. 3 (where it is a dissyllable) O'Dav. 101.

luath, adj. *fleet, swift* (ON. fljot-r), acc. pl. f. luatha Sep. 9, cognate with luam (gl. celox) Z². 22, root PLU ? see luid infra.
Lucas, Mar. 15, gen. sg. lucais, lucae Oc. 1, the evangelist.
lucell, Oc. 6, epithet of abbot Colmán, Mart. Don. It seems an adjective meaning *bright* or *shining*.
Luceri, gen. sg. a mistake for Gluceri, Glyceri, Jan. 14.
1. lucht, s. m. (W. llwyth, ex PLUG-tu?) *folk, people*, (collective) Jan. 17, Ep. 49, gen. lochta, dat. sg. lucht Ep. 48, acc. pl. luchtu Ep. 147.
2. lucht, *a load* (ex TLUC-ta): uair dind lucht *a bit from the caldron's charge*, Broc. h. 47.
luchtlach, luchtloch, *a multitude*, Ep. 21.
Lucia, Feb. 6, a Sicilian virgin and martyr temp. Diocletian: when Paschasius ordered her to be dragged away to martyrdom, "she became suddenly by the power of God immoveable. They brought ropes, fastening them to her waist, her arms and legs, and men and oxen pulled with all their might, but in vain." Jameson S. & L. Art, 614-5: the words *whom thousands moved not* refer to this legend.
Lucianus, priest of the Church of Antioch, mart. at Nicomedia, temp. Maximini, Jan. 7, Feb. 24, Dec. 24.
Lucilia, Mar. 2. A saint Luciosa martyred in Portu Romano, is mentioned by Boll. at this day.
Lucius, Mar. 4. A Lucius, bishop and martyr at Rome, Boll.
lúd, see luth.
Lugaid, gen. lugdach, Prol. 208, probably the king who was killed by lightning for having insulted Patrick, 4 MM., A.D. 503.
Lugdach, bishop, latinised Lugnidus, Reeves' Col. 51, Oc. 6.
luid, *irit* (root PLU? Ebel, cf. aller from adnare), a t-pret-rite Jan. 1, Ap. 19, 28, May 20, June 4, 6, 15, 19, July 13, Aug. 23, 27, Sep. 15, Nov. 8, 19, 22, 25, 3 pl. lotar (= luthatar) May 5, Aug. 2, Dec. 20, compounded with do : dolud-sa *iri* LU. 25ᵃ. dolluid *irit* Pref. 92, óthuid = ó dolluid Prol. 128 A, atuluid, mad tuluid, maiterlaid, = nuath-do luid July 12. Other forms of this verb (which belongs to the in-conjugation) are no-luinn *ibam*, as-lui *excedit*, asluat *deserunt*, as-ru-ludus *effugi*, as-luiset *evaserunt*.
lúirech, lúrech s. = lorica, *hauberk, corselet*, Ep. 78, 197.
luithe, s. *swiftness* (deime, 3 Ir. Gl. 65, 127, i. lúas O'Cl.) dat. sg. Prol. 287, 299.
lúithige, a.f. *gladness*, in the phrase co luithigi altae Ep. 134, seems a deriv. from lúthach = *glad*. P. O'C. It occurs in LU. 112ᵃ.: ar denmi ind aicnid 7 lúthige ind láthair 7 méit na gailo.
Lupus, B. Lumbus A. July 29ᵇ, Ep. confessor Trecis (Troyes) in Gallia,' Boll.
Luscai, Lusk, co. Louth, Sep. 6, lusca .i. teach talman, O'Cl.
luth, (read lúth ?) *pleasure, delight*, acc. sg. Oc. 8, compare is lúud leu teistiu fuile *they have a longing to shed blood*? Z². 25. luth *longing, yearning*, P. O'C. dobhi a croidhe ag lúth *his heart was longing*, Gen. xliii. 30. Luth (with short u) is explained '*agitation, emotion, passion, affection*,' by P. O'C.

m corresponds with the Greek, Latin, and Gothic m: mathir, marb, medón, menme, mí, mil.
m, before b and m instead of n.
m, infected, for b infected: promam *probamus*, Prol. 143.
1. m infixed and suffixed personal pron. of the 1st sg. See mm.
2. m, possessive pronoun of the first person, before vowels see mo.
ma, conj. *if*, Prol. 186, Mar. 2, Nov. 15, Ep. 102, ma-no-d-techtaid *if ye have it* Ep. 389.
na (má ?) (μή, Skr. mā́) seems a negative particle with imperfect and preterito, July 4, Ep. 128.
mac, macc, s.m. (O. W. map) *son, child*, Aug. 4, 18, gen. sg. maicc, meicc, micc, mcc, June 24, Oc. 26, Ep. 428, 429, dat. sg. macc, mac, Prol. 148, acc. sg. mac-n, Prol. 56, May 22. voc. sg. amic Pref. B. n. pl. mcc, meic, meicc (O. Ir. maicc Z². 225) Prol. 134, Mar. 15, June 18, Nov. 28, gen. pl. macc-n Ap. 21, Aug. 1, Sep. 26, dat. pl. maccaib

June 16, maccaib Z^2. 227, acc. pl. maccu Ep. 507, Z^2. 227. Compounds: see banmac, fermac.
Mac caille, a bishop, Ap. 25.
Mac Comain, Nov. 21.
Mac Congraid or Conchraid, Nov. 21.
Mac Cuilind of Luscae, Sep. 6.
Mac Cula [' nomen matris eius' Mart. Tall. xx], Ap. 5.
Mac hui Beona, Jan. 28.
Mac hui Birn, June 14.
Mac hui Chuinn, Feb. 7.
Mac hui Dalann, Oct. 11.
Mac hui Guala (Gualae, Gaili), Oct. 30.
Mac hui Láne, Dec. 6.
Mac Lenini, Leneni, Nov. 24.
Mac Lonain, Dec. 24, i.e. Mochua.
Mac nissi, abbot of Clonmacnois, June 13. Mac nisse of Conderi, Sep. 3.
Mac óige, Dec. 3.
Mac tàil, June 11. ('M. T. cille cullinn qui et Eoghan prius dictus est') Mart. Tall. xxvi.
macán, maccán s.m. dimin. of mac, Prol. 137, June 15, gen. sg. macáin July 16, n. pl. macain. maccáin Aug. 2, Sep. 4, Dec. 28.
maccrad, s.f. *children* (collective) gen. sg. macraide Fiacc h. 16, dat. sg. macraid Feb. 12. acc. sg. maccraid, maccraith Aug. 22.
maccu, is, I believe, the true reading for mac hui in Jan. 22, Feb. 7, June 14, and Oc. 30, Dec. 6; as it certainly is in Oc. 11, where Mac hui dálann is = the Mocu Dalon of Reeves' Adamnan, 220. The change of the Old Irish maccu or mocu (= Gaulish maccaus? Glück, Renes &c. 4) into mac h(ui) is not uncommon in Middle Irish MSS. Thus the Dubthach macculugir or Dubthoch macculugil *Dubthach of the gens of Lugar* of the Book of Armagh, becomes Dubthach m. huilugair *son of Lugar's descendant* in the preface to Fiacc's hymn, Lib. Hymn. 15, ib. In June 14 (nem maccu-birn brigach) and Dec. 6 (maccu laindrech láine) maccu must be the nom. sg. or gen. pl.
Mache, Machae, Macha, gen. sg. Prol. 168, May 28, Nov. 27.
macru (in Momaeru Mar. 3.) is for m'sacru, mo-sacru, Mart. Don. xxliii.
mad, *si id est* Feb. 27, B. June 6, July 24, Ep. 173, see id supra.
mad, for math q.v. in mad-génair *bene natus est*, Prol. 251. mad tulaid, ma tuluid, July 12.
madae, mada, adj. (= μάταιος) *idle, useless*, Ep. 227. the adv. inmadae (gl. sine causa) Z. 563. mada (gl. sine causa) 564, so in Ml. 98: nfba madae dam m(f)óisitiu (gl. frustrata non erit meorum confessio uotorum).
Madian, Feb. 23, the apostle Mathias, chosen to fill the place of Judas. Martyrised in Judea. As to the form Madian see Todd Lib. Hymn. 78, note.
mael (W. moel) *bald, tonsured*, and hence *seruant*.
Maelaithgin, June 6, B (Maelaithgen, A, Maelaithchen D).
Maelduh, Moelduh, Oc. 20.
Maclodran, Dec. 2, latinised Mailodranus, Reeves' Columba, p. 50.
Maelruain, Pref. 105. B. Prol. 225, July 7. Dec. 18 A, Ep. 64. gen. sg. Mailruain Pref. B. The Maelruain in Prol. 225, Ep. 64, was the founder of Tallaght, Co. Dublin. He died A.D. 792.
Maelrubai, Ap. 21.
mag, s. neut. s- stem, Z^2. 271 (Gaulish magos, W. ma) *field, plain* gen. sg. maige, muige Sep. 10. Oc. 5. dat. sg. maig Nov. 7. (muig Pref.), acc. sg. mag Tirech. 6. loc. sg. maig, muig in desmaig, desmuig Prol. 226. n. pl. maige (ni nchtat oen maige mór mairg, Amra Chol.), gen. pl. maige-n (ad regiones callrigi tre maige, Lib. Armach. 15. a. 1, Bran tri

maige Corm. s.v. edel), dat. pl. maigib (ms. mnigib) ib. s.v. Tamlachta. acc. pl. maige (ranic maige mós nad genetar ciuil. Amra Chol. totegtis na tuatha im- muige móra, Corm. s.v. Tamlachta), dat. dual maigib, Tirech. 8.
Mag Abnae, Oc. 5, now Mowney, a parish in the barony of Slieveardagh, Co. Tipperary.
Mag Bile, Sep. 10, now Movilla, near Newtonard, Co. Down, Mart. Tall. 44.
Mag Rechet, Pref. 88. 93, now Morett.
Magdalena, Mar. 28, July 22.
Magnus, Feb. 4, martyred at Forum Sempronii (Fossombrone) Aug. 19 : at the latter day Boll. gives two saints of this name, one a bishop and martyr in Italy, the other a martyr in Cappadocia.
Mái. *May*, gen. sg. Máy 1, 31.
Maiguend Dec. 18 = Magniu. Magnenn in Rawl. 505.
máin, s. (= moenus, munus), Oc. 12. pl. máini *dona, pretiosa* Z^2. 30: cf. moin - deinmidetu, *munificentia*.
Mainchine, Manchene (leg. Mainchíne, Manchéne ?), Jan. 2.
máinech, adj. *precious, treasurous*, Feb. 19, Ap. 11, May 18. gen. sg. m. mainig, mainich, Oc. 27. dat. sg. f. máinig (leg. móinig to rhyme with Bóiti ?) Dec. 7.
mainistir =monasterium, gen. Manistrech, LU. 53ª. dat. sg. Dec. 7.
Mainistir-Buiti. now Monasterboice, co. Louth, Dec. 7.
mair, see ceinmair.
Maire, Mare (corruptly Muire) f. = Maria, July 1. 22. Sep. 8. gen. sg. maire Prol. 56, 338, Jan. 19. May 3. Sep. 15. Ep. 384. dat. sg. mairi Dec. 25 B. acc. maire-u, leg. mairi n, Ep. 252. At Nov. 22 I take maire to be an ejaculation like the English *marry*. So dó máir *great God!* in Fiacc's hymn, 9. At Jan. 19 Rawl. 505 has Etsecht maire martha coningum nodnaili, *the death of Marius and Martha, the conjuges whom thou beseechest*, and the gloss is .i. marius et martha uxor eius qui rome cum duobus filiis audifax et ambacuc (leg. Abacuc, Habacuc?) martirio coronati sunt ut Grigorius in romano marterilogio sapit. With this agrees Ob. & Mart. p. 80. The Mary celebrated at July 1 was sister of Moses and Aaron, Boll.
mairg, maire, Prol. 57, where it is used as an interjection : as a substantive it occurs in LU. 33ª: biaid andsin mairg 7 iachtad. gol 7 egnech. cnet 7 greeach cach oen beoil. As an adj. in LU. 51, 52b: am mairg-sea desede or mugain.
Mairge, Mairce, gen. sg. Jan. 2, now the barony of Slievemargy, in the S.E. of Queen's County.
mairt, s. *March*, gen. sg. marta Mar. 1, 31.
maisse, maise, s.m. (n.?) (gl. decor, gl. pulchritudo) Ir. Gl. p. 110. dat. sg. maissi, massi, Ep. 218, 334, for O. Ir. maissiu, cf. tuisled ho ermaissiu fírinne Z. 1064.
maith, adj. i-stem, *bonus*, Feb. 11. Mar. 13. June 5. Dec. 18. Ep. 379. gen. sg. m. maith May 18. voc. sg. m. (fir)maith, Prol. 10. n. pl. f. maithi da noi mili maithi *eighteen good thousands*, if we follow B at July 23, but da noi miled maithe *two nines of good soldiers ;* if we follow A. Here A seems right. Other instances of the gen. pl. of an adjectival i- stem ending in - e are arside *veterum* and connailte *quictorum*, Z^2. 237. So áille (ex áilne, nom. álind), Ep. 83, and blaithe, Sep. 18. In Mid. Ir. the -e is dropt : cf. coimmned teora mbliadan mbind, LU. 9ª 2. oc cantain salm mbuan mbind, note to Félire, Feb. 17. crocui locg n-allaid ba hé a étach, ib. Mar. 5.
maith, s. *bonum* Prol. 267 (where for immaith we should probably read ammaith). gen. sg. n. maith Feb. 5, where már governs the genitive, as in mór n-amri. mór n-uile Z^2. 916.
maithem, s. f. acc. sg. maithim in the phrase cen maithim, inathim Nov. 28, *without abatement*, which is also in Broc. h. 7. maitheamh *abatement*, P. O'C.
mall, v. inmall.
Mammes, July 16, Aug. 17, gen. mammetis, July 16, passus est imperante Aureliano, Ob. & Mart. 146. The Mammes mentioned at July 16 is said to have been martyred at

2 P

Caesarea in Cappadocia. The Mammes at Aug. 17 is said by Boll. to be an Alexandrian martyr.

manach, s.m. = monachus (W. mynach, monach) Prol. 97, gen. sg. manaig Jan. 17, July 27, Aug. 17, gen. pl. manach-n, Ep. 273.

mani, *nisi*, Prol. 313, June 13, July 19.

mann, s.m. *manna* ('cibus celestis', O'Dav. 105), see glanmann, nom. sg. nipu imdu do in mann *non fuit abundantius ei manna*, Z. 593. acc. sg. cen-mand cin bin *without fodder, without food*, 1 S.M. 270. Probably a loan. If Celtic cf. mandere, Goth. matjan.

manod = ma-no-d, Ep. 389.

Mansuetus, Dec. 30. 'in Alexandriä', Ob. et Mart. p. 193.

mar, conj. *if*, Feb. 27. (mor, A.)

maraim, *maneo*, 3d sg. pres. indic. act. (conjunct form) -mair Prol. 199, 203. Z². 430. -muir Prol. 60 B. (absol. form) mairid Prol. 204. 252. = maraid Prol. 168. 244. 3d pl. mairit Prol. 194 B. marait Prol. 88. 3d pl. rel. mairte (ms. mairde) Prol. 194. A. 3d sg. redupl. fut. abs., méraid Prol. 174. 3d sg. pret. act. romar Prol. 135. Cognate with Lat. mora. root SMAR, as maneo with root MAN, Curtius Gr. Et. 96.

már, adj. *great* (W. mawr) Prol. 226. Jan. 6. 11. gen. sg. m. máir Pref. 39. gen. sg. f. máire, máre Dec. 6. dat. sg. m. (n. ?) már June 20. acc. sg. m. már, mór Dec. 17. dat. pl. máraib Sep. 3. gen. pl. m. már-n, mór-n Feb. 1. Compounds : már-rath June 8. see mór.

márnim, *I magnify*, 3d pl. pret. pass. romártha Prol. 236 : see moraim.

marb, adj. *dead*, dat. pl. marbaib Ep. B. 192 (where A has the acc. pl. m. marbu). The b in marb is a v, as we see from the modern marbh and the W. marw: cf. μαῦρος from μαρτος.

marbdae, adj. *deadened*, n. pl. m. marbdai, Sep. 8.

Marc, Marc I. the Evangelist, who by command of Peter preached the Gospel in Egypt and founded the church of Alexandria, where he was martyrised, Ap. 25. July 10.
II. a bishop or martyr (gen. sg. maire, mairec) May 18, June 10, Oc. 3. acc. sg. marc-n Oc. 7, Ep. 260.

Marcell, gen. sg. marcill, maircill, an African martyr, Feb. 19. Sep. 28. Oc. 13. The Marcill (*sic*) at Oc. 13 is Marcellus apparently martyred at Chalcedon, Boll.

Marcellosa, Marcellossus, May 20, seem corruptions of Marcelliosa, an African martyr, Boll.

Marcellus, Feb. 14, Oc. 4, where note the transported n after the Lat. acc. Marcellum. The Marcellus at Oc. 4 was a pope, Boll.

Marcianus, an Egyptian martyr, June 5.

margan, s.m. = Lat. margin(em), dat. sg. Prol. 307.

Martain, Martinus of Tours. Nov. 11. acc. sg. mártain Ep. 275, but mártan Ep. 547, which points to a nom. sg. martan, whence the gen. sg. martain July 4. A pig called Lupait, was slain on Martin's festival, O'Dav. 103.

martar, s.m. = *martyr* : gen. sg. martir, mairtir Jan. 11. Ap. 8. June 7. July 21. Aug. 19. 26. 27. gen. pl. martar-n July 10. see martir.

martarlaic, s. *martyrology*, Ep. 140. O'D. Supp. cites martarluic fireoin, which he renders 'the relics of the just.'

Martha, sister of Lazarus, gen. sg. Jan. 19.

Martinianus, a Roman martyr. Boll. July 2. where Oengus writes, metri gratia, Martiani.

martir, mairtir, s.m. = *martyr*, Feb. 4. May 21, July 17. Aug. 13. 17. Oc. 2. 17. Nov. 13. Ep. 87. dat. sg. martir, mairtir, July 5. gen. pl. martrai (leg. maitrae) Dec. 23, but martir-n, mairtir-n Jan. 30. Feb. 1. 2. July 4. Sep. 8. 13. Oc. 5. Ep. 249.

martre, martra s. (gl. martyrium) Ir. Gl. p. 91. Jan. 7. 12. June 5. July 3. gen. sg. martra (leg. martrai ?) Jan. 30, Feb. 12, Dec. 6. dat. sg. martra Nov. 22, acc. sg. martrai-n martra-n, Ap. 17. 28, July 11. Nov. 6, martra Ep. 267. 511. The phrase luid martrai, Ap. 28, Sep. 15 is = drebuing martm, Ap. 17, dochuaid martra, Ep. 267, where the accusative comes after a verb of motion. So in do dul martre. Z². 484. ránic tir, r. iath. r. maige, Amra Chol. and in Latin : revertère domum (= taucatur atech, Brocc. h. 54), and in Homer οἶκονδε ἵκει.

mas (see rindmas), adj. *beautiful*, dat. pl. massaib, Goidil. 39. compar. maissiu, Goidil. 38. W. maws *pleasant*.
masu, máso (=má-is-u) *if it is*=masa Z. 671.=mása O'D. Supp. But in June 24 it seems to mean *if thou art*.
mat (=má-it), *si est* Ep. 178 A. Mid. Ir. for mad.
math, mad adj. *good*, mad-génair *bene natus est* Prol. 251. mad-tulaid, matulnid *bene ivit*, July 12, bá mad tulad dot brethir *it was well I went to thy word*, L.U. 114ᵃ. ni ma lodmar LL. 45ᵃ. mad-bocht .i. maith roboinged Br. h. 29. u. pl. m. maith Aug. 2. This is the W. mad, Gaulish matos in Teuto-matus.
Matha, the Evangelist, July 1. Sep. 21. Oc. 22.
máthir, s. f. r-stem, *mother* Z². 262. 2 Beitr. 163. gen. sg. mathar Jan. 18. Ep. 174, but (with passage to the á-declension) máithro Ep. 474 B, 526. dat. sg. máthair Ap. 21.
-med, *announces*, *says* (W. medd), daith-medh .i. uaire aisneid, H. 3. 18. p. 69. 3d sg. pres. indic. pass. medair, Prol. 219 B. (medar A.)
medair, s.m. (n ?) *eloquence*, *utterance*, acc. sg. Nov. 11. So in Z. 929: fommchain cói menn medair mass : meadhair *speech*, *talk*, P. O'C.
mátuluid, see mad, math.
Mauri, Oc. 15. 'ss. ccclx mm. Mauri Coloniae Agrippinae,' Boll.
Maxim, Maximus May 8. The name occurs in the acc. sg. at Oc. 25 and Nov. 19. At May 8 Maximus a Byzantine martyr is mentioned by Boll. At Oc. 25 S. Maximus Millenarius, a Roman martyr (Boll.) is referred to.
mebrugud, -ud, s.m. *remembering* Pref. B., deriv. from mebuir, *in memoria*, Z². 251.
mebraigiur, *I remember*, 2d. sg. pres. conjunctive mebraigther Mar. 2, where B. has mebraigter, D. memraigter, *are remembered*.
Medcoit (see Inis medcoit), is perhaps a gen. sg. Metcaud, Medcaut are the forms in Nennius, Reeves Col. 374.
medón, s. *medium* (W. mewn), dat. sg. medon Ep. 343 : compound : medón-rand *middle part*, acc.—r(a)ind Pref.
medrach, adj. *mirthful*, *merry*, *elated*, Ep. 362, a derivative from medair=meadhair *mirth*, *joy*, P. O'C.
Medran, gen. medrain, June 8.
meirb, adj. *weak*, June 13, July 19. nirbat lesc arnarbat meirb, LU. 48ᵇ.=meirbh *weak*, *feeble*, P. O'C. The b in meirb represents v, and is regularly vocalised in W. merw *flaccid*, *flat*, *insipid*, A.S. mearu 'mürbe :' a sister form merb occurs at July 19 D, and in LU. 47³: is merb is ismarb uno guth *my voice is weak and dead*.
meirbléu, s. m. (n. ?) *weak woe*, acc. sg. Jan. 24 : compounded of merb and lén.
meirlech, s. f. Pref. 61, *a thief*=fúr, O'Dav. 84, .i. gadaidhe P. O'C.
méit, s. f. (W. maint), Med. Ir. méid (gl. magnitudo) Jan. 16, dat. sg. méit Prol. 6. There seems also to have been a fem. á-stem, mét, whence gen. méite (= méti Pref.) Z². 251.
mélacht, s. f. *reproach*, acc. sg. Nov. 19, Ep. 70, nom. sg. ba mór a mélacht lea techt cosinfer in imdái ossi alacht, LU. 128ᵇ. conérget intalnaig imónrig iar mélacht forro, LU. 132. cf. méala .i. athais, O'Cl. Gl. bá mela léo, LU. 65ᵃ.
melim (gl. molo) Z². 429, 2 Beitr. 163, 3d sg. pret. pass. (absolute form) melaid July 12, and cf. perhaps frismelat.
mell, s. *error*, Pref. B. mealladh *a deceiving*, *cheating*, *defrauding*, P. O'C.
Mellán, Feb. 7, prob. from Meldán (Meldanus, Reeves' Col. 45).
Mellain (Mellan B.) Oc. 26.
memra, membra, s. f. *a shrine* (membra .i. sgrin no coimhed a mbid taise *a shrine or a case wherein are relics*, O'Cl. Gl.), dat. sg. isamlaid din ata corp Cianain cenlegad isin membrai, note to Fél. Nov. 24, acc. sg. teit Adomnan isinmbemrai (sic ?) ib. gen. pl. membra-n Prol. 224 (.i. adhnacul 3 Ir. Gl. 126), dat. pl. memraib Prol. 80. From Lat. memoriae, which, like μαρτύρια, meant the tombs of martyrs and confessors.
Mena ' pontis,' gen. sg. Sep. 16.

menann, menand, adj. (.i. follus O'Dav. 98) *clear, manifest*, Prol. 285.
menice, menic, adv. *often* (W. mynych, Corn. menough), Jan. 17: cognate with min *often*, annin *seldom*, and see 2 Beitr. 171—2.
menme, menma, s. f., *mind* Z². 264, Prol. 141, Ep. 362, gen. sg. menman June 1, dat. menmain Z². 265, dat. pl. menmanaib 267.
mer, adj. *mad, foolish*, June 13, A, (B and D have meirb). Hence mire μωρία.
merbae, s. f., *error, falsehood*, acc. sg. merbai, merbae Ep. 150. This is .i. mearbhall no brig, O'Cl. Gl., and see 3 Ir. Gl. 140.
Mérnóc (= m' érnóc) Aug. 18. Hic erat Erneneus, filius Craseni, postea per omnes Scotiae ecclesias famosus et valde notissimus, Reeves' Col. 25.
Merobius (mss. Merobus, Meropus, Morepus) a Nicomedian saint, Dec. 4.
Messorianus, an African martyr, Jan. 28.
methel, meithel s.f. (W. medel) *a party of reapers*, Corm. gen. sg. methle, meithle Oc. 31, acc. sg. meithil-n, Dec. 28, Cognate with meto.
metrapoil, metrapoli s. *metropolis*, Aug. 3.
mi, s. n-stem (W. mis, μήν) *month*, May 31, Z². 271, gen. sg. mis, Mar. 1, gen. pl. mis-n, Prol. 301, 321. See 2 Beitr. 163.
miad, s. *pride* (gl. fastus) Sg. 106ᵇ, Prol. 170, gen. miada, dat. huanmiad (gl. fastu) Ml. 82ᵇ. dimiad *dishonour*, B. of Moira, 30, gen. dimiadha, ib. 42, nach miadh doridhnacht dia do foroscla(dh) aire, *every honour which God had bestowed on him was taken away from him*, O'Dav. 84. Old-Breton mocot in ammoet (gl. fastu). Hence miadhach .i. uallach, O'Dav. 104.
Michel, chief of the three archangels and conqueror of Lucifer, gen. sg. michil May 9, dat. sg. michel, Sep. 29, acc. sg. michel-n, Ep. 234. As to the vision of Michael descending on Monte Galgano, to which Oengus refers, May 9, see Jameson S. and L. Art 97. Bui din araile fer soinm isintsleib .i. Garganus ainim infirsin 7 isuad rohainmniged insliab .i. sliab ngarga(i)n. Isann roboiside isheantraig dimad ainm seponte. Fecht ann tarb tarb do indilib Gargain. Dochoid (.i. gargan) tra commogadaib diaiarnd comusfuair indorus nahuama innachtar intsléibi. Focherd iarum gargan saigit forsinanmunna, uair ba fergach diatheslad. Tanic immurro chuca féu forcelu asaigit curnsgeognin fodessin 7 niceoemnacu(i)r ni donannmunna custolad. Bamachtad mór laccoemthecchtaislib gargain innisin. IArsin tra ateés inscelsin do episcop nacatrach, forereongairside curnainitis ulifernib macaib umaib, curafoillsige dia doib cia ardhe forcoemnacuir isinnmaiginsin. Orafurbad intredan cusinnine donarfaid michel do unsalepscop nacatrach .i. sepunte ifis, et dixit michel frisin pscup. Babe fotruair tidecht dontsaigit forculu onanmunna cogargan, cusiufcr rola 7 asbert michel combad uttrab dó italuain intinabsin. *Now there was a certain wealthy man on the mountain, Garganus was that man's name, and from him the mountain was named, to wit, Mount Gargan. He was then biding in the city called Seponte. A bull was once missing from Gargan's herds. He went with his servants to seek it, and found it in the entrance of the cave at the top of the mountain. Then Gargan shot an arrow at the beast, for he was angry at losing it. Howbeit, back to him came his arrow, and wounded him, and nought could it do to the beast unto which it was sent. Great marvel thereat had Gargan's servants. So then that tale was told to the bishop of the city, and he ordered that they should all fast, men, chi'dern, women, that God might manifest to them what sign had happened in that place. When three days' fasting was completed, Michael appeared in a vision to the high bishop of the city Seponte, and said that it was he that had caused the arrow to go back from the beast to Gargan, the man who had shot it; and Michael said that that place was his abode on earth*, LB. 73ᵇ.
Mide, *Meath*, gen. sg. midi, Prol. 226, June 28.
midchuairt, s. *midcourt*, gen. sg. midchuarta, B. of Moira, 6n. dat. sg. Ep. 94, so iarmedón midlái, LU. 78ᵃ. mid-nocht, *midnight*, Reeves' Culdees 86, Lat. medius, μέσος, madhva.
1. mil, s.m. t-stem=*miles* (W. milwr) Z². 255, Feb. 12, June 3, 17, Sep. 29, acc. sg. mil (for

mílid) Ep. 275, n. pl. milid Prol. 73, 77, gen. pl. miled-n Mar. 9, 18, April 28, Z². 232. In July 23 and Sep. 18 miled is perhaps a mistake for mile. Compounds: see cathmil.

2. mil, s. n. *beast* (W. mil, Gr. μῆλορ), gen. sg. a brá mil móir, Colm. h. 37, n. pl. mila Ep. 219.

milach, adj. *abounding in beasts*, πολυκήτης, June 21, where muir milach is = Horace's beluosus Oceanus.

míle, s. f. *a thousand*, Ap. 6, n. pl. míli, Jan. 16 A. (Feb. 6), July 10, gen. pl. mile-n Prol. 72, Jan. 16, Mar. 17, Ap. 24, May 24, 31, June 2, July 31, Aug. 1, Dec. 6, 13, dat. pl. mílib Prol. 212, Sep. 3, Ep. 28, 29, acc. pl. míli Sep. 1, Dec. 26, dat. dual dib mílib Sep. 22. In Zeuss' glosses this numeral is always fem., and the form tri-mile (not teora mili) in Jan. 16 A. is a Middle Irish corruption. So in Fis. Ad. trinuile cheól necsamail *three thousand of various melodies*, LU. 28ᵃ.

Milit (milid)=Miletus or Meliton, bishop of Laodicea, Jan. 10.

milis, adj. *sweet* (W. melys), July 13, Corm. 30, acc. pl. biada milsi, Z². 227.

millim, *I destroy* (root mard?), 3d sg. pret. pass. romilled Prol. 213 : milled s. *destruction*, Corm.

mílte, s. f.=militia, *warfare*, gen. sg. Nov. 12.

minann, adj., *little*, Dec. 31. This is the reading of the Franciscan copy, cf. μινυ-ϝθα.

1. mind, s. n., *diadem*, Jan. 2, Feb. 6, 12, 19, Mar. 23, May 18, June 10, July 22, Oc. 22, Nov. 3, 27, 29, Dec. 18 (in mind-sa, A and B but am-minn-sa D,). The neuter gender also appears from mind-n Feb. 19 D. March 23 D. May 18 D. June 10 D. Aug. 13, 16, mind u-óir, Tochmarc Bec Fola. dat. sg. foa mind, Prol. 257. In a secondary sense minn .i. uasal no sui, *noble or a sage*, O'Dav. 104.

2. mind, s. *a reliquary*, n. pl. minda, Pref. B.

mírbuil, mírlail, adj., *mirabilis*, Jan. 27, May 21, June 15, Aug. 13, Dec. 3.

Miserianus, Jan. 28, A, a corruption of Messorianus q. v.

mithich, mithig (corruptly mithid), adj. *timely*, Ep. 394, Z². 234, ba mithig em, LU. 44ᵇ. is mithig techt, LU. 47ᵇ.

mm, m, the infixed and suffixed pers. pron. of the 1st sg.

I, infixed, ni-m-toersa Prol. 322 B. fo-m-ruirmius Ep. 38, ro-m-bith beo Ep. 39, ro-m-berthar, Prol. 3, ro-m-ain, ro-mm-ain Prol. 18, Ap. 11, B. Oc. 29, Dec. 22. Ep. 226. do-m-r-orbai, Prol. 25, ro-m-snaidet, Ep. 47, do-m-r-airbera, Ep. 65, do-mm-ainic, do-m-anic, Ep. 93, ro-m-saera, Ep. 441, and perhaps do-mm-itecht, Ep. 561.

II, suffixed, di-m. Prol. 223, form Ep. 380, frim Aug. 4, frimsa Dec. 18, lim Ep. 494=lium, Ep. 367, 423.

mo, pron. poss, *my*, Prol. 1, June 16, Ep. 47, 94, 162, 297, 369, 370. Before a vowel the o is elided : m'aite Ep. 65, m'ainim Ep. 297, m'annuain 442, 546.

In Irish, as in Spanish—cf. mio Cid—this pronoun is often employed "comme indiquant l'amitié de celui qui l'emploie et la distinction à l'égard de celui qui en est gratifié," Jacquemont, *Récits Espagnols*, 44, n. Thus :—

mo-beóc, mo-beóóc, mo-phióc, Dec. 16.
mo-biu, mobí, July 22.
mo-bii, mobí, Oc. 12.
mo-chellóc, Mar. 26.
mo-choe, mo-chue, June 23.
mo-choemi, mo-choimi, May 1.
mo-choemóc, Mar. 13.
mo-cholmóc, July 25, also called Colmán.
mo-choummóc, Dec. 26.
mo-chritóc, May 11.
mo-chua, Mar. 30, Aug. 6, Dec. 24.
mo-chuae, May 4.
mo-chnaróc, Feb. 9, May 7.
mo-dímóc, Dec. 10.
mo-domnóc, Feb. 13, May 18.
mo-ecca, mo-ecca, Jan. 20.
mo-éda, moida (=mo-fiada), Jan. 27.
m' oedoc, m' fiedóc, Ap. 11.
mo-gobnait, mo-gobnat, Feb. 11.
mo-luchtóc, Mar. 19.
mo-líba, mo-liba, Feb. 18.
mo-luóc, June 25.
mo-m' acru, mo-acru, Mar. 3, see macru.
mo-máedóc, mo-m'óedóc, Mar. 23, May 18, Aug. 13.
mo-silóc, July 13.
mo-themnóc, mo-themnióc, Dec. 23.
m'eiltóc, mo-eltóc, Dec. 11.
m'ernóc, Aug. 18.

GLOSSARIAL INDEX.

Compounded with prepositions mo loses its vowel but retains its power to aspirate:—
  ama' *for my*, Prol. 15.
  com' *to my, with my*, Jan. 21, Ep. 46, 51, 52, 327.
  dom' *to my*, Jan. 21, 24, Nov. 12, Ep. 271, 287, 363.
  frim' *to my*, Dec. 12, 19, Ep. 296, *at my* Ep. 71.
  im' *in my*. Ep. 126.
  lam' *with my*, June 25, July 13, Dec. 23, 24.
mo, mu a verbal prefix, originally meaning *soon* (Ir. mó, Lat. mox): mo-ling, see note on June 17, mu-riissi farnilochum *I should soon come to you*, Z^2. 418. mu-s-creitfet *mox credent id*, ib. asbert mo-sn-icfed patraice *dixit quod cito venturus est ad eos*.
mó, *major, majus*, cum dat. vel abl. Ap. 1, Sep. 24, Nov. 10, Ep. 28, 127, Z^2. 276, 917.
Mochabae, *Maccabaeus*, Aug. 1, where the poet refers to the seven Jewish brethren celebrated in the second book of Maccabees.
mochtae, mochta, p. part. p. = W. maith, Lat. mactus, *magnified, glorified*, gen. sg. m. mochtai May 6, Aug. 12, acc. sg. mochta Dec. 2, gen. pl. Mar. 18.
Mochtae of Louth (Maucteus, Reeves' Col. 6) Mar. 24, Aug. 19, ob. A.D. 534.
mod, s.m. = *modus*, Oc. 26, dat. mud, múd Z^2. 224.
Moel, Mel, a bishop, Feb. 6.
Moelanfaid, Maelanfaid, Jan. 31.
Moelruain, Maelruain, Prol. 225.
mog = mug q.v.
mogad ? s.m. *slave*, gen. sg. mogaid Pref. B.
Móinán, móenán, gen. moenain June 18, B.
Móinend, móenenn, Mar. 1, Sep. 16.
Moisi, Moysi) *Moses* Mar. 1, Ep. 502: see Diez Gr. II. 9, as to the form moisen, if indeed it
Moisen, Moysen) be not Latin here.
molad, s.m. *praise* (W. molawd), gen. sg. molta, acc. sg. molad-n Nov. 27.
molatha, molotha, Sep. 2, seems an archaic form of the part. prot. pass. of molur, q.v.
molbthach, adj. *praiseworthy*, ba molbthach inmind, LU. 51ᵇ, gen. pl. June 2.
Moling Luachair, June 17.
molmae = molnae .i. molta *praised*, O'Cl. Gl. gen. sg. f. Aug. 31. This seems a participle passive of molur, q.v., the - mae being a *weiterbildung* of - ma as -tae of ta, cf. the Old Bulgarian and Lith. part. pres. pass. in - *mu*. Schleicher Compendium pp. 417, 418.
molur, *laudo*, Z. 989, pres. pret. nomolur, romolur Prol. 13. nomolur A. 1st pl. pres. indic. no-s-mohammar, molamar,-molomar, Jan. 17, co molait són (gl. ut psallant) Ml. 259.
mong, s.f. *hair of the head* (buinne oir inmá moing, LU. 25ᵃ). = W. mwng, Br. moe, 2 Beitr. 176: also *mane* (graig ngabor nglas brec a mong, LU. 48ᵃ).
mongach, adj. *hairy*, gen. sg. m. mongaig Aug. 14, gen. sg. n. marcach in mara mongaig *the rider of the crested sea*, Sgl. Conc.
Moninde, Moninne, July 6. (Is the mo- here the pron. poss.?)
1. mór, adj. *great*, (= inár q.v.) Prol. 148, 168, Jan. 18, May 6, July 2, Nov. 8, gen. sg. m. móir Mar. 29, June 7, Aug. 12, dat. sg. m. mór Sep. 15, dat. sg. f. móir June 28, acc. sg. m. (n. ?) mor-n Jan. 15 (mór trom tredan), acc. sg. f. moir-n Aug. 2, acc. sg. n. mór-n Jan. 15 (mór-ngur ngalar) voc. sg. m. móir Ep. 312, 313, n. pl. m. móir Prol. 149, June 5, n. pl. n. móra Ep. 387, gen. pl. mór-n Prol. 301 : comparative mó q.v.
mór adv. *greatly* (cf. Lat. magnum clamat) Sep. 4.
  In composition:—
  mór-bail, s. *great goodness*, June 15.
  mór-bruth, s. *great fervour*, Oc. 29.
  mór-buiden, s.f. *a great troop*, dat. sg. mórbuidin, Mar. 18, July 19.
  mór-chlíar s.f. *a great train*, dat. sg., morchléir, June 4, Nov. 4.
  mór-chroch, s.f. *a great cross*, dat. sg. mór-chroich, Aug. 25.

mór-drem, s. *a great party*, May 21.
mór-féil, s.f. *a great festival*, dat. sg. Aug. 15.
mór-fert, s.m. *a great miracle*, n. pl. mórfertai, mórferta, Ep. 506.
mór-féssiur, mór-séisir s.n. *seven persons*, (lit. *great-six-persons*), Aug. 7, dat. sg. July 18.
mór-flaith, s.f. *a great prince*, Sep. 4, *a great kingdom*, Nov. 10.
mór-gal, s.f. *great valour*, dat. sg. June 15, B.
mór-gním, s. *a great deed*, June 6, dat. June 7.
mór-grían, s.f. *a great sun*, July 27, Dec. 18, B.
mór-lith, s. *a great festival*, Sep. 9.
mór-martra, s. *a great martyrdom*, Jan. 3.
mór-nert, s. n. *great virtue*, Ep. 155.
mór-pairt, s. *a great tome?* acc. pl. mórpartae, Ep. 136.
mór-phían, s.f. *great pain*, acc. sg. mórphéin, Aug. 17.
mór-rí, s.m. *a great king*, n. pl. mór-ríg, Prol. 61, D.
mór-scél, mórsceol, s. n. *a great story*, Prol. 138.
mór-serc, s.f. *great affection*, acc. sg. mórseircc July 5.
mór-sliab, s. n. *a great mountain*, n. pl. mórslébe Prol. 237.
mór-slóg, mór-slúag, s.m. *a great host*, Ap. 2, May 29, dat. sg. Mar. 9, 20, n. pl. morslúaig Sep. 22.
mór-slúagad s.m. *a great hosting*, dat. sg. mórslúagud Aug. 20, acc. sg. morsluagad-u, July 7.
mór-throm, adj. *great-heavy*, n. pl. m. mórthruim, June 27.

2. mór, n. *much*, governing the gen. (like *par, proprium, simile, commune*): mór maith Feb. 5, mór ndelma Ap. 7, mór mbuaide Mar. 21, mór mbríge Aug. 1, mór n-duba Ep. 377, cf. mór-n-amri, mór-n uile Z. 889, mór saido, Cod. Boern. In mór do rígaib, Prol. 52, the prep. do seems used for di: cf. mór di maid, Z. 599.

móraim, *I magnify*, 3d sg. pres. indic. with -us suffixed: morth-us Prol. 132 A. 3d pl. mórait Prol. 116, Feb. 1. 3d sg. pres. a-conj. act. ro-n-móra Mar. 28. 3d pl. ro-n mórat July 17, Ep. 59. 2d sg. s-pret. romorais (gl. mirificasti) Ml. 37ᵃ. 3d sg. s-pret. mórais Aug. 18: with -us suffixed: mórs-us Prol. 132 B, Jan. 30, June 5, 3d sg. pret. pass. romórad Prol. 103.

mórad, s.m. *a greatening, magnifying*, Jan. 18, dat. sg. do-mórad dáe (gl. in gloriam dei) Z². 239.

mórdae, adj. *haughty*, n. pl. m. mórdai, Mar. 1.

morepus, Dec. 4, a mistake for Merobius.

mos, mus, mus, an adverb=Skr. makshu, Lat. mox, only found in composition with verbs: mos-ricub mo mochlige *I shall soon reach my early grave*, Longes Mac n-Usnig: fomentar mo rigtin-se mos-riccubsa *expect my coming. I shall soon come*, Z². 418. dochum niuue mos-rega *to heaven thou shalt soon come*, Fiacc h, 50. mus creitfet *mox credent*, or perhaps *mox credent id*, Z². 418. mos-tic cach notuaile *mox bene, venit omnis quisquis eum petit*, July 9. Mós taircella ém súil tar sodain, LU. 68ᵇ. ni-mos-tias .i. ni rop moch thias, Lib. Hymn. 28ᵃ.

muad, adj. Ep. 362. O'Clery gives four meanings: uasal *high*, maith *good*, mór *great*, maoth *soft, tender*.

múchaim *I smother*, 3d pl. s-pret. rumúgsat (gl. suffoderunt, Z². 464. 3d sg. pret. pass. romúchad Prol. 169. pl. romuchtha Prol. 233. hoc nad muchtha dóine impu, Táin bó Fr. inmusmuchat *suffocant* ib. formúicthib (gl. subfucatis) Lib. Arm. 181. a, 1.

mug, mog, s.m. (Goth. magus, Corn. maw, W. meu in meu- dwy) *slave, servant*, Pref. gen. moga, dat. mug, n. pl. moge, mogi, Z². 227, 238, 239.

Mugnae, Dec. 11.

Muine, s.f. *Menevia, St. Davids*: Cell muine, Mar. 1.
muinter, munter, múinnter, s.f. *familia, household*, Prol. 284, May 11 (where it is wrongly rendered) Aug. 9, gen. sg. muintire, muntaire Z². 242. dat. sg. muintir Pref. and Tir. 11. acc. muintir-n, muntir-n, Ap. 8.
muir, s.n. *sea* (Ganlish mori, Z². 13. Gl. K.N. 33. Lat. mare, Gr. πλημμυρίς, Ebel) June 21, Ep. 30, Z². 233. gen. sg. mora, Z². 234. acc. sg. muir-n Feb. 13. isam-muir *in mare*, Tur. n. pl. mora Z. 236. dat. pl. murib Br. h. 18.
Muiredach, bishop of Killala (cell-alad), gen. muiredaig, muredaig Aug. 12=Muiredaich, Goidil. 39, Muiredachi Reeves Col. 40, now 'Murray.'
Muirdebar, Nov. 3. According to Laud 610 iferann Martain ata ifail Ducain, *in Martin's territory he is, near Buchan*, 7 Oenglais nomen loci eius nunc.
muirgeu s. *seabirth, a mermaid*, according to O'Curry, acc. sg. Jan. 27. She was Liban, daughter of the Echaid Find mac Mairedn from whom Lough Neagh (loch n-Echach) is named. Isi raboí xxx. bliadan illoch échach conasrugaib beoan iascaire comgail inaliu 7 corosbaist comgall, *it is she that was 30 years in Lough Neagh, and Beóán, Comgall's fisherman, caught her in his net and Comgall baptized her*, et narravit ei omnia que accederant sibi in aquis, Rawl. 505. See the story in Lebor na huidre, pp. 39, 40, where it is said that Murgen (.i. gein in muru) or Muirgeilt (.i. geilt in muru) was the name given to Liban after her baptism, and that half of her was as a salmon and the other half as a human being. Irish words for mermaid or siren are murdhuchu, suire .i. murduchann O'Cl., samhghubha .i. anmann na murduchan bhios isin bfairrge *ib.* muirmóru (gl. siren) Z. 28=W. morforwyn.
Muma, s. *Munster*, gen. sg. muman, Jan. 15, acc. sg. mumain Pref. B.
múr, s.m.=mūrus, Jan. 24, Sept. 15, 21. Dec. 6, Ep. 151, n. pl. uii. múir, LU. 114ᵇ, acc. pl. nochlaided na mura, LU. 109ᵇ.
múr, s. (.i. iomad *abundance*, O'Cl.), dat. sg. muir Prol. 126 : leg. múr and cf. Dia mar mo anaccol do múir theindtide, *great God be my protection from the fiery abundance!* Anra Chol. LU. 7ᵃ. doronsat mic mílid imarbaig imrama ac tiachtain coroeustar Ir mac Miled muir-cet(h) do gach luing. mur innat 7 ceth .i. tonn *the sons of Miled rowed a race when coming, so that Ir son of Miled brought many a wave to each ship*, Gl. 688.
Murchú, ('*sea-hound*') son of Hua Mactein, Todd L. H. 165. gen. sg. murchon June 8.
Muric, Sep. 22=Mauricius, Mauritius, the commander of the Theban Legion (which numbered 6666), and the patron saint of footsoldiers.
Muri, Oc. 15, leg. Mauri q.v.
Maxentius, Jan. 12, for Maxentius ?

n corresponds with Latin, Greek and Gothic n : nascaim, nél, nói-n, nua.
n- (m before b) case-ending (=Skr. and Lat. m) transported to the following word :—
n. sg. neut. síl n-ádaim Prol. 131, Ep. 439. síl m-buadach Feb. 13. all n-glaine Jan. 6. comeit n-glaine Ap. 1. mór ndelma Ap. 7. ilar m-buada June 5. mór n-didnad June 8. atach m-bille July 3, Aug. 8. mór mbrige Aug. 1. mind n-goedel Aug. 13. mind n-uaghailee Aug. 16. ler m-buade Oc. 30. mor n-gur n-galar Nov. 16. buaid n-icthbritain, Dec. 8, Franciscan copy, saerchetul m-buan Ep. 158. mór n-duba Ep. 377.
acc. sg. each n-aidid, Prol. 49. each m-bais Ap. 4. erch n-airim July 15. each n-gabud, Oc. 29. each n-oen Ep. 114. mór n-gnim n-gaile, Prol. 54. each m-bordgal, Ep. 206. each n-duine Ep. 215. firthuillem m-buide Prol. 55. saethar n-gor. 59. each n-duil, 91. loc n-úire 128. slóg n-aingel 132. sessilbe m-buada 183. sluniged n-án 303. tormach n-colais 317. mór n-gur n-galar Jan. 15. muir n-gledend Feb. 13. martra m-buade Ap. 17. cléir n-apreil Ap. 30. cléir n-gelmair May 13. bith (f)laith m-buadaig May 16. cléir m-buada June 2. crich

n-érenn June 3. parthalon m-bresta June 13. benedicht m-buadach June 14. Ep. 264. sil n-adaim July 15. nóem n-áilme Aug. 5. nóem n-dóe Aug. 27. ualerau n-idan Aug. 11. ethri n-august Aug. 31. feil n-ailbe Sep. 12. cingid m-báge Sep. 13. diis m-bodmair Sep. 14. coisecrad m-baislicc Sep. 15. sossad n-ard n-oiblech Sep. 21. draic n-dálach Sep. 29. ancrist n-irach ib. mare n-epscop Oc. 7. baethine m-brignach Oc. 6. fonmbith m-buidnech Oc. 15. ocm n-uasal Oc. 24. bendacht m buada Nov. 2. coisecrad n-eclas Nov. 18. rigmac n-ainglech Nov. 22. émin n-geldae Dec. 22. dith n-dorchae Dec. 25. incop n-ordan Dec. 27. Ep. 256. coemthur n-dile Ep. 66. abraham n-amra, 244. cech n-audpairt 345. uuall m-buada 349, noebspirut n-delbda 354. itche n-aile 413. iferud n-gér n-ginach, 538. cech n-dligail 516.

gen. pl. martir nar n-gledenn Feb. 1. cailech n-érenn ib. bech n-érenn Feb. 13. noebáng n-ennae Ap. 9. mac n-ennac Ap. 24. martir n amra July 4. Oc. 5. miled m-blaithe Sep. 18. ban n-goedel Sep. 23. mac n-érend Sep. 26. fátha n-érenn Nov. 29. mór n ard n-aille, Ep. 83. lebur n-érenn, Ep. 141. nasalnoeb n-érenn, 277, noeb n-albau, 280. noeb n-érenn 284. noem n-eorapa, Ap. 20.

In marcellum n-epscop, Oc. 4, the n is merely syntactical.

In intorgam .c. mbuada, Mar. 12 A. the m is a mistake.

For instances of the transported n after numerals which originally ended in nasals, see secht, ocht, nói, deich.

n, infixed relative pron.: for-n-osna Prol. 5. ro n-glea Jan. 5. do-n-arlaid Dec. 8. ro-n-uc Dec. 14. fo-n-d-rúair Ep. 97. ro-n-gádsa Ep. 421. uo-n-ailiu 559. Before c, t, p, f, and s it is recognisable from the absence of infection, e.g. ata secoil ro-clotha Aug. 24. docuissin Ep. 443. rocráite Ep. 269. ro-eruide Ep. 136. in grafand rofersam Ep. 73. Before r it is assimilated: do-r-rime, Sep. 5.

n' infixed pers. pron. of the 3d sg.: dia-n-promam (=dian-n-promam) Prol. 143. o do-n-ánic Ap. 14. no-n-áilem July 14. ro-n-fethis June 24. Aug. 7. at-n-rocham Dec. 21.

n, for nn, infixed pers. pron. of the 1st pl. see nn.

1. na, no, *vel, sive*, Z². 699. Prol. 136. nocom ... na, Prol. 135 na .... na Ep. 121 A, ni ... na Prol. 108, Ep. 129. 135. In Ep. 478, if the true reading be *ar each nole nn druchrad*, na seems to mean *and*.

2. na, *tῆς*, gen. sg. fem. of the article
3. na, *τούς, τάς, τά*, acc. pl. of the article
4. na, for na-n, inna-n, *τῶν*, gen. pl. of the article
5. na, for nab, *τοῖς, ταῖς*, dat. pl. of the article } see ind.

6. na. *not* (in a subjoined or relative sentence) Prol. 201, 204. Feb. 9. Mar. 18. Ap. 9. Nov. 10. Ep. 122. arna Prol. 297 (= aran-na), arnái-p Prol. 323. Compounded with -ch and -d', it means *that not, that is not*: na-ch-at-risad Prol. 284. na-ch-am-tecma, na-ch-in-tecma Jan. 10. na-d soréid Prol. 30. na-d charam Prol. 134. ná-d céla'm, Prol. 142. Ep. 86. nad-chunuscaigset, Feb. 6. na-d aithbi Ap. 15. Aug. 12. nad-chelar, Aug. 11. nad char, Aug. 16. na-d duthain (= na-ch duthain B.) Nov. 28. na-d donai (= na-ch dona, B) Sep. 16. na-d chlithi Dec. 9, Ap. 306. nad-labrai Dec. 22. na-d ránic Ep. 17. For na-d we find na-t: na-t cumscaigset, Feb. 6 A, na-t char (nad char B.) June 22. nat-car, Aug. 16 B, n-at celar. Aug. 11. na-t labrai, Dec. 22 A, nat-rainic, Ep. 17 D.

Nabeodon, Nábgodon, Prol. 94, shortened from the Nabuchodonosor of the Vulgate.

nach, with a subst. adj. or pron. Z². 361, *any*, Ep. 337. gen. sg. nach-hé, acc. sg. cen nach tuisel July 8. *every*, nom. nach ainim, Ep. 53. nach mac 267. nach ní 360. nach bág 361.

nach, } see na, and Z². 741.
nad, }

nair, Jan. 8, for anáir *from the East*, Feb. 13: cf. nambuiduib Ep. 295, for in am - buidnib.

námae, náma, s.m. nut-stem, *foe*, Z³. 255. dat. sg. námait Feb. 15. acc. pl. náimtea (ms. náimtiu) Prol. 231. Z². 258.

naptar, nabdar; *quorum . . . non fuerunt* (na-batar), Mar. 18.

nárach, adj. *shameful*, from nár *shame*, acc. sg. m. Mar. 8, where, however, the glossographer regards nárach as the gen. sg. of the name of Senan's smith. If so, the translation should be *gibbeted Nára's foe*. The story is told in prose LD. 271 a, and in verse Laud 610, fo. 63 b.

násad, s. Oc. 26 (nassan B) .i. clú *fame:* Three Ir. Gl. 137, gen. pl. comsid na náem násad nan, LU. 40ᵃ.

Nascae, Oc. 25. May 12, at May 12 the glossographer in Rawl. 505 explains nascai by nasc uobi fámgait cen isiud alainu coathrucud, *a tie that was on his neck while he was in the river bathing:* cognate probably with nascim, = *nexere,* or rather the Lucretian *nexare:* nascair, *nexitur,* 1 S.M. ar-ob-rói-nasc *vos enim despondi,* Z². 813, a frequentative from NAGH, Skr. nah.

nát, see ná.

Nathí (Nahū A), Aug. 9.

nathir, naithir, s.f. c-stem (matrix, 2 Beitr. 168, W. neidr, Br. azr) Z². 259. *snake, serpent,* gen. sg. nathrach, Z². 260, gen. pl. nathrach-n, Ep. 480. acc. pl. nathracha (gl. aspides) Tur. 11.

Natsluag, gen. natsluaig, Pref.

Nazair, July 12 = Nazarius, a Milanese martyr? Or is it a mistake for Nabor, who is bracketed with Felix in Boll. at this day? But cf. Boll. "Nazarius de Lieth, qui scandit ad angelorum consortium, in omni coetu celebris, ut inquit Ængussius, Gormanus legit. Nasan alienus a crimine. Nomina patria Hibernica sic Latine reddita sunt, ut ex varia inflexione facile multiplicentur."

nd for nn: indtliucht Prol. 298, (inntliucht, 318), rand Jan. 10. laindi Feb. 21, condeuch (= con-neuch) Feb. 23, ceand, cind Feb. 25, 27, cend Ap. 23, July 24, Aug. 10. Nov. 29, Dec. 18. Ep. 8, 164, 414, rétlaind Mar. 3, feraind, colaind, Mar. 12, endag Ap. 9, endac Ap. 24, tuind Ap. 23, June 3, thondaib Nov. 23, forcendait Ap. 30, forcenda Ep. 282, craind May 3. anmand May 19, iohandis June 26 B. brainlib June 29, indoeiun Aug. 22, caimlech Oc. 11, dírmand Oc. 11, Ep. 143, árnind, érind Nov. 21. goband Nov. 25, glanmand Dec. 19, fairind Ep. 51. rochindset Ep. 108, doruirmind Ep. 128, comand Ep. 189, fírendgu Ep. 322, ifernd Ep. 482-538. for nt in loanwords: tend, cland.

nds for ns: andsa, Ap. 12, tindsean, May 1, Nov. 14, 15, indse, Feb. 7, Mar. 8. indsi, July 7.

ndt for nt: Findtain, Feb. 17, 21. Falland.

nech, pron. *aliquis*, Z². 362, gen. sg. neich ib. dat. sg. neoch Prol. 146, July 30, neuch (in comdeuch, leg. conneuch) Feb. 23.

necht, adj. *clean* (W. nith, Skr. nikta in nirnikta) Corm. s.v. Cruithnecht. Hence perhaps Nechtán, of Dungiven, Jan. 8, Nechtán mac Lemna (gen. sg. nechtáin) May 2.

neim, s. m. (n. ?) *poison,* gen. sg. ind neime Z². 10, dat. sg. neim Ep. 480.

Neir, *Nero.* Prol. 113, gen. sg. neran 112, but nerain, nerainn 121, dat. sg. néran, nernino 117.

neit, Ep. 314 A, a mistake for chneit acc. of cnet q.v.

nél, s.m. *cloud,* (W. niwl, νεφέλη, nebula, 2 Beitr. 164) gen. pl. nél, nell, Feb. 16, May 11. Ep. 398, dat. pl. nélaib Prol. 22, Nov. 20, Ep. 347, 566, nellaib F.D.G. 76, acc. pl. niulu Z². 20, néolu LU. 23ᵃ.

nélach, adj. *cloudy* (W. niwlog). gen. sg. m. nélaig Prol. 187, acc. sg. n. nélach 280, riced a barr nem nelach. Vis. Cath. Mór.

1. nem, s.n. s-stem, *heaven* (= W. nef, νέφος, Skr. nabhas, 2 Beitr. 178, au-nem adchianni Ml. 42ᵇ), gen. sg. nime May 17, Nov. 7, Ep. 85, 96, 196, 233, 373, nime locharnaig *caeli lucernosi,* Colm. h. 31, a ri nime glais o *rex caeli caerulei!* Three Fragments, &c. 60, dat. sg. nim Ep. 294. acc. sg. nem-n Prol. 216, Aug. 26. Oc. 24. Ep. 25, loc. sg. nim (Ebel Beitr. v. 225), gen. pl. nime-n, Prol. 2, Ep. 120. 401, dat. pl. nimib, Sanct. h. 19, acc. pl. nime, 1 s. M. 30.

2. Nem maceu Birn. June 14.

3. nem-, a negative prefix = (O. Ir. neb-, neph-), nemchorp *non-body,* nemchorpdae *non-corporal,* Pref.

nemde, nemdae adj. *heavenly,* Z². 229. Oc. 17, acc. sg. m. Ep. 356, n. pl. m. nemdai, Z². 226.

nert, s. n. *strength, virtue* (W. nerth, Gaul. nerto-) Prol. 253, 256, gen. sg. nebrt Ml. 80, dat. sg. neort Prol. 163 B (nert A), niurt 219, atomriug niurt *me alligo ad virtutem,* Patr. h. = neurt, Z². 223. acc. pl. tnithaid nerta lochmamat, LU. 109ᵃ. Hence éuirt, sonairt.

nertflaith, s. f. *a strong prince*, acc. sg. Ep. 170.
nessa, (corruptly nessu) *weaver*, Prol. 217. Z². 277. W. nés.
Nessán, gen. sg. nessáin, nessáin, nesáin, Mar. 15, Aug. 8, Dec. 1, acc. sg. nessán July 25 : a diminutive of ness '*weasel*.'
nethehoemi, May 1.
n–b for nn : an hualann Sep. 26 A. so in Fiacc h. 65 : con-hualai, and in Cornish in-hans, in-both, an-bethek, an-hethys, lanherch, canhagowe.
–ni, –ne, suffix of the first pers. pl. ar-rig-ne, Prol. 256, uain-ni, Jan. 28, almi-ni, Jan. 10 B. sloind-fim-ni, sluindfemne, Prol. 287.
ní, ni *not*, Z. 701, ni trebthair (ni threbthair B) Prol. 176. ni beir 223. ni fil, ni fuil 281. ni femd-ibther 260. ni bruifem 304. nídlig Ap. 25, ní foigbe Ep. 147 B, ni promfat (ni fhromat B.) Ep. 219. ni lobfat Ep. 220: ni . . . na Ep. 129. 135. With *is* omitted : ni léim Dec. 31, ní gó Ep. 27. ní tiamdai Prol. 259. ní diultach Ep. 371, ni eslind 397. And see nidat, nimta, ninse, nip, nis, nit, na-ni.
ní, s.n. *thing*, Prol. 185. 217. Sep. 24 D, Ep. 360. Z². 364.
Niall, Frossach (the showery) Pref. 19. Ob. A.D. 778, Reeves' Col. 67. 387. Niall, spelt ncel in Lib. Arm. 10 a. 2, is the Njal of the Sagas.
Nicodimus, Necodimus, *Nicodemus*, Oc. 17.
nidat, *non sunt*. Jan. 17.
nimand? Dec. 31. leg. minann?
nimtá, *not so is*, Prol. 97. 129. 137. 185 : pl. nimtát, Prol. 77 = ni + imta *so is*, Senchas Már, III. 30.
nínach, adj. *delightful* (Three Ir. Gl. 126. nionach .i. aoibhinn, O'Cl. Gl.), an epithet of heaven Prol. 108. (cf. W. nen *heavens*, O Br. ninou gl. laquearibus), *forky* (gablach) an epithet for a cross, Mar. 31, from nin *fork* ut in ussu dicitur hit arda nin na garmna *high are the forks of the weaver's beam*, ar nin isint (s)engoedile gobul sin indiu *for nin in the oti Gaelic is* gobul '*fork*' *to-day*, Rawl. 505.
ninse, = ni-anse *not difficult*, Pref. written nin.
Ninuen, Ninuén, *Nineveh*, acc. Ep. 401.
nip, *ne sit*, Ep. 417.
nis, *non eos*, May 19.
nit (= ní-it, Z². 488) *non sunt*, Prol. 76. Mar. 1. Ep. 16. In Sep. 8 the sense seems to require *non-es* (ní-at, Z². 487).
nnt for nt : tenntib Prol. 39, gennti Prol. 61.
1. no, conj. *or* (W. neu) Prol. 222. Ep. 562. Z². 699. see na.
2. no, verbal prefix, Z². 415. = ro, Ebel. no-molar Prol. 13. no-sretha 138. no-rádi Feb. 18. no rádiu Ep. 338. no-chantais July 30. nuchartais Nov. 16. With infixed pronouns :— notlomaim (=no-d-dlomaim) no-n-dlomaim Prol. 315. no-d-techtaid Ep. 389. no-do-snaidfea Ep. 260. no-n-ailem July 14. no-n-ailiu Ep. 559. no-s-tnirfem Prol. 289. no-s-molamar Jan. 17. no-s-gebad Pref. no-t-guidin Prol. 265, Ep. 37. 312. 313. not-caru Ep. 311. not-carnim Ep. 50. no-tn-ali Feb. 7. no-dn-ali July 9. no-t-géba Ep. 114. 173 B. =no-d-gela 166. 180. no-d-guidiu Ep. 337.
nochon, *not*, noc(h)on-fiu *non est dignum*, Prol. 111. noe(h)onfess, 135. nochon saethar madæ. *non est labor vanus* Ep. 227. nochon-esracht necch arae(h)inn istaig acht dubthach macculugair namma *no one arose before him within save D.M. only*, Trip. Life, Eg. 3. b. 1. nochon-étammar, olsiat, LU. 3ᵃ. Apparently a formation from nocho (O'Don. Gr. 268): noco-raibo usci occai *there was not water with him*, Leb. Breec cited Todd L.H. 28.
Nóe, Noah, Ep. 237. 451.
1. nóeb, (noem, naem) adj. *holy*, Prol. 337. Jan. 14. Ep. 178. gen. sg. m. nóib, Aug. 22. gen. sg. f. nóebe Prol. 338 B. (noeime A), voc. sg. m. noeb Ep. 37, acc. sg. m. noeb-b Aug. 5, dat. pl. noclaib Ep. 348. compar. noebu Jan. 20. May 27 D. superl. naebem, noemem July 14. Old Persian naiba *fair, good* (Zimmer).

In composition :—
nóeb-ainm, s.n. *a holy name*, Prol. 109, acc. sg. Prol. 99.
nóeb-apstal, s.m. *a holy apostle*, May 30.
nóeb-arbar, s. *a holy troop*, dat. pl. nóebairbrib, Ep. 344.
nóeb-clecheng, s. *a holy pair of champions*, Nov. 21.
nóeb-epscop, s.m. *a holy bishop*, gen. sg. noibepscoip, Mar. 20. gen. pl. noeb-epscop, Ep. 253.
nóeb-gérait, s. *a holy champion*, Aug. 4.
nóeb-itge, s. *a holy prayer*, July 19.
nóeb-máthair, s.f. *a holy mother*, Aug. 16.
nóeb-muinter, s.f. *a holy household*, May 13.
nóeb-relic, s. *a holy relic*. gen. pl. noemreilec, Oc. 1.
nóeb-spírut, s.m. *a holy spirit*, acc. sg. Ep. 354.
nóeb-úag, s. f., *a holy virgin*, n. pl. nóebúaga, Feb. 28. gen. pl. nóebúag-n, Ap. 9, Ep. 252.
2. nóeb (noem, naem) s.m. *a saint*, Feb. 9, Ep. 178, n. pl. noeim, Pref. gen. pl. nóeb-n Ap. 20, Ep. 131, 277, 280, 284, dat. pl. nóebaib Aug. 30, Ep. 112, 288, acc. nóebu Ep. 357. Compounds : noeb-onorátus, Ep. 261, noeb-thomás, Dec. 21.
nóebaim (noemaim), *I hallow, I sanctify*, 3d sg. a- conj. ronóeba, Ep. 436, 3d pl. ronóebat, Ep. 59, 3d sg. pret. pass. ronóebad. Ap. 11, Ep. 438.
nóebad, s.m. *sanctification*, Ep. 183, 203.
nóebán, s.m. *a saintling, a little saint* (hypocoristic), Ep. 99.
nóebdae (noemdae), adj., *holy (hallowed)*, Mar. 7, July 18, gen. sg. m. noebdai noemdai July 13, June 11, acc. sg. May 12, compar. noemdu, May 27, B.
nóebe, nóibe (noeme, noeime), s. f., *holiness*, Z^2. 212, gen. sg. nóebe Sep. 13, dat. sg., nóebi Jan. 19, Feb. 18, Aug. 3, 22.
Nóendruim (*nine-ridge*, ix. udruimne fil isinbaile ita a chell), June 23, an island, now Inishmahee, in Strangford Lough, Co. Down, gen. sg. mochoe nóindrummo Z. Pref. xv. Todd. LII. 100, Joyce, 137. Naomdruim .i. ainm cille .i. nai tulcha isau iudsi nafail, O'Mulc. Gl. 834.
nói-n, nóe-n, nái-n, *nine*, la nái n-grad, Ep. 235, dá nói, *two nines*, July 23, noi-cet, nóe-chét '900.' Aug. 29.
nóidiu, s., *a babe, an infant*. Z^2. 264, gen. sg. noiden, Z^2. 265, gen. pl. nóiden, nóeiden, July 14.
Nóis, gen. sg. (a dissyll.), Prol. 184.
Nola, Jan. 14, a city of Campania.
noll (nóll ?) adj. *great*, July 29, Aug. 8, where B has the gen. sg. m. nuill. In Prol. 54, nuall-sa is glossed by oll indso *great this*, nall .i. uasal, LU. 120ᵃ.
nóna, s. *nonae*, Prol. 305.
notlaic, notlaicc, nodlaig. s. f. natalicia (W. nadolig) *christmas*, dat. sg. Nov. 13, Dec. 24, 25.
nouimber, s.m. *November*, gen. sg. Nov. 30.
nua (O. Ir. nue Z^2. 56, nauc, W. newydd) adj. *new, fresh*, Jan. 5 : as this is a dissyll. cf. Skr. navya, Lat. novius, Gaul. novio- rather than nava, novus, νέ(F)ος.
nualann, adj. Feb. 1, Sep. 26, Nov. 29, subst. Feb. 13. This seems an old participle in -ndo meaning *to be applauded, laudandus, laudandum*, root NU *to cry*, (Skr. nauti, navate) whence Skr. nava, navana *praise*, Lat. nenia (Froehde), Ohg. niu-món *to praise* (Fick). Hence also
nuall, s. n. *clamor*, Sep. 16, Nov. 8, Dec. 28. Ep. 163, 406, acc. sg. nuall-n, Prol. 304, Ep. 349. In Early Middle Irish this word was fem. cf. airlitiud co nuaill, Vis. Cath. Mór.

o corresponds with the Latin and Gr. o : ocht = octo, ὀκτώ, oll = πολλός, roth = rota : o from u by breaking : cloth from *cluta κλυτός.
o for a : colléec Prol. 239, domair Feb. 16 A.
ó from á : mór ; from au : pól, ór.
ó, ua, prep. *a, de*, cum dat. abl. Prol. 122, 251. Ap. 7, 10, June 18, 23, Aug. 6, 8, Sep. 3, 12, 25, 26, Nov. 25, 28, Dec. 7, 16, 25, 28. In Mar. 23, ó should perhaps be rendered *by*

means of, or *of*: cf. illeth o mathair *on (his) mother's side* LU. 14ᵇ. With the article ónd, óu, Prol. 325, Mar. 15, Oc. 16, Ep. 1. ó-sin immach *thenceforward*, Pref.

ó conj. *when*, before a verb, ó bebais, o mbebais Prol. 95. ótluid (=ó dolluid) Prol. 128, o donánic Ap. 14, cf. ó donanicc foirbtheu *ex quo venit mihi firmitas* Z. 678.

oc (ac, ic), prep. cum dat. *at*: oc cuinchid Prol. 329, with the article ocunt-sle(i)b-sin, Oc. 20, with the pers. pron. ocum Pref. B. with the poss. pron. 1 acom, ocam, ocum Ep. 44, 292, 293, icom 299. 3 ocá aca *at his*, Prol. 227, occa-n *at their*, Prol. 47. This prep. is written ucc in Tír. 11 and may come from oneva = Goth. nehva, Eng. nigh.

oche, s. f. *armpit*, gen. sg. oiche, ocha, Aug. 4.

ocht-n, *eight*, W. wyth, Jan. 28, June 22, Sep. 22, gen. Dec. 23.

ochtmoga, *eighty*, Feb. 14.

óc, adj. *young*, abridged from óoc, q.v.

óeri, s. m. *a young king, prince* (MSS. ocgri, og ri) Prol. 92, where the reference is to Apoc., i. 5 : Jesu Christo ... primogenito ex mortuis et regum terrae principe.

ócrígan, s. f. *a young queen, princess*, Oct. 13.

Octimper, Octimber, Ochtimber, s.m. *October*, Oct. 1. 31. gen. sg. Octimbir. This is the vulgar Latin Octember, O. French Octembre.

1. ocus, adj. (onevastu) *near, close* Ep. 230. dat. sg. ocus (leg. acus) Ep. 110.

2. ocus, conj. *and*, Prol. 85. June 29, Ep. 442 : usually denoted by the siglum 7.

Odran, Oc. 27 : see Reeves' Columba 203-4.

óeded, áided, s. f. *death by violence* (οἶτος) (oidheadh, oidhidh P. O'C.) : ni fess an oidhead coranic Lugaid *their death was not known till L. came*, acc. sg. óedid (MS. oedig), áidid Prol. 49. n. pl. oitte O'Curry Lect. 587.

óei, umlaut of the diphthong óe : nocime Prol. 338. nocim Aug. 12. cló́eine Ep. 424. cocircch Feb. 9. docine Ep. 152.

óen, áen *one* (=oinos, únus) Jan. 21. dat. sg. Ep. 20. Compounded : oenchói, aenchae June 10. óeulith Jan. 20. Feb. 26. June 14. Aug. 23.

Oengus, gen. sg. oengusa, Pref. n. dat. oengus, Pref. 46. Oengus céle dé, the alleged author of the Félire, Mar. 11, where his name occurs in the text both in A and B. The true reading is possibly this : It coimti ar fladat isind flaith uas flaithib librén senán suthain constantin rí raithin. W. Ungust, Lib. Land. 201. Latinised Aeneas, Ir. Gl. No. 342.

óentu, s. m. *unitas*, Z². 225. (W. undawd), gen. sg oentath, ointad ib. dat. oentid 256. acc. sg. óentaid (ms. oentaig) Pref.

Oenu, moeu loigse, second abbot of Clonmacnois, Jan. 20. Reeves' Col. 211. ⁸.

óg, úag, adj. *perfect, virginal*, gen. sg. f. óige, húaige, Mar. 17. s.f. *virgin*, gen. sg. uage, áighe, Oc. 4. dat. sg. óig, úaig Feb. 16. acc. pl. ógu, uaga Sep. 20. = oga gl. virgines, Gild. see uag. Compounds : óg-céssad, huag-césad, June 6.

oi for ai : iloind, Dec. 15. coindlech, Dec. 16. coibtell, Ep. 100.

ói, umlaut of ó : póil, antóin, bróige.

óiblech, adj. *sparkling* (W. ufelawg) Nov. 26, gen. sg. n. óiblig, áiblig. Prol. 80 (.i. alaiun no solustu, O'Dav. 105), acc. sg. m. (n. ?) oiblech, aiblech Sep. 21. The acc. pl. of the noun whence óiblech is derived occurs in the Trip. Life, Eg. 1 b, rothuim a laim isin uisci 7 dorep(r)ensat cóic banna a mérail[b] patricc 7 doronai coic oibli dib focétóir *he dipt his hand into the water and five drops flowed from P.'s fingers, and he made five sparks thereof at once.*

Oiblen, gen. sg. oiblein, Pref. n.

oid, s. f. *heed, care*, June 1, where oid menman is = oid menmain (gl. ecce) Ml. 24 c. 13. Compare tabair det óid (gl. intellige) LB. 72 a. 9. intan doshéra dia oid saine cech datha friaruile dib, LB. 108 a.

oifrend, s. m. (n. ?) *a mass*, borrowed (like W. offeren) from offerre : gen. pl. oifrend, nifrend, aifrenn, Ep. 177.

óige, s. f. *virginity* = óge, Z². 247. gen. sg. Ep. 131. dat. sg. óighi, Ep. 107, 131 B.

Oileeb, Pref. 79.

Oimne (if this be the reading) a man's name, Oc. 12.
óinme, Oc. 2. onme, Oc. 12 seems (notwithstanding the notes) an adverb meaning *together* or *at the same time*. In the Martyrology of Tallaght, p. xxxv, we have oinmine glossed by simul and by Ginllan. dialotar incóicter eucaiseom ïón óinme : *when the five men went to him at the same time*. LU. 77ᵃ. onnue .i. inalle, O'Dav. 110. óinne .i. maille O'Cl.
oipne, oibne, s.f. *subdeaures* (deriv. from opunn), acc. sg. May 30, Nov. 4, where in Three Ir. Gl. 137 opni is glossed by ferg *anger*.
oirdnide, p. part. p. *ordinatus, electus*, Pref. B. = oirdnithe Z². 479, oirdnibliu .i. ongthu (gl. christo) Ml. 48ᵇ.
oirther = s. m. *eastern part, forepart*, gen. sg. (or loc. sg. ?) oirthir (airthair B. airthir D) Dec. 9. acc. sg. arindi atrefea nirther (gl. eous) *because he inhabits the East*, Z². 275. airther also means *a person dwelling in the East*, n. pl. airthir " anteriorum qui scotice indairthir nuncupantur," Reeves Col. 204.
1. ol, *saith*, Pref. 96, 97, 98. so in Z. 602. 991 : ol. ihu *inquit Jesu*, olse *inquit ille*, ol cess *inquit pes*.
2. ol, conj. *because, for*, Z². 715. Prol. 14. 26. 259. Ap. 11. June 26. Ep. 42. 330. 335. 379. 382. 534. 554. In Ap. 30 ol seems to mean *and* (ol .i. ocus, O'Dav. 109) or *therefore*. In Ep. 399. it seems to mean *yet*.
olc, adj. *bad*, dat. sg. n. ule, Ep. 422. 443. n. pl. n. uile, Z². 226. acc. pl. m. ulcu, ib. 227 : see elc.
oll, adj. *great, ample* (= πολλός, Lat. poll-ex ὁ μέγας δάκτυλος). compar. uilliu pref. B. huilliu *plus* Z². 273. Hence ollaigthe (gl. amplion) Ml. 70ᶜ. no ollaiged (gl. ampliauit) Ml. 61ᵃ. Compounds : oll-chésad. s. *a great passion*, Dec. 2. oll-muir, s. n. *a great sea*, Feb. 17. so oll-ár, *a great slaughter*, oll-arbhar *a great troop*, O'Cl.
-om, -am (from -um) infixed pron. *me, to me*, con-om-raib, con-am-rafb *ut mihi sit*, Prol. 11.
omun, omon, oman (= W. ofn. Gl. K.N. 191), s. *fear* (.i. ecla O'Dav. 109), acc. sg. July 5. Ep. 202. compound unr-omun q.v. Hence nammigiu *terreo*.
on, s. *blemish* (.i. ainim O'Dav. 109), = W. anaf) acc. sg. Pref. 40, cen on cen ainim Tir. 11.
Onchu (son of Blathmac B), gen. onchon, July 9 : see Three Ir. Gl. 133. s. v. membro.
ónd, ón, *from the*, Prol. 325. March 15, Ep. 1.
onoir, s.n. *honour*, dat. sg. Pref. B.
Onorátus, Ep. 261 : this is probably Honoratus, bishop and confessor, whose day in Ob. and Mart. is xii Kal. Jan.
óoc, s. adj. (= W. ieuanc. Corn. iouenc, jouone, 2 Beitr. 162 = juvencus *a youth*. Eng. young), gen. pl. óoc, óuc Sep. 22. where it is a dissyllable. The oldest form is óac: Sg. 38ᵃ. Z². 812. cid óac in duine, Sg. 38ᵃ. ni theit oac and re siun, LU. 131ᵇ. Comparative oa = W. iau, superl. oam = W. ieuaf. The subst. óc. like the Latin iuvenis, often means simply *a soldier* (cf. magnâ iuvenum stipante catervâ, Aen. i. 497, iuvenum manus, ib. vi. 6, iuvenum corpora, Liv., lib. 1, c. 31. Hence O'Clery : oig [leg. óic] .i. gaisgeadhaigh.
opair, s. = *opera*, Corm. 33, acc. sg. Ap. 12.
or for ar, conj., *for*, Ap. 11 B.
ór, conj. *for, because*, Pref. B.
ór, s. n. = *aurum*, W. aur, gen. sg. óir Prol. 80, Jan. 24, Feb. 10, Mar. 16, April 25, June 17, July 28, Nov. 11, 26, Dec. 12. Compound: firór q.v.
orbae, orba, orbba, s.n. *heritage* (Goth. arbi, 2 Beitr. 173) Jan. 8: so in 1 S.M. 136, gen. sg. orpi Tir. 6. O'Dav. 109, explains orba by feranu. ind flaith issed a orbae, St. P. cf. comarba, indarpu.
orcaim *I slay*, 3d sg. t-pret. ro-dus-ort-sam Prol. 57 (where ort is for orct), ro-órt *delevit*, Ml. 48ᵃ, pret. pass. 3d sg. ort Oc. 22. 3d pl. orta, ortai, Prol. 36, 65, Jan. 26, 3d sg. 2dy pres. pass. orta Mar. 6, Sep. 7. See asore, ascomore supra, and cf. Skr. arça.
ord, s.m. *order* (Br. urz, W. urdd) Pref. 12, Prol. 333. Ep. 101. gen. uirdd, uirt Z². 60. dat. sg. urd, Prol. 279. acc ord-n, Prol. 314, 332, in ordd cóir (gl. in ordinem) Z². 235.

órdae, adj. *golden*, Ep. 250.
ordan, orddan, s. *preeminence, supremacy, sovranty, primacy*, Prol. 96, 121, Feb. 6, 22, Mar. 23. Fiacc h. 25. dat. sg. ordun, ordan, ordon, Prol. 276, Mar. 30, acc. sg. ordan, Mar. 15, gen. pl. ordan-n Dec. 27. Ep. 208, 256. In Ult. h. 7 (con orddain adbail) ordan is declined as if it were fem. Compounds, see cáin-ordan, dag-ordan. O'Dav. explains ordan by uasal.
organ, s.m. = organum, W. organ, *instrument*, Mar. 12.
orlau, adj. for forlan q.v.
oscar, s.m. *an ignorant, inexperienced person*, (osgar .i. aneolach O'Dav. 109), dat. pl. oscraib, Ep. 77, dat. sg. dond oscar (gl. idiotae) Z. 232, oscar cách i cerd araili *ignorant is every one in another's art*.
osnad, s.f. *a sigh*. (W. ochenaid, uchenaid), acc. pl. osnada, Ep. 326 : có osnada (gl. usque ad suspiria) Ml. 31ᵇ. acc. sg. osnaid, LU. 29ᵇ. dat. pl. trom-osnadaib, LU.
Osualt, Aug. 5, *Oswald*, a king of the Northumbrians, slain by Penda, the Southumbrian, at Maserfield, A.D. 511, " whose holiness and miracles were afterwards variously made known throughout this island," A.S. Chronicle ed. Thorpe.

p for b in loan words: Iacóp, Parthalon, Barnaip, Morepus, Sapaist: for pb : pilip, Oc. 18, in certain forms of the verb biu : rop, ropu, ciaptar : napta, níptar (poi *fuit* seems to occur on two Ogamic inscriptions): after r and l (comarpi, gulpan): after d and th in composition : (topur, epiur).
pairt s. = pars (Corn. 36) W. and Corn. parth, Br. parz. *a tome*, Ep. 137. gen. pl. partae, Ep. 136. dat. pl. fotbúilliud in ilpartib, LU. 69ᵇ.
paiss, pais, s.f. = passio, undeclined, nom. sg. Jan. 14, Feb. 24, Ap. 24, May 9, 30, June 20, 26, 28, July 2, 21, 22, Oc. 1, 20, Nov. 5, Dec. 1, gen. sg. Aug. 26, dat. Mar. 2, 3, May 4, July 26, acc. Jan. 26, Feb. 19, 24, Mar. 25, May 31, June 11, Aug. 9, 23, Sep. 17, Oc. 2, 8, 18, 22, Dec. 7.
Pampil, Aug. 20, Pamphilus a martyr or confessor at Synnada in Phrygia, Boll.
Pancratius, Dec. 1 (Pancrazio, Pancras), beheaded temp. Diocletian.
Pantaleon of Nicomedia, a martyr, July 28, Sep. 22. The P. mentioned at July 28, is celebrated in Boll. at July 27.
pardus s.m. = pardisus (W. paradwys, Br. baradoes), gen. sg. parduis, Tur. dat. sg. pardus, parrdus Ep. 39.
Parmenius, an Alexandrian martyr, July 7, Dec. 2.
Parthalon, Parrthalon, Parrtalon = Bartholomaeus the apostle, June 13, Aug. 25, Bartholon (gen.-oin LU. 15.), mac Sera.
Pátricc, Pátraic, Pátraicc = Patricius, undeclined, nom. Mar. 17, Nov. 2, gen. Prol. 171, Ap. 5, May 2, 28, Nov. 27, dat. Ap. 14, acc. Ep. 278, 551.
Pauliu, Aug. 31=S. Paulinus ep. Trevirensis, in Phrygia, Boll. Paulinus, Oc. 14, ep. in Cantia, Boll.
Paulus, a bishop, Jan. 29, an African martyr, Feb. 19, June 26. The Paulus (Pól) celebrated at June 7, was Patriarch of Constantinople (Boll.). The Paulus (Pól) celebrated at June 20, was martyred at Tomae in Scythia, Boll. As to the Paulus mentioned at June 26, see Johannes.
pauper, s.m. .i. bocht, O'Cl. pl. puipir, S.M. III. 18. Hence the diminutive
pauperán, s.m., Ep. 408, *a mendicant* (bhikshu).
peccad, s.m. (= peccátum, W. pechod, Corn. peghes, Br. pechet) Ep. 460, gen. sg. pectho, Z². 239, gen. pl. peethe-n, Tur. dat. pl. peethaib Ep. 460 B.
Pelait, Pilait. *Pilate*, undeclined, Prol. 85, gen. Prol. 126 (piláit, O'Cl. pioláit, is from palatium).
Perpetua, Mar. 7 (" dispersos capillos infibulavit ; non enim decebat martyrem dispersis capillis pati, ne in sua gloria plangere videretur ") Nov. 4 = Vivia Perpetua, Jameson, S. & L. Art. 564.

persa, s. from *persona* (with change to the n-declension), Pref. 2, 3, 90, n. pl. persin, Z^2. 245.
Petar=Petrus, gen. sg. petair, Prol. 109, 116, Jan. 11, 18, Feb. 22, Ap. 12, 17, June 29, Aug. 1, B. Nov. 18, acc. petar Ep. 245, 254, 515, 535. In Nov. 4 the Latin gen. Petri is used. As to Deacon Peter commemorated at Ap. 17, see Reeves' Columba, 304. He was martyred at Antioch.
Petronilla, Patroinilla, Paternélla, May 31, daughter of S. Peter, Jameson, S. & L. A. 210.
ph for infected b: saph Oc. 17, Mo-phiéc, Dec. 16.
pian, s.f.=*poema* (W. poen, Br. poan), gen. sg. péine, péne, Prol. 118, dat. péin, Z^2. 243, n. pl. piana, Prol. 74, 88, Z^2. 244, acc. pl. piana, Mar. 28, May 5, Oc. 19.
Pictavi, Jan. 13, now Poitou.
Pilipp, Pilip=Philippus the apostle, not declined, Ap. 22, gen. sg. May 1, Oc. 18: episcopus et martyr, Firmi in Piceno (Boll.) Oct. 22.
pit, s.f. (Corm. s.v. fogamur) in terc-phit q.v. pid .i. proind bec, L.Lec. Voc. 537, ferr do anmain in phit bee min quam in phit mór annain, LB. 11ᵃ. gen. sg. tormach pite. ib. W. peth. See Romance words in Diez s.v. pito.
plág, s.f., *plague*, (W. pla), gen. sg. pláige, Ep. 492.
plágaim, *I plague*, 3d pl. pret. pass. rophágtha, Prol. 234.
pleo, s. Ep. 258, probably a loan from the low-Latin blavium *wheat*. Compare Matth. 3, 12. 13, 30. Luke 3, 17.
Pól=Paulus, Prol. 119. Jan. 25. Ep. 247. gen. póil, Prol. 23. Feb. 25. June 7, 20, 29. Aug. 22. Nov. 18. Z^2. 223. see Seu-pól.
Pól, deochain Ap. 13 : A martyr named Paulus is mentioned at this day by Boll. But he does not appear to have been a deacon. Can Oengus have intended Deacon Papylus, martyred at Pergamos, and also celebrated on 13 Ap.?
Pól, martir, June 7, bishop of Constantinople, Oh. and Mart. p. 123.
Polio, Palio, Pullio (leg. Pollio 'lector in Cibaliis et Martyr, Boll.) May 29.
Policarpus, Poilicarpus, (leg. Polycarpus) bishop of Smyrna Jan. 26, Dec. 7, burnt alive temp. Marcus Aurelius.
Policronius (leg. Polycronius) Mar. 20, bishop of Babylon, stoned temp. Decius.
Pont Philait, Phelait, *Pontius Pilate*, Prol. 85, 126 (pont .i. borb, O'Cl.)
popul, s.m.=*populus* (W. pobl), gen. sg. popuil Prol. 115, p. 12, Ml.—37. Z^2. 225, dat. popul, Nov. 26. Compound, see cain-popul.
port, s.m. = *portus*, Corm. 35. dat. sg. purt, Ep. 187. acc. sg. port, Tir. 13.
Praxedes, gen. sg. pais fraxidis, fraxitis, July 21, probably the well-known Roman virgin, (Jameson S. and L. Art. 622). But Oengus regards the name as that of a male.
predchim, Z^2. 434,=*praedico*, 3d sg. imperf. pridchai, Prol. 164.
precept, s.f.=*praeceptum*, May 1, gen. sg. precepte Z^2. 242, dat. precept 243, acc. precept-n 214, n. pl. precepta 244. W. pregeth.
prím (W. prif)=primus, occurs in the following compounds :—
  prím-airce prím-airece, s. *first finding*, May 3.
  prím-chésad, s.m. *chief suffering*, Oc. 15.
  prím-drecheng, prím-trecheng, s. *chief champion-triad*, Nov. 28.
  prím-féil, s. *chief festival*, June 10. nom. dual, May 31.
  prím-locc, s.m. *chief place*, n. pl. prímluicc, Pref.
  prím-martir, s.m. *chief martyr*, Oc. 18.
  prím-slóg, prím-slúag, prímluag, s.m. *chief host*, Feb. 12. dat. sg. Ap. 13.
  prím-suide, s. *chief seat*, Prol. 117.
prímdae, prímda, adj. *primarius, excellent* (.i. ergna, Three Ir. Gl. 131) Mar. 7. Ap. 5. 15. Nov. 2. 4. Ep. 247. 258.
Priscus, Oc. 1, mart. Tomis in Moesia Inferiore, Boll.
Processus, July 2 : see Boll. July 2, p. 295.

prolach (brolach B) s.m. =prologus, Prol. 144. W. prol.
promaim = probo: 1 pl. conj. promam, Prol. 143. 3d pl. b-fut promfat Ep. 219, 3d pl. pret.
    pass. ropromtha, rofromtha, June 27. p. part. pass. promthae, promtha, Feb. 12. May
    9. Oc. 21. promthe in briss (gl. probus in Christo) Z². 67. W. profi, Br. prouffafl.
Protasius, May 20, June 19. see Gervasius.
Prothus, Sep. 11=Protus, see Iacinthus.
púdar (gl. error) pref. means *hurt, harm, injury*, gen. púdra, borrowed from *pútor*: ni dernai
    pudar dóib *it, the poison, did them no harm*, Goidel. 134. crochad pylipp pudar mór
    I"s crucifixion, a great harm, Harl. 1802. 9. b. bid lanpudar LU. 56ª. ann romaoite an
    mor-phúalhar *there the great injury was inflicted*, Circ. of Ireland, 98. is lethfinach dia ti
    pudur de *it is half fine if injury comes from it*, 1 S.M. 178. mad fofath pudra doguether
    if it be done for purpose of injury, ib. In the Highlands the adj. pudharnch means 1.
    damnosus, 2. *ulcerosus*.
Purtinatus (Fortunatus B.) Aug. 23.

Quadratus, Cadratus, Ap. 9. Quadrati sanguis dicitur adhuc remanere, Boll., referring to ms.
    Tamlactense.
Quintinus, Oc. 31, son of Zeno, martyred at Augusta Veromanduorum (now St. Quintin in
    Belgium), Butler and U's.
Quintus, a martyr, Aug. 26: a Lucanian martyr (U's.), Oc. 29.
Quiricus, Ciricus, gen. Ciricii, Ep. 265 B. see Ciric, Giric.
Quirinus, Cirinus, Ap. 30, a Roman martyr, Ob. and M. 111. St. Quirinus Episcopus in
    coemeterio Romano Praetextati, Boll.

r corresponds with the r of the other Indo-European languages: rádiu, ri, rigim, rún, sruaim, dair.
-rad (see caratrad, drochrad, ingenrad, macrad, rígrad), is used to form abstract substantives,
    Z². 856.
rád, s. *a saying*, Jan. 18.
-rádiu, -ráidiu (= Goth. rodja), *I say, I relate*, Ep. 358. 2d sg. pres. indic. act. no-rádi, Feb.
    18, 3d sg. ni radi ni tri thalmadchi *amal dundchuirethar inna beulu non loquitur quid
    repentine prout adlescicit in labia sua*, Ml. 35d: radid ncheist *he tells his quest*, Táin bó
    Fráich : intan radar nech insci a belrai fesin, Ml. 42ª: 2d sg. imper. ráid, Sep. 17,
    Nov. 19, emphatic form, ráite Dec. 18. 1st sg. s-pret. ro-ráidius, Jan. 29, 2d sg. ro-ráidis
    (= roradis gl. dixisti; Rawl. 505) Jan. 9 : part. fut. pass. ráti (raite) Ap. 9.
1. raith, s. *grace, prosperity*, in the phrase dia raith-sium *for his sake. on his behalf*, Ep. 165.
    Raith no doráith .i. arsou, O'Cl. Compare rath infra.
2. raith, raid *cucurrit*, Sep. 19, Oc. 16, Nov. 22 D., .i. doreimnigh no docheimnigh, O'Cl. 3d sg.
    redupl. pret. of rithim, q. v. The 3d pl. is rathatar, Sep. 18.
ráith, s. f. *a stronghold, fort*, Prol. 177, gen. sg. rátha Prol. 200 B. dat. hir-ráith chungi, Lib.
    Arm. 11 b. 2 : acc. pl. rathi ib. 6 b. 1. The acc. sg. of the Gaulish form of this word—
    ratin—seems to occur on the Poitiers stone.
Ráith Cruachan, Prol. 177, now Ratheroghan, near Belanagare, co. Roscommon.
rán, adj. *very splendid*, ran-togu, Jan. 6, rán baile, Ap. 20, rán clochar, Aug. 15. gen. sg. m.
    imrordus ríg richbi ráin, LU. 40ª. voc. sg. tucc a rí rán do grad cogribh, *give, O noble
    King, thy love quickly!* Goidil. 94, gen. pl. rán, Sep. 19. ran .i. maith no togaide, LLec.
    Voc. 134 : probably from ro + áu, as rard, *very high*, and rísil, *very low*, are formed
    from ro-ard and ro-ísil, Gl. 610, 611.
ránic (ro-ánic), *venit*, May 2, Ep. 17. See ic.
1. rann, rand, s. f. *part, share*, Prol. 258, gen. sg. rainne, Z². 242. acc. rainn-n, ib. 244. Com-
    pounds, see droch-rann. W. rhan.

2. rann, rand, s. m. *a quatrain, verse*, dat. sg. runn, rund, LU. 6ᵇ, but rann, Pref. dat. pl. rannaib Prol. 38, Dec. 21, acc. pl. rannu, LU. 40ᵃ. Compounds, see leth-rann.
ráth, s.n. *grace, favour* (W. rhad) May 15, gen. sg. raith, Aug. 18, Z². 223, dat. sg. rath Nov. 5, and cf. ro rath, Prol. 99, n. pl. ratha Pref. acc. pl. ratha ib. Hence rathach, rathmar.
1. ráith, s. n. *stronghold, fort*, gen. sg. ráith, Prol. 200, n. pl. rátha. Prol. 176.
2. ráith, s. m. *a guarantor, surety*, Ep. 164, 165.
rathach, adj. v. il-rathach.
rathaigim, *I perceive*, 3d sg. s.pret. abs. rathaigis, Pref. B. Cognate with raith, *percepit*, Beitr. vii. 12, which Windisch (Beitr. viii. 11) connects with Goth. frathja *verstehe, erkenne*.
rathatar, *cucurrerunt*, Sep. 18, v. rithim.
Rathin, Raithin, gen. sg. Mar. 11, May 14, Nov. 28, now Rahin, near Tullamore, in King's County, where there was a celebrated monastery, as to which see Petrie R. T. 242, 243.
rathmar, adj. *gracious* (W. rhadfawr), gen. sg. m. rathmair, Ep. 235. voc. sg. m. rathmar (for rathmair), Ep. 458.
re=Skr. *ri*, in do-breth (suffix tá), sreth (suffix ti).
ré, ria, prep. cum dat. *before*, Prol. 340, Jan. 1, Mar. 12, July 15, Nov. 13, Dec. 24.
réa (?) gen. sg. v. Duibréa.
recht, s. m. (also n.), *law*, gen. rechto Z². 230, dat. recht Sep. 10 B (riacht A), acc. recht-n, Jan. 1, cen recht, Pref. n. pl. recte Z². 240. W. rhaith, Lat. rectus, Goth. ruihts, 2 Beitr. 168.
recomarc, s. *a dissyllable* (Corm. G. s. v. déach), Pref. 53.
réde, s. f. *smoothness*, gen. sg. réde (rédi A.), Prol. 120, acc. rédi, Ep. 132.
rega, *I will come*, regmai, *we will come*, Prol. 291, do-ragat, *they will come*, Ep. 115.
reiclés, s. *a little cell* (roclusum), dat. sg. Pref. B., Reeves' Col. 277, dub-reicles *cellula nigra*.
réid, adj. *smooth, easy* (W. rhwydd ?), Nov. 18 B, Ep. 133, dat. sg. m. Nov. 28. See soréid.
réid-riunard, s. *easy rinnard*, Pref. 55: cf. ni réid chene gl. magnus poeta Virgilius fuit, *not easy, however*, Sg. 238ᵇ.
réil, adj. *clear, manifest*, Nov. 18, gen. sg. a rí richid réil, LL. 19 a. v. See ro réil.
réim, rém, s. n. *cursus*, Prol. 107, 306, Jan. 18 B, 21, July 23, Ep. 54, acc. sg. réim Z². 269, Oc. 16. From *ran-men?
rélad, s.m., *manifestation*, dat. sg., Prol. 278, -réla *manifestat*, Z². 434.
relic, relice, reilic, s. (gl. simitherium), *graveyard*, Ap. 16, 'a reliquiis sanctorum,' says Cormac.
rem, *ante* = Lith. pirm *vor* (Windisch in Curtius, G. E. No. 380). Hence
remain, adj., *preëminent*, Jan. 1, 31, gen. sg. m. Sep. 19, acc. sg. Ep. 6 (where it is used as a subst.), acc. dual f. Mar. 3.
remthechtas, s. *a preceding*, gen. sg. remthechtais Pref.
reraig, s. *patriarch*, P. O'C.'s rearaidh .i. seanóir no duine aosta, *a senior or aged man*, nom. pl. reraig, faithi cen dibad, Colm. h. 44, gen. pl. reraig, reraich, Ep. 237, (where B has rerach l. riarach), remthus rerig, LU. 104ᵇ. The declension is quite irregular.
resmai, *ivvrimus*, Prol. B. 257, 1st pl. s-fut. act. of rega.
rét, s. m. *thing*, Z. . 238, Pref. gen. sg. réto, acc. pl. rétu Z². 442.
réthannach (leg. rétglannach?), adj., *starry*, July 29 B, from
rétlu (leg. rétglu?), retla, s. f. *star*, Feb. 10, retla (gl. stella), Ir. Gl. gen. sg. retlainde, LU. 36ᵃ. n. pl. (irregularly) retlainne July 29 (rétglanna in the Franciscan copy), retlanna in Rawl. 505), acc. dual dí réthaind, da retlainn, Mar. 3 B (but da retgla in the Franciscan copy), gen. pl. rétland LU. 36ᵃ. acc. pl. nóairmebad retlanna nime, *he would reckon heaven's stars*, LU. 11ᵇ. dat. pl. retglannaib, St. Paul codex.
rí, s.m. (=rex, Gaul. rix, reix) Z². 259, Jan. 1, g.n. sg. ríg, Prol. 27, 187, Dec. 14, Ep. 18, 61, 91, 96, 159, 161, 235, 398, dat. sg. rig, June 19, acc. sg. rig-n, Prol. 22, 93, Jan. 26, Ep. 46, voc. sg. ri, Prol. 4, 7, 10, Ep. 37, n. pl. ríg, Prol. 83, 149, Ep. 85, gen. pl. rig-n, Aug. 15, Sep. 19, dat. pl. rígaib, Prol. 36, 52, Jan. 27, Oc. 9, acc. pl. ríga, Sep. 9, Ep. 32 B and D, 36. Compounds: ard-rí, gorm-rí, óc-rí, and

ríg-epscop, s.m. *king-bishop*, Ap. 14.
ríg-féil, s.f. *royal feast*, Nov. 29.
ríg-flaith, ríg-laith, s.f. *royal kingdom*, Oc. 23, Dec. 14, Ep. 334 : *royal Prince*, Ep. 310.
ríg-gein, s. *royal birth*, June 24.
ríg-macc, s.m. *royal son, prince*, gen. sg. ríg-maicc Aug. 16, acc. sg. ríg-macc-n Nov. 22.
riacht, Sep. 10, is possibly = riacht (i.e., ro-sincht *assecuta est*, Z. 445, a t-preterite like doriacht. In B, however, the reading is recht .i. soiscela.
riachtain (richtain A.) s. *a reaching*, acc. sg., Mar. 12.
ring, s. f. *a gibbet, torture*, July 2, gen. sg. bithnitreb péne 7 rege, LU. 17ᵇ. acc. pl. ringa, Feb. 23, Oc. 19, (gl. patibulum). Z. 21 .i. césad, O'Dav. 11. régh .i. croch, dobenrar é dochum a réghe .i. dochum a chroiche, O'Cl. roriaghadh .i. do erochadh, ibid.
1. ríagail, s.f. *a rule* (regula, W. rheol)Pref. 40. riagoil Z². 226. dat. sg. Ep. 96. = riagoil Z². 243,
2. riagail, (riga, B.) Ep. 32, seems = reguli.
Riagail of Mucinis, Oc. 16. Riaguil of Tech Riagla, Sep. 17.
riam, adv. *aforetime, formerly*, Z. 568. Prol. 52, where it is a dissyllable.
1. ría-n, prep. enm dat. *before*, Prol. 248. Ep. 64. also ré-n, q.v. riana-n *before their*, Prol. 31 B.
2. ría-n for fria-n, Ep. 107.
riar, s.f. *will, liking*, acc. sg. réir Pref. 57 B., Prol. 269 B, perhaps from *prērā, root pri.
riarach, s. Ep. 237 B.
riched, s.m. (n. ?) *heaven*, gen. sg. atrab ind richith, Book of Dimma, dat. sg. richiud, Feb. 23, acc. riched Prol. 6, 120, May 22, July 7, Sep. 18, Nov. 6, Ep. 54, 222, 311, 466. Compounds: ard-riched q.v. Coguate with richis (gl. carbo) Z². 273.
richt, s.m. (n. ?) *form* (W. rhith), dat. sg. richt Pref. B. O. Ir. dat. hir-riucht essu *in formā Esau*, Tur.
richtain, s. *a reaching*, dat. sg. Mar. 12, Ep. 223.
ríguim, *I make a king, I crown*, 3d sg. pret. pass. rorígad, Prol. 104, May 18, Aug. 25, Ep. 263. 3d pl. rorigtha, Prol. 235.
rigain, s.f. *regina*, Prol. 125, gen. sg. rigna July 11, 18, dat. sg. rigain Prol. 105. gen. pl. rignæ, St. Paul codex.
rigan, s.f. *regina*, Corm. 39, Sep. 20, and see óe-rígan.
rigdae, rigda, adj. *kingly, royal*, Feb. 9, Mar. 5, Ap. 10, Aug. 4. gen. sg. m. rígdai, July 2, Nov. 18. acc. sg. Mar. 4, Ap. 16, Ep. 260, nom. pl. rígdai July 29.
ríge, s. n. (m. ?) *kingdom*, Prol. 158, gen. sg. rígi Feb. 6, Oc. 8, 22, dat. sg. rigiu, Ep. 359, rign Jan. 23, acc. sg. rige-n Prol. 70, Jan. 16.
rigrad, s t. *king-folk, kingry*, Prol. 13, 20, 82, 278, Ep. 41, 300, 564, dat. sg. rigraid Prol. 12, Dec. 23, acc. sg. rigraid Prol. 21, 271, July 13, Nov. 10, Ep. 229, 301, rigrad Ep. 565.
rím, s.n. (W. rhif) *a counting, numbering*, Prol. 268, gen. rímæ, Z². 935 n. Hence rímire *computator* ibid., and
rímim, *I reckon*, 2d sg. depon. rimther Prol. 286. Ep. 46. 3d sg. pret. pass. rorímed Mar. 18. Compare ad-rímiu, do-rímin supra and aram *numerus*.
1. rind, s. m. *a point, headland*, (W. rhyn *promontory*), in riund *aculeus*, Z². 64. (gl. cacumen) Ir. Gl. p. 117, acc. pl. rindi Ap. 26, rinde Aug. 27, dat. pl. rindib, rinnib Prol. 37, 238, renna 7 benna aunsanna do armaib, H. 3. 18, p. 51 b.
2. rind, s. n. acc. pl. rinde Ep. 84, seems here to mean *harmonized melodies*: Rinn .i. [cool]co-cuibdius ina aghaidh, *melody with harmony over against it*, O'Dav. 110. Rinn .i. colus. ut est aircital .i. in rind robui ac Amirgin 7 ic Roighne rinn aire 7 rinn molta, O'Dav. 111. Rinn .i. cool, Rinn .i. cos, rinne .i. cos, O'Cl.
3. rind, s. *a star*, Jan. 30, Z². 233. Rinn .i. relta, rinn solus .i. relta solusta, O'Cl.
rindach, rinnach, adj. *starry*, acc. sg. m. (n.?), May 22, from 3. rind, q.v.
rindard, rinnard (rind+ard), s.f. the name of the metre in which the Félire is written, Pref. gen. sg. rinnairde, dat. rinnaird, ib.
rindmas, adj. *beautiful with constellations*, Ep. 378.

rinduem, s.n. *starry heaven*, dat. sg. rindnim, May 29 : Rinn-nimh .i. neamh rennach no rèltanach, O'Cl.

ringim, *I torture*, 3d sg. pret. pass. roringed, Feb. 14 (.i. roriagad, Rawl. 505), 3d pl. roringthe, Prol. 37.

rith, s.m. *a running, course, race, career*, Prol. B. 28, dat. sg. dind riuth *de cursu*, Z. 211, n. pl. retha, Ep. 274, dat. pl. rethib, Prol 69 B. W. rhed.

rithim, *I run* (Lith. ritù *ich rolle*, Windisch), rethi *curris*, rethess *qui currit*, rethit *currunt*, Z². 429, 430, 3d sg. redupl. pret. raith, raid, Jan. 6, Sep. 19, Oc. 16, Nov. 22 D. 3d pl. rathatar Sep. 18. See adreith, doreith, fris-reith.

rius, *I should come*, 1st pl. s-conj. co-risam, Dec. 17, 3d sg. 2dy. s-conj. nach-at-risad, rissed Prol. 284, 3d sg. redupl. fut. pass. rigthir (leg. rigthir) Z². 475. Compare ὀ-ρίγω, rego, e-rigo, por-rigo.

1. ro-, r', verbal prefix (=pro. Umb. pru, προ) Z⁴. 411, Prol. 29, 32, 33, 37, 84, 89, 101, ro-gbus Prol. 18, do-ro-chair Nov. 17, con-om-rai-b Prol. 11, do-r-aius Prol. 15, im-ro-rdus Prol. 20, do-ró-sat Prol. 91, do-ro-dimd Prol. 96, r-ancatar Prol. 78. có-r-bo Prol. 93, at-r-annad Ap. 5. as-r-éracht Prol. 92, ní-r-athgab Prol. 107, cota-r-nieset May 8. do-r-ortad May 27. With infixed pronouns : ro-m-berthar Prol. 3, ro-mm-ain Prol. 18, ro-n-beth Prol. 241, ro-n-bia Jan. 13, ro-n-snádat Jan. 23, ro-n-ain Aug. 28, ro-s-tuirius June 26, ro-dau-ort-sam Prol. B. 57, ro-dus-ort-sam Prol. A. 57, ro-tus-crochsat Prol. 73.

2. ro-, r', intensive prefix, Z². 864, Glück K.N. 67. see rochned, rochnet, roe, roglach, rolaind, romaith, romar, romuir, romith, roreil, rotenu, ráu.

roach, s. Ep. 129 .i. roseacha tindain no roseacha briathar, O'Dav. 110 and O'Don. Supp. icthar a leth do rathaib do roachaib, Senchas Már, iii. 6. Meaning doubtful : possibly *multiloquium* or *verbositas*, ex ro-fach or ro-sach ?

rochned (ro-chned), s.f. *a great wound*, acc. sg. rochneid, Aug. 28.

rochnet (ro-chnet), s.f. *a great sigh*, dat. sg. rochneit, Ep. 171.

rochtain, s. *a reaching*, Aug. 4 A. (the other mss. have richtain, richtu).

Rodauis, Rodamais, leg. Rhodonis, gen. sg. of Rhodon, Jan. 3.

róe, roi, s.f. (.i. magh, O'Cl.) *field, arena, battle*, ind roi, Ml. 133ᵇ (rue .i. fearann, rae .i. cath, O'Cl.) gen. sg. fobith na roe fochtae *because of the foughten field* 1 S.M. 250, dat. sg. roi, Feb. 14. isind roi (gl. scammate) Lib. Hymn. 3. W. rhae.

róe, (dissyll.) adj. *very sharp* (ro-aith) according to the glossographer : acc. pl. roi, Ap. 26, roe, Aug. 27.

roen, s.m. *road*, acc. pl. roenu May 27, June 19, Ep. 322. mor naithe udermarai dorochratar bir-menu romaidmai indásin, LB. 266 a. Lata et speciosa est via quae ducit ad mortem .i. as lethon sochair in raon gabthar cusan ubas, H. 3. 18, p. 796. doghabhadar an raon direach *they took the straight way*, O'Brien.

rogdac, adj. *chosen, choice*, Prol. 221, derived from rogu *electio*, Z². 270.

roglach (ro-galach) adj. *very valiant*, Prol. 94, gen. sg. m. roginig, Prol. 170. O'Cl., however, glosses by feargach, *wrathful*.

roiceu, *adeo*, 2d sg. s fut. rois (dissyll.) *adieris*, Ep. 146. So in Sg. 229 ni róis chluiu na coleaid.

roichim, *adeo, porrigo*, 3d sg. pres. indic. act. roich Z². 431. 3d pl. rochet. 3d sg. pres. indic. pass. roichthir (gl. porregitur) Ml. 55d. In Prol. 257 rosme may be the absolute form of the 1st pl. s-fut. act. ; but the true reading is doubtful, as B has resmai.

rolaind (ro-laind) adj. *very vehement, eager, zealous*, Mar. 12, May 21, Nov. 24.

Roma, Ep. 253, and perhaps Sep. 20. See ruam.

romaith, romaid (ro-maith), adj. *very good, excellent*, Ap. 10, Ep. 161, acc. sg. f. Sep. 17.

romár, romór (ro-mår), adj. *very great*, gen. sg. m. romair Ep. 236 ; dat. sg. f. romoir Jan. 31.

romuir (ro-muir), s.n. *a great sea*, dat. (abl.) Ep. 42, acc. sg. Nov. 3, 11, Dec. 8.

Romula, July 20. A ' Romula virgo' is commemorated in Us. at 24 June.

Ronáin, bishop, of Lessmór, Feb. 9.

Ronán of Liath-ross, April 30. Ronán Find May 22 ; Ronán mac Beraig, Nov. 18.
rop, rob, *sit*, Jan. 24, Mar. 17, Oc. 19, Dec. 19, pl. ropat Dec. 18.
ropu, *esset?* Pref. 1.
rorath (ro-rath). s. *great grace*, dat. sg., Prol. 99.
roréil (ro-réil), adj. *very clear*, dat. sg., Aug. 26.
ross, ros, s. m. .i. *a wood* Corm. 38, (vṛkshá, varesha, Bugge) : 2. *a promontory*, gen. sg. rois, ruis, Jan. 30, roiss, ruiss Sep. 6, dat. rus Ap. 10 B.
  Ross Cáin, in Cluain Fergaile in Delbna of Tír-dá-loch, Dec. 16 B, where the elements of the name are transposed (cáin rois).
  Ross Crée, Ap. 28, now Roscrea, co. Tipperary.
  Ross Eó, Ap. 10, now Rush, co. Dublin.
  Ross Glandae, Sept. 6, now Donaghmore in Tyrone, Reeves' Col. 172, from Glan, the name of a well there, Mart. Don. p. 238.
  Ross Liath, Ap. 30 = Liathros, Mart. Don. 114.
  Ross mór, Jan. 30, now Rossmore, co. Wexford.
  Ross Tuire, Sep. 17.
rosmc, see ruichim.
Rossa, gen. sg. Pref. B.
rót, s.m. = *road*, (O. Fr. rote, via *rupta*) Corm. 38, acc. pl. rotu, Prol. 29.
rothenu (ro-tenu), adj. *perrigidus*, dat. pl. rotennib, Prol. 38.
rr from rs : fuirre : for r before g and infected t and d : Parrtholon Aug. 25, parrdus Ep. 39, fairrge Ep. 536, ferrda Feb. 8, ferrdu Aug. 20.
rúad, adj. (W. rhudd, Lat. rufus from roudhus. Ohg. rót) *red*, Prol. 94, 221, dat. sg. f. ruaid Oc. 16 : see ruidiud.
Rúadún, Ap. 15. This name is prob. a dimin. of the adj. rúad. The noun ruadhan is explained as meaning *red wheat*, O'Dav. 112.
rúadgorm, adj. *fiery-red*, acc. sg. m. Ep. 260. See gorm, and cf. gormrúad an epithet for a spear, LU. 89ᵃ.
rúnim, s.f. *a burial-ground*, Prol. 195 (ruam B).
1. rúam, s.f. *a burial-ground* (cf. Goth. rûma, *raum*, *room?*) July 23, Oc. 28.
2. rúam = Róma, Corm. 39, gen. sg. ruama, Mar. 12, dat. sg. ruaim, róim Jan. 18, Mar. 4, Ap. 30, June 27, July 23, also *a city* Prol. 192, u. pl. ruama Prol. 71, 211.
rúamach, adj. *city-having*, Mar. 5, July 20 (.i. catharda, 3 Ir. Gl. 134), Aug. 6.
rúamda, adj. Ap. 16, .i. catharda no uasal *city-like or noble*, Three Ir. Gl. 131, which seems a mere guess. Can it be cognate with Goth. rûma, *roomy*, räumlich?
rúanaid, adj. .i. laidir, O'Cl. *strong*, Prol. 256. As a subst. robo dord niad 7 robo rig ruanada, LU. 59ᵇ.
ruc, rucc (ro-uc), *tulit* Aug. 6, 4 Beitr. 175, 176, ro-n-uc *quem peperit* Dec. 14, ru-s-fuc B, with prothetic f : roucc D, 3d pl. r-aucsat *tulerunt eam* Z². 464. 3d pl. pret. pass. rouctha, douetha, Prol. 45.
rudrach, s. Ep. 129 B., meaning doubtful. Possibly, like the corrupt 'ruadrac,' equivalent to rudrad, q.v.
rudrad (ro-durad) s. *great duration, prescription?* Prol. 206, where the meaning seems to be that the heathen had possessed their cities so long as to have acquired a prescriptive ownership. Ep. 129, where rudrad seems to mean *tediousness*. So in Ep. B. 145. See Corm. 39, O'Dav. 111, rúdrad .i. róduradh .i. anadh fota for tír nach aile *long remaining on another's land*, Gl. 609.
Rufin, Rupliiu A. Aug. 27 = Rufinus Marsorum episc. et mart.?
ruidiud, s. m. (u. ?) [ruidhealh .i. indeargadh O'Cl.] *a reddening, blushing*, and hence *reproof*, rudiud roálaind fo gráad cechtar na, LU. 90ᵇ. acc. sg. ruidiud Ep. 145. Cognate with rubor (ex * rufor, rudhor), ἐρύθημα. See rúad supra.

ruire, ruri, s. m. *lord, chieftain,* Z². 259, Prol. 14, ruri Colm. 29, voc. sg. a ruire, a ruri, Prol. 285, gen. sg. mathair mo ruirech Broce. h. 4, hi tig ruirech LU. 46ᵇ, dat. sg. dasind rurig LU. 91ᵃ, acc. sg. cach drong immá rig, cach réim immá rurig, cach buden immá tuseeh, gen. pl. ite seo ammandside imma rurech LU. 80ᵇ. Cognate according to Glück, K. N. 142, with Raurici n. pl. of Raurieos ; but this would be rúarech in Irish. A form rurech occurs in the nom. sg. bamsa rurech do thretaib tore berend, *I was lord of the herds of the wildboars of Erin,* LU. 16ᵃ.

rún, s. f. *mystery* (W. rhin, Goth. runa, 2 Beitr. 177), dat. sg. ruin, Ap. 22, acc. ruin, Z². 243, gen. pl. rúnn Z². 245, dat. pl. runaib, July 30, Nov. 20, Z². 245, acc. pl. rúna, ib. 246 and Jan. 12, B. and D.

rúnach, adj. *mysterious,* acc. sg. m. (n.?) Nov. 6, gen. sg. m. ind ríg runaig .i. ind ríg taitnemaig hicotaat rúna, Lib. Hymn. 28 b. 1.

rúnda, adj. *mysterious,* voc. sg. Ep. 458, n. pl. Ep. 274.

s initial corresponds, 1. with Greek, Latin, and Gothic s : saigim, samail, seeh, seeht, sé, sen, sreth, su- ; 2. with original sv : siuur, solus ; 3. in loanwords, with Latin f : slechtain, sroiglithe.

s seems to occur as a suffixed pers. pronoun of the 3d sing. m. in ass, fris, lais, tairis. Infixed, it menus cam (ni-s-tarca June 29, ro-s-tuirius June 26, do-s-rimemar Ep. 6) or eos (ni-s-gignetar, May 19, no-s-tuirfem, Prol. 289, no-s-molammar Jan. 17, fo-s-dail July 15). A form with a nasal occurs in ro-sm-lé Ep. 56 B. It sometimes stands for the infixed relative -sn : la-s-r-orta Prol. 65 B, la-s-r-ort Prol. B.

-sa, -sea, -se, a demonstrative adverb used (1) after a substantive or adjective (in rig-sa, in slóg-sa, Prol. 27, 28, na mís mór-sa, Prol. 301, druing-sea, Ep. 285, iarsinm-baig-se, Ep. 315), and (2) to strengthen the 1st pers. sg. (am trög-sa Prol. 26, ro beo-sa Prol. 271, trim-sa Dec. 18, mo der-sa Ep. 400).

1. **sab, saph,** adj. *firmus,* Oc. 17, Dec. 14 : cf. Fiacc's h. 23. O'Clery writes sab (with uninfected b) .i. sonairt *firm,* no láidir, *strong.*
2. **sab, saph,** s. m. Z². 255, Ap. 12, June 23, July 1, Sep. 21, Nov. 10, Ep. 272. Here the meaning is, apparently, *a champion.* The n. pl. is sabaidh, O'Dav. 114, where sabb is glossed by trenn. So sabuid .i. trén, *great or powerful persons.* O'Don. Supp.

Sabina, July 20, ex Sabino Hieronymianorum efficta, Boll.

sacart, s. m. *priest,* borrowed from sacerdos, Corn. 40, acc. sg. Ep. 548, gen. pl. Ep. 269.

Sacru, see Macru. Teach Sacru is now Sagart, near Tallaght, co. Dublin.

saegul, s. n. borrowed from saeculum : is garait ar saigul (gl. exigui temporis uita nostra est) Ml. 59ᶜ, gen. sg. saegail.

saer, s. m. *artifex, wright,* Ir. Gl. p. 132, gen. sg. sdeir, saír Aug. 14, Sep. 9. W. saer.

saethar, s. n. *labor,* Ep. 227, gen. sg. saithir, Lib. Arm. 184 b, acc. sg. saethar, Prol. 59, Ep. 298.

saichim, soigim *attingo,* gl. adeo Z². 259, *consequor,* an ā-stem (isse do-dob-saig, LU. 56ᵃ, do-scieb *persequitur,* Z². 130), 2d sg. conj. saiche Prol. 298, 318, 3d pl. s- pret. saichsiot .i. rangadar no tangadar, O'Cl. pret. part. pass. saigthe, Prol. B. 162. Root SAK.

saidbir, adj. *wealthy,* May 15, gen. sg. m. doclum laich saidbir, LU. 15ᵇ.

saidbre, s. f. *wealth,* Prol. 162, dat. sg. saidbri Nov. 9.

Saigir, gen. Saigre, Mar. 5, Saigir-Ciarain, now Seirkieran, the name of a parish near Parsonstown, King's Co.

saigthiu, a mistake for saithin, Mar. 31 A.

sáilu, s. m. (n. ?) *sea,* gen. sg. sáili, July 9 : for tuind int-saili, Petrie's Tara, 111 : cf. sál.

sáilim (v. fris-sailiu), now saoilim, *I think;* cognate with Goth. saivala, Eng. séola, soul?

-sain, a demonstrative suffix, Ep. 29, 30, 32, = -sin, q.v.

sair, adv. (s-air, cf an-air) *eastwards* Nov. 11, snaitid Liban sair siar sunchan tar cach trethain L. *will swim to east, to west, to and fro, over every sea,* LU. 39ᵇ, a nigod sairi LU. 50ᵇ.

sairde, adj. *eastern,* March 5.

sáire v. sóire.
saithe, sathe, s. m. (n. ?) *a swarm, a multitude*, Jan. 25, May 28, July 23, dat. sg. saithiu, saithin Mar. 31, acc. sg. sathe Aug. 6, dat. pl. saithib Sep. 30 : saithi .i. sochaide LLec. Voc. 113, W. haid, Br. hed
sál, s. m. (n. ?) *sea*, acc. sg. Mar. 5, Aug. 25, Sep. 10 : tar sal, O'Mulc. 276.
salland, sallann, s. (.i. radh no cantain, O'Cl.), *a saying, a singing*, Prol. 322. Root SVAR, whence A.S. svarian *to speak*, Eng. an-swer.
salm, s. m. borrowed from psalma, Prol. 218, Sep. 11, Ep. 155, gen. sg. sailm, Z^2. 231, dat. salm Z^2. 223, dat. pl. salmaib, Ep. 190 B, where A has, wrongly, the acc. salmu.
sálmuir, s. n. *mainsea*, gen. pl. salmnire, Ep. 238.
Salvator, Mar. 14, Corn. sylvador, D. 304.
-sam for -som, an intensive suffix for the 3d sg. masc. and neut. and the 3d pl. of all genders: ro-dus-ort-sam Prol. 57, it-cocm-sam, it-soer-sam, Sep. 2.
samail, s. *similitude*, Nov. 11, acc. sg. June 16. W. hafal *similar*.
Samson, Ep. 543.
Samthann, Samthand, Samdann, of Cluáin Brónaig, Dec. 19.
samuin, samain, s. f. *All Saints Day*, gen. sg. lathe na samna LU. 43ᵃ. aidchi samna LU. 126ᵃ. dat. areech samain LU. 52ᵃ. acc. sg. Nov. 1, Three Ir. Gl. 137, lathi nand resint-samfuin aile cind bliadna, LU. 44ᵃ. bahisede caise nangente *the easter of the heathen*, LU. 52ᵃ.
-san, -sa, an, the relative pronoun, for-sa-torchair Ep. 361. See an, n, and s. In form it is identical with the nom. and acc. sg. neut. of the article.
sanas, s. f. *susurrus, whisper, muttered prayer*, acc. sg. sanais, Mar. 15, Corn. hanas. For the use of the prep. fri after sanas, cf. itge frissin-deacht Z^2. 650, diucrae friusom Z^2. 651. For the use of sanas to mean *muttered prayer*, cf. Lucan 5, 104 : tacito mala vota susurro concipiunt.
sanct = sanctus, W. sant, Corn. 39, Nov. 11, Ep. 283. dat. pl. sanctaib Br. b. 94. See diau-sanct lethan.
Sanctlethan, Santlethan, June 12.
Sapaist, Sabbaist, Sabaist, Jan. 20 = Sebastianus (defensor ecclesia Romanae) mart. temp. Diocletian.
sar, s. n. (W. sar) *outrage, disgrace*, nom. sg. Z^2. 16, is mor-sa-sar-sa for coimdid nime 7 talman, Lambeth ms. (MacDornan's Gospels), dat. aramarad a slicht and cobráith ar-sár for ultu, LU. 65ᵇ. acc. sg. sar, Jan. 6, foruair sar for sochaidhi *he brought disgrace on many*, O'D. Supp. tár ib.=do-sár.
Sarán, of luis-mór, May 15, gen. saráin, Lib. Arm. 16, b, 2, A Sarán is mentioned in Lib. Arm. 16, 6, 2, as one of the principes uenerantes sanctum patricium et successores eius.
Satharn, gen. sg. din sathairn *Saturday*, Pref.
sathe, see saithe.
Saturniu, May 2=Saturninus, ' Mart. Alexandriae,' Boll.
Saul, Ep. 524, gen. sg. de lamaib sauil *de manibus Saulis*, Ml. 117.
Saxan, Sachsan, *Saxonum*, gen. pl. Aug. 5.
scarad, s. m. *separation* (W. esgaru) Ep. 368, 424, na scarad *us secedat*, Z. 708. Root SKAR, Curtius, No. 56.
sceithim, *vomo*, 3d sg. pret. sceith, Feb. 16, cognate with W. chwydu as scél with chwedl.
scél, s.n. *tidings, a saying, a story*, Feb. 20, Mar. 27, May 9, July 12, Dec. 21, Z^2. 223, n. pl. scéla Z^2. 226. and Aug. 21 D (sceoil A. and B), dat. pl. scélaib Sep. 24, Z^2. 240.
sceoil = scél supra, acc. Feb. 16, cf. the dat. ibar-scéuil-si *in nuntio vestro*, Z^2. 224, and the acc. hi nephchendil (gl. in non gentem) Z^2. 225.
sceol = scél supra, Prol. 138 A.
Sciath, name of a virgin, gen. scéithe (scethi A) Sep. 6, Mart. Don. p. 238.
Scillitae, Scellitae, Chellitae, July 17 = the Scillitani of the Ob. and Mart., twelve martyrs in Carthage.

Scire, name of a virgin, Mar. 24, Mart. Don. 86.
scith, sceith, adj. *weary*, Dec. 31, B and D.
scis. s.f. *weariness, fatigue*, dat. sg. Ep. 38. cf. íar scís imgona 7 imforrain LU. 21b. gen. sg. lotor hi tír do chor a scísi 7 do chumsanad Egerton 93, fo. 2 b, 2.
scor. s. *a multitude* (.i. iomad O'Cl. Gl.) *a herd*, dat. pl. scoraib Prol. 81.
scorim, scuirim, *I unharness, unyoke, desist*, 3d pl. s-pret. scorsit, scuirset, May 17, pres. indic. 3d pl. scorit a cairptiu, LU. 111 b, a denominative from scor (fri scor fri imthecht Z². 649) and cognate with κείρω, skiriů, etc. Curtius. No. 76.
scríbaim, *scribo*, 3d sg. s-pret. roscríb. May 6.
scríbend, s. *writing*. (Corn. scriuen, W. ysgrifen), gen. sg. scribind Pref. B. scribinnd Z². 11.
scríbnid, s.m. *a scribe*, July 8, (=W. ysgrifenydd), gen. sg. ar ainmain in scribneda *for the scribe's soul*, Cod. Maelbrigte, 156 b.
scrútaim, *scrutor*, 1st sg. s-pret. roscrútas Ep. 109, ara scrúta *ut scrutetur* Z. 680.
scuchaim, *I depart, I vanish*, 3d sg. redupl. pret. ro-scáich Prol. 121, ro firscáich supra : with suffixed pron. ro-scáich-e, Prol. 177, 193. Windisch compares A.S. scóc, O. Sax. skók *ist geschwunden*.
Scuithíne, Scothéine, Scoithíne, Jan. 2=Sguithin, Mart. Don. Tech Scuithin, now Tiscoffin, Co. Kilkenny. Mart. Tall. p. 50.
sé. *six*, May 13, nom. dual dá sé *two sixes*, (bis sex, Acu. xi. 9) July 10.
1. sech, prep. cum acc. *praeter, ultra, supra*, sech piana Mar. 28, May 5, Oc. 19, sech ingra Ep. 119, W. hep, hob. Lat. secus : sech infects in Mar. 28, May 5, (sech phiana) ; so sechani Z². 653, not sechsani.
2. sech, conj. *quatenus, siquidem, quoniam, nimirum*, Z². 717. Pref. So perhaps in Ep. B. 195.
sechim, s. *sequi, imitatione consequi* Pref. 6. See saichim supra.
Sechnall, Nov. 27. His hymn Audite omnes is printed in Todd's Lib. Hymn. pp. 1–23.
secht-n=*septem*, undeclined, June 27. gen. Prol. 2, Ap. 9, Ep. 126. dat. Oc. 10. acc. Ep. 125.
sochtae, adj. *having seven things, septenarius*, 1 S.M. 96. gen. sg. m. sechtai May 15.
sechtmoga, *seventy*, Ap. 3, Nov. 19.
Secundus, martyred in Narbona civitate. Boll., Mar. 22 : an African martyr, Nov. 15.
Segéne (=Seighin, Mart. Don.), fifth abbot of Hi, ob. A.D. 652. gen. sg. segeni, Aug. 12. ségeni, Lib. Arm. 16. b. 2. Seginius, Reeves' Col. 373, a diminutive of segh .i. agh allaid O'Cl. Gl.
seimle, semle, July 4, is perhaps =*simile-eo*, a combination of samail q.v. and the suffixed pron. e. But the reading in Rawl. 505, O'Dav. 116 and Three Ir. Gl. 133 is soimle .i. innis *declare, relate*.
séis, borrowed from Lat. sensus, Ep. 138. gen. seasa, O'Dav. 86. adgenammar a séis, Z. 682. rofes ruaim rofés séis, Amra Chol. LU. 10ª, where sess is glossed by solis .i. lis ecnai 7 fáitsine *knowledge of wisdom and of prophecy*.
séiser, sesiur, s. *six persons*, May 13.
selaim, see arsclaim.
sellaim, *I see* (W. sylhu), 2d pl. pres. pret. rosellaib *vidistis* July 4 : cf. the deponential forms r-élnebair-se *polluistis* LB. 42ª, donuinebhair, Four Masters A.D. 876, do dechabair, do dechobair *venistis* Trip. Life. tancabair, *venistis* : cf. also the s-prets. rolínsib, rodúnsib LB. 141. a. With deponential ending rodoirtsibar ib. the t-pret. rofetubar LB. 37ª, rofetalursi, ib. 49ª. Here b comes from sv (W.-ch, Goth. izvis), whence also the s of roûtis *scitis*. Cognate are silleadh .i. féghain, sillis .i. fenchais, O'Cl. gl. sella *oculos*, O'Dav. 83. s.v. forann. scall .i. súile, O'Cl.
-sem, suffixed pronoun 3d pers. Z². 326. 337. dia-tháin-sem, Ep. 524.
Semeon ('qui stetit in columpna,' Ob. and Mart. 76), gen. sg. semeoin, Jan. 5.
Semplex, semplix, July 29 = Simplicius, a Roman martyr, Ob. and Mart. 140. Boll.

sen, adj. *sen-ex, retus*, 2 Kuhn's Beitr. 165. Glück K.W. 124. compar. siniu Z². 275. Compounds: sen-chathir s.f. *retus ciritas*, n.pl. senchathraig, Prol. 205, and see Sen-Phátric, Sen-Phól.
sénaim, (W. syno), *signare, to sain, to charm*, 2d sg. imperat. Prol. 1 (sén .i. bennachad, O'Dav. 116. séona saebha .i. draoidheacht, O'Cl.), 3d sg. n=conj. ro-n-séna Mar. 28. íarn dosenad lían druidib *iron was sained by their druids*, dobretha luchta a iarn senta lais *L. brought his charmed iron with him*, Book of Ballimote cited by Hennessy, 10 Proc. R. I. A. 42. cumcumla .i. baile sentæ lasna gente a conruicced dias *a place sained by the heathen wherein two used to fight*, Gl. 186.
Senach, of Clonard, Aug. 21. of Cluain Foda fine, Mart. Don.
senad (senod, Corm.), s.m.=*synodus* (W. senedd, Corn. sened) Prol. 110. Ep. 93. gen. sg. sennid July 12, Nov. 3. senadh .i. coinnhthionól, O'Cl.
senán (gl. senecio Z². 293.), gen. Senáin, Mar. 3.
    Senán of Inis Cathaig, Mar. 1, 8.
    Senán. (=Mošensc beitheach, Mart. Don. 74.), Mar. 11.
    Senán of Laithrech Briuin, Sep. 2.
sennath, sennad, s. *persecution*, Prol. 46 : ar dufesatar asennad Ml. 24ᵇ. audumsennat (gl. persequentes me) Ml. 39ᵃ. do-sefainn, do-sephainn, *persecutus est* : cf. Skr. súd (from svand, Windisch) *to kill, to hurt ?*
Sennis, July 30. Ennis A. sennes Ob. and Mart. 141. a subregulus martyrized at Rome under Decius. The name is Sennen in Boll.
Senóc (*senecio*), Mosenoce Mughna, Mart. Don.), Dec. 11.
senóir, s.m. *senior, an old man*, Pref. 95.
Senotus, Zenotus, Sep. 7, a mistake for Sinotus ' Martyr et verisimiliter episcopus Capuae in Campania Italiae.' Boll.
Sen-Phátric (*old Patrick*) Aug. 24. S. Patrick's tutor at Glastonbury. See Fiacc's h. 65.
Sen-Phól (*old Paul*), an Egyptian monk, called ' Monachus' and ' Simplex' (ὁ ἀπλοῦς, Smith, Dict. Biog. iii. 152). Prol. 97, Ep. 251, gen. sg. senphóil Jan. 19, Mar. 2. As to Jan. 19, note that the Bollandists say S. Paulus Thebaeus, primus Eremita, colitur hoc die ab ecclesia Tornacensi in Belgio.
séol, s. (W. hwyl) *a course*, Prol. 43. fo seol na haimsire imbiat *according to the course of the time in which they will be*, O'Dav. 115.
Septim, Ap. 18. = Septimus, a deacon, martyred at Salona, in Dalmatia, Boll.
September, Septimper, s.m. *September*, Sep. 1, 30.
serb, adj. *bitter, sharp*, (W. chwerw), serbaigthir (gl. amaricatur) Tur. Compounds : serb-charcar s.m. *a bitter dungeon*, acc. pl. serbcharcru, Oc. 15. serb-chroch s.f. *a bitter cross*, dat. pl. serbchrochaib May 15. serbgábud s. *bitter danger*, dat. pl. serb-gaibthib, Dec. 2.
serc, serce, s.f. *love*, W. serch m., Skr. sprhā, int serc gl. affectus Ml. 278, Prol. 148, 186, Ep. 12, 210, gen. sg. serce Z². 242. acc. sg. seirc, scirce, Feb. 11, May 8. Compounds, see mórserc.
sercach, adj. (W. serchog), *loving, amorous*, Jan. 14. gen. sg. m. sercaig, Sep. 25.
sernaim cognate with the verbal noun scarnadh (sernad), which O'Clery glosses by sgaoileadh, 3d pl. pres. indic. act. sernait Aug. 31, Oc. 31. 2d sg. imperat. seiru, sernd Mar. 15 But sérnn (gl. studé) Ml. 56 c.
sert, ro-n-sert Ep. 11. (.i. roesreith no ronnert, 3 Ir. Gl. 139) seems to mean *nos firmavit* : cf. scirt (.i. neart *strength*, O'Cl.)
sesca, *sixty*, conjunct. form, acc. sg. la sescait soer slechtae, Dec. 23.
sescat, *sixty*, absolute form, coic cnibtil. . . . . sescat ar tri octaib, Prol. 327. dá cét sescat, Oc. 30.
séssilbe, séselbe (= seiseilbhe .i. caint, O'Cl. séselbe LU. 87ᵃ), s.f. *any repeated sound* (πίτυλος), *the plash of oars, a chant*, dat. sg. con gráin moir 7 séssilbi, LB. 210 b. acc. sg. Prol. 183. intan tra atchuala hec. nuairn 7 sésilbi intslóig, LL. 181. a. 1.
1. sét, s. (=séd .i. samhail, O'Cl.) *likeness*, June 16, from sim-ta (-ti, -tu ?), Lat. simitu, sinul :

cf. ὁμοιότης. Skr. samatā *sameness, equality.* With the phrase nifrith sét na samail dó cf. uipu séit samil 7 ind lithæ ueteris, Lib. Arm. 170 b. 2.
2. sét, s.m. (W. hynt, Goth. sinths 2 Kuhn's Beitr. 177) *way,* Corm. s.v. rot: dat. sg. dind séit Z². 212. n. pl. séti Z². 215. dat. pl. sétaib Ap. 3. iarsetaib Prol. 326, May 13, Sep. 8, Oc. 9. In Old Celtic this word was a neuter o-stem, if Glück K.N. 43, is right in explaining Gabrosentum by 'via caprilis.' With Oengus, like other mediæval writers, 'the way' was the technical theological expression for this mortal life.
sethir, s.f. *sister,* gen. sg. sethar Z². 262. nom. pl. sethir, seithir, Sep. 30. dat. pl. sethraib, Aug. 30; seems cognate with ἕταρος, ἑταῖρος, 2 Beitr. 164.
Sétna, gen. sg. Prol. 204.
Seuer, gen. seuir, Oc. 24. = Severus, a Nicomedian martyr, Boll.
Seuerianus, Jan. 23, a Mauritanian saint, burnt alive with his wife Aquila, Ob. and Mart. 82.
sex, *sextus*: hi sex-kalainn apreil, Mar. 27.
si, pron. pers. *she* (W. hi), is-si a chland Prof. 71. is-si in brig uile Prol. 147.
-si, intensive pronom. suffix: a rím-si *this counting,* Prol. 268. lib-si *apud uosmet,* Ep. 397. in forn-gnáis-si, Ep. 375.
siachtatar, *they reached or attained* 3d pl. t-pret. Prol. 70. 3d. sg. rosiacht corrici nem a trocaire *ascendit usque ad coelum misericordia eius* Ml. 55ᵈ. siacht .i. tainice, siachtadar .i. tangadar, O'Cl. Gl. r. SAK.
sian, s. .i. glór, O'Cl. Gl. (W. huin). Hence
sianach, adj. *noisy, loud-sounding,* dat. sg. f. sinnaig, Nov. 1.
siar (s-iar), adv. *west,* Nov. 11. *versus occidentem,* Z. 567. also *retro:* trilis tara haiss siar, LU. 55ᵇ.
síd, síid Z². 21. s.m. (n. ?) *peace,* (W. hedd), gen. sg. side Z². 21, intsida LU. 86ᵇ. acc. sg. sid n Sep. 21 B and D Ap. 2. July 5. 18. dogeni sid n-etarro, LU. 83. doroni find 7 goll sid iartain LU. 42ᵇ. Root SAD, sed-ero.
side, pron. demonstr. Sep. 10.
sídflaith, s.f. *peace-kingdom,* acc. sg. May 10, July 13.
sidit, forsidit, adv. (gl. cito) Ap. 16. .i. forrith .i. collnath, Rawl. 505: cf. W. hed *flight ?* or Lat. sedulus, Curtius Gr. Et. No. 281.
síl, s.n. (W. hil) '*sē-men.*' 2 Beitr. 172. Prol. 131. Feb. 13. Ep. 439. Z². 223. gen. sg. sil Nov. 10. Dec. 25. Z². 223. acc. sg. Prol. 340. Jan. 1. July 15. dat. pl. sílaib LU. 35ᵇ.
sillab, s.f. *syllaba* (W. sillaf, silles, sill), n. pl. sillæba Pref.
Sillán, (from Silvanus?) gen. silláin, Feb. 28.
  Sillán, abbot of Bennchor, Feb. 28: obiit A.D. 610: called Silauus (leg. Silnanus?) in the Antiphonary of Bangor, Reeves' Col. 77.
  Sillán, deacon, May 4, Silvanus, bishop of Gaza, mart. in Palestina, Boll.
  Sillán of Imbliuch Cassain, Sep. 11.
Sillóc, see Mosiloc.
Silvester, Dec. 31, pope, il primo ricco patre.
Simeon Stylita, gen. semeoin, semioin, July 27.
Simfronius, Simproinius, Feb. 3: see Symphronius.
Simon Cannaneus, the apostle, July 1, Oc. 28. celebrated with S. Thaddeus or Jude.
Simplex, Feb. 12, a translation of the Irish dinit, i.e. bishop Modiuit of Kilmude in Hy Many, Mart. Don. 46.
Simplice, Simplicius, see semplex.
-sin, -sain, a demonstrative suffix used (like French -là) after substantives (buaid-sin June 20, Aug. 2. Oc. 12. liu-sain, sluag-sain Ep. 31, 32) and adjectives (már-sin, án-sin June 20. moir-sin, maith-sin, Aug. 2; cain-sin Oc. 12. buan-sain Ep. 30) Z². 347.
Sinchell, gen. sg. sinchill June 25, gen. dual da sincholl Mar. 26 A. See the Four Masters ed. O'Don. at A.D. 548 and A.D. 982.

sinde, pron. pers. 1st pl. = sinn + ni, *we*, Prof. D.
Sinech, (daughter of Fergna) Oc. 5, gen. sinche (of Cluain Leith tengad) Nov. 9.
sinnad, s. *reviling* (W. senu, senw) dat. sg. Prol. 47, 3 Ir. Gl. 116. fal scote sinnath, sinnad .i. aora(d), O'Dav. 85. sionnadh .i. caineadh, O'Cl.
Sión, Prol. 270 .i. cathair nimhe *city of heaven*, O'Cl. Gl.
sír, adj. (W. hir, Lat. sērus) *long* (.i. fada, O'Cl.), dat. pl. f. sírnib May 13. Compar. sia = W. hwy. Compounds:—sírchnet, s.f. *a long sigh*, dat. sg. sírchneit May 2. see cnet, rochnet.
sírecht, s. (W. hiraeth) *longing* ('*pity, grief, sorrow,*' P. O'C.) acc. Ep. 332, sirechta .i. geis no fuachtain, O'Dav. 118. sirechtach tuile, ib. 117.
Siric, Sirice (bishop of Magh Bolc) Nov. 26.
Sisinnius, Sisennius, an Alexandrian martyr, July 19.
Sistán (an Irish dimin. of Sixtus) Aug. 6. Sixtus II. bishop of Rome and martyr.
sith, s. *length*, W. hyd, adj. *long*, compar. sithither, Corm. prull: cf. sioth bhallraidh .i. boill fhada *long limbs*, O'Cl. Gl.
sithbe, s. (.i. táoiseach, O'Cl.) *a chieftain*, Aug. 19. in sithbe óir dar in clár findruini, LU. 52ᵇ. O'Dav. 116 explains by sithbeo .i. fota a clu *long his renown*, and by taiseoch *leader, chieftain*: sithbe cruaidh catha *hard chieftain of battle*.
-siu, pronom. suffix (1) after possess. pron. 2d sg. do-rer-siu, fort láim-siu, Prol. 269, 273. duit-siu Ep. 335, 338. (2) after verb in 2d sg. (roere-siu Ep. 427. 431). In mo neit truaig-siu, int-sluaig -siu Ep. A. 314, 316, it is wrongly written for -sea ex -sa.
-sium from som, pronom. suffix to 3d pers. (q.v.) by progressive umlaut: an-guin-sium Prol. 58, am-bunid-sium Sep. 2. (-scom B.), dia raith -sium Ep. 165.
siuur, siur, s.f. *soror, sister*, July 6, Dec. 14, in both places a dissyllable. Another form is fiur, both from SVAsar = Skr. svasr, Zend quaṅhar, W. chwaer (W. chwiawr seems to point to an indoceltic svasár).
Sláine, now Slane, in co. Meath· gen. sg. Nov. 2.
slaine, slane, adv. Oc. 30, *integre, wholly, entirely*.
slán, adj. (ex salan) *salvus, integer* (gl. sanus, gl. sospes Z². 16) Jan. 6, Mar. 2, Aug. 10, Sep. 30, Ep. 173. n. pl. m. sláin Z². 226.
slánaigim, *sano*, 2d pl. imperat. slánaigid, Ep. 383. 403.
slánchotlad, s. m. *sanct dormitio*, Dec. 27.
r. SLEC (Goth. slah-), *to cut down, slay*, 3d sg. redupl. pret. act. roselaig (=roseślaig) Prol. 101. 3d pl. roselgatar Prol. 29, iarsin roselachsa *postquam eum occidi*, Siaburcharpat Coinc. 1st pl. redupl. s-fut. silsimini, LU. 58ᵃ. 3d sg. pret. pass. slecht Feb. 20, June 16. 3d pl. slechta Nov. 5. Dec. 23 .i. romarbtha O'Dav. 117. 3d sg. 2dy. pres. pass. slechta Feb. 12 (or is this the 3d pl. pret. pass., prímslóg being a noun of multitude?) conruslenchta *deleti fuerunt*, Ml. 53ᵈ. huare roslechta *quia destructi fuerunt* Ml. 48ᵈ.
sléchtaim, *flecto*, 3d sg. pres. slechtid isserninus dupatrice Tir. 10, 3d sg. s-pret. slechtais *genuflexit* Prof. B. The cognate subst. da cét déc slechtan '210 *genuflexions*,' LU. 9ᵃ.
slemon, slemun (W. llyfn ὁ·λυβρός) adj. *smooth*, July 5. n. pl. n. slemna (gl. levia) Z². 226. 236 slemuin (gl. lubricus) Ir. Gl. p. 84.
sliab, s.n. (an s-stem Z². 270) *mountain*, Nov. 11. gen. sg. int-sléibe July 6, Ep. 556. dat. sléib Ap. 7. Ep. 76, Oc. 20. acc. sg. sliab 1 S.M. 68. n. pl. iuna slebe Ml. 81ᵃ, sléibe Prol. 240 B (A here has the modern form sleb-t-i).
  Sliab Bladma (Bladma), now Slieve Bloom, in King's county, Ap. 7.
  Sliab Cuilinn, now Slieve Gullion, co. Armagh, July 6.
  Sliab Tábair, Mount Tabor, July 26.
slicht, s. *a track*: the nom. pl. slechta is perhaps in Sep. 7; but the passage is very obscure.
slige, s. *a road*, Nov. 7. Corm. s.v. rot, Z². 255. gen. sliged : cf. SLEC and arslig.
slis, s. (W. ystlys) *side, flank*, slios .i. taobh, O'Cl. Hence
slisgel, adj. *whitesided*, Sep. 29.

GLOSSARIAL INDEX.

slóg, sluag, s.m. (W. llû, Gaulish slógos, Skr. sarga?) *a host, a throng*, Prol. 28, Jan. 28. Feb. 2. Mar. 6. Ap. 3. June 15, 16, Oc. 7, 22, 28, 29. Nov. 20. Dec. 17. 30. gen. sg. sloig, slúaig, Feb. 15, 28. Mar. 29. 31. July 27. Aug. 24. Ep. 316. dat. sg. slóg, sluag Jan. 31. Mar. 4. Ap. 26. June 1. July 12, 15, 16, 30. Dec. 11. 29. Ep. 104. Sep. 15. acc. sg. slóg-u slúag-n Prol. 132. July 17. Aug. 10. n. pl. sloig, slúaig Prol. 47. 63. Jan. 26. July 31 A. Sep. 7 A, Nov. 1. gen. pl. slog-n, sluag-n Prol. 266, Ep. 32. dat. pl. slógaib, sluagaib Prol. 33, June 19, Ep. 62, acc. pl. sluagu, Nov. 30.

slógad, sluagad, s.m. (W. lluad) *a hosting, a thronging*, May 17, gen. sg. slógaid Dec. 19. dat. sg. slógud, slúagud July 28. Nov. 15, acc. sg. sluagad-n, July 7.

slóglae, slúagda, adj. *hostful*, Mar. 21. gen. sg. f. July 11.

slóiged, slúaiged, s. *a thronging, a multitude* (.i. inad, Three Ir. Gl. 139)=slógad q.v. Feb. 3. May 17. July 18. Ep. 33. 141. acc. sg. sluaiged-n Prol. 303 Jan. 31, June 30: bí-sluaiged=faibuthraibna.

sloudim, *I declare, I name*, 3d sg. pres. indic. rel. sloindes Ep. 155. 2d sg. imperat. sluind Jan. 31. Feb. 19. Mar. 4. 30. May 26. July 10. Nov. 3. Dec. 1. B-fut. act. 3d sg. sluinddid Prol. 320. 1st pl. sluindfemne Prol. 287. sloindfimmi 3d pl. sluinnfet Prol. 300=sloindit B. 3d sg. pret. pass. slondad June 12. oc slund *significando*, Z². 230. O.W. istlinnit .i. loquitur=O. Ir. sluindith. The verbal noun is slonniud, LU. 15ᵇ. cf. aslondad supra.

slúag, sluagad, sluagda, sluaiged see slóg, slógad, slogda, sloiged.

slúagach, adj. *hostful, troopful*, Mar. 5 (.i. buidhnech, Three Ir. Gl. 130) May 10, June 14, 21, Sep. 21, 29, Ep. 262.

-su, infixed pron. see s.

snádim (W. noddi), *I protect, I give refuge*, 3d sg. a- conj. ron-snáidea, ron-snaide, ron-snada, Feb. 23, Mar. 14, May 10, Sep. 20, Oc. 19. ron-snádea Mar. 28. May 28, July 14. ronsnáide Mar. 13 (ronsnáde B), Dec. 17. rosnaidhe .i. go ndidne O'Cl. 3d pl. ron-snáidet Ep. 47. 51. ron-snaidet Mar. 6. ron-snádat Jan. 23. 29. May 29. June 9. Sep. 27. Ep. 563. B-future 3d sg. nodo-snaidfea, snáidfid-i, Ep. 160. S-conjunctive 3d sg. snaid-sium July 18. Sep. 21 (snaid-sjuud B).

snádud, s. (W. noddad, nawdd) *protection*, dat. sg. Jan. 21. snadhadh .i. comairce, O'CL .i. ditin 3 Ir. Gl. 130. fri snádud neich dothissad conairectul, LU. 61ᵇ.

snai, Prof. 29, reading and meaning doubtful.

snámach, adj. *buoyant?* Oc. 27. acc. sg. m. Aug. 6. acc. sg. f. snámaig snámaich, Sep. 12. Root SNA, Skr. snāti. νάμα, nāre, W. nofio. When used as an epithet for a saint, snámach has perhaps a technical meaning: cf. the Skr. snātaka (lit. *one who has bathed*) from the same root, which is applied to the pupil who has finished his apprenticeship to his spiritual guide. As a subst. snamach glosses suber: snob (gl. suber) Sg. 64ᵃ W. nof.

snigim, *I drop*, redupl. pret. 3d sg. senaig, senaich (=seśnaig) May 15, 3d sg. b-fut. snigfid crú, LU. 56ᵃ. Zend çnigh *to snow*, Lith. snigti.

sním, s. *sadness* (sniomh .i. tuirsi O'Cl.), dat. sg. Ep. 407. acc. sg. Prol. 223, saire cen saethar cen sním, LU. 33ᵇ. So imsniomh .i. tuirsi no brón O'Cl.

so-, see su-

soud, s. *a turning, a change*, Ap. 19, better soud : is lond in fer so ol maui la soud úad, LU. 71ᵃ., [soadh 7 sodh .i. tionutódh no claochlodh. O'Cl. sodh fri nois, *turning to custom* .i. an feinechas do chor ar geul, *to put aside the lex scripta*,] ib. Root su, whence many Irish words cited by Ebel, 4 Kuhn's Beitr. 172, 173, to which add nosoc (gl. averti soles) Ml. 44ᵇ. indi sons (gl. uersantis) Ml. 64ᵇ. soit *vertunt* Fis. Ad. impaid *vertit* ib. comthoither *convertetur*, LU. 8c. na eserge, and sous infra. Hence also Lat. su-cula *windlass*.

soas, s. (lit. versutia?) *science* (.i. fios maith, *good knowledge*, O'Cl.) Nov. 12, Ep. 89. gen. sg. soais, sois, Ap. 4, dat. sg. soas, Mar. 13, Ep. 124, acc. sg. soas-n, Ep. 132 = sous .i. dán, Br. h. 37.

sobail, adj. Prol. 218, June 16, Ep. 234. In the first place it is an epithet for a psalm, in the second for a holy host, in the third for an archangel : la suid saer sobail, LB. 101, lower margin. It is the opposite of dobail (ferais echt ndochlae ndobail, LU. 19ᵇ, 81ᵇ), which seems to mean *dark, evil*: cf. φαλαρός.

sóbis, sóibis, suabais, adj. (.i. sobesach *well-mannered*, O'Dav. 116), *good, gentle,* Jan. 13, dat. sg. m. July 16, voc. sg. m. Ep. 502, gen. pl. Feb. 2, suabais .i. sobesach, L.Lec. Voc. 115, suabh .i. sobésach, H. 3, 18, p. 51ᵃ. ('suab in aithne ambi intarg'). Root subh ?

sobarthan, s. *good luck, prosperity, benefit,* Ep. 57, O'Dav. 116, explains sobartan by soaraide : bnaid a soborthon 7 abal form ancebtair, Goidel. p. 180 ; sobharthain *happiness,* P. O'C. biaid inmed lenda 7 biad 7 sobarthan isincathraig, Trip. Bodl. 27 b. 1. tria sobarthain mBrigte, LB. 64ᵇ. ar a sruithe sobartan in athur, 3 Senchas Mar, 64.

sochlae, sochla, adj. (opposite of dochlae ἐυσκλεής, and = εὐκλεής, Skr. suçravas *famous, glorious*), Prol. 163, Jan. 13, Ap. 24, May 9, June 21, 23, Ep. 262, gen. sg. m. sochlai Aug. 12, dat. Dec. 29. voc. Ep. 502 : sochla .i. maith, O'Dav. 115.

sochlach, adj. Jan. 14, dat. sg. n. Sep. 19. Same meaning as sochlae.

sodan, adj. Aug. 10, D. *prosperous, happy,* .i. sona, O'Cl.

sodath, sodad, adj. *beautiful* (εὔχροῖς), acc. sg. m. Aug. 10. Nov. 27, B.

soce, gen. sg. Ep. 126, seems = sous supra.

soegal, s. n. = saeculum, Ep. 424 C.

sóer, saer, adj. *free, noble,* (=Skr. su-víra, opp. to dóir) Z². 31, Ap. 12, July 20, Oc. 24, 27, Nov. 11, 27, Dec. 31, acc. sg. m. Ap. 2, Aug. 10, acc. sg. f. Dec. 7, gen. pl. Dec. 4 (or should we here read sóer-sruithe?), dat. pl. sóeraib, saeraib, Aug. 30, Ep. 286. Comparative, soiriu Z². 275. Compounds:—

    sóer-búaid, s. n. *a noble victory,* acc. sg. July 8.
    sóer-chetul, s. n. *a noble song,* Ep. 158.
    sóer-choinnel, s. f. *a noble light,* acc. pl. soerchoinnle, soercoindli, Prol. 288.
    sóer-deochain, s.m. *a noble deacon,* Ap. 3.
    sóer-gein, s. *a noble birth.* Oc. 3.

sóeraim, *I free, ennoble,* 3d sg. pres. indic. act. soerait(h) Ap. 1, 3d pl. pres. indic. act. soerait. sseruit Nov. 1, 2d sg. a-conj. act. soirnsiu (gl. liberato) Ml. 61ᶜ. 3d sg. ro-n-soera, Mar. 14, Oc. 19. Ep. 435, rom-soera, Ep. 441, 445 etc. s-pret. abs. 2d sg. soersi, soersai, saersu. Ep. 447, 451, subjoined ro-soerus, Ep. 486, 3d sg. abs. saerais, Sep. 25, subjoined rosaer Pref. 3d sg. pret. pass. rosoerad, Ep. 440, 3d pl. rosaertha Pref.

sóerad, saerad, s. *liberation,* Sep. 23. ara soirad són dinaib fochaidib, *for his deliverance from the tribulations,* Z². 216.

sóerdae, saerdae, adj. *free, noble,* acc. sg. f. July 13, 18, gen. pl. Aug. 5.

sóeth, sáeth, s.m. *tribulation, affliction,* gen. sg. mor saido, Cod. Boern., gen. pl. Ap. 3, dat. pl. saethaib .i. saothraibh O'Cl., Prol. 69, acc. pl. soethu (.i. pianu), Prol. 32 = saethu LU. 9ᵇ. O'Dav. 117. has saoth .i. galar *disease* (no easlainte O'Cl.), and this is its meaning in the Amra Chol. (LU. 13ᵃ) fo lib lige a ai ar cech sœth, *good with you (is his) grave, O sages, against every disease.*

sóethar, see saethar.

soimle (.i. innis *declare thou*) July 4, D, and Thrge Ir. Gl. 133.

soinmech, somnech, adj. *prosperous,* May 28, soinmhsach *happy, charming,* P. O'C.

solad, s. *solatium,* Prol. 11, Nov. 27.

solus, adj. (gl. clarus) *bright, shining,* Jan. 30, n.pl. soilsi, soillsi, suillse, Sep. 7. Cormac's solas, compar. soillsithir, Fis. Ad. soillsi (gl. clarior) Ir. Gl. 129, root SVAR, Windisch 21 Kuhn's Zeits. 428.

-som, pron. used as an intensive suffix after 3d sg. m. and n., and 3d sg. pl. fo a mind-som, Prol. 257, a rann-som, 258, it soer-som, it coem-som, Sep. 2, ar-ruam-som, a sluag-som, Oc. 28. See -sem, -sium.

són, pron. demonst. *that* (= s' + ón) Prol. 124, 172, Z². 353.
sonae, sona, adj. *happy, prosperous*, June 23, Sep. 16, Oc. 3, dat. sg. m. Ap. 13.
sonairt, adj. *firm* (W. hynerth), Prol. 261, compar. sonortu, Z². 276.
sonn, s. (=W. ffon, *staff, cudgel*) .i. cuaille, *a stake*, O'Cl. Hence
sonnaim, *I impale*, 3d pl. pret. pass. rosunnta, rosuindtea, Prol. 33.
sorchae, adj. (su-riche, opposite of dorchae) *luminous*, Dec. 25, 26, acc. sg. f. sorchai Sep. 12, compar. sorchu, Mar. 9.
soréid, adj. (su-réid) *very smooth*, Prol. 30.
sorn, s.m.=*furnus* (W. ffwrn, Corn. forn), dat. sg. surn, April 24, Colm. h. 29, acc. pl. surnu Prol. 44.
sossad, s.m. (n. ?) *statio*. acc. sg. sossad-u. Feb. 26, Sep. 21, Z². 337. W. go-sod. Hence
sostan, s. July 10, i. cunsanadh *rest*. O'Dav. 116, sostain *a ceasing, stopping, desisting*, P. O'C. min böjeste ro.
sotal, adj. .i. uallach no dimsach O'Dav. 116, .i. dimmasach no urisa a thoil co drochni. L.L. Voc. 130. (But sotal .i. olc, Three Ir. Gl. 132 : sotal .i. moidlamheach, O'Cl.) Hence
sotlae, sotla, s.f. *vainglory* : ceu sotlai Ap. 28, Sept. 15, Ep. 135, W. ffothyll=spustula : cf. μεγαφυσᾶr, magnum spirare, u. pl. sotli (gl. animositates) Wb. sotlae .i. sothol, Three Ir. Gl. 139, sotlacht LU. 21ᵇ.
sothnge, adj. *well tongued*, Jan. 13, Sep. 30. O'Cl. explains .i. soitheangthach .i. breitheamh *a judge*, and quotes adcodu sothnge siodhughadh *a judge obtains, brings about, peacemaking* : suithnge .i. sothengaidh .i. maith a crlabra, *bono loquela ejus*, O'Dav. 117.
spírut, s.m.=*spiritus*. gen. sg. spírta May 15, spiurto Tur. acc. pl. spirtu, Z. 333.
sreim, *sterno*, 3d sg. pr. ind. act. manraid slúagu sreid múine, 3d sg. pret. pass. rosreth, Aug. 25 3d sg. 2dy. pres. pass. nosretha. Prol. 138.
sreith, s. (gl. strues) Z. 984, acc. sg. sreith-n Aug. 24, gen. pl. sreithe, Dec. 4, sreith (gl. pratum) Sg. 20ᵃ, both connected with στόρνυμι, sterno, &c.
sreth, s. *a rank*, Z. 992, acc. pl. sretha, Ep. 238, Lat. ser-ies, Gr. σειρά, Skr. sarat. sarit, are cognate.
sroigell, s. (W. ffrowyll)=*flagellum*. Hence
sroiglim=*flagello*, 3d pl. pret. pass. sroiglithe, Prol. 43 .i. do sgiursadh, O'Cl.
srúaim, sróin, s.n. *stream*, (.i. sruth, O'Dav. 115, 116) Ap. 4, Nov. 27, isiede ind ail rúnda asatorómed a srúaim mór indforcitil spirdáldi (?) arrodibaid itith indisrahel spiurdalti innanoib, *this is the mystical rock whence brake forth the great stream of the spiritual teaching which quenched the thirst of the spiritual Israel of the Saints*, Z². xxxvi. n. sruam .i. imad, Ll.ec. Voc. 126, dat. pl. sruamannaib, O'Dav. 52. 117=fluminibus : cf. O.N. straumr, Στρύμων. Rúmen the old name of the Tiber, Corssen, i 364.
srúamach, adj., *streamy*, (.i. srothach P. O'C.) Nov. 26, acc. sg. m. (n. ?) Aug. 25, acc. sg. f. sruamaig. Dec. 7, O'Cl. explains by slunghach and P. O'C. has sruam .i. sluagh.
sruith, s. *an elder, a sage*, Prol. 97 B, Nov. 2, sruith ath. (gl. patronus Sg. 12ᵇ. gen. sg. srotha Jan. 5, Aug. 24, n. pl. sruithe (=O.W. stratin) Ep. 47. gen. pl. sruithe-n Prol. 167, May 28, July 1, 23, Dec. 4, Ep. 272. inna sruthe (gl. veterum) Ml. 55r. sruith .i. cagnaid, L.Lec. Voc. 317. The gender seems fem., at least cf. epscop sanctan sancta sruith. It occurs as an adj. in the superl. in L.B. 123ᵇ, line 2 : intan ba sruithem 7 ba fírrosta he fodessin fri derm·ad a óesi, *when he himself was very old and truly aged at the end of his life*.
Stellain, of Tír dáglas (Terryglas), May 26.
Stephanus, Stephanus, Zefanus, Steffan, Stefan, deacon and protomartyr, Aug. 3, Dec. 26. Ep. 249.
Stolus, June 30, (Zoilus B), a name for S. Paul the apostle.
su-, so- (W. hu-, ho-, he-, hi-, hy-)=Skr. su-, Gr. ἐΰ-, Glück K.N. 48, see sobail, sochla, sodath, suba, suilbir, etc.
suabais, adj. see sóbis.

suacht, s.f. Ap. 19, *sickness? weakness?* The root may be suk, whence NIIG. schwach and perhaps goth. sinkan, siuks, Fick³ i, 801, 802.
Suanach, a man's name, *sleepy?* gen. suanaig. May 16.
súas, adv. *upwards*, (sursum) Z. 567. ruc suas, Aug. 6, cechaing suas, Oc. 9. s-úas.
suba, s. (subha .i. sublhachas *hilaritas*, O'Cl.), *gladness, joy.* Jan. 6, 11, gen. sg. subai, April 21, B. acc. suba, Dec. 17, abl. suba, sube, Ap. 1.
subach, adj. *happy, joyful*, ('Hilarius,' Mart. Dom. 472), acc. sg. m. **Ap. 2.** Hence the demonstrative verb sabaigit (gl. gaudent) Ml. 61ª.
subaich, adj. Ap. 10 A, seems=subach, q.v. The other MSS. have subaid.
súi, s.m. *a sage*, (* su-vit?) Z². 255, Sep. 10, 30, gen. sg. suad, Corm. prull, acc. sg. suid (la suid saer sobail), L.B. 101, lower marg. acc. pl. súide Ep. 81, voc. pl. a suide aille erenn, L. Br. sui (now saoi, as druí is now draoi) is the opposite to dui (= *du-vit?), gen. duad, dat. duid *a fool*.
1. suide, s.n. *sedes, sessio*, gen. sg. suidi Z². 230, Ap. 12, dat. sg. suidiu Z². 225. acc. suide ib. 231. Compounds: see prímsuide and for dib rigsuidib déc, *on twelve thrones*, LU. 32ᵇ.
2. suide (=so-de) pron. demonst. Z². 349-350, dat. sg. m. (n.?), suidiu, Prol. 122, dat. pl. suidib suidib Prol. 84.
súil, s.f. *eye*, Corm. 39, gen. súla, dat. súil, Prol. 218, n. pl. súli Z². 251, gen. dat. sule, **sulib,** 252, Cognate with Skr. sûri, Lat. sôl, Goth. sauil, Root SVAR.
suilbir, adj. *eloquent*, Aug. 21, Ep. 126=sulbair q.v.
suilge, s. Nov. 9, B. is fuilge in A. Meaning obscure.
suilgind. Ep. 126, B. Obscure and probably corrupt.
suirge. s. Ep. 135. The meaning is obscure. P. O'C. has suirghe *courting, wooing*, cf. suirgech (gl. procus) Ir. Gl. In Three Ir. Gl. it is glossed by suaire *pleasant.* But this meaning will not suit here. I suspect a connection with suirigh *doctors, kings, princes.* O'Don. Supp.
súithe, s.f. *wisdom:* gen. sg. suithe Amra Chol. acc. sg. suithi, Nov. 12 raleg súidi nglan, Klosterneuburg codex: (su-vitja? root vit. Zend with *wissen gewahr werden*, Justi 275?)
sulbair, adj. (= su-labair, W. helafar) *eloquent*, Aug. 21. B. =sulbir Z². 233.
Sulpic, Sulpice, Jan. 13 '.i. qui libros martini fecit,' Rawl. 505.
1. sum, a suffixed pron. of the 1st pers. sg., which by assimilation becomes -sium: see examples infra s.v. -um.
2. -sum = -som, Prol. 59.
sund, sunt, sunn, adv. *here* Sept 6, Ep. 378, 391, 395. Z². 355.
sunn, suffixed personal pron. of the 1st pl., which by assimilation becomes siunn: see examples infra s.v. -unn.
sunnraid, adv. Pref. 97: O.Ir. sainriud *particularly, especially.* ocus ó dainiul sainriud tuc, Lib. Hymn. ed. Todd, p. 205.
sunt, adv. see sund.
Susanna, Ep. 187, where the poet alludes to the Hist. of Sussanna, v. 60.
Sussius, Oc. 19, Nov. 20, for Susius, a martyr, Boll. Oc. viii. p. 381.
suthin, suthain, adj. *diuturnus, perennis* (opposed to duthain) Z². 233. Mar. 11, May 14, Sep. 30, Nov. 28, Dec. 28. gen. sg. m. suthain Mar. 26, gen. m. dual Mar. 26 A, suthain .i. buan, LLec. Voc. 388.
Symphronius, a martyr in Africa, Feb. 3.

t expresses original t: táid, tál, tá, te, tech, temel, teor, treb: t for the d of the prep. do in composition: to-t-ic, May 25, and perhaps othuid=ódulluid Prol. 128. t = dd: notlomaim Prol. 315: t for d in loanwords: tese, Trursus, Fraxitis, Osualt.
t, pron. poss. *thy*, before a vowel: t'aiccept *thy lesson*, Pref. B: before t: th-erta, Ep. 558 B: suffixed: dot chobair, July 24.
-t, suffixed pron. pers. of 2d sg. see duit, it: infixed pron. do-t-ic May 25, do-t-icfa July 16, no-t-guidiu Ep. 37: infixed pron. of 3d sg. no-t-géba, Ep. 114, 173: no-t-gesed, F p. 217.
tá, *is*, táimne, táam *we are*, Prol. 157, 161. Root sta.

tabairt, tabart, s.f. *a giving* (see firthabairt).
Tabúr; sliab tabóir July 26. isleib tabór, Z^2. 271.
tabur, (do-ath-beru) *I give,* Z^2. 428. 2d sg. imperat. tabair Pref. B.
tachor, s.m. *a combat* (tachar .i. deabaidh no comhrac, O'Cl.). In June 24 A it is a mistake for tathchor q.v.
tadlach, taidlech, s. acc. sg.Oc.15, .i. tuilleadh uile, s. *an addition of evil*: no dochamhail *affliction,* O'Cl. But in Three Ir. Gl. 137 it is explained by (1) ammus *temptation,* (2) *a wringing which is given a fisher's net,* (3) *affliction.* I conjecture that it is cognate with tadall (do-da-aidlen *adit eam,* Z^2. 434) and means *a visitation.* P. O'C. explains tadhlach by *touching:* also *a pain in the wrist from hard labour.*
taerthim, tairthim, s. acc. sg. Prol. 166, seems to mean *splendour* and to be=tairthim, LU. 33ᵇ. tairthim llatho, ib. 132.
táid s.m. (gl. fur) Z^2. 273. Cognate with *rárdw l rob,* O. Slav. tati *thief,* and
táide, táthe, s.m. *stealth, concealment,* acc. sg. Prol. 71. Oc. 10.
taile, adj. .i. daingin, (O'Dav. Hence talce, tailce q.v.
taimthene, tamthine, s. f. *death,* gen. sg. Oc. 29.
taimthin, s. *death* (from sickness?) June 30, July 2, 27, Aug. 17, gen. sg. taimthen? root TAM (Skr. tamyati), whence the noun tám .i. bás and the verb tathaim *obiit,* pl. tamatar.
táin, s. *a spoiling, driving, pursuit,* dat. sg. Ep. 524.
tair, adv. *in the east,* Ep. 70 B.
tair, s. *insult,* see dithair.
tairic (do-air-ic) .i. tig, O'Cl. taric, July 19. 3d sg. pret. do-r-araice, Aug. 1. 2d sg. s-conj. tair *come,* Pref. B. 3d pl. s-conj. tairset, Dec. 13 = doairset, Sep. 20.
tairm, prep. praef. *trans,* Z^2. 879.
tairmrith, tarmrith, s. *transcursus,* July 3 B. acc. sg. June 4 B. where O'Dav. 122 explains tairmrith martini by '*his relics were taken from the monastery wherein he died, to the city.*'
tairugertaid, (do-air-chon-gertaid), s.m. *prophet* Pref. B. cf. dumirugirtsiu *promisisti* Ml. 74ᶜ. and see 3 Kuhn's Beitr. 280.
taise, taisse, tasse, s.f. *a relic,* May 20. n. pl. taisi, taissi, Ep. 220. acc. pl. taissi, tassi, Ep. 336.
taispenim (do-as-benim = ἐκ-φαίνω) 3d sg. pres. indic. taispenaid Pref. B. 3d sg. s-pret. rothaispen *ostendit,* Pref. 22. 45. cf. doad-badar *ostenditur,* Z. 471.
taispenad, s.m. *monstratio, expositio,* Pref. B. gen. taispenta, Ir. Gl. p. 106.
taithlech, s. (.i. ceannsa no sith *peace,* O'Cl. and see O'Dav. 123) Sep. 19. rothathlaigh .i. dochennsaigh, O'Cl.
taithmet (do-aith-men-t) s. *commemoration, memorial,* Ep. 131, Br. h. 94, Colm. h. 18. O'Clery's taithmhead .i. cuimhniughadh: cf. do-aithminedar *commonet,* Z^2. 438.
taitnem, s. *radiance, brightness,* Prol. 330: taitnem (gl. lucina) Sg. 37ᵃ, toitnem (gl. candela) Sg. 37ᵃ. Hence taitnemach (gl. candidus).
tál, s. m. (n.?) *adze,* gen. táil, June 11=O.Slav. tesla, Ohg. dehsala.
talam, s. *the earth* as opposed to the sky and the sea, *land,* gen. sg. talman, Prol. 245. Mar. 27. Z^2. 264. dat. sg. talmain May 20, June 6. July 27. Ep. 294, 441. short form talam, Prol. 130. acc. sg. talmain-n Ep. 434. short form talam, Prol. 216.
talce, tailce, s.f. (= Nhg. stärke?) *strength,* dat. sg. tailci, talcai, Ap. 28. June 7, Sep. 15.
talland, s. n. *talent,* Dec. 31, borrowed from Lat. talentum: the double l is due to the accent. The gen. pl. occurs in LU. 114ᵇ: uii. cét talland argait báin im secht cét talland óir, 700 *talents of white silver, with 700 talents of gold.*
talgud, s. *appeasing* or *quieting,* P. O'C (.i. ceannsughadh no crithnughadh, O'Dav. 122: talgud a brotha LU. 127ᵃ, acc. sg. Oc. 29: the cognate verb is in O'Dav. Three Ir. Gl. 163, amail do-n-ailge in duilem in muir mór *as the Creator quiets the great sea.*
Tamlachta (gen.-tan, dat.-tain) Pref. Tallaght, Co. Dublin.
tamthine, see taimthine.
tan, adv. *when,* Ep. 470, 561. see iartain, intain. As a subst. it occurs in Lib. Hymn. ed. Todd. p. 20: indaratan is desillachtach . . . . . intan ele is tresillabach, and in LU. 96ᵇ: nach

tan tosnaidle suil indrig tibid, *every time the King's eye visits them, he smiles*: cf. Skr. -tana in nūtana *new, young*. Lat. tino in diutinus, crastinus, pristinus.
tánise, *second*, Pref.
tánic, táinic (do-ánic) *euuit*, Jan. 11. ó do-n-ánic. ó donánaic *cum uenit*, Ap. 14.
tar, dar, prep. cum acc. *over*, Sep. 9. 10. Nov. 3. Dec. 8. 11. Ep. 238.
taraill, *adiuisti*, Pref. B.
tarca .i. derrscugudh *an excelling*, O'Dav. 122. ni-s-tarca deilm catha, *noise of battle does not excel it*, June 29. cf. dofairci, dofarcat supra.
Tarcelli, Darcelli, Feb. 26. I cannot identify this name.
tarcenn, prep. nom. Ep. 414, *for sake of*, Z^2. 658.
taric, see tairic.
tarla, (do-ar-la) *adit*, 3d sg. t-pret. do-n-arlaid *qui adiit* Dec. 8. 1st pl. conj. tarlam *adeamus*, Prol. 319 B.
tarmbreth, s.f. *translatio*, July 3, acc. sg. tarmbreith-n, June 4.
tarmchruthud, s. m. *transfiguration*, July 26, gen. sg. tairmchrutto, Z^2. 184.
tasc, Jan. 18, B. R. and Rawl. 505, *report, tidings*: tasc mor .i. in hoc die ad romam tasc báis maire *tidings of M's death* peruenit, Rawl. 505.
tascnaim, *adeo*, see doascnaim.
Tassach, bishop of Ráith Cholptha (Raholp), Ap. 14.
tasse, see taisse.
Tatha = Thaddaeus, July 1, Oc. 28.
tathchor, s. m. (n. ?) *removal, transfer, transposition*, June 24, reuolutio .i. tathchor na hanma hi corpaib cesamhaib, LU. 36ᵇ. In June 24 the allusion is to the return of S. John after Domitian's death, from his exile in Patmos to his church in Ephesus.
táthum, *est mihi*, Prol. 217 = tatham .i. atá liom *I have*, O'Cl.
táthunn, *est nobis, we have*, Prol. 217 B.
táthut, *est tibi*, July 24. tathus *est ei* Feb. 5. tathai *est ei*, Crith Gabl. p. 487: cf. tathad (leg. tathat) .i. atá leó *they have*, O'Cl.
Taulchán, Telchán, gen. taulchain, telchain, Oc. 21.
té, adj. *hot*, (rothe *very hot*, LU. 33ᵇ.) n. pl. téit (=tepentes) Z^2. 69. dat. pl. (luach-) tétib Prol. 40.
Tecla, Feb. 22, a virgin martyred at Antioch, June 1, Nov. 17, Ep. 471. See her legend, Jameson S. and L. Art, 556.
techt, s.f. (do-ic-tá) *a going*, (itio), gen. techta riana techt, Prol. 31. oc techt, Pref. B. re techt fo bathis, Tur. In friscillin do thechta, Ep. 560, we seem to have the gen. sg. cf. tairmthechta *transgressions*, imthecht.
techta, adj. *due*, Ep. 390.
techtaim, *I have*, 2d pl. ma no-d-techtaid *si id habetis*, Ep. 389. 2d sg. techtai-si ór .i. atá ór agadsa, O'Cl. cognate with τίκτω and Ohg. digiu *obtineo, impetro!*
tecmung, *accido*, tecmaing *accidit*, Z^2. 431. (=do-aith-cum-aing), do-n-ecmaic, dondecmaic, *qui evenit*, Dec. 24. 3d sg. s-conj. nach-in-tecma, arnan-tecema, nachaun-tecma, Jan. 10. do-nd-ecmai Dec. 29 R. cf. na thecmung (gl. ab eventu) Z^2. 224.
teg, tech, s.n. (an s-stem = τέγος, 2 Reitr. 165), gen. sg. tige (= τέγεος) Ep. 94. dat. tig, taig, acc. teg, toch, Z^2. 271.
teglach, s.n. *household*, Ep. 364. luid ailill 7 medb 7 ateglach n-uli LU. 107ᵃ. gen. sg. teglaig Ep. 550. óis teglig Z^2. 74. lín a teglaich, Táin bó Fr. dat. sg. i tegluch, ib. donteghuch LU. 108ᵃ. acc. sg. teglach, Prol. 95.
teidm, s.n. *disease*, gen. sg. tedma, Ep. 200, 518, Ult. h. 4. dat. ontedmaim (gl. tabe) Z^2. 269. acc. pl. tedmann, Colm. h. 8.
Teimnen, see Temnen.
teine, see tene.

tét, *to go*, 3d sg. pres. indic. téit Prol. 248 = do-éti, Beitr. viii. 3.
Telle (mac Seigin) gen. sg. Teilli, Telli, June 25.
Temair. *Tara*, latinised Temoria, Lib. Arm. 3. b. 2. gen. sg. temrach, Pref. temra, Prol. 165. temro Lib. Arm. 10ª. 2, dat. temraig. Ep. 552.
temel, s. f. *darkness*, gen. sg. teimle, July 4, W. tywyll, Lat. tenebrae (from temefrae), Skr. timira.
temen, teimen, adj. *dark gray*, Corm. s. v. teim. Hence the diminutives
Temnen, Teinmen (monk and martyr), gen. Temnein, Aug. 17 B, and
Temneóc, Temnióc, (cook of S. Mochua of Clonfert), Dec. 23.
tempul, s. m. = *templum* (whence also W. teml, Corn. and Bret. tempel), gen. sg. tempuil, Ap. 8. May 10, Dec. 15; Tur. 80. dat. sg. tempul, Feb. 2.
tend, tenn, adj. *stiff, rigid*, dat. pl. rotennib Prol. 38. cf. ar biastaib ilardaib imdubaib imthennaib, LU. 15ª. Borrowed, like W. tyn, Corn. ten, Br. tenn, from Lat. teutus.
tendri, s.m. *ex rigidus*, Pref., where it is written tendrig.
tendal, s. Corm. *a firebrand*, acc. pl. docuiredar teinnte 7 tenndála innte, Trans. Gael. Soc. 100. Hence the adjective
tendalach, used as an epithet for Flaud, Pref.
tene, s.m. (a t-stem) *fire*, Z². 255. cf. τε-ράν ? Feb. 26. gen. sg. tened, teined Prol. 44, Ep. 540. = teneḋ. Z². 256. dat. tenid, acc. tria thenid imbrátha *per ignem judicii*, LU. 34ª. dat. pl. tentib, tennatib Prol. 39.
tenge, s.m. (a t-stem) *tongue* Z². 255. gen. sg. tengad, 256. dat. tengaid, ib. dat. pl. tengthaib Vis. Ad. acc. pl. tengtha Ep. 125. See sothnge, and cf. Lat. ta-n-go. O'Clery's ting .i. teanga may be cognate with Lat. tingo, τέγγω.
Teolis, Teoilis, Feb. 25. gen. sg. I cannot identify this name.
Teophil, Teophail, July 28, = Theophilus, mart. at Laodicea, Boll.
teor, *three*, acc. fem. Sep. 1. The usual form is teora ; but teor is exactly the Skr. tisras.
Teothota, Aug. 2, Sep. 2, = Theodota, burnt alive with her three sons, temp. Diocletian, at Nicaea in Bithynia.
Teraeus, Ciraeus, gen. sg. May 13, leg. Ceratus, a martyr celebrated at June 6, or Theraclius at July 9 ?
terca, (tarea A) June 29 B, v. tarca.
terc, adj. *scarce, rare, scant* = teirc (gl. rarus) Ir. Gl. No. 672. Hence
tercae, s. *scarcity, rareness*, acc. sg. tercai, May 6 : teirce (gl. raritudo) Ir. Gl.
terephit, s. f. *a scanty bit*, dat. sg. Sep. 8 : cf. lethphit Reeves' Culdees 90. in phit beac ib. 91. gen. sg. pite ib. bheith for teirefit .i. ar phroinn mbig, O'Cl. s. v. Fit proinn.
ternaim, (do-erna- : cf. ὄρνυμι ?) *evado* 3d sg. pret. (impf. ?) ternai Ep. 544. tearnaigheam, *I depart*, P. O'C.
tescaim, (do-esc-, do-sec-) *seco, lacero*, 3d. pl. pret. pass. rotesctha Prol. 238.
téte, s. f. *warmth, comfort, delight*, dat. sg. téti (.i. aibnius), Prol. 25. derivatur from the adj. té = tepens. It is glossed by aibnius in Three Ir. Gl. 125.
th for dh : Hiruath Prol. 85=, for dd: Tatha July 1, Oc. 28, therta for de ferta, Ep. 558 B.
thiar, (do-iar) adv. *in the west*, Ep. B. 70.
1. tinchra, .i. duilge *affliction*, Ap. 29, .i. a gorti, Rawl. 505, *anger, peevishness, frowardness*, P. O'C.
2. tinchra, s. m. (n?) .i. glicus Three Ir. Gl. 138 ; *sharpness, shrewdness, prudence*, gen. sg. tinchrai, Nov. 12. deriv. from tinchair .i. glic O'Dav. 65. .i. goirt L. L. Voc. 131. ti[a]-chair (gl. acer) Sg.
tiagu, tiagaim (= στείχω, Goth. steiga) Z². 429. 3d pl. pres. indic. tiagat Ep. 58. tiagait Z². 433. 3d sg. s-conj. absolute téis Pref. subjoined form arna-te, *ne eat*, Ml. 36ª. 2d sg. 2dy. s-conj. tiastae Ep. 470, 3d. sg. teised Ap. 27.
tiam, Oc. 26, is glossed by úain *time, leisure ;* lase bas n-uáin do (gl. cum ei vacuum fuerit Z². 22.

1. tiamdae, adj. *afraid* (meata O'Dav. 122) Prol. 259. ba tiamda .i. ba merbh, H. 3. 18. p. 51ᵇ.
2. tiamdae, adj. (.i. dorcha *dark* O'Dav. 122) Prol. 294.
Tiamdae, 'Timotheus' (alumnus Pauli ap.) Mar. 18. 'mart. Syrmii in Pannonia' (Boll.) May 15. June 30. Diac. in Britannia martyr May 21, Boll. A Roman martyr, Aug. 22. A martyr at Antioch Sep. 8, Boll.
Tiburtius (Tributius A) a Roman martyr, Boll. Aug. 11.
tic, (do-ic) *venit*, July 9, 3d sg. b-fut. do-t-icfa *tibi veniet*, July 16. 3d pl. s-conj. tisat, do-mm isat, tisset, Ep. 23. 36. 295.
tíchtu, s.f. *a coming*, Z². 624, Ep. 394, acc. sg. tichtin Z². 266.
tidnacim, *I give* (do-aith-nanc), 3d sg. pret. pass. do-r-idnacht Nov. 12 : root NAK, Skr. naç *assequi*.
Tigernach (*lordly*) acc. sg. Ap. 4, bishop of Cluain-eonis in Fermanagh. For cognate words see Glück KN. 179, 180.
tim, adj. *timid*, Prol. 259.
timne, timnae s.n. *a precept, a mandate* (.i. aithne O'Dav. 122) Z². 229, timpne Z². 231. dat. sg. timnu ib. 230. gen. pl. comét timnae mdae (gl. mandatorum custodia) Ml. 45. dat. pl. timnaib Prol. 27. From do-imm-ane : cf. co immánad *ut delegaret*, 4 Beitr. 378.
tinbuanad (do-in-b.) s. m. *a making permanent* (buan), Ep. 204.
tindscanim, tinscanim, *I begin*, 2d sg. imperat. tindscan May 1. Nov. 14. 3d sg. s-pret. rothinscain Pref. intinscana *incipit*, intinscantar *incipitur*, tindarscam, intindarscan *incaepit*, Tur.
tindscetal, s. n. *a beginning*, Pref. B.
tinde, tinne. I *a ring* (tinne óir, Mart. Don. 172), *a link*, II *a bar*, Ap. 25.
tir, s.n. *land*, Z². 233, gen. sg. tíre Prol. 160, May 24, Nov. 2, Z². 234. n. pl. tíre Prol. 161. Should we compare Osc. teram, or Skr. tīra from *tārā *shore, bank*?
Tír dá glas, Terryglass (in Upper Ormond, Tipperary), May 24.
tirbaid, tairbaid, s. *tribulation*? Prol. 169. pl. tirbithi Z². 637, where it is rendered 'angustiae'.
tís (do-ís) adv. *below*, Ep. 70. Z². 612.
titecht, *adveniet*? (do-aith-tect), do-mm-itecht *shall come to me*? Ep. 561. cf. titacht *adventus*.
tlacht, s. m. *a robe* (.i. brat O'Cl. .i. édach O'Dav. 119) ; os talman tlacht, H. 2. 16. col. 392. dat. pl. tlachtaib Prol. 246, and I.U. 23. a. 37. acc. pl. tlachtu Jan. 4. See bán-tlacht.
-tn-, infixed pers. pron. 3d sg. (= dn), for-tn-iadae May 31 = fortniada July 31. no-tn-aile July 9 A. In mani-t-frescai July 19 A. no-t-carmim Ep. 50. fo-t-ruair Ep. 97 B. either the n is dropt before f and r or we have examples of t for d.
tú-, to-, a prefix = do + fo.
Tóbe, Tóba, Ep. 511, – Tobit, though the Irish form is equivalent to Tobias.
tócuired, (do-fo-ad-gared) s. *an invocation* Ep. 212. tochuirimm (gl. postulo) Corm. s.v. apstal.
todiuscud, toduscad, s. *an awakening*, Ep. 193, a m. as ndínim lanech todiusgud nach aili ásuan *sicut est facile cuique expergefacere alium a somno*, Ml. 61ᵇ.
tóeb, s.m. (W. tu) *a side*, acc. pl. taebu, tóeba, Ep. 324.
tóebán, s.m. *a little side*, acc. sg. Oct. 23. Ep. 352.
togairm (do-fo-g.) s.n. *a calling*, Jan. 5. Feb. 21. 26, May 16. June 7. Aug. 12. Dec. 15. dat. sg. togarmaim Z². 269 : 'a *summons*, or *citation*, also *an invocation or prayer*', P. O'C.
1. togu, corruptly togu, toge, s.n. *a choice*, Prol. 123. Jan. 6, Nov. 7, togu Z². 270 (= do-fo-gus) : cf. tníese infra.
2. togu, *eligo*, Z². 429. 1st sg. reduplicated 2dy fut. dogéugainn (ex dogeuguinn, *do-eggusinn), dogeguind Pref. see toga 2d sg. pret. do-r-roega *quem elegisti*, Fiacc.
toich, (do-tech, do-frech ?) adj. *pleasing* July 24 : matoich .i. madail, Three Ir. Gl. 134.
tóid, *to come*, 3d sg. imperat. act. táided, táided, Prol. 340, Jan. 1. .i. ticed. Laud 610.
1. tóiden, s. *a coming*, .i. tidhnacht no thachtain, O'Dav. 122.
2. tóiden, tóeden, toeiden, s. July 7. Aug. 13. Sep. 23. may come from root tu, and means perhaps *troop, host* (buiden, sluag). See O'Dav. 123. ferus failte frisna cliarcho sochla taidben, H. 2. 16. col. 392.

3. tóiden, tóeden, s. (.i. toitnem, Three Ir. Gl. 139) *sheen, radiance*, Ep. 142 in Three Ir. Gl. 139. na-rind astoidet (gl. signa radiantia) Z. 257 : cf. ρυν-θός, taeda. But here, as in July 7 and Sep. 23, tóiden probably means *a troop, a company*.

tóidlech, toeidlech, adj. *shining, radiant*, Sep. 21, 23. Ult. h. 2 (=taidleach .i. loinderda, LL.c. Voc. 60) acc. sg. f. tóidlig-n Prol. 78. Feb. 22.

toirm, tairm, torm, s. (W. twrf) *noise*, May 10 (.i. molad no gloir, O'Dav. 122.) Cognate, perhaps, with Eng. storm. Nhg. sturm.

toisc, s. see toscai.

tóisech, s.m. (n.?) *beginning*, dat. sg. toissich Pref. 21. W. tywysog *leader*.

tol, s.f. (do-vola?) *will, desire* Prol. 267. gen. sg. tuile Ap. 20, Ep. 184. Z^2. 242. n. pl. tola May 19. acc. sg. toil Z^2. 244. gen. pl. tol Z^2. 249. dat. pl. tolaib Prol. 83. Z^2. 249. acc. pl. tola Ap. 15, Z^2. 246.

Tóla, bishop of Disert Tóla in Thomond, gen. sg. Tolai, Mar. 30.

tolgdae, tolcda, adj. *haughty* (dímsach, O'Dav. 122) Prol. 125.

Tomás, (Didymus) S. Thomas, gen. sg. tomais May 30, Dec. 21. The Thomas celebrated at July 3, was martyred at Constantinople, Boll.

tonn, tond, s.f. *wave* (W. ton), dat. sg. tuinn, tuind Prol. 250. Ap. 23, acc. sg. tuind-n June 3. n. pl. tonna Z^2. 244. dat. pl. tonnaib, tondaib Nov. 23, Ep. 536.

tonnad, s.m. (n.?) gen. sg. deoga tonnaid *drinks of death*, LU. 90ᵇ, dat. tonnud Ep. 552 : tonnadh .i. neimh no deoch ina mbí neimh *poison, or a drink wherein is poison*, O'Cl.

tor, s.m. (W. twr) *tower*, July 28, Dec. 12. gen. sg. immedón in tuir LU. 38ᵃ. dat. sg. on tur ib. acc. sg. cosin tur, ib. A pl. tuirid occurs LU. 47ᵇ and Reeves' Col. 277.

tor-, a prefix=do + for.

torann, s. (W. taran, toni-tru, τον-θρύς) *thunder*. Hence the name Torannán, *Boanerges*, June 12. See Ob. and Mart. p. 166. n. (4).

torbe, torba, tarba, s.m. (n.?) *profit*, Prol. 143. Ep. 77. dat. sg. torba (leg. torbu ?) Ep. 76. acc. torbe-n, Z^2. 230.

torbenim *I profit* : torban *prodest* Z^2. 636, 3d sg. s-conj. do-m-r-orbai, domrorba *may it profit me*. Prol. 25.

torc, s.m. (W. twrch) *boar*, Corm. 41. torc allid (gl. aper) Sg. 37ᵃ, gen. sg. tuirc, tuirce, Sep. 17.

torchair, *cecidit*, Ep. 361 .i. do tuith O'Cl. 3d pl. torchartar, Tir. 12. contorchratar (gl. concidcrunt) Ml. 48ᶜ. The present indic. has not been found, but was probably torchrinim.

tormach (do-for-mag) s.n. *increase* Z^2. 223. dat. tormuch ib. 224, acc. sg. tormach Prol. 317, .i. medughadh O'Cl. tormaig *auget* Z^2. 430. cia doromnai a eneclann *though his honourprice may increase*, Crith Gablach, 490 : cf. a már thormachtai (gl. macte), magisancte) Z^2. 231.

toscai, s. acc. sg. July 19, seems cognate with toisc (gl. voluntas hominis) Corm.

toscclad, s. m. (=do-fo-scélad) *a shewing forth*, Ep. 80.

tossach, tosach, s.n. *beginning*, dat. sg. tosuch Tir. 1. tossuch, tossoch, tossug, tosug, Z^2. 224. acc. sg. Jan. 7 : see toisech.

tothla, adj. acc. pl. f. Ap. 15. *pressing, urgent*. Hence tothlaigim .i. altaighim, O'Dav. 122. tothlai(g)ther *postolas*, tothlugud *postulare*.

tr from dr : trén, tróg, trom and the loanword Trursus, Dec. 4.

tra, adv. *ergo, igitur* Pref. Z^2. 659.

traite, s. P. O'C.'s traide *quickness, readiness, activity*, Pref. a derivation from traid .i. luath no obann *swift or sudden*, O'Cl. treit .i. luath, H. 3, 18, p. 51ᵇ. is machtad ol ailill athraite robíth incethror, LU. 58ᵃ. on traite .i. on luas Gl. 871. tiefa i traide .i. colúath, Gl. 883.

tráth, s.m. gen. trátha, *a time, an hour*, acc. temporis : in trath-sa, Ep. 411.

tré, tria (O. W. trui) prep. cum acc. (aspirating) *through* June 27, Aug. 27, Nov. 6. Ep. 352. tre-bithu tria bithu *per secula*, Prol. 156. Mar. 31 : with suffixed pronouns : triut *through thee*, Ep. 438. tria *through his*, Oc. 9. tria-n trén-n *through their*, Jan. 4. Ep. 324. triana *through his*, Pref. triasin-n *per quem*, Pref. 50 : with the article triasna *through τούς*, Prol. 44.

treb, s.f. (W. tref, O. W. treb, Goth. thaurp, Eng. thorp Corm. 12) *homestead, household, hamlet*, gen. sg. treibe 1 S.M. 122. cethar-trebe Fiacc 5. dat. sg. treib Ap. 9. acc. sg. treib-n Prol. 78. bith-aittreb Oc. 8. Cognate are the Gaulish Con-trebia and A(d)-trebates (Glück, K.N. 38, 39).

trebaim, *I make a home* (W. trefu) *I inhabit*, 3d sg. pass. trebthair (which should be 3d pl. pass. trebtair) Prol. 176 : cf. ad-ro-threb *habitavit* Z^2. 866. 868.

trebar, adj. *prudent, wise*, Aug. 11. gen. pl. Feb. 20. Ep. 142 : compar. trebairiu Z^2. 275. Hence trebaraigim, trebraigim (gl. sapio, prudens sum) Z^2. 435.

trecheng, s. (tregeng D, drecheng A.) Sep. 16, B, *three chiefs*.

tredan, s. *a three days' fast* (treadhan .i. trosgadh O'Cl.), acc. sg. Jan. 15, Mar. 24, Nov. 16. gen. pl. Ep. 186. cf. iciunia triduana, Hieron. Ep. 54, 10. Hence

trednach, adj. *abstemious, abstinent*, Oc. 21, Dec. 13, gen. sg. m. trednaig Feb. 25, dat. sg. f. trednaig, Oc. 18.

trén, adj. (ex tresna, W. tren) *bold, valiant*, Aug. 11, Sep. 21, Oc. 21, Dec. 11, Ep. 151. gen. sg. m. triuin, treoin, Feb. 25. = triuin Z^2. 223. dat. sg. f. triuin Oc. 18 B, seems cognate with Skr. drishau, Gr. θρασύς. The compar. tressa (W. trech) Z^2. 277, and superl. tressam 278 may be cognate with Skr. dhríshta, Lat. *fortis* from *forstis*.

trenfer, s.m. (vir fortis) *a champion*, gen. pl. Feb. 20. nom. pl. dociuchratar a trenfir, LU. 51ª.

tres, tress, *third*, Pref. The oldest form seems triuss, Z^2. 309, where it is called an ablative.

trét, s. n. *a flock, a herd*, gen. sg. treoit, nom. pl. tréta, Prol. 230 B.

trethan, s. m. *sea*, (gl. gurges) Z^2. 264, *wave* (.i. tonn, O'Cl.), gen. sg. trethain (.i. mara, Three Ir. Gl. 133) Nov. 23, acc. sg. trethan Prol. 216. Dec. 11. abl. sg. trethan Ap. 22. n. pl. trethain June 27. What seems a gen. sg. of an n-stem (n. tredhn?) trethan occurs in June 3, from this may come the acc. sg. trethain, supra s. v. sair. A connection with Trita áptya, Ἀμφιτρίτη and Τριτο-γένεια is possible. With the Vedic Tretana, Zend Thraetaona, Cormac's triath *sea* may be cognate.

trí, τρεῖς, *three* m. Aug. 2: tri, τρία, *three* neuter, when neuter it aspirates : tri chét June 2, gen. tri-n, Ap. 24. dat. pl. trib, Sep. 8, Oc. 9, acc. n. la tri choice(t)a naga, Dec. 10 B.

tria, triana, triasiu-n, triasna, see tré.

triamuin, triamain, adj. *weary, sad*, Prol. 26, (triamhain .i. tuirseach O'Cl. .i. toirrsech, 3 Ir. Gl. 225.) = trémuin Z^2. 18, where it is wrongly rendered *infirmus*.

tricha, τριάκοντα, triginta, *thirty*, Feb. 20. Sep. 1. dat. sg. trichait Ap. 24. see certricha.

trilech, s. f. seems *a song*, acc. sg. trílig Pref.

1. trilis, Ap. 23 (nas tuind trilis) is either an adj. agreeing with, or a noun governed by, tuinn. As the deriv. trilsen means *facula*, I conjecture that trilis here either means *sparkling, shining* or *of sheen*. An adj. trillsech *sparkling* (= P. O'Cl.'s trilsench *splendid, brilliant*) occurs in D. E.

2. trilis, s. *tress, hair*, dat. sg. Mar. 15 : lir nas trilis .i. nas moing in mara *over the sea's hair*, Three Ir. Gl. 130.

trírech, s. some kind *of song* or poetical composition, Pref. trírech inna néu, Z^2. 994. cf. trilech.

triur, s. *a set of three persons*, gen. sg. tríur Oc. 11. A (where it is a dissyllable), dat. sg. triur, triuur, Jan. 24. Dec. 14. dat. pl. tríríb Prol. 210.

triut, see tré.

trocthaim, *I abate*, 3d sg. s-pret. abs. troethais, Nov. 16 A : with suffixed pron. troeths-us ib. B. arrathroith (gl. comprimente) Ml. 38ᵈ.

troethad, traethad, s. m. *an abating*, Ep. 184.

Trofin, Trophin, acc. sg. Nov. 28 = Trophimus, a Syrian saint, a disciple of St. Paul (Acts xx. 4, xxi. 29).

tróg, trúag adj. (W. tru) *wretched, pitiable*, Prol. 26, 157, Ep. 399, 408, 409, acc. sg. f. truaig-n Ep. 314. Hence

tróige, trúaige, s. f. *wretchedness*, gen. sg. truaige, Mar. 17 D, dat. sg. tróige (leg. trúigi) Ep. 482. abl. tróige, Ep. 512. acc. sg. tróigi, trógi, Feb. 3.
trom, tromm adj. *firm, heavy, grievous* (W. trwm) Prol. 165. Jan. 15. July 7. Ep. 380.
Trophima, Trifonia, Treofonia, Oc. 18. (spelt Tryphonia by Boll.) the wife of the emperor Decius, 'que, uiro suo, post interfectionem Sixti et Laurentii, diminitus punito, peciit se baptizari, cum filio Decii Cirilla, a Iustino presbitero, et alia die defuncta est, ac iuxta sanctum Ypolitum in cripta sepulta,' Ob. et Mart. 168.
Trursus, Drursus, Dec. 14, a blunder for Drusus q. v.
tt for t: marttra, Ep. 267.
1. tú, *thou*, Prol. 14 = Skr. tvā *thee*.
2. tú, *I am*, for táu, tú-sa, Ep. 385.
tue, adj. *silent*, gen. sg. Dec. 22, a nickname for a saint named Ultán, Mart. Don. p. 342. mac dá thó *filius duorum silentium* Z². 228. W. taw.
tuarcaib, tuargaib, *surrexit*, Mar. 9.
túas, (do-úas) adv. *up* Ep. 70. Z². 612. In Dec. 28 A tuas seems a mistake for duas, the reading of R. (duais B, D).
túaslucud, s. m. (do-oslucud) *an opening, freeing*, dat. sg. Mar. 27.
tuath, s.f. *a people, a tribe* (root TU), 2 Beitr. 165. dat. sg. tuaith pref. 7. Ep. 396. abl. sg. tuath Prol. 142. (where *a* seems the possess. pron. 3d sg. used pleonastically) dat. pl. tuathaib June 17. acc. pl. tuatha Nov. 8. Ep. 33.
tuathach, adj. May 24. P. O'C. gives three meanings 1. *country-like, rural*. 2. *lordly*. 3. *sinistrous, awkward*. The second suits best here.
tuath, s. *the north, the left*, antúaid *a septentrione* Z². 612, tuathbel *sinistrorsum*, tuathum *ad sinistram meam*, Sanct. h. 2. All from a compound of du- and savia=Skr. savya, Zend. havya, Welsh aeu.
tuathmag, s.n. *north plain*, loc. sg. tuathmaig Dec. 11: cf. desmaig Prol. 226.
tuba, s. *a thin sod for thatching*, tuba tire O'Dav. 119. acc. sg. luid fo thalmain tuba *went to a shelter under ground*, June 6, where the glossographer explains tuba by *in a house or under shelter* In B and D the reading is tugai *thatch*.
1. tuc, *to understand* (do-ucc-): tucu, *intelligo* 2d sg. conj. mani thucai Prol. 313; tucsat intellexerunt, Z². 464. Hence the English slang word *twig*.
2. tuc, *to bring, give*, (do-ucc) 1 pl. s-pret. abs. -tucsam Ep. 31. 3d pl. pret. pass. douctha, rouctha, Prol. 45. na tuic sétchi *noli ducere uxorem*, Z². 443.
tucaith, s. *cause* Pref. 8. 16. tucsait (gl. causa est) Ml. 58ᶜ.
tuchtach, adj. *shapely*, Three Ir. Gl. 134. maccaim tuchtach .... atotchomnaic, L U. 68ᵇ. acc. sg. f. tuchtaig-n July 21, derived from tucht (tucht arandalfarsa, Táin bó Fráich): tucht animroma, H. 2. 16. col. 392.
tudrach, s. (gl. irritamen) Z². 810. acc. sg. Ep. 329. cf. dodúrget *pellicium*, Z². 433, todurgim, totúrgim (gl. irrito, gl. pellicio) Z². 42. intudmchtai (gl. inviti) Ml. 46ᶜ. At Ep. 329, B has dudrach .i. miscais .i. tromdacht, mere guesses.
tuichse, part. pret. pass. *chosen* (=do-fo-guiste, Ebel, cf. toga supra). gen. sg. m. tuicsi Oc. 25. superl. du thuichsimem (gl. acceptissimi tui) Ml. 71ᵇ.
tuidme, s. *a binding together, union*, Oc. 17. acc. sg. Ep. 355. tuidhme .i. coimhcheangal, P. O'C. oc tuidme Corm. s.v. essem. a ligo o thuidmi H. 2. 16, tuidmide (gl. fixum) G.C². 984, where it is wrongly taidmide. The root of tuidme (= do-fo-de-mia) seems da (Skr. dā, dāmān, dāma, Gr. ἔω, ἐέ-σις, ἐε-σ-μός).
tuile, s.n. *flood, abundance*, Z². 229, gen. sg. tuili (ms. tuile, tuiliu) Prol. 250. dat. sg. tuilin Prol. 124, 247, Ep. 310.
tuillem, s.n. *addition, enhancement*, for tuilnem, do-fo-lan-em: do fuilled *ad amplificationem*, Z². 353. see firthuillem, and cf. tuilled *derbtha more proof*, fuillim *addo* ex fuilnim.
tuir, s. *pillar*, Ap. 8. dat. sg. turid Corm. s.v. tuirgin: for *stuir, cognate with σταυρός?

1. túirim, *I scrutinize*, 3d pl. pres. indic. passive tuirtir Prol. 230. 2d sg. imperat. túir Prol. 331. 1st pl. b-fut. no-s-tuirfem Prol. 289. 1st sg. s-pret. ro-s-tuirius June 26. 1st pl. s-pret. rotbuirsium, rotúirsem Ep. 75. 143. 3d pl. rutuirset (gl. scrutati sunt) Ml. 44ᵈ.

tuirem, tuirim, s. *a recounting* .i. airemuh, *a reckoning or counting, repeating or reciting*, P.O'C. dat. sg. Pref. 98. Ep. 231. 305. 390.

tuirenn, tuirend, s. m. (n. ?) *wheat*: gen. sg. tuirind, May 21. dat. sg. tuirind (for *tuiriunn) Aug. 18, Nov. 24.

tuirmim, *I recount, I declare*, 2d sg. conj. tuirme (.i. aisneid, Three Ir. Gl. 136) Sep. 17. 3d sg. pres. indic. pass. tuiremar Z². 652. (trissinprecept bésti ituiremar bestatu cáich ' **per doctrinam moralem in quâ denuntiatur moralitas cuiusvis** '), 3d sg. pret. pass. ro-tuirmed, Ep. 122.

tuisel, s.m. *a falling* (*do-fo-PAT-tila, cf. πίτνημι, πίπτω), dat. sg. tuisiul Z². 211. acc. sg. tnisel-n July 8. acc. pl. tuisliu Z². 15. dofuislim (gl. labo) Z². 435, hotuislider (gl. quo laberis) 438. dufuisledor (gl. ut relabatur) ib. dufuisledar 442.

tus, infixed pron. *them*, Prol. 73=-das-, B, -dus-, Prol. 57.

u expresses Indo-European u : sruth.

u for a in Lebar Brecc : rosischtutar Prol. 70. fiadu 86. piunn May. 5. firendgu Ep. 322. osnadu Ep. 326. brigu Prol. 87. nessu 217. carum 264. denum, -snadut, rathutar &c. : from o by assimilation : urd Prol. 279, surn Ap. 24, Furtunatus June 11, purt Ep. 187.

for i : um Feb. 8 : for -iu : dorimu Ep. 317, rigu Jan. 23 : for infected a before r : ardrriice Ap. 19 D.

-u, suffixed pers. pron. of 3d pl. acc. friu.

ú generally expresses the ú of other Indo-European languages : dún, rún. In dúil *elementum* (dhā-tu) and gnús *mos* it seems to have come from ā. In clú, núe, súil it represents av.

ua, úai from ó, ó i : trúag=trogas, slúag=slōgas, Hiruath=Heród, búaid=bódi, crúaid=cródi.

ua, hua, s.m. *nepos* (=O. Ir. aue, haue = πάϊς) Ap. 11, where it is a dissyllable. The gen. sg. hui, ui, Jan. 23, Feb. 7, June 14, Oc. 11, 30, Dec. 6, is treated as a monosyllable, and is therefore, I think, a Middle-Irish corruption of the last syllable of maccu.

úabair, adj. *haughty*, Prol. 199, cognate with uabar *vana gloriatio* Z². 22 and ὕβρις. Hence the verb ru-n-naibrigistar (gl. profanauerat) Ml. 73ᵇ.

1. úag, húag, óg, adj. *integer* (root ug, whence Skr. ojas, ojman, Lat. aug-men, aug-ustus, aug-eo, Goth. aukan, Lith. augu, áug-ti *wachsen*) Jan. 8, Aug. 30. Oc. 30, gen. sg. f. uaige May 3. n. pl. f. uagn June 5. acc. pl. n. uaga Dec. 10 (where A has uagne), compar. uagu Nov. 30. comp. huag-césad June 6, and see óg. In Ep. 358 anuag no-raidiu seems *ro integrum quod dico* !

2. úag, s.f. *virgo*, gen. sg. uage Oc. 4 (óighe A.), gen. pl. uag-n Jan. 28. dat. pl. uagaib Jan. 27. acc. pl. uaga Sep. 20 (ogha D.). See nóebúag : uag from ug=virgo from vargh (vrh)= Ohg. magad (Eng. maid) from ma(g)h.

úagbail, s. *perfect goodness*, dat. sg. Dec. 3.

úagbailce, adj. *perfectly strong*, Aug. 16.

úagdae, adj. *virginal*, dat. sg. fem. uagdai July 29, acc. dual ógda, Dec. 10 D.

úage, úaige, s. f. *wholeness, virginity*, gen. sg. húaige, óige, May 25, Dec. 6, dat. sg. uaigi, uagi, corruptly uage, Prol. 255, Mar. 29, April 6, June 4, 18, Aug. 29, Sep. 1, Oc. 8, 14, Nov. 14, 18, Dec. 30. acc. sg. uaigi, Sep. 26.

úai, umlaut of úa, ó : tuai, rúaim, únige.

úaib, *e vobis*, Ep. 374.

úainn, huaind, uain, uan, huan, *e nobis*, April 21, June 11, 13, Dec. 20. With the suffix -ni : uainni, huanni, Jan. 28.

uair, conj. *quia*, Pref.

úaitne, uatne, s.m. (n. ?) *a pillar, column*, Ap. 29, dat. sg. úaitniu, dat. pl. úaitnib, LU. 23ᵃ.

húalann, Sep. 26, nualann? P. O'Cl. nalland .i. uasal.
uall, s. f. *superbia* (gl. elatio) Z². 232. gen. sg. uáille, Z². 242. Hence
uallach, adj. *proud*, Prol. 189, huallach (gl. arrogans) Ml. -41. n. pl. m. uallaig Prol. 245=huallaig (gl. elati) Z². 55. Hence uallchar *arrogance*, LU. 21ᵇ.
1. uar, s. f. = hóra (W. awr, O. Bret. aor), gen. sg. uare, orr, la braíud noen-úaire, LU. 31ᵇ. dat. sg. in cech uair, Dec. 29.
2. uar, adj. *cold* (W. oer), nom. f. gáeth ard huar isel grían LU. 11ᵇ. gen. sg. f. uare, Ap. 17, uaire, Ep. 331. Cognate perhaps with Zend aota.
úas, prep. (W. uch, 2 Beitr. 176) cum dat. *above, over*, Prol. 22, 23, 30, 155, 179, 250, Mar. 15, Ap. 23, June 17, Aug. 30, Dec. 12, Ep. 566. With the article: uasin lige Pref. uasna flaithib Ep. 542: with pronouns, uas-barn, uas forn, *over your*. Ep. 63, uassa, *above it*, Pref. B.
úasal, uassal, adj. (W. uchel) *high, noble*, Feb. 4, Ap. 25, 27, Sep. 23, gen. sg. m. uasail Feb. 24, Ap. 3, July 22, Sep. 24, gen. sg. f. uaisle, Feb. 7, dat. sg. m. uasal June 1, Aug. 13, acc. sg. n. uasal-n Oc. 24, voc. sg. m. uasail Ep. 462 A, n. pl. m. uasail, Prol. 327. Compar. uaisliu, uasliu, Prol. 151, 263, Jan. 7, 18, 21, Mar. 19, May 1, Oc. 23, Ep. 11, 55, 319, 395, superl. huaislimem (gl. altissimum) Z². 278.
úasalathair, s.m. (gl. patriarcha: cf. AS. heahfäder), n. pl. uasalathraig Ep. 13, 243, gen. huasalathrach, dat. húasalathrachaib Z². 261.
úasaluóeb, s. m. *a noble saint*, gen. pl. uasaluoeb-n, Ep. 277.
úatiu, Ep. 395 B, compar. (used as a superl.) cognate with úaithed *paucitas*, Z². 24.
uce, = ἴχε in ἤγγιχον, Ebel, 1 Beitr. 175, see cotarnicset and tuc supra.
ucut, adv. *there*, isin lige ucut *in the grave there*. rath na meti ucut *grace of that greatness*, Pref. 95, 102.
ui, 1. umlaut of u (popuil, nom. popul. buidin, cruiche), 2, umlaut of o (cuirp nom. corp, muir =mori, metrapuil), 3. for ai (muig, muige, nom. mag, Muire=Maria), for i : fuil Prol. 281 A.
úi umlaut of á (clúime, dúine, nom. sg. clúm, dún).
uib, suffixed pron. 3d pers. pl. fiad-uib.
uile, adj. pron. *every, all*, Prol. 141, 147, 201, Z². 229, 360, gen. sg. f. uile Ap. 20, n. pl. uile (for uili), Prol. 53, 264, gen. pl. mac nanule ndana *filius omnium artium*, Book of Leinster 149, a. 3, acc. pl. Ep. 486.
uis, adj. .i. umhal *humilis*, O'Cl. .i. coir, LLec. Voc. 69, .i. conuidais no umal, ib. 133, n. pl. m. uissi, ussi, June 19.
uissen, gen. sg. July 8, Glenn Uissen.
Ulaid, *Ulstermen*, gen. pl. ulad-n Dec. 1 [cf. fines ulathorum Lib. Arm. 2 b 2. ad regiones ulothorum. ib. 3 a 2], dat. pl. ultaib, acc. pl. ultu Lib. Arm. 8 b 1. Z². 961. In the second edition of the Gramm. Celtica p. 258, this word is wrongly placed under the consonantal declension.
ule, s. *evil*, acc. sg. Ep. 478. see ole.
Ultan of Ard Breccain, Sep. 4.
um, prep. for imm, imb, q. v. Feb. 8 A, May 8 A.
un, an infixed and suffixed personal pronoun of the first person. The class to which it belongs is as follows:—

sg. 1. um, om : with prefixed s, sum   pl. unn : with prefixed s, sunn*.
    2. ut, ot   ub, ob
    3. us.   usu, osn

Examples: (a) infixed : (1) inun um-ruidbed *circumcisus sum* Z². 328, ar-om-foimfea acc

---

* Absolute forms with prefixed s are : ol-smé *say I*, II. 2. 16, col. 388, and (ro)laimir-sni (gl. audemus) Wb. 15 cited Z¹. 325.

piet me ib. dian-un-soirac *si me salvas* Ml. 19 r. imm-un-rordad *memorati sumus*, Z². 328, ar-un-utangar (gl. adficiemur) Ml. 47 r. ar-un-tāia, Z. 577. (2) ar-ot-naisc *dó bind thyself for it*; Táin bo Fráich (-dut, -dot- formed by prefixing do, are more frequent). ar-ob-rói-naso *ros despondi*, Z². 813. ad-ob-rogart *vos fascinavit*, Z². 330. (3) No examples in the sg. of -us infixed: pl. imm-us-acaldat (gl. se adloquuntur) Ml. 61 r, imm-us-asenat (gl. obviaverunt sibi) South. Ps. imm-us-comarc *cos rogavit*, Corm. s.v. prull, imm-os-tuaircet, Tochmarc Bec Fola.

(b) suffixed: (1) táth-um *est mihi*, Prol. 217 A, bith-om-sa *sit mihi* and (with progressive assimilation) aiussium Jan. 30. suáidium July 18, Sep. 21. Colm. h. snad-sium ar cel LU. 15ᵃ. táth-und *est nobis* Prol. 217 B. and (with progressive assimilation) snaid-siunn *servet nos*, Colm. h. 38, snaid-siund July 18 B. Sep. 21. B. ainsiunn *protege nos*, Sanct. h. 14. (2) táth-ut *est tibi* July 24. tri-ut *per te*, fri-ut, cuc-ut *ad te*, iarm-ut (gl. post te) Ml. 70ᵃ. er-ut-su, tor-ut-su, cen-ut-su Z². 334. air-iub-si *pro vobis* Z. 334. (3) sg. sex-us *investigavit ille* Amra Chol.. táth-us *est eae* Feb. 5, mors-us *magnificavit illum*, Prol. 132. slocc-us *obruit illa* Trip. Eg. 2. b. 2. gabs-us *cepit illud ni*, Táin bó Fráich: with progressive assimilation: glins-ius *dilucidavit ille* Amra Chol., sluins-ius *significavit ille* ib. cuills-ius *destruxit ille* ib. cluids-ius *superavit ille*, ib. Pl. mórs-us *magnificavit illos*, Jan. 30. troeths-us *oppressit illos* Nov. 16 B, dlomth-us *denunciat illos* Feb. 17. cars-us fiadu *illos amavit dominus* 11. 2. 16 col. 393. mairtid-us *occidet illos*, LU. 19ᵃ. with progressive assimilation: guids-ius *rogavit illos*, 1 S.M. 250. The form with n seems found in LU. 111ᵇ: má-s-tat carait co-ná-m-usn-ágat. ma-s-tat námait co-m-os-r-alat *if they are friends, let them not fight me; if they are foes, let them come to me* and in LL. 184ᵇ 1, imm-osn-acaillet iarum ailill 7 medb *A.* and *M. then converse with each other*.

umal, adj. = *humilis*, gen. sg. m. umail, humail, Sep. 28, Dec. 8.
Umbanius, Dec. 5. = Ambonius, a Roman saint, Ob. and Mart. Dec. 1, celebrated with Filatus [R. has Humani.]
-unn, see -um.
úr, s.f. *earth*, *mould*, *clay*, Corm. 45. gen. sg. úire, húre, Prol. 128, Ep. 219.
Urban, gen. Urbain, May 19 = 'S. Urbanus papa et confessor,' Boll.
urdraice, adj. Ap. 19 B. = *audire*, *ordaire* q. v.
-us, see -um.
-ut, see -um.
Valentinus, Feb. 14 (where seven Valentines, all martyrs, are mentioned by the Bollandists). A Ravenna martyr, Dec. 16, Us. At xvi. kal. Martis (= Feb. 14) two Valentines are celebrated, one a Roman priest, beheaded under Claudius Cæsar, the other a martyr, Bishop of Interamnes.
Valeran, Valiran, Valerianus. Aug. 11.
Valerius (Varilius), Bishop of Cæsaraugusta (Saragossa), Jan. 22.
Victor, Dec. 29. gen. sg. Uictoir Dec. 17. Victor Maurus martyred at Milan, May 8. Victor an Alexandrian martyr, May 17.
Victorinus (Vichtorinus B), Mar. 6, a Nicomedian saint who died in prison, Ob. and Mart. 93.
Vincentius, July 23 (Mart. Romæ seu via Tiburtina, Boll. July 24). The Vincentius at Aug. 21 was a deacon of Saragossa, martyrised temp. Diocletian. See his legend Jameson S. and L. Art. 549.
Virulus, Feb. 21, a corruption of Verulus, name of a martyr who suffered at Adrumetum in Africa.
Vitális (Vitalais, A), Jan. 9. martyr. The Bollandists mention at this day two martyrs named Vitalis. One died in Africa, the other at Smyrna.
Vitus (Victus, B. and D.), June 15. a Sicilian boy-martyr, temp. Diocletian, Jameson S. and L. Art. 554.
Zofan, acc. sg. Ep. 249 = Stephanus q. v.
Zenatius, Zenotius, Stenonius, Aug. 24, mistakes for Zenobius, martyred at Antioch ł
Zoilus, June 30 B. (stolus A. solus B), an African martyr, Boll.

2 u

GEOGRAPHICAL INDEX

TO THE NOTES.

Achad Aball (*Aghowle*), clvi.
Achad Bó Cainnig (*Aghabo*), cxlii, clvi.
Achad Callten, clxviii.
Achad Cille Clochair, cxlvii.
Achad Conairi (*Achonry*, in cos. Sligo and Mayo), cxxx.
Achad Deo (dá eo ?), clviii.
Achad Fiuniche (on the Dodder), lxxxv.
Achad Raithin, clxxiii.
Achad úr (*Freshford*), lxiv.
Achaia, clxxiii.
Afraic (*Africa*), cxxxiii.
Airdne Coemáin (*Ardcavan*, on Wexford Bay), cii, where Airne is misprinted for Airdne.
Airgéill (*Oriel* in Ulster), lxxii.
Airgiallaich, lxiv.
Airic, xxxi.
Airtech (in co. Roscommon), liii.
Alba (*Scotland*), lxxv, cii, cvi, cxv, clvi, clxxx.
Alexandria, lxxvi.
Ambiani, clxi.
Antiochia, cii, cxxi. Antuach (Antioch) xxxix, liii, lxxii.
Aporcrossan (*Applecross*), lxxv.
Aráip, Araib (*Arabia*), cxv, cxxxiii.
Ard, clxix – Ard Ulad.
Ardachad (*Ardagh*), xlviii.
Ardbó on Loch n-Echach (*Arboe* in Tyrone ?) lii.
Ard Camroiss (Cáinroiss), clxxxii.
Ard Carna (*Ardcarne*), lxii.
Ard Finnin (*Ardfinnan*), lxxvii.
Ardgal, cvii.
Ard Macha (*Armagh*), lxxvi, ciii, cliv, clv.
Ard maic Nascai, clix.
Ard Mail, lxiii.
Ardmór in Desib Muman, cxx.
Ard na sruithe, l.
Ard Sratha (*Ardstraw*, co. Tyrone), clxvii.
Ard Ulad (*The Ards*, co. Down), xci, cxlvii.
Armenia, lxvi, cxxvii.
A'ru, a hill, clxx.
A'ru airthir (*Inisheer*), clxx.

A'ru (A'rann), *Aranmore*, l, lxiv, cii.
Asia Minor, xxxiv.
A'thcliath (*Dublin*), clxxxiii.
A'th dá loarg (*Boyle*, co. Roscommon), clxxix.
A'th Duirn Buidi, xlviii.
A'th Truim húi Loegairi (*Trim*) lii, clv, clvi,

Bairche, lxxxvi.
Balla in Cera, lxvi.
Banua (the river *Bann*), clxxx.
Becc-E'riu (*Beggery Island*, *Wexford*), lxxvi.
Belach Conglais (*Baltinglass*, co. Wicklow), clxxi.
Belach Gabrain (*Gowran Pass*), clxxxiv.
Belach Mugna (*Ballaghmoon*), clxxxi.
Bennchor (*Bangor*), liv, lxvi, lxxv, lxxxv.
Berba (the river *Barrow*), l, clxviii, clxxxi. clxxxiii.
Bethlehem, cxlviii, clxxxiv.
Bithynia, cxxvii.
Birra (*Birr*), clxxiii.
Bó-chluain, clxix.
Bóind (the river *Boyne*), lxxxiii.
Brechmag (*Breaffy*), xc.
Brechmag in huib Torta, cxvii.
Brefne Connacht, cxlii.
Brega, lxxiv, lxxxiii, clx, clxvii, clxx, clxxxiii.
Bretain, xxxix.
Bretain Corn (*Cornwall*), lxxxvii.
Brig Ele (*Croghan Hill?* King's county), xlvi.
Brí Gobann (*Brigown*, near Mitchelstown, Cork), clxxii.
Brosnachae, clxxiii.

Caille Fallamain (in co. Westmeath), cxlv.
Cairpre hua Ciarda (*Carbury*, co. Kildare), lx, xcix.
Caitt(?), lxxxiv.
Caluc(?), xxxiii.
Campain, (*Campania*), xxxiv.
Carthago, cxxxiii, cxlv.
Cassan Linne, lxvi, cxxxi.

2 *n* 2

Cathair Conchaid, lxv.
Cell Abbain (*Killabban*, Queen's county), clx.
Cell Achid Sinchill (*Killeigh*, King's co.), cvii.
Cell A'ir i Midi (*Killare*, in Westmeath), clxviii.
Cell Airnd, cxv.
Cell Biesige (*Kilbixy*, Westmeath), cliv.
Cell Brige, xl.
Cell Céit Christ (inHúib Dunchada), lx.
Cell Chére (*Kilkeare*, Upper Ormond), xxxiii.
Cell Conainn, lxii.
Cell Cuiliud (*Kilcullen*), lxxvii.
Cell da Chelléc (*Kilmallock*), lxv.
Cell dá less, lxxxv.
Cell dara (*Kildare*), xl, xlvi, lxxii, lxxxiii.
Cell Dolga in Ardgal (*Kildalkey?*), cvii.
Cell Derbiled (*Kildervila* or *Termondervila*), cxxviii.
Cell Draignech (*Kildreenagh*, co. Carlow), cxxxi.
Cell Faelain i Laigis (*Ballyheyland*), cvi.
Cell Finche (*Killinny*), xlviii.
Cell Findich, xlviii.
Cell Finninaige, lxxvii.
Cell Fortchirn, clv.
Cell Fuinchi, lxxxiii.
Cell Gabra (?) cxli.
Cell Garad, cxlii.
Cell Giallain, cliv.
Cell Ingen Aillén, xci.
Cell Ingen Ailella, clxxxi.
Cell Ingen Iaráin, clix.
Cell Iugine Branin, lxiv.
Cell I'tu (*Killeedy*), clxix.
Cell Lamraige (*Killamery*), clxxx.
Cell Macc Cathail, clxxxiv.
Cell Macc Thaidg, clvi.
Cell Maelocoisne, cxxxi.
Cell Maigneun (*Kilmainham*), xxxv, clxxxiii.
Cell Manach, clxxxiv.
Cell Manach in iarthar Osraige (*Kilnamanagh*), cxxi, clxxxiv.
Cell modluit, li.
Cell Mór Airthir Fine, clxix.
Cell Mór hua Nialláin, lxxii.
Cell Mosflóic, cxviii.
Cell Muine (*St. David's*), xxxix, xl.
Cell uan-Ingen, clix.
Cell Rignonaig (*St. Andrew's*) clvi.
Cell Roiss, xxxix.
Cell Ruaid (*Kilroot*), clvi.

Cell Scire (*Killskeery*, in Meath), lxiv.
Cenannus (*Kells*), lxxxvii, clx, clxxxix.
Cenél Conaill (*Donegal*), cxix.
Cenél Dobtha (in the east of Co. Roscommon), lii.
Cenél Eogain, Tyrone, Londonderry, and the baronies of Inishowen and Raphoe, co. Donegal, lxxv, cxlvi.
Ceungarad (*Kingarth*, in Bute), cxxx.
Cenn Saile i Fini Gall (*Kinsaley* north of Dublin), cxviii.
Cenn Saile indescirt Erenn (*Kinsale* in Cork), clxxxii.
Cera (*Carra* in Connaught), lxvi, xc, clxxxi.
Cianachta Glinne Geimin (*Keenaght* in Ulster), xxxiii, clxxx.
Ciarraige Ai, xc.
Ciarraige Luachra (*Kerry*), lxxiv, clv.
Claonad (*Clane*), clxxxiii.
Clann Lugdach maic Itha, lxi.
Clochar (*Clogher*), lxiv.
Clochar Duilig, clxix.
Cluain Aithchein, liii, clv.
Cluain Boirenn, l.
Cluain Brónaig (*Clonbroney*, co. Longford), clxxxiii.
Cluain Bruices, clxvii.
Cluain Cáin (*Clonkeen*), xxxviii, clv.
Cluain Cáin A'rad, clxxxi.
Cluain Cairpti (*Kilbarry*), lii.
Cluain Conairi Tomain (*Cloncurry*), cxlvi.
Cluain Conlaid, clvi.
Cluain Credail (*Killeedy*, co. Limerick), xxxiv.
Cluain Crucha Coirpre, clxxii.
Cluain dá u-Annaba, clxxxii.
Cluain Dolcain (*Clondalkin*), cxxx.
Cluain E'idnech (*Clonenagh*), liii, lx, xc, clix, clxvii, clxix, clxx.
Cluain Eoais (*Clones*), lxxii.
Cluain Ferguile, clxxxii.
Cluain Ferta Brenainn (*Clonfert*), liii, lx, lxxiii.
Cluain Ferta Molua (*Clonfertmulloe*, in Ossory), xxxiv, cxxxviii, clxxxiii.
Cluain Ferta Mugaine, cxli.
Cluain Fota Boetain Aba (*Clonfad*, co. Westmeath), l.
Cluain Fota Fine (*Clonfad*), cxxxii.
Cluain Fota i Laigis, clxvii.
Cluain Fota Libréin, cxxxii.
Cluain i Laigis, cxxxii.

GEOGRAPHICAL INDEX.   cccxxxiii

Cluain Immorroiss, clviii.
Cluain Imorchuir, cxlvi.
Cluain Iraird (*Clonard*, in Meath), l, cxlvii, clxxxii, clxxxiv.
Cluain na Lántan, xc.
Cluain Lethtengail, clxviii.
Cluain Luicell, clv.
Cluain Molocóc, xc.
Cluain Moesene, xxxiii.
Cluain Mór, cxviii.
Cluain Mór Maedóic (*Clonmore*, in Leinster), xlix, clvi.
Cluain mór Main, lxxiv.
Cluain Sosta (*Cloonsast*, King's county), clxxx.
Cluain Uamai (*Cloyne*, in Munster), clxxi.
Coinderi (*Connor*), cxlii.
Conailli Muirthemni (co. Louth), lxxvii, clxix, cxxxi.
Congbail Glinne Suiligo (*Conwal*, in Tirconnell), xlix.
Coningnig, lxxvii.
Conmacni Mara (*Connamara*), cxxx.
Connacht (*Connaught*), xxxv.
Corcach (*Cork*), xxxii, lxiv.
Corco-Baiscinn (*Corcovascin*, in Thomond), xxxix, cxlvii.
Corco-Duibne(*Corgaguiny*, in Kerry), liii, lxxiii, lxxiv, clix, clx, clxxiii.
Corcofirtri (in Sligo), clvi.
Corco Luigde (in co. Cork), lxi.
Corn, lxxxvii.
Crích Coirpri, clxxxiii.
Croch, a river, clxxii.
Cruachan Brig Eli (*Croghan Hill*, in Offaly), lxxvi.
Cruachan Maige Abna, cliv.
Cruachu Connacht (*Rathcroghan*), liii.
Cuailnge (*Cooley*, in co. Louth), cxliv.
Cuan Airbre, cxviii.
Cúil Bennchoir i Lurg, clv.
Cúil Bennchoir in huib Failgi (*Cool Banagher*), clv.
Cúil Muilt, clxxii.
Cuilenn, a mountain, clxxi.
Cuirenc (barony of *Kilkenny West*, in Westmeath), clvi.
Cúl Raithin (*Coleraine*), clxviii.

Daiminis Ulad (*Devenish*), cxlv, clxxix.
Daire (*Londonderry*), lxxxiii.
Daire Eidnech, clv, clxix.

Daire Ingen Aillen, xci.
Daire maic Dímmai, clxvii.
Daire Maic Marga, xcix.
Daire Mochua, clv.
Daire Mór i Maig Airb (*Derrymore?*) cxxi.
Daire na Fland (*Derrynavlan*, co. Tipperary), clv.
Dairinis, xl, cxxxi.
Dairmag, Daurmag, Dermag, Dirmag (*Durrow*), cvi, cvii.
Dairmag hua n-Duach, clviii.
Dál-n Araide (in the east of Ulster), xxxix, lxxxiv, cxlvi, clvi, clxviii, clxix.
Dál Birnn, lx, cii.
Dál Buindi (on the Lagan), xci.
Dál Cais (in N. Munster), lxxxviii, cxvii.
Dál Cethern, cxlii.
Dál Mesincorb (in co. Wicklow), lxxxix, cxlv.
Dál Riata, lxxxiv.
Dalpia(?), cxxxvii.
Damascus, cviii.
Delbna Ethrai (*Delvin-Mac-Coghlan*, in King's county), cvii.
Delbna Tíre dá Locha, clxxxii.
Dési, xxxiv, cxv.
Dési Muman (*Decies*, co. Waterford), l, lxv, cxvii, cxviii, clxxiii.
Disert Bricín, cxlii.
Disert Cumín, liv.
Disert Diarmata (*Castledermot*), cvi.
Disert Garad, cxli.
Disert i Maig Raigne, clxix.
Disert maic Conlocha, cxviii.
Disert maic Cuilind, xxxi.
Disert Muirdelair, clxviii.
Disert Tola (*Dysart O'Dea*, co. Clare), lxvi.
Díram, clvii.
Doel, name of a river, cxlv.
Doim-liac Cianain (*Duleek*), clxx.
Domnach maige Imchlair (*Donaghmore*, in Tyrone), cxliii.
Domnach Sechnaill (*Dunshaughlin*), clxxiii.
Dorn Buide, xlviii.
Dothair (the river *Dodder*), lxxxv.
Drochait, in Aird Ulad, cxlvii.
Druim bó (*Drumbo*), cxxx.
Druim Cliab hi Cairpri (*Drumcliff*), cii.
Druim Dáganda, clxix.
Druim Daliter, clxix.
Druim Derg, xlvi.
Druim Dubáin, lxxiii.

Druim Eneselainne (*Drumiskin*, co. Louth), clxix.
Druim Fertain, lx.
Druim Fota talman, cxxxii.
Druim Indbir (*Dromincer*, in Tipperary), clxxix.
Druim Ingard, clv.
Druim Láigille, lxxxv.
Druim Mór in Húib Echach Ulad (*Dromore*), xcix.
Druim Raithno, cxxxii.
Druim Snechtai i Fernmaig (*Drumsnat*, co. Monaghan), cxxviii.
Dub Arda, clxxxiii.
Dubthor, l.
Dún Bláain (*Dumblane*), cxxx.
Dún-Blesce, xxxiii.
Dún dá én (*Duneane*, in Antrim), clxi.
Dún Flesce, clxvii.
Dún-geimin (*Dungiven*, co. Londonderry), clxxx.
Dún Rechet, clxxi.

Echdruim Breccáin, lxxxiv.
Edessa, lx, cxv.
Ega (*Eig*), lxxiv.
Egypt, Egipt, Egept, xxxiv, lx, lxxvi, cliv.
Eli, cxxi, clxxiii.
Eli thuascirt, cxxvii, clx.
Enach Dairen, lxvi.
Enach Truimn (*Annatrim*, in Upper Ossory), clxix.
Eoganacht Chaisil, xxxviii, lx, lxxiv, cliv, clviii, clxix.
Eoganacht Locha Léin, clxix.
Ephesus, cvii, cxxix.
Eriu (*Ireland*), lxxiv, lxxvi, cii, cxxxiv, cxliv, clix, clxxx.
Eriu, a hill ('in Ui-Faelain, in the plain of the Liffey,' O'Don.), clxx.
Ernaide (*Urney*, in Tyrone), xxxviii, clvi.
Ess mac n-Eirc (on the river Boyle), lxii.

Fabar (*Fore*, in Westmeath), xxxvii.
Faeldruim (*Feltrim*, near Swords), clxix.
Fánait (a territory in Tirconnell), cxxxiv.
Féile (Fial?), clv.
Feraun Duin, cxx.
Ferna (*Ferns*), xxxix.
Fornmag (*Farney*, co. Monaghan), cxxviii.
Forta for Feirc (*Slane*), clxvii.
Fia, lxxiii.
Fid Cuillinn in búib Faelain (*Feighcullen*), cxxx.

Fid Duin in Osraigib (*Fiddown*), lxxxviii, cxxxi.
Fid Ela, lxxxvii.
Fid Lothan at Less Mór, lxiv.
Fidarta, lxxxiv.
Fidbad Dáil Araide, clxi.
Findabair Aba (*Fennor*, on the Boyne), lxxxiii.
Findmag i Fothartaib, lx.
Findtracht Gléri, lxi.
Fine Gall (*Fingal*, North Dublin), cxviii, clxix.
Fir Arda (*Ferrard*, co. Louth), xxxii, lxiv.
Fir Bile (*Farbill*, co. Westmeath), l.
Fir Cell (*Fircall*, King's County), clxxiii.
Fir Cúla Breg, lxxiii, clxxiii.
Fir Luirg (*Lurg*, co. Fermanagh), xxxix.
Fir Maige Féne, or Fir Maige (*Fermoy*), xxxvii, clxxii.
Fir Tulach (*Fartullagh*, co. Westmeath), xxxiii, xlviii, cxxxii.
Flesc, a river, xxxiii, clxvii.
Fotharta, lx.
Fotharta Laigen (*Forth*, co. Carlow?), cxxxi.
Forthuatha Laigen (in the co. Wicklow), lxxvii.
Frainc (*the Franks*), cvii, cxxxi.
Futerna (*Whiterne*), cxlvii.

Gailenga (*Morgallion*, co. Meath), clvi.
Gailfine, clxi.
Gaill = Fine Gall, q. v., clvi.
Gaill Iudbir Domnand, l.
Gair maic moga, clx.
Galile, cxxi.
Gallia, cxv.
Gallia Lugdunensis, clxviii.
Gallgoedil (*Dano-Irish*), lxxv, cxxx.
Garganus, lxxxv, cxlviii.
Glan, cxliii.
Glas Mór, l.
Glas Nóiden (*Glasnevin*), clvi.
Glastonbury, cxxxii.
Glenn dá locha (*Glendalough*), xcviii, clv.
Glenn Faidble, xxxix.
Glen Gemin (*Glengiven*), xxxiii.
Glenn Rige, *Glenree*, (the valley of the Newry river), l.
Glenn Suilige (*Glenswilly*, in Tirconnell), xlix.
Glenn Uissen (*Killushinn*, near Carlow), liv, cxvii.
Gloinestir, cxxxii.
Goedil, lxiii, cxxxii.

Heliopolis, xxxiv.
Hermopolis, xxxiv.
Hí (*Iova*, corruptly *Iona*), liv, lx, lxiii, lxiv, c, cxxx, cxlvi.
Húi Bairrchi (= *Slievemargy*, Queen's county), lxxii, cxvii, clxxxiv.
Húi Briuin Chualann (part of the counties of Dublin and Wicklow), xlvi, xc.
Húi Cairpri n Mumain (in Limerick), lxv.
Húi Caitrenn, clxxx.
Húi Chernaig (in co. Limerick), lxxxvii.
Húi Chonin, lxxxvii.
Húi Cellaig Chualann (in Leinster), clxvii.
Húi Cennselaig (in Leinster), lxxvi, cii. cxviii, clx, clxxxix.
Húi Cinnselaig, cxxxi.
Húi Conaill Gabrai (*Conello*, in co. Limerick), clxviii, cixix.
Hui Dega, xxxix.
Húi Degad (in co. Wexford), cxviii.
Húi Donnchada (in Kerry), lxxxv.
Húi Dortain (in Meath), xxxiii.
Húi Drona (*Idrone*, co. Carlow), l, xci, cxxxi, cxlii. Húi Drona Laigen, clv, clvi.
Húi Dunch (*Idough*, co. Kilkenny ?), clviii.
Húi Duib Dunnach, clviii.
Húi Dunchada (in co. Dublin), lx, clx, clxxxiv.
Húi Echach Muman (the country of the O'Mahonys, co. Cork), clxxxi.
Húi Echach Ulad (*Iveagh*, co. Down), liii, lxxvi, lxxxix, clix, cxvi, clxxx.
Húi Enechelais (in co. Wicklow), lxxvii H ui Fenechlais ?
Húi Faeláin (*Offelan*, in co. Kildare), lxxxviii, xcix, cxxx, cxxxv, cxli, cxlvi, clx, clxxxiii.
Húi Failge (*Offaly*, in Leinster), lxv, lxvi, lxxvi, cvii, cviii, clxxx.
Húi Felmeda (in co. Wexford), cii.
Húi Fenechlais (in the barony of Arklow), clxix.
Húi Firb, lx.
Húi Fidgente (in co. Limerick, round Croom), cxx.
Húi Forchelláin (*Offerrilan*, Queen's county), cxli.
Húi Garrchon, lxiv, lxxiii, cxv, cxxxi, cxlv.
Húi Gilli Suanaig, lxxxvii.
Húi Liathain (in co. Cork), lxxxvi, cvi, cxliii, clxxi.
Húi Luchtai, lxxiv.
Húi Maic-Caille (*Imokilly*, co. Cork), lxxxvi, clxxiii.

Húi Maic-Uais (*Moygish*, in Westmeath), xlix, cvii, cliv.
Húi Mail (*Imaile*, in co. Wicklow), clv.
Húi Maine (territory of the O'Kellys, in Galway and Roscommon), l, lxii, cxxxi.
Húi Muirednig, cvi, cliv, clx.
Húi Núill, xlvi.
Hui Sellain, xlviii.
Húi Ségain, clv.
Húi Torta, cxvii.

Ierusalem, liii, lxxvi, clvii, clxxxiv.
Imbliuch (*Emly*, co. Tipperary), xc.
Imbliuch Cassain, cxliv.
Imbliuch Fia (*Emlagh*, in Meath), lxxiii.
Imbliuch Ibair (*Emly*, co. Tipperary), cxlv, clxxxiv.
Inber Domnann (*Malahide Bay*), l.
Inber Mara (*the Straits of Gibraltar ?*), xlvii.
India, cxv, cxxxiii.
Inis Aingin (*Inchinneen*, Hare Island, Lough Ree), clxxix.
Inis Airther, ci.
Inis Bó finde (*Inishboffin*, co. Mayo), cxxx.
Inis Boethfui (*Inishboheen*, co. Wicklow), lxxxix.
Inis Cail (*Inishkeel*, in Tirconnell), lxxxvi.
Inis Cáin Dega (*Iniskeen*, in co. Louth), cxxxi.
Inis Cathaig (*Scattery Island*, in the Shannon), xxxix, lx, lxii.
Inis Celtra (*Iniscaltra*, in Lough Derg), lxiv, clxxxii.
Inis Clothrann (*Iniscloghran*, in Lough Ree), xxxviii.
Inis Cusernid (*Inishcoursey*, co. Down), cxx.
Inis Maccu Cuinn, xxxv, lxix.
Inis Medcoit (*Lindisfarne ?*), cxxxv.
Inis Mocholmóic, clxix.
Inis Mór of Loch Uair, xlix.
Inis Mór in Húi maic Caille or in Húi Liathain, lxxxvi.
Inis Muiredaig (*Inishmurray*, in co. Sligo), cxxx.
Inis Pátric (Inishpatrick, near Skerries, co. Dublin), xxxiv.
Inis Teimle (*the Little Island*, near Waterford), cxv, clxviii, clxxix.
Inis Uachtair, lx.
Inis Ulad, clxxix.
Iosafath (in ualle), lxxxiii.
Irarda, xlix.
Italia, xxxiv.

GEOGRAPHICAL INDEX.

Lacus Christinae, cxix.
Láichis = Láigis (q.v), clxix.
Laigin (*Leinstermen, Leinster*), lx, cxv, clxxi.
Laid Treoit, clxxx.
Láigis (*Leix*, in Queen's county), xxxi, xxxviii, liii, lx, lxiv, lxxii, ci, cii, clvi, clxix.
Láine, clxxx.
Land Becuir, xxxvii.
Land Ela (*Lynally*, in King's county), xc, cxlvii, cliv.
Land Luachain, cvi.
Land Maic Luachain (in Meath) lxvi, lxc, ciii.
Land Ronain find (*Magheralin*, co. Down), lxxxix.
Lathrach Briuin (*Laraghbrien*), cxli.
Laodicea, xxxiv, clxxx.
Lec Cassain Linne, lxvi.
Lemchoill, liii.
Less Longarad, cxli.
Less-Mór, xxxix, xl, xlviii, lxiv, lxxxvi.
Less Mór in Albain, cvii.
Less Mór Mochua, cvii.
Less mór Mochuda (*Lismore*, co. Waterford), xl, l, cxx, clxxix.
Leth Cathail (*Lecale*, co. Down), lxxiv, cxlvi.
Leth Cuinn (*Conn's half*, the northern half of Ireland), cliv.
Letha, a forest, lxv.
Letha (*Latium*) lxiii.
Lethglenn (*Leighlinn*, co. Carlow), liii, lxxv, cxliv, clxviii, clxxviii.
Letir Dálaraide, xxxix.
Letracha Odrain (*Latteragh*, co. Tipperary), cxliv, clx.
Liamain, lxxxiv, clxxxi.
Liath in Eblinn, cxviii.
Liath Mór Mochoemóic (*Leamokevoge*), cxviii.
Liconium (?), cii.
Life (*the river Liffey*), xlvi.
Lilgach (Lilcach ? in Meath), clxxxiii.
Linn Luachan, cxxxi.
Loch Bricrenn (*Loughbrickland*, co. Down), clix.
Loch Carman (*Wexford Haven*), cii.
Loch Cuan (*Strangford Lough*), cvii, clxix.
Loch Dergdeirce (*Lough Derg*, on the Shannon), cxlvi, clvi.
Loch Erni (*Lough Erne*), xxxviii, xxxix, l, cxlv, clv.
Loch Garman (*Wexford Haven*), clxxxii.
Loch Gerg (Loch Derg, co. Donegal), clxxxii.

Loch Láig (*Belfast Lough*) clvi, clix.
Loch Léin (*Killarney Lakes*), lxxiii.
Loch Lemnachta, xlvi.
Loch n-Echach (*Lough Neagh*), xxxix, lii.
Loch Oirbsen (*Lough Corrib*), xxxv, xlix.
Loch Rib (*Lough Ree*), xxxviii.
Loch Rudraigi (*Dundrum Bay*), cxxxiv.
Loch Seimne, cxviii.
Loch Silenn (*Lough Sheelin*), lx.
Loch Uair (*Lough Owel*, Westmeath), xlix.
Longbaird (*Lombards*), cxv, cxxxi.
Luachair Masue, cvii.
Luachar Dedad, ciii.
Lugmad (*Louth*), lxiv, cxxxii, cxlii.
Luigni Connacht (*Leyny*, co. Sligo), cxxx, clvi.
Lurg (in Fermanagh), clv.
Lusca (*Lusk*, co. Dublin), cxliii, cxliv.

Macha = Ardmacha (*Armagh*), cxxxiii.
Mag Aei (in co. Roscommon), lxxxiv, clxxxiv.
Mag Airbh (in co. Kilkenny), cxxi.
Mag Arnaide (*Moyarney*, in Wexford), clx.
Mag Bolg (*Moybolg*, in Meath), clxxiii.
Mag Breg (*Moy Bray*), cxlvi.
Mag Elta (the plain of Clontarf), clxix.
Mag Eó in Dál Cais (*Moyna*, co. Clare?) lxxxviii.
Mag Eó na Saxan (*Mayo*), clxxxi.
Mag Garad, cxli.
Mag Itha (in barony of Forth, co. Wexford), xxxviii, clxviii.
Mag Laigen (the plain of Leinster), xxxiv, lxxxviii, ci.
Mag Lifi (in Kildare), clxxxi.
Mag Locha inn-Brogaib (in the county Kilkenny), lxxiv, xcix, cxxxii.
Mag Lundat (co. Tyrone), clx.
Mag nAilbi (*Moynalvy*), clxxxii.
Mag nAllain (?), clxxxii.
Mag Raigne (in barony of Kells, co. Kilkenny), cxlvi, clxviii.
Mag Rechet (*Morett*, Queen's county), clvi.
Mag Tuathat, cxli.
Mainister Bóiti (*Monasterboice*, co. Louth), clxxx.
Mairge, cxx.
Mediolanum (*Milan*), lxxii.
Men, cxlvi.
Men-Droichet (*Monadroghid*, in Leix), cxlvi.
Mide (*Meath*), xlix, l, lxiv, cxviii.
Míliuc (*Meelick*), l.

GEOGRAPHICAL INDEX.

Moethail Broccáin (*Mothel*, in Waterford), cxvii, cxviii.
Móin Fathnig (*Boughna Bog*, in Offaly?), xlvii.
Mucc-inis (on Lough Derg), cxlvi, clvi.
Mucraime, lxxxiv.
Mugduirn, clxxii.
Mugduirn Maigen (*Cremorne barony*, co. Monaghan), clxxxiii.
Muimnig (*Munstermen*), clxxxiii.
Muinter Chuanna, clviii.
Muinter Maelduib, clviii.
Muir n-Icht, xlvii.
Muir Torrén (*the Mediterranean*), xlvii.
Muma, Mumu (*Munster*), cxx, clxx, clxxxi.
Mumain (*Munster*), lxiii.
Mungairit (*Mungret*, co. Limerick), cxxi.
Muscraige Breogain (in the S.W. of the co. Tipperary), xc.
Muscraige Tíre (in co. Tipperary), xxxiii, clx.
Muscraige Trí-maige (in Barrymore, Cork), cxliii.

Nás (*Naas*, co. Kildare), clxx.
Nephtalim, cxxi.
Nicomedia, cxxi.
Noendruim (*Nendrum* or *Inishmahee*), cvii.
Noile, xxxiv.
Nola, xxxiv, cxxxv.

Omin, clvi.
Osraige (*Ossory*), xlviii, li, lx, lxxxviii, cii, cxxi, cxliii, clviii, clxxx.

Parona (*Peronne*), xxxv.
Plea, xlvii.

Ráith Blathmaic (*Rath*, in the south of the barony of Inchiquin, co. Clare), cxvii.
Ráith Cholpa (*Raholp*), lxxiv.
Ráith E'renn, cvi.
Ráith Maige Tuaiscirt, clv.
Ráith Mór una Clochar, lxxii.
Ráith Noe (*Rathnew*, in Wicklow), cxxxi.
Raithin (*Rahin*, King's county), lxiii, lxxvi, cxliv.
Relic Aingel, xlix.
Relic Odrain (in Iona), clx.
Róm (*Rome*), xxxii, xxxvi, liii, lxxxiv, cxix, cxxix.
Rómáin (*Romans*), cvii.
Ross, cxliii.

Ross Airther (*Rossorry* in Fermanagh), xxxviii.
Ross Commain (*Roscommon*), clxxxiv.
Ross Conaill, clxxxi.
Ross Corcumruad, cxxvii.
Ross Corr, lxxxvii.
Ross Cré (*Roscrea*, co. Tipperary), liv.
Ross Dela (*Rosdalla*, co. Westmeath), cxxxii.
Ross Ech i Midi (*Russagh* in the parish of Diamor), cxlv.
Ross Gialláin, cxliii.
Ross Glaisse, 1, clxxxiii.
Ross Liac, cxlv.
Ross mór mo-Mernoc, xxxix.
Ross Uainni, lxxvii.

Saig, lxi.
Saigir (*Seirkieran*, in King's county), lx, lxi.
St. Andrews, clvi.
Saxain (*Saxons*), cxxxii, Saxain bicc, cxxxv
Scíaich Condlaid, lxxxiii.
Scilla, cxix.
Sebastia, cxxxiii, cxxxv.
Senar, clvii.
Senbotha Fola, clx.
Senbuaile, lxxvii.
Sendless, xlix.
Sid Trudum (near Slane, in Meath), clxvii.
Sinand (the river *Shannon*), l.
Sinda, gen. sg. *the Shannon* (cf. sindhu), l.
Slaine (*Slane* in Meath), clx. clxvii.
Slebti (*Sletty* in Queen's county), clvi.
Sliab Bladma (*Slieve Bloom*), cxxviii.
Sliab Cua (*Slieve Gua*, co. Waterford), xxvii.
Sliab Cuilind (*Slieve Gullion*, co. Armagh). cxvi.
Sliab Eblinne (*Slieve-Phelim* mountains, co. Tipperary), lxxxv.
Sliab Gargain (*Mount Gargunos*), cxix.
Sliab Guairi (*Slieve Gory*, co. Cavan), clvi.
Sliab Liac (*Slieve League*, in Donegal), clxviii.
Sliab Mairge (*Slieve Margy*, Queen's county), xxxii, xlviii, cxli.
Smyrna, xxxix.
Sogan (in N.E. of co. Galway), li, lvi.
Somna flumen, clxi.
Sord Coluimb Chille (*Swords*, co. Dublin), l. lxv, cxviii, clxix.
Syria, cxv.

Tabor, cxxi.
Tamlachta Findlogain, xxxiii

Tamlachta Maelruain (*Tallaght*, co. Dublin), cxvii, cxxx, cliv.
Tamlachta Menann, clix.
Tarsus, cviii.
Tebtha, Tefa (a territory in Longford and Westmeath), clxxxiii.
Tech Airerain, cxxx, clx.
Tech Boethin i Midi (*Taghboyne*), liii.
Tech Boethin in Airtiuch (*Tibohine*), liii.
Tech Boethin i Tir Conaill (*Taughboyne*), liii.
Tech da-Goban (now *Seagor, Suide-Goba*, in Armagh), clxxx.
Tech Fleide, cxlv.
Tech húi Chonaill, xc.
Tech Ingen mBoiti, lxv.
Tech Maelaithgin, xcix.
Tech maic Dimmai, clxvii.
Tech Mochua (*Timahoe*, Queen's county), clxxxiv.
Tech Moling (*St. Mullin's*, co. Carlow), cxx.
Tech Riagla (*Tyrella*, in Down), cxlvi.
Tech Saxan, clxxxi.
Tech Scothíni (*Tiscoffin*, Kilkenny), xxxii.
Tech Tacra, lx.
Tech Telli (*Tehelly*, near Durrow, King's co.), cvii.
Tech Tuae (*Taghtoo*, co. Kildare), clxxxiii.
Teg nam-Bretan, clx.
Telach Dubglaisse, xcix.
Telach min Molaga (in Fermoy, Cork), **xxxvii**.
Telach na n-escop (*Tully*, near Kingstown), xlvi.

Tibra Fachtnai (*Tibraghny*, Co. Kilkenny), li, lxxxviii.
Tir Cell, xc, cliv.
Tir Conaill (*Tirconnell*, Donegal), xxxiv, xxxvi.
Tir dá glas (*Terryglas*, in Lower Ormond), lxxxiii, xc, clxxxii.
Tir Eogain (*Tyrone*), xxxiv, cxliii.
Tir húa Cennselaig, cxv.
Tir hua nDuach, liii.
Tir Lugdach (in Tirconnell), cxix.
Tir Ratha, xxxviii.
Torinis (*Tours*), cxv, clxviii.
Trudraige (*Tradry*, co. Clare), lxxxv.
Tréfot (*Trevet*, in Meath), clxvii.
Tuaim dá Gualann (*Tuam*), clxxxiv.
Tuaim Drecain (*Toomregan*, co. Cavan), cxlii.
Túaim Findlocha (*Toomfintough*, co. Clare), lxxvii.
Tuaim Gréne (*Tomgraney*, co. Clare), clxvii.
Tuaim Iudbir, clxxix.
Tuath dá-maige (in the King's county), xlvi.
Tuatha fer tire, xc.
Tugmad (?), cxxxii.
Tuilén (*Dulane*, near Kells), lxxxvii.
Tulach Fortchirn (*Tullow*, co. Carlow), cii.
Tulach leis na Saxan (*Tullabease*, co. Cork), clxxxi.
Tulach Tinn, lxi.

Uachtarnird (*Oughterard*, co. Kilkenny ?), clxxxii.
Ulaid (*Ulstermen*), l, clvi.

INDEX OF PERSONS

MENTIONED IN THE NOTES.

Aaron, clxxxvi. Aron, cxv.
Abbán, li, lxiii.
Abbán, son of Laignech, clx.
Abdinago ('Abhedh Něghó), lxxvi.
Abdon, cxxi.
Abel, clv.
Abra, son of Branán, clxxiii.
Abraham, clv. clxxxv.
Acarias ('Azaryâh), lxxvi.
Aculius, xci.
Adam, lii, lxv.
Adamnán, St., lxiv, cxlvi, cxlvii, clxxi.
Aed álaind, clvi.
Aed-béo, lxii.
Aed Cobran, clxxiii.
Aed cumnail, lxxxiii.
Aed (MacCarthann), cli.
Aed Slaine, lxxxviii.
Aed, son of Ainmire, xc.
Aed, son of Artchorp, cxxxii, cxxxv.
Aed, son of Brecc, clxviii.
Aed, son of Dallan, cxv.
Aed, son of Fergus, xci, clxxii.
Aed, son of Setna, xxxix.
Aedán, son of Iacop, clxx.
Aedán, son of Lugar, cxxxv.
Agatha, xcix, cxv, cxxxv.
Aibenn, xcviii.
Aiche, xlix.
Aidbe, Aidben, xc.
Ailbe, cxxxii.
Ailbe of Emly, cxlv, clxxxiv.
Ailgel, son of Idnac, clvi.
Ailill Mór, son of Breccán, xcix.
Ailill, son of Dunlang, clxxxi.
Ailill, son of Fergus, lxv.
Ailill Telldub, clxxxii.
Aillen, son of Baedan, xci.
Ainliairr, cxlv.
Ainle, cvi.
Ainmire, king of Fir Arda, lxiv.
Ainmire, son of Sétna, xc.

Aircran, cxxx, cxxxiv, clxxxiv.
Alexander, cii.
Amalgaid, son of Fothad, clviii.
Amalgad, son of Muiredach, xxxix.
Amantius, xcix, clxxx.
Ambrois, lxxii.
Ambrosius, clvii.
Ananias (Hanányâh), lxxvi.
Anna, clxxxvi.
Anatherius (Anterinus, A.), lxxxiv.
Andreas, cviii.
Andud, son of Fothad, clviii.
Anesus, lxvi.
Antoninus, lxxxvi.
Apollonaris, xcviii.
Apolloin, cxx.
Araide, clxix.
Arou, cxv.
Artchorp, clvi.
Artchorp, son of Fiacha Suigte, cxv, cxx, clxxxiv.
Artchorp, son of Niacorp, cxxxii, cxxxv.
Athrne, son of Luguae tri n-og, clvi.
Augustin, clxix.
Augustin, bishop of the Saxons, lxxxix.
Augustinus of Africa, cxxxiii.
Axal, xcix.

Balmill, xxxix.
Baedan, son of Echaid, xci.
Baeth Bannach, xxxiv.
Baethan, of Cluain, clxxxii.
Baethin, Boethin, cvi, cxlii.
Baethine, Baethine, son of Brenann, liii, xcix, ci.
Baethine mac Alla, liii, clv.
Baethine, son of Cuana, liii.
Baethine, son of Finda, liii, lxxxix.
Baite (Bóite ?), lxv.
Bairre, cxlvii.
Balar, son of Cas, clxxx.
Balbina, cliv.
Banban, of Leighlin, clxxiii.
Barr, king of Laigis, ci, cii.

INDEX OF PERSONS.

Barra, of Cork, xxxii.
Barrac, lxxxvii.
Barrfind, clxviii.
Barrfind, of Druim Cuilind, lxxxviii.
Barrfind, son of Aed, cxv.
Beccan, son of Lugaid, xci.
Becenat, Becenait, lxxiii.
Benedicht, Benidecht, xxxiv, lxiv.
Berach, son of Crimthann, clxix.
Berach, son of Nemnann, li, lii.
Berchan, clvi.
Berchan, of Clonsost, clxxx.
Beóán, clix.
Beóán, son of Bresal, clvi.
Beóán, son of Nessán, cxxx.
Biccsech, cliv.
Bláán, cxxx.
Blaisse, daughter of Comgall, xxxix.
Blathmac, son of Aed Slaine, lxxxviii.
Blathnait, xlvi.
Blesc, xxxiii.
Bochra, clxxiii.
Boga, daughter of Comgall, xxxix.
Boite, son of Brónach, clxxx.
Boz, cviii.
Bran Becc, lxxxviii.
Bran (?) of Clacnad, clxxxiii.
Branán, son of Oengus, clxxiii.
Brandan, lxxxvi.
Brandub, bishop, lxxv.
Branin, lxiv.
Brece, son of Artchorp, cxv, cxx.
Brecc-buaid, cxliii.
Breccán, son of Fiacc, xcix.
Breccán, of Echdruim B., lxxxiv.
Bregdolb, clvi, clxxxiii.
Brenaind, xxxii, lxxiii, cxviii.
Brenainn, son of Findloga, clxxiii.
Brenann, of Clonfert, lxxxvi.
Brenann, son of Fergus, xcix.
Bresal, son of Ailgel, clvi.
Bresal, son of Dén, lii.
Brian, son of Echaid Muidmedon, li, cxlvii, clviii.
Brian, son of Enna, xci.
Bricem, cxliii.
Bríg, xl.
Brigit, lii, lxxii, lxxiii, lxxvi, lxxxiv, cxv.
Briun, son of Echaid, lxxii.
Briun, son of Eogan, cxv, cxx.
Broccán, cxvii.
Broicsech, cxvii.

Brolchan, clxxxv.
Bronach, son of Balar, clxxx.
Buaidbeó, son of Lugaid, clxix.

Caecilius, cxlv, clxx.
Cael (Coel?), son of Aed, cxxxii, cxxxv.
Cailchin, lxxxvii.
Cailchine, lxxv.
Cain, lii.
Cainnech, lxxxvii, cxviii.
Cainnech macu Dalann, clvi.
Cainndech, son of Corp, cxxxii.
Cainnech, son of Ceise, clxxxii.
Cainnech, son of Imchath, clx.
Cainree (?), clxxiii.
Cailodran, lxv.
Cairech Dergain, l.
Cairell, cxlvi.
Cairisim, lxxiv.
Cairnech moel, lxii.
Cairnech of Tuilén, lxxxvii, clxx.
Cairpre fili, son of Ailill Mór, xcix.
Cairpre Ua Ciardai, xl.
Callistus (better Callistus), pope, A.D. 218, clvi.
Calpurn, lxxxiii.
Cámin of Inis Celtra, lxv, clxxxii.
Canannan, son of Ailill, lxv.
Candida, cliv, clxxix.
Capitolinus, clxxxi.
Carthach, son of Find, lx.
Carthann, son of Colla Uais, xxxix.
Cas, son of Fiacha Araide, cxvi.
Cas, son of Nia, clxxx.
Cathach, lxii.
Cathal, son of Blathmac, lxxxviii.
Cathbad, cxx.
Cathbad (?), son of Echaid, xci.
Cathar Mór, lxiv, lxxii.
Cathchú, son of Oengus, xxxiv.
Carthach, of Rathin, lxxxvi.
Cecilia, Valerian's wife, cxxx.
Ceise, son of Lugaid, clxxxii.
Céle Crist, lx.
Cellach, clv.
Cellán, son of Tailcenn, lx.
Celtcar, son of Uitecar, clxxxii.
Cennfaelad, son of Maelcaba, xc.
Cerball, lxxxviii.
Cernach sotal, lxxvii.
Christ, lxv.
Christina, cxix.

INDEX OF PERSONS.

Cian, son of Ailill Aulum, clxxi.
Ciannait, lxiv.
Cianan, of Duleck, clxx, clxxi.
Ciar ingen Duibréa, xxxiii.
Ciardac, xl.
Ciaran, lxi, lxii, lxxv, cxviii, cxliii.
Ciarán, of Cluain, xxxvii, xxxviii, lxxxiv.
Ciarán, of Saigir, lx, cii.
Ciarán mac int-sáir, ci.
Cillín, lxv.
Cindech, li.
Cirillus, lxxvi.
Cirine, pope, lxxvii, cxlviii.
Cirion, cxv.
Ciriens, cii.
Ciríacus, lxxxvi.
Claudiens, clxxx.
Clement, clxix, lxx.
Clidna, lxiv.
Cnes, cxlii.
Coechlamair, lxxiii.
Coel, clix, clx.
Coem, son of Enna, liii.
Coemán, xcviii, cii.
Coemán Brecc, cxlii, cxlv.
Coemán of Inis Airther, ci.
Coemán of Enach Truimm, clxviii.
Coemell, xcviii.
Coengel, clxviii.
Coengen, li, xcviii.
Coengen of Glendalough, clxviii.
Coemlog, clxviii.
Coingell, clix, clx.
Coirell, son of Laisre, xxxviii, xxxix, cxxxii.
Coirpre, son of Fergus, lxxii.
Coirpre, son of Niall, lxxvi.
Colgan (Colcu ?) son of Tuathal, lxxxix.
Colla dá Chrich, lxxxix.
Colla derg, lxiii.
Colla Uais, xxxix.
Colmán Cuile, son of Muiredach, clxix.
Colmán Duib-Chuilinn, clxxi.
Colmán Ela, xc, cxix, cxlvii, cliv.
Colmán, father of Maelruain, cxvii.
Colmán hua Fiachrach, clx.
Colmán hua Liathan, cxx.
Colmán of Inis Mocholmóc, clxix.
Colmán lobar, lxxxviii.
Colmán Mór Mide, xc.
Colmán of Airer, cxx.
Colmán of Glenn Delmaic, clxviii.

Colmán of Laau Mic Lunchau, lxvi.
Colman of the Gaillduc, clxi.
Colmán, son of Aed, lii.
Colmán, son of Cathbad, clvi.
Colmán, son of Comgall, lii.
Colmán, son of Comínán, clxx.
Colmán, son of Cuil, clv.
Colmán, son of Dimma, clxvii.
Colmán, son of Findchad, clxvii.
Colmán, son of Lenín, clxxi.
Colmán, son of Luachan, xc, ciii.
Colmán, son of Oengus, cxxi.
Colmán Stellain, xc.
Colmóc, lxvi.
Colomb, Abbot of Tír dá glas, xc.
Colomb Cille, l, li, liv, lxxiv, xcix, c, ci, civ, cxxxiv, cxli, cxliv, clxxi.
Colomb Croxaire, cxliii.
Colomb of Donnach Maige Inclair, cxliii.
Colomb of Ross, cxliii.
Colomb of Tír dá glas, clxxxii.
Colomb, son of Nindid, lxxxviii.
Coma, daughter of Comgall, xxxix.
Comchaide, cxlii.
Comgall, xxxiii, lxxv, cxviii.
Comgall of Bennchor, lxxxv, cxxviii, clxx, clxxii.
Comgan, cxvii.
Comgan of Cluain Conlan, clvi.
Commán of Arnu, clxx.
Commán of Ross-Commáin, clxxxiv.
Conach, lxxvii.
Conaire Mór, xxxiii.
Conall, lxi.
Conall Derg, l. lxiv.
Conall glún, clviii.
Conall Gulban, xc, xcix.
Conall of Inis Cael, lxxxvi.
Conall, son of Niall núigiallach, lxxxviii.
Conandil, lxii.
Conchad, lxv.
Condlaed, lxxxiii.
Condla, son of Tadg, clxxi.
Concrad, son of Daircell, clxxxii.
Congrad (Conchrad ?), clxx.
Coningen, lxxvii.
Conluch, cxviii.
Conmac, lxxxv.
Conn, cliv.
Conn cét-chathach, clxxxi.
Consatín=Constantinus, lxxxiii.
Constantín, xxxvi.

INDEX OF PERSONS.

Constantín of Rathin, lxiii.
Constantinus, filius Elenae, cxxx.
Constantinus Martius, cxxix.
Core of Cell Mór hua Niallain, lxxii.
Corerán, clv, son of Echaid, liv.
Corcnutan, clxviii.
Cormac cruimther, lxxxv.
Cormac of Durrow, cvi.
Cormac, Patrick's successor, lii.
Cormac, son of Cúchorb, li, clx, clxxxii.
Cormac, son of Ocugus, lxxxiv.
Cornelius, cxlv.
Corp, son of Fergus, cxxxii.
Corona, lxxxvi.
Cosmas, cxlvii.
Créd, lxxxix.
Cremthannan, son of Cathar Mór, clxxxii.
Cresine, cxxxi.
Crimthann, Colomb Cille's first name, xcix.
Crimthann, King of Airgiall, lxxii.
Crimthann, son of Cathar Mór, lxiv, lxxxviii.
Crimthann, son of Echaid, clv, clxxxii.
Crimthann, son of Erc-loga, clxix.
Crispinus, clxxx.
Crist, xxxiv, lii.
Cristifer, lxxvi.
Critán, cxlv.
Cronan, l, lxxvii.
Cronan mac Netscmon, l.
Cronan, Mochua's first name, cxxix.
Cronan of Ferns, cv.
Cronan of Tuaim Gréne, clxvii.
Cruindbél, son of Fedlimid, lxxxix.
Crumine, cviii.
Cuan Airbre, cxviii.
Cuana, xlviii.
Cuana, son of Coem, liii.
Cuangus, lxiii.
Cuanna, son of Andud, clviii.
Cuunna, son of Midorn, xxiv.
Cúchorp, xxxii, li, clx, clxxxii.
Cúchorp, son of Coirpre, lxxvi.
Cuil, son of Midgnae, clv.
Cuinuid, cxlvii.
Cuitbriet (?). clxxxi.
Cula, lxxiii.
Cumain, xci.
Cumall, clxxii.
Cumine Fota, clxviii.
Cumine, sister of Colomb Cille, xci
Cumine, son of Dinertach, liv.

Curufin, cxx.
Cyprianus, cxlv.
Cyrinus, cxlvi.

Dabid of Cell Muine, xl, lx.
Dabid, son of Jesse, clv.
Da-Chellóc, lxv.
Dachua of Druim Bó, cxxx.
Dagan, cxlv.
Da-Goban, clxxx.
Daig of Inis Cain Dega, cxxxi.
Daig Derg (?) lxxvii.
Daig, son of Coirell, xxxviii.
Dairchell (Moling's first name), ciii.
Dairchen, ci.
Daireill, son of Senach, clxxxii.
Daire Barrach, lxxii, cxix.
Dal, son of Laidir, xxxii.
Dallan, son of Eogan, xxxix, cxxxii.
Dallan, son of Liathan, cxv.
Damán, li.
Damasus, clxxxi.
Damianus, cxlvii.
Daniel, cxx.
Daráne, Dairine, cxxi.
Darbilin, clix, clx.
Darerea, xlviii, xlix, cxvi.
Darí, lxiv, cxlvii, cxlviii.
Darnuil, clix, clx.
Dartinne, cxv.
Dec (Decius), lxxvi.
Declan of Ardmór, cxx.
Decius, cxxx.
Dectir, lxxxv.
Deda, lxiii.
Delbna Mac Eoin, lxxxvii.
Demosthenes, cxx.
Dén, lii.
Derbfraich, lxxii, lxxiii.
Dergan, ci.
Dianarau, son of Ferdomnach, clxxxiii
Diarmait = Modimóc, cxvii.
Diarmait of Disert D., cvi.
Diarmait, son of Aed, clxxxii.
Diarmait, son of Luguae, xxxiv.
Dichuill, clxxxiii.
Dichú, son of Trichem, clxxxiii.
Dima mac noc, xcix.
Dinertach, liv.
Dionis, xc.

INDEX OF PERSONS.

Dionysius, cxxix.
Dioscorus, cxxxii.
Dobaid (?) son of Oengus, li.
Do-choll (?) clxix.
Domangort, lxv.
Domene Doimargait, l.
Domitianus, lxxxiv, xc.
Domnall Mór Ua Briain, clxxxvii.
Domnall, son of Murchad, lxxxvii.
Domninus, clxviii.
Donnán of Eig, lxxiv.
Doroma (?) clxvi.
Drúna, son of Tigernach, clxxi.
Drusus, clxxxii.
Duach (?) son of Mac-niad, lxxv.
Dubán, li.
Dubdliged, xxxvii.
Dub-dimach, son of Andew, clviii.
Dubthach, father of Brigit, xlvi, xlvii.
Dubratha, son of Enna, lxxiv.
Duibréa, gen., xxxiii.
Duilech, clxix.
Dunchad, son of Blathmac, lxxxviii.
Dunchad, son of Cennfaelad, xc.
Dunlaing, lxxiv.

Echaid (a quo Ui-Echach Ulad), lxxvi.
Echaid Doimplen, lxxxix.
Echaid Gunnat, xci.
Echaid Láinderg, lxxxiv, cxxxii.
Echaid Muidhedoin, lxv, cxxxii, cxlvii, clxxiii.
Echaid Mundremair, cxlii.
Echaid, son of Bresal, lii.
Echaid, son of Brian, xci.
Echaid, son of Conall, lxxxviii.
Echaid, son of Crimthann, lxxii, clv.
Echaid, son of Daire Barrach, lxxii.
Echaid, son of Setna, lxxxiv.
Ecne, son of Aeltae (?) lxxxvii.
Egbert, clxxx.
Eilténe, clxxxii.
Ela, cxlvii.
Elena (Helena), lxxxiii.
Eleutherius, cliv.
Elizabeth, lxxii, clvii.
Emelianus, cxxxii.
Emene of Rossa Glaisse, clxxxiii.
Enán, cxlvi.
Enán of Druim Raithne, cxxxii.
Enda, clxxxiv.

Enna, liii.
Enna of Aran, lc, lxiv.
Enna, son of Cathbad, xci.
Enna, son of Lachan, lxxii.
Enna, son of Niall, lxxiv.
Eochaid, son of Barr, ci, cii.
Eochaid, son of Oengus, clxxxii.
Eogan of Ard Sratha, clvxii.
Eogan, son of Bishop Erc, cxxxii.
Eogan, son of Brecc, cxv, cxx.
Eogan, son of Cniudech, cxxxii.
Eogan, son of Canannan, lxv.
Eogan, son of Dergán, ci.
Eogan, son of Niall, xxxix.
Eogan, son of Niall Nóigiallach, xci, cxxxii.
Eoin, liv, cxlvii.
Eoin Baubtaist, liv.
Eoin Cassion, clxxii.
Eoin, son of Usalec, lxxxvii.
Eolang of Achad Bó, cxliii.
Epectinus, lxxxix.
Erasmus, xcviii.
Erc Derg, son of Brian, li.
Erc-logn, son of Ernaide, clxix.
Erc of Domnach Mór, clx.
Erc, son of Brian, clxxiii.
Erc, son of Echaid Mundremair, cxlii.
Erc, son of Feradach, xxxix.
Erc, son of Mac Niad, cxx.
Erc of Slaine, cxxxii, clxvii.
Erc, son of Tren, lxxv.
Ermis (Hermes), cx.
Ermogin (Hermogenes), lxxv.
Ernaide, son of Muirene, clxix.
Ernín of Leighlin, liii.
Ernín, son of Cael, cxxxii, cxxxv.
Ernín, son of Findchan, clxix.
Erníne, cxxxi.
Essodir, xxxi.
Estamon, son of Mugh Toeth, lxxxvii.
Etech, nurse of the Fiann, lxxiii.
Etheen (Etchein?), l.
Ethiar dub, lii.
Etine, son of Cairpre, xcix.
Ethne, lxv.
Ethne, daughter of Dima mac noe, xcix.
Eugenia, lxiii.
Eugitianus, clix.
Euphemia, cxviii, cxlvi.
Eusebius, cxlvii, cliv.
Eustochium, cxlviii.

INDEX OF PERSONS.

Eutychius, clviii.
Eva, lii.
Evagair, lxxii.

Fachtnae, cxxxi.
Fachtnae, son of Rossa, lxxv.
Fachtna of Ross Ailithir, lxi.
Faelan, xxxiii.
Faelchú, clxxxiv.
Failbe, lxiv.
Faillén, ciii.
Faustinus, clxxxii.
Fechine of Fore, xxxvii, clviii.
Fedelm, daughter of Ailill, clxxxi.
Fedlimid, liv.
Fedlimid Rechtmar, cxx, clxxxiv.
Fedlimid, son of Cas, cxvi.
Fedlimid, son of Fergus, xcix.
Fedlimid, son of Fiacha Cassan, lxxxix.
Feradach, lxiv.
Feradach, son of Fiachra, xxxix.
Ferb, lx.
Ferbla, lxxxvii.
Fer dá chrich, clv.
Fer-dá-chrich of Dairinis, cxxxi.
Ferdomnach, son of Dichú, clxxxiii.
Fergna Brit, lx.
Fergus Cennfota, xc.
Fergus mac Roig, xxxii.
Fergus mac Rossa, lxxxvii.
Fergus, son of Ailill Telldub, clxxxii.
Fergus, son of Conall Gulban, xcix.
Fergus, son of Echaid Muidmedoin, lxv.
Fergus, son of Enna, lxxii.
Fergus, son of Eogan, xci.
Fergus, son of Fothad, cxxxii.
Femme, cxlvi.
Femin, xxxviii.
Fer-tlachtga, xxxii.
Fiace, xci, clvi.
Fiace, son of Imchath the Proud, clxxi, clxxxiii.
Fiace, son of Daire Barrach, xcix.
Fiacha, clxix.
Fiacha Araide, cxvi.
Fiacha Cassan, lxxxix.
Fiacha mac Mailebressi, lxxxvii.
Fiacha, son of Niall, clxviii.
Fiacha, son of Niall Nóigiallach, lxxxix.
Fiacha Suigde, cxx.
Fiachna, a monk, lxxvii.

Fiachra, xxxiv.
Fiachra of Congbail, xlix.
Fiachra, son of Amalgad, xxxix.
Fiachrac, son of Fiace, clvi.
Fiachu mac Fiachach, lxxxvii.
Fidairle, lxxxvii.
Fidchure, son of Delbna, lxxxvii.
Fidrumine, lxxxvii.
Figus, lxxxvii.
Finan camm, lxxiii, lxiv.
Finan lobar, xlix, cxvii, cxviii.
Find, son of Cumall, clxxii.
Find, son of Nóe, lx.
Finda (Findach ?) lxxxix.
Findbarr, cxliv, clvi, clxviii.
Findbarr, son of Aed, cxv.
Findbarr, son of Fraech, xxxiv.
Findchad mac Gossa, lxxxvii.
Findchad, Sinell's father, lxxiii.
Findchán, clxix.
Findchath, lxiv.
Findchoem, son of Fiace, clxxi.
Findchú Brí Gobann, clxxii.
Findchua, cxix.
Finlech Duirn, xlviii.
Findén, cxxxii.
Findén, son of Finntan, clxxxiii.
Findia, cxlvii, clvi.
Findlug, xxxiii.
Findlug, father of Brenainn, lxxiv.
Findlug maccu Allta, lxxxvi.
Findsech, clvi.
Finnén, cxviii.
Finntan, xxxiii.
Finntan, abbot of Tír dá glas, xc.
Finntan, son of Conerad, clxxxiii.
Finntan, son of Gabréne, lii, Gabrán.
Finntan, son of Mal, li.
Fintan, clvi, clix.
Fintan Maeldub, clviii.
Flaccus, xci.
Fland Fina, cxxix.
Fland Léna, lxxxvii.
Flandán, son of Toirdelbach, cxlvi.
Flavianus, cviii.
Fled, cxlv.
Fobrece, cxliii.
Foelan, cvi.
Foelan, Fursae's brother, clxi.
Fortchern, son of Loegaire, clv.
Fothad, son of Conall glún, clviii.

INDEX OF PERSONS.

Fothad, son of Echaid Laimderg, lxxxiv, cxxxii.
Fraech, son of Cathchú, xxxiv.
Fraecháu, clxix.
Fuinche, daughter of Coirell, xxxviii.
Furodran, cvi.
Fursae, xxxv, xxxvi, cxlii.

Gabrán, liii.
Gaible, son of Ecne, lxxxvii.
Gaibréne, son of Corcrán, lii.
Gallicamus, cvii.
Gamuled (Gamaliel ?), cxxxviii.
Garbán, cxviii.
Garb-daire, cxlv.
Gelaisse, xlviii.
Germained, xxxix.
German, xci, cliv.
German cruimther, lxxvii.
Gervais, cvi.
Gille Suanaig, lxxxvii.
Glanna (?), clvi.
Gobbán, clxxx.
Gossa (!) mac Gaible, lxxxviii.
Grigoir, lxiii, lxiv, lxvi, lxxxix.

Heli, cxxxv.
Hermes, cxxxiii.
Herentius, cxxix.
Hilarius, clxviii.
Hilarius, ep. et mart., lxxxiv.
Hieronymus, cxlviii.
Hippolytus, cxxx.
Hiruaith (Herod), clxxxiv.
Hua Annóc, etc., see Ua.
Hyacinthus, cxliv

Iachem, clxxxvi.
Iachtadu (?) son of Morna, clxxii.
Iacobus, frater Domini, lxxxiii.
Iacop, lxiii.
Iacop Alphei, cvii.
Iacop glúinech, lxv
Iacop (son of Zebedec), lxxv, cxxi.
Ibair, bishop, cii.
Idnae, son of Athrae, clvi.
Iguatius, clxxxiii.
Imchad, son of Fedlimid, cxvi.
Imchath, li, clxxxiii.
Imchath, son of Condla, clxxi.

Imchath, son of Cormac, clx
Imrossa Nith, xxxii.
Iob, lxxxv.
Iohannes apostolus, lxxxiv, clxxxiv.
Iohannes baptista, cxxxiii, cxxxiv.
Iohannes euangelista, xc.
Iohannes, one of the seven sleepers, cxxix.
Iohannes, son of Zebedee, cvii.
Ioel, cxvii.
Iosep, lxiv.
Isaias, cxvii.
I'su, lxiv. I'sucán, xxxv.
I'te, lx ; of Cluain Credal, xxxiv.
Ith, lxi.
Itharnaise, clxxxiii.
Iubar, bishop, lxxvi.
Iudas, lii, ciii.
Inil, lxxiv, cxv.
Iuliana, lii.
Iulita, ciii.
Iunell, cxlvii.
Iust, deacon, lxxxiv.

Labraid, li.
Labraid, son of Cormac, clxxxii.
Lachtain of Achad-ur, lxiv.
Laeban, son of Brinn (Brian ?), lxxii.
Laideenn, clxxiii.
Laidcenn, son of Baeth Bannach, xxxiv.
Laignech, li.
Laignech, son of Cainnech, clx.
Laisre, son of Dallan, xxxix, cxxxii.
Laisrén, abbot of Hi, cxlvi.
Laisrén=Molaisse, lxxv, cxxx, cxlv.
Laisrén, son of Nascae clix.
Laisrén, son of Ua Loegairi, cxlvi.
Lallóc, xlix.
Landan, xc.
Lassair, daughter of Branin, lxiv.
Laurint, liii.
Laurentius, cxxx.
Lenin, clxxi.
Levi, clxxxvi.
Lindnine, lxi.
Liumain, xlviii, lxxxiii, clxxiii.
Liathan, son of Briun, cxv.
Liatheú, son of Araide, clxix.
Libren, lxiii.
Lilnch, son of Lugaid, cxvi.

INDEX OF PERSONS.

Lithgen, li.
Lochan, lxxv, clxxxiv.
Lochine, xxxvii.
Loegaire, son of Niall Nóigiallach, clv, clxix.
Loman, lxix, clvi.
Lonan, clix.
Louán, son of Senach, clxxxiii.
Lonan, son of Talmach, clxvii.
Lonan, son of Telchán, clxvii.
Longarad, cxli.
Longinus, clix.
Loth, clxxxv.
Luachan, xc.
Lucas, lxxii, cliv.
Luchdaigirn (?), lxxvii.
Lucianus, cxxviii.
Lugaid, son of Findbarr, xxxiv.
Lugaid, son of Ith, lxi.
Lugaid, son of Labraid, clxxxii.
Lugaid, son of Liatheú, clxix.
Lugaid, son of Macnach, lxxv.
Lugaid, son of Rossa, cxvi.
Lugaid, son of Tuathan, xci.
Lugas, son of Ernin, cxxxiv.
Lugdach, clv.
Lugna, lxxv.
Lugna, father of Ciaran, lxi.
Lugna, son of Bregdolb, clxxxiii.
Lugnae, son of Lugaid, xxxiv.
Lugnae tri n-og, clvi.
Luicell, clv.
Luimnech, xxxi.
Lumbus v. Lupus.
Lupait, xlviii.
Lupus (Lumbus A.), cxxi.

Mac Caine, xlvii, xlviii, lxxvi.
Mac Carthainn, xlix, lxiv, clv.
Mac-con, son of Lugaid, lxxv.
Mac Conglinne, cxlv.
Mac Cula, lxxiii.
Mac Cuilinn, xxxi.
Mac Cuilind of Lusk, cxliv.
Mac Iairnn, clxi.
Mac Lanchan, lxvi.
Mac Maildalua, lxxiv.
Mac niad, son of Brinn, cxx.
Mac nind, son of Mac-con, lxxv.
Mac nisse, cxlii.
Mac-óige, clxxix.

Mac Rustaing, cxv.
Mac Samain, cxlv.
Mac Tail, lxxvii, ci, cxxi.
Madian, liii.
Maedóe hua Dunlaing, xlix.
Maedóe of Chuan Mór M., lxxiv.
Maedoc of Ferus, xxxix, xl, cvii.
Maedóe, son of Midgna, lxiv.
Maelaithgen, xcix.
Maelanfaid, xl.
Maelbresail, lxxxvii.
Maelbressi, lxxxvii.
Maelcaba, son of Aed, xc.
Maelcoisne, cxxxi.
Maeldub, xc.
Maeldub, son of Amalgaid, clviii.
Maelgetirid, lxxxv.
Maelisu hua Brolchan, clxxxv.
Maelodrain, lxxxviii, clxxix.
Mael, son of Iuchtadu (?), clxxii.
Maelruain, cxvii, clv, cxxxi.
Maclrubai, lxxv.
Masnach, son of Fachtnae, lxxv.
Maigneun of Kilmainham, xxxv, clxxxiii.
Maine Cerr, lxi.
Maire, cxv, cxliii, cliv.
Malchus, cxxix.
Mal nae Dobtha, li.
Mammes, cxix, cxxxi.
Manchine of Cúl Caiss, lxxv.
Mansuetus, clxxxiv.
Matha, lxxxiv, cxv.
Matha, evangelist, cxlvi.
Mathias, apostolus, lxxxiii.
Marc, cxviii, cliv.
Marc, the evangelist, lxxvi, lxxxviii.
Marcán Laginiensis, lxxxviii.
Marcellus, cxlvii, clvi.
Marcellosus, lxxxviii.
Marcianus, xcix, cxxix.
Maria, lxxii.
Maria, mater domini, cxx.
Maria, mater filii Alphei, cxx.
Maria, mater filiorum Zebedei, cxx.
Maria Magdalena, lxv, cxx.
Martha, xxxvii.
Marticianus, cxv.
Martin, lxxv, xcviii, cxv, clxviii.
Maxia, lxxxiv, cxlvi.
Maximinianus, cxxix.
Medran, xcix.

INDEX OF PERSONS.

Mell, li.
Mellan, xlix, clix.
Mellan, father of Cronan, l.
Mellan, son of Ua Cuinn, xxxv.
Melchisidech, clxxxvi.
Mernóc, lii, cxxxi.
Merobins, clxxx.
Mess Buachaille, xxxiii.
Messencorb, Messencorp, lxxxiv, cxxxii.
Metan, clxix.
Mete, son of Nindnid, lxiv, lxxxviii, clv.
Miada, li.
Michel, lxxxv, lxxxviii, cxlviii, clviii.
Midgnae, son of Mete, lxiv, lxxxviii, clv.
Midorn, son of Dubratha, lxxiv.
Milid, xxxiii.
Minchloth, xcix, clxxxii.
Misahel (Mishaél), lxxvi.
Misac (Méshakh), lxxvi.
Mite, lx.
Mo-Beoóc, clxxxii, of Lough Gerg, clxxxii.
Mobi, cxviii, clvi.
Mo-Bióc, clxxxii.
Mochabae, cxxvii.
Mo-chelloc, lxv.
Mochoe of Noendruim, cvii.
Mochoem, lii.
Mochoeme, xcviii, lxxxiii.
Mochoeme of Tirdáglas, clxxxii.
Mocholmóc of Clonard, l.
Mocholmóc of Druim Mór, xcix.
Mocholmóc of the Laun, clxi.
Mo-chommóc, clxxxiv.
Mochonda, lxxxiii, clxix.
Mochonna of Inis Pátric, xxxiv.
Mo-chritóc, lxxxv.
Mo-coemóc, lxiii.
Mochtae, son of Cuinnid, cxlvii.
Mochta, son of Lilach, cxvi.
Mochta of Louth, lxv, cxxxii.
Mochua, deacon, cxxxii.
Mochua mac Cuinn, lxxxiv.
Mochua of Les Mor Mochua, cvii.
Mochua of Miliuc, l.
Mochua, son of Lugaid, cxxix.
Mochuaróc, l.
Mochuda, lx, lxxvi, lxxvii.
Mochuda of Raithin, cxliv.
Mochumma, clxix.
Modíchú, clxxxiii.

Modimóc, cxviii, clxxxi.
Modiuit, li.
Modomnóc, li, lxxxviii.
Moel, bishop, xlvii, xlviii.
Moelchu, liv.
Moeldub, liv.
Moenán, cvi.
Mo-elteóc, clxxxii.
Mo-Gobnait, l.
Mo-laca, xxxvii.
Molaise, lxxv, of Leighliu, cxliv.
Molaise of Men Droichet, cxlvi.
Molilat, liii.
Moling, ciii, civ, cv.
Molna, xxxiv, lxxv.
Molua mac Ochai, xl, cxxviii, cxxix.
Molua of Clonfert, clxxxiii.
Moluoc of Lismore, cvii.
Moineun, lx, of Chuain Conairi Tomain, cxlvi.
Mo-macru, lx.
Monaedoc, lxxxviii, of Fid duin, cxxxi.
Mo-m-Ernóc, xxxix.
Moninne, cxvi.
Monisia, lxiii.
Morna, clxxii.
Moses, lx.
Mosilóc, cxx.
Mothoren, cii.
Mugain, clxix.
Mugna (Mugain ?), daughter of Ailill, clxxxi.
Mug Toeth, lxxxvii.
Muirdebar, clxviii.
Muiredach Munderg, lxxxv.
Muiredach, son of Carthann, xxxix.
Muiredach, son of Echaid, lxxxviii.
Muiredach, son of Fiacha, lxxxix.
Muiredach, son of Loegaire, clxix.
Muire = Marius, xxxvii.
Muirene, son of Sechnasach, clxix.
Mundu, clix.
Murchad, lxxiii.
Murchad ua Cailchin, lxxxvii.
Murchú, xcix.

Nabeudon, lxxvi.
Nachor, cviii.
Narach, lxii.
Natenim, lxviii.
Nateneim, abbot of Tirdáglas, xc.
Natfraech, cvi, cxviii, Molaise's father, cxlv.

INDEX OF PERSONS.

Nathí, son of Fiachra, xxxiv.
Nazair, cxviii.
Nazar, son of Crimthann, lxxxviii, clxxxiii.
Nechtan, Patrick's pupil, lxxxiii.
Nem, cii.
Nemnainder, son of Erc, cxlii.
Nemangen, son of Finntan, li.
Nemnann, son of Nemangen, li.
Nero, xci.
Nesloga, lxiii.
Nessán, lxiii.
Nessán, father of Beóán, cxxx.
Nessán of Cork, lxiv, clxxix.
Nessán of Mungairit, cxxi.
Nessán of Ulster, clxxix.
Nia, son of Airmedach, clxxx.
Niall Nóigiallach, lxxiv, lxxxvii, xc, cxxxii.
Niall, son of Echaid, lxxvi.
Niallán, lxxii.
Nindid, cxviii ; son of Nazar, lxxxviii ; son of Star, lxiv, clv.
Nine (Ninnine) éces, cxvi, clxxxi.
Nisse, son of Nemainder, cxlii.
Noe, lxxvii ; son of Cellán, lx.
Nos, cxliii.

Octauin, August, clvii.
Odran, clx ; of Lettracha Odrain, cxliv.
Odran, the Master, clxxxii.
Oengus, lxiii, ci.
Oengus Goibniu, cxvi.
Oengus of the Children of Lugaid mac Itha, lxi.
Oengus, son of Creunthannán, clxxxii.
Oengus, son of Echaid, lxxxiv.
Oengus, son of Erc the Red, li, clxxiii.
Oengus, son of Lugna, clxxxiii.
Oengus, son of Natfraech, cvi, cxxi.
Oengus, son of Nathí, xxxiv.
Ogaman, son of Fidchure, lxxxvii.
Oimne, cliv.
Olchu, son of Ogama, lxxxvii.
Onchu, xlix ; son of Blathmac, cxvii, cxviii.
Osa, cxxix.
Osualt, cxxix.

Palladius, cii.
Pátraic, xlvi. xlviii, lxi, lxiv, lxxiii. lxxiv, lxxvi, xci, cxvii, cxxxiii, cxlii, cxlvii, clxvii, clxxi.
Parmenius, clxxix.

Panchratus, clxxix.
Pamphilus, cxxxii.
Pantaleo, cxxi, cxlvi.
Parthalon, cii, cxxxiii.
Paula, cxlvii.
Paulus, cviii.
Petar, lxxxviii, cliv.
Petar Apstal, xxxvi, xxxvii, xlvii, liii, liv.
Petar deochan, lxxiv.
Petronilla, xci.
Pilip, clviii. Pilip (apostle), lxxxiii.
Pól, lxxiv, xci, cliv ; Pól apstal, xxxvi, xxxvii, xlvii.
Policronius, lxiv.
Polycarpus, clxxx.
Porian, son of Echaid Muidmedon, clxxiii.
Priscus, cliv.
Protasi, cvi.
Protus, cxliv.

Quiriacus, cxxxiii.
Quintinus, clxi.
Quintus, cxxxiii.

Restitutus, clxxiii.
Riagail, cxxxiv, cxlvi ; of Muc-inis, clvi.
Ricell, xlviii.
Romula, cxx.
Ronain, bishop, l.
Ronait, cxlvi.
Ronán, king of Leinster, lxxxix.
Ronán of Ross Cainni, lxxvii.
Ronán, son of Berach, clxix.
Ronán, son of Saran, lxxxix.
Ronchend, lxxxiii.
Rossa, son of Erc, lxxv.
Rossa, son of Iuchad, cxvi.
Ruadan, lxxiv, cxviii.

Sabaist, xxxviii.
Salome, cxxxv.
Samthan of Cluain Brónaig, clxxxiii.
Samuel, clxxxv.
Samuel, father of Sanctain, lxxxv.
Samuel, propheta, cxxxii.
Sanct, cxxi.
Sanctain, lxxxv.
Sanctlethan, cii.
Sarán, lxxxvi ; son of Colgan (Colen ?), lxxxix.
Sarbile, cxvi.

INDEX OF PERSONS.

Sciath, cxliii.
Scíre. lxv.
Scothín, Scuithéne, xxxii.
Sechnall, cliv ; son of Restitutus, clxxiii.
Sechnasach, son of Colman Uaile, clxix.
Secundinus=Sechnall, clxxiii.
Sedrach (Shadhrakh), lxxvi, clvii.
Segéne, cxxx.
Semeon, cxxi.
Sen, lxiii.
Senach, bishop, cxxxii.
Senach garb, lii.
Senach, son of Diarmait, clxxxii.
Senach, son of Oengus, clxxxiii.
Senan, lx, cxli.
Senchaid of Dub Aeda, clxxxiii.
Senchán, li.
Sennis, cxxi.
Senóe, clxxxi.
Senpátraic, cxxxii, cxxxiii.
Septim, lxxv.
Serapion, cxxix.
Sesnan, son of Drona, clxxi.
Setnae, father of Comgall, lxxv.
Setnae, son of Abra, clxxiii.
Setnae, son of Erc, xxxix.
Setnae, son of Fergus. xc.
Setnae, son of Fothad, lxxxiv.
Setuae, son of Trebthach, xxxii.
Sillán, cxliv ; of Bennchor, liv.
Sillán (Silvanus), lxxxiv.
Silóe, cxviii.
Silnestar, xxxvii, clxxxiv.
Simon Cannaneus, cxv.
Simon Petrus, cviii.
Simplex, cxxi.
Sinchell, lxv ; of Cell Achid S., cvii.
Sinech, xcix, cliv, clxviii.
Sinell, son of Findchath, lxiv, lxxiii.
Sinotus, cxliii.
Siric of Mag Bolg, clxxiii.
Sisennius, cxix.
Sistan, cxxix.
Sixtus, cxxx.
Sodelb, lxv.
Star (Zar), son of Crimthann, lxiv, clv.
Stephanus, cxxviii, clxxxiv.
Stolus, cviii.
Suanach, lxxxvii.
Subthan, lxxv.

Tadg, son of Cian, clxxi.
Tailcenn, son of Ferb, lx.
Talmach, clxvii.
Tara, cviii.
Tarcairtenn, clxxxiii.
Tassach, lxxiv.
Tatha, cxv, clx.
Tecla, xcviii.
Telchán, clxvii.
Telle, cvii.
Temnén, cxxxi.
Temneóc, clxxxiii.
Teophil, cxxi.
Teracus. lxxxvi.
Ternóc, xlix.
Thecla, clxix.
Theodota, cxxxvii, cxli ; Theodote, cxlvii.
Tiamda, lxiv, lxxxvi, lxxxviii.
Tigernach of Clones, lxxii.
Tigernach Bairche, lxxxvi.
Tigernach, son of Findchoem, clxxi.
Tigris, xlviii.
Titus, lxxxiii.
Toimdenach, li.
Toirdelbach, cxlvi.
Tomas, xci, clxxxiii.
Torannan (Palladius), cii.
Tuathal, son of Cruindbél, lxxxix.
Tuathan, son of Aed, xci.
Tulchan, clix.
Traian, liii, Traianus, clxxxiii.
Trebthach, son of Dal, xxxii.
Tren mac Duach, lxxv.
Trichem, son of Fiacc, clxxxiii.
Trophimus, clxxiii.
Tryphonia, clviii.
Tulodran, lxv.

Ua Annóe, clxxxvii.
Ua Beona, xxxv.
Ua Cellchín, clxxxvii.
Ua Cormaic, lxiii.
Ua Cnind, xxxv.
Ua Glesain, clxxxvii.
Ua Laigse, xxxvii.
Ua Sunnaig, lxxxvii.
Ua Sluasti, clxxxvii.
Uachall, lxvi.
Uaininn, clvi.
Uitecar, clxxxii.

Ultán, cxlii ; the Silent, clxxxiii.
Unniut (?), cxxxii.
Urbanus, lxxxviii.
Usalec, son of Eslamon, lxxxvii.

Valentinus, li, clxxxii.
Velerianus, cxxx.
Vespasianus, lxxxiii, cxx.

Victor, lxxxiv, lxxvi, clxxxiii, clxxxiv
Victorinus, lxii.
Vincentius, cxxxii.
Vitus, cii.

Zacharias, cxxxv, clvii.
Zeno, clxi.
Zenobius, cxxxiii.

INDEX OF THINGS.

Adze, ci.
Age of Saint Abban (317 years), lxiii, clx.
—— Senchell (330 years), lxv.
—— Cruméne (180), cvii.
—— Moninne (180), cxvi.
Ambrosius, cited, ccxxvi.
Anchor, xlvii.
Angels, v, viii, xl, lxxii, xcix, cxix, cxxviii, clxxx.
Apostles, clxxxvii; of Ireland, cxviii.
Architecture:—
  bend in daurthige, xxxii.
  bendchopar in daurthigi, xlvii.
  daurthach made of wood, lxxiii.
Armpit (ocha), cxxviii.
Asceticism, clviii. Findchú's, cxlxxii. Ultan the silent, cxlxxiii.
Assimilation, ccxii ; of n, ccxxix.
Austerities of Fintan, lii ; of Ciaran, lxii.
Baculus pastoralis, clxxxvi.
Baptism, clxx.
Barley-bread, lxii.
Bathing-tub, clxx, clxxi.
Bees, xlii.
Bell, lxxiv, cxxxi, clvii.
Besom out of Fanait, cxxxiv.
Blood, leprosy healed by children's, xxxvi.
Bird lamenting Molua, xl ; singing fifty years, cvii. See *Pet.*
Bisextus, liii, liv.
Bishop's orders (*gradu escuip*), xlviii.
Boat (*curach*), clxxiv.
Booksatchels, cxli.
Books of Longarad, cxli.
Buide Chonuill, cxlii.

C in loanwords for p, ccxxxiii.
Calligraphy, lvii, cxxxi.
Cardinal, theft of his horses, &c., clxxxvii.
Casting lots, xlvii.
Cattle of Ciaran, lxi ; their fear of Mac-Oige, clxxix.
Cause, one of the four requisites, iii, viii.
Céli dé (Culdees), civ.
Celláir, clviii.
Children in Bethlehem, clxxxiv.
Christ appearing as an infant, xxxv ; crucifixion of, clix ; King of the stars, clviii.
—— in the wilderness, reasons for worshipping, clxxxvii.
Church undiscovered in wood, lxxxiv.
Clapper (*bascheann*), xlvi.
Clergy freed from raiding, iii, viii.
Clerics, duty of, clxxxvi, clxxxvii.
—— not to be slain, lxiv.
Conception from a star, lxi ; from a salmon, lxxiii ; of a dead woman, clvi ; star making manifest, clxxx ; of Boethine, lxxxviii.
Continence, proof of, xxxii.
Coracle (curchan), clxxv.
Cormac, etymologies of, lxxxv.
Corpse, lying with, clxxii.
Creed, Apostles', clxxxvii.
Crepitus ventris, cxlv.
Cross, finding of, lvi.
Croziers, cxxxi, clxxxvi.
Culdee, see Céli dé, civ.
Curse, cvi. See *Left hand.*
Daurthach, lxxiii.
Decay, saint's body free from, cxlxx.
Demon, xliii, lii, lxvi.

INDEX OF THINGS.

Devil, his interview with Muling, civ.
—— cannot kneel, cv.
Dew of grave, cxcv.
Diadem (*mind*), xli, xliii, lviii, lxxx, cxi, cxxiii, cxxiv, cli, clxii, clxv, clxvi.
Dive, miraculous, xxxviii.
Dogs, lxxxv.
Dove, cxix.
Dress, lxii.
Drúi, wizard, lxxv.
Ducange, cited, ccxxvi.
Ducks, unboilable, clx.
Dumb poet, cxvi.
Encelann, lxi.
Epenthesis, ccxiv.
Eric (mulct), lxxxvii.
Exchange of diseases, xxxv.
Exorcist, clv.
Exposing infants, cxxviii.
Fasting, cxvi, cxliv, cxlxx; to cut short Ciaran's life, cxliv.
Fer dá chrích, clv.
Fer dá lethe, clxxx.
Fiann, Nurse of the, lxxiii.
Fiery column, xlvii.
Fire carried in chasubles, xxxii.
Fish, see *Salmon*.
Flame (*breo*), lxix, lxx, xcii, cxxiv.
—— (*lassar*), lxix.
—— (*lith*), cxxvi.
Food, lxii, in lent xl, see *Pottage*, *Watercress*.
Fornication, lx.
Fostering, cxxi, cxlii.
God, King of the white sun, xiii; King above clouds, xiii; King of clouds, lxxix, cxxv, lei.
Gold, glowing mass of, xxix, xlii, xlxv; flesc óir, lxx.; doss óir, lxxx. And see cli, doss ordai, cxcvi; sliab nóir, clxii.
Gospel, Christ's successor, civ, made by Daig, cxxxi.
Grave, MacRustaing's, cxlv.
Hair cut before entering God's service, xxxviii; of Peter cut, liii; deadly, cxliv.
Harlot, lxiii.
Hart ploughing, li.
Heavens, seven, xiii, ccii.
Helmet, xxvii.
Honey, civ.
Hornce, ccxciii.
Horses used in tillage, lxi.
Hostages, cliv.

Hosting, lxxx.
Illuminated book, lxii.
Incest between Mugain and her father, clxix. suspected, l.
Ink, clxxi.
Juvenal, cited, ccxxv.
Kiln-drying, viii, cxxxii.
Kings of the Pagans, xv.
Lamp, xix, xli.
Lark, lxvi.
Larra, ccxiii.
Law, see *Eric*, *Securities*.
Left hand used in malediction, cxlii.
Lent, clxxxiii.
Leper, lvii, lxxx, clxix.
Leprosy, clix; healed by children's blood, xxxvi.
Life, respect for, xl.
Light (*les*), lvii.
Little-finger, clix, cvi.
Lousing heads, l.
Manuscript, wondrous, lxii.
Martyrdom, kinds of, xiv, red, lxxiv.
Metre of the Félire, iv, ix.
Milk, miraculous increase of, xlvi, mixed with pottage, c.
Mill, lxxxviii.
Miracle, death without corruption, cvii, cxx.
Moon, Rhodon, xxvi.
Monster (*béist*), lxii.
Mother's son, *Mac Lémna*, lxxxiii.
Names, changed in token of union, clix; origin of, xxxvii, xxxviii, lxxiv; (my kick, &c.), cxxviii; Giallan, cliv; Mo-ling, ciii; son of Adze, ci; son of Cunlenn's ink, cxlxxi.
Nettlepottage, c.
None, celebration of, l.
Nollaic mór (Great Christmas), clxxxiv.
Oratory, lxxiii.
Orders of penitence (*grada aithrige*), xlvii, xlviii; episcopal, see Bishop; sacerdotal, li.
Oxen, not to be stolen, lxiv.
Penancer, viii. See *Asceticism*.
Person, one of the four requisites, iii, viii.
Pet scallerow, lxxiii.
Pigs, clxviii.
Pilgrimage to Rome, lx; to Clement's relics, cxlxx; from the east, clxi.
Pillar (*áge*), xvii, xlii, lvii, lxxviii, lxxxi (bis), *naitae*, lxxi, cix, cxiii, cliii, clxii.
Pillow, clviii.

INDEX OF THINGS.

Place, one of the four requisites, iii, viii.
Pledges (*coir*), liii.
Ploughing without a share, li.
Pope, Ireland's tribute to, clxxxvii.
Pottage, c.
Priest's orders (*grada sacairt*). li.
Prophecy, by Moling. cxxxiv.
Psalmist (*salmchétlaid*), lx.
Proverb, xlvi, (*loimm de romuir*), clxxxix, *is colunn cea chenn duine cen anamcharait*, xlvi, cxxix ; *bot fo brega*, clxxxi.
Rampart (*már*), cxxxvii. cxxxviii, clxxiv.
Red martyrdom, lxxiv.
Reduplicated future, ccx, ccxliv.
Relics, collection of, xlix, cvi, clx : of Paul and Peter, liv, cvi.cliv; of Colomb, cvi, clxxxii; of Finan and Onchu, cxviii.
Rithairec, cxlxxii.
Rock, xxvi.
Rules (*cána*) of Ireland, lxiv.
Saints are God's wheat, cxxxi. Their age, see *Age*. Their vengeance, cxvii. Unity of. lxxxvii. Curses of, lxxxiv. Visiting burial place of, xx. Exchanging diseases, xxxv.
Salmon, conception from, lxxiii.
Satirists, lxxxvii.
Saxons have tribute and right over Ireland, clxxxvii.
Scribe. cxxxi.
Sea (*ler*), lvii.
Sea, lviii. Church in, xxxii. Saint walking on, xxxii. City under, clxx. Rising against a saint, cvi.
Securities (*ratha*), liii.
Seven Sleepers, cxxix. cxxx.
Share, li.
Shrine of gold, xv.
Sickle (*corran*) of iron, cxlvi, clxxii.
Slavery, cii.
Soldiers of Jesus, xv.
Soulfriend (*anamchara*), xlvi, lxxiv. cxxix.
Stagbeetle, (*Joel*). xxxiv.

Star, xlii. lv, cxii. Falling into Liadaine's mouth, lxi. Manifesting conception, clxxx.
Stone tomb (*ilad, ulad*), cxxxiii.
Squinting. lxxiv.
Sun, King of the. xiii.
Sun, saints called, Maelruan, xx. Ciar. xxvi. Ite, xxviii. Cronan, xiii. Patrick, lvii. George, lxx. German, lxxxi. Moling, xciv. Moelruain, cix. Diarmait, cx. Simeon, cxii. Longarad, cxxxvi. Malthaeus, cxxxviii ; and see clxix (*bis*). cli. clxii, clxxv, clxxvi, clxxvii.
Sunday, rule of, lxiv.
Superstitions, see *Left-hand*.
Swineherd of king, xxxiii.
Testament (*udacht*), lxxxiii.
Tithe, clxxxv. clxxxvi.
Time, one of the four requisites, iii. viii.
Tond Clidna, lxiv.
Tongue, preaching after excision of, clix.
Tool, see *Adze, Share, Sickle*.
Tower, lxviii, cxii, clxxv.
Tree, enormous, clxxxi ; worshipped, lxxv.
Triads, Conall's three manly deeds, l.
——— three worst counsels, cxliv.
Tribute of Ireland, clxxxvii.
Type of darkness, xxxiv.
Union of Saints. iv.
Vengeance of Moelruain, cxvii.
Vision of Boethine, ci.
Watercress, lxxxix.
Wave, see *Tond Clidna*.
Well, cxliii.
Wheat, red, lxxxviii.
White battle, xciii.
Will, xlvi, lxxxii.
Wolf suckling a girl, lxxvii : devouring Condlaed, lxxxiii.
Wolves, cxliii.
Woman in guise of a monk, lxiii : fighting, cxlvi : not to be slain, lxiv.
Writing of Cianan, clxxi ; of Cairnech, lxii.
Yew, of Mugna. clxxxi.

www.ingramcontent.com/pod-product-compliance
Lightning Source LLC
Chambersburg PA
CBHW022334230426
43664CB00040B/484